COMPANION TO
SCOTTISH LITERATURE

COMPANION TO SCOTTISH LITERATURE

TREVOR ROYLE

GALE RESEARCH COMPANY
BOOK TOWER · DETROIT, MICHIGAN 48226

© The Macmillan Press Ltd, 1983

All rights reserved. No part of this publication may be reproduced
or transmitted, in any form or by any means, without permission.

This edition is published in the United States, its possessions and Canada
by the GALE RESEARCH COMPANY, Book Tower, Detroit, MI48226.

Library of Congress Cataloging in Publication Data

Royle, Trevor.
    Companion to Scottish literature.

    British ed. published under title: The Macmillan companion to Scottish
literature. London: Macmillan Reference Books, 1983.
    Includes index.
    1. Scottish literature – History and criticism.
2. English literature – Scottish authors – History and criticism. I. Title.
PR8511.R67 1983b   820'.9'9411   83-5493
ISBN 0-8103-0519-4

Filmsetting by Vantage Photosetting Co. Ltd,
Eastleigh and London

Printed in Hong Kong

Contents

Acknowledgements

First and foremost I wish to thank the general editor of this *Companion* and its 'onlie begetter', Professor A. N. Jeffares of the University of Stirling, both for his useful advice and helpful criticism and for his unfailing support throughout the project. I owe debts of gratitude, too, to the following friends who have helped on several matters through conversations or correspondence: Dr Ian Campbell, University of Edinburgh; Douglas Gifford, University of Strathclyde; Professor Francis Russell Hart, University of Massachusetts; and Dr Roderick Watson, University of Stirling. I was also greatly assisted by the many writers and publishers who replied to my requests for biographical or bibliographical information; and I was fortunate in having such a tolerant publisher. It would be invidious of me not to acknowledge the courtesies and encouragement afforded to me by Shaie Selzer and Mara Vilčinskas of Macmillan and I should like to thank Rosemary Roberts for editing the copy. Professor William Gillies, of the University of Edinburgh, kindly read the sections relating to Gaelic literature and suggested improvements and alterations. Walter Perrie assisted with the correction of proofs and helped in many other untold ways; to him go my thanks, although all errors in the text must remain my responsibility. No book of this kind could have been attempted without the excellent services of the National Library of Scotland and throughout I have been both assisted and heartened by the helpful ministrations of its staff. Likewise, the staffs of the Scottish and the Edinburgh Rooms of the Edinburgh Central Library, and of the Mitchell Library in Glasgow, offered their customary friendly help and advice.

Introduction

The purpose of this *Companion* is to provide an alphabetical list of references to Scotland's literature from earliest times to the present day. Its backbone is supplied by the biographical essays devoted to the principal poets, novelists, dramatists, critics and men of letters who have written in English, Scots or Gaelic and whose work constitutes the main corpus of Scottish literature. Also included are a number of historians, philosophers, divines, diarists and other occasional writers who may be considered to have made their own contribution through the literary worth of their writings. Where writers have pseudonyms these are listed but the reader is referred back in each case to the writer's real name. Working outwards from the biographical essays through a system of cross-referencing there are further essays which cover the following fields: principal literary works, institutions, literary movements, historical events and personalities, printed ephemera and publishing.

The length of an essay must of course to some extent be determined by its subject's worth, but the reader should not use bulk as a guide in every case. Some writers led fuller, better-documented lives and published more books than others: of necessity their entries are longer than those on equally important writers, the facts of whose lives may be more obscure. In each entry I have tried to provide the date and place of birth and death and the principal facts of the writer's life. Most writers were born and brought up in Scotland or could claim Scottish nationality through parentage, but I have not allowed myself to be over-dominated by the claims of nationhood. Several writers spent most of their working lives outside the country of their birth and never returned. Others who stayed were not always completely under the influence of Scotland, its culture and its traditions. A handful of writers of nationalities other than Scottish spent their lives in Scotland and through their writings added to the heritage of their adopted land. I have chosen to include all three types. In the space available it has not been possible to provide original literary criticisms, although by way of aesthetic comment I have attempted to give a critical viewpoint of the writer or the work under discussion.

The impingement of history on the nation's literature could not be ignored. Thus cognisance is taken of the kings and queens, the statesmen and the main events that have influenced in some way the world of letters. Similarly the religions of Scotland and the writings inspired by their espousal find a place, as does the law, which has played such an influential role in shaping Scotland's intellectual traditions. There are also essays devoted to the Scottish philosophers, particularly to those associated with the Scottish Common-Sense school.

Gaelic created a different problem. Although it is now a minority language, its literature, especially its poetry and its song tradition, has made a signal contribution to Scotland's literature. Not being a Gaelic speaker I am denied access to many of the texts, other than to those published with English translations. As a consequence, the references to Gaelic writers and to Gaelic literature may appear to be restricted but the diligent reader will discover that many of the main writers are included. Following the example of Professor Derick Thomson in his *Introduction to Gaelic Poetry* (London, 1974), the Gaelic writers have been listed under their Gaelic names. Duncan Ban MacIntyre appears under 'Mac an t-Saoir, Donnchadh Bàn'; but where the writer has used Gaelic and English in equal measure, he is entered under the English form of his name ('Iain Crichton Smith' is preferred to 'Iain Mac a'Ghobhainn').

During the preparation of the *Companion*, the standard of choice and selection was always under review and several writers on the fringe were omitted because it was felt that their work had been too marginal. With contemporary writers, no one has been included who was born after 1950 and in most cases caution has been preferred to commitment in offering a literary judgement. The process of any literature is bound to be continuous and those writers will one day find themselves subjected to different standards of selection and compilation in future companions to Scottish literature.

Finally, this *Companion* will have served something of its purpose if it can act as a companionable guide and introduction to Scotland's own very distinctive voice as reflected in its national literature.

Trevor Royle
Edinburgh, August 1982

Bibliographical Information

The biographical essays are based in the main, though not exclusively, on entries in the *Dictionary of National Biography* and on *Who's Who* for the relevant years. The other main works consulted were: D. Irving, *The Lives of the Scottish Poets* (Edinburgh, 1804); R. Chambers, *A Biographical Dictionary of Eminent Scotsmen*, 4 vols. (Edinburgh, 1832–4); W. Anderson, *The Scottish Nation*, 9 vols. (Edinburgh and London, 1882); *Scottish Biographies 1938* (London, 1938); and G. Donaldson and R. S. Morpeth, eds., *Who's Who in Scottish History* (Oxford, 1973). Wherever possible, reference has been made to the publications of the Scottish Text Society, the Association for Scottish Literary Studies and the Scottish Gaelic Text Society. These provide admirable critical introductions to the principal texts of Scotland's literature.

At the conclusion of each writer's biographical essay are listed his or her book publications, but in some cases complete or collected editions of works, have been preferred to a listing of individual titles. Plays are dated according to their first production but when published, the date of publication has been given in the 'Works' section. The main critical and biographical studies have also been listed (in the 'References' section) but lack of space prevented reference to individual critical essays in literary magazines and journals.

The following books provided the main body of critical study and should be consulted in addition to those individual studies referred to in the text.

Aitken, A. J. and McArthur, T., *The Languages of Scotland* (Edinburgh, 1979)
Bold, A., *The Ballad* (London, 1979)
Buchan, D., *The Ballad and the Folk* (London, 1972)
Campbell, I., ed., *Nineteenth Century Scottish Fiction* (Manchester, 1979)
Collinson, F., *The Traditional and National Music of Scotland* (London, 1966)
Craig, D., *Scottish Literature and the Scottish People* (London, 1961)
Daiches, D., *The Paradox of Scottish Culture* (Oxford, 1964)
Daiches, D., ed., *A Companion to Scottish Culture* (London, 1981)
Davie, G., *The Democratic Intellect* (Edinburgh, 1961)
Fulton, R., *Contemporary Scottish Poetry: Individuals and Contexts* (Loanhead, Midlothian, 1974)
Glen, D., *A Bibliography of Scottish Poets from Stevenson to 1974* (Preston, 1974)
Grierson, H. J. C., ed., *Edinburgh Essays on Scots Literature* (Edinburgh and London, 1933)
Hart, F. R., *The Scottish Novel: a Critical Survey* (London, 1978)
Henderson, T. F., *Scottish Vernacular Literature: a History* (London, 1900)
Jack, R. D. S., *The Italian Influence on Scottish Literature* (Edinburgh, 1970)
Kinsley, J., ed., *Scottish Poetry: a Critical Survey* (London, 1955)
Lindsay, M., *The Burns Encyclopaedia* (London, 1959; rev. 1980)
——, *History of Scottish Literature* (London, 1977)
Mackenzie, A. M., *An Historical Survey of Scottish Literature to 1714* (London, 1933)
Maclean, M., *The Literature of the Highlands* (London, 1925)
McNeill, F. M., *The Silver Bough*, 4 vols. (Glasgow, 1957–68)
MacQueen, J. and Scott, T., eds., *The Oxford Book of Scottish Verse* (Oxford, 1965)
Millar, J. H., *A Literary History of Scotland* (Edinburgh and London, 1903)
Muir, E., *Scott and Scotland* (London, 1936)
Shire, H. M., *Song, Dance and Poetry of the Court of Scotland under King James VI* (Cambridge, 1969)
Smith, G. G., *Scottish Literature: Character and Influence* (London, 1919)

Smith, J. M., *The French Background of Middle Scots Literature* (London, 1934)
Speirs, J., *The Scots Literary Tradition* (London, 1962)
Thomson, D., *An Introduction to Gaelic Poetry* (London, 1974)
Wittig, K., *The Scottish Tradition in Literature* (Edinburgh, 1958)

Abbreviations

ASLS Association for Scottish Literary Studies
DNB   Dictionary of National Biography
OED   Oxford English Dictionary
SGTS Scottish Gaelic Text Society
SND   Scottish National Dictionary
STS   Scottish Text Society

A

Abbotsford. The home of Sir WALTER SCOTT, purchased from Dr Robert Douglas, minister of Galashiels, in 1811. It was originally called Cartleyhole but because of its proximity to a ford on the River Tweed and because it had associations with the Abbey of Melrose Scott changed its name to the more romantic Abbotsford. It was improved and rebuilt between 1818 and 1824 to include many features such as an armoury which reflected Scott's interest in history; the house was one of the first in Scotland to use oil-gas for lighting. By 1820 Scott's estate extended to 1400 acres and included houses for his son-in-law JOHN GIBSON LOCKHART at Chiefswood and his friend ADAM FERGUSON at Huntlyburn. Among the prominent visitors to Abbotsford during Scott's lifetime were Maria Edgeworth, William Wordsworth and Washington Irving. The house has remained in the Scott family as a memorial to the man and a museum of his work.

Abbotsford Club. A publishing society founded in Edinburgh in 1833 in memory of Sir WALTER SCOTT, with the express purpose of printing 'miscellaneous pieces, illustrative of history, literature and antiquities'. The club was never formally dissolved but it was declared by its secretary in 1866 'to have reached its termination'. It was one of the most prolific of all the Scottish 19th-century publishing societies in the number and variety of its publications; of especial interest is the reprinting of the ecclesiastical records of the early church of Scotland.

Abercrombie, John (i) (1726–1806). Horticulturalist. He was born in Edinburgh, the son of a gardener. After an apprenticeship with his father, he moved in 1744 to London where he was employed as a gardener in the royal palaces. He became well-known for his land-

scaping and was employed as a landscape gardener by several noble families in England. Among his publications may be mentioned *The Universal Gardener and Botanist* which went into several editions, *The Gardener's Pocket Dictionary* and *The Garden Vade Mecum*.

WORKS: *The British Fruit Gardener and the Art of Pruning* (1779); *The Complete Forcing Gardener* (1781); *The Complete Wall Tree Pruner* (1783); *The Propagation and Botanical Arrangement of Plants and Trees* (1784); *The Gardener's Daily Assistant* (1786); *The Gardener's Pocket Dictionary* (1786); *The Garden Vade Mecum* (1789); *The Hot House Gardener* (1789); *The Universal Gardener's Kalendar* (1789); *The Universal Gardener and Botanist* (1797); *The Garden Mushroom* (1802); *Every Man his Own Gardener* (1803)

Abercrombie, John (ii) (1781–1844). Physician. He was born on 11 November 1781 in Aberdeen, the son of a minister. He studied medicine at the University of Edinburgh and after graduating in 1803 lived in London for a year before being admitted to the Royal College of Surgeons on 12 November 1804. He returned to Edinburgh to a general practice and gained a reputation as a writer on medical and moral matters. His two most important books, *Inquiries Concerning the Intellectual Powers and the Investigation of Truth* (1830) and *The Philosophy of Moral Feelings* (1833), deal with the vexed problem of the marriage of scientific discovery with Christian doctrine, and in their day enjoyed considerable popularity. He died on 14 November 1844.

WORKS: *Inquiries Concerning the Intellectual Powers and the Investigation of Truth* (1830); *The Philosophy of Moral Feelings* (1833); *Observations on the Moral Condition of the Lower Orders in Edinburgh* (1834); *The Culture and Discipline of the Mind* (1836); *Think on These Things* (1841)

REFERENCE: D. MacLagen, *Sketch of the Life and Character of Dr John Abercrombie* (London, 1854)

Abercromby, Patrick (1656–1716). Historian. He was born in 1656 in Forfar, the third son of Alexander Abercromby of Fetternair in Aberdeenshire. He was educated at the Universities of St Andrews and Paris and practised as a doctor in Edinburgh, before being appointed physician to James II, a post he held until the Revolution of 1688. He lived in Europe for some years before returning to Scotland during the reign of Queen Anne, when he became an opponent of the pro-Union party. He died in poverty, probably in 1716.

In 1707 Abercromby published his translation of Beaugue's *L'histoire de la Guerre d'Ecosse 1556* as *The History of the Compagnes 1548 and 1549; being an exact account of the martial expedition performed in those days by the Scots and French on the one hand, and the English and their foreign auxiliaries on the other; done in French by Mons. Beaugue, a French gentleman; with an introductory preface by the Translator.* The work stresses the importance of the AULD ALLIANCE and is an account of the French soldiers who fought against the Protector Somerset; it was reprinted by the BANNATYNE CLUB in 1823. Abercromby is best remembered for his two-volume *The Martial Achievements of the Scots Nation; being an account of the lives, characters and memorable actions of such Scotsmen as have signaliz'd themselves by the sword at home and abroad; and a survey of the military transactions wherein Scotland or Scotsmen have been remarkably concern'd, from the first establishment of the Scots monarchy to the present Time* (1711–15) which was printed by THOMAS RUDDIMAN.

WORKS: *The Advantages of the Act of Security* (1706); trans., Beaugue, *L'histoire de la Guerre d'Ecosse 1556*, as *The History of the Compagnes 1548 and 1549* (1707); *The Martial Achievements of the Scots Nation*, 2 vols. (1711–15)

Aberdeen. A city situated in the north-east corner of Scotland, where it has enjoyed for centuries the twin advantages of an agrarian and maritime economy. Aberdeen was established during the reign of MALCOLM III (Malcolm Canmore); it received special privileges of the acquisition of farmland, the so-called Freedom Lands, from ROBERT I (Robert the Bruce), and the 15th century saw the construction of the Cathedral of St Machar and of the university buildings in the area now known as Old Aberdeen. Its two universities, King's College (1494) and Marischal College (1593), were not joined until 1860, but both places of learning, and their links with the surrounding area, helped to give education an imposing

stature in the north-east from the 15th century onwards. The historian HECTOR BOECE was the first principal of King's and others associated with the university have been the philosophers ALEXANDER BAIN and JAMES BEATTIE, who helped to evolve the distinctly Scottish Common-Sense school of philosophy in the late 18th century.

Aberdeen's great years of expansion occurred during the first half of the 19th century. Two architects, Archibald Simpson (1790–1847) and John Smith (1781–1832), endowed the city with domestic and public buildings of neo-classical grace and charm, constructed out of the native stone that gives Aberdeen its nickname, 'the Granite City'. The discovery of oil in the North Sea during the 1970s and the development of Aberdeen as a centre for its exploitation inevitably changed the face of the city, but the spirit of the surrounding region has remained remarkably unmoved by sudden wealth and the introduction of foreign values.

A distinguishing feature of the literature of the north-east is the abiding concern for the land and a sense of belonging to it. Nowhere is that deep attachment better expressed than in the trilogy of novels by LEWIS GRASSIC GIBBON, A SCOTS QUAIR, although it also informs novels such as JOHNNY GIBB OF GUSHETNEUK by WILLIAM ALEXANDER (ii), *Shepherd's Calendar* by IAN MACPHERSON and *Farmer's Boy*, a study of boyhood by JOHN ROBERTSON ALLAN. Likewise it has inspired much of the poetry of the area, and the poets who have or have had their roots in Aberdeenshire and the surrounding counties include ARTHUR JOHNSTON, ALEXANDER ROSS, VIOLET JACOB, CHARLES MURRAY, FLORA GARRY, ALEXANDER SCOTT (ii) and GEORGE BRUCE.

Aberdeen Press and Journal. A newspaper founded as *The Aberdeen's Journal and North British Magazine* on 5 January 1748 in Aberdeen by James Chalmers. It remained in the hands of the Chalmers family until May 1876 when a new company was formed and it became a daily publication. A daily evening newspaper, the *Evening Express*, was added in January 1879. In 1922 the company amalgamated with the *Aberdeen Free Press* to publish the paper under the title *Aberdeen Press and Journal*, and subsequent owners have been Lord Kemsley (1928–59) and Lord Thomson of Fleet, who purchased the paper in 1959 and whose company still owns it. Among the writers who have worked as journalists for the *Press and Journal* during the 20th century are JAMES LESLIE MITCHELL, ERIC LINKLATER and JAMES KENNAWAY; under the editorship of Cuthbert Graham the weekly review has published dialect poetry from the north-east of Scotland.

REFERENCES: G. Fraser and K. Peters, *The Northern Lights* (London, 1978); C. Graham, ed., *North East Muse Anthology* (Aberdeen, 1977)

Act of Union. The Treaty of Union, made law on 1 May 1707, which united the parliaments of Scotland and England and created the Parliament of Great Britain. Under its terms Scotland retained her own Church, law and justiciary system and a complicated financial system of 'equivalents' was created, mainly to compensate Scotland for her involvement in the National Debt. There was considerable opposition to the Union, especially in the cities, and during the debate on the Treaty by the Scottish Parliament in 1706 there was a voluminous publication of strongly worded pamphlet literature. Some of the regret felt in Scotland for the passing of the Treaty can be gained from the novels WAVERLEY and THE HEART OF MIDLOTHIAN by Sir WALTER SCOTT.

Adam, Alexander (1741–1809). Rector of the HIGH SCHOOL OF EDINBURGH from 1768 until his death. A much respected man, Adam taught most of Edinburgh's leading literary and legal figures and Lord Cockburn described him as 'a warm encourager by praise, play and kindness; and constantly under the strongest sense of duty'. He was the author of a *Latin Grammar* (1762) which became a standard school textbook, a popular antiquarian study *Roman Antiquities* (1791), and *A Compendious Dictionary of the Latin Tongue* (1805).

WORKS: *Latin Grammar* (1762); *The Principles of Latin and English Grammar* (1772); *The Rudiments of Latin and English Grammar* (1786); *Roman Antiquities* (1791); *A Summary of Geography and History* (1794); *Classical Biography* (1800); *A Compendious Dictionary of the Latin Tongue* (1805)

REFERENCE: A. Henderson, *An Account of the Life and Character of Alexander Adam* (Edinburgh, 1810)

Adam, Jean (1710–65). Poet. She was born in Greenock, the daughter of a shipmaster. Orphaned at an early age she became a governess and later established a school for girls in Greenock. Her only collection of poems, *Miscellany Poems*, was published in 1734, but she is best remembered as the supposed author of 'The Song of the Mariner's Wife' or, as it is better known, 'There's nae luck aboot the hoose', which was included in his collection of 1776 by DAVID HERD. After living in poverty in London, Jean Adam died in a Glasgow poorhouse on 2 April 1765.

Adam, Robert (1728–92). Architect. He was born on 3 July 1728 in Kirkcaldy, Fife, the son of William Adam (1689–1748), an architect who was responsible for a number of 18th-century Scottish houses, including part of Hopetoun House. Adam enjoyed a classical education which included visits to Italy and Dalmatia to study Roman architecture; the drawings he made there were to have an effect on his style of architecture. On his return to Britain he was made architect to GEORGE III and, with his brother James, he wrote the influential three-volume *Works on Architecture* (1778–1822). Adam designed several striking buildings in London, including Syon House and the Adelphi Theatre, and in Edinburgh he completed the designs for Register House and the Old College of the University as well as the unified buildings on the north side of Charlotte Square. The Adam style, as it has come to be known, is popularly associated with his interior designs which combine the Gothic with the neo-classical of the 18th century.

REFERENCE: J. Fleming, *Robert Adam and his Circle* (London, 1962, 2/1978)

Adam of Dryburgh [Adam the Scot] (*c* 1140–1212). Divine. He was a native of Berwickshire. In 1184 he was made Abbot of Dryburgh and during his period of tenure he won a popular following for his style of preaching. But four years after his election he sought seclusion in a Carthusian monastery at Witham in Somerset in order to devote his time to scholarly religious writing. The earliest edition of his work is dated at Paris in 1518 and includes 24 sermons, *Liber de tripartite tabernaculo*, and *Liber de contemplationis*, interpretations of Old Testament teaching. A second collection of his work was published in 1659 by Peter Bellerus of Amsterdam, to which was added Adam's *Soliloquium de instructione*, a Platonic dialogue between the Soul and Reason. All the writings show a keen mind at work and one that was thoroughly versed in the classical texts of the Premonstratensian order.

REFERENCE: J. Bulloch, *Adam of Dryburgh* (London, 1958)

Adamson, Patrick (1537–92). Divine. He was a native of Perth and was educated at the University of St Andrews, from which he graduated in 1558. Between then and 1566, when he travelled to Paris and Italy as a private tutor, he was minister of the parish of Ceres in Fife. His first verses, written in Latin, were strenuous, if conventional, attacks on excesses in the Catholic Church, and his Protestant leanings were strengthened during his stay in Europe. Among his sacred works were translations of the book of *Job* into Latin hexameters and a Latin translation of the Scottish Confession of Faith. By 1571 he was back in Scotland to take the charge of Paisley and over the next 20 years he was drawn increasingly into Scottish church politics. To the disgust of many of his more extreme colleagues he accepted the archbishopric of St Andrews in 1576 and later historians, such as DAVID CALDERWOOD, went out of their way to misrepresent him as a licentious buffoon. ANDREW MELVILLE, Principal of St Mary's College in St Andrews, became a feared opponent in debate as he constantly quizzed Adamson's adherence to Episcopalianism. Having relied for many years on the support of JAMES VI, Adamson was dismayed to find that by 1590 the king had switched his allegiance to Melville; the final years of his life were spent in poverty and disgrace. He died on 19 February 1592.

As most of the facts about Adamson's life come from biased accounts in Calderwood and from the diary of the reformer JAMES MELVILLE (ii), it is difficult to form a firm judgement of his ability and influence. He made accomplished translations of biblical texts into Latin and enjoyed a substantial reputation as a Latinist in Europe; but today, perversely, he is remembered best of all as the butt of a furious verbal assault by ROBERT SEMPILL (i) in the satire *The Legend of the Lymmaris Lyfe* (1584).

EDITION: T. Wilson, ed., *Poemata sacra cum aliis opusculis* (London, 1619)

Address to the Deil. A poem by ROBERT BURNS in which the Devil takes on the aspect of the devils of folklore and popular superstition (*see also* TAM O'SHANTER). The headnote to the poem is quoted from *Paradise Lost* but Burns's Devil lacks the lofty grandeur of Milton's Satan and is instead a mischievous prankster whose only harm is 'to skelp and scaud poor dogs like me/An hear us squeal'.

Admirable Crichton, The. The name given to the 16th-century poet and scholar JAMES CRICHTON of Cluny. It is also the title of a play by J. M. BARRIE, first produced in 1902, in which Crichton, an imperturbable butler, is forced to take command when his patrician masters are wrecked on a desert island. Once back in civilization the positions are again reversed and the old order restored, but Barrie was at pains to emphasize that Crichton maintained his position of pre-eminence on the island by virtue of his own abilities.

Advocates, Faculty of. The Scottish Bar, whose membership of advocates enjoys exclusive right of audience in the Scottish Supreme Courts. During the 18th century the Faculty was an intellectual and social élite and attracted to it many of the great thinkers and writers of the day. The library of the Faculty of Advocates, founded by Sir GEORGE MACKENZIE (ii), of Rosehaugh, was presented to the nation in 1925 and forms the basis of the NATIONAL LIBRARY OF SCOTLAND.

Ae Fond Kiss. A song written by ROBERT BURNS in December 1791 on the conclusion of his epistolary relationship with AGNES M' LEHOSE. With its heartfelt sentiments of regret and spent passion it is one of the great Scottish love-songs. It was first published in THE SCOTS MUSICAL MUSEUM to the older tune 'Rory Dall's Port'.

Aiken, Robert (1739–1807). Lawyer in Ayr. As patron of ROBERT BURNS he collected 145 subscriptions for the KILMARNOCK EDITION of the poet's work, issued in 1786. Burns dedicated 'The Cotter's Saturday Night' to Aiken and enjoyed a close friendship with him, despite a temporary rupture when Aiken and James Armour mutilated Burns's declaration of intent to marry JEAN ARMOUR. Most of Aiken's correspondence with Burns was unfortunately destroyed after the poet's death.

Ainslie, Robert (1766–1838). Lawyer. He was a close friend of ROBERT BURNS, whom he accompanied on a tour to the Borders during the summer of 1787. Ainslie shared Burns's

delight in carousing and song and was a confidant in Burns's affair with AGNES M'LEHOSE.

Aird, Thomas (1802–76). Poet. He was born
on 28 August 1802 at Bowden, Roxburghshire.
He was educated locally and at the University
of Edinburgh, and during his student days
became acquainted with THOMAS CARLYLE
and JAMES HOGG. Aird became a regular contributor to BLACKWOOD'S MAGAZINE and
through the influence of JOHN WILSON (iii)
was appointed editor of the *Dumfries and Galloway Herald* in 1835. He died on 25 April 1876
in Dumfries.

Aird's poetry is mostly concerned with nature, treated in a Wordsworthian vein, and
Carlyle said of it: 'he found everywhere a
healthy breath as of mountain breezes'. His
collections are: *Murtzoufle: a Tragedy in Three
Acts and Other Poems* (1826), *The Captive of
Fez* (1830) and *Poetical Works* (1848). Among
his prose works are a memoir of DAVID MAC-
BETH MOIR and a popular but sentimental
description of Scottish country manners, *The
Old Bachelor in the Scottish Village* (1845).

WORKS: *Murtzoufle: a Tragedy in Three Acts and Other
Poems* (1826); *Religious Characteristics* (1827); *The
Captive of Fez* (1830); *Orthuriel and Other Poems*
(1840); *The Old Bachelor in the Scottish Village*
(1845); *Poetical Works* (1848)

A. K. H. B. Pen-name of A. K. H. BOYD.

Akros. A literary magazine, first published in
August 1965 and edited by its founder, DUN-
CAN GLEN. With a firm commitment to publishing new work by Scottish poets and with a
particular emphasis on poetry in Scots, *Akros*
became a vital forum for the discussion of
literary topics; its early issues featured in particular the work of Hugh MacDiarmid
(CHRISTOPHER MURRAY GRIEVE), ALEXAN-
DER SCOTT (ii), SYDNEY GOODSIR SMITH,
NORMAN MACCAIG and GEORGE BRUCE.
Akros Publications, the literary press run also
by Duncan Glen, became one of Scotland's
leading poetry publishers and set new standards
in typography and design.

Alasdair Mac Mhaighstir Alasdair (Alexander
Macdonald) (*c*1695–*c*1770). Poet. He was a
native of Moidart, but very little is known
about his early life. He was the son of the
Episcopalian minister of Ardnamurchan and
he may have studied at the University of Glasgow. In 1729 he is first mentioned as being in

the employment of the Society for Propagating
Christian Knowledge (SPCK) at Islandfinnan,
Ardnamurchan, where he remained as a
teacher until the JACOBITE rising of 1745. He
was commissioned into the Clanranald Regiment, and tradition claims that he was responsible for teaching Gaelic to Prince CHARLES
EDWARD STUART. After the rising he was
bailie to the Clanranalds on the island of
Canna, but his standing within the clan allowed him to return to Moidart around 1752
and he lived near Arisaig until the end of his
life.

In 1741 Alasdair produced a Gaelic–English
dictionary for the SPCK, and his poetry was
published in 1751 in *Ais-eiridh na Sean Chánain
Albannaich*. Such was the supposed potential
for treason in the nationalist poems contained
in it that the volume was reputedly burned by
the hangman in Edinburgh. Alasdair considered himself a propagandist for the Jacobite
cause; his patriotism was not, however, confined to an espousal of the Stewarts but was
extended to include the interests of the Gaelic-
speaking peoples of Scotland. The title of his
collection means 'Resurrection of the ancient
Scottish tongue' and Alasdair was stalwart in
his defence of the language. He also satirized
those who had failed to support the Jacobite
uprising, especially the Campbells, and he reserved particular scorn for the Hanoverian
dynasty in 'A Chanibal Dhuidsich', in which
George III is hailed as a cannibal from
Germany.

Alasdair's greatest single work is *Birlinn
Chlann Raghanill* ('The Birlinn of Clanranald')
which describes a voyage by sea from South
Uist to Carrickfergus in Ireland. It was translated by Hugh MacDiarmid (CHRISTOPHER
MURRAY GRIEVE) in 1935 and a vivid picture
emerges from it of the sights and sounds of a
journey over a treacherous sea. To this poem
Alasdair brought a sure eye for detail and a
meticulous power of observation, and added to
these virtues a steady rhythm, rather like the
beating of oars on sea water. The poem opens
with the blessing of the ship in verse couched
in traditional terms; it continues with a description of the rowers and their task and then
of the voyage itself as the ship runs through a
storm to the culmination of safety in port.

Alasdair is also remembered for his poem in
pibroch measure, 'Mòladh Moraig' ('In praise
of Morag'), and for his nature poetry, which
closely resembles THE SEASONS of JAMES

THOMSON (i). He influenced other later 18th-century Gaelic poets, including DONNCHADH BÀN MAC AN T-SAOIR, and his innovative use of language and rhymes and his disciplined intellect make him one of the finest Scottish poets of his day.

EDITION: A. and A. Macdonald, eds., *The Poems of Alexander Macdonald* (Inverness, 1924)

Albany, James. Pen-name of HUGH C. RAE.

Alexander, Sir William (i), Earl of Stirling (*c* 1567–1640). Poet. He was born at Menstrie in the parish of Logie, Clackmannanshire, and after the death of his father was placed in the care of his granduncle, James Alexander, a merchant in Stirling. He was educated there and at the universities of Glasgow and Leiden and later became a tutor to the Earl of Argyle, who introduced him to the court of JAMES VI in Edinburgh. There he became tutor to Prince Henry and was associated with the CASTALIAN BAND of poets who surrounded James. Political and social preferment followed his departure with the court to London after the Union of the Crowns in 1603: he was knighted in 1609; in 1621 he was granted the plantation of Nova Scotia and established the ill-advised baronetcies, a scheme that was foiled by the intervention of French interests in the area; five years later he became Secretary of State for Scotland; and in 1633 he was created Earl of Stirling. Towards the end of his life he encountered severe financial difficulties and he died in poverty on 12 September 1640 in London.

Alexander became one of the most powerful men of his generation but because of his involvement in political affairs he was unpopular in Scotland, where he attracted the scorn of many of his fellow countrymen. As a poet he wrote a number of tolerable sonnets, elegies and songs in *Aurora* (1604), and for Prince Henry he wrote the four *Monarchicke Tragedies* (1607) – *Darius* (1603, rev. 1607), *Croesus, The Alexandrian* and *Julius Caesar* – which lack any dramatic form owing to their over-rhetorical style, and are now little more than literary curiosities. His long poem of over 10,000 lines *Doomes-day* (1614) is an elaborate and tedious examination of sin, damnation and man's fall from grace.

WORKS: *Darius* (1603); *Aurora* (1604); *A Paraenesis to the Prince* (1604); *The Monarchicke Tragedies* (1607); *An Elegy on the Death of Prince Henry* (1612); *Doomes-day* (1614)

EDITION: L. E. Kastner and H. B. Charlton, eds., *The Poetical Works of Sir William Alexander, Earl of Stirling*, 2 vols. (Edinburgh and London, 1921–4)

Alexander, William (ii) (1826–94). Novelist. He was born in Chapel of Garioch, Aberdeenshire, in 1826 and was given a rudimentary education at the parish school. He worked as a farm-boy and ploughman until a farming accident in his early 20s caused him to have a leg amputated. Unable to work on the land he moved to Aberdeen, where he tried to earn a living from journalism. Although his early attempts brought only a modest income, he persevered with his writing and enjoyed his first success with the serialization between 1869 and 1870 in the *Aberdeen Free Press* of his novel JOHNNY GIBB OF GUSHETNEUK. With its scenes of country life and manners, told both in English and a vigorous, racy Scots, it enjoyed a wide popularity and was published in book form in 1871. Alexander lived to become editor of the newspaper that had given him so much encouragement and he continued to write in the vein that had brought him success. *Johnny Gibb of Gushetneuk* was reprinted several times during Alexander's lifetime; his other work of note is *Sketches of Life Among my Ain Folk* (1875).

WORKS: *Johnny Gibb of Gushetneuk* (1871); *Sketches of Life Among my Ain Folk* (1875); *Notes and Sketches* (1876); *Twenty-Five Years: a Personal Retrospect* (1878); with J. G. Mackie, *Memoir of the Late Andrew Jervie,* (1879); *Mrs Garden: a Memorial Sketch* (1887); *The Making of Aberdeenshire* (1888)

Alison, Sir Archibald (1792–1867). Historian. He was born on 29 December 1792 at Kenley, Shropshire, the son of a parson. In 1800 his family moved to Edinburgh and between 1805 and 1813 he was educated at the University of Edinburgh, where he read law. Called to the Bar on 8 December 1814, he became a financially successful advocate and was appointed Advocate-Depute in 1822. During this period he travelled extensively and enthusiastically in Europe. He married Elizabeth Glencairn, the niece of Lord Woodhouselee, on 21 March 1825. The defeat of Wellington's ministry in November 1830 ended Alison's hopes of political and legal advancement but in 1834 he accepted the office of Sheriff of Lanarkshire and settled at Possil House near Glasgow, which remained his home for the rest of his life. A popular figure in Glasgow, he was elected Lord Rector of its university in 1850, in preference to Lord Palmerston. He died on 23 May 1867.

Alison is best known as an author for his ten-volume *History of Europe*, begun early in 1829 and completed on 6 March 1842. The work enjoyed great popularity in its day, being translated into most European languages, and despite the extreme conservatism of Alison's attitudes it remains a useful summary of European history. Alison was also a regular contributor to BLACKWOOD'S MAGAZINE, for which he wrote a series of profiles of famous historical figures and a political column which denounced parliamentary reform. In 1861 he published *Lives of Lord Castlereagh and Sir Charles Stewart*. His autobiography, edited by his wife, appeared in 1883.

WORKS: *Principles of the Criminal Law of Scotland* (1832); *Practice of the Criminal Law in Scotland* (1833); *History of Europe during the French Revolution*, 10 vols. (1832–42); *The Principles of Human Population*, 2 vols. (1840); *England in 1815 and 1845* (1847); *Free Trade and Fettered Currency* (1847); *The Military Life of John, Duke of Marlborough* (1848); *Essays, Political, Historical and Miscellaneous*, 3 vols. (1850); *The Life of John, Duke of Marlborough*, 2 vols. (1852); *Lives of Lord Castlereagh and Sir Charles Stewart*, 3 vols. (1861); *Memoir of Patrick Fraser Tytler* (1873); Lady Alison, ed., *Some Account of my Life and Writings*, 2 vols. (1883); *The Old Scots Parliament* (1892)

Allan, David (1744–96). Artist, known as 'the Scottish Hogarth'. He was born in Alloa and educated at the Academy of Art founded by ROBERT FOULIS and forming part of the University of Glasgow from 1754 to 1775. Allan enjoyed the patronage of several noble families and studied in Rome before being appointed Director of the Trustees of the Academy of Art in Edinburgh in 1786. He was best known for his pastoral work – his illustrations to THE GENTLE SHEPHERD by ALLAN RAMSAY made him a household name. Through his friendship with GEORGE THOMSON Allan illustrated *A Select Collection of Original Scotish Airs*, work which Robert Burns admired greatly: 'He is the *only* Artist who has hit *genuine* Pastoral costume.' He also made engravings for Burns's TAM O'SHANTER and THE COTTER'S SATURDAY NIGHT. Other work illustrated by Allan included THE SEASONS by JAMES THOMSON (i).

Allan, John Robertson (*b* 1906). Journalist. He was born in Udny, Aberdeenshire, and was educated at the University of Aberdeen. His autobiographical story of the farming communities of the north-east of Scotland, *Farmer's Boy* (1935), is a classic study of childhood and is richly evocative of a bygone age. Allan worked as a journalist in Glasgow but returned later to his native Aberdeenshire to farm at Methlick. Most of his published work has been devoted to agricultural subjects but his *North-east Lowlands of Scotland* (1952) is a loving, though utterly unsentimental, account of the topography and history of the land of his birth.

WORKS: *A New Song to the Land* (1931); *Farmer's Boy* (1935); *Down on the Farm* (1937); *Scotland* (1938); *Summer in Scotland* (1938); *England Without End* (1940); *North East Lowlands of Scotland* (1952); *The Seasons Return* (1955); *Crombies of Grandholm and Cothal* (1960)

Alloway Kirk. A church at Alloway, Ayrshire, built in the early 16th century. It was last used for worship in 1756 and quickly became a ruin. ROBERT BURNS used it as the setting for the satanic happenings in his long narrative poem TAM O'SHANTER; his father WILLIAM BURNS lies buried in the churchyard.

Ambrose's Tavern. A tavern at 15 Picardy Place, Edinburgh, which became the meeting-place for many of the writers associated with BLACKWOOD'S MAGAZINE in its early days. It provided the setting for the fictitious 'NOCTES AMBROSIANAE', the monthly articles in *Blackwood's*, which purported to describe the dinners and highjinks enjoyed by JOHN WILSON (iii) ('Christopher North'), JAMES HOGG ('The Ettrick Shepherd') and ROBERT SYM ('Timothy Tickler'). The site of Ambrose's Tavern is now covered by West Register Street near the present-day Café Royal.

Ancient and Modern Scottish Songs. An anthology of Scottish songs and ballads made by DAVID HERD and published in two volumes in 1776. Herd was an enthusiastic collector of ballads, and his manuscript, which provides the basis for the collection, is the single most important store of surviving Scottish traditional songs. Both ROBERT BURNS and Sir WALTER SCOTT stated their debt to Herd's work, Scott calling it 'the first classical collection of Scottish songs and ballads' (*Introductory Remarks on Popular Poetry* (1830)). Like other 18th-century collectors, Herd published the songs and ballads without music, though he did give an indication of the tunes that were meant to be used. Herd's manuscript collection is divided between the British Museum and the library of the University of Edinburgh.

Ancrum, Earl of. *See* KER, ROBERT.

Anderson, Alexander ['Surfaceman'] (1845–1909). Poet. Alexander Anderson, who wrote under the name 'Surfaceman', was born on 30 April 1845 at Kirkconnel, Dumfriesshire, but spent most of his childhood at Crocketford in Galloway. He was educated at the local school but spent his spare time gaining a fluent knowledge of German, French and Spanish. Through his self-education Anderson was able to leave his work as a railway navvy or surfaceman, and in 1881 he was appointed assistant librarian at the University of Edinburgh, becoming librarian in 1901. He died on 11 July 1909. Anderson wrote four collections of light verse and is best remembered for his 'cuddle doon' poems (lullabies for children), and his poems celebrating the railways in *A Song of Love and Labour* (1873) and *Songs of the Rail* (1878).

WORKS: *A Song of Love and Labour and Other Poems* (1873); *The Two Angels* (1875); *Songs of the Rail* (1878); *Ballads and Sonnets* (1879)

EDITION: A. Brown, ed., *Later Poems of Alexander Anderson* (Glasgow, 1912)

REFERENCE: A. Brown, *Surfaceman: a Biographical Sketch* (Glasgow, 1912)

Anderson, Willa ['Agnes N. Scott'] (1890–1970). Novelist and translator. She was born and brought up in Shetland, and studied classics at the University of St Andrews, where she also taught for a period after graduation. In 1918 she became Vice-Principal of Gipsy Hill Training College in London, and it was at that time that she met EDWIN MUIR, whom she married on 7 June 1919. With Muir she translated works by Franz Kafka, Lion Feuchtwanger and several other contemporary European novelists, and she was a constant source of encouragement to her husband during the frequent tribulations of his literary career. After his death she published a moving memoir of their life together, *Belonging* (1968), and, using her husband's notes, she wrote *Living with Ballads* (1965). Several of her translations were published under the name

'Agnes N. Scott'. Under he own name she wrote two original novels: *Imagined Corners* (1931) and *Mrs Ritchie* (1933). She died on 22 May 1970.

WORKS: *Imagined Corners* (1931); *Mrs Ritchie* (1933); *Mrs Grundy in Scotland* (1936); *Living with Ballads* (1965); *Belonging: a Memoir* (1968)

Andrew, St. The fourth in rank of the apostles of Jesus Christ and the adopted patron saint of Scotland. Andrew plays a small part in the Gospels; tradition claims that he was martyred at Patras in Achaia on the *crux decussata*, the image of which – an X-shaped cross in white on a dark blue background – forms the Scottish 'saltire' or national flag. During the early Middle Ages the church in Scotland propagated the story that Andrew's relics had been brought to Scotland by St Regulus, or St Rule, and that the burial place at Kilrymont in Fife had become the site of the Cathedral of St Andrews. These claims have no basis in fact and may have their origins in the desire to reinforce the story, related by JOHN OF FORDUN and others, of the appearance of St Andrew's cross in the sky before a Pictish victory over the Anglian King Athelstane in present-day East Lothian. More obviously, they may have gained a wider currency through the Church's ambitions to reinforce the primacy of St Andrews as an ecclesiastical centre. St Andrew's Day, or ANERMAS, is principally celebrated by expatriate Scots.

Andrew of Wyntoun (c1355–1422). Historian. He held the position of canon regular at St Andrews, and between 1395 and 1413 he was Prior of St Serf's Inch, the island on Lochleven where MARY, Queen of Scots, was later imprisoned. At the request of Sir John Wemyss, his patron, he wrote at the end of the 14th century his ORYGYNALE CRONYKIL OF SCOTLAND, a history of Scotland from the Creation to his own times, in which he also established the nature of Scottish independence. Written in rhyming couplets of eight syllables, the chronicle sheds an interesting light on earlier periods of Scotland's history for which there is little contemporary evidence.

Anermas [St Andrew's Day]. The Feast of St Andrew, which falls on 30 November. Although no longer a popular festival, it is still celebrated overseas by expatriate Scots.

Angus, Marion (1866–1946). Poet. She was born in Aberdeen but spent her childhood in Arbroath, where her father was a minister. Most of her adult life was spent in Aberdeen but she also lived in Helensburgh and Edinburgh and was an early member of Scottish PEN. She died on 18 August 1946 in Arbroath.

Most of Marion Angus's poetry was influenced by traditional ballad material, and her best work is in Scots, especially in poems dealing with unrequited love such as 'Mary's Song' and 'Think Lang'. Her best-known poem is the often anthologized 'Alas, Poor Queen', a lament for MARY, Queen of Scots. Her *Selected Poems* (1950) were edited by MAURICE LINDSAY.

WORKS: *The Lilt and Other Poems* (1922); *The Tinker's Road* (1924); *Sun and Candlelight* (1927); *The Singin' Lass* (1929); *The Turn of the Day* (1931); *Lost Country* (1937); M. Lindsay, ed., *Selected Poems* (1950)

Annals of the Parish. A novel by JOHN GALT, first published in 1821. It is more a series of sketches or scenes from country life than a novel with a plot, and from his *Autobiography* we know that Galt had intended to write 'a book that would be for Scotland what *The Vicar of Wakefield* is for England'. The narrator of the annals is the Revd Micah Balwhidder, who records the history of the village of Dalmailing from 1760 to 1810; during that period several significant changes are set in train: agricultural methods improve, a cotton mill is established, a turnpike road is opened, and a stage-coach runs to Glasgow. Although Balwhidder is at pains to note the passing of the seasons with their timeless, simple ceremonials, and to include the trivia of everyday life, the village is no cut-off rural backwater. The impact of the outside world is continually felt as young men emigrate or prepare for hostilities during the French Revolution. The telling of the life of the village assumes a universality and Dalmailing becomes the centre of its own cosmos. Throughout the novel Galt paints in the finer details of the people's lives and the background in which they live. Something of that concern for detail is captured in the painting *The Penny Wedding*, executed by Galt's friend DAVID WILKIE to illustrate a scene from the novel. The publication of the *Annals of the Parish* established John Galt as a novelist of the first order.

Annand, J(ames) K(ing) (*b* 1908). Poet. He was born on 2 February 1908 in Edinburgh and was educated there at Broughton Secondary School and at the University of Edinburgh. While a schoolboy he edited the *Broughton Magazine* which published some of the early work of Hugh MacDiarmid (CHRISTOPHER MURRAY GRIEVE), including 'O Jesu parvule' in 1925. After graduating in 1930 Annand taught in schools in Edinburgh and Whithorn, Wigtonshire. During World War II he served with the Royal Navy between 1941 and 1946. Although never a prolific poet, Annand's work is written in an aggrandized Scots which has been enriched by his careful scholarly learning. He has translated work from German and medieval Latin into Scots, and his *Songs from Carmina Burana* (1978) captures much of the earthy humour of the original. However, Annand is no mere pedant and, like WILLIAM SOUTAR, has given endless delight to children with his bairn-rhymes, collected in three volumes: *Sing it Aince for Pleisure* (1965), *Twice for Joy* (1973), *Thrice to Show Ye* (1979). He has been an editor of LINES REVIEW and has edited the magazine of the Scots Language Society, *Lallans*, since 1973.

WORKS: *Sing it Aince for Pleisure* (1965); ed., *Early Lyrics by Hugh MacDiarmid* (1968); *Two Voices* (1968); *Twice for Joy* (1973); *Poems and Translations* (1975); *Songs from Carmina Burana* (1978); *Thrice to Show Ye* (1979); ed., *A Scots Handsel* (1980)

Anster Fair. A poem by WILLIAM TENNANT, first published in 1812; it takes its theme from the earlier poem by FRANCIS SEMPILL, 'Maggie Lauder'. A mock-heroic comedy, it follows the traditional Scottish theme (compare 'HALLOW FAIR' by ROBERT FERGUSSON and 'THE HOLY FAIR' by ROBERT BURNS) of country people celebrating a traditional festival, in this poem at Anstruther, Fife. Written in English, but with a Scots accent never far away in its comic rhymes, the poem uses a stanza form that was later taken up by Lord Byron in *Don Juan*.

Antiquary, The. A novel by Sir WALTER SCOTT published in 1816. In the Preface Scott stated his intentions: 'The present Work completes a series of fictitious narratives, intended to illustrate the manners of Scotland at three different periods. *Waverley* embraced the age of our fathers, *Guy Mannering* that of our youth, and *The Antiquary* refers to the last ten years of the eighteenth century.' The hero of novel is Jonathan Oldbuck, the Laird of Monk-barns, whose historical and antiquarian inter-ests hark back to the Scotland of long ago. He was based on Scott's friend George Constable, but his antiquarian hobbies mirror many of those held by the author himself, and he re-mains one of the most endearing and true-to-life portraits created by Scott.

The plot of *The Antiquary*, like that of its predecessor GUY MANNERING, is taken up with the theme of the 'missing heir'. An English-man, Major Neville, having wooed his loved one, Isabella Wardour, unsuccessfully, as-sumes the name 'Lovel' and pursues her to Scotland. There he turns out to be the heir to the estate of Glenallan and is free to marry Isabella, whose father, the pompous Sir Ar-thur, removes all objections to the match. Before that happy ending can be achieved, Neville fights a duel with Oldbuck's nephew Hector M'Intyre, rescues Isabella and saves Sir Arthur from ruin at the hands of the rascally Dousterswivel. As a result he enjoys the friend-ship of Oldbuck and of Edie Ochiltree, a sturdy character from stoic farming stock. *The Anti-quary*, which Scott admitted to be his favourite novel, displays a sure ear for the cadences of poor country life.

Aphelli. *See* UP-HELLY-AA.

Arbroath, Declaration of [Declaration of In-dependence]. A Letter of April 1320 to Pope John XXII, produced by the clergy of Scotland and assented to by the nobility, stating their allegiance to ROBERT I (Robert the Bruce) as King of Scots. Three years later the pope gave Bruce the title of king but the bull granting his anointing did not arrive until after Bruce's death in 1329. BERNARD DE LINTON, Robert's chancellor, is thought to have been the princi-pal author of the document, which is com-posed in the rhythmical *curseus* of medieval Latin. The Declaration remains the most pow-erful statement of the concept of Scottish independence: 'For so long as there shall be but one hundred of us remain alive, we will never consent to subject ourselves to the dominion of the English.'

Arbuthnot, Alexander (i) (*d* 1585). Printer. Alexander Arbuthnot, who has often been confused with his namesake (*see* ARBUTHNOT, ALEXANDER (ii)), was a Burgess of the City of Edinburgh. With his partner THOMAS BASSEN-DYNE, he printed the first Bible in Scotland. Following its success Arbuthnot was appointed printer to the church for the production of Bibles on a large scale; in this work he was greatly helped by the act of 1579 which com-pelled every householder to possess a copy of the Bible. He also printed the first volume of *Rerum scoticarum historia* by GEORGE BUCHANAN.

Arbuthnot, Alexander (ii) (1538–83). Poet. He was a leading member of the Reformation movement in Scotland and one of the early theorists with ANDREW MELVILLE of church government. He was twice Moderator of the General Assembly and between 1569 and his death on 10 October 1583 he was Principal of King's College, Aberdeen. He wrote a Latin treatise on church law, and three of his poems in Scots, 'On Luve', 'The Miseries of a Pure Scholar' and 'The Praises of Women' (a poem that established womankind as the object of God's praise, and perhaps his best-known work), were published in *Ancient Scottish Poems* by JOHN PINKERTON in 1786.

Arbuthnott, John (1667–1735). Physician and satirist. He was born on 29 April 1667 in Kincardineshire and was educated at the uni-versities of Aberdeen, Oxford and St An-drews. He settled in London and was appointed physician to Queen Anne. He died on 27 February 1735. A close friend of Jonathan Swift (1667–1745) and Alexander Pope (1688–1744), he was the main author of the *Memoirs of Martin Scriblerus* which was pub-lished with Pope's *Works* in 1741. He was an advocate of the ACT OF UNION of 1707, and in 1706 wrote a satirical essay in its support – *A Sermon Preached to the People at the Mercat Cross, Edinburgh.*

WORKS: *An Essay on the Usefulness of Mathematical Learning* (1701); *A Sermon Preached to the People at the Mercat Cross Edinburgh* (1706); *The History of John Bull* (1712); *Law is a Bottom-less Pit* (1712); *A Treatise on the Art of Political Lying* (1712); *An Invitation to Peace* (1713); *A Review of the State of John Bull's Family* (1713); *A Farther Continuation of the History of the Crown Inn* (1714); *A Fourth and Last Part of the History of the Crown Inn* (1714); *A Postscript to John Bull* (1714); *The Present State of the Crown Inn* (1717); *Tables of Ancient Coins* (1727); with Alexander Pope, *Esther, an Oratoric or Sacred Drama* (1732); *An Essay Concerning the Effects of Air on Human Bodies* (1733); *Critical Remarks on Dr Gulliver's Travels* (1735); *An Essay Concerning the Nature of Aliments* (1735); with Alexander Pope, *Memoirs of an Extraordinary Life* (1741)

EDITIONS: *The Miscellaneous Works of the Late Dr Arbuthnott*, 2 vols. (Glasgow, 1751); G. Aitken, ed., *The Life and Works of John Arbuthnott* (Glasgow, 1892)

Archer, William (1856–1924). Critic. He was born on 23 September 1856 in Perth and was educated there and at the University of Edinburgh. After graduating he studied for the English Bar but by then he had turned to journalism for a living. He worked first for the *Evening News* in Edinburgh, and between 1879 and 1881, by which time he had moved to London, he was employed as the drama critic of *Figaro*. From then until the end of his life Archer devoted himself to the theatre through his work as a critic for *The World*, *The Nation*, *Tribune*, the *Morning Leader* and the *Manchester Guardian*: he became one of the most influential critics of the day with a firm belief in good dramatic structure and high standards of stagecraft. He died in London on 27 December 1924.

Although he did much to revitalize the English theatre through his outspoken criticism, it is as the translator of the works of the Norwegian playwright Henrik Ibsen (1826–1906) that Archer is best remembered; it was in his translations of the prose dramas, collected in four volumes (1890–91), and the complete works, published in 11 volumes (1906–7), that Ibsen's work was introduced to the theatre in England. In 1923 Archer's own play *The Green Goddess* was staged successfully in London, two years after it opened in New York. His other dramatic works are *War is War*, *Martha Washington*, *Beatrice Juana* and *Lidia*. Many of his journalistic writings were collected in book form and among his writings on the theory of theatre may be mentioned *Masks or Faces* (1888) and *Play-making* (1912), which were considered the standard works on the art of stagecraft and plot. Archer was also a campaigning journalist with interests in criminology, rational humanism and race relations, and with Harley Granville-Barker (1877–1946) and others he was active in the drive to create a national theatre.

WORKS: with R. W. Lowe, *The Fashionable Tragedian* (1877); *English Dramatists of Today* (1882); *Henry Irving: a Critical Study* (1883); *Henry Irving: Actor and Manager* (1884); *About the Theatre* (1886); *Masks or Faces* (1888); *William Charles Macready* (1890); *Study and Stage* (1899); *America Today* (1900); *Poets of the Younger Generation* (1902); *Real Conversations* (1904); *Shirking the Issue* (1904); *A National Theatre: Scheme and Estimates* (1907); *Through Afro-America* (1910); *The Life, Trial and Death of Francisco Ferrer* (1911); *Play-making* (1912); *Fighting a Philosophy* (1914); *The Thirteen Days: 23 July – 4 August 1914* (1915); *Colour-blind Neutrality* (1916); *Knowledge and Character* (1916); *501 Gems of German Thought* (1917); *God and the Wells* (1917); *India and the Future* (1917); *Six of One and Half-a-dozen of the Other* (1917); *The Villains of World Tragedy* (1917); *The Peace-President* (1918); *The Pirate's Progress* (1918); *War is War* (1919); *The Green Goddess* (1923); *The Old Drama and The New* (1923); *Three Plays* (1927); *The Great Analysis* (1931); *On Dreams* (1935)

EDITION: J. M. Robertson, ed., *William Archer as Rationalist* (London, 1925)

REFERENCE: C. Archer, *William Archer, Life, Work and Friendships* (London, 1931)

Aretina. A novel by Sir GEORGE MACKENZIE (II), of Rosehaugh, published in 1660. It is generally considered to be the first novel published in Scotland and is one of the rare printed books in the NATIONAL LIBRARY OF SCOTLAND. 447 pages long, the volume includes a dedication 'To all the Ladies of this Nation', two Royalist poems, and an 'Apologie for Romance' in which Mackenzie set out his aims – to compose a serious romance in the classical Greek tradition and the later European romance tradition. The plot is simple and conventional. Monanthropus, the Chancellor of Egypt, witnesses the rescue of two ladies (who play no further part) by two knights, Megistus and Philarites. At his house Philarites falls in love with Aretina, as does Megistus, later, with Agapeta. Through their new found friendships the knights are drawn into political intrigue in Egypt, as Sophander, a corrupt favourite, plots with the Persians to overthrow the throne of Egypt. After several battles, virtue triumphs and Sophander is led away for execution. The third book is a coded history of the civil war in Scotland. In the fourth book Mackenzie returns to Aretina's story in a romance of intrigue as Monanthropus tests the lovers' affections by arranging a mock kidnapping. Interspersed in the narrative of all the books are Mackenzie's discourses on such diverse subjects as life at court, physiognomy and madness. Although the romance of *Aretina* has only a certain curiosity value the coded history contained in book 3 is a useful personal account of events which were close to Mackenzie's own lifetime; it is similar in effect to *Euphormionis satyricon* (1603), a coded satire on the Jesuits written in France by John Barclay (1582–1621).

Argyll, 2nd Duke of. *See* CAMPBELL, JOHN.

Argyll, 8th Earl and 1st Marquis of. *See* CAMP-BELL, ARCHIBALD.

Armour, Jean (1767–1834). The wife of ROBERT BURNS, whom she met in 1784 in Mauchline. When she became pregnant in 1785 Burns offered her a written declaration of intent, which then formed a marriage contract, but this was mutilated by her father and the Ayr lawyer ROBERT AIKEN. After appearing before WILLIAM AULD, the minister of Mauchline, Burns was declared a single man but Jean Armour's father was intent on enforcing payment for the unborn child. Burns went into hiding and contemplated emigration to the West Indies, but the success of the KILMARNOCK EDITION of his poems in 1786 partially reconciled the Armours to Burns. By April 1788, after two sets of twins had been born to them, Burns acknowledged Jean as his wife, despite several mystifying letters that imply the contrary; she bore him nine children. Burns wrote 14 songs for her of which the best known is *Of a' the airts the wind can blaw*.

Armstrong, John ['Launcelot Taylor'] (1709–79). Poet. He was a native of Castleton, Roxburghshire. He studied medicine at the University of Edinburgh, graduating in 1732, and set up in practice in London. There he became a friend of DAVID MALLOCH and began writing verse, much of it inspired by medical subjects. In 1746 he became physician to the Hospital for Lame, Maimed and Sick Soldiers in London, and he was appointed physician to the British Army in Germany in 1760. Ten years later he was back in London and that was to be his home until his death on 7 September 1779. Armstrong destroyed much of his work during his own lifetime; although there is a light Augustan touch to his verse epistle, 'A Day' (inscribed to John Wilkes, 1727–97), most of his extant work is little more than pastiche, full of pseudo-scientific jargon. *The Art of Preserving Health* contains much sensible medical advice but it is stilted and uninspired poetry.

WORKS: *The Art of Preserving Health* (1744); *Taste: an Epistle to a Young Critic* (1753); *A Day: an Epistle to John Wilkes* (1761); *Miscellanies* (1770)

REFERENCE: W. J. M. L. Maloney, *George and John Armstrong of Castleton* (Edinburgh, 1954)

Armstrong, William ['Kinmont Willie'] (*fl.* 1590). Border reiver. He took his nickname, 'Kinmont Willie', from his keep at Kinmont near Canonby in Dumfriesshire. Armstrong stole cattle from his English neighbours on a grand scale but he was not above raiding his own country – in 1585 he took part in the sacking of Stirling during the Earl of Angus's campaign. He is best remembered for his 'illegal' capture and imprisonment in Carlisle following a truce on 17 March 1596. The failure of diplomacy to secure his release led to a raid on Carlisle Castle by his kinsman Walter Scott of Buccleuch who freed him on 13 April 1596; this incident is skilfully, if bombastically, retold in the ballad 'Kinmont Willie', which Sir WALTER SCOTT included in the MINSTRELSY OF THE SCOTTISH BORDER.

Arnot, Hugo (1749–86). Historian. He was born on 8 December 1749 in Leith, the son of a merchant named Pollock. Arnot changed his name in early life in order to take over his mother's estate at Balcomo in Fife. He trained as an advocate but ill health forced him to interrupt his studies and he turned to historical research and writing. He lived in Edinburgh until his death on 20 April 1786. His most influential work is his meticulously researched *History of Edinburgh* (1779), which remains a standard reference book. His other work of importance is *A Collection of Celebrated Criminal Trials in Scotland with Historical and Critical Remarks* (1785).

WORKS: *Juridica* (1772); *An Essay on Nothing* (1776); *A Letter to the Lord Advocate of Scotland* (1777); *The History of Edinburgh* (1779); *A Collection of Celebrated Criminal Trials in Scotland with Historical and Critical Remarks* (1785)

Asloan Manuscript. A manuscript collection of Middle Scots poems made in 1515 by one John Asloan, the first of the large 16th-century manuscripts. It was in the library of Sir ALEXANDER BOSWELL of Auchinleck and later that of Lord Talbot de Malahide, who presented it to the NATIONAL LIBRARY OF SCOTLAND. The SCOTTISH TEXT SOCIETY published the manuscript in two volumes in 1923–5.

EDITION: W. A. Craigie, ed., *The Asloan Manuscript*, 2 vols., STS (Edinburgh and London, 1923–5)

Association for Scottish Literary Studies. A publishing society founded in 1970 to promote the study, teaching and writing of Scottish literature and to further the study of the languages of Scotland. The Association edits and publishes an annual volume of out-of-print literary texts and is the publisher of the *Scottish Literary Journal*.

Athens of the North, the. A name used of Edinburgh during the 18th century and still in common use. The first reference to a comparison between Edinburgh and Athens is in James Stuart's *Antiquities of Athens* (1762), but according to Lord Cockburn the name came into popular usage only from about the beginning of the 19th century when Edinburgh began to take an interest in the construction of grand civic buildings (as had happened during the age of Pericles in Athens). Its use was also allied to the building of the Georgian New Town, the intellectual mood of the SCOTTISH ENLIGHTENMENT and the increased interest in commerce, law and education during that period.

Auld, William (1709–91). Presbyterian minister in the village of Mauchline. In the summer of 1786 he publicly reproved ROBERT BURNS for his fornication with JEAN ARMOUR. He appears as Father Auld in the head-note to Burns's 'HOLY WILLIE'S PRAYER' and as Daddy Auld in 'The Kirk's Alarm'.

Auld Alliance. The name given to the treaties drawn up between Scotland and France; it is also used more informally to describe the cultural and historical links between the two countries. The first evidence of a formal alliance is found in a series of treaties, the first of which was signed in 1295 by John Baliol and Philipe de Bel and ratified in 1326 by ROBERT I (Robert the Bruce). It was renewed in 1359 by David II, and it became an important tenet of the Stewarts' domestic and foreign policies to maintain the French connection. JAMES IV invaded England in 1513 to uphold his treaty obligations, and his son JAMES V married two French wives, Madeleine de Valois and, after her death, Mary of Guise-Lorraine. The official alliance was dissolved in 1560 but the two countries continued to maintain powerful cultural links during the 17th century; after 1746 France became the centre for JACOBITE sympathies following the failure of THE FORTY-FIVE rebellion. The links between the two countries provided a cross-fertilization of ideas, and the French influence in Scotland has been felt in the nation's vocabulary, architecture and literature, as well as in its culinary habits. Scots mercenaries fought in France and the Garde Ecossaise was the bodyguard to the French throne. Tradition has it that the Auld Alliance had its origins in the reign of Charlemagne who became a popular folk figure in Scotland and who makes an appearance in the anonymous alliterative poem RAUF COILZEAR.

Auld Farmer's New Year Morning Salutation to his Auld Mare Maggie, The. A poem by ROBERT BURNS, 'on giving her the accustomed ripp of corn to hansel in the New Year'. It takes the form of a monologue between the farmer and his old mare on New Year's morning as he remembers her in her prime and himself in his youth. Despite the keenly felt emotion of their fondly remembered companionship, Burns avoids sentimentality by presenting a realistic picture of the farmer's attitude to his work which is never pathetic or self-pitying.

Auld Lang Syne. Song of remembered friendship used throughout the English-speaking world as a communal farewell. Variations have appeared in the folk tradition and in broadsides, and it has been reworked by several poets including Sir ROBERT AYTON and ALLAN RAMSAY. The best-known version is by ROBERT BURNS, who never claimed it as his own but, in a letter to Mrs Dunlop of Dunlop of 17 December 1788, stated that he had amended the fragment of a 'heaven-inspired poet' and had sent it to JAMES JOHNSON for inclusion in the fifth volume of THE SCOTS MUSICAL MUSEUM.

Auld Licht Idylls. A collection of stories of Scottish village life written by J. M. BARRIE from 1884 and published in 1888. The first story, *An Auld Licht Community*, had been published in the *St James's Gazette* by Sir Frederick Greenwood in November 1884, and it was followed, at the editor's insistence, by other stories set in Thrums, the thinly disguised Kirriemuir of Barrie's childhood. Most of the stories were based on the memories of Barrie's mother, Margaret Ogilvy, and their publication met with instant acclaim among the London literary critics, who saw in them an accurate reflection of Scottish pastoral life. In reality the stories that make up *Auld Licht Idylls* were exaggerated pastiches, whimsically told and imbued with the pawky sense of humour that characterized so much of Barrie's later work. The characters are nothing less than caricatures and an atmosphere of mockery runs through the accounts of the villagers' lives, loves and deaths. The publication of Barrie's book prompted numerous imitations and placed Barrie firmly in the KAILYARD school of sentimental story-telling. The 'Auld Lichts' of the title refers to the seceders of 1733 within the Church of Scotland who upheld the Solemn League and Covenant. Barrie wrote as a sequel a further collection of stories, *A Window in Thrums* (1889), also prompted by his mother and set in Kirriemuir.

Auld Reekie (i) ('Old Smokey'). A name by which Edinburgh is known. Tradition claims that the inhabitants of Fife, on the other side of the Firth of Forth, could tell the time of day from the smoke of the city's chimneys when cooking for dinner began. ROBERT CHAMBERS in his *Traditions of Edinburgh* (1824) dates the phrase from the reign of Charles II but it was probably in use before then.

Auld Reekie (ii). A poem of 328 lines by ROBERT FERGUSSON, published in 1773. It was first produced as a pamphlet, and 40 lines were added to it in the posthumous edition of Fergusson's *Poems* (1779) by WALTER RUDDIMAN. *Auld Reekie* gives an evocative portrait of Edinburgh, its citizens and its low life; Fergusson describes in detail the city's night life, the taverns and clubs, Sunday afternoon walks and the debtors' sanctuary at Holyrood. Although the city is chided for its dirt and smells, the poem is Fergusson's hymn of praise to Edinburgh and he pays particular tribute to the Lord Provost George Drummond who was largely responsible for the construction of the New Town. The poem was the first part of a planned comedy of Edinburgh life which was cut short by Fergusson's death in 1774.

Ayton [Aytoun], Sir **Robert** (1570–1638). Poet. He was born at Kinaldie near St Andrews and was educated at St Andrews University between 1584 and 1588. During a Continental tour he studied law in Paris, returning to Scotland in 1603 to become a member of the court of JAMES VI. He followed James to London and enjoyed a number of public honours, including the post of secretary to the queen. He was knighted in 1612 and after his death in Feb-

ruary 1638 he was buried in Westminster Abbey.

Ayton wrote a number of poems in the style of the English metaphysical poets but he lacked their brilliant technical ability and most of his work has been forgotten. He also contributed a number of Latin poems for state occasions to Sir JOHN SCOTT of Scotstarvit's DELITIAE POETARUM SCOTORUM (1637). He is justly remembered for his songs and his easy ability to wed court song to native air. In the 18th century, JAMES WATSON, in his CHOICE COLLECTION OF COMIC AND SERIOUS SCOTS POEMS, credited Ayton with a version of the song AULD LANG SYNE, which was later reworked by ALLAN RAMSAY and, more successfully, by ROBERT BURNS.

EDITIONS: C. Roger, ed., *Poems of Sir Robert Ayton* (Edinburgh, 1844); C. B. Gullans, ed., *The English and Latin Poems of Sir Robert Ayton*, STS (Edinburgh and London, 1963)

Aytoun, William Edmonstoune (1813–65). Poet and humorist. He was born on 21 June 1813 in Edinburgh. His father was a WRITER TO THE SIGNET and one of the founders of the Edinburgh Academy, to which Aytoun was sent in 1824. Between 1828 and 1833 he studied law at the University of Edinburgh, and he published his first collection of poems, mainly romantic pastiches, *Poland, Homer and Other Poems* in 1832. On graduating he travelled in Germany before joining his father's law firm. In 1836 he made his first contributions to BLACKWOOD'S MAGAZINE, associating himself with its conservative politics; for *Blackwood's* he wrote over 200 poems, political articles and short stories, including 'How we got up the Glenmutchkin Railway' (October, 1845), a droll exposé of railway mania which indicted both unscrupulous speculators and gullible buyers, and 'How I stood for the Dreepdailly Burghs' (September, 1847), a satire on political sycophancy. Aytoun formally joined the staff of *Blackwood's* in 1844 and the following year he was appointed Professor of Rhetoric and Belles Lettres at the University of Edinburgh. On 11 April 1849 he married Jane Emily, the daughter of JOHN WILSON (iii). He continued to practise at the Bar and for his support of Protectionism, Derby's government rewarded him with the Sheriffship and Lord Admiralty of Orkney and Shetland in 1852.

With Sir THEODORE MARTIN Aytoun wrote *The Book of Ballads edited by Bon Gaultier*

(1845), 'Bon Gaultier' being the pseudonym that Martin had used previously. The ballads are parodies and burlesques of contemporary poems such as Tennyson's 'Locksley Hall' and Hunt's 'Rimini' which had appeared originally in *Fraser's Magazine* and TAIT'S EDINBURGH MAGAZINE. They were added to and republished in 1857 and are known popularly as 'THE BON GAULTIER BALLADS'. Aytoun's best-known work is LAYS OF THE SCOTTISH CAVALIERS AND OTHER POEMS, published in 1849, which became a Victorian bestseller. The ballad romances, written in the style of Sir WALTER SCOTT and Thomas Babington Macaulay, deal with such historical subjects as the BATTLE OF FLODDEN, the pilgrimage of THE BLACK DOUGLAS to the Holy Land to bury the heart of ROBERT I (Robert the Bruce), and an account of exiled soldiers of JOHN GRAHAM, 'Bonnie Dundee', fighting in the service of the French.

As a critic for *Blackwood's* Aytoun attacked the so-called Spasmodic school of poets, P. J. Bailey (1816–1902), Sydney Dobell (1824–74) and ALEXANDER SMITH, who were popular in the 1840s. In their work, the poet–heroes lead lives of mysterious spiritual insularity which force them to commit bizarre acts in striving to discover the secrets of the universe. In the May 1854 issue of *Blackwood's* Aytoun published a burlesque review, with copious extracts, of an imaginary Spasmodic poem, *Firmilian: or the Student of Badajoz, a Spasmodic Tragedy* by T. Percy Jones, and he followed up the review by actually writing the poem *Firmilian* and publishing it in *Blackwood's* three months later. The hero, Firmilian, is engaged in writing a tragedy about Cain and in

order to equip himself for the task he embarks on a series of crimes with absurd results. The publication of *Firmilian* and its success as a parody effectively destroyed the popularity of the Spasmodics.

In 1856 Aytoun published *Bothwell*, a long poem about the events surrounding the relationship of MARY, Queen of Scots, with her third husband JAMES HEPBURN, 4th Earl of Bothwell. Written in ballad form, it is marred by historical inaccuracy and its dependency on the monologue of its hero. Aytoun also published *The Ballads of Scotland* (1858), a collection of 139 carefully excised Scottish ballads. His autobiographical novel, *Norman Sinclair*, was published four years before his death on 4 August 1865. A memoir of his life was published by his friend and collaborator Sir Theodore Martin in 1867.

WORKS: *Poland, Homer and Other Poems* (1832); *The Life and Times of Richard the First* (1840); *Our Zion, or Presbyterian Popery, by ane of that Ilk* (1840); *The Drummond Schism Examined and Exposed* (1842); *The Book of Ballads edited by Bon Gaultier* (1845); *Lays of the Scottish Cavaliers and Other Poems* (1849); *Firmilian: or the Student of Badajoz by T. Percy Jones* (1854); *Bothwell: a Poem* (1856); ed., *The Ballads of Scotland*, 2 vols. (1858); with Theodore Martin, *Poems and Ballads of Goethe* (1859); *Inaugural Address to the Associated Societies of the University of Edinburgh* (1861); *Norman Sinclair*, 3 vols. (1861); ed., *The Poetical Works of Thomas Campbell* (1862); *Nuptial Ode on the Marriage of His Royal Highness the Prince of Wales* (1863)

EDITIONS: F. Page, ed., *Poems* (Oxford, 1921); W. L. Renwick, ed., *Stories and Verse* (Edinburgh, 1964)

REFERENCES: E. Frykman, *W. E. Aytoun: Pioneer Professor of English at Edinburgh* (Gothenburg, 1963); M. A. Weinstein, *William Edmonstoune Aytoun and the Spasmodic Controversy* (New Haven, Conn., and London, 1968)

B

Bachelors' Club. A debating club founded on 11 November 1780 by ROBERT BURNS and a group of friends in the village of Tarbolton. Burns was elected its first chairman and among the subjects debated were questions involving love, friendship and liberty. The club, which was never to exceed a membership of 16, continued for several years after Burns's death and its meeting-place has been preserved as a museum.

Baillie [née Home], Lady **Grizel** [Grisell] (1665–1746). Songwriter. She was born on Christmas Day 1665, the daughter of Sir Patrick Home, a noted Covenanter. Much of her youth was spent enduring the persecution of her family who had sheltered Robert Baillie of Jerviswood, the Covenanting scholar and scientist whose brother George she later married. She was with her father in exile in Utrecht until the Restoration, when her family was able to return to Scotland. Lady Grizel was the first in a long line of 18th-century songwriters and is best known for her song, 'Werena my heart licht I wad die' which was published in 1724 in the collection THE TEA-TABLE MISCELLANY by ALLAN RAMSAY. She was also a patron of JAMES THOMSON (i). Her domestic memorabilia were collected and published under the title *The Household Book* in 1911.

EDITION: R. Scott-Moncrieff, ed., *The Household Book of Lady Grisell Baillie, 1692–1733* (Edinburgh, 1911)

REFERENCE: Countess of Ashburnham, *Lady Grisell Baillie: a Sketch of her Life and Character* (London, 1893)

Baillie, Joanna (1762–1851). Poet and dramatist. She was born on 11 September 1762 at Bothwell, Lanarkshire, the daughter of a minister. In 1778 her father died and six years later the family moved to London to the house of their cousin Dr William Hunter (1718–83).

Her first collection of poems, *Fugitive Pieces*, was published anonymously in 1790 and her other collections are *Metrical Legends* (1821) and *A Collection of Poems* (1823). Although most of her poetry is in the minor key, she had a sure use of Scots and wrote a number of memorable songs including 'Woo'd an' married an' a'' and 'It fell upon a mornin' when we were thrang'.

Joanna Baillie enjoyed a greater reputation as a dramatist and her work was admired by Sir WALTER SCOTT. Her first works, a series called *Plays of Passion*, which included *The Tryal* and *De Montfort*, were published in 1798, but her development of character lacked stagecraft and the plays were less successful on their first production in London in April 1800. A second series, which included *Hatred* and *Ambition*, were also stage failures, though she continued to receive generous notices for her literary style and praise for her efforts to restore the dramatic grandeur of true tragedy. More successful, from the theatrical point of view, was *The Family Legend* about the Argyle family, which was produced in Edinburgh in 1810 with a prologue by Scott. A third series of plays was published in 1836. She died on 23 February 1851 in London.

WORKS: *Plays of Passion* (1798); *Metrical Legends of Exalted Characters* (1821); *A Collection of Poems* (1823); *The Martyr* (1826); *The Bride* (1828); *A View of the General Tenor of the New Testament* (1831); *Lines on the Death of Sir Walter Scott* (1832); *Miscellaneous Plays* (1834); *Dramas*, 3 vols. (1836); *Dramatic and Poetical Works* (1836); *Fugitive Pieces* (1840); *Ahalya Baee* (1849); *The Family Legend* (1870)

REFERENCE: M. S. Carhart, *The Life and Work of Joanna Baillie* (New Haven, Conn., 1923)

Baillie, Robert (1602–62). Divine. He was born in 1602 in Glasgow, the son of a merchant. He was educated at the University of Glasgow, graduating in 1620, and remained there as a Regent in Divinity until 1625 when he was appointed minister of Kilwinning in Ayrshire. Baillie supported the COVENANTERS and was a member of the General Assembly of 1638. Although he acted as chaplain to the Covenanting army in 1639–40, by 1649 he was a 'Resolutioner', prepared to negotiate with Charles II. In 1642 he became Professor of Divinity at Glasgow and was principal between 1660 and his death in 1662. His writings on Scottish church matters include *The Canterburians Self-Conviction* (1640) and *A Parallel of the Liturgy with the Masse Book* (1642), but he is best remembered for his *Letters and Diaries*, republished by the BANNATYNE CLUB in 1841–2, which are valuable source books for the period of Baillie's life and career in the Church of Scotland.

WORKS: *The Canterburians Self-Conviction* (1640); *An Antidote against Armenianism* (1641); *The Unlawfulness and Danger of Limited Episcopacie* (1641); *A Parallel of the Liturgy with the Masse Book* (1642); *The Life of the Archbishop of Canterbury Examined* (1643); *Satan the Leader as Chief to all who Resist the Reparation of Sion* (1643); *A Dissuasive from the Errors of Time* (1645); *Errors and Induration* (1645); *A Historical Vindication of the Government of the Church of Scotland* (1646); *A Review of Dr Bramble* (1649)

EDITION: D. Laing, ed., *Letters and Diaries of Robert Baillie*, 3 vols. (Edinburgh, 1841–2)

Bain, Alexander (1818–1903). Philosopher. He was born on 11 June 1818 in Aberdeen, the son of a weaver, a career he followed himself before winning a bursary to study at Marischal College. After graduating he became an assistant to the Professor of Moral Philosophy and was appointed to the Chair of Logic in 1860. He remained in Aberdeen until his death on 18 September 1903. Early in Bain's career he visited London and was befriended by THOMAS CARLYLE and by John Stuart Mill (1806–73), who was to exert a seminal influence on his philosophy and writings. He later wrote a biography of Mill and he was a leading Utilitarian, although he expanded Mill's doctines by emphasizing the importance of the will and the emotions in human behaviour. Bain was also one of the first British philosophers to investigate the physiological influence of the nerves and the brain on man's philosophical make-up. His *Autobiography*, published posthumously in 1904, is an evocative account of his life, in which he rose from poverty and obscurity to become one of the leading men in his profession.

WORKS: *Astronomy* (1848); *Electricity* (1848); *Well Being* (1848); *The Sense and the Intellect* (1855); *The Emotions and the Will* (1859); *On the Study of Character* (1861); *An English Grammar* (1863); *English Composition and Rhetoric* (1866); *Mental and Moral Science*, 2 Vols. (1868–72); *Logic*, 2 vols. (1870), *A First English Grammar* (1872); *Mind and Body: the Theories of their Relation* (1873); *A Companion to the Higher English Grammar* (1874); *Education as a Science* (1879); *James Mill* (1882); *John Stuart Mill* (1882); *Practical Essays* (1884); *On Teaching English* (1887); *Dissertations on Leading Philosophical Topics* (1903); W. L. Davidson, ed., *Autobiography of Alexander Bain* (London, 1904)

Balfour, Alexander (1767–1829). Poet and novelist. He was born on 1 March 1767 in the parish of Monikie near Forfar. For a number of years he was a successful merchant in Arbroath but he was made bankrupt in 1815, when he moved to Edinburgh to become a clerk in the publishing house of WILLIAM BLACKWOOD. He was stricken with paralysis in 1819 and died on 12 September 1829. Among his works are the sentimental novels *Campbell* (1819), *The Farmer's Three Daughters* (1822) and *The Smuggler's Cave* (1823), and a collection of poems *Contemplation and Other Poems* (1820). His memoir, *Weeds and Wildflowers*, was edited by DAVID MACBETH MOIR.

WORKS: *Campbell, or the Scottish Probationer* (1819); *Contemplation and Other Poems* (1820); *The Farmer's Three Daughters* (1822); *The Smuggler's Cave* (1823); *Characters, and Other Tales* (1825); *Highland Mary* (1826); D. M. Moir, ed., *Weeds and Wildflowers* (1830); *King Robert Bruce's Breakfast* (1835), *The Old Maid and the Widow* (1835)

Ballad. Originally a song composed to accompany a dance (Old French *ballade*); 'ballad' later came to be the generic term for any popular song. From this definition came its modern usage: 'a simple spirited poem in short stanzas, narrating some popular story' (*OED*), or a folk-song, transmitted by word of mouth, that tells a story. The songs flourished in nonliterate communities and told, invariably in a dramatic and highly-stylized form, stories connected with the community, which were then retold within accepted rules of construction and composition.

The origins of the Scottish ballads are a cause of much speculation; some are related to ballads in other European countries, but in their finest and most enduring form they have existed for centuries in the north-east – in Aberdeenshire, Banff, Moray and the Mearns of Kincardineshire. In his major collection, *English and Scottish Ballads* (1882–98), the

American, F. J. Child (1825–96) noted that a greater quantity of ballads and more variants originated in the remote agrarian society of the north-east than elsewhere, because literacy was slow in arriving. The two most important collections of ballads from that area are contained in the manuscripts of Mrs Gordon (Anna Brown of Falkland, 1747–1810) and GAVIN GREIG; after Greig's death part of his collection was published in *Last Leaves of Traditional Ballads and Ballad Airs* (1925), edited by Alexander Keith, and it has now appeared in its entirety (1981–2).

However, for most people Scottish ballads are synonymous with Border ballads. There, in the frequently embattled borderland between Scotland and England, are the origins of the great 'riding' ballads which tell the story of warfare and cattle raiding and of the fierce independence of the Border folk. Among these are such well-known ballads as 'Johnnie Armstrong', 'Kinmont Willie', 'The Battle of Otterbourne' and 'Jock o' the Side'. A tradition shared by the Borders and the north-east are the ballads that deal with the supernatural, such as those concerned with the legend of THOMAS OF ERCELDOUNE (Thomas the Rhymer) and those dealing with stark human tragedy such as 'Sir Patrick Spens', 'The Twa Corbies', 'Lord Randal' and 'The Wife of Usher's Well'. Many have a common provenence and it has been shown (Buchan, *The Ballad and the Folk*, p.6) that many of the Border ballads are based on ballads from the north-east and that Sir WALTER SCOTT in THE MINSTRELSY OF THE SCOTTISH BORDER used variants of north-east ballads and attributed them to the Borders.

Increased literacy in the 18th and 19th centuries, and a curiosity about the country's past, led to the printing of ballads in chapbooks and broadsides and to their collection by poets and editors anxious to capture the dramatic effects and contrasting imagery of the traditional ballad. The most enduring collections are: DAVID HERD, ANCIENT AND MODERN SCOTTISH SONGS, 2 vols. (1776); Sir Walter Scott, *The Minstrelsy of the Scottish Border*, 3 vols. (1802–3); George Ritchie Kinloch, *The Ballad Book* (1827); and WILLIAM MOTHERWELL, *Minstrelsy, Ancient and Modern* (1827). Many of the early collectors felt it necessary to anglicize the texts, change words and phrases and even add verses of their own composition, and many ballads were printed without reference

being made to their tunes. Nevertheless, this far from systematic collection, carried out by enthusiasts and containing many mistakes in transcription and attribution, has served as a reminder of the richness of the nation's poetic and linguistic heritage. Collection of folksongs and ballads in Scotland has been continued in the 20th century by the research fellows of the SCHOOL OF SCOTTISH STUDIES within the University of Edinburgh.

REFERENCES: D. Buchan, *The Ballad and the Folk* (London, 1972); J. Reed, *The Border Ballads* (London, 1973); A. Bold, *The Ballad* (London, 1979)

Ballantine, James (1808–77). Artist and man of letters. He was born in Edinburgh. He worked for a period as a house-painter before studying drawing at the Trustee's Gallery in Edinburgh and interesting himself in the revival of glass-painting. After the publication of his *Stained Glass, Showing its Applicability to Every Style of Architecture* (1845) he was commissioned to execute the stained-glass windows in the House of Lords. Ballantine was connected with the WHISTLE-BINKIE poets and he published volumes of poems in 1856 and 1866, *The Gaberlunzie's Wallet* (1843) – his best-known collection of prose and sentimental verse – *The Miller of Deanhaugh* (1845), and *Lilias Lee* (1871) a tale in Spenserian verse. He died in December 1877.

WORKS: *The Gaberlunzie's Wallet* (1843); *The Miller of Deanhaugh* (1844); *Stained Glass, Showing its Applicability to Every Style of Architecture* (1845); *Essay on Ornamental Art* (1847); *Poems* (1856); *Chronicle of the Hundredth Birthday of Robert Burns* (1859); *Verses for the Burns Centenary Banquet* (1859); *The Life of David Roberts* (1866); *One Hundred Songs* (1866); *Lilias Lee and Other Poems* (1871); *A Short History of Church Stained Glass* (1911)

Ballantyne, James (1772–1833). Printer. He was born in Kelso and educated at the Grammar School, where he met WALTER SCOTT in 1783. He attended the University of Edinburgh between 1785 and 1786 and became a solicitor's apprentice, before establishing his own law office in 1795. The following year he undertook the printing and editing of the *Kelso Mail* and his friendship with Scott enabled him to print the first two volumes of THE MINSTRELSY OF THE SCOTTISH BORDER in January 1802. After its success Scott persuaded Ballantyne to set up a business in Edinburgh by lending him £500 and procuring him legal printing work; Scott became a partner in the firm and principal shareholder (though this was not made public). He also established the publishing and bookselling firm run by JOHN BALLANTYNE, James's brother; although this failed, the printing business was a great success and gained a reputation for the fineness and accuracy of its work. As well as printing Scott's work, Ballantyne acted as an editor and made several alterations to mistakes in the texts of the novels. The printing firm of James Ballantyne was involved in the financial crash of the publisher ARCHIBALD CONSTABLE in 1826 and was forced to declare itself bankrupt. Ballantyne died on 17 January 1833.

Ballantyne, John (1774–1821). Publisher. He was the younger brother of JAMES BALLANTYNE and was born in Kelso. He worked for a period in a merchant bank in London, before entering his brother's printing business as a clerk in 1805. In 1808 he became head of the publishing and bookselling business of John Ballantyne, which was established by Sir WALTER SCOTT. Although the business failed, he and Scott remained firm friends until his death on 16 June 1821. The latter years of his life were spent as an auctioneer. He wrote a sentimental novel *The Widow's Lodgings* (1812).

Ballantyne, R(obert) M(ichael) (1825–94). Writer of adventure stories for children. He was born on 24 April 1825 in Edinburgh, the son of Alexander Thomson Ballantyne, the youngest brother of JAMES BALLANTYNE and JOHN BALLANTYNE, printers and publishers to Sir WALTER SCOTT. He was educated at home by his mother and between 1836 and 1838 at the Edinburgh Academy, but most of his childhood was overshadowed by the financial difficulties caused by the crash of 1826 in which his family was involved with Scott and ARCHIBALD CONSTABLE. In 1841 Ballantyne entered the service of the Hudson's Bay Company, and between then and 1847 he worked as a clerk in their office at the Red River Settlement in northern Canada. On his return to Edinburgh in 1848 he was employed as a clerk with the North British Railway in order to support his mother and his five sisters; in 1852 he was appointed a partner in the publishing house of Thomas Constable.

Ballantyne's first book, *Hudson's Bay, Everyday Life in the Wilds of North America*, a collection of letters and illustrations sent to his family, was published privately and reprinted

by WILLIAM BLACKWOOD. Encouraged by its success, Ballantyne rewrote (1853) for children *A Historical View of the Progress and Discovery of the more Northern Coasts of America* (1832) by PATRICK FRASER TYTLER, but his first successful adventure story for children was *The Young Fur Traders* (1856), an autobiographical, but fictionalized, account of life with the Hudson's Bay Company. As with all Ballantyne's stories there is little plot, but the appeal of the book lies in the accuracy of the background and in the vividly described adventures of its hero, Charles Kennedy. His next book in the same vein was his most successful: *Coral Island* (1858) told the story of three boy castaways and their adventures on a south Pacific island. There followed a succession of adventure stories set in the American west, at sea and in the African jungle, all of which enjoyed great popularity and, like *Martin Rattler* (1859), echoed the growing enthusiasm for service to the ideals of the British Empire.

Ballantyne continued to live in Edinburgh until 1875, when he moved to France and then to Harrow in England. He died in Rome on 8 February 1894. His latter years were spent as a public lecturer on travel and adventure and in writing numerous books for boys, of which the more durable were: *The Dog Crusoe* (1861), *The Red Eric* (1861), *Erling the Bold* (1869) and *The Rover of the Andes* (1885). His autobiography, *Personal Reminiscences in Book-making*, was published in 1893.

WORKS: *Hudson's Bay, Every-day Life in the Wilds of North America* (1848); *Mabel Grant* (1854); *The Young Fur Traders* (1856); *The Life of a Ship* (1857); *Ungava* (1857); *Coral Island* (1858); *The Environs of Edinburgh* (1859); *How Not to Do It* (1859); *The Lakes of Killarney* (1859); *Martin Rattler* (1859); *Mee-a-ow: Good Advice to Little Kittens* (1859); *Mr Fox* (1860); *Three Little Kittens* (1860); *The Volunteer Force* (1860); *The Dog Crusoe* (1861); *The Golden Dream* (1861); *The Gorilla Hunters* (1861); *The Red Eric* (1861); *Away in the Wilderness* (1862); *Fast in the Ice* (1862); *Fighting the Whales* (1863); *Man on the Ocean* (1863); *The Wild Man of the West* (1863); *The World of Ice* (1863); *Gascoyne the Sandalwood Trader* (1864); *The Lifeboat* (1864); *Freaks on the Fells* (1865); *The Lighthouse* (1865); *Silver Lake* (1867); *Shifting Winds* (1868); *Chasing the Sun* (1869); *Erling the Bold* (1869); *Hunting the Lions* (1869); *Lost in the Forest* (1869); *Over the Rocky Mountains* (1869); *Photographs of Edinburgh* (1869); *Saved by the Lifeboat* (1869); *Sunk at Sea* (1869); *Up in the Clouds* (1869); *The Floating Light of the Goodwin Sands* (1870); *The Iron Horse* (1871); *The Norsemen in the West* (1871); *Black Ivory* (1873); *Life in the Red Brigade* (1873); *Chit-chat by a Penitent Cat* (1874); *The Ocean and its*

Wonders (1874); *The Pirate City* (1874); *Rivers of Ice* (1875); *Under the Waves* (1876); *The Settler and the Savage* (1877); *In the Track of Troops* (1878); *Philosopher Jack* (1879); *The Pioneers* (1879); *Six Months at the Cape* (1879); *The Story of the Rock* (1879); *The Lonely Island* (1880); *Post Haste* (1880); *The Collected Works of Ensign Sopht* (1881); *My Doggie and I* (1881); *The Butterfly's Ball and the Grasshopper's Feast* (1882); *The Giant of the North* (1882); *The Kitten Pilgrims* (1882); *The Battery and the Boiler* (1883); *Battles with the Sea* (1883); *The Madman and the Pirate* (1883); *The Thorogood Family* (1883); *Dusty Diamonds Cut and Polished* (1884); *The Middy and the Moors* (1884); *The Young Trawler* (1884); *Fighting the Flames* (1885); *The Island Queen* (1885); *The Rover of the Andes* (1885); *Twice Bought* (1885); *The Lively Poll* (1886); *The Prairie Chief* (1886); *Red Rooney* (1886); *The Big Otter* (1887); *The Fugitives* (1887); *Blue Lights* (1888); *Blown to Bits* (1889); *The Crew of the Water Wagtail* (1889); *Charlie to the Rescue* (1890); *The Eagle Cliff* (1890); *The Garret and the Garden* (1890); *The Buffalo Runners* (1891); *The Coxswain's Bride* (1891); *The Hot Swamp* (1892); *Hunted and Harried* (1892); *Personal Reminiscences in Book-making* (1893); *The Walrus Hunters* (1893); *Wrecked but not Ruined* (1895); *Reuben's Luck* (1896); *Deep Down* (1912); *The Jolly Kittens' Book* (1926)

REFERENCE: E. Quayle, *Ballantyne the Brave* (London, 1967)

Bannatyne, George (1545–1608). Collector of poems. He was born on 22 February 1545, the son of an Edinburgh lawyer, James Bannatyne of the Kirktown of Newtyle in Forfarshire. He worked as a merchant in Edinburgh and owned considerable property in the city; he was created a burgess in October 1587. His chief claim to fame is his compilation of the 800-page manuscript collection of early Scottish poetry now known as the BANNATYNE MANUSCRIPT, which is in the possession of the NATIONAL LIBRARY OF SCOTLAND. In September 1568, when plague struck Edinburgh, Bannatyne retired to his father's estate where he compiled the manuscript, styled by him 'Ane most godlie, mirrie and lustie Rapsodie maide be sundrie learned Scots poets and written be George Bannatyne in the tyme of his youth'. By his industry he collected together work that might have been lost – the poetry of WILLIAM DUNBAR, ROBERT HENRYSON, Sir DAVID LYNDSAY and ALEXANDER SCOTT (i) as well as work by lesser-known and unknown makars of the 15th and 16th centuries. The manuscript was preserved in his daughter's family until the 18th century when parts of its contents were printed by ALLAN RAMSAY in THE EVER GREEN. It was edited more completely by DAVID DALRYMPLE, Lord Hailes,

in 1770. Bannatyne was adopted as patron of the BANNATYNE CLUB, founded in 1823 under the presidency of Sir WALTER SCOTT, who also edited the *Memorials of George Bannatyne* (1829).

Bannatyne Club. A publishing society founded in 1823 for the purpose of editing and printing Scottish literary and historical texts. It was named after the 16th-century Edinburgh merchant and anthologist GEORGE BANNATYNE. Sir WALTER SCOTT was the club's first president and it was dissolved in 1861.

Bannatyne Manuscript. A collection of early Scottish poetry made by the Edinburgh merchant GEORGE BANNATYNE, subtitled 'Ane most godlie, mirrie and lustie Rapsodie maide be sundrie learned Scots poets and written be George Bannatyne in the tyme of his youth'. The manuscript was compiled from September 1568, when plague in Edinburgh forced Bannatyne to retire to his father's estates in Forfarshire, where he was able to indulge his interests in Scots poetry by transcribing the work of its foremost practitioners. It provides the largest collection of the work of the makars, especially of ROBERT HENRYSON, WILLIAM DUNBAR, Sir DAVID LYNDSAY and ALEXANDER SCOTT (i) as well as work by other, lesser-known poets, and is the single most important source for definitive texts. After Bannatyne's death the manuscript remained in his daughter's family and in the 18th century it was lent to the poet ALLAN RAMSAY for his collection of Scots verse, THE EVER GREEN. It was first edited more completely by DAVID DALRYMPLE, Lord Hailes, in 1770; between 1873 and 1901 it was published in 11 parts by the HUNTERIAN CLUB of Glasgow.

EDITION: W. T. Richie, ed., *The Bannatyne Manuscript Written in Tyme of Pest 1568 by George Bannatyne*, 4 vols., STS (Edinburgh and London, 1928–30)

Bannerman [née Boog Watson], **Helen** (1862–1946). Children's writer. She was born on 25 February 1862 in Edinburgh, the daughter of a minister of the Free Church of Scotland. Part of her childhood was spent in Madeira and she was educated privately in Edinburgh. In 1887 she was awarded an external degree from the University of St Andrews. Following her marriage to Dr Will Bannerman in 1889, Helen lived in India until 1918, and it was from there that she began writing the illustrated letters to her children that culminated in the publication in 1899 of *The Story of Little Black Sambo*, the story of a black boy and his adventures with the tigers. The loss of her copyright allowed the book and its illustrations to be pirated in other countries, with the result that the book assumed racist overtones that were not in the original edition. Helen Bannerman wrote nine further illustrated books for children on similar themes. She died on 13 October 1946 in Edinburgh.

WORKS: *The Story of Little Black Sambo* (1899); *Thee Story of Little Black Mingo* (1901); *The Story of Little Black Quibba* (1902); *The Story of Little Degchiehead* (1903); *Pat and the Spider* (1904); *The Story of the Teasing Monkey* (1906); *The Story of Little Black Quasha* (1908); *The Story of Little Black Bobtail* (1909); *The Story of Sambo and the Twins* (1936); *The Story of Little White Squibba* (1966)

REFERENCE: E. Hay, *Sambo Sahib: the Story of Little Black Sambo and Helen Bannerman* (Edinburgh, 1981)

Bannockburn, Battle of. A battle fought on 24 June 1314 at Bannockburn near Stirling between a Scottish army under ROBERT I (Robert the Bruce) and an English force, mainly consisting of cavalry and archers, under Edward II. It was the decisive battle in the war against England waged by Bruce, who had been crowned King of Scots in 1306, and the Scottish victory rallied the country behind their king. Bruce's victory owed much to his use of guerilla tactics and to the construction of deep pits to restrict the movement of the English cavalry; with the English archers unprotected, the way was open for the Scottish spearsmen to advance on the opposing army and to claim a complete victory. There is a vigorous description of the battle in THE BRUCE by JOHN BARBOUR, and the Scots victory has been the theme of many poems and songs, notably canto vi of *The Lord of the Isles* by Sir WALTER SCOTT and 'Bruce's Address to his Troops at Bannockburn', more commonly known as SCOTS WHA HAE, by ROBERT BURNS.

Bannock Night. *See* FASTERN'S E'EN.

Barbour, John (*c* 1320–95). Poet, churchman and scholar. He was probably born in Aberdeen and certainly spent most of his life there. His name is first mentioned as Archdeacon of Aberdeen in August 1357 and he held the post until his death on 13 March 1395. In 1357 and again in 1364 he was granted a free pass by Edward III of England to study at Oxford; and in 1365 and 1368 he was granted free passage to

study in Paris. In 1372 he was appointed Clerk of Audit in the household of Robert II and Auditor of the Exchequer; there are several mentions in the Exchequer Rolls of Scotland of the pensions paid to him at the king's behest.

From his admirer ANDREW OF WYNTOUN we learn that Barbour wrote two long poems, now both lost: *The Brut*, which chronicled the history of the Britons from the time when Aeneas's descendant Brutus landed in England from Troy; and *The Stewartis Original*, a companion piece that relates the fictitious pedigree of the Stewarts back to Banquo and his son Fleance. In 1377 Robert II awarded Barbour a gift of £10 for his long patriotic poem THE BRUCE; the poem supplies some of the facts of the life of ROBERT i (Robert the Bruce), many of which are told in a spirited anecdotal style, but Barbour's main intent in relating Bruce's exploits in freeing Scotland from English domination is patriotic. The poem is exceptional for its vivid descriptions, especially of the BATTLE OF BANNOCKBURN, and above all for its famous expression of freedom:

> A! Fredome is a noble thing!
> Fredome mayss man to haiff liking,
> Fredome all solace to man giffis;
> He levys at ess tha frely levys.

EDITIONS: W. Skeat, ed., *The Bruce*, 2 vols., STS (Edinburgh and London, 1894); M. P. McDiarmid and J. A. C. Stevenson, eds., *Barbour's Bruce*, vols 2 and 3, STS (Edinburgh, 1980)

Barclay, John (1582–1621). Poet. He was born on 28 January 1582 at Pont-à-Mousson in France, where his father was Professor of Civil Law. Until the accession of JAMES VI to the throne of England as James I of England, Barclay remained in France; he failed to find a source of patronage when he arrived in London and in 1616 he retired to live in Rome, where he died on 28 July 1621. He wrote two prose works in Latin in the style of Petronius: *Euphormionis Lusini satyricon* (1603), and *Argenis* (1611), a romance that enjoyed a wide currency, being translated by Ben Jonson (1572–1637), among others. A selection of Barclay's Latin poems appeared in the DELITIAE POETARUM SCOTORUM of 1637.

REFERENCE: D. Dalrymple, *Sketch of the Life of John Barclay* (Edinburgh, 1786)

Barclay, Robert (1648–90). Divine. He was born on 23 December 1648 at Gordonstoun near Elgin and was educated at the Scots College in Paris. He returned to Scotland in 1664 and followed his father into the Quaker faith, becoming one of its principal apologists. Barclay's publications on Quakerism are: *Truth Cleared of Calumnies* (1670), *A Catechism and Confession of Faith* (1673) and, his most important work, *An Apology for the True Christian Divinity* (1676), which is dedicated to Charles II. He was imprisoned several times for his beliefs but he eventually found a protector in James II, and in 1682 he was appointed nominal governor of the state of East New Jersey, which had been established as a Quaker colony. He died on 3 October 1690.

WORKS: *Truth Cleared of Calumnies* (1670); *William Michel Unmasked* (1672); *A Catechism and Confession of Faith* (1673); *An Apology for the True Christian Divinity* (1676); *Universal Love Considered* (1677); *Epistola amatoria* (1678); *Theologiae vere Christianae apologica* (1678); *Possibility and Necessity of Inward Immediate Revelation of the Spirit of God* (1686); *Truth Triumphant through Spiritual Warfare* (1692); *Theses theologicae* (1711); *Serious Considerations on Absolute Predestination* (1741); *An Anarchy of the Ranters* (1771)

REFERENCE: M. C. Cadbury, *Robert Barclay: his Life and Work* (London, 1912)

Bard. A word used to describe the poet of a clan or tribe in Celtic Scotland and Ireland; the position was hereditary. The bard was a highly specialized poet who wrote verse according to the strict linguistic and metrical rules laid down by bardic colleges, which came into being during the 12th century. Within the community the bards' function was to provide praise poems for the chief, laments, incitements to battle and satire, but they also enjoyed great temporal power and were often wealthy men owning land and property. The best-known bardic family in Scotland was the MACMHUIRICH family, who were descended from the Irish bardic family, the O'Dalaighs. Much of the best extant Scottish bardic poetry is preserved in the 15th-century BOOK OF THE DEAN OF LISMORE. The term came to be used as a romantic word for a poet, and ROBERT BURNS is often referred to as 'Scotland's national bard'.

Barke, James (1905–58). Novelist. He was born at Tullieallan, Clackmannanshire, though in his collection of sketches of childhood, *The Green Hills Far Away* (1940), he refers to a 'Borders birthplace'; his parents were farm-workers from Galloway. He worked for a time as an engineer in the years after World War I, but turned to writing and editing for a living after the publication of his first novel *The World his Pillow* (1933).

Barke's best novel is *The Land of the Leal* (1939), a thinly disguised autobiographical novel which traces the journey through life of Jean Ramsay, an aggressively practical woman from a peasant background, and her weak-willed, poetic husband, David. It spans three–quarters of a century of Scottish life and Barke traces the couple's wanderings from the idyll of their childhood in Galloway, through work for the landed gentry in the Borders and Fife, to their fall from grace in the depression years in industrial Glasgow. Inevitably, as their children are born and grow up and as the years slip away, their rural background becomes another Eden, but Barke keeps sentimentality in check in his reflective description of the changing face of Scottish society. Jean and David are 'pawns in the development of economic cause and political effect'; Barke had already explored this theme in *Major Operation* (1936), which examines the industrial system in Glasgow from a worker's and a businessman's point of view.

Barke edited the works of ROBERT BURNS and was responsible, with SYDNEY GOODSIR SMITH, for the definitive edition of THE MERRY MUSES OF CALEDONIA; he also wrote a series of five novels about Burns's life, which was published under the title *Immortal Memory* (1946–54).

WORKS: *The World his Pillow* (1933); *The Wild Mac-Raes* (1934); *The End of the High Bridge* (1935); *Major Operation* (1936); *The Land of the Leal* (1939); *The Green Hills Far Away* (1940); *The Wind that Shakes the Barley* (1946); *The Song in the Greenthorn Tree* (1947); *The Wonder of All the Gay World* (1949); *The Crest of the Broken Wave* (1953); *The Well of the Silent Harp* (1954); *Bonnie Jean* (1959)

Barrie, J(ames) M(atthew), Sir (1860–1937). Dramatist and novelist. He was born on 9 May 1860 in Kirriemuir, Angus, the ninth child of a weaver. When Barrie was seven, David, his older brother and his mother's favourite son, was killed in a skating accident; from that date Barrie strove to fill the vacant place in his mother's affections and he became exceptionally close to her. In later life he told the story of that relationship in a sentimental biography, *Margaret Ogilvy* (1896). Between 1867 and 1871 he was educated at the Glasgow Academy where his oldest brother, Alexander, was a master, and subsequently at Forfar Academy and Dumfries Academy from 1873 to 1878, when he matriculated at the University of Edinburgh. There he studied English in the class of Professor DAVID MASSON and he became a regular reviewer of theatre for the *Edinburgh Courant* and of books for THE SCOTSMAN. In 1882 he was appointed a leader-writer on the *Nottingham Journal* and he held the post until 1884 when he returned home to Kirriemuir. From there he began contributing to Sir Frederick Greenwood's *St James's Gazette* and *Cornhill Magazine* the stories of Scottish village life, its characters and religious principles, told to him by his mother. These were later published in AULD LICHT IDYLLS (1888) and they present a humorous, but sentimental, caricature of rural manners in Thrums, the village that disguised the reality of Kirriemuir. Their cloying picture of rural life belongs properly to the KAILYARD school of writing. A second collection, *A Window in Thrums*, was published in 1889.

In 1885 Barrie moved to London to work as a journalist and he started writing, under the pseudonym Gavin Ogilvy, for the *British Weekly*, which was edited by WILLIAM ROBERTSON NICOLL. Barrie's growing success was consolidated by his second novel *When a Man's Single* (1888) (*Better Dead*, his first novel, had been published at his own expense in 1886 and it was reissued in 1888), *An Edinburgh Eleven: Pen Portraits of College Life* (1889), his reminiscences of university life in Edinburgh, and his most successful novel *The Little Minister* (1891), which he dramatized for the stage in 1897. Barrie married the acress Mary Ansell on 9 July 1894 but their marriage seems never to have been consummated and it broke up in 1909 when Mary left him for Gilbert Canaan, a barrister and secretary to Barrie's Censorship Committee. Something of the futility of Barrie's marriage can be seen in two novels, *Sentimental Tommy* (1896) and its sequel *Tommy and Grizel* (1900).

Barrie visited America in 1896 and on his return he met the Llewellyn Davies family with whom, especially the children, George, Jack, Peter, Michael and Nicholas, he was to enjoy a close relationship. For the boys he wrote *The Little White Bird* (1902), a fantasy set in Kensington Gardens, and out of that book and out of their close relationship he wrote his best-known work, *Peter Pan, or The Boy who*

Wouldn't Grow Up (1904): 'I suppose I always knew that I made Peter Pan by rubbing the five of you violently together, as savages with two sticks produce a flame. I am sometimes asked who and what Peter is, but that is all he is, the spark I got from you.' (Unpublished draft of the dedication to a performance of *Peter Pan* in 1926.) The play was Barrie's greatest success and has remained popular with children ever since, with its make-believe world of fairies, pirates and Red Indians in the Never-Never Land inhabited by Peter Pan. It also contains elements of Barrie's own obsession with mother love and with the lost world of childhood. The story of the play was published in book form in *Peter and Wendy* in 1911.

Barrie's first successful play was *The Little Minister* (1897), and from the beginning of his theatrical career he demonstrated a command of language and grasp of stagecraft, allied to an ability to create rounded, realistic characters. His principal plays were as follows (here and throughout this paragraph dates given are those of first performance): *Quality Street* (1901), a love story set in the Napoleonic Wars; THE ADMIRABLE CRICHTON (1902), a comedy about the effects of a butler becoming a dictator when a family is shipwrecked; *What Every Woman Knows* (1908), which suggests that behind every successful man is a stalwart, charming wife like Maggie, who in the memorable first act questions her position as an appendage to her husband; *A Kiss for Cinderella* (1916), an attempt to revive the fantasy of *Peter Pan*; *Dear Brutus* (1917) which with its famous, sentimental scene in Lob's wood explores the theme that people can be given a second chance in life; *Mary Rose* (1920), a whimsical story about a dead mother's love for her son; *Shall We Join the Ladies?* (1921) an uncompleted murder mystery; and his last play, an unsuccessful religious drama, *The Boy David* (1936). Barrie's other work for the theatre includes: *Becky Sharp* and *Ibsen's Ghost* (1891), *Walker, London* (1892), *The Professor's Love Story* (1894), *The Wedding Guest* (1900), *Little Mary* (1903), *Alice-Sit-By-The-Fire* (1905), *Josephine* and *Punch* (1906), *Old Friends, The Twelve-Pound Look* and *A Slice of Life* (1910), *Rosalind* (1912), *The Will, The Adored One, Half Hours* and *The Dramatists Get What They Want* (1913), *Der Tag* (1914), *The New Word* and *Rosy Rapture, Pride of the Beauty Chorus* (1915), *The Old Lady Shows her Medals* (1917), *A Well Remembered Voice* (1918), *The Truth about the Russian Dancers* (1920) and *Barbara's Wedding* (1927).

After the deaths of Arthur Llewelyn Davies in 1907 and his wife in 1910, Barrie's relationship with their sons grew even closer and he became their guardian and unofficial stepfather. He also befriended the family of Captain Robert Scott (1868–1912), the Polar explorer. Barrie's adoration of attractive women and their children was to remain an obsession throughout his life; he also enjoyed the friendship of many of the leading political and literary men of his time. His services to literature were rewarded with a baronetcy in 1913 (he had turned down a knighthood in 1909), and other public honours, including the Order of Merit in 1922, the year that, as Rector of the University of St Andrews, he gave his rectorial address on 'Courage'; he was also Chancellor of the University of Edinburgh. He died on 19 June 1937.

Barrie was one of the most successful and popular dramatists of his day but none of his plays has withstood the test of time. In some works such as *The Admirable Crichton* and *What Every Woman Knows,* he questioned social mores, but in weak endings he allowed the *status quo* to prevail (Crichton returns to his position as a butler, Maggie takes up her wifely duties), although in the latter play his portrait of a Scotsman 'on the make' is perfectly drawn. As his career progressed he became increasingly involved in the worlds of fantasy and faery and in the search for the lost world of childhood, and he is still best remembered for the creation of Peter Pan. In his early Scottish stories sentimentality and bathos are occasionally kept at bay by his pawky humour and social observation, but at heart the *Auld Licht* stories, set in Thrums, are artificial and devoid of life. His other novels and works of non-fiction are: *My Lady Nicotine* (1890), a novel extolling the joys of smoking; *Courage* (1922), the text of his St Andrews rectorial address; *The Greenwood Hat* (1930), a privately printed collection of autobiographical sketches; and *Farewell Miss Julie Logan* (1932), a love story set in Scotland.

WORKS: *Better Dead* (1886); *Auld Licht Idylls* (1888); *When a Man's Single* (1888); *An Edinburgh Eleven: Pen Portraits of College Life* (1889); *A Window in Thrums* (1889); *My Lady Nicotine* (1890); *The Little Minister* (1891); *Richard Savage* (1891); *A Holiday in Bed* (1892); *Allahakbarries* (1893); *An Auld Licht Manse* (1893); with Arthur Conan Doyle, *Jane Annie* (1893); *A Lady's Shoe* (1893); *A Tillyloss Scandal* (1893); *Two of Them* (1893); *The Sabbath Day* (1895); *Scotland's Lament* (1895); *Margaret Ogilvy* (1896); *Sentimental Tommy* (1896); *The Allahakbarrie Book of Broadway Cricket for 1899* (1899); *Life in a Country Manse* (1899); *Tommy and Grizel* (1900); *The Wedding Guest* (1900); *The Little White Bird* (1902); *Peter Pan in Kensington Gardens* (1906); *Walker, London* (1907); *George Meredith* (1909); *Peter and Wendy* (1911); *Quality Street* (1913); *The Admirable Crichton* (1914); *Der Tag* (1914); *Half Hours* (1914) *Pantaloon* (1914) *Rosalind* (1914); *The Twelve-Pound Look* (1914); *The Will* (1914); *Charles Frohman* (1915); *Shakespeare's Legacy* (1917); *Who was Sarah Findlay? by Mark Twain. With a Suggested Solution of the Mystery* (1917); *Echoes of the War* (1918); *The New Word* (1918); *The Old Lady Shows Her Medals* (1918); *A Well Remembered Voice* (1918); *What Every Woman Knows* (1918); *A Kiss for Cinderella* (1920); *Courage* (1922); *Dear Brutus* (1923); *Mary Rose* (1924); *Neil and Tintinnabulum* (1925); *Shall We Join the Ladies?* (1927); *The Greenwood Hat* (1930); *Farewell Miss Julie Logan* (1932)

EDITIONS: *The Novels, Tales and Sketches of J. M. Barrie,* 8 vols. (New York, 1896); *The Plays of J. M. Barrie,* 12 vols. (London, 1918–38); *The Works of J. M. Barrie,* Uniform Edition, 4 vols. (London, 1925–32); V. Meynell, ed., *The Letters of J. M. Barrie,* (London, 1942)

REFERENCES: W. A. Darlington, *J. M. Barrie* (London and Glasgow, 1938); D. Mackail, *The Story of J. M. B.* (London, 1941); J. Dunbar, *J. M. Barrie: The Man Behind the Image* (London, 1970); A. Birkin, *J. M. Barrie and the Lost Boys* (London, 1979)

Basilicon doron. A guide to kingship and statecraft written by JAMES VI in the summer of 1598 and first published in the spring of the following year, 1599. The original manuscript is now in the British Library (MS Royal 18 B.xv). It was written by James for his son Prince Henry and when James became King of England in 1603 it was translated into French, German, Dutch and Swedish for the benefit of the courts of Europe. The work contains a revealing description of Scottish affairs as James perceived them at the end of the 16th century; though most readers would find it tantalizingly short, this forms the most interesting part of the book. The remainder is a set of precepts for his son to follow, based largely on earlier works on kingship, and it ends with a vituperative attack on the more militant Scottish church leaders. Although the manuscript is written in Scots, later published versions appeared wholly in English.

EDITION: J. Craigie, ed., *The Basilicon doron of King James VI,* 2 vols., STS (Edinburgh and London, 1944–50)

Bassendyne, Thomas (*d* 1577). Printer of the first Bible printed in Scotland, known commonly as the Bassendyne Bible. A burgess of the City of Edinburgh, Bassendyne studied the art of printing in Leiden and set himself up as a printer in 1567. He produced the *Works of David Lyndsay* (*see* LYNDSAY, DAVID) in 1574 and two years later received a licence under the Privy Seal to print a Bible in association with ALEXANDER ARBUTHNOT (i). It appeared in its final form in 1579, after Bassendyne's death.

Baxter, Charles (1845–1919). Lawyer, and friend of ROBERT LOUIS STEVENSON. He was born on 27 December 1848. He met Stevenson while they were pupils at the Edinburgh Academy and their friendship continued at the University. Baxter shared many of Stevenson's low-life adventures in Edinburgh while they were students, and it was during that period that they assumed their alter egos of Thomson and Johnstone; they used these names in later correspondence, written in broad Scots, which is notable for Stevenson's evocative and nostalgic portrayal of the Edinburgh of their youth. Baxter became Stevenson's legal adviser and loyal friend, and it was to him that Stevenson first confided his early love for FANNY OSBOURNE. In *The Wrong Box* Baxter appears in the character of Michael Finsbury. He died on 29 April 1919 in Edinburgh.

REFERENCE: D. Ferguson and M. Waingrow, eds., *Stevenson's Letters to Charles Baxter* (New Haven, Conn., 1956)

Beattie, James (1735–1803). Poet and philosopher. He was born on 25 October 1735 in Laurencekirk, Kincardineshire, the son of a shopkeeper. He was educated at the village school and in 1749 he matriculated at Marischal College, Aberdeen. Between 1753 and 1758 Beattie taught at the village school at Fordoun, before becoming a master at Aberdeen Grammar School; he was unexpectedly appointed Professor of Moral Philosophy at the University of Aberdeen in 1760, a post he held for 30 years. He became a close friend of JAMES BURNETT, Lord Monboddo, and was a frequent visitor to London, where he enjoyed a high standing in literary and political circles. In his latter years Beattie was incapacitated by rheumatism and was awarded a state pension. He died on 18 August 1803 in Aberdeen. His biography was written by Sir William Forbes in *Account of the Life and Writings of James Beattie, LL.D.*

Beattie first came to public attention as a poet through the publication of his long poem *The Minstel*, written in two books in 1771 and 1774. It is in Spenserian stanzas and Beattie described it as 'a moral and serious poem'; it follows, in fashionable, high-flown Augustan tones, a poetic visionary's symbolic journey from chaos to a true understanding of art. His other works, parodies and satires in the style of Alexander Pope, have been long forgotten, though his epistle 'To Mr Alexander Ross' was often anthologized in the 19th century. His reputation as a poet has also been tarnished by his support for the OSSIAN poems by JAMES MACPHERSON.

As a philosopher Beattie enjoyed some success in his day for his attack on DAVID HUME (ii) in *Essay on . . . Truth* (1770), a work that has long been discredited by metaphysicians. His other philosophical works are, principally, *Elements of Moral Science* (1790–93), *Dissertations, Moral and Critical* (1783) and *The Evidences of the Christian Religion Briefly and Plainly Stated* (1786), all of which echo Beattie's interest in religion and its application to philosophy. In 1779 he published his *Scoticisms, Arranged in Alphabetical Order, Designed to Correct Improprieties of Speech and Writing*, which was produced originally for his students, who had 'no opportunity of learning English from the company they kept', but which is also an indication of the desire of many of the intellectuals of Beattie's period to speak correct, Augustan English.

WORKS: *Original Poems and Translations* (1760); *The Judgement of Paris* (1765); *Poems on Several Subjects* (1766); *An Essay on the Nature and Immutability of Truth* (1770); *The Minstrel*, 2 vols. (1771–4); *Essays on Poetry* (1778); *Scoticisms, Arranged in Alphabetical Order, Designed to Correct Improprieties of Speech and Writing* (1779); *Dissertations, Moral and Critical* (1783); *The Evidences of the Christian Religion Briefly and Plainly Stated*, 2 vols. (1786); *Elements of Moral Science*, 2 vols. (1790–93)

EDITIONS: A. Dyce, ed., *The Poetical Works of James Beattie* (London, 1831); R. S. Walker, ed., *James Beattie's Day-Book, 1773–1778* (Aberdeen, 1948); R. S. Walker, ed., *James Beattie's Diary 1773* (Aberdeen, 1948)

REFERENCES: M. Forbes, *Beattie and his Friends* (London, 1904); E. H. King, *James Beattie* (Boston, Mass., 1977)

Beith, John Hay ['Ian Hay'] (1876–1952). Novelist. John Hay Beith, who wrote under the pen-name 'Ian Hay', was born on 17 April 1876 in Manchester, the son of a cotton merchant. He was educated at Fettes College, Edinburgh, and St John's College, Cambridge, and returned to Edinburgh twice, in 1901 and 1906, to teach at Fettes before becoming a full-time writer in 1912. During World War I he served with the Argyll and Sutherland Highlanders and from his war experiences he wrote the successful novel *The First Hundred Thousand* (1915) which captured the buoyant mood of the first conscript army. His other war novels were *Carrying On* (1917) and *The Last Million* (1918) and he also wrote a number of light but shrewdly observed novels of public school life. Beith was rightly praised during the 1930s as a collaborator in the theatre with authors such as Stephen King-Hall and P. G. Wodehouse. He died on 22 September 1952 in Petersfield, Hampshire.

WORKS: *Their Name Liveth* (1931); *The Royal Company of Archers, 1676–1951* (1951) as Ian Hay: *Pip* (1907); *A Man's Man* (1909); *A Safety Match* (1911); *Happy-go-lucky* (1913); *A Knight on Wheels* (1914); *The Lighter Side of Life* (1914); *The First Hundred Thousand* (1915); *Carrying On* (1917); *The Last Million* (1918); *Tilly of Bloomsbury* (1919); *The Willing Horse* (1921); with Seymour Hicks, *Good Luck* (1922); *The Happy Ending* (1922); *The Shallow End* (1924); *The Sport of Kings* (1924); *Paid with Thanks* (1925); *Half a Sovereign* (1926); with P. G. Wodehouse, *A Damsel in Distress* (1928); *The Poor Gentleman* (1928); with P. G. Wodehouse, *Baa-baa Blacksheep* (1929); with P. G. Wodehouse, *Leave it to Psmith* (1930); *The Middle Watch* (1930); *A Song of Sixpence* (1930); *Mr Faintheart* (1931); *The Midshipmaid* (1932); *Orders are Orders* (1932); *The Great Wall of India* (1933); *A Present from Margate* (1933); with Stephen King-Hall, *Admirals All* (1934); *David and Destiny* (1934); *Lucky Dog* (1934); *The Frog* (1936); *Housemaster* (1936); *The King's Service* (1938); *The Gusher* (1939); *Stand at Ease* (1940); *Little Ladyship* (1941); *America Comes Across* (1942); *The Unconquered Isle* (1943); *Peaceful Invasion* (1946); *The Post Office Went to War* (1946); with Stephen King-Hall, *Off the Record* (1947); *R.O.F.* (1948); with L. Du Garde Peach, *The White Sheep of the Family* (1951); *Cousin Christopher* (1953); *100 Years of Army Nursing* (1953)

Bell, Henry Glassford (1803–74). Poet and man of letters. He was born on 8 November 1803 in Glasgow. He studied law at the University of Edinburgh and was called to the Scottish Bar in 1832. Between 1833 and 1852 he was Sheriff–Substitute of Lanarkshire before becoming Sheriff of Lanarkshire in succession to ARCHIBALD ALISON; he held the post until his death on 7 January 1874. Bell's literary tastes were developed while he was a student and his first poems were published as early as 1824. By editing a number of short-lived literary magazines he made the acquaintance of many of the writers of the day and he was a well-known figure in Edinburgh literary circles. A lifetime spent editing books and indulging his own antiquarian interests earned him the title of the 'last of the literary sheriffs'. Little of his own work has survived, though his verse romance *Mary Queen of Scots* was once popular and he published a spirited and well-argued defence of the queen in his two-volume *Life of Mary Queen of Scots* of 1831.

WORKS: *Poems* (1824); *Selections of the Most Remarkable Phenomena of Nature* (1827); *Life of Mary Queen of Scots*, 2 vols. (1831); *Summer and Winter Hours* (1831); *My Old Portfolio* (1832); *On the Bankruptcy Law of England and Scotland* (1860); *Romances* (1868)

REFERENCE: A. M. Stoddart, *Henry Glassford Bell: a Biographical Sketch* (Edinburgh, 1892)

Bell, John Joy (1871–1934). Novelist. He was born on 7 May 1871 in Glasgow, the son of a tobacco manufacturer. He was educated in Glasgow at Kelvinside Academy, in Perthshire at Morrison's Academy, and at the University of Glasgow, where he studied chemistry. There is a tell description of his childhood days in the Scotland of the 1880s in his volume of reminiscences *I Remember* (1932), and its sequel, *Do you Remember?* (1934), takes the story up to the years after World War I. Bell spent most of his later years in Aberdeen and he remained a lifelong friend of the novelist and editor NEIL MUNRO. He died on 14 November 1934.

Most of Bell's early writing was in journalism and it was from a series of sketches published in the *Glasgow Evening Times* between 1901 and 1902 that he came to publish, at his own expense, *Wee MacGreegor* (1902), a pawky novel about a small boy and his adventures in Glasgow. With its sentimental and stylized picture of working-class life in Glasgow, *Wee MacGreegor* was an instant success; it sold over a quarter of a million copies and was pirated in North America. Bell followed the successful formula in its sequels *Wee MacGreegor Again* (1904) and *Wee MacGreegor Enlists* (1915). In 1909 he introduced another *enfant terrible*, Christina, in *Oh, Christina*, which was followed by *Courtin' Christina* (1913). Glasgow figures as a backdrop to most of Bell's novels, and even as the school of fictional realism grew in the 1920s and 1930s Bell continued to publish novels of urban KAILYARD sentimentality, such as *The Braw Bailie* (1925). A volume of his verse, *Clyde Songs*, was published in 1906.

WORKS: *The New Noah's Ark* (1899); *Jack of All Trades* (1900); *Wee MacGreegor* (1902); *Ethel* (1903); *Jess and Co.* (1904); *Mistress McLeerie* (1904); *Wee MacGreegor Again* (1904); *Mr Lion of London* (1905); *Mr Pennycook's Boy* (1905); *Clyde Songs and Other Verses* (1906); *Thou Fool* (1907); *Joseph Redfern* (1908); *Whither thou Goest* (1908); *Oh, Christina* (1909); *Dancing Days* (1910); *Jim Crow* (1911); *A Kingdom of Dreams* (1911); *Courtin' Christina* (1913); *Bobby* (1914); *The Whalers* (1914); *Wee MacGreegor Enlists* (1915); *Cupid in Oilskins* (1916); *Kiddies* (1916); *Little Grey Ships* (1916); *Five and Twenty Turkeys* (1917); *Kitty Carstairs* (1917); *Till the Clock Stops* (1917); *All Ages* (1918); *Atlantic Gold* (1918); *Johnny Pride* (1918); *The Middle Ship* (1919); *Jimmy, Jimmy* (1921); *Secret Cards* (1922); *Wee MacGreegor's Party* (1922); *The Nickums* (1923); *Some Plain, some Coloured* (1923); *Thread o'Scarlet* (1923); *The J. J. Bell Reader* (1924); *Mr Craw* (1924); *Those Class Distinctions* (1924); *The Braw Baillie* (1925); *The Invisible Net* (1925); *Wolves* (1925); *Exit Mr McLeerie* (1926); *The Laird's Lucky Number* (1926); *Mr and Mrs Craw* (1926); *Billy* (1927); *Meet Mr Craw* (1927); *Hoots!* (1929); *Gambler's Hope* (1930); *Good Morning, Sir John!* (1930); *A Relapse of Consuls* (1930); *Laird of Glen Laggan* (1931); *The Glory of Scotland* (1932); *I Remember* (1932); *Scotland's Rainbow West* (1933); *The Women* (1933); *Breaking Point* (1934); *Do you Remember?* (1934); *Hamish* (1934); *Scotland in Ten Days* (1934)

REFERENCE: H. von Baur, *Der Dialekt von Lanarkshire, Glasgow und Umgegund und die Dialektdichtung 'Wee MacGreegor'* (Leipzig, 1933)

Bellenden, John (*fl* 1533). Poet. Very little is known with any certainty about the life of John Bellenden, other than that he may have been educated at the universities of St Andrews and Paris. His main claim to fame is his translation into Scots of *Scotorum historiae* by HECTOR BOECE, which he made in 1536 on the commission of JAMES V. From the title-page we learn that Bellenden was at that time 'archdene of Murray and channon of Ros', that is, a priest of some authority in the county of Moray in north-east Scotland. Bellenden continued to receive royal patronage; in the King's Treasurer's Accounts he is sometimes referred to as 'Ballentyne'. His other work of note is his translation of Livy's *History of Rome*. He was a straightforward translator, not given to the use of Latinate rhetorical devices of the king that distinguish many examples of early Scots prose. The prologue to *Papyngo* by Sir DAVID

LYNDSAY describes him as a poet 'quhose ornat workis my wit can nocht defyne'.

EDITIONS: W. A. Craigie, ed., *Livy's History of Rome Translated into Scots by John Bellenden*, 2 vols., STS (Edinburgh and London, 1901–2); R. W. Chambers, E. C. Batho and H. W. Husbands, eds., *The Chronicles of Scotland, Compiled by Hector Boece and Translated into Scots by John Bellenden*, 2 vols., STS (Edinburgh and London, 1936–41)

Beltane. A festival celebrating the beginning of summer; it was one of the two great fire festivals in the early Celtic world, the other being *Samhuinn* or HALLOWE'EN. Traditionally the Fianna left the people and went out to hunt, flocks and herds were put out to pasture and the seed was sown. Beltane was marked by the lighting of sacred fires in supplication to the sun which fertilizes the earth. The festival and its rites continued in some parts of the Highlands until the early 19th century and it is now the May Day holiday in Scotland.

Bernard de Linton (*d* 1331). Abbot of Arbroath. Nothing of Bernard de Linton's life is known before his appointment as parson of Mordington near Berwick in 1296. After the coronation of ROBERT I as King of Scots he was appointed chancellor, and he was elected Abbot of Arbroath in 1311, a post he held until 1328 when he resigned the chancellorship and became Bishop of the Isles. As well as advising Robert on matters of state, he was responsible for drafting the DECLARATION OF ARBROATH in 1320. Written in the rhythmical *cursus* of medieval Latin, the Declaration of Arbroath has remained a powerful statement of the concept of Scottish independence.

Bisset [Bysset], **Habakkuk** (*fl* 1610). Historian. He was the son of a caterer to MARY, Queen of Scots. According to his own word he was a lawyer and his life seems to have been interrupted by personal litigation of various kinds. His principal work, *Rolment of Courtis*, is a compilation of his legal writings and among the first known pieces of prose in Scots.

EDITION: P. J. Hamilton-Grierson, ed., *Bisset's Rolment of Courtis*, 3 vols. (Edinburgh and London, 1920–26)

Black, Adam (1784–1874). The founder of the publishing house of A. and C. Black. He was born on 20 February 1784 in Edinburgh, the son of a master-builder. He was educated at the HIGH SCHOOL OF EDINBURGH and at the age of 15 was apprenticed to John Fairburn, an Edinburgh bookseller. In 1804 he went to London, where he worked with Thomas Sheraton on his *The Cabinet-maker and Artist's Encyclopaedia* (1791–3), and thereafter with the publishers Lackington Allen and Co. He returned to Edinburgh in 1807 and set himself up as a bookseller at 57 South Bridge, where he remained until 1818, when he moved to larger premises at 27 North Bridge; in 1846 the firm moved to its last Edinburgh address, 6 North Bridge, before moving to London in 1890.

Black started publishing political pamphlets, educational books and a series of travel books in 1817. He bought the rights to publish the ENCYCLOPAEDIA BRITANNICA in 1826 and the following year he took over the publication of the *Edinburgh Review* (see EDINBURGH REVIEW (ii)) following the financial ruin of ARCHIBALD CONSTABLE. His nephew Charles (1804–54) joined the firm in 1834, and in 1854 they bought the rights to the novels of Sir WALTER SCOTT. They also published *Memorials of his Time* (1856) by HENRY THOMAS COCKBURN and his *Life of Lord Jeffrey* (1852).

A Whig in politics, Black held a number of important public posts in Edinburgh. He was Commissioner of Police in 1822 and Lord Provost between 1843 and 1848. He died on 24 January 1874, a few weeks before his 90th birthday. His successor was his son, James Tait Black (1826–1911), whose wife endowed the James Tait Black Prize for fiction and biography, awarded annually by the Regius Professor of English at the University of Edinburgh.

Black, David Macleod (*b* 1941). Poet. He was born on 8 November 1941 in Wynberg, South Africa, the son of a Scottish academic. He was educated at Trinity College, Glenalmond, and the universities of Edinburgh and Lancaster. He lives and works in London where he is a Jungian analyst. Black's early poetry, written in a surrealist free verse, is dramatic and beguiling, creating a fantastic world of space and time travel, peopled by dwarfs, judges, eunuchs and executioners. His skilful manipulation of the narrative in the dream-like sequences of much of the poetry in *From the Mountain* (1963) and *With Decorum* (1967) led to his first long dramatic narrative poem *Anna's Affairs*, published in *The Educators* (1969); this has become a favoured poetic form. *The Hands of Felicity, Urru and Uppu* and *Notes for Joachim*,

published in *Gravitations* (1979), mark Black as one of the few contemporary poets able to sustain the traditional long narrative poem while introducing his own linguistic, psychological and allegorical innovations. Black's insistence on the power of words and his ability to control audacious rhyming schemes give his work an instantly recognizable and highly original voice.

WORKS: *Rocklestrakes* (1960); *From the Mountain* (1963); *Theory of Diet* (1966); *With Decorum* (1967); *A Dozen Short Poems* (1968); with Peter Redgrove and D. M. Thomas, *Penguin Modern Poets 11* (1968); *The Educators* (1969); *The Old Hag* (1972); *The Happy Crow* (1974); *Gravitations* (1979)

Black, William (1841–98). Novelist. He was born on 9 November 1841 in Glasgow and was educated there at the School of Art. Abandoning art for journalism, he moved to London in 1864 and served as a war correspondent during the Austro-Prussian War of 1866 and the Franco-Prussian War of 1870–71. Black's first novel *James Merle* (1864) sank without trace, but he made his name with *A Daughter of Heth* (1871) which established him as writer of popular Gothic romances in the Celtic revival style of his contemporary WILLIAM SHARP ('Fiona Macleod'). It was followed by a succession of novels, usually set in the Highlands, which follow a stylized plot: that of the marriage of a beautiful outsider into an exotic society. Most successful of these were *A Princess of Thule* (1874), *Macleod of Dare* (1878), *In Far Lochaber* (1888) and *Donald Ross of Heimra* (1891). Black's novels were collected in 26 volumes during his lifetime (1894) but they have long since disappeared into literary obscurity and he is remembered mainly for his notorious, overwritten descriptions of Hebridean sunsets. He died at the height of his popularity on 10 December 1898 in Brighton.

WORKS: *James Merle* (1864); *Love or Marriage?* (1868); *In Silk Attire* (1870); *A Daughter of Heth* (1871); *The Monarch of Mincing Lane* (1871); *The Strange Adventures of a Phaeton* (1872); *The Maid of Killeena* and *The Marriage of Moira Fergus* (1874); *A Princess of Thule* (1874); *Three Feathers* (1875); *Lady Silverdale's Sweetheart* (1876); *Madcap Violet* (1876); *Green Pastures and Piccadilly* (1877); *Goldsmith* (1878); *Macleod of Dare* (1878); *Sunrise* (1880); *White Wings* (1880); *The Beautiful Witch* (1881); *Adventures in Thule* (1883); *Shandon Bells* (1883); *Yolande* (1883); *Judith Shakespeare* (1884); *White Heather* (1885); *The Wise Women of Inverness* (1885); *Sabina Zembra* (1887); *In Far Lochaber* (1888); *The Strange Adventures of a Houseboat* (1888); *The Penance of John Logan* (1889); *Nanciebel*

(1889); *The New Prince Fortunatus* (1890); *Donald Ross of Heimra* (1891); *Stand Fast Craig-Royston* (1891); *The Magic Wish* (1892); *Wolfenburg* (1892); *Highland Cousins* (1894); *Briseis* (1896); *Wild Eelin* (1898); *With the Eyes of Youth* (1903)

REFERENCE: T. W. Reid, *William Black: Novelist* (London, 1902)

Black Douglas, the. The name given, principally, to Sir James Douglas (1286–1330), the friend and confidant of ROBERT I (Robert the Bruce); the name is also applied to the later Sir William Douglas, Lord of Nithsdale. Sir James Douglas successfully harried the English borderlands in 1319 and thus helped to bring about the treaty between Robert and England's king, Edward II. It was due to the ferocity of his army's depredations that he earned his nickname. On Robert's death Douglas is supposed to have taken the king's heart with him on a crusade to the Holy Lands, a pilgrimage that was cut short when he was killed fighting the Moors in Andalusia. In Scotland he is known as 'The Good Sir James Douglas' and his escapades feature in *Castle Dangerous* by Sir WALTER SCOTT.

Blackie, John Stuart (1809–95). Scholar. He was born on 28 July 1809 in Glasgow, the son of a banker who moved to Aberdeen during his son's infancy. Blackie was educated at Aberdeen Grammar School and the University of Edinburgh, and thereafter he studied theology at Aberdeen with the intention of entering the ministry of the Church of Scotland. However, having completed his training at the age of 19, he was considered to be too young to preach, and his father sent him to Germany and Italy for a further period of study. In 1831 he returned to Scotland to study law in Edinburgh and, although he was never to practise, he was called to the Scottish Bar in 1834. He also began at that time his association with BLACKWOOD'S MAGAZINE, to which he continued regularly to contribute until his death on 2 March 1895. Between 1841 and 1852 he was professor of humanities at Aberdeen and until his retirement in 1882 he held the Chair of Greek at Edinburgh.

Blackie was a tireless translator of work from the classics and he also wrote on the history and philosophy of Greece and Rome. A nationalist and firm supporter of Presbyterianism, he was also an enthusiastic champion of university reform who did much to bring about the foundation of a Chair of Celtic Language

and Literature at Edinburgh. His autobiography, *Notes of a Life* (1910), draws an entertaining, though at times self-satisfied, picture of his life and times.

WORKS: *Classical Literature and its Relation to the Nineteenth Century* (1852); *The Pronunciation of Greek* (1852); *Lays and Legends of Ancient Greece* (1857); *Lyrical Poems* (1860); *The Gaelic Language* (1864); *The Constitutional Association* (1867); *War Songs of the Germans* (1870); *Four Phases of Morals* (1871); *Greek and English Dialogues* (1871); *Lays of the Highlands and Islands* (1872); *Horae hellenicae* (1874); *On Self Culture* (1874); *The Language and Literature of the Scottish Highlands* (1876); *Songs of Religion and Life* (1876); *The Natural History of Athens* (1877); *The Wise Men of Greece* (1877); *The Nile Litany* (1878); *Gaelic Society: Highland Depopulation and Law Reform* (1880); *Lay Sermons* (1881); *Altavona* (1882); *Democracy* (1885); *The Scottish Highlands and Land Laws* (1885); *Messiae vitae* (1886); *The Life of Robert Burns* (1888); *Scottish Song* (1889); *Essays on Subjects of Moral and Social Interest* (1890); *A Song of Hermes* (1890); *Greek Primer* (1891) *A Plea for Scottish Home Rule* (1892); *Christianity and the Ideal of Humanity in Old Times and New* (1893); *Selected Poems* (1893); *Glencoe: an Historical Ballad* (1912)

EDITONS: A. S. Walker, ed., *The Letters of John Stuart Blackie* (Edinburgh, 1909); A. S. Walker, ed., *Notes of a Life* (Edinburgh, 1910); A. S. Walker, ed., *The Day Book of John Stuart Blackie* (London, 1912)

REFERENCE: J. G. Duncan, *The Life of John Stuart Blackie* (Edinburgh, 1895)

Blacklock, Thomas (1721–91). Poet. He was born in Annan, Dumfriesshire, the son of a bricklayer. At the age of six months he became ill with smallpox and as a result he lost his sight permanently. Through the patronage of an Edinburgh doctor, he was brought to the city to complete his education at the University. There he was befriended by the philosopher DAVID HUME (ii), who arranged for Blacklock to be introduced to Joseph Spence (1699–1768), the Professor of Poetry at Oxford and friend of Alexander Pope. In 1754 Spence collected together Blacklock's poems and organized the publication of an edition, together with notes on the text and a biographical sketch of the author. Blacklock was licensed as a preacher in 1759 and became minister of Kirkcudbright, but his blindness had already increased the timidity of his personality and he returned to Edinburgh in 1764 to earn his living by tutoring. He was made a Doctor of Divinity of the University of Aberdeen in 1767 and he died on 7 July 1791.

The publication of *A Collection of Original Poems* (1760), mainly bad imitations of genteel Augustan verse, made Blacklock one of the leading members of the Edinburgh *literati* during the period of the SCOTTISH ENLIGHTEN-MENT, paradoxically at the same time that ROBERT FERGUSSON was writing and publishing his vigorous poetry in Scots. But it was largely due to Blacklock's letter of praise to George Lawrie on the publication of the KIL-MARNOCK EDITION of poems by ROBERT BURNS that Burns abandoned his plans to emigrate to Jamaica and decided to move instead to Edinburgh. Blacklock's other work of note was a heroic ballad, *The Graham* (1774). His poems were collected after his death and published in 1793 with a biography by HENRY MACKENZIE.

WORKS: *Poems on Several Occasions* (1746); *An Essay on Universal Etymology* (1756); *A Select Collection of Psalms* (1756); *A Collection of Original Poems* (1760); *Revealed Religion Proper Consolation of Human Life* (1767); *The Graham* (1774)

EDITIONS: J. Spence, ed., *An Account of the Life, Character and Poems of Mr Blacklock* (Oxford, 1754); H. Mackenzie, ed., *Poems Written by Thomas Blacklock* (Edinburgh, 1793)

Blackwood, William (1776–1834). The founder of the publishing house of William Blackwood and Sons. He was born in Edinburgh on 20 November 1776. At the age of 14 he was apprenticed to the Edinburgh booksellers Bell and Bradfute, and after a spell in Glasgow he formed a partnership with Robert Ross in Parliament Close, Edinburgh. In 1804 he established himself as a bookseller and publisher at 64 South Bridge and was one of the first to move to the Georgian New Town, to 17 Princes Street in 1816. The following year he began to publish BLACKWOOD'S MAGAZINE as a Tory rival to the Whig *Edinburgh Review* (*see* EDINBURGH REVIEW (ii)) and until his death on 16 September 1834 he was at the forefront of Edinburgh publishing.

Blackwood's early catalogues showed a leaning towards antiquarian books, but after he had become John Murray's Edinburgh agent he joined in the contemporary practice of sharing publishing costs and co-operated with Murray in publishing the works of Byron, Shelley and Hazlitt. Encouraged by his success both as a magazine owner and a literary entrepreneur, Blackwood published many of the leading authors of his day: SUSAN EDMONSTOUNE FERRIER, JOHN GALT, JAMES HOGG, ARCHIBALD ALISON and MICHAEL SCOTT (ii).

Blackwood was succeeded by his sons, the second youngest of whom, John Blackwood (1818–79), published, among many other leading authors, George Eliot. A grandson, William Blackwood (iii) (1836–1912), took over in 1879 and was the first British publisher of Joseph Conrad.

REFERENCE: M. Oliphant, *William Blackwood and his Sons: the Annals of a Publishing House*, 2 vols. (Edinburgh, 1897) [vol.3 by Mrs Gerald [Mary] Porter (Edinburgh, 1898)]

Blackwood's Magazine. A magazine published in Edinburgh by the bookseller and publisher WILLIAM BLACKWOOD from 1 April 1817 and originally named the *Edinburgh Monthly Magazine*. For the first six, monthly issues it was edited by JAMES CLEGHORN, a farmer and later editor of the *Farmer's Magazine* published by ARCHIBALD CONSTABLE, and THOMAS PRINGLE. Blackwood established his magazine as a Tory rival to the *Edinburgh Review* (*see* EDINBURGH REVIEW (ii)) set up by FRANCIS JEFFREY and by Constable; when he realized that Cleghorn and Pringle were incapable of editing the magazine in such a way as to challenge the *Edinburgh Review* strongly he dismissed them and employed two young advocates, JOHN WILSON (iii) and JOHN GIBSON LOCKHART. With the help of JAMES HOGG they published in the October 1817 issue the 'CHALDEE MANUSCRIPT', a scurrilous attack, couched in the language of the Old Testament, on Scotland's leading Whigs and all those associated with the *Edinburgh Review*. With this issue the magazine was renamed *Blackwood's Magazine*. The magazine had a *succès de scandale* overnight and the editors followed up their initiative with a critical broadside on the Cockney school of poetry and on Samuel Taylor Coleridge's *Biographia literaria*. There followed similar attacks on John Keats, Leigh Hunt and William Wordsworth which, together with the editors' aggressively pro-Tory stance, earned *Blackwood's* a notorious reputation in its early years.

Lockhart left Edinburgh in 1825 to edit John Murray's *Quarterly Review*, and Wilson remained as the main contributing editor with DAVID MACBETH MOIR. From 1822 to 1835 Wilson was the author of the 'NOCTES AMBROSIANAE', a series of imaginary accounts of nights spent in AMBROSE'S TAVERN, which appeared at regular intervals in the magazine, featuring Wilson as 'Christopher North' and

Hogg as 'The Ettrick Shepherd'. By the 1830s *Blackwood's Magazine* was a spent force as a critical journal but it continued to publish the leading authors of the day. George Eliot's novels, with the exception of *Romola*, appeared in serial form between 1856 and 1876, and among its main contributors were JOHN GALT, Thomas De Quincey, A. W. Kinglake, Lord Lytton, Charles Whibley, NEIL MUNRO, Joseph Conrad and, between 1898 and 1939, JOHN BUCHAN. By the beginning of the 20th century *Blackwood's* had become something of an anachronism, publishing military memoirs and tales of travel and adventure among its book reviews and right-wing editorials. But it continued publication until December 1980.

Blackwood's Magazine was also known by two nicknames: 'Maga', from William Blackwood's pronunciation of 'magazine', and 'Ebony', from the 'Chaldee Manuscript'.

REFERENCE: M. Oliphant *William Blackwood and his Sons: the Annals of a Publishing House*, 2 vols. (Edinburgh, 1897) [vol3. by Mrs Gerald [Mary] Porter (Edinburgh, 1898)]

Blair, Hugh (1718–1800). Divine. He was born on 7 April 1718 in Edinburgh, the son of a merchant. He was educated at the HIGH SCHOOL OF EDINBURGH and the University and was licensed to preach in 1741. Turning to teaching in 1759 he was made Professor of Rhetoric and Belles Lettres at the University of Edinburgh in 1762, an appointment that brought him the friendship of DAVID HUME(ii), WILLIAM ROBERTSON, ADAM SMITH, and other members of the Edinburgh *literati*. Blair's sermons enjoyed an unprecedented popularity during his lifetime and were collected in five volumes published between 1777 and 1801. His *Lectures on Rhetoric and Belles Lettres* (1783) also attracted admirers and helped to set the tone for the Edinburgh literary establishment, but his ornate, somewhat pompous prose style makes his published work little more than a literary curiosity today. As a critic he admired the Augustan prose of Addison and Swift, to which he directed his students 'as a proper method of correcting any peculiarities of dialect'–like many other Scots of the period he was acutely aware of the SCOTICISMS in his speech. In academic and political circles he enjoyed considerable influence but his reputation has been tarnished by his unqualified support for the OSSIAN poems of JAMES MACPHERSON. He retired from public life in 1783 and died on 27 December 1800 in Edinburgh.

WORKS: *The Wrath of Man Praising God* (1746); *The Importance of Religious Knowledge to the Happiness of Mankind* (1750); *A Critical Dissertation on the Poems of Ossian* (1763); *Sermons* (1777); *Lectures on Rhetoric and Belles Lettres* (1783); *Conclusion of a Sermon Preached on the Occasion of the Death of Dr Robert Walker* (1785); *On the Duties of the Young* (1793); *The Compassion and Beneficence of Duty* (1796); *The Beauties of Blair* (1810); *Advice to Youth* (1813); *The Hour and the Event of all Time* (1857)

REFERENCE: R. M. Schmitz, *Hugh Blair* (New York, 1948)

Blair, Robert (1699–1746). Poet. He was born in Edinburgh, the son of a minister of the Church of Scotland, a calling he himself followed after studying at the University of Edinburgh. Between 1731 and his death on 4 February 1746 he had the charge of Athelstaneford in East Lothian (he was succeeded there by JOHN HOME). His son Robert was a distinguished judge, who later became Lord President of the Court of Session. However, it is not merely to these relationships that Blair owes his place in Scottish letters. In 1743 he published his one long poem, *The Grave*, a didactic work of 767 lines which meditates on death and its mysteries and the mournful aftermath of loss and bereavement. The poem is too long and uneven to have survived its immediate publication, but it has been praised for Blair's insights and for the occasional skilfully made line in his blank verse. It was later illustrated by William Blake (1757–1827), who also produced illustrations for *Night Thoughts* by Edward Young who was thought to have influenced the creation of Blair's poem.

WORKS: *A Poem Dedicated to the Memory of the Late Learned and Eminent Mr William Law* (1728); *The Grave* (1743)

EDITION: R. Anderson, ed., *The Poetical Works of Robert Blair* (London, 1794)

Blake, George (1893–1961). Novelist. He was born on 28 October 1893 in Greenock and was educated at the University of Glasgow, where he studied law. During World War I he was wounded at Gallipoli and thereafter turned to journalism, first with the *Glasgow Evening News*, where he succeeded NEIL MUNRO, and later in London as editor of *John o' London's Weekly* and the *Strand Magazine*. In 1930 he became a director of the publishing house of Faber and Faber, and their incorporation of the

Edinburgh company the Porpoise Press took Blake back to Scotland in 1932. From then until the end of his life on 29 August 1961 he lived in Helensburgh and Glasgow, apart from a period during World War II when he worked for the Ministry of Information in London.

Blake is remembered for his novel of the depression period, *The Shipbuilders* (1935), which portrays sympathetically the problems faced by a community when a shipyard closes; it contrasts the fortunes of Leslie Pagan, the owner's son, and Danny Shields, a riveter. Like all his work it is notable for the evocation of Glasgow life and his ability to draw strong, true-to-life characters. He wrote a number of other fine novels about Glasgow, including *Mince Collop Close* (1923), *The Wild Men* (1925), *Young Malcolm* (1926), *David and Joanna* (1936) and *The Peacock Palace* (1958). No less successful are his novels about small-town life and society in the fictional Garvel (Greenock) of *The Valiant Heart* (1940), *The Constant Star* (1945), *The Westering Sun* (1946), *The Paying Guest* (1949) and *The Voyage Home* (1952). Blake also wrote criticism of the 20th-century Scottish novel in *Barrie and the Kailyard School* (1951), and an autobiographical sketch, *Down to the Sea* (1937).

WORKS: *The Mother* (1921); *Clyde Built* (1922); *Vagabond Papers* (1922); *Mince Collop Close* (1923); *The Weather Vessel* (1923); *The Wild Men* (1925); *Young Malcolm* (1926); *Paper Money* (1928); ed., *Scottish Treasure Trove* (1928); *The Coasts of Normandy* (1929); *The Paths of Glory* (1929); *The Press and the Public* (1930); *The Seas Between* (1930); *Returned Empty* (1931); ed., Neil Munro, *Sea Tangle* (1932); *The Looker-On* (1933); *The Heart of Scotland* (1934); *Rest and Be Thankful* (1934); *The Shipbuilders* (1935); *David and Joanna* (1936); *R. M. S. Queen Mary* (1936); *Down to the Sea* (1937); *The Valiant Heart* (1940); *Big Ships, Little Ships* (1944); *The Constant Star* (1945); *British Ships and Shipbuilders* (1946); *The Westering Sun* (1946); *The Five Arches* (1947); *Scottish Affairs* (1947); *Scottish Enterprise and Shipbuilding* (1947); *The Paying Guest* (1949); *Mountain and Flood* (1950); *The Piper's Tune* (1950); ed., *The Trials of Patrick Carraher* (1951); *Barrie and the Kailyard School* (1951); *The Firth of Clyde* (1952); *The Voyage Home* (1952); *The Innocence within* (1955); *The Ben Line* (1956); *Clyde Lighthouses* (1956); *The Last Fling* (1957); *The Peacock Palace* (1958); *Lloyd's Register of Shipping 1760–1960* (1960); *The Loves of Mary Glen* (1960); *Gellatly's 1862–1962* (1962); *The Gourock* (1963)

Blind Harry (c1440–c1492). Poet. Little is known with certainty about the life of Blind Harry who wrote a long poem, WALLACE, about the life of the Scottish patriot Sir WIL-

LIAM WALLACE. Blind Harry was mentioned in 'Lament quhen he was seik' by WILLIAM DUNBAR and in *Historia Majoris Britanniae* by JOHN MAJOR, and there are references to five payments made to 'Blind Hary' by JAMES IV in the Accounts of the Lord High Treasurer of Scotland between April 1490 and January 1492. Early scholars assumed that Harry had been blind since birth but it is unlikely that a blind man would have conceived with such passion the vivid descriptions of warfare which make up the bulk of *Wallace*. From his knowledge of the topography of Scotland it would seem that he was a native of the central belt in which most of Wallace's adventures took place; his familiarity with contemporary scholarship suggests a burgh grammar school education; and his opposition to the pro-English politics of JAMES III would place him as a member of a family from the old landed gentry such as those of Sir William Wallace of Craigie and Sir James Liddale of Creich, at whose instigation he wrote *Wallace*. There is circumstantial and unconvincing evidence from Blind Harry's most recent editor, M. P. McDiarmid (*Hary's Wallace*, vol. 1, pp.cviii–cxxxii) that he also wrote the anonymous *Ballet of the Nine Nobles*, *Rauf Coilzear* and *Golagros and Gawane*.

Harry probably composed *Wallace* about 1477. Written in 12 books, the purpose of the poem was to present in heroic terms the life of Wallace and the story of his struggle against the English. The central character emerges as a man of selfless honesty and, in spite of Harry's distortion of historical fact and his exaggeration of Wallace's prowess, the poem is both a statement of nationhood and a source of information about Wallace's life.

EDITION: M. P. McDiarmid, ed., *Hary's Wallace*, 2 vols., STS (Edinburgh and London, 1968–9)

Blue and Yellow, the. The nickname given to the *Edinburgh Review* (see EDINBURGH REVIEW (ii)). After its first publication in October 1802 it adopted a blue and yellow cover, the election colours of the Whig Party to which the magazine owed political allegiance.

Bochanan, Dùghall [Dugald Buchanan] (1716–68). Poet. He was a native of Ardoch in Strathyre, Perthshire. His education at the parish school was rudimentary and at the age of 14 he left Strathyre to live in Stirling and then in Edinburgh, where he remained until he was

18. He was then apprenticed to a carpenter and after marrying he returned to his native parish, but his new occupation offered little inner satisfaction. During this period the religious manifestations that had haunted him as a child became an obsession, and his diary, kept between 1741 and 1750, contains frightening descriptions of his spiritual struggles between good and evil. He became a travelling teacher and his work as an evangelist led to his being licensed as a preacher in 1753. He assisted with the publication of the first edition of the Gaelic New Testament and his own poems were published in 1767, a year before his death from fever in Kinloch Rannoch.

All Bochanan's poems and songs reflect his fascination for subjects religious and moral, and his long poem *Là a Bhreitheanais* ('The Day of Judgement') is preoccupied with the origin of evil and with the terrors that face the damned. There is little of the milk of human kindness or the balm of God's mercy in the poem, which is, nevertheless, made vivid and alive by Bochanan's lovingly described vision of the torments of the souls in hell. His songs, though didactic, offer a more contented view of the human condition and advocate a personal morality which eschews avarice and ambition and turns instead to the precepts of the scriptures.

EDITION: D. Maclean, ed., *The Spiritual Songs of Dugald Buchanan* (Edinburgh, 1913)

Boece [Boethius], Hector (c1465–1536). Historian. He was born in Dundee, a son of the Laird of Panbride. He was educated at the universities of St Andrews and Paris, and between 1492 and 1498 he was a Professor of Philosophy at the College of Montacute, where he made the acquaintance of Erasmus. His friendship with Bishop Elphinstone, the founder of King's College, Aberdeen, led to his appointment as the college's first principal. Boece's *Vitae Episcoporum Murthlacensium et Aberdonensium* was published in Paris in 1522, but his fame rests on his *Scotorum historiae* (Paris, 1526), which emulates the earlier work by JOHN MAJOR. The *History* was translated into Scots by JOHN BELLENDEN in 1536 and much of it passed into Holinshed's *Chronicle*, but Boece was an inaccurate historian, his account of the early centuries of Scottish history owing more to imagination than to fact. Shakespeare based his tragedy *Macbeth* (*see* MACBETH) on information which Holinshed

had gleaned from Boece. For his work Boece received a crown pension and on his retirement he had the living of a church sinecure in Fyvie, Aberdeenshire.

WORKS: *Vitae Episcoporum Murthlacensium et Aberdonensium* (1522); *Scotorum historiae a prima gentis origine cum aliarum et rerum et gentium illustratione non vulgare* (1526)

EDITIONS: J. Moir, ed., *Lives of the Bishops of Aberdeen*, Translated from Hector Boece, New Spalding Club (Aberdeen, 1894); G. Watson, ed., *The Mar Lodge Translation of the History of Scotland by Hector Boece*, STS (Edinburgh and London, 1946)

Bogan of Bogan, Mrs. Pen-name of CAROLINA OLIPHANT.

Bold, Alan (*b* 1943). Poet. He was born on 20 April 1943 in Edinburgh and was educated there at Broughton High School and at the University. After a variety of jobs, including a year in journalism, he became a full-time writer and now lives at Markinch in Fife. Bold has produced a number of notable anthologies and his critical work includes studies of Scottish literature, Hugh MacDiarmid (CHRISTOPHER MURRAY GRIEVE) and GEORGE MACKAY BROWN. His early poetry expresses his suppressed anger with a society that he believed would not support real values. Although he shows a tendency to allow his poems to become overdidactic, there is a noble dignity in his rage at 'the human lack' in 'June 1967 at Buchenwald' and in his moving poem on his father's suicide, 'A Memory of Death'. Since the mid-1970s Alan Bold has become more interested in the visual, creating a series of stylistically rewarding 'illuminated poems': in his latest collection, *This Fine Day* (1979), he shows a new observation of natural objects without losing sight of his social conscience. As a literary critic he contributes to several newspapers and magazines and is one of the most prolific writers in Scotland today.

WORKS: *Society Inebrious* (1965); *The Voyage* (1966); *To Find the New* (1968); with Edward Braithwaite and Edwin Morgan, *Penguin Modern Poets 15* (1969); *A Perpetual Motion Machine* (1969); *The State of the Nation* (1969); ed., *The Penguin Book of Socialist Verse* (1970); *The Auld Symie* (1971); *A Century of People* (1971); *He Will Be Greatly Missed* (1971); *A Pint of Bitter* (1971); *A Lunar Event* (1973); with David Morrison, *Hammer and Thistle* (1974); ed., *The Cambridge Book of English Verse, 1939–75* (1976); ed., *The Martial Muse: Seven Centuries of War Poetry* (1976); *Thom Gunn and Ted Hughes* (1976); *George Mackay Brown* (1978); ed., *Making*

Love: the Picador Book of Erotic Verse (1978); *Scotland Yes!* (1978); *The Ballad* (1979); ed., *The Bawdy Beautiful: the Sphere Book of Improper Verse* (1979); *This Fine Day* (1979); ed., *Mounts of Venus: the Picador Book of Erotic Prose* (1980); ed., *Tobias Smollett* (1982)

REFERENCE: T. Royle, ed., *Jock Tamson's Bairns: Essays on a Scots Childhood* (London, 1977)

Bonar, Horatius (1808–89). Divine. He was born on 19 December 1808 in Edinburgh and was educated at the HIGH SCHOOL OF EDINBURGH and the University, where he studied divinity. He was licensed as a preacher and was minister in Kelso from 1837 to 1866, when he returned to Edinburgh as minister of the Chalmers Memorial Church. In 1883 he was Moderator of the Assembly of the Free Church, having joined it at THE DISRUPTION of 1843. An evangelist, Bonar wrote numerous religious tracts; he was an energetic preacher and writer of hymns such as 'Glory be to God the Father' and 'I heard the voice of Jesus say'. His *Hymns of Faith and Hope* (1857) was one of the most popular collections of his day and 18 of his compositions were included in the *Scottish Hymnary*, the standard hymnbook of the Presbyterian Churches.

WORKS: *The Door of the Closet Shut* (1838); *Can We Remain in the Church?* (1842); ed., *The Bible Hymnbook* (1845); *The Night of Weeping* (1846); *Truth and Error* (1846); *Prophetical Landmarks* (1847); *The Story of Grace* (1847); *The Blood of the Cross* (1849); *The Coming of the Kingdom of the Lord Jesus Christ* (1849); *Daniel Rowlands* (1850); ed., *Kelso Tracts* (1850); *The Morning of Joy* (1850); *Songs for the Wilderness* (1850); *The Grace the Service and the Kingdom* (1851); *Man his Religion and the World* (1851); *The Sin of our Holy Things Borne by Christ* (1851); *Words of Welcome* (1851); *Forty-fifth Thousand* (1853); *A Stranger Here* (1853); *The Eternal Day* (1854); *The Way of Life* (1855); *The Desert of Sinai* (1857); *Hymns of Faith and Hope* (1857); *The History of Simeon Rosenthal* (1858); *Jerusalem and the Christians there* (1858); *A Land of Promise* (1858); ed., *Lays of the Holy Land* (1858); *Service and Strength for it* (1859); *The True Heart* (1859); *Christ is All* (1860); *Earth's Thirst* (1860); *The Unwritten Words of the Grace of Christ* (1860); *Words to Winners of Souls* (1860); *God's Way of Peace* (1862); *Family Sermons* (1863); *God's Way of Holiness* (1864); *The Word of Promise* (1864); *Catechisms of the Scottish Renaissance* (1866); *Days and Nights on the Cross* (1866); ed., *Lyra consolationis* (1866); *Words Old and New* (1866); *Twenty-first Thousand* (1868); *The Life and Work of the Rev. John Milne of Perth* (1869); *The Nun* (1869); *Light and Truth*, 5 vols. (1872); *The Song of the New Creation* (1872); *The Everlasting Righteousness* (1873); *The Christ of God* (1874); *Follow the Lamb* (1874); *Earth's Morning* (1875); *The Banished One Bearing our Banishment* (1875); *The Love of the Spirit* (1875); *The Rent Veil* (1875); *Believe and Live*

(1876); *The Blood Covenant* (1876); *Brief Thoughts Concerning the Gospel* (1876); *Christ the Cleanser* (1876); *The Cross of the Lord Jesus* (1876); *The Divine Banquet* (1876); *Herod's Ball Room* (1876); *Kept from Falling* (1876); *The Light in the Dark Place* (1876); *The Righteousness of God* (1876); *The Sight of Jesus* (1876); *God's Glory Discovered* (1877); *My Old Letters* (1877); *Does God Care for our Great Cities?* (1880); *Songs of Gladness* (1880); *The White Fields of France* (1880); ed., *Communion Hymns* (1881); *A Home for Eternity* (1881); *How Shall I Go to God?* (1881); *The Life and Work of the Rev. G. Theophilus Dodds* (1884); *Songs of Love and Joy* (1888); *Crowned with Light* (1889); *The Treasures of the Gospel* (1889); *The Light of Dawn* (1895); *Hymns of the Nativity* (1897); *The Land of Light* (1912)

REFERENCE: W. Ewing, *Memories of Dr Horatius Bonar* (Edinburgh, 1909)

Bone, Sir **David William** (1874–1959). Novelist. He was born in Glasgow and between the ages of 15 and 22 served as a sailor in the merchant marine, working on square-rigged sailing ships. In 1899 he joined the Anchor Line, rising to the rank of Commodore, but the publication of his novels about the sea, among which should be mentioned *The Brassbounder* (1910), *Broken Stowage* (1915) and *The Lookoutman* (1923), brought him to public attention and he became a well-known authority on maritime matters. His *Merchantmen at Arms* (1919) was a moving account of the merchant marine during World War I and it was lovingly illustrated by his brother the artist Muirhead Bone. They had previously collaborated, together with Archibald H. Charteris, to produce *Glasgow in 1901* (1901), an enthusiastic, factual description of the city at the turn of the century, produced under the collective pseudonym 'James Hamilton Muir'. Bone was knighted in 1946 and his autobiography, *Landfall at Sunset*, appeared in 1955, four years before his death on 17 May 1959.

WORKS: with Archibald H. Charteris, *Glasgow in 1901* (1901); *The Brassbounder* (1910); *Broken Stowage* (1915); *Merchantmen at Arms* (1919); *The Lookoutman* (1923); *Capstan Bars* (1931); *Merchantmen Re-armed* (1949); *The Queerfella* (1952); *Landfall at Sunset* (1955)

Bon Gaultier Ballads, The. The popular title of a collection of light poems, parodies and burlesques of popular verse written by WILLIAM EDMONSTOUNE AYTOUN and Sir THEODORE MARTIN and published in 1845 under the title *The Book of Ballads edited by Bon Gaultier.* 'Bon Gaultier' was the pseudonym under which Martin wrote for *Fraser's Magazine* and TAIT'S

EDINBURGH MAGAZINE, and many of the ballads appeared in those publications between 1841 and 1844. It is taken from Rabelais' *Prologue to Gargantua: 'A moy n'est que honneur et gloire d'estre dict et repute Bon Gaultier et bon compaignon; en ce nom, suis bien venu en toutes bonnes compaignies de Pantagruelistes.'* Among the parodies are those of Tennyson's 'May Queen' and 'Locksley Hall', Hunt's 'Rimini', Macpherson's OSSIAN poems, Scottish ballads and popular Victorian verse. The ballads are both an attack on exaggerated Romantic sensibility and a satire on the obscurity and egotism of the poets whom Aytoun connected with the so-called Spasmodic School (*see* AYTOUN, WILLIAM EDMONSTOUNE). In their day the ballads enjoyed great popularity and they mark the beginning of the Victorian interest in literary parody. The first edition contained 39 ballads and the final, authorized edition (1857) 56. Although the title remained *The Book of Ballads*, it was known popularly as 'The Bon Gaultier Ballads'.

Bonnie Dundee. *See* GRAHAM, JOHN.

Bonnie Prince Charlie. *See* STUART, CHARLES EDWARD.

Book of Deer. A ninth-century manuscript associated with the Cistercian Abbey of Deer in north-east Aberdeenshire. Written in Latin, it contains the Gospel of St John, parts of the Gospels of Matthew, Mark and Luke, and the Apostles' Creed. It would have been of little value or interest but for the 12th-century additions in Gaelic; the monks' intention in writing the Gaelic notes was to provide a record of grants of land and immunities awarded to their monastery, and in so doing they bequeathed to posterity a valuable social document. Not only do the notes give solid documentary evidence about the tenor of the monks' lives, but they also give a good indication of the kind of Gaelic spoken by the upper classes of northern Scotland during that period. Also included in the notes is the legend of the founding of the monastery by ST COLUMBA and his pupil Cosgrach. The manuscript was acquired by Cambridge University Library (MS I.i.6.32) in 1715, but no attention was paid to it until 1860 when information about its existence was passed to, among others, COSMO INNES. He mentioned it in a postscript to *Scotland in the Middle Ages* (1860) and published it with a translation in his edition of the *Facsimiles of the National Manuscripts of Scotland* (1867).

REFERENCE: K. H. Jackson, *Gaelic Notes in the Book of Deer* (London, 1970)

Book of the Dean of Lismore. A collection of poems in Gaelic compiled by JAMES MACGREGOR, Dean of Lismore in Argyll, and his brother Duncan, who also contributed five poems of his own creation. The verse falls into three parts: bardic/panegyric/formal; occasional/miscellaneous/informal, and heroic poetry from the Ossianic cycle (*see* OSSIAN) common to both Scotland and Ireland. Although the phonetic method of transcription led to the mutilation of several of the works, the *Book of the Dean of Lismore* is a rich source of Gaelic verse before 1500 and its rediscovery in the middle of the 18th century proved the range and catholicity of early Scottish Gaelic bardic verse. Of the 88 poems in the first group the subject matter ranges from praise poems, laments, satires, clan poetry and love songs to poems commenting on contemporary society. They were composed from the early 14th century to the time of the compilation of the book (between 1512 and 1526), mainly by professional bards but also by clan chiefs and others such as Finlay, chief of Clan MacNab, and Isabella, Countess of Argyll.

REFERENCES: W. J. Watson, ed., *Scottish Verse from the Book of the Dean of Lismore*, SGTS (Edinburgh, 1937); N. Ross, ed., *Heroic Poetry from the Book of the Dean of Lismore*, SGTS (Edinburgh, 1939)

Boswell, Sir Alexander ['Simon Gray'] (1775–1822). Antiquary and songwriter. He was born on 9 October 1775 at the family home of Auchinleck in Ayrshire. His father was the biographer JAMES BOSWELL and his grandfather the judge Lord Auchinleck (1706–82). After a tour of Europe during which he studied at Leipzig, Boswell returned to Scotland and took up residence at his family seat, where he interested himself in the collection of traditional Scots songs. He contributed to the *Select Collection of Original Scotish Airs* (1817) by GEORGE THOMSON, and before that, on his own account, he had written and published his *Songs, Chiefly in the Scots Dialect* (1802), which contains the popular airs 'Jenny's Bawbee' and 'Jenny dang the weaver'. At Auchinleck he established his own printing press in 1815 and set about printing his own antiquarian works, as well as reprints of Scottish historical documents and poems. Among his own publications *The Spirit of Tintoc or Johnny Bell and the Kelpie* (1803), a folk ballad, and *Edinburgh or the Ancient Royalty: a Sketch of Former Manners* (1810) written under the pseudonym 'Simon Gray', are perhaps the best known.

Boswell enjoyed an esteemed place in Ayrshire society and he was responsible for the erection of the monument to ROBERT BURNS on the banks of the River Doon. His involvement in Tory politics led to a duel with his neighbour James Stuart of Dunearn, during which he was mortally wounded and he died on 27 March 1822. Stuart was subsequently tried for murder but was acquitted following a skilful defence by HENRY THOMAS Lord COCKBURN and FRANCIS JEFFREY. Sir WALTER SCOTT used the facts of the duel for a scene in his novel *St Ronan's Well* (1824).

WORKS: *Cold in this Tomb the Dust of Werter Lies* (1800); *Jenny's Bawbee* (1800); *Songs, Chiefly in the Scots Dialect* (1802); *Epistle on the Edinburgh Reviewers* (1803); *The Spirit of Tintoc or Johnny Bell and the Kelpie* (1803); *Epitaph on the Late Alexander Wood* (1807); as Simon Gray, *Edinburgh or the Ancient Royalty: a Sketch of Former Manners* (1810); *Clan Alpin's Vow* (1811); ed., *Frondes caducae*, 7 vols. (1816–18); *If your Hobby's Unsound* (1816); *Skeldon Haughs* (1816); *The Woo-Creel or the Bill o'Bashan* (1816); *Bar-tho-lo-me-o* (1820); *Epitaph on Lord President Forbes* (1820)

EDITION: R. H. Smith, ed., *Poetical Works of Sir Alexander Boswell* (Glasgow, 1871)

Boswell, James (1740–95). Biographer. He was born on 29 October 1740 in Edinburgh, the son of an advocate, Alexander Boswell (1706–82), who was later to become Lord Auchinleck, a distinguished Lord of Session. He was educated privately in Edinburgh and by a tutor until he was 13, when he matriculated at the University of Edinburgh. While a student he started writing poetry, Augustan pastiches, for the SCOTS MAGAZINE AND GENERAL INTELLIGENCER, and verse writing was to remain an interest throughout his life. The theatre, too, became a passion, and Boswell's interest in it (his first publication, *A View of the Edinburgh Theatre* was published in 1759) and his tendency to philander led to a breach with his father, culminating in his banishment to Glasgow to study law in 1759. In the summer of the following year he ran away to London, where he became a Catholic and attempted to

find the necessary political patronage to join a guards' regiment, but through his father's influence he returned to Edinburgh to resume his legal studies. During this period he enjoyed the friendship of Lord Kames and Lord Hailes, two leading Edinburgh *literati* who also became father figures to the young Boswell. He furthered his legal studies in Utrecht and was called to the Scottish Bar in 1766. While in Europe (1763–5) he visited Germany and Italy, and through his persistence engineered visits to Jean-Jacques Rousseau (1712–78) and Voltaire (1694–1778), meetings which satisfied both his lifelong need to make the acquaintance of great men and also his genuine intellectual curiosity. In 1759, at the end of his tour, he was in Corsica where he met the patriot Pasquale Paoli and gained the material for his successful book on Corsica's plight, *An Account of Corsica* (1768).

For 17 years Boswell practised at the Scottish Bar, making frequent visits to London to pursue his literary and political ambitions and to keep up his friendship with Samuel Johnson (1709–84) who helped him in 1773 to join The Club, later The Literary Club. Boswell had first met Johnson on 16 May 1763 in Thomas Davies's Bookshop in Russell Street, and, although he was at first rebuffed by the great English man of letters, Boswell pursued his claim and the two quickly became close acquaintances.

Boswell began to keep a journal in 1762 and for the rest of his life he retained an ability to summon up scenes and conversations from his many meetings in London, Edinburgh and Europe, which were to be of use to him in his published writings. At their best, Boswell's journals and letters to friends such as John Johnston reveal him as an inquisitive, perceptive recorder of the society of his age and a writer of great verbal dexterity; at their worst they betray him to have been a self-centred seeker after personal glory, much given to lascivious behaviour. The combination of those two opposites in his private writing provided most of the material he needed for his two great works, his journal of the tour he made with Johnson through Scotland to the Western Isles in 1773, which came out in 1785 but which was not published in its entirety until 1936 (as *Boswell's Journal of a Tour to the Hebrides with Samuel Johnson LL.D. Now First Published from the Original Manuscript*), and his *Life of Samuel Johnson LL.D.* (1791), generally held to be the greatest biography in the English language. In both books Boswell's power of recall and his vivid narrative present an irresistible picture of Dr Johnson and his social milieu. Although Boswell had courted Johnson's friendship and continued to be jealous of it throughout his life, his portrait is not that of a sycophant and Johnson is presented in all his differing moods and failings.

Johnson's visit to Edinburgh in 1773, en route for the Western Isles, was a high point in Boswell's career and one that enabled him to give full vent to his pride in his native country in front of the famous Scotophobe. Boswell was split in his attitudes to Scotland: on the one hand he was fiercely proud of his lineage and of the traditions and history of Scotland, on the other he preferred the metropolitan culture of London to what he saw as the provincial narrowness of Edinburgh, and like many other *literati* of his generation he was concerned to rid his speech of SCOTICISMS. His hopes for political advancement in Scotland were dashed by his arguments with the powerful secretary of state HENRY DUNDAS, Viscount Melville, and by his increasingly irresponsible behaviour in public. In 1786 he finally settled in London and attempted, unsuccessfully, to make a living at the English Bar and to prepare his biography of Dr Johnson. He was appointed Recorder of Carlisle in 1788 under the patronage of the Earl of Lonsdale but relinquished the post a year later. The final years of his life were spent in sad dissipation in London where he died on 19 May 1795. Boswell had married his cousin Margaret Montgomerie (*d* 1789) in November 1769 and they had four children, one of whom, Alexander (*see* BOSWELL, ALEXANDER), became a well-known antiquary and songwriter.

The recovery of many of Boswell's letters from Malahide Castle in Ireland in 1926, 1937, 1939, and 1948, and from Fettercairn in 1930 has thrown new light on his private life, as well as providing a compelling picture of the age in which he lived, its personalities and manners. Their discovery has also allowed complete editions of the *Tour* and the *Life* to be published (in 1936 and 1934–40). The letters and other previously unpublished papers are being published by Yale University Press under the editorial chairmanship of F. A. Pottle. Boswell also contributed several essays of an introspective nature to the *London Magazine* under the pseudonym 'Hypochondriak', and

his other works of note are a prose romance, *Dorando* (1767), *The Essence of the Douglas Cause* (1767), *A Letter to the People of Scotland on the Present State of the Nation* (1783) and *A Letter to the People of Scotland on the Alarming Attempt to Infringe the Articles of Union* (1785); the last two are cogently argued epistles aimed (unsuccessfully) at furthering his political ambitions.

WORKS: *A View of the Edinburgh Theatre* (1759); *Elegy on the Death of an Amiable Young Lady* (1761); *Ode to Tragedy* (1761); *The Cub at New-Market* (1762); *Critical Strictures on the New Tragedy of Elvira* (1763); *Letters between James Boswell and the Hon. Andrew Erskine* (1763); *Dorando* (1767); *The Essence of the Douglas Cause* (1767), *An Account of Corsica* (1768); ed., *British Essays in Favour of the Brave Corsicans* (1769); *On the Profession of a Player* (1770); *Letter to Robert MacQueen, Lord Braxfield* (1780); *A Letter to the People of Scotland on the Present State of the Nation* (1783); *Ode by Dr Johnson to Mrs Thrale* (1784); *Journal of a Tour to the Hebrides* (1785); *A Letter to the People of Scotland on the Alarming Attempt to Infringe the Articles of Union* (1785); *Conversation between His Most Sacred Majesty George III and Samuel Johnson* (1790); *the Life of Samuel Johnson LL.D*, 2 vols. (1791); *No Abolition of Slavery* (1791); *Ode to Mr Charles Dilley* (1791)

EDITIONS: T. Secombe, ed., *Letters of James Boswell to the Rev. W. J. Thrale* (London, 1908); C. B. Tinker, ed., *Letters of James Boswell*, 2 vols. (London, 1924); M. Bailey, ed., *The Hypochondriak*, 2 vols. (London, 1928); M. Bailey, ed., *Boswell's Column, being his Seventy Contributions to the London Magazine* (London, 1931); G. Birbeck Hill, ed., rev. L. F. Powell, *The Life of Samuel Johnson LLD*, 6 vols. (Oxford, 1934–40); F. A. Pottle and C. H. Bennett, eds, *Boswell's Journal of a Tour to the Hebrides with Samuel Johnson LL.D. Now first published from the Original Manuscript* (New York and London, 1936); F. A. Pottle, ed., *Boswell's London Journal 1762–1763* (London, 1950); M. Bishop, ed., *The Journal of a Tour to Corsica; and Memoirs of Pascal Paoli by James Boswell Esq.* (London, 1951); F. A. Pottle, ed., *Boswell in Holland 1763–1764* (New York and London, 1952); F. A. Pottle, ed., *Boswell on the Grand Tour, Germany and Switzerland, 1764* (New York and London, 1953); F. A. Pottle, ed., *Boswell on the Grand Tour: Italy, Corsica and France, 1765–1766* (New York and London, 1954); F. Brady and F. A. Pottle, eds., *Boswell in Search of a Wife, 1766–1769* (New York and London, 1957); W. K. Wimstatt and F. A. Pottle, eds., *Boswell for the Defence* (New York and London, 1960); C. Ryskamp and F. A. Pottle, eds., *Boswell: the Ominous Years, 1774–1776* (New York and London, 1963); R. S. Walker, ed., *The Correspondence of James Boswell and John Johnston of Grange* (New Haven, Conn., and London, 1966); M. Waingrow, ed., *The Correspondence and Other Papers of James Boswell Relating to the Making of the 'Life of Johnson'* (New Haven, Conn., and London, 1969); C. M. C. Weis and F. A. Pottle, eds., *Boswell in Extremes 1776–1778* (New York and London, 1971); J. W. Reid and F. A. Pottle, eds., *Boswell:*

Laird of Auchinleck, 1778–1782 (New York and London, 1977)

REFERENCES: F. A. Pottle, *The Literary Career of James Boswell* (New York and London, 1929); F. Brady, *Boswell's Political Career* (London, 1965); F. A. Pottle, *James Boswell: the Earlier Years* (New York and London, 1966)

Bothwell, 4th Earl of. *See* HEPBURN, JAMES.

Bower, Walter (1383–1437). Historian. He was born in Haddington and educated at Paris and St Andrews before being appointed Abbot of the island of Inchcolm in the Firth of Forth in 1418. In 1424 he was one of the commissioners appointed to raise the ransom for the release of JAMES I. He continued what is now known as the SCOTICHRONICON by expanding on the *Chronica gentis Scotorum* of JOHN OF FORDUN, extending the history from 1383 to 1437. Like John he had access to documents and other materials which have since been lost and the *Scotichronicon* has become one of the most important source books for Scottish historians. Several manuscript copies were made but it was not published in its entirety until 1759.

Boyd, A(ndrew) K(ennedy) H(utchison) (1825–99). Divine and essayist. He was born on 3 November 1825 in Glasgow. After a period spent studying for the English Bar he returned to Glasgow to study for the ministry of the Church of Scotland. In 1865 he became a minister in St Andrews; he enjoyed a good deal of success in church life by publishing sermons and doctrinal essays, and in 1890 he was elected Moderator of the General Assembly of the Church of Scotland. Boyd was a regular contributor to a number of literary periodicals, writing under the pseudonym of his initials, and a selection of his well-told stories, consisting of reminiscences and gossip about country matters, was published in *The Recreations of a Country Parson.*

WORKS: *Spiritual Insensibility* (1859); *The Commonplace Philosopher in Town and Country* (1862); *The Graver Thoughts of a Country Parson* (1862); *Leisure Hours in Town* (1862); *The Recreations of a Country Parson* (1862); *Counsel and Comfort Spoken from a City Pulpit* (1863); *The Autumn Holidays of a Country Parson* (1864); *The Practical Service of Imperfect Means* (1864); *The Critical Essays of a Country Parson* (1865); *Sunday Afternoon at the Parish Church of a University* (1866); *Lessons of Middle Age* (1868); *Changed Aspects of Unchanged Truths* (1869); *The Place of Ritual* (1869); *Present Day Thoughts* (1871);

Seaside Musings on Sundays and Weekdays (1872); *A Scotch Communion Sunday* (1873); *Landscape Churches and Moralities* (1874); *From a Quiet Place* (1879); *Towards the Sunset* (1883); *Our Little Life* (1884); *A Young Man* (1884); *What Set him Right* (1885); *Our Homely Comedy and Tragedy* (1887); *The Best Last* (1888); *East Coast Days and Memories* (1889); *To Meet the Day Through the Christian Year* (1889); *Church Life in Scotland* (1890); *The Mother of us All* (1890); *Twenty-Five Years of St Andrews* (1892); *St Andrews and Elsewhere* (1894); *Occasional and Immemorial Days* (1895); *The Last Years of St Andrews* (1896); *Sermons and Stray Papers* (1907)

REFERENCE: D. R. Hutchison, *Anecdotes and Recollections of A.K.H.B.* (Edinburgh, 1900)

Boyd, Mark Alexander (1563–1601). Poet and scholar. He was born on 13 January 1563 at Penkill, Ayrshire. After his father's early death he was educated under the care of his uncle James Boyd, who was consecrated Archbishop of Glasgow in 1573. Boyd's headstrong temper and predilection for fighting duels forced him to flee to Paris in 1581 (it was during this period that he added the martial 'Alexander' to his name). He studied there and then took civil law at Orleans and Bourges before plague drove him to Italy, where he remained until 1587. During the civil war in France he fought as a soldier of fortune in the army of Henri III and was wounded at Toulouse. For the rest of his period in France he alternated between his legal studies and his career as a soldier, believing that a knowledge of military affairs was essential for the complete man. The story of his wanderings in France and Italy is told in his letters, printed with his poems in Latin in Antwerp in 1592. In 1596 he returned to Scotland and attempted to join the court of JAMES VI. He died on 10 April 1601 in Ayrshire.

Boyd wrote his poetry in Latin in the style of Ovid, and his *Hymni* are concerned with the legends surrounding various plants and flowers. Together with his *Epistolae heroidum* they were published in the DELITIAE POETARUM SCOTORUM published in Antwerp in 1637 edited by Sir JOHN SCOTT of Scotstarvit and ARTHUR JOHNSTON. Boyd's one poem in Scots, an Italianate sonnet 'Fra banc to banc, fra wod to wod, I rin', is considered one of the finest love-poems in Scots.

WORKS: *M. Alexandri Bodii Epistolae heroides et Hymni* (1592)

REFERENCE: D. Dalrymple, *Sketch of the Life of Mark Alexander Boyd* (Edinburgh, 1787)

Boyd, Zachary (c1585–1653). Poet. Zachary Boyd was educated at the universities of Glasgow and St Andrews and he studied subsequently at the Protestant college of Saumur in France. In 1623 he returned to Glasgow as a minister of the Church of Scotland and until his death in 1653 he was deeply involved in the affairs of the University of Glasgow to which he bequeathed his substantial manuscript collection. Boyd printed a number of quaint prose works between 1629 and 1650 and produced a series of evangelical poems, now long forgotten. His name has been preserved, though, through *Zion's Flowers*, a collection of Bible stories turned into frequently execrable verse, and for his attempts to produce metrical versions of the PSALMS in Scots. In later years the piety of Boyd's work was often the butt of parody, especially by Samuel Colvill in *The Whig's Supplication*.

WORKS: *The Balme of Gilead Prepared for the Sicke* (1629); *The Last Battell of the Soule in Death* (1629); *Two Orientall Pearles* (1629); *Two Sermons* (1629); *Rex pater patriae* (1633); *A Cleare Form of Catechising* (1639); *The Battle of Nevvburne* (1643); *Crosses, Comforts, Counsels* (1643); *The Sword of the Lord and of Gideon* (1643); *The Garden of Zion* (1644); *Zion's Flowers* (1644)

Brandane, John. Pen-name of JOHN MACINTYRE.

Braxfield, Lord. *See* MACQUEEN, ROBERT.

Brewster, Sir David (1781–1868). Natural philosopher. He was born on 11 December 1781 at Jedburgh and was educated locally before enrolling at the University of Edinburgh in 1793 to study for the ministry of the Church of Scotland. To make ends meet Brewster found employment as a private tutor to a Peeblesshire family and he also began contributing articles on various scientific subjects to Edinburgh literary journals. In March 1804 he was licensed as a preacher in Edinburgh, but his nervousness in the pulpit forced him to return to private tutoring and he began to press his claims for an academic appointment. Despite a plethora of honorary degrees he failed to gain a chair in a Scottish university and was forced to make his own way in the world. His interests turned to the polarization of light, and following time spent in Switzerland and London he produced a number of papers on the subject; he also invented the kaleidoscope for his own and others' amusement. His researches into the science of optics led him to report officially on new systems of illumination for lighthouses; they were the means of his meeting early photographers and he was an enthusiastic supporter of the work of D. O. Hill (1802–70) and Robert Adamson (1821–48), the Scottish calotype pioneers.

Brewster received international acclaim for his scientific work and he was knighted in 1831. He was invited to become the editor of the *Edinburgh Encyclopaedia*, a task that was to take up 22 years of his life, and he was a founder-member of the Royal Scottish Society of Arts. Between 1837 and 1859 he was Principal of the united colleges of St Salvator and St Leonard in St Andrews and then Principal of the University of Edinburgh until his death on 10 February 1868. Although his career as a divine had been cut short, Brewster was an ardent supporter of the Free Church of Scotland after THE DISRUPTION of 1843. His fame ultimately rests on his scientific work on the nature of optics, with special regard to the invention of the stereoscope and the introduction of new and improved systems of light projection for British lighthouses.

WORKS: *The History of Free Masonry* (1804); *A Treatise on the New Philosophical Instruments* (1813); *A Treatise on the Kaleidoscope* (1819); *A Life of Sir Isaac Newton* (1831); *Letters on Natural Magic* (1832); *A Treatise on Magnetism* (1837); *The Martyrs of Science* (1841); *More Worlds than One* (1854); *Memoirs of the Life, Writings and Discoveries of Sir Isaac Newton*, 2 vols. (1855); *The Stereoscope, its History, Theory and Construction* (1856); *On the Life Boat, the Lightning Conductor and the Light House* (1859); *Introductory Address on the Opening of the Session, 1859–1860* (1859)

REFERENCE: M. Gordon, *The Home Life of Sir David Brewster* (Edinburgh, 1869)

Bride [Brigit, Bridget, Brighde], **St.** There are three versions of the story of St Bride, corresponding with the different forms of her name. The pre-Christian Celtic Brigit, daughter of Dagda and wife of the sea giant Bress, was known as a powerful fire goddess. The historical St Bridget of Kildare (452–524) was associated with the religious settlement on the Curragh in Ireland, which became one of the great Irish monastic foundations; Bridget was the patron saint of the newly-sown crops. From the fusion of pagan goddess and Christian saint the figure of St Bride emerged in Scotland, where she is worshipped in some of the Hebridean islands as *Muime Chriosd,* the foster-mother of Jesus Christ. Her Saint's day is 1 February, the old Celtic festival of Spring and the day before the Christian feast of CAND-LEMAS.

Bride of Lammermoor, The. A novel by Sir WALTER SCOTT, first published in 1819 in the third series of TALES OF MY LANDLORD. It tells the story of the Ravenswood family, dispossessed of their East Lothian estates through the legal machinations of Sir William Ashton, the Lord Keeper. Old Lord Ravenswood dies leaving his son Edgar to avenge the family's honour. After a chance encounter with Ashton and his daughter Lucy, during which Edgar rescues them from a wild bull, Ashton, a Whig, sees the opportunity of restoring his favour with the Tories by relenting towards the Ravenswood family. His chosen instrument is Lucy, who has fallen in love with Edgar. Any hope of an engagement is dashed by Lady Ashton who arranges a marriage for Lucy with the wealthy Laird of Bucklaw. Ravenswood is sent on a diplomatic mission overseas and his correspondence with Lucy is intercepted. Lucy is married unwillingly to Bucklaw whom she murders on their wedding night; she then dies in a fit of insanity. On his return Ravenswood prepares to fight a duel with Lucy's brother but is accidentally drowned in the quicksands of Kelpie's Flow, thus fulfilling an ancient prophecy of doom. Caleb Balderstone, steward to the Ravenswoods, belongs to Scott's gallery of grotesque minor characters, and it is his place in the novel to act as a reminder of the past glories of his master's family.

Much of the novel was written while Scott was unwell and taking drugs, and on rereading it in health he disclaimed all knowledge of having written some of the gloomier episodes. The atmosphere, perhaps because of Scott's physical and mental state, is dark, lowering and portent-laden, with violent motifs from Scotland's past, in this case the later 17th century. But beyond the doomed inevitability of the fates of the central characters, Scott drew a finely resolved picture of the passion felt for each other by Edgar and Lucy. The novel was made into an opera, *Lucia di Lammermoor,* by Donizetti.

Bridie, James. Pen-name of O. H. MAVOR.

Brigs of Ayr, The. A poem by ROBERT BURNS,

first published in the Edinburgh edition of Burns's poems in 1787. It is written in the form of a dialogue between the old bridge of Ayr and its modern successor, built in the autumn of 1786, and is modelled on the dialogue 'Mutual Complaint of Plainstanes and Causey, in their Mother Tongue' by ROBERT FERGUSSON.

Brodie, William (*d* 1788). Edinburgh town councillor, who held the post of Deacon of Wrights and Masons. He led a notorious double life as head of a gang of burglars by night; after an unsuccessful attempt to rob the General Excise Office in Chessel's Court, he was betrayed by an accomplice and although he fled to Holland he was arrested in Amsterdam and brought back to Edinburgh to face trial. He was executed on a gallows of his own design on 1 October 1788. He is the subject of a play by ROBERT LOUIS STEVENSON and W. E. Henley (1849–1903), *Deacon Brodie, or The Double Life* (1880), and the duality of his character, sober citizen by day, outlaw by night, was a source of inspiration for Stevenson's novel THE STRANGE CASE OF DR JEKYLL AND MR HYDE.

Brougham,   Henry   Peter, 1st   Baron (1778–1869). Lawyer and journalist. He was born on 19 September 1778 in Edinburgh and was educated at the HIGH SCHOOL OF EDIN-BURGH and the University. He was called to the Scottish Bar in 1800 and to the English Bar ten years later, and much of his early life was spent enjoying the success of a highly regarded barrister. He was Queen Caroline's defence counsel in 1820 when she was accused of adultery, and his liberal sympathies led him to espouse the cause of popular education and the abolition of slavery. In 1830 he entered on a political career and was made Lord Chancellor but he quarrelled with his colleagues and never reached higher office. His interests in education attracted him to the Society for the Diffusion of Knowledge, a philanthropic group which helped to establish the Mechanics' Institutes; he was also a founder of the University of London.

Brougham is perhaps best remembered as an associate of Sydney Smith and FRANCIS JEF-FREY, the founders of the *Edinburgh Review* (*see* EDINBURGH REVIEW (ii)). He wrote widely on legal and political matters during his lifetime but none of his writings has withstood the test of time; it is probable that he wrote the review of Byron's *Hours of Idleness* in 1808 which provoked the publication of Byron's famous reply in *English Bards and Scotch Reviewers* (*see* BYRON, GEORGE GORDON NOEL). Brougham was caricatured as 'the learned friend' in the satirical novel *Crotchet Castle* (1831) by Thomas Love Peacock (1785–1866), and his features were well-known from the cartoons of *Punch*. His *Complete Works* were published in 11 volumes (1855–61) and his autobiography appeared in the year of his death.

REFERENCES: F. Hawes, *Henry Brougham* (London, 1957); C. W. New, *The Life of Henry Brougham to 1830* (London, 1961)

Brown, George Douglas ['Kennedy King'; 'George Douglas'] (1869–1902). Novelist. He was born on 26 January 1869 in Ochiltree, Ayrshire, the illegitimate son of a farmer. He was educated at the village school and between 1884 and 1887 at Ayr Academy, where he was greatly influenced and encouraged by its rector William Maybin. In 1887 he matriculated at the University of Glasgow and in 1891 he won a Snell Exhibition which took him to Balliol College, Oxford, where he remained until 1895. His mother's death that year cut off many of his links with Ayrshire and he settled in London, earning a living from tutoring and literary journalism.

Brown's first book, a boy's adventure novel set in the Afridi War, *Love and Sword* (1899), was published under his pseudonym 'Kennedy King', the name which he used for most of his lighter journalism. Through his friendship with David Meldrum, Blackwood's literary adviser, he contributed a telling article on ROBERT BURNS to the August 1896 issue of BLACKWOOD'S MAGAZINE, and a glossary to Blackwood's republication of the novels of JOHN GALT, a writer whom Brown particularly admired. In 1900 he began work on the novel for which he is best known, THE HOUSE WITH THE GREEN SHUTTERS, published in 1901 under his pseudonym 'George Douglas'. Written in opposition to the KAILYARD school of rural sentimentality, *The House with the Green Shutters* traces the fall of John Gourlay, a self-made man with vaulting ambitions, in the claustrophobic small town of Barbie. Much of the novel came from Brown's childhood memories of village life and in the powerful portrayal of John Gourlay there is evidence of Brown's hatred of his illegitimate relationship

to his own father, an overbearing Ayrshire farmer. Brown intended to follow up his success with two novels, *The Incompatibles* and *The Novelist*, both of which existed in note form and are loosely autobiographical, but he died of pneumonia on 28 August 1902 after returning to London from a visit to Ayrshire. His early death removed from Scottish literature one of its richest talents.

WORKS: as Kennedy King, *Love and a Sword* (1899); as George Douglas, *The House with the Green Shutters* (1901)

REFERENCE: J. Veitch, *George Douglas Brown* (London, 1952)

Brown, George Mackay (*b* 1921). Poet and novelist. He was born on 17 October 1921 in Stromness, Orkney, the youngest son of a postman. He was educated at Stromness Academy between 1926 and 1940 but after leaving school illness prevented him from working and he spent a period in hospital suffering from tuberculosis. In 1957 he entered Newbattle Abbey College, a residential adult education college near Edinburgh, where EDWIN MUIR was Warden. Brown's first poem was published while he was a student and he enjoyed the support and encouragement of Muir, who also contributed an introduction to Brown's first collection of poems, *The Storm* (1954). Further illness prevented Brown from completing the course at Newbattle, but he returned in 1956 to prepare himself for matriculation at the University of Edinburgh. He graduated in 1960 and returned to Edinburgh between 1962 and 1964 to do post-graduate work on Gerard Manley Hopkins. Since then he has lived at Stromness in Orkney.

A second collection of poems, *Loaves and Fishes* was published in 1959, while Brown was a student at Edinburgh. The book is arranged in three sections, 'The Drowning Wave', 'Crofts along the Shore' and 'The Redeeming Wave', but the collection exists as a unity through its religious perspective, a concern with death and resurrection, themes which are central to his poetry. There is also a fine delineation of the wind-swept Orkney landscape and its people, both real and mythical; in 'Hamnavoe' (which came to be the fictional name of Brown's Stromness) a tribute to his father turns into an evocation of a day in the life of the town of his childhood. in *The Year of the Whale* (1965), published after Brown's conversion to Catholicism (in 1961), there is a preoccupation with faith and its renewal, by which man is able to overcome death and defeat. Brown's only long poem (to date), *Fishermen with Ploughs*, was published in 1971, but it is more of a sequence of interdependent poems than a continuous narrative. Many of Brown's favourite images are present in the poem, which follows the history of the valley of Rackwick on the island of Hoy from the time of the early settlers to its final destruction in the name of progress: the happy simplicity of the Viking settlers, the renewal of life through the planting of seed and its harvest, and Christ's passion in counterpoint to the suffering of man. The Christian theme is extended in *Winterfold* (1976) which begins and ends with a religious sequence, the stories of the nativity and the crucifixion. As in most of his religious and historical poems, Brown uses the technique of weaving together past and present, the mythical with the contemporary. In all his poetry there is a natural fluency, which extends from the directness of the lyric to an ornate form with intricate internal rhymes, which he uses especially in his religious work.

Many of Brown's favourite poetic themes recur in his short stories which are firmly rooted in the communal life of Orkney. The tales are told with a simple lyrical intensity; they are concerned both with the matter of everyday life and with the rich heritage of Orkney's history, the two frequently being interwoven. *A Calendar of Love* (1967) was his first collection and its title story is rich with the symbolism of seed-time and harvest and with the renewal of life through pain and suffering; the collection contains *Witch*, a horrifying story of witch-hunting in 16th-century Orkney. His second collection, *A Time to Keep* (1969), contains his two best short stories, *Celia*, a sensitive study of alcoholism and loneliness, and *The Eye of the Hurricane*, in which an old sea captain drinks himself to death in despair. Brown's interest in the story of his native islands comes alive in *Hawkfall* (1974), which ranges from the Bronze Age to the present day, and *The Sun's Net* (1976), which contains the story of John Gow, the Orkney pirate. There are also two collections of stories for children: *The Two Fiddlers* (1974) and *Pictures in the Cave* (1977).

Greenvoe (1972), Brown's first novel, is a sequence of six portraits of the imaginary community of Greenvoe on the island of Hellya. The final destruction of the island by a military–technological project, Operation Black Star, is preceded by a series of loving pictures of the island and its people, the action frequently being seen from multiple viewpoints. His second novel, *Magnus* (1973), retells the story of the murder of ST MAGNUS from the ORKNEYINGA SAGA by intertwining past and present and overlaying the action with Catholic doctrine in the martyrdom of Magnus. Brown has written a play for radio, *A Spell for Green Corn* (1970), and several of his short stories have been dramatized. He has won several literary prizes and was made an Officer, Order of the British Empire in 1974.

WORKS: *Let's See the Orkney Islands* (1948); *The Storm* (1954); *Loaves and Fishes* (1959); *A Calendar of Love* (1965); *A Calendar of Love* (1967); *Twelve Poems* (1968); *An Orkney Tapestry* (1969); *A Time to Keep* (1969); *A Spell for Green Corn* (1970); *Fishermen with Ploughs* (1971); *Lifeboat and Other Poems* (1971); *Poems, New and Selected* (1971); *Greenvoe* (1972); *Magnus* (1973); *Hawkfall* (1974); *The Two Fiddlers* (1974); *Edwin Muir: a Memoir* (1975); *Letters from Hamnavoe* (1975); *The Sun's Net* (1976); *Winterfold* (1976); *Pictures in the Cave* (1977); *Selected Poems* (1977); *Witch and Other Stories* (1977); *Portrait of Orkney* (1981); *Andrina* (1983)

REFERENCE: A. Bold, *George Mackay Brown* (Edinburgh, 1978)

Brown, Isaac. Pen-name of WILLIAM MOTHERWELL.

Brown James ['J. B. Selkirk'] (1832–1904). Poet. He was born in Galashiels and his childhood was spent in the neighbouring Border town of Selkirk, which was to be his home for the rest of his life. Coming from a mill-owning family, Brown entered his father's tweed-manufacturing business, after being educated at Selkirk Grammar School and Edinburgh Institution, but he was unsuited to a career in commerce. He retired early after the collapse of his firm in 1870, and until his death on 25 December 1904 his life was spent in local civic affairs. Taking the name of his adopted town as his pseudonym, Brown became a frequent contributor to BLACKWOOD'S MAGAZINE and CHAMBERS'S JOURNAL on a variety of religious and poetic topics; his study *Bible Truths with Shakespearean Parallels* was published in 1857. His collections of verse of 1883 and 1896 enjoyed a wide popularity for their simple and unaffected descriptions of Border landscapes and for Brown's homely sentiments on such moral matters as the sanctity of family life, the purity of love, and spiritual devotion. The death of his wife in 1874 cast a gloom over his life and the poems in her memory, such as 'Time's Test' and 'Broken Strings', have a poignancy that never allows false sentimentality to intrude. His best poems, though, deal with the countryside of the Borders and episodes from Border history.

EDITION: W. Sorley Brown, ed., *The Complete Poems of J. B. Selkirk* (Selkirk, 1932)

Brown, John (1810–82). Essayist. He was born on 22 September 1810 in Biggar, Lanarkshire, the son of a minister and biblical scholar of the same name. In 1822 the family moved to Edinburgh and Brown was educated at the HIGH SCHOOL OF EDINBURGH and the University, where he studied medicine; Edinburgh was to remain his home until his death on 11 May 1882.

During his lifetime Brown lived two lives: he was a well-respected general practitioner and an essayist with a wide circle of literary friends. Renowned as a brilliant conversationalist, something of that easy, flowing style can be found in his essays, published in *Horae subsecivae* in 1858. He wrote on a variety of subjects, medical and religious, but the volume achieved its greatest fame through Brown's diverting essays on the human nature of dogs, 'Rab and his Friends' and 'Our Dogs'. Brown also wrote about the child author MARJORY FLEMING, whom he christened 'Pet Marjorie', and he was one of the first to promulgate the legend that she and Sir WALTER SCOTT were intimate friends. Several of the essays were published later in individual volumes and among his other works are *Health: Five Lay Sermons to Working People* (1862), *John Leech* (1877) and *Thackeray: his Literary Career* (1877). In all his work Brown was able to write candidly, yet delightfully, about human nature, and his essays have been compared to those of Charles Lamb (1775–1834).

WORKS: *Horae subsecivae*, 3 vols. (1858–82); *Rab and his Friends* (1859); *Letter to Dr Cairns* (1860); *Health: Five Lay Sermons to Working People* (1862); *Our Dogs* (1862); *Marjorie Fleming* (1863); *Minchmore (1864)*; *Jeems the Doorkeeper: a Lay Sermon* (1864); *Locke and Sydenham* (1866); *On the Deaths of the Rev. J. M. Gilchrist, J. Brown and J. Henderson* (1867); *John Leech* (1877); *Thackeray: his Literary Career* (1877); *Something About a Well with more of our Dogs* (1882)

Brown, Thomas (1778–1820). Philosopher. He was born on 9 January 1778 in the parish of Kilnabreck, the son of a minister, whose death in 1780 forced him to be educated with relatives in England. In 1792 he returned to Edinburgh to study in the class of DUGALD STEWART, the Professor of Moral Philosophy whom he was to succeed in 1810. Brown held the chair until his death on 2 April 1820 while on a visit to London. After a precocious education in his childhood Brown grew up to be a mature philosopher, a critical disciple of DAVID HUME (ii) and one of the last of the Common-Sense school of Scottish philosophy. Apart from his philosophical writings he published a number of sentimental poems in the Romantic style and he was a founder-member and early supporter of the *Edinburgh Review* (*see* EDINBURGH REVIEW (ii)).

WORKS: *Poems*, 2 vols. (1804); *Observations on the Nature and Tendency of the Doctrine of Mr Hume* (1805); *The Renovation of India* (1808); *The Paradise of Coquettes* (1814); *The Wanderer in Norway* (1816); *Agnes* (1818); *Inquiry into the Relation of Cause and Effect* (1818); *Lectures on the Philosophy of the Human Mind* (1820)

REFERENCES: D. Welsh, *Account of the Life and Writings of Thomas Brown* (Edinburgh, 1825); L. von Dobrzynska-Rybicka, *Die Ethik von Thomas Brown: ein Beitrag zur Geschichte des Intuitonismus* (Posen, 1909)

Bruce, George (*b* 1909). Poet and critic. He was born on 10 March 1909 in Fraserburgh and was educated at the University of Aberdeen. After a period spent teaching, he joined the BBC in 1946 and served as a general talks producer with responsibility for the arts until 1970. Since his retirement he has held several creative writing posts in Scotland and in the USA.

Bruce's first collection of verse, *Sea Talk*, was published in 1944 and it was followed by *Selected Poems* (1947). There was a gap of 20 years before *Landscapes and Figures: a Selection of Poems* appeared in 1967; his *Collected Poems* was published in 1970. Bruce's work owes much to the imagery of the rugged land and seascapes of his native north-east Scotland, and his craft of versification was influenced by Ezra Pound (1885–1972), especially by his *Hugh Selwyn Mauberley* (1920). His is a personal vision of the permanency of the land and the durable qualities of its people; and in a group of poems, 'Tom and His Toys', 'Tom on the Beach', 'Tom in Bed' and 'Tom Discovers', the symbolism of childhood and its immutability is an important motif. The inexorable, yet ordered, march of history is another favourite image, especially in his poem about St Andrews, ' A Gateway to the Sea', which contrasts the city's ancient ecclesiastical history with the agelessness of the sea and man's struggle against it. Bruce has also written a number of critical works including *Ann Redpath* (1974) and *Festival in the North: the Story of the Edinburgh Festival* (1975).

WORKS: *Sea Talk* (1944); with T. S. Halliday, *Scottish Sculpture* (1946); *Selected Poems* (1947); ed., Maurice Lindsay, *The Exiled Heart* (1957); ed., with Maurice Lindsay and Edwin Morgan, *Scottish Poetry 1-6* (1966–72); *Landscapes and Figures: a Selection of Poems* (1967); ed., *The Scottish Literary Revival: an Anthology of Twentieth Century Poetry* (1968); *Collected Poems* (1970); ed., *A Fatal Tree* (1971); *Neil Miller Gunn* (1971); *Some Practical Good* (1973); *Ann Redpath* (1974); *Festival in the North: the Story of the Edinburgh Festival* (1975); *Pitlochry's Festival Theatre* (1976)

Bruce, James (1730–94). Explorer. He was born at Kinaird in Stirlingshire and, after failing to finish his legal studies at the University of Edinburgh, became a wine merchant in London. He was for a time the British consul in Algiers; from there he set out in 1768 to explore Abyssinia, and two years later he reached the source of the Blue Nile, which he supposed, incorrectly, to be the spring of the main river. His five-volume *Travels to Discover the Source of the Nile* (1790) contained much new information (largely disbelieved by Bruce's contemporaries) about Abyssinia, though as a reference book it was superseded by records of later explorations in the 19th century. Bruce returned to live in Scotland and died as the result of a fall on 27 April 1794.

WORKS: *An Interesting Narrative of the Travels of James Bruce into Abyssinia* (1790); *Travels to Discover the Source of the Nile 1768–1773*, 5 vols. (1790); *Travels between the Years 1768 and 1773* (1805); *Bruce's Travels through Abyssinia* (1806)

EDITION: C. F. Beckingham, ed., *Travels to Discover the Source of the Nile* (Edinburgh, 1964)

Bruce, Michael (1746–67). Poet. He was born on 27 March 1746 in Kinnesswood, Kinross, the son of a weaver, Alexander Bruce; from his father he gained an early knowledge of the songs and stories of the folk tradition, as well as a grounding in the teaching of the Secessionist Church. After an education at the village school, he matriculated at the University of Edinburgh in 1762 and later became a teacher in the village of Gairney Bridge, where

the Secessionist Church had been founded in 1721 by Ebenezer Erskine (*see* ERSKINE, RALPH). In 1766 Bruce studied for the ministry and attended the Burger Synod Theological Hall in Kinross. He taught again at the end of that year at Forest Mill near Tillicoultry, but illness forced him to return home early in the following year. He died of consumption on 5 July 1767.

Although most of Bruce's poetry is juvenilia his 'Elegy to Spring', a melancholy lament for his own early death, is worthy of attention. He also improved a number of paraphrases, including the stirring Paraphrase 18 of *Isaiah* 2. 2–6. After Bruce's death his college friend JOHN LOGAN collected his poems for publication in 1770. In later years he claimed that Bruce's best-known poem, 'Ode to the Cuckoo', was his own, and for a time controversy surrounded the authorship of the poem, which was popular for the clarity of its language and the bittersweet sadness of its imagery.

WORKS: *Poems on Several Occasions* (1770); *The Buchanshire Tragedy* (1776); *Sir James the Ross* (1805); *Lochleven* (1822); *An Elegy to Spring* (1833)

EDITIONS: A. B. Grosart, ed., *The Works of Michael Bruce* (Edinburgh, 1865); J. G. Barnet, *Life and Complete Works of Michael Bruce* (London and Edinburgh, 1930)

REFERENCE: T. G. Snoddy, *Michael Bruce: Shepherd Poet of the Lomond Braes* (Edinburgh, 1947)

Bruce, The. A poem in 20 books and 13,550 lines, by JOHN BARBOUR, completed by c 1375. It concerns the life and struggles of ROBERT I (Robert the Bruce) to free Scotland from the domination of England. The intention of the poem was patriotic and it is suffused with Barbour's portrayal of Bruce's moral and physical defiance; but Barbour was also at pains to depict Bruce as a real man and not as a mythical hero. Although *The Bruce* draws on the marvellous story-telling tradition of the Middle Ages, Barbour extended that tradition by telling his 'romanys' (I, 446) in the octosyllabic couplets more usually suited to the telling of straight history.

Barbour relates most of the main events of Bruce's life in the early books of the poem, and in his descriptions of the military campaign he shows a sure eye for detail, especially in his spirited record of the Battle of Methven (II, 346ff) and the taking of the castles of Linlithgow (X, 137ff), Roxburgh (X, 352ff) and Edinburgh (X, 507ff). The poem reaches its zenith in the vigorous account of the BATTLE OF BANNOCKBURN, as Barbour builds up layers of atmosphere, with cross-references from the minutiae of the soldiers' trappings to the overall plan of battle. But *The Bruce* is famous above all for Barbour's immortal expression of individual freedom, which man should value above all else. Into the account of the Wars of Independence Barbour inserted several anecdotes which betray both the temper of the times and a grim, sardonic humour: for example, when the Irish king O'Dymsy tries to drown the Scottish guests, Barbour remarks that at least they had had plenty to drink; and Douglas's larder is a mixture of meal, malt, wine and the blood of beheaded prisoners. The other hero of *The Bruce* is Sir James Douglas, 'THE BLACK DOUGLAS', Bruce's lieutenant, who, in the final stages of the poem, carries the dead king's heart with him on his crusade against the Saracens.

While there may be some doubts about the historical accuracy of the poem, *The Bruce* remains a monumental retelling of a famous period in Scottish history and a patriotic account of the life of the hero–king, Robert the Bruce. Barbour's love of action and his sharp eye, both for detail and for the nobility of his protagonists, was to have no parallel in Scottish literature until the historical compositions of Sir WALTER SCOTT. The poem exists in manuscript in the library of St John's College, Cambridge, and in the NATIONAL LIBRARY OF SCOTLAND. Part of it was printed in 1571, ANDRO HART issued it in 1616 and it was reprinted several times during the 18th century. *The Bruce* was edited by W. W. Skeat in 1894 for the SCOTTISH TEXT SOCIETY, by W. M. Mackenzie in 1909, and by Matthew P. McDiarmid and James A. C. Stevenson (again for the STS) in 1980 (*see* BARBOUR, JOHN, for further details).

Brunton, [née Balfour], **Mary** (1778–1818). Novelist. She was born on 1 November 1778 in Orkney, the daughter of an army officer. In 1798 she married the Revd Alexander Brunton and the couple settled in the parish of Bolton near Haddington, East Lothian; between 1803 and her death on 7 December 1818 she lived in Edinburgh, where her husband was minister of the Tron Kirk. After his wife's death Alexander Brunton wrote her biography (1819). He survived her by 40 years, becoming in later life Professor of Oriental Languages at the University of Edinburgh. Mrs Brunton made her name with her first novel, *Self Control* (1810), which was dedicated to her lifelong friend JOANNA BAILLIE. It was followed by *Discipline* in 1814. Both novels were popular 'improving' works in their day and were reprinted several times. After a visit to England in 1815 she planned a series of sketches of middle-class manners, but only one, *Emmeline* (1819), reached fruition before her death.

WORKS: *Self Control* (1810); *Discipline* (1814); *Emmeline* (1819); *The Works of Mary Brunton*, 7 vols. (1820)

Buchan, Anna ['O. Douglas'] (1877–1948). Novelist. She was the sister of JOHN BUCHAN and shared his childhood in Fife, the Borders and Glasgow, where she was educated at Hutchesons' Grammar School. She lived most of her life in Peebles, at the family home, Bank House, which became the 'Priorsford' of many of her novels, *Penny Plain* (1920) being perhaps the best-known. Her first novel, *Olivia in India* (1913), was written after a visit to her brother William, who was in the Indian Civil Service. *The Setons* (1917), her second, is a well-observed and sympathetic view of Glasgow middle-class manners; its companion piece, *Ann and her Mother* (1922), is an autobiographical novel set in a Glasgow manse before World War I. *Unforgettable, Unforgotten* (1945) is an autobiographical book about the Buchan family, and a memoir of her life was published in *Farewell to Priorsford* (1950).

WORKS: *Olivia in India* (1913); *The Setons* (1917); *Penny Plain* (1920); *Ann and her Mother* (1922); *Pink Sugar* (1924); *The Proper Place* (1926); *Eliza for Common* (1928); *The Day of Small Things* (1930); *Priorsford* (1932); *Taken by the Hand* (1935); *Jane's Parlour* (1937); *People Like Ourselves* (1938); *The Home that is our Own* (1940); *Unforgettable, Unforgotten* (1945); *Farewell to Priorsford* (1950)

Buchan, John, Lord Tweedsmuir of Elsfield (1875–1940). Novelist, critic and editor. He was born on 26 August 1875 in Perth, the son of a Free Church of Scotland minister. He was educated at Hutchesons' Grammar School, Glasgow, and between 1892 and 1895 at the University of Glasgow. His parents' families had homes at Peebles and Broughton Green in the Scottish Border country and, as a child, most of his summers were spent visiting his grandparents and tramping the Border hills. The knowledge he acquired during those years of Border history and balladry, and of the delineation of the countryside, was to have a great influence on his later writing. After graduating from Glasgow he went up to Brasenose College, Oxford, on a Junior Hulme Scholarship, and he took a first in Greats in 1899. There followed a short career as a barrister and journalist and in 1901 he joined the staff of Lord Milner, who had been appointed High Commissioner of South Africa with responsibility for the reconstruction of the Transvaal and the Orange Free State. In 1903 he returned to Britain and pursued several careers, each with varying success: journalist with the *Spectator*; director of the publishing company Thomas Nelson and Sons; Director of Information in the Lloyd George government during World War I; and Tory Member of Parliament for the Scottish Universities (1927–35). In 1935 he was appointed Governor-General of Canada, taking the title Lord Tweedsmuir of Elsfield.

Buchan started writing while still an undergraduate at Glasgow, his first book being a critical introduction to the works of Francis Bacon, *Essays and Apothegems of Francis Lord Bacon* (1894). He went on to write 30 novels, 7 collections of short stories, 66 non-fiction books, 26 pamphlets, 63 contributions to other books and a host of articles and assorted pieces of journalism for a wide variety of magazines and journals. Much of his early story-telling owes a debt to the craft of ROBERT LOUIS STEVENSON, whom Buchan admired. His second novel, *John Burnet of Barns* (1898), belongs to a romantic historical genre to which he was later to return in novels such as *Witch Wood* (1927) and *The Blanket of the Dark* (1931).

Before the outbreak of World War I Buchan became ill with an intestinal complaint and he was to be a partial invalid for the rest of his life. He used this opportunity to turn to writing the popular thrillers – or 'shockers' as he called them – for which he is best known. *The Power-House*, written in 1913 for BLACKWOOD'S MAGAZINE, was the first, followed by THE THIRTY-NINE STEPS in 1915; this introduced one of his main protagonists, Richard Hannay, who also appears in *Greenmantle* (1916), *Mr Standfast* (1919), *The Three Hostages* (1924), *The Courts of the Morning* (1929) and *The Island of Sheep* (1936). He wrote a thriller a year between 1922 and 1936, from which he derived his main income as a writer. Implicit in all Buchan's thrillers is a belief that civilization

is a thin veneer, a sheet of glass which is easily shattered, allowing chaos to rule. His heroes are men of resolution who are called to dedicate themselves to the maintenance of law and order by the responsibility of their positions. Buchan has been accused, unjustly, of being a jingoistic imperialist and a social snob, yet in all his heroes there is an awareness that privilege has to be earned by duty and hard work and cannot be attained merely by blood or breeding.

Buchan's contribution to Scottish letters is also noteworthy. He edited the *Scottish Review* in 1907 and an anthology of verse in Scots, *The Northern Muse*, in 1924, and he wrote biographies of Sir WALTER SCOTT (1932) and JAMES GRAHAM (*Montrose*, 1928), a Presbyterian cavalier whom he admired. In 1925 Hugh MacDiarmid described Buchan as 'Dean of the Faculty of Scottish letters' (*Scottish Educational Review*, June 1925).

Buchan died in Canada on 11 February 1940. His last novel, *Sick Heart River* (1941), was published posthumously and was written out of his Canadian experiences, following a journey he made down the Mackenzie River. His autobiography, *Memory Hold-the-door*, was published in 1940.

WORKS: *Essays and Apothegems of Francis Lord Bacon* (1894); *Sir Quixote of the Moors* (1895); *Scholar Gipsies* (1896); *Brasenose College* (1898); *John Burnet of Barns* (1898); *Grey Weather* (1899); *A Lost Lady of Old Years* (1899); *The Half-Hearted* (1900); *A Watcher by the Threshold* (1902); *The African Colony* (1903); *The Law Relating to the Taxation of Foreign Income* (1905); *A Lodge in the Wilderness* (1906); *Some Eighteenth Century Byways* (1908); *Prester John* (1910); *The Moon Endureth* (1912); *Andrew Jameson, Lord Ardwall* (1913); *Nelson's History of the War*, 24 vols. (1915–19); *Salute to Adventurers* (1915); *The Thirty-nine Steps* (1915); *Greenmantle* (1916); *The Power-House* (1916); *Poems, Scottish and English* (1917); *The Island Of Sheep* (1919); *Mr Standfast* (1919); *These for Remembrance* (1919); *Francis and Riversdale Grenfell* (1920); *The History of the South African Forces in France* (1920); *The Path of the King*, 4 vols. (1921–2); *Book of Escapes and Hurried Journeys* (1922); *Huntingtower* (1922); *The Last Secrets* (1923); *Midwinter* (1923); *Lord Minto* (1924); *The Northern Muse* (1924); ed., *The Three Hostages* (1924); *The History of the Royal Scots Fusiliers* (1925); *John Macnab* (1925); *The Dancing Floor* (1926); *Homilies and Recreations* (1926); *Witch Wood* (1927); *The Marquis of Montrose* (1928); *The Runagates Club* (1928); *The Causal and the Casual in History* (1929); *The Courts of the Morning* (1929); *Castle Gay* (1930); *The Kirk in Scotland* (1930); *The Blanket of the Dark* (1931); *The Novel and the Fairy Tale* (1931); *The Gap in the Curtain* (1932); *Julius Caesar* (1932); *The Magic Walking-Stick* (1932); *Sir*

Walter Scott (1932); *The Massacre of Glencoe* (1933); *A Prince of the Captivity* (1933); *The Free Fishers* (1934); *Gordon at Khartoum* (1934); *Oliver Cromwell* (1934); *The House of the Four Winds* (1935); *The King's Grace* (1935); *The Island of Sheep* (1936); *Augustus* (1937); *Canadian Occasions* (1940); *Comments and Characters* (1940); *Memory Hold-the-door* (1940); *The Long Traverse* (1941); *Sick Heart River* (1941)

REFERENCES: J. A. Smith, *John Buchan* (London, 1965); D. Daniell, *The Interpreter's House* (London, 1977); J. A. Smith, *John Buchan and his World* (London, 1979)

Buchan, Peter (1790–1854). Antiquary and collector of ballads. He was born in Peterhead and, after a rudimentary education, trained as a printer in Edinburgh. In 1816 he returned to his home town and set himself up in business as a printer, but an expensive lawsuit in 1852 forced him to retire to live in Leitrim, Ireland, and he died on 19 September 1854 while on a visit to London. Buchan's fame rests on his collection of over 40 north-east ballads, which he published in 1828 as *Ancient Ballads and Songs of the North of Scotland*. A later collection, *Scottish Traditional Versions of Ancient Ballads*, appeared in 1845. He also published several collections of minor verse and pro-Tory pamphlets, but these are negligible in comparison with the painstaking work of his collections of ballads from oral sources.

WORKS: *Songs and Verses in the Scottish Dialect* (1814); *Annals of Peterhead* (1819); *An Historical Account of the Ancient Earls of Keith* (1820); ed., *Ancient Ballads and Songs of the North of Scotland* (1828); *The Peterhead Smugglers of the Last Century* (1834); *The Eglintoun Tournament and Gentlemen Unmasked* (1839); *An Account of the Chivalry of the Ancients* (1840); ed., *Scottish Traditional Versions of Ancient Ballads* (1845); *Man: Body and Soul* (1849)

Buchan, Tom (*b* 1931). Poet. He was born on 19 June 1931 in Glasgow and was educated there and at Aberdeen Grammar School. After graduating from the University of Glasgow in 1953 he taught in Scotland and India and he has been a full-time writer since 1971. His best poetry is contained in *Dolphins at Cochin* (1969) and in his selected poems of 1972, both of which display his interest in the imagery of science and contemporary means of communication. In poems such as 'Polemical Elegy for Reinhardt Heydrich' and 'Submarine', which deal with different aspects of man's inhumanity, indignation is kept in careful check by his unadorned language, which does not have to descend to mere rhetoric to achieve its effect.

Much of Buchan's most recent work has been done for the theatre and for multi-media entertainments.

WORKS: *Ikons* (1958); *Dolphins at Cochin* (1969); *Makes you Feel Great* (1971); *Exorcism* (1972); *Poems 1969–72* (1972)

Buchanan, Dugald. *See* BOCHANAN, DÙGHALL.

Buchanan, George (1506–82). Scholar. He was born in February 1506 at Moss near Killearn in Stirlingshire. His father died when Buchanan was a child and the five sons and three daughters were brought up in much reduced circumstances by their mother Agnes Heriot. Buchanan was educated at the local grammar school and at the age of 14 his aptitude was such that his uncle James Heriot sent him to study at the University of Paris, where he remained until 1522. The following year he returned to Scotland and enlisted in the army of the regent Albany, which harried the keeps on the English border. In the spring of 1525 Buchanan's name appeared as a pauper student at the University of St Andrews, where he studied under JOHN MAJOR whom he accompanied to Paris in 1526 to complete his education; between 1528 and 1537 he taught at the College of Sainte Barbe in Paris.

In 1537 JAMES V appointed Buchanan tutor to one of his natural sons, but his stay in Scotland was short owing to his boisterous, and frequently coarse, satire against Cardinal Beaton, *Franciscanus* (published 1567). Condemned as a heretic, he fled to England and then on to Bordeaux, where he taught until 1547, when he moved to Portugal to teach at the University of Coimbra. The Inquisition imprisoned him for his heretical beliefs and it was during this period that he translated the PSALMS into Latin. Set free in 1553, he spent the years until 1560 in France and Italy in further study, and on his return to Scotland the following year he was appointed tutor to MARY, Queen of Scots, despite his rationalist leanings towards Protestantism. He was awarded a pension from the Abbey of Crossraguel and in 1566 he was appointed Prihcipal of St Leonard's College in St Andrews. His friendship and liking for the queen came to an end after the murder of Lord Darnley in 1567, but by that time he had already become alienated from the court because of his membership of the newly founded General Assembly of the

Church of Scotland. In 1567 he was appointed its moderator and between 1570 and 1578 he was Keeper of the Privy Seal and tutor to the young JAMES VI. Much of his time during that period was spent in pamphleteering against the queen and in preparing the frequently scurrilous accusations which appear in *De Maria Scotorum Regina*; this was translated in the year of its publication (1571) as *Ane Detectioun of the Duings of Mary Quene*. Buchanan continued to play a prominent role in religious affairs until his death on 29 September 1582. He is buried in Greyfriars' Churchyard in Edinburgh.

Buchanan wrote most of his work in Latin and he was considered to be one of the finest Latin prose stylists of his day; he also wrote two vernacular works in 1570, *Ane Admonitioun Direct to the Trewe Lordis*, an attack on the Hamilton family for their part in the murder of the regent Moray, and *Chamaeleon*, a satire on the machiavellian role played in Scottish politics by William Maitland of Lethington (*c* 1525–73). He composed four plays: *Medea* and *Alcestis* are translations from Euripedes, and *Jepthes sive Votum* (1557) and *Baptistes sive Calumnia* (1578) are original tragedies. Buchanan's chief works, though, were his *De juri regni apud Scotos* (1579), which was written to justify Mary's deposition and enjoyed a substantial reputation among European reformers, and *Rerum scoticarum historia*, a 20-volume history of Scotland completed shortly before his death. His other work of note is *De sphaera*, an attack on contemporary science, especially on the Ptolemaic system. Although he never preached, Buchanan was one of the leading reformers and he played an important role in providing an intellectual backbone to the Reformation movement in Scotland.

WORKS: *Rudimenta grammatices* (1533); *Medea* (1544); *Alcestis* (1556); *Jepthes sive Votum* (1557); *De caleto* (1558); *Psalmorum Dauidis* (1566); *Anent the Reformation of the University of St Andrews* (1567); *Elegiae, sylvae endecasyllabi* (1567); *Franciscanus* (1567); *Tragodiae selectae* (1567); *An Admonitioun Direct to the Trewe Lordis* (1570); *The Chamaeleon* (1570); *De Maria Scotorum Regina* (1571); *Baptistes sive Calumnia* (1578); *De juri regni apud Scotos* (1579); *Rerum scoticarum historia*, 20 vols. (1582); *De sphaera* (1586); *Selectorum carminum ex doctiis* (1590); *De prosodia libelles* (1595)

EDITION: T. Ruddiman, ed., *Opera omnia, ad optimorum lodicum fidem sumno studio recognita et castigata*, 2 vols. (Edinburgh, 1715)

REFERENCES: P. H. Brown, *George Buchanan* (Edinburgh, 1890); R. Wallace and J. C. Smith, *George Buchanan* (Edinburgh, 1899); I. D. Macfarlane, *Buchanan* (London, 1981)

Buke of the Howlat, The. Middle Scots alliterative poem in rhyming stanzas, which exists in the ASLOAN MANUSCRIPT and the BANNATYNE MANUSCRIPT. It is the work of Sir RICHARD HOLLAND and was probably composed in the year 1450 for his kinswoman, the Countess of Moray. Like its English equivalent, Chaucer's *Parlement of Foules*, the poem is an allegory in which the birds of the air and field are given human status. In this case the owl bemoans its tawdry appearance and appeals to the peacock, the pope of the birds. A conference of birds is called and having decided that they cannot interfere with nature they pass the matter to the eagle, the emperor of the bird kingdom. After a grand feast, Dame Nature descends and allows every bird to award one feather each to the owl, but in its newfound glory the owl overreaches itself with pride. Dame Nature retaliates by restoring it to its former state and the owl is left with the poet to moralize on the dangers of vaulting ambition. Introduced into the poem is a passage of praise for the Douglas family, especially for the deeds of Sir James Douglas, 'THE BLACK DOUGLAS', who carried with him to the Holy Land the heart of ROBERT I (Robert the Bruce).

Burke, William (1792–1829). Murderer who, with William Hare, was the instigator of 16 sensational murders and underwent an equally sensational trial at Edinburgh. He was a native of Ulster. After a period of service as a soldier with the Donegal Militia he drifted to Scotland, working as a navvy on the Union Canal. He ended up in Edinburgh and in 1827 he met Hare, in whose lodging-house he stayed with his mistress Helen MacDougal. For the anatomist Dr Robert Knox they provided cadavers for medical study, and they turned to murder to meet the demand. Their partnership came to grief when they murdered their 16th victim, an old Irish woman called Mary Docherty, and left evidence of their crime. Although they were both arrested, with Helen MacDougal, the Crown had difficulty in presenting the case and Hare was persuaded to turn king's evidence to save his own neck. Burke was tried on Christmas eve 1828 and sentenced to death, while the case against MacDougal was not proven. The trial caused a furore in

Edinburgh and Burke was hanged in front of an enormous crowd on the morning of 29 January 1829. The events of the Burke and Hare case provide the background for the play *The Anatomist* by James Bridie (O. H. MAVOR). Burke added a new verb to the English language, 'burke': 'to smother, hush up' (*OED*).

REFERENCE: O. D. Edwards, *Burke and Hare* (Edinburgh, 1979)

Burn, William (1789–1870). Architect. He was a friend of Sir WALTER SCOTT and designed the tombstone for the grave of Helen Walker, the model for Jeanie Deans in THE HEART OF MIDLOTHIAN. He also designed the Custom House in Greenock.

Burnes, William (1721–84). Gardener. Father of ROBERT BURNS. He changed the family name to 'Burns' after leaving his native north-east and settling in Ayrshire. Despite the financial hardships he suffered in his farming enterprises he made sure that his children received a knowledge of the Scriptures and a solid educational grounding.

Burnet, Gilbert (1643–1715). Historian and divine. He was born on 18 September 1643 in Edinburgh, the son of a lawyer. He studied in Aberdeen and Amsterdam; on his return to Scotland he became an Episcopalian minister at Saltoun and in 1669 Professor of Divinity at Glasgow University. Thereafter Burnet enjoyed a somewhat chequered career: his friendship with Charles II took him to London but he was out of sympathy with James II's policies and was forced into exile in Europe until the Glorious Revolution of 1688. Although he was appointed Bishop of Salisbury that year, his middle-of-the-road attitude towards the Episcopalian succession and the Covenanting opposition won him few friends. He died on 7 March 1715. Burnet was an energetic and racy commentator on the events of his lifetime, and his main work, *History of my Own Times* (1723), is written with all the freshness, and justifiable bias, of the live witness of important national events. He also wrote learned works on church law and a memoir of the Dukes of Hamilton.

WORKS: *Vindication of the Authority, Constitution and Laws of the Church and State in Scotland* (1672); *Memoirs of the Dukes of Hamilton* (1677); *History of the Reformation of the Church of England*, 3 vols.

(1679–1714); *Exposition of the 39 Articles* (1699); *Some Passages in the Life and Death of Lord Rochester* (1680); *History of my Own Times* (1723)

REFERENCE: T. E. S. Clarke and H. C. Foxcroft, *Life of Gilbert Burnet* (London, 1907)

Burnett, James, Lord Monboddo (1714–99). Judge and philosopher. He was born on 25 October 1714 on the family estate of Monboddo in Kincardineshire. He was educated at the parish school in Laurencekirk and at King's College, Aberdeen, leaving in 1732 to study law in Edinburgh and at Groeningen between 1733 and 1736. Called to the Scottish Bar in February 1737, Burnett rose steadily through the legal hierarchy. He became Sheriff of Kincardine in 1760 and was made a Lord of Session in 1767, taking the title 'Lord Monboddo'. Edinburgh's social and intellectual life also claimed him: he was a supporter of the theatre, a member of the social and debating club the SELECT SOCIETY, and, through his 'learned suppers', a friend of the leading *literati* of the period. JAMES BOSWELL was for many years an especial friend and confidant.

Burnett's first work, *Of the Origin and Progress of Language*, was published in six volumes between 1773 and 1792. When the first volume appeared it caused a sensation because of the author's claims that men in the Nicobar Islands had tails and that the orang-outan was a class of the human species, lacking only speech. The later volumes dealt with the natural history of language, which Monboddo claimed had its origins in necessity and was not a gift of God. His *Antient Metaphysics* (1779–99), also in 6 volumes, advanced a general theory that the sciences and philosophy had to co-exist in harmony for the proper advancement of culture. In volume 4 he returned to his argument that the orang-outan stands at the beginning of man's history.

Although his views were attacked in Scotland, particularly by his rival JAMES BEATTIE of Aberdeen, Burnett enjoyed considerable prestige in London, which he visited once a year, travelling on horseback until he was 80. One of the great learned eccentrics of the SCOTTISH ENLIGHTENMENT in Edinburgh, he died on 25 May 1799 and was buried in an unmarked grave in Greyfriars' Churchyard.

REFERENCES: W. A. Knight, *Lord Monboddo and some of his Contemporaries* (London, 1900); H. G. Graham, *Scottish Men of Letters in the Eighteenth Century* (London, 1901); W. F. Gray, *Some Old*

Scots Judges (London, 1914); E. L. Cloyd, *James Burnett, Lord Monboddo* (Oxford, 1972)

Burns, Gilbert (1760–1827). Brother of ROBERT BURNS and his partner at Mossgiel Farm, which he kept until 1798. After Burns's death he became a factor in East Lothian. He failed to correct the picture of his brother as a besotted womanizer painted by Dr JAMES CURRIE in the first biography and collected poems (1800).

Burns, Robert (1759–96). Poet and songwriter. He was born on 25 January 1759 at Alloway, Ayrshire, the eldest son of WILLIAM BURNES and Agnes Brown. At the age of six Robert and his brother Gilbert were sent to the school of John Murdoch at Alloway Mill, where Robert was influenced by reading Arthur Masson's *Collection of Prose and Verse* and the modernized translation by WILLIAM HAMILTON (i) of Gilbertfield of WALLACE by BLIND HARRY. At home his father instilled religious belief, and from his mother and her cousin's widow, Betty Davidson, he gained an early knowledge of the folk tradition which he admitted in later life 'cultivated the latent seeds of Poesy'. In 1765 William Burnes rented the farm of MOUNT OLIPHANT and in 1768 his sons ended their education with Murdoch, although Robert was to return to him briefly in 1773 as a boarder in Ayr. Although the farm was unsuccessful William Burnes still attended to his sons' education, and in 1775 Robert was sent to a school at Kirkoswald kept by Hugh Rodger. It was during this period that he wrote his first love-song, *O, once I lov'd a bonnie lass*, for Nelly Kirkpatrick of Dalrymple.

In 1777 William Burnes moved his family to a farm at Lochlie near the village of Tarbolton, where Robert and some friends, including DAVID SILLAR and John Rankine of Adamhill, founded a debating society, the Tarbolton BACHELORS' CLUB. Burns became a Freemason on 4 July 1781. Between 1781 and 1782 he worked in Irvine as a flax dresser, but a disastrous fire and his father's ill health brought him back to Lochlie, where his father died, after a court action with his landlord, in February 1784. Robert and Gilbert rented from a Liberal lawyer, GAVIN HAMILTON, the farm of MOSSGIEL near Mauchline, where Burns lived until 1786. He entered into a relationship with Jean Armour whose father issued a writ against him when Jean's pregnancy became known in 1786;

Burns was almost forced to emigrate to the West Indies as a result of this episode. Jean bore him two sets of twins before he married her in 1788. Burns had other affairs, with Elizabeth Paton and MARY CAMPBELL (the 'HIGHLAND MARY' of Burns legend).

Between April 1783 and October 1785 Burns kept his first commonplace book, in which he kept notes and entered poems; he began a second in April 1787. During this period he wrote some of his best satirical poetry, directed against the rigid Calvinists of the local community: 'The Holy Tulzie', in which two quarrelling ministers are represented as country herds; 'HOLY WILLIE'S PRAYER', one of his finest poems and a bitter attack on religious hypocrisy and the Calvinist theory of predestination; and 'THE HOLY FAIR', which celebrates a popular country event and was much influenced by ROBERT FERGUSSON who was to have a great effect on Burns's writing. In the winter of 1785–6 he wrote the 'cantata' THE JOLLY BEGGARS, which he may have conceived in Poosie Nansie's alehouse in Mauchline. Its praise of the freedom man could enjoy if he was freed from responsibility is taken up in 'THE TWA DOGS', in which Caesar, a rich man's dog, and Luath, a farmer's tyke, discuss their masters' way of life. The 'Epistles' written to his friends (*see* EPISTLES OF ROBERT BURNS), usually in the verse form STANDARD HABBIE (among which may be mentioned 'Epistle to Davie', 'Epistle to J. Lapraik', 'Epistle to William Simpson of Ochiltree' and 'Epistle to James Smith'), reveal Burns's personal and private feelings about love, independence, politics and the lot of poor people, subjects dear to his heart.

On 31 July 1786 Burns's *Poems, Chiefly in the Scottish Dialect* was published by a Kilmarnock printer, JOHN WILSON (ii), and was an immediate success (*see* KILMARNOCK EDITION). The poems had been chosen with care and reveal Burns as a craftsman with an intimate knowledge of literary style. Although he omitted several poems in Scots, including 'DEATH AND DR HORNBROOK', some of his best poems are included in the Kilmarnock edition: 'The Twa Dogs', 'The Holy Fair', 'ADDRESS TO THE DEIL', 'The Death and Dying Words of Poor Mailie', 'Mailie's Elegy', 'THE AULD FARMER'S NEW YEAR MORNING SALUTATION TO HIS AULD MARE MAGGIE', 'THE COTTER'S SATURDAY NIGHT', 'TO A MOUSE' and 'TO A LOUSE'. The book's success – HENRY MACKENZIE hailed

Burns as the 'heaven-taught ploughman' in the December issue of THE LOUNGER – took Burns to Edinburgh on 27 November 1786, where he was lionized as a social phenomenon and as a 'ploughman poet'. A second edition of his poems was published on 21 April 1787 by WILLIAM CREECH and printed by WILLIAM SMELLIE, Burns's friend in the convivial drinking club the CROCHALLAN FENCIBLES.

Despite his social success, Burns failed in his intention to find a patron in Edinburgh, and during the summer of 1787 he visited the Borders and the Highlands, returning to Edinburgh in late October. There he began work on the editing of the collection by JAMES JOHNSON of Scottish songs, THE SCOTS MUSICAL MUSEUM (1787–1803), which contained about 160 of Burns's own songs. He also involved himself in a romantic affair by exchange of letter with AGNES M'LEHOSE in which he took the sobriquet 'Sylvander' and she 'Clarinda'. The affair ended in 1791 and is celebrated by Burns's haunting song 'AE FOND KISS'.

Burns's song work fuses poetry and music into an inseparable unity, reflecting many different moods: celebration of the countryside (*Ye banks and braes o' bonnie Doon*), sentimental Jacobitism (*Charlie, he's my Darling'*), love and passion (*O my luve's like a red, red rose* and *Corn Riggs*), carousing and friendship (*Willie brew'd a peck o' maut* and AULD LANG SYNE), and nationalism (SCOTS WHA HAE). Many of Burns's songs were of his own creation, set to old airs, others were traditional songs which he refashioned, but in all he demonstrated a sure ear for the setting of words to music. He also composed a number of boisterously earthy songs which are included in his collection of bawdy verse THE MERRY MUSES OF CALEDONIA.

In June 1788 Burns took over the lease of the farm of Ellisland, which he kept until November 1791, when he moved with his family to the neighbouring town of Dumfries. He was an excise officer in September 1789 and held the post until his death, from rheumatic fever, on 21 July 1796. In 1793 his outspoken support for the French Revolution led to an official inquiry in to his loyalty. During the latter years of his life Burns concentrated on song writing and collecting, working for GEORGE THOMSON who produced the *Select Collection of Original Scottish Airs* (1793–1841). In 1790 Burns wrote TAM

O'SHANTER for the picture of ALLOWAY KIRK in Grose's *Antiquities of Scotland* (April 1791). A dramatic narrative poem which involves the reader both in the cosy world of the tavern and in the horrors of devilry at Alloway Kirk, *Tam o'Shanter* is Burns's most assured piece of work, with its deft changes of mood and a vital, racy language.

After Burns's death attempts were made to expurgate his more earthy poetry and his first biographer, JAMES CURRIE, was also the first of many commentators to cast him in the role of a drink-besotted womanizer. It is only in fairly recent years that the balance has been restored and that Burns's vast output as a poet and songwriter has been properly assessed. The myth of the 'ploughman poet' lived on, but Burns was a highly cultivated intellectual whose poetry, with its vigorous language and colourful imagery, stands in line with that of ROBERT HENRYSON and WILLIAM DUNBAR, the medieval makars. He remains Scotland's national bard, a poet whose achievement was great and far-reaching, and he is celebrated each year on 25 January – BURNS NIGHT – by Scots the world over. In his nature poems he captured the unsentimental nuances of life in pre-industrial Scotland; he espoused individual liberty and praised love and lust. His songs revitalized the folk tradition, and in all his work he demonstrated a sure ear for the authentic use of Scots.

WORKS: *Poems, Chiefly in the Scottish Dialect* (Kilmarnock, 1786); *Poems* (Edinburgh, 1787, 2/1793)

EDITIONS: J. Barke and S. G. Smith, eds., *The Merry Muses of Caledonia* (London, 1965); J. Kinsley, ed., *The Poems and Songs of Robert Burns* (Oxford, 1968); D. Daiches, ed., *The Selected Poems of Robert Burns* (London, 1979)

REFERENCES: C. Carswell, *Life of Robert Burns* (London, 1930); F. B. Snyder, *The Life of Robert Burns* (London, 1932); H. Hecht, trans. J. Lymburn, *Robert Burns* (London, 1936); T. Crawford, *Burns: a Study* (Edinburgh, 1960); D. Daiches, *Robert Burns* (London, rev. 2/1966); M. Lindsay, *Burns: the Man, his Work, the Legend* (London, rev. 2/1971); D. A. Low, ed., *Critical Essays on Robert Burns* (London, 1974); M. Lindsay, *The Burns Encyclopaedia* (London, rev. 3/1980); R. D. S. Jack and A. Noble, eds., *The Art of Robert Burns* (London, 1982)

Burns Cottage. The birthplace of ROBERT BURNS in Alloway, Ayrshire. The poet spent the first seven years of his life there before moving to the farm of MOUNT OLIPHANT. In 1781 the cottage was bought by the Incorporation of Shoemakers at Ayr who sublet it to a publican. The Alloway Burns Monument Trustees bought it in 1881 and restored it to its original proportions. It is now a museum of Burns's life and work.

Burns Night. An annual celebration of the birth of ROBERT BURNS on 25 January 1759. Within five years of Burns's death the first club in his honour had been founded in Greenock and the records of the Kilmarnock Burns Club go back to 1808. The first Burns Supper in Edinburgh was held in 1815 and it is described in PETER'S LETTERS TO HIS KINSFOLK by JOHN GIBSON LOCKHART. The principal fare at the supper is the haggis which is hailed with Burns's poem 'Address to a Haggis'; the supper is followed by an entertainment of Burns's songs and poems.

Burton, John Hill (1809–81). Historian. He was born on 22 August 1809 in Aberdeen, the son of an impecunious army officer. He studied law at the University of Aberdeen and was called to the Scottish Bar in Edinburgh, where he lived for the rest of his life. To supplement his income he published numerous historical essays in literary magazines and encyclopaedias and he also contributed to legal textbooks. His reputation as a writer was confirmed with the publication of biographies of DAVID HUME (ii) in 1846 and of Lord Lovat and Duncan Forbes in 1847. He became a regular contributor to THE SCOTSMAN and to BLACKWOOD'S MAGAZINE, for which he wrote a series of entertaining essays collected in *The Book Hunter* (1862) and *The Scot Abroad* (1864). What Burton lacked in imagination he made up for with a pleasing, if solid, literary style and by a devotion to accurate research. For many years his nine-volume *History of Scotland* (1853–70) was a standard work and he was appointed Her Majesty's Historiographer for Scotland in 1867. Political patronage came to him in 1854 with his appointment as Secretary to the Prison Board of Scotland and he became a commissioner to that body in 1877. Burton's first wife died in 1847 and he married the daughter of COSMO INNES in 1855. He died after a long illness on 10 August 1881.

WORKS: *A Manual of the Law of Scotland* (1839); *On the State of Law* (1840); *The Law of Bankruptcy* (1845); *The Life and Correspondence of David Hume* (1846); *The Local Taxes of Scotland* (1846); *Lives of Simon Lovat and Duncan Forbes* (1847); ed., *Letters of Eminent Persons Addressed to David Hume* (1849);

Political and Social Economy (1849); *Narratives from Criminal Trials in Scotland*, 2 vols. (1852); *Black's Picturesque Guide to the Trossachs* (1853); *The History of Scotland*, 9 vols. (1853–70); *The Book Hunter* (1862); *The Cairngorm Mountains* (1864); *The Scot Abroad*, 2 vols. (1864); *Convicts* (1866); *The Emigrants' Manual* (1867); *Memorandum of the Collection and Arrangement of the Judicial Statistics of Scotland* (1868); *History of the Reign of Queen Anne* (1880)

Byron, George Gordon Noel, 6th Baron (1788–1824). Poet. He was born on 22 January 1788 in London. At birth he was found to have a club foot, a deformity that was to cause him both physical and mental suffering throughout his life. His early childhood was clouded by debt caused by his father's profligacy and most of it was spent in straitened circumstances. At the age of four Byron was taken to Aberdeen so that his mother could be closer to her relatives, the Gordons of Gight, an old Aberdeenshire landed family. He received his education at Aberdeen Grammar School, and summer visits to relatives on Donside provided him with the imagery for his early poem 'Lachin y Gair', which records his memory of the mountain Lochnagar which dominates the district. In 1798 Byron succeeded to the family title, having become heir apparent in 1794 on the death of the 5th baron's grandson. He left Scotland, never to return, although he was to remain romantically proud of his Scottish parentage, claiming in *Don Juan* (X, 17): 'But I am half a Scot by birth, and bred/A whole one.'

In 1801 Byron was sent to Harrow School and four years later he went to Trinity College, Cambridge. His lifelong interest in swimming and shooting and his indulgence in the sophisticated social life of a man about town began during his two years at Cambridge. When his collection of juvenilia, *Hours of Idleness* (1807), was savaged in the *Edinburgh Review* (*see* EDINBURGH REVIEW (ii)) Byron's retort was a heated attack on most of the poets of the day and on FRANCIS JEFFREY, the magazine's editor; it was published in 1808 under the title *English Bards and Scotch Reviewers* and was written in a cleverly reconstructed version of the heroic couplets used by Byron's admired model Alexander Pope.

Between 1809 and 1811 Byron travelled widely in Europe and the Near East, an experience that gave rise to the publication of *Childe Harold's Pilgrimage*, cantos 1–11, a long poem written in Spenserian stanzas; this began

Byron's habit of presenting himself in his poetry in the guise of a world-weary cynic, and the *persona* of Childe Harold is the first of several Byronic heroes. The publication of the poem caused a sensation and Byron compounded its success with a number of Romantic narrative poems, set in exotic surroundings and involving fantastic adventures. These include *The Bride of Abydos* (1813), *The Giaour* (1813) and *The Corsair* (1814). Byron became a literary lion and was introduced to London society, which took him to its heart even though his affair with Lady Caroline Lamb became a public scandal. In 1815 he made an ill-advised marriage to Anne Isabella Milbanke but parted from her a year later. Their separation and the rumours of an incestuous relationship with his half-sister, Augusta Leigh, were instrumental in forcing Byron to leave England for ever on 25 April 1816.

In Switzerland Byron befriended the poet Percy Bysshe Shelley; he then moved to Italy and entered into a happy relationship with the Countess Teresa Giuccioli. In 1823 his interests turned to the Greek revolution against the overlordship of the Turks and he committed himself to the Greeks' cause. At the beginning of the following year he arrived in Missolonghi to train Greek soldiers and it was there that he died of rheumatic fever on 19 April 1824.

Although Byron was made famous in his day by the composition of his melodramatic narrative poems and by his creation of gloomy, profligate, misanthropic, romantic heroes, his reputation as a poet must ultimately rest on three long poems, *Beppo* (1818), *The Vision of Judgement* (1822) and *Don Juan* (1819–24). The last work is written in *ottava rima*, an elegant rhyming verse scheme that lends great ease and fluency to Byron's burlesque retelling of the adventures of Don Juan. Byron was admired greatly in Europe and he also influ-enced the development of the Romantic movement, his work being seen as a counterpoint to Shelley's more ethereal ideals. In Greece his death was seen as a martyrdom in the cause of the country's independence.

WORKS: *Hours of Idleness* (1807); *Poems on Various Occasions* (1807); *English Bards and Scotch Reviewers* (1808); *Address for the Opening Day of Drury Lane Theatre* (1812); *Childe Harold's Pilgrimage*, cantos I–II (1812); *The Curse of Minerva* (1812); *The Bride of Abydos* (1813); *The Giaour* (1813); *Waltz* (1813); *The Corsair* (1814); *Lara* (1814); *Ode to Napoleon Buonapart* (1814); *Hebrew Melodies* (1815); *Childe Harold's Pilgrimage*, canto III (1816); *Fare thee Well* (1816); *Monody on the Death of R. B. Sheridan* (1816); *Parisina* (1816); *Poems* (1816); *The Siege of Corinth* (1816); *A Sketch from Private Life* (1816); *The Lament of Tasso* (1817); *Manfred* (1817); *Beppo* (1818); *Childe Harold's Pilgrimage*, canto IV (1818); *On John William Rizzo Hoppner* (1818); *Don Juan*, cantos I–II (1819); *Mazeppa* (1819); *Cain* (1821); *Don Juan*, cantos III–IV (1821); *The Irish Avatar* (1821); *Marino Faliero* (1821); *The Prophecy of Dante* (1821); *Sardanapalus* (1821); *The Two Foscari* (1821); *The Vision of Judgement* (1822); *The Age of Bronze* (1823); *Don Juan*, cantos VI–XIV (1823); *The Island* (1823); *Werner* (1823); *The Deformed Transformed* (1824); *Don Juan*, cantos XV–XVI (1824); *Observations upon Observations* (1834); *Ode to the Framer's of the Frame Bill* (1880)

EDITIONS: E. H. Coleridge, ed., *Byron's Works: Poetry*, 7 vols. (London, 1898–1904); R. E. Prothero, ed., *Byron's Works: Letters and Journals*, 6 vols. (London, 1898–1901); J. J. McGann, *Lord Byron: The Complete Poetical Works*, vol. 1 (Oxford, 1980); L. A. Marchand, ed., *Byron's Letters and Journals*, 12 vols. (London, 1973–81)

REFERENCES: H. Nicolson, *Byron: the Last Journey* (London, 1924); I. Origo, *The Last Attachment* (New York, 1949); P. Quennell, ed., *Byron: a Self-Portrait*, 2 vols. (London, 1950); G. W. Knight, *Lord Byron's Marriage* (London, 1957); L. A. Marchand, *Byron: a Biography*, 3 vols. (London, 1957); W. Marshall, *The Structure of Byron's Major Poems* (New York, 1961); A. Rutherford, *Byron: a Critical Study* (Edinburgh and London, 1961)

Bysset, Habakkuk. *See* BISSET, HABAKKUK.

C

Cadell, Robert (1788–1849). Publisher and partner (from 1811) of ARCHIBALD CONSTABLE. He was born on 16 December 1788 at Cockenzie, East Lothian, and he died on 20 January 1849 at Ratho, West Lothian. After Constable's financial crash of 1826, which ruined Sir WALTER SCOTT, Cadell set about republishing Scott's novels in uniform editions and was the publisher of the last novels; by becoming Scott's sole publisher he was able to revive his own and Scott's fortunes. JOHN GIBSON LOCKHART in his *Memoirs of the Life of Sir Walter Scott* (1837–8) wrote of Cadell's 'delicate and watchful' attention to his author.

Caird, Edward (1835–1908). Philosopher. He was born on 22 March 1835 at Greenock, the son of a shipbuilder and was educated at Greenock Academy, the University of St Andrews and Balliol College, Oxford, where his tutor was Benjamin Jowett (1817–93). He was elected a Fellow of Merton College, a post that he held until 1866 when he became Professor of Moral Philosophy at the University of Glasgow. In 1893 he returned to Oxford to succeed Jowett as Master of Balliol and he remained there until his death on 1 November 1908. As a philosopher Caird published pioneering monographs interpreting the work of Kant and Hegel, and like his brother John Caird (1820–98) he wrote on the evolution of Christianity.

WORKS: *Ethical Philosophy* (1866); *A Critical Account of the Philosophy of Kant* (1877); *The Problem of Philosophy at the Present Time* (1881); *Hegel* (1883); *The Social Philosophy and Religion of Comte* (1885); *The Critical Philosophy of Immanuel Kant*, 2 vols. (1889); *Essays on Literature and Philosophy*, 2 vols. (1892); *The Evolution of Religion*, 2 vols. (1893); *The Evolution of Theology in the Greek Philosophy*, 2 vols. (1904)

REFERENCE: H. Jones, *The Life and Philosophy of Edward Caird* (Glasgow, (1921)

Calderwood, David (1575–1651). Historian. Little is known with certainty about David Calderwood's early life except that he was educated in Edinburgh and was minister of Crailing, Roxburghshire, from 1604 to 1619. An opponent of Episcopalianism, Calderwood was eventually forced to flee to Holland, where he wrote several tracts in defence of Presbyterianism. He returned to Scotland in 1625, when he began work on his massive and well-documented *True History of the Church of Scotland* (1678). From 1637 he took part in the resistance against Charles I and the following year he became minister of Pencaitland in East Lothian.

WORKS: *De regimine ecclesiae scoticanae* (1618); *Perth Assembly* (1619); *A Defence of our Arguments against Kneeling in the Act of Receiving the Sacramental Elements* (1620); *A Dialogue Betweixt Cosmiphilus and Theophilus* (1620); *Parasynagina perthense* (1620); *Beloved Children* (1620); *Scoti Paracelsis* (1622); *A Dispute upon Communicating at our Confused Communions* (1624); *An Epistle of a Christian Brother* (1624); *An Exhortation of the Particular Kirks of Christ* (1624); *The Pastor and the Prelate* (1628); *The True History of the Church of Scotland* (1678); *Altare Damascenum* (1708)

EDITION: T. Thomson, ed., *The History of the Kirk of Scotland*, 8 vols., Woodrow Society (Edinburgh, 1842–9)

Caledonia. The name given by the Romans to the northern part of Britain which corresponds to present-day Scotland. It was occupied by a tribe called the Caledones and to defend their northern frontier the Romans were forced into a position in which the country had to be invaded. The invasion was carried out in 82 by Julius Agricola and he defeated the Caledones at the decisive Battle of Mons Graupius; present-day Perthshire was the limit of his advance. The Forth Valley was invaded in 142 and the Romans remained in the area with an army of occupation until the third century. The name 'Scotland' originated in the 11th

54

century when the south-western Scots, who had emigrated centuries earlier from Ireland, became the dominant tribe in the country. 'Caledonia' continued in use as a poetic or romantic name for Scotland, as in the long poem by Sir WALTER SCOTT, THE LAY OF THE LAST MINSTREL (canto VI, ii):

> O Caledonia! stern and wild,
> Meet nurse for a poetic child!
> Land of brown heath and shaggy wood,
> Land of the mountain and the flood,
> Land of my sires!

Caledonian antisyzygy. A phrase coined by G. Gregory Smith in his study *Scottish Literature: Character and Influence* (1919) to describe the 'zigzag of contradictions' which he claimed provided the dynamic qualities of Scottish literature. As expressed by Smith, in the Caledonian antisyzygy 'we have a reflection of the contrasts which the Scot shows at every turn, in his political and ecclesiastical history, in his polemical restlessness, in his adaptability, which is another way of saying that he has made allowance for new conditions, in his practical judgement, which is the admission that two sides of the matter have been considered.' This intellectual and emotional dualism was claimed by Hugh MacDiarmid (CHRISTOPHER MURRAY GRIEVE) to be 'one of the quintessential principles of the [Scottish Renaissance] Movement' (*Voice of Scotland,* vol. 1, p. 3, p. 16). Certainly the sudden clash of opposites is present in his long poem A DRUNK MAN LOOKS AT THE THISTLE in which it becomes an essential theoretical prop, allowing him to exclaim:

> I'll hae nae hauf-way hoose, but aye be whaur
> Extremes meet – it's the only way I ken
> To dodge the curst conceit o' bein' richt
> That damns the vast majority o'men.

By arguing that his poem had to be taken to extremes, MacDiarmid was able to contain within it concepts of time and space to express his wide-ranging thoughts on the process of creativity, as well as limiting his argument to the detritus of everyday life in provincial Scotland. MacDiarmid also saw the Caledonian antisyzygy, the hypothetical balancing of opposites, as an integral part of Scotland's culture and history.

Caledonian Hunt. An association of noblemen and country gentry who, through the influence of JAMES CUNNINGHAM, Earl of Glencairn, subscribed to 100 copies of the second, 'Edinburgh', edition of the poems of ROBERT BURNS. Burns dedicated the volume to the members of the Hunt and was himself enrolled a member on 10 April 1792.

Caledonian Mercury. A newspaper first published in Edinburgh on 28 April 1720 and printed by William Rolland in Parliament Close. Initially it was published three times a week with abstracts of news from the London press, but when THOMAS RUDDIMAN took over the printing it also published local news and advertisements. Rolland died in March 1729 and the *Mercury* passed into the hands of the Ruddiman family who owned it until May 1772. During the JACOBITE rising of 1745–6 the paper covertly supported Prince CHARLES EDWARD STUART, and it has been suggested that Ruddiman's son acted as printer to the Jacobite army. In 1776 the third owner, John Robertson, attempted unsuccessfully to increase the publication to five days a week. In 1790 the *Mercury* was bought by Robert Allan. The first recognized editor was David Buchanan, between 1810 and 1827, and he was succeeded in turn by James Browne, James Dundas White, W. Downing Bruce and James Robie. The last owner was William Saunders who sold the paper to THE SCOTSMAN in April 1867. There had been considerable animosity between the two newspapers, which had resulted in a duel between Browne and Maclaren of THE SCOTSMAN on 12 November 1829.

Calgacus [Galgacus] ('the swordsman'). The leader of the tribe of Caledones who were defeated at the Battle of Mons Graupius in 82 by the invading Romans of Julius Agricola. That we know anything about him or his fellow tribesmen is due to the industry of the historian Tacitus, Agricola's son-in-law. To Calgacus he ascribed the noble words '*Solitudinem faciunt, pacem appellant*' ('They create a desert and they call it peace)'.

Caller Herrin'. A song by CAROLINA OLIPHANT, Lady Nairne, depicting the street cries of the fisherwomen from the village of Newhaven near Edinburgh. In their picturesque shawls and laden with creels, they were a common sight in Edinburgh as they walked the streets selling their wares with the cry 'Wha'll buy my caller herrin'?' ('Who'll buy my fresh herrings?'). As was the case with many other composed songs of the period, *Caller Herrin'* quickly assumed the status of a traditional folk-song.

Calvin, Henry. Pen-name of CLIFFORD HANLEY.

Calvinism. A system of theology, evolved by the Swiss reformer John Calvin (1509–64), which forms the basis of the Presbyterian Church in Scotland. Calvinism has three main, but related, tenets: the majesty and power of God and the weakness and futility of man; the authority of the Bible and the unquestionable nature of divine law; and forgiveness of sins through love of Jesus Christ. In Scotland during the 17th century Calvinism was modified and strengthened to include the dogma of predestination, the belief that a man was either one of the 'elect' or a 'reprobate'; that is, either marked for salvation or doomed for eternity. That brand of Calvinism has had a marked effect, for good and ill, on the Scottish character. In its more extreme form it has led to the hypocrisy of the elect who believe that all their actions are justified whether right or wrong, a belief characterized in the poem 'HOLY WILLIE'S PRAYER' by ROBERT BURNS and the novel THE PRIVATE MEMOIRS AND CONFESSIONS OF A JUSTIFIED SINNER by JAMES HOGG. The concept of God as an all-powerful, stern father is reflected in many novels that deal with father and son relationships in which the father is a manifestation of the divine ideal: for example, WEIR OF HERMISTON, GILLESPIE and THE HOUSE WITH THE GREEN SHUTTERS. Although Calvinism is held to have been an authoritarian, pleasure-denying and colourless influence, it would be wrong to overemphasize its drawbacks or to hold it to blame for every shortcoming in the national temperament. Many of the Scots' more extreme characteristics were shaped by no less powerful forces, such as politics, economics and geography, and Calvinism is generally held to have shaped many of Scotland's positive attitudes towards education, law and politics. The apostle of Calvinism in Scotland was the reformer JOHN KNOX.

Cameron, Norman (1905–53). Poet. He was educated at Fettes College, Edinburgh, and at Oriel College, Oxford, where he became a lifelong friend of the poet Robert Graves (*b* 1895). In 1929 he was appointed an education-al officer in Nigeria, a post he held until 1932, when he went to live in Mallorca with Graves and Laura Riding. A clash of personalities forced him to return to Britain where he lived in London, earning a living as an advertising copywriter. During World War II he served as a political officer in North Africa, an experience that gave rise to two of his best poems, 'Green, green is El Aghir' and 'Black Takes White'; both are ironic statements on the futility of war. In 1946 he returned to advertising. He died in April 1953 shortly after being converted to Catholicism. Part Presbyterian moralist and part pagan poet in his attitudes to life and art, something of that paradox can be felt in poems like 'Forgive me, Sire' and 'Nunc scio quid sit amor'.

WORKS: *Collected Poems*, with an introduction by Robert Graves (London, 1957)

Cameronians. A sect formed by the followers of the Covenanting leader, Richard Cameron, after the Battle of Bothwell Bridge in 1679. It rejected the indulgences offered to the COVENANTERS and renounced allegiance to the king, Charles II. The Cameronians continued the practice of holding field conventicles, open-air religious services, but the death of their leader at Aird Moss in June 1680 and the subsequent execution of his principal lieutenant, Hackston of Rathillet, were a sore blow to their cause. Although it was no longer a potent opposition, its members continued to be persecuted by government troops, especially in the wake of the Test Act of 1681, which required an oath of allegiance to the king and the recognition of the Protestant faith. During that period, which came to be known as the 'Killing Times', the Cameronians were put down with much ferocity by the Lord Advocate, Sir GEORGE MACKENZIE (ii) of Rosehaugh, and by JOHN GRAHAM of Claverhouse. A sympathetic account of the Cameronians appears in OLD MORTALITY by Sir WALTER SCOTT. Later, the Cameronians gave their name to the 26th Regiment of Foot which was raised by William of Orange in 1688.

Campbell, Archibald, 8th Earl and 1st Marquis of Argyll (1607–61). He was educated at the University of St Andrews. He joined the Covenanting party in November 1638 and was a supporter of the Parliamentary party during the Civil War. He was created 1st Marquis of

Argyll in 1641. Between 1644 and 1645 his army was defeated three times by the Highland and Irish force under the command of his rival JAMES GRAHAM, the Marquis of Montrose. Argyll played a devious role in Scottish politics and at the Restoration he was arrested and executed in Edinburgh in 1661. He figures in the novel *John Splendid* by NEIL MUNRO.

Campbell, Donald (*b* 1940). Poet and dramatist. He was born on 25 February 1940 in Wick, Caithness, but most of his life has been spent in Edinburgh, where he has been a full-time writer since 1974. Most of his poetry is written in an eloquent colloquial Scots, reminiscent of the voice of his fellow Edinburgh poet, ROBERT GARIOCH SUTHERLAND, and it is remarkable for its conversational ease. That, together with the sensitivity of his poetic response to the human condition, has made Campbell one of the most interesting dramatists writing in Scotland, notably in plays such as *The Widows of Clyth* (1979), which examines the impact on a small community of a fishing tragedy and the plight of the surviving womenfolk.

WORKS: *Poems* (1971); *Rhymes 'n Reasons* (1972); *Murals* (1974); *The Jesuit* (1976); *Somerville the Soldier* (1978); *The Widows of Clyth* (1979)

REFERENCE: T. Royle, ed., *Jock Tamson's Bairns: Essays on a Scots Childhood* (London, 1977)

Campbell, John, 2nd Duke of Argyll (1678–1743). He trained as a soldier and served under Marlborough in his European campaigns, commanding the allied forces in Spain in 1711. He was appointed Commander-in-Chief in Scotland in 1714 and put down the JACOBITE uprising of 1715. As a politician he supported the ACT OF UNION of 1707 and the later part of his life was spent in building up his family's political power in Scotland. He figures in THE HEART OF MIDLOTHIAN by Sir WALTER SCOTT and the novel *The New Road* by NEIL MUNRO.

Campbell, John Francis (1822–85). Folklorist. He was born on 29 December 1822 on the island of Islay and was educated at Eton and the University of Edinburgh. His family's aristocratic connections brought with them the benefit of patronage and their eldest son became in turn a groom-in-waiting at court, secretary to the Lighthouse Commission and secretary to the Coal Commission. In his spare time Campbell collected a large number of traditional

fairy-tales, which he published in four volumes in *Popular Tales of the West Highlands* (1860–62). The tales were translated into English but Campbell was careful to give Gaelic variants and to name the provenance of his collection. His knowledge of Gaelic gave him easy access to the folk tradition of the islands and West Highlands, and his most enduring monument is *Leabhar na Feinne* (1872), a collection of Ossianic ballads in which he also attacked the authenticity of the OSSIAN poems by JAMES MACPHERSON. Campbell enjoyed foreign travel and he was also something of an inventor and a dabbler in the natural sciences – he invented an apparatus for measuring the sun's rays. He died on 17 February 1885 in Cannes, France.

WORKS: *Popular Tales of the West Highlands*, 4 vols. (1860–62); *Frost and Fire* (1865); *A Short American Tramp in the Fall of 1864* (1865); *Leabhar na Feinne* (1872); *My Circular Notes* (1876); *The Parallel Roads of Lochaber* (1877); *Time Scales* (1880); *Thermography* (1883); *The Celtic Dragon Myth* (1911)

EDITIONS: J. G. Mackay, ed., *Ancient Legends of the Scottish Gael, from the Manuscript Collection of J. F. Campbell* (London, 1914); W. J. Watson, ed., *More West Highland Tales, from the Manuscript Collection of J. F. Campbell* (Edinburgh, 1940)

Campbell, Mary (1763–86). The 'Highland Mary' of Burns legend. Little is known of Mary Campbell's life; she was born in Auchamore by Dunoon and was employed as a nursery maid to GAVIN HAMILTON in Mauchline, and later as a dairymaid at Coilsfield. She met ROBERT BURNS during the period of his estrangement from JEAN ARMOUR and according to tradition she and Burns exchanged Bibles on the banks of the River Ayr on the second Sunday of May 1786. Mary Campbell died in Greenock in October that year, either as a result of typhus fever or in childbirth; Burns's song 'Will ye go to the Indies, my Mary' suggests that he may have asked her to emigrate to the West Indies with him. In later life Burns was stricken with remorse over the affair and he wrote for her the song 'The Highland Lassie O' and a sentimental poem 'To Mary in Heaven'.

Campbell, R. T. Pen-name of RUTHVEN TODD.

Campbell, Thomas (1777–1844). Poet and journalist. He was born on 27 July 1777 in Glasgow and was educated there at the University. After a period spent tutoring in Mull, he went to study law in Edinburgh but failed to make any headway in the subject. In 1803 he moved to London and remained there until shortly before his death in Boulogne on 15 June 1844. During his long period of absence from Scotland he maintained his links with his homeland through his friendship with Sir WAL-TER SCOTT, whom he had met while a law student in Edinburgh; he was also three times Lord Rector of the University of Glasgow. Although his literary interests in London led to the publication of long poems like *Gertrude of Wyoming* (1808) and *Theodoric* (1824), he is best remembered for his composition of such stirring ballads as 'Hohenlinden' and 'Lord Ullin's Daughter', which were popular repetition pieces in schools and drawing-rooms during the Victorian period; but Campbell never realized the full potential of his first poem *The Pleasures of Hope* (1799), which contains the oft-quoted line ''Tis distance lends enchantment to the view'. As a critic, his *Specimens of the British Poets* (1819) was highly regarded in his day.

WORKS: *The Pleasures of Hope* (1799); *Poems* (1803); *Annals of Great Britain from the Accession of George III to the Peace of Amiens* (1807); *Gertrude of Wyoming* (1808); *Specimens of the British Poets* (1819); *Theodoric* (1824); *Life of Mrs Siddons* (1834); *Letters from the South* (1837); *Life of Petrarch* (1841); *The Pilgrim of Glencoe* (1842); *Frederick the Great: his Court and Times* (1842); *History of our Own Times* (1843)

EDITION: J. L. Robertson, ed., *Complete Works of Thomas Campbell* (Oxford, 1907)

Canadian Boat Song. A song, of disputed authorship, published in the 'NOCTES AM-BROSIANAE' of the September 1829 issue of BLACKWOOD'S MAGAZINE. This 'oar song', supposedly sung in Gaelic by Scottish exiles in Canada, is introduced by 'Christopher North' (JOHN WILSON (iii)), who claims to have received the verses from 'a friend of mine now in Upper Canada'. As the 'Noctes' were the work of several hands, including those of Wilson, JOHN GIBSON LOCKHART and JAMES HOGG, it is impossible to ascertain the creator of this beautiful song of exile and longing, and its genesis remains a mystery. In his *The Canadian Boat Song: its Authorship and Associations* (Stirling, 1935) Edward MacCurdy has suggested that the author was DAVID MACBETH MOIR, who was at that time in correspondence with JOHN GALT, then in the employment of the Canada Company in Upper Canada.

Candlemas. The Feast of the Purification of the Virgin Mary, celebrated on 2 February. The candles burned in her honour are the legacy of a Roman pagan festival for Februa, the mother of Mars. In Scotland the day before Candlemas was dedicated to ST BRIDE, the successor to a Celtic goddess of the same name, and the Day of Bride was the old Celtic festival of spring.

Cape Club. A literary club formed in Edinburgh about the year 1764 for the purpose of debate in convivial surroundings. It formulated its laws in 1769 when it was agreed that members should adopt fanciful titles of knighthood. Thus a founder-member of the club, James Aitken, became 'Sir Poker' and by 1800 the club's minutes recorded that 650 'knighthoods' had been granted. The Cape Club's most famous member was the poet ROBERT FERGUSSON, who took the title 'Sir Precenter'; other notable members were the artists ALEX-ANDER NASMYTH, ALEXANDER RUNCIMAN and HENRY RAEBURN. The club was dissolved in 1841.

Caraid nan Gaidheal ('Friend of the Highlanders'). The name by which NORMAN MAC-LEOD (i) was known.

Carlyle, Alexander (1722–1805). Divine and man of letters. He was born on 26 January 1722 in Cummertrees, Dumfriesshire, the son of the parish minister, and was educated at the universities of Edinburgh and Glasgow, then for a time in Leiden, Holland. His whole life was devoted to the ministry of the Church of Scotland and from 1748 until his death on 25 August 1805 he held the charge of Inveresk, near Musselburgh. As a churchman, Carlyle was of the moderate party and he gained a good deal of notoriety for his defence of his friend JOHN HOME when his play DOUGLAS was first performed in Edinburgh in 1756. Carlyle enjoyed the friendships of the leading *literati* of the day and something of his shrewd, intelligent and always delightful observation of the scene around him can be found in his *Autobiography* (1860), which was edited after his death by the historian JOHN HILL BURTON. Because of his imposing appearance he was nicknamed 'Jupiter Carlyle'. He belongs to that small, though important, group of Scottish men of letters whose private writings illuminate the age in which they lived.

Carlyle, Jane (Baillie) Welsh (1801–66). Wife of THOMAS CARLYLE. She was born on 14 July 1801 in Haddington, East Lothian, the daughter of a doctor. Her tutor was the Secessionist EDWARD IRVING and it was through him that she met Carlyle, whom she married on 17 October 1826. From then until her death on 21 April 1866 she was Carlyle's constant support and, although their marriage was brittle and frequently tormented, Jane and her husband relied heavily on each other for mutual comfort; she helped Carlyle to survive the difficult years in Edinburgh and at Craigenputtoch before his literary success in London. Although she was prompted by Carlyle and others to write herself, she never did, but through her letters a vivid and affectionate, though at times angry and ironic, picture emerges of her life and times. Though she did not become a novelist her letters reveal her to have been a fascinating teller of good stories. After her death, Carlyle wrote an anguished memoir of her which was published in *Reminiscences* (1881).

EDITION: A. and M. McQueen Simpson, eds., *I too am Here: Selections from the Letters of Jane Welsh Carlyle* (London, 1977)

Carlyle, Thomas (1795–1881). Historian and essayist. He was born on 4 December 1795 at Ecclefechan in Dumfriesshire. His father, James, was a stonemason who later became a farmer, and from him Carlyle gained a rudimentary practical education which was augmented at the village school. From there he went to Annan Academy and in 1809 he matriculated at the University of Edinburgh. Although Carlyle was to complain later, in his *Reminiscences* (1881), that his childhood was starved of poetry and imaginative literature, religion and the Bible played an important part in the Carlyle household and his parents were strict members of the Secessionist Church. While a student in the arts faculty at Edinburgh, Carlyle read widely and concentrated on the study of mathematics in the class of Professor John Leslie. On graduating in 1813 he was uncertain of the direction that his career should take, and after a year spent in studying for the ministry of the Secessionist Church in Edinburgh, he became a teacher, first at Annan Academy and then between 1816 and 1818 in Kirkcaldy. There he met the revivalist minister EDWARD IRVING who was to become a lifelong friend, despite the irregulari-

ty of his later religious beliefs in 'the gift of tongues', which he took to be a manifestation of divine will.

In December 1818 Carlyle gave up the 'schoolmaster trade' and moved back to Edinburgh to study law; but this course of study did not suit him and he turned to private tutoring to earn his living. Ill health and depression dogged him during this period – this was partially exorcised in *Sartor Resartus* (1833–4) by the denial of the Everlasting NO as the centre of the universe – but by 1823 he was beginning to make a name for himself through his translations of Goethe's *Wilhelm Meisters Lehrjahr* (1824) and *Wilhelm Meisters Wanderjahre* (1827), and his *Life of Schiller* (1825). In 1824 he visited London and Paris, and between 1825 and 1826 he lived at Hoddam Hill near his parents' farm at Ecclefechan. In 1826 he married Jane Welsh (see CARLYLE, JANE WELSH) and from then until 1828 the couple lived in Edinburgh. They made the acquaintance of FRANCIS JEFFREY who accepted Carlyle as a contributor to the *Edinburgh Review* (see EDINBURGH REVIEW (ii)), but Carlyle could not make a living from his writing and in May 1828 he moved to Craigenputtoch, a farm near Dumfries which belonged to Jane's family. He remained there for six years but visits to Edinburgh and London convinced him that he had to move out of country isolation, and in June 1834 he took up residence at 5 Cheyne Walk in Chelsea, London; the rest of his life was to be spent there and in later life he was known as the 'Sage of Chelsea'.

Carlyle's first task on his settling in London was to complete *The French Revolution*, which was eventually published in 1837 in spite of its loss in manuscript while in the hands of John Stuart Mill. He also embarked on a career as a public lecturer and a collection of his lectures, *On Heroes, Hero Worship and the Heroic in History* was published in 1841. In *Chartism* (1839) and *Past and Present* (1843) he turned his attention to political matters, and taking his cue from the events of the French Revolution he opposed a policy of *laissez-faire* and advocated instead the government of society by a strong, just man whose election would not be subject to the laws of democracy. In that way individual freedom, a concept dear to his heart, could be preserved. A natural consequence of that line of thought was his edition, published in 1845, of Oliver Cromwell's letters and speeches; it also led to Carlyle's being viewed with distrust in some quarters as an opponent of Liberalism. *Latter Day Pamphlets* (1850), a collection of eight essays, advocated, among other ideas, application to duty, punishment as opposed to blandishments and obedience to the rules of a society that would be ruled by a heroic leader. This period also saw the beginnings and completion of his six-volume *History of . . . Frederick the Great* (1858–65), a study remarkable both for the impeccability of his research and for his unbounded admiration for the autocratic ruler of Prussia.

In April 1866 Carlyle was installed as Lord Rector of the University of Edinburgh, but his pleasure at the appointment was marred by the death of his wife that same month. She had been a mainstay of his life, and his writing and her own letters and diaries present a vivid insight into their relationship and the workings of Carlyle's mind. After her death Carlyle wrote little of importance: 'Shooting Niagara – and After?', published in *Macmillan's Magazine* (August 1867), is a further unpleasant manifestation of his tendency towards racism, and *The Early Kings of Norway* (1875) is a minor piece of historical writing which reflects his interests in Scandinavian mythology. Carlyle died after a short illness on 5 February 1881, an honoured and respected 'grand old man' of British letters.

Carlyle's *Reminiscences* was published in 1881 by his disciple James Anthony Froude (1818–94), who acted as his literary executor between 1881 and 1884 and whose frank revelations of some aspects of Carlyle's private life in the official *Life* provoked a good deal of antagonism and controversy. That picture of the Carlyles' unhappy home life was partially balanced by D. A. Watson's six-volume biography of 1923–9; Carlyle's life and literary career have been the subject of considerable critical interest and further biographical research. His and Jane's letters have been much published and are the subject of a research and publishing undertaking shared by the University of Edinburgh and Duke University, North Carolina, USA.

During his lifetime Carlyle enjoyed enormous prestige as a social prophet, even though there were those who disagreed with his increasingly obdurate right-wing views. There have also been arguments about his literary style: he has been praised for his graphic descriptive powers and yet the density and un-necessary obscurity of much of his writing have annoyed many of his critics. This is especially true of *Sartor Resartus* which was published in *Fraser's Magazine* in 1833–4 and as a separate volume in Boston, Massachusetts, in 1836, the first British edition appearing in 1838. The work was influenced by the writings of the German novelist Johann Paul Friedrich Richter (1763–1825) and it falls into two parts. Firstly, there is a satirical discourse on clothes, in which Professor Teufelsdröckh comes to the conclusion that all human values are based on clothes and are therefore temporary; but the second half is largely autobiographical, as Teufelsdröckh traces his development from the Everlasting NO to the Everlasting YES through the Centre of Indifference, from uncertainty to an awareness that life has a deeper set of values.

That revelation gained through the writing of *Sartor Resartus* provoked in Carlyle a belief that religion was an important counterbalance to the growing industrialization of the late 19th century, and although he rejected the Calvinism of his childhood years, he believed that Christianity and application to duty formed a secure basis for life. Against the background of those beliefs it is possible to see in a proper perspective Carlyle's ideas about the emergence of the hero as ruler and the protection of individual freedom in a universe in which disorder is kept firmly at bay. However tortuous may be his theories and the ways in which they were expressed, Carlyle was one of the few British thinkers to attempt to come to an understanding of the problems created by the new industrial society.

Carlyle wrote one uncompleted novel, *Wotton Reinfred* (1827); he also published essays on ROBERT BURNS and Sir WALTER SCOTT, and an affectionate biography of his friend John Sterling (1851) which also contains a finely written portrait of Samuel Taylor Coleridge (1772–1834).

WORKS AND EDITIONS: *Wilhelm Meister's Apprenticeship: a Novel from the German of Goethe*, 3 vols. (1824); *The Life of Schiller* (1825); *German Romance*, 4 vols. (1827); *Sartor Resartus* (1836); *The French Revolution: a History*, 3 vols. (1837); *Critical and Miscellaneous Essays*, 4 vols. (1838); *Lectures on the History of Literature* (1838); *Chartism* (1839); *On Heroes, Hero Worship and the Heroic in History*, 2 vols. (1841); *Past and Present* (1843); *Oliver Cromwell's Letters and Speeches*, 2 vols. (1845); *Latter Day Pamphlets* (1850); *Life of John Sterling* (1851); *The History of Friedrich II of Prussia, Called Frederick the Great*, 6 vols. (1858–65); *The Early Kings of Norway:*

also an Essay on the Portraits of John Knox (1875); J. A. Froude, ed., *Reminiscences* (1881); J. A. Froude, ed., *Reminiscences of my Irish Journey in 1849* (1882); H. D. Traill, ed., *Centenary Edition of Carlyle's Works*, 30 vols. (1896–9); J. A. Froude, ed., *Last Words of Thomas Carlyle* (1898); S. A. Jones, ed., *Collectanea Thomas Carlyle 1821–1855* (1903); R. A. E. Brooks, ed., *Journey to Germany, Autumn 1858* (1940); H. Shine, ed., *Carlyle's Unfinished History of German Literature* (1951).

REFERENCES: J. M. Sloan, *The Carlyle Country* (London, 1904); T. Holme, *The Carlyles at Home* (London, 1965); G. B. Tennyson, *Sartor called Resartus* (London, 1965); J. S. Collis, *The Carlyles* (London, 1971); J. P. Siegel, *Carlyle: the Critical Heritage* (London, 1971); I. Campbell, *Thomas Carlyle* (London, 1974)

Carnegie, Andrew (1835–1919). Philanthropist. He was born on 25 November 1835 in Dunfermline, Fife, the son of a poor linen weaver. In 1848, during the depression that hit the linen trade, the Carnegie family emigrated to the United States where they lived in Allegheny City, Pennsylvania. There young Carnegie took to the weaving trade but, despairing of advancing in life, he moved to Pittsburgh to work as a telegraph messenger boy. A free library scheme in the city allowed Carnegie the opportunity of study but it was a timely investment in a railway company that put him on the road to gaining an immense fortune. He quickly acquired interests in railways, locomotive construction and iron works, and by dint of making sound investments, and exploiting an ability to foresee technological innovations, he had by 1901 amassed a private fortune of £60 million.

By that time Carnegie's interests were changing from the making of money to its equal distribution among his fellow men, and he published his ideals in his credo *The Gospel of Wealth* (1900). First and foremost funds were set aside for the establishment of libraries in the United States and Britain on condition that they would be maintained by the local authority. Six separate funds were established in the United States for educational advancement and in Britain he founded the Carnegie Trust for the Universities of Scotland, the Carnegie Dunfermline Trust, the Carnegie Hero Trust and the Carnegie United Kingdom Trust. Carnegie received several public honours, including the Lord Rectorship of the Scottish universities; he bought the estate of Skibo in Sutherland as a summer retreat. His passionate concern for international peace resulted in the foundation of the Palace of Peace in The Hague in 1903 but the outbreak of World War I dashed his ideals and put an end to his promotion of Kaiser Wilhelm II of Germany as 'a man of destiny'. Carnegie died on 11 August 1919 at Lennox, Massachusetts.

WORKS: *An American Four Hand in Britain* (1883); *Round the World* (1884); *Triumphant Democracy* (1886); *The Gospel of Wealth* (1900); *The Empire of Business* (1902); *Life of James Watt* (1905); *Problems of Today* (1908); J. van Dyke, ed., *Autobiography of Andrew Carnegie* (1920)

Carruthers, Robert (1799–1878). Editor and man of letters. He was born on 5 November 1799 in Dumfries, the son of a smallholder. He was apprenticed to the *Dumfries Courier* and after a short period in England he became editor of the *Inverness Courier* in 1831 and subsequently its proprietor. There he was able to publish the early work of HUGH MILLER, who was to become a lifelong friend. Carruthers contributed many scholarly essays to the eighth edition of the ENCYCLOPAEDIA BRITANNICA, and with ROBERT CHAMBERS he edited a bowdlerized version of the works of Shakespeare (1861–3). But he is best remembered for his his four-volume edition of the life and works of Alexander Pope (1688–1744), which was published in 1853. He died on 26 May 1878 in Inverness.

Carswell [née Macfarlane], **Catherine Roxburgh** (1879–1946). Novelist and critic. She was born on 27 March 1879 in Glasgow, the daughter of a merchant with interests in shipping. She was educated at the Park School and, between 1896 and 1898, at the Schumann Conservatorium in Frankfurt-am-Main. Although she retained a lifelong interest in music, on returning to Glasgow she turned to lecturing on art. In 1903 she made her first marriage to H. P. M. Jackson, which was annulled after an early separation. She became drama critic of the GLASGOW HERALD in 1907, but lost her post in 1911 after reviewing D. H. Lawrence's banned novel *The Rainbow*. The death of her mother in 1912 completed the break-up of her family home in Glasgow and she moved to London to become a reviewer and drama critic of *The Observer*. In 1917 she married DONALD CARSWELL, a fellow journalist and critic. During this period she became friendly with D. H. Lawrence who encouraged her to complete her first novel *Open the Door!* (1920), a thinly disguised autobiographical work, which is memorable for the description of the escape of the heroine, Joanna, from the confines of a middle-class, Calvinistic Glasgow family. *The Camomile: an Invention*, a less successful sequel, was published in 1922. Like many other writers of her generation she had to remain in London to make a living from her literary earnings, and among her friends there were JOHN BUCHAN and Hugh MacDiarmid (CHRISTOPHER MURRAY GRIEVE). She died on 19 March 1946 and her autobiography, *Lying Awake*, which is also a summary of her literary aspirations, was published in 1950.

It is as a critic that Catherine Carswell is best remembered, even though her *Life of Robert Burns* (1930) was badly received by Burns scholars, especially in Scotland. She was one of the first critics to return to original sources in her treatment of Burns's relationships with MARY CAMPBELL and JEAN ARMOUR and the publication of the KILMARNOCK EDITION of his poems. She claimed, in a letter of 19 July 1929 to F. Marian McNeill, that her method would bring Burns 'out of the mist they have loved to keep about him'. After Lawrence's death in 1930 she wrote a personal view of their friendship, *The Savage Pilgrimage: a Narrative of D. H. Lawrence* (1932), which was initially suppressed in publication as being libellous. In 1937 she published a biography of Boccaccio, *The Tranquil Heart*. With her husband she compiled an anthology of Scottish writing, *The Scots Weekend*.

WORKS: *Open the Door!* (1920); *The Camomile: an Invention* (1922), *Life of Robert Burns* (1930); *The Savage Pilgrimage: a Narrative of D. H. Lawrence* (1932); *Robert Burns* (1933); ed., with Donald Carswell, *The Scots Weekend* (1935); *The Tranquil Heart* (1937); *Lying Awake* (1950)

Carswell, Donald (1882–1939). Critic. He was a native of Glasgow, where he was educated at Glasgow Academy and later at the University. On graduating he became a journalist with the GLASGOW HERALD and during World War I he moved to London to work for *The Times*. In 1917 he married Catherine Roxburgh Macfarlane (*see* CARSWELL, CATHERINE), a fellow journalist from his time in Glasgow. Between them Donald and Catherine Carswell attempted to earn their living from writing, but Donald's insistence on revision and on polishing his style lost him several commissions. His painstaking methods are reflected in the books that he did write:

Brother Scots (1927) is an elegant study of Scots Presbyterianism during the 19th century as reflected the lives of HENRY DRUMMOND, JOHN STUART BLACKIE, KEIR HARDIE, WILLIAM ROBERTSON NICOLL, William Robertson Smith (1846–94) and Lord Overtoun (1843–1908); and *Sir Walter: a Four Part Study in Biography* (1930) contains much useful information on the literary background to Scott's career, with separate essays on JAMES HOGG, JOHN GIBSON LOCKHART and JOANNA BAILLIE. Shortly before the outbreak of World War II Carswell secured employment as a civil servant. He was killed in a motoring accident in October 1939.

WORKS: *Brother Scots* (1927); *Sir Walter: a Four Part Study in Biography* (1930); *Count Albany* (1933); *Trial of Guy Fawkes and Others* (1934); *A Virtuous Widow and Others* (1940)

Castilian Band. The name given to the group of poets at the court of JAMES VI, formed by the king himself in 1583. Among its more prominent members were WILLIAM FOWLER, ALEXANDER MONTGOMERIE and JOHN STEWART of Baldynneis. In his lament for Montgomerie, James made fond reference to the Band and to the esteem in which he held it:

> What drousie sleep doth syle your eyes allace
> Ye sacred brethren of Castilian band
> And shall the Prince of Poets in our land
> Goe thus to grave unmurned in anie cace?

The Band had its origins in the king's reorganization of his court, following his year's imprisonment by the Scottish nobles after the Raid of Ruthven in 1582. It was his intention to attract to the court musicians and poets, who were encouraged to make translations, experiment with metrical forms and to collaborate in the composition of poetry and songs. The group was to centre on the Apollo figure of the monarch himself, and James's REULIS AND CAUTELIS laid the ground rules for the hoped-for literary revival. But all was not harmony and there were splits within the Band itself: Montgomerie was banished on account of his religious beliefs and there were disputes over the compilation of a collection of PSALMS. With the removal of the court to London in 1603 the influence of the Castilian Band was effectively at an end.

REFERENCE: H. M. Shire, *Song, Dance and Poetry of the Court of Scotland under King James VI* (Cambridge, 1969)

Celtic Twilight. Originally the title of a collection of Irish stories (1893) by W. B. Yeats (1865–1939), it has become a generic phrase used, often pejoratively, to describe the late 19th-century movement of Scottish and Irish story-writing that exploits the Celtic mysticism of the folk heritage in those countries. Implicit in this genre of writing is a belief in ghosts, spirits, fairies and ancient heroes and gods; its chief practitioners in Scotland were WILLIAM SHARP ('Fiona Macleod'), WILLIAM BLACK and, to a lesser extent, NEIL MUNRO.

Chaldee Manuscript. Published in BLACK-WOOD'S MAGAZINE on 21 October 1817, the 'Translation from an ancient Chaldee Manuscript, supposed to have been written by Daniel' purported to be a translation of a manuscript discovered in the Bibliothèque Nationale, Paris (Salle 2d, no.53, B.A.M.M.). It was in fact a satirical attack, couched in the language of the Old Testament, on Blackwood's Whig rivals, the publishers of the *Edinburgh Review* (*see* EDINBURGH REVIEW (ii)); its publication caused a scandal in Edinburgh and London, adding greatly to the magazine's popularity and to its readership. JAMES HOGG, who was closely associated with the Blackwood group, claimed responsibility in later life for its composition, but it seems likely that although he may have conceived the original idea additions were made by to the text before publication by the contributing editors JOHN WILSON (iii) and JOHN GIBSON LOCKHART. In later editions of the October issue the 'Chaldee Manuscript' was deleted, but its publication did much to set the aggressively satirical anti-Whig attitude of *Blackwood's Magazine* in its early days.

Chalmers, George (1742–1825). Historian. He was born at Fochabers, Moray, and was educated at the University of Aberdeen before studying law at the University of Edinburgh. From 1763 to 1775 he practised as a lawyer in Baltimore, Maryland, returning to live in London on the outbreak of the American War of Independence. His early work was concerned with colonial policies and in 1786 he was appointed chief clerk to the Committee of Privy Council for Trade and Foreign Plantations. After publishing biographies of Daniel Defoe (*c* 1660–1731) and Thomas Paine (1737–1809), Chalmers turned his attention to Scottish antiquarian studies; he printed editions of the poems of Sir DAVID LYNDSAY and

ALLAN RAMSAY, but he is best remembered for the ambitious *Caledonia* in which he proposed to publish the entire history of Scotland and its antiquities (six volumes were planned but only three appeared). Chalmers died on 31 May 1825 before the project could be completed.

WORKS: *Political Annals of the Present United Colonies from the Settlement to the Peace of 1768* (1780); *An Estimate of the Comparative Strength of Great Britain* (1782); *An Introduction to the History of the Revolt of the Colonies* (1782); *The Propriety of Allowing a Qualified Export of Wool Discussed Historically* (1782); *Opinions on Interesting Subjects of Public Law and Commercial Policy* (1784); ed., *Historical Tracts of Sir John Davie* (1785); *Life of Daniel Defoe* (1786); *A Collection of Treaties between Great Britain and other Powers*, 2 vols. (1790); *Life of Thomas Paine* (1793); *Life of Thomas Ruddiman* (1794); *Prefatory Introduction to Dr Johnson's 'Debates in Parliament'* (1794); *Apology for the Believers of Shakespeare's Papers* (1796); *Observations on the State of England in 1796* (1796); *Vindication of the Privilege of the People in Respect of the Constitutional Right of Free Discussion* (1796); *A Supplemental Apology* (1799); ed., *The Poems of Allan Ramsay*, 2 vols. (1800); *Life of Sir David Lyndsay of the Mount*, 3 vols. (1807); *A Chronological Account of Commerce in Great Britain from the Restoration to 1810* (1810); *Considerations on Commerce* (1811); *Historical View of the Domestic Economy of Great Britain and Ireland* (1812); *Points of English Jurisprudence* (1814); *The Author of 'Junius' Acclaimed* (1817); *Churchyard's Chips concerning Scotland* (1817); *Comparative Views of the State of Great Britain and Ireland since the War* (1817); *Life of Mary Queen of Scots*, 2 vols. (1818); ed., Robert Henryson, *Robene and Makyne and The Testament of Cresseid* (1824)

Chalmers [Hay], **Margaret** (*d* 1843). The daughter of a farmer, Margaret Chalmers was related to the Mauchline lawyer GAVIN HAMILTON, a friend of ROBERT BURNS. There is little doubt from their letters that Burns was in love with Margaret, or 'Peggy', and she later told the poet THOMAS CAMPBELL that Burns had proposed to her at her parents' house of Harviestone, Clackmannanshire, during his Highland tour of 1787. She married a banker, Lewis Hay, in December 1788 and died in Switzerland on 3 March 1843.

Chalmers, Thomas (1780–1847). Divine. He was born on 17 March 1780 in Anstruther, Fife, and was educated at the University of St Andrews. He became minister of Kilmeny in Fife in 1803 but transferred to Glasgow in 1815 at a time when he was building his reputation as a powerful and persuasive preacher. In 1823 he returned to St Andrews as Professor of Moral Philosphy and in 1828 he became Professor of Divinity at Edinburgh. Between 1833 and 1843 Chalmers was involved in the conflicts between Church and State over the appointment of ministers; following THE DISRUPTION of 1843 he became the first Moderator of the General Assembly of the Free Church of Scotland and the principal of its theological college. A committed and internationally known philanthropist, Chalmers devoted much of his life to the problems caused by poverty in industrial areas. His chief works were devoted to theology, political economy and scientific development, of which the most lasting are *A Series of Discourses* (1817) and *On Political Economy* (1832). After his death, on 30 May 1847, his works were collected and published in 34 volumes and a memoir of his life by William Hanna appeared in four volumes between 1845 and 1852.

WORKS: *An Enquiry into the Extent and Stability of National Resources* (1808); *The Evidence and Authority of the Christian Revelation* (1814); *The Influence of Bible Societies* (1814); *The Duty of Giving an Immediate Diligence to the Business of Christian Life* (1815); *Thoughts on Universal Peace* (1816); *The Utility of Missions Ascertained by Experience* (1816); *Scripture References* (1817); *A Series of Discourses on Christian Revelation* (1817); *A Doctrine of Christian Charity* (1818); *The Application of Christianity* (1820); *The Doctrine of the Eleventh Article* (1820); *The Importance of Civil Government to Society* (1820); *The Christian and Civic Economy of Large Towns* (1821); *On the Advantages of Local Parish Schools* (1824); *A Few Thoughts on the Abolition of Colonial Slavery* (1826); *On Cruelty to Animals* (1826); *The Effect of Man's Wrath* (1827); *On the Use and Abuse of Literary and Ecclesiastical Endowments* (1827); *On Political Economy* (1832); *On the Power, Wisdom and Goodness of God* (1833); *Churches and Chapels* (1834); *On the Evils which the Established Church has suffered in Edinburgh* (1835); *The Right Ecclesiastical Economy of a Large Town* (1835); *Church Establishments Defended* (1837); *A Conference with Certain Ministers and Elders* (1837); *The Consequences of Sowing to the Flesh* (1837); *Five Lectures on Predestination* (1837); *Lectures on the Epistle of Paul the Apostle* (1837); *The Messiah's Duty Considered* (1837); *Lectures on the Establishment and Extension of the National Church* (1838); *What ought the Church and the People of Scotland to do now?* (1840); *On the Sufficiency of the Parochial System* (1841); *Address Delivered at the first General Assembly of the Free Church* (1843); *On the Economics of the Free Church of Scotland* (1845); *On the Evangelical Alliance* (1846); *The Efficacy of Prayer* (1849); *Horae biblicae quotidianae* (1853); *Select Sermons* (1859); *The Reign of Grace* (1865); *Modern Science and the Bible* (1872)

EDITIONS: *Sermons Preached on Public Occasions* (Glasgow, 1823); *Speeches and Tracts* (Glasgow, 1824); *The Works of Thomas Chalmers*, 25 vols. (Glasgow, 1836–42); W. Hanna, ed., *Posthumous Works of Thomas Chalmers*, 9 vols. (Edinburgh,

1847–9); Hanna, ed., *Selected Works of Thomas Chalmers*, 12 vols. (Edinburgh, 1856)

REFERENCES: W. Hanna, *Memoirs of Thomas Chalmers*, 4 vols. (Edinburgh, 1845–52); H. Watt, *Thomas Chalmers and the Disruption* (London, 1943)

Chambers, Robert (1802–71). Author and publisher. He was born on 10 July 1802 in Peebles, the son of a wool manufacturer; the family moved to Edinburgh in 1814. Robert joined his brother, WILLIAM CHAMBERS, in the bookselling trade and they branched out later into publishing, establishing the firm of W. and R. Chambers, which produced CHAMBERS'S JOURNAL. Chambers became a prolific producer of reference books; as well as editing the *Chambers's Encyclopaedia* (1859–68) and *The Cyclopaedia of English Literature* (1842), he wrote three important works of his own: *A Biographical Dictionary of Eminent Scotsmen* (1832–4), which contains much standard information about the lives of leading men and women in Scotland's history; *The Book of Days* (1863), an almanac of historical, religious and social data; and *Domestic Annals of Scotland* (1859–61), a collection of extracts from Scottish historical source material. He also wrote on Edinburgh: his *Traditions of Edinburgh* (1824) is a personal and entertaining record of the city and its history, written at a time when many of the antiquities and memories of past years were in danger of being forgotten; and his *Walks in Edinburgh* (1825) reflects his intimate knowledge of the city of his adoption. His other works of interest are *The Popular Rhymes of Scotland* (1826), *History of the Rebellion in Scotland 1745–6* (1828), and *The Vestiges of the Natural History of Creation*, published anonymously in 1844, which was one of the precursors of the theories of Charles Darwin (1809–82). Chambers died on 17 March 1871.

WORKS: *Traditions of Edinburgh* (1824); *Illustrations of the Author of Waverley* (1825); *Walks in Edinburgh* (1825); *The Popular Rhymes of Scotland* (1826); *The Picture of Scotland* (1827); ed., *The Scottish Ballads* (1829); *History of the Rebellion in Scotland 1745–6* (1828); *History of the Rebellions in Scotland under the Marquis of Montrose and Others 1638–60* (1828); ed., *The Scottish Songs* (1829); *The Life of King James the First*, 2 vols. (1830); *A Biographical Dictionary of Eminent Scotsmen*, 4 vols. (1832–4); *Scottish Jests and Anecdotes* (1832); *Minor Antiquities of Edinburgh* (1833); *History of the English Language and Literature* (1836); ed., *Cyclopaedia of English Literature*, 2 vols. (1842); *The Vestiges of the Natural History of Creation* (1844); *Ancient Sea-Margins* (1848); *The History of Scotland*, 2 vols. (1849); *Tracings of North Europe*

(1850); *Tracings of Iceland and the Faroes* (1856); *Domestic Annals of Scotland from the Reformation to the Revolution*, 2 vols. (1859–61); ed., *Chambers's Encyclopaedia* (1859–68); *Edinburgh Papers*, 5 vols. (1859); *Domestic Annals of Scotland from the Revolution to the Rebellion of 1745* (1861); *The Book of Days*, 2 vols. (1863); *Smollett* (1867); *Life of Sir Walter Scott* (1871); *The Threiplands of Fingask* (1880)

REFERENCE: W. Chambers, *Memoir of Robert Chambers* (Edinburgh, 1872)

Chambers, William (1800–83). Publisher. He was born on 16 April 1800 in Peebles, the son of a wool manufacturer. In 1814 his parents moved to Edinburgh where he was apprenticed as a bookseller, and in 1819 he set up his own bookselling business with his brother ROBERT CHAMBERS. They branched out later into publishing and the firm of W. and R. Chambers became one of the country's leading publishers, publishing CHAMBERS'S JOURNAL from 1832. Chambers was Lord Provost of Edinburgh between 1865 and 1868 and he was renowned as a philanthropist with interest in slum clearance and town planning. He contributed a major sum to the restoration of the High Church of St Giles and to his native town of Peebles he presented a museum library and art gallery. As a publisher Chambers encouraged the production of reference books and inexpensive educational material. Among his own publications are *The Book of Scotland* (1830) and the *History of Peeblesshire* (1864). His *Memoir of William and Robert Chambers* (1883) gives a vivid impression of the Edinburgh of his period and of the rise of commercial publishing during the 19th century. He died on 20 May 1883.

WORKS: *The Book of Scotland* (1830); *A Tour in Holland* (1839); *Truth and Trust* (1848); *Fiddy* (1851); ed., *Poems for Young People* (1851); *Things as they are in America* (1854); *Peebles and its Neighbourhood* (1856); *American Slavery and Colour* (1857); *The Youth's Companion and Counsellor* (1858); ed., *Chambers's Social Science Tracts*, 6 vols. (1860–63); *Something of Italy* (1862); *A History of Peeblesshire* (1864); *Chambers's Historical Questions* (1865); *Chambers's Social Science Tracts*, 6 vols. (1860–63); *Light and Descriptive* (1866); *France, its History and Revolutions* (1871); *Memoir of Robert Chambers* (1872); *A Week at Welwyn* (1873); *Wintering at Mentone* (1876); *Kindness to Animals* (1877); *Stories of Old Families* (1878); *Stories of Remarkable Persons* (1878); *The Story of St Giles Cathedral Church* (1879); *The Story of a Long and Busy Life* (1882); *Memoir of William and Robert Chambers* (1883); *The Life and Anecdotes of David Ritchie* (1885); *Exploits and Anecdotes of Scottish Gypsies* (1886)

Chambers's Journal. Literary magazine first published as *Chambers's Edinburgh Journal* on 4 February 1832 by the publishing house founded by WILLIAM CHAMBERS and ROBERT CHAMBERS. It quickly achieved a circulation of 30,000 readers. The first editor was William Chambers, whose editorial taste reflected many of his philanthropic interests: the magazine would only publish 'original and select papers on Literary and Scientific objects including articles on the Formation and Arrangements of Society', and the articles in the early editions were deliberately educative in content. In 1833 Robert joined his brother in editing the *Journal*. Gradually he assumed full control and changed the editorial tenor by publishing literary and philosophical essays. He encouraged HUGH MILLER and Robert Gilfillan and the literary reputation of the magazine prospered. Later in the century Thomas Hardy (1840–1928), ARTHUR CONAN DOYLE and JOHN BUCHAN contributed their early work and the tradition of encouraging younger writers continued into the 20th century when NEIL M. GUNN became a regular contributor. *Chambers's Journal* was published monthly until 1956, when it ceased publication.

Chapman [Chepman], **Walter** (c1473–c1538). Printer. He was born in Edinburgh during the reign of JAMES III and first appears as a clerk in the royal household of JAMES IV in 1494. He was a wealthy Edinburgh merchant and owned considerable property in the city, including the estate of Prestonfield. In 1507 he obtained the royal patents to set up Scotland's first printing press in the Cowgate, Edinburgh. The printers and their machines were brought over from France and they were directed by Chapman's partner, the bookseller Andrew Myllar. Their first productions, a selection of poems by ROBERT HENRYSON and WILLIAM DUNBAR appeared in 1509, but most of their publications were instigated by William Elphinstone, Bishop of Aberdeen, including the *Aberdeen Breviary* and the two volumes of *Legends of the Saints* (both 1510). Chapman and Myllar retained the monopoly of printing books in Scotland until 1536, when Thomas Davidson printed John Bellenden's translation into Scots of *Scotorum historiae* by HECTOR BOECE. In 1513 Chapman founded the chaplaincy of St John the Evangelist in the Church of St Giles, and between 1514 and 1515 he was Dean of the Guild of Edinburgh.

Charles Edward Stuart. *See* STUART, CHARLES EDWARD.

Chepman, Walter. *See* CHAPMAN, WALTER.

Cherrie and the Slae, The. A poem by ALEX-ANDER MONTGOMERIE, first published in two versions in 1597 by Waldegrave. In 1615 ANDRO HART published another version containing a further 47 verses of Montgomerie's composition, reflecting the poet's increasingly devout Catholicism. Other versions were printed in 1636 and in 1724 in THE EVER GREEN by ALLAN RAMSAY. At the beginning of the poem the poet stands in idyllic surroundings of great natural beauty when Cupid appears before him to offer him the use of his wings to fly 'as Icarus with borrowed flight'. Let down heavily on earth again after a fruitless flight, the poet scolds himself for his rashness and lack of reason. Then he becomes aware of a cherry tree high on the crag above him, and below sees a bush of bitter sloe berries. There follows a discussion between Courage and Hope who urge him to attempt to win the cherries, and Dread and Despair who argue that he should settle for the more accessible sloes. Other emotions join in: Will counsels that he should try for the cherries despite the recent disaster with Cupid, Wit and Skill show how the crag may be climbed, and Reason works out a plan. In the midst of their several discussions, however, the cherries fall, the poet is refreshed and thanks God 'who did mine health to mee restore'. Unlike earlier dream allegories in the medieval tradition, the poet is not asleep or in a trance, and his emotions are not characterized but remain states of his subconscious mind. Nevertheless, there are many levels of meaning in Montgomerie's allegory, the most acceptable being the opposing forces of Catholicism (the cherries) and Protestantism (the more accessible sloes). Like most of Montgomerie's work, *The Cherrie and the Slae* is written in a strict rhyming scheme that suggests that it was composed for singing, probably to a dance tune.

Choice Collection of Comic and Serious Scots Poems. An anthology of Scots poems and songs comprising three volumes, published in 1706, 1709 and 1711 by the Edinburgh printer JAMES WATSON. The volumes contained an odd assortment of 16th- and 17th-century verse, mixing together the classical work of the makars with comic songs, dog-Latin rhymes and more contemporary poems and songs. Watson's intention in publishing the volumes was patriotic in origin, and the *Choice Collection* was to become a helpful source book, and an inspiration, for the 18th-century revival of interest in poetry written in Scots. But the anthology also served to emphasize the debilitation of literary Scots as a spoken language since its heyday during the 16th century. Among the longer poems published in the collections were versions of CHRISTIS KIRK ON THE GREEN and THE CHERRIE AND THE SLAE.

Christis Kirk on the Green. A burlesque poem attributed to both JAMES I and JAMES V, which appears in the Maitland Folio Manuscript (*see* MAITLAND MANUSCRIPTS), and the BANNATYNE MANUSCRIPT. It marked the start of a Scottish tradition of composing humorous poems about popular events, in this case a peasant festival seen through the amused eyes of an upper-class poet. It is notable both for its vivid and evocatively expressed wealth of description and for its metrical brilliance. Each stanza has two quatrains and a repeated closing line and within the stanzas there is a rhyming scheme, *abab/abab/c/d*, in which *c* is called the 'bob' and the repeating closing line *d* the 'wheel'.

> Was never in Scotland hard nor sene
> Sic dansing nor deray
> Nother in Falkland on the Grene
> Nor Peblis to the Play,
> As was of wowaris as I wene
> At Chrystis Kirk on ane day.
> Thair come our Kittie wesching clene
> In hir new kirtell of gray
> Fullgay,
> At Chrystis Kirk on the grene.

The fast-moving metre and the exuberant language allow the poet to pass deftly from one scene to the next, thus building up a solid canvas of moods and physical impressions.

The bob – wheel stanza was adapted by later poets, most tellingly by ALLAN RAMSAY, who added verses to the poem, and ROBERT FERGUSSON and ROBERT BURNS, both of whom continued the comic tradition of poems in this genre in, respectively, 'HALLOW FAIR' and 'THE HOLY FAIR'.

Chronicles of the Canongate. The title of two series of novels by Sir WALTER SCOTT, published in 1827 and 1828. The first series contained THE HIGHLAND WIDOW, THE TWO

DROVERS and THE SURGEON'S DAUGHTER; and the second, THE FAIR MAID OF PERTH. As with all Scott's novels, the conceit of the well-told tale allowed him to pretend that the books had been written anonymously, in this case by Chrystabel Croftangry, who had been told the stories by a resident of the Canongate in Edinburgh, Mrs Bethune Baliol.

Clarinda. The name adopted by AGNES M'LEHOSE to sign the letters that she wrote to ROBERT BURNS during their epistolary relationship from 1787 to 1791.

Clark, Rev. T. Pen-name of JOHN GALT.

Clear, Claudius. Pen-name of WILLIAM ROBERTSON NICOLL.

Clearances. A term used to describe the enforced migration of a large section of the population from the Highlands in the years following the JACOBITE rebellion of 1745, which continued throughout the 19th century. The reasons for the clearances can be partly ascribed to the failure of the rebellion, the government's consequent desire to curb the power of the clan chiefs and the break-up of the clan system of land ownership; but the first clearances, in Sutherland, were as a result of a move by the landowners to introduce new methods of agriculture and land usage. Crofters (small farmers), holding no rights to their land, were removed to the coastal strips to make way for the introduction of sheep farming in the more fertile glens. However, the new mixed economy and the introduction of industries such as fishing and linen manufacture did not provide a secure basis for the population, and throughout the 19th century absentee landlords encouraged emigration, especially to North America. Many of the evictions were carried out with a brutality that has become part of Highland mythology and folk memory, and there was some spirited resistance to the clearances in Skye through strikes and land raids. Security of tenure was granted to the crofters only by the Napier Commission of 1886, but by then the population of the Highlands had dwindled. The clearances changed the face of the Highlands, encouraged absenteeism among landlords and helped to weaken Gaelic culture and language, although its literature is rich in their condemnation. THE SILVER DARLINGS by NEIL GUNN is a portrayal of life in a post-clearance fishing village; other novelists who have written about the clearances are THOMAS DOUGLAS MACDONALD ('Fion MacColla') and IAIN CRICHTON SMITH.

Cleghorn, James (1778–1838). Editor. He was a native of Duns in Berwickshire and for the early part of his life he worked there as a farmer. In 1811 he became editor of the *Farmer's Magazine* and with Thomas Pringle he edited the first six issues of the *Edinburgh Monthly Magazine* which was published by WILLIAM BLACKWOOD between April and September 1817 and which subsequently became BLACKWOOD'S MAGAZINE. Cleghorn's only other editorial appointment was with the SCOTS MAGAZINE AND GENERAL INTELLIGENCER. He had trained as an actuary and between 1822 and his death on 27 May 1838 he worked as an accountant with several leading insurance firms.

WORKS: *On the Depressed State of Agriculture* (1822); *Thoughts on the Expediency of a General Provident Institution* (1825)

Clerk, Sir John, of Penicuik (1676–1755). Politician and patron of the arts. He was born in Edinburgh and studied law at Glasgow and Leiden, although he was destined never to practise. While abroad his interests turned to music and architecture, and his travels in Italy between 1697 and 1700 awakened classical tastes. On his return to Scotland he became a Commissioner for the ACT OF UNION of 1707 and spent some time at the court of Queen Anne. After the passing of the Act he received the sinecure of Baron of the Exchequer and retired to his seat at Penicuik to enjoy the pleasures of a literary and antiquarian life and the cultivation of his large garden. Like many other Augustan squires he composed a number of rounded verses and produced books on scientific and classical literary subjects. Among those who enjoyed his patronage were the poet ALLAN RAMSAY and the architect ROBERT ADAM.

EDITION: J. M. Gray, ed., *Memoirs of Sir John Clerk of Penicuik* (Edinburgh, 1892)

Clouston, J(oseph) Storer (1870–1944). Novelist. He was born on 23 May 1870 in Cumberland, into an old-established Orkney family. He was educated in Edinburgh and Oxford and was called to the English Bar although he never practised as a barrister. Most of his life was spent in Orkney and during World War I he was Sub-commissioner for Orkney and Shetland under the National Services Department. Clouston was a prolific writer and in 1899 his first comic novel, *The Lunatic at Large*, became a popular success; it was followed by a series of equally successful sequels: *Count Bunker* (1906), *The Lunatic at Large Again* (1922), *The Lunatic Still at Large* (1923) and *The Lunatic in Charge* (1926). Among his many other publications may be mentioned two spy thrillers, *The Spy in Black* (1917) and *The Man from the Clouds* (1918), and *A History of Orkney* (1932). He died on 23 June 1944.

WORKS: *Vanrad the Viking* (1898); *The Lunatic at Large* (1899); *The Duke* (1900); *The Adventures of M. D'Haricot* (1902); *Our Lady's Inn* (1903); *Garmiscath* (1904); *Count Bunker* (1906); *A County Family* (1908); *The Prodigal Father* (1909); *The Peer's Progress* (1910); *His First Offence* (1912); ed., *Records of the Earldom of Orkney 1299–1614* (1914); *Two's Two* (1916); *The Spy in Black* (1917); *The Man from the Clouds* (1918); *Sermon* (1919); *Carrington's Cases* (1920); *The Lunatic at Large Again* (1922); *The Lunatic Still at Large* (1923); *Tales of King Fido* (1924); *The Lunatic in Charge* (1926); *Mr Essington in Love* (1927); ed., *The Orkney Parishes* (1927); *The Jade's Progress* (1928); *After the Deed* (1929); *Colonel Dam* (1930); *Virtuous Tramp* (1931); *Best Story Ever* (1932); *A History of Orkney* (1932); *Button Brains* (1933); *The Chemical Baby* (1934); *Real Champagne* (1934); *Our Member Mr Mittlebery* (1935); *Scotland Expects* (1936); *Scots Wha Hae* (1936); *Not Since Genesis* (1938); *The Man in Steel* (1939); *Beastmark the Spy* (1941)

Cockburn [née Rutherford], **Alison** (c 1712–94). Songwriter. She was a daughter of Robert Rutherford of Fairnielee, Selkirkshire, and a distant relation of Sir WALTER SCOTT. In 1731 she married Patrick Cockburn, the son of Lord Ormiston the Lord Justice Clerk, and she quickly became known in Edinburgh both for her beauty and for the wit and elegance of her entertaining. Her husband died in 1753 but she remained in Edinburgh, where she befriended many of the leading *literati*, especially DAVID HUME and JAMES BURNETT, Lord Monboddo, and later Sir WALTER SCOTT. Alison Cockburn's chief claim to fame is her version of THE FLOWERS OF THE FOREST, which was written not as a lament for the BATTLE OF FLODDEN but, according to Scott, as a result of a financial disaster to lairds in the Ettrick valley. She died on 22 November 1794 in Edinburgh.

EDITION: T. Craig-Brown, ed., *Letters and Memoirs of her own Life, by Mrs A. Rutherford or Cockburn* (Edinburgh, 1900)

Cockburn, Henry Thomas, Lord (1779–1854). Judge and man of letters. He was born on 26 October 1779 in Edinburgh. His father, Archibald Cockburn, was a Sheriff of Midlothian, a Baron of the Court of Exchequer, a close friend of ROBERT MACQUEEN, Lord Braxfield the Lord Justice Clerk, and first cousin to HENRY DUNDAS, Viscount Melville, Pitt's 'manager for Scotland'. Between 1787 and 1793 he was educated at the HIGH SCHOOL OF EDINBURGH and at the age of 14 he entered the University of Edinburgh to study law, becoming an advocate in 1800. It was during this period that he renounced his family's Tory politics and became a Whig. He was a frequent contributor on legal matters to the newly founded *Edinburgh Review (see* EDINBURGH REVIEW (ii)) and was a lifelong friend and colleague of its editor FRANCIS JEFFREY, whose biography he wrote in 1852. Despite his abandonment of Tory politics, Dundas appointed him Depute to the Lord Advocate in 1807, and he held the post for three years.

In 1811 Cockburn married Elizabeth Macdowall and took up residence in Charlotte Square and at Bonaly House in the lee of the Pentland Hills. Throughout his life he was a critic of Edinburgh's expansion and a believer in the public control of the environment, aspects of his work which are commemorated in the name of the Cockburn Association, a leading Edinburgh amenities society. In 1823, with Sir WALTER SCOTT, he helped to found the Edinburgh Academy, a boys school with a bias towards the teaching of the classics.

Cockburn was an accomplished pleader of criminal cases. He is best known for the opening speech in 1821 in his defence of James Stuart of Dunearn who had killed Sir ALEXANDER BOSWELL in a duel, and for his defence in 1828 of Helen MacDougal, the common-law wife of WILLIAM BURKE, in the Burke and Hare case. He was a critic of the method by which a judge could choose his jury and he argued that the Lord Advocate's powers should be confined to legal matters and should not embrace the political powers of a Secretary of State for Scotland. Like Jeffrey and other leading Whig advocates, he wrote several pamphlets urging the extension of the parliamentary and municipal franchise, and he was responsible for the drafting of the Scottish Reform Bill in 1832 and the Burgh Reform Bill in 1833. Although he was an ardent reformer he could not countenance universal emancipation but believed that the vote should be entrusted to the intelligent and the prosperous. Cockburn was appointed Solicitor-General in 1830 and a Lord of Session in 1834 after the return of the Whigs to power. He died on 26 April, 1854.

As a writer and a chronicler of his times Cockburn is best remembered for his *Memorials of his Time* (1856), an autobiography interspersed with intimate descriptions of the manners and events of his life, together with generous character sketches of his contemporaries. This was followed by his *Journal*, published in 1874 after his death, which is a more austere work in the form of a diary of the years 1831–44. Together they form a continuous account of the main events of his lifetime. In much of his writing Cockburn betrays the dilemma faced by his contemporaries of an attachment to a romantic view of Scotland's past while accepting the advantages of Hanoverianism and union with England. His *Circuit Journeys*, an account of his travels in Scotland as a circuit judge, was published in 1888.

WORKS: *Inaugural Address at the University of Glasgow* (1839); *Life of Lord Jeffrey* (1852); *Memorials of his Time* (1856); *Lord Cockburn's Works*, 2 vols. (1872); *Journal of Henry Cockburn* (1874); *Circuit Journeys* (1888); *An Examination of the Trials for Sedition*, 2 vols. (1888)

REFERENCES: K. Miller, *Cockburn's Millenium* (London, 1975); A. Bell, ed., *Lord Cockburn: a Bicentenary Commemoration* (Edinburgh, 1979)

Cocker, W(illiam) D(ixon) (1882–1970). Poet and dramatist. He came from a long line of Glasgow merchants, but it was not to the city of his birth that he owed his poetic inspiration, rather to the countryside of Strathendrick in Stirlingshire. There his mother's family were farmers and most of Cocker's mature poetry takes its imagery from the remembered sights and sounds of his boyhood days in the countryside. In later life Cocker became a journalist with the *Daily Record* in Glasgow, but his memories of rural scenes and of the language of the country people were to suffuse all his work. Like his fellow Glasgow journalist NEIL MUNRO, Cocker was fascinated by the history and the lore of the Gaels, and his collection of short stories *Brave Days of Old* (1926) are clever pastiches of Munro's and

Stevenson's romance style. His poetry is written in a meticulous, though often stilted, archaic Scots, and he was one of the minor, and unjustly forgotten figures associated with the aims of the SCOTTISH RENAISSANCE Movement. His many one-act historical plays are little more than literary curiosities.

WORKS: *The Dreamer and Other Poems* (1920); *Dandie and Other Poems* (1925); *Brave Days of Old* (1926); *The Bubbly-Jock and Other Poems* (1929); *Graham of Claverhouse* (1929); *Patterson Paints Parrots* (1931); *Auld Robin Gray* (1932); *Go to Jericho* (1932); *In the Spring o' the Year* (1932); *Poems, Scots and English* (1932); *The Spaewife* (1932); *Further Poems, Scots and English* (1935); *Many Happy Returns* (1935); *Cupid and Cupidity* (1937); *The Lass that loo'd the Tinkler* (1940); *The Wooin' o' it* (1942); *The Folk frae Condie* (1949); *New Poems* (1949); *Loch Lomond* (1951); *The Firth of Clyde* (1952); *Gretna Green* (1953); *Random Rhymes and Ballads* (1955)

Colkelbie's Sow. An anonymous 15th-century poem found in the BANNATYNE MANUSCRIPT. It tells the story of Colkelbie, a simple rustic who sold his black sow for three pennies, and of what became of him thereafter. The second penny (although it is the first to be discussed), is lost, then found by a man who buys one of the sow's piglets, only for it to be stolen by a harlot. As it is about to be slaughtered, the piglet is rescued by its mother and the pig family makes off amidst scenes of boisterous hilarity. Colkelbie gives the first penny to an old blind man for his beautiful daughter, who comes to live with him and eventually marries his son. So virtuous and beautiful are the couple that they are rewarded by an earldom from the King of France. Colkelbie hides away the third penny until it can be used to buy two eggs for Cockalb, his godson. The gift is spurned, but from the eggs is hatched a large progeny of hens and Colkelbie becomes the richest man in the country. From the three stories and their short 'Prohemium' a moral emerges about the usefulness of money and the dangers it can bring. *Colkelbie's Sow* was a nationally known poem (both WILLIAM DUNBAR and GAVIN DOUGLAS make mention of it), popular both for its irregular, alliterative couplets, which help to adorn the extravagant plots, and for the bawdy, rumbustious nature of the story-telling.

Collins, William (1789–1853). Publisher, and the founder of the publishing house that bears his name. He was born on 12 October 1789 in Eastwood, Renfrewshire. His early training was in the weaving trade and in 1800 he became a clerk in a cotton mill, where he established a rudimentary form of evening classes for the workers. By 1813 he felt confident enough in his own abilities to open a private school for the poor in Glasgow and he became an elder of the Tron Church at what was then considered to be the early age of 25. Through his philanthropic works Collins became a close friend of the evangelist THOMAS CHALMERS with whose brother Charles he set up in business as a bookseller, printer and publisher in September 1819. Collins's early publications reflected his personal interest in the evangelical movement and his enthusiasm for Scottish church history, and he was also one of the first publishers to exploit the growing market for school textbooks. Among his first authors were ROBERT POLLOK and EDWARD IRVING, but the firm prospered in those early years by being the sole publisher of Thomas Chalmers's bestselling works. Collins died on 2 January 1853 leaving the publishing and printing business to his son William. It still maintains many of the publishing interests of its founder and although its main editorial base is in London, the firm still keeps an office and its printing works in Glasgow.

REFERENCE: D. Keir, *The House of Collins: the Story of a Scottish Family of Publishers, from 1789 to the Present Day* (London, 1952)

Columba [Columkille], **St.** He was born in Gartan in Donegal and was educated at the great Irish centres of monastic learning at Magh Bile, Clonard and Glasnevin. His early life was devoted to the foundation of religious centres in Derry and other parts of Ireland, which supplanted the older Patrician monasteries. In 563 he moved to Iona, the island on the west coast of Scotland from which his monks began the evangelization of many parts of mainland Scotland. Columba, the most inspiring of the saints of the early church in Scotland, died on 9 June 597, and the second Thursday on each June is still celebrated as his saint's day in many parts of the Western Isles. The religious centre on Iona, originally 'Hii' in Gaelic, was developed and expanded in later years and the medieval abbey was restored by the Church of Scotland at the beginning of the 20th century. The saint's relics were translated to Ireland in the 9th century but were mostly lost during the Viking invasions 200 years later. St Adamnan, a 7th-century monk who

also lived on Iona, wrote the first life of Columbia, which is one of the key reference works in the history of the early Church in both Scotland and Ireland.

Common Ridings [Riding the Marches]. A series of festivals held in several Scottish burghs in June, originally deriving from the BELTANE celebrations. The main feature of the ceremony is the riding of the burgh's common lands on horseback, which has its origins in the ancient need to mark out the boundaries of the burgh. The festival is particularly strong in the Border towns, where the ceremony has been influenced by the symbolism of the defeat of the Scottish army at the BATTLE OF FLODDEN in 1513.

Complaynt of Scotland, The. The most important of the early prose writings in Scots, *The Complaynt of Scotland* was long considered to be if not anonymous then at least of doubtful authorship. Its most recent editor, A. M. Stewart, has provided evidence, apparently conclusive, that it was composed by Robert WEDDERBURN of Dundee, one of the brothers responsible for the compilation of the GUDE AND GODLIE BALLATIS. The framework for *The Complaynt of Scotland* is taken from Alain Chartier's 15th-century French polemic *Le quadrilogue invectif* (1422), the best-known work in the European tradition of writing 'complaints' against tyranny.

Wedderburn's work falls into four parts: a 'Dedicatory Epistle', a 'Prologue to the Reader' and the two parts of the 'complaynt', the first headed 'Monologue Recitative'. The 'complaynt' consists of a dream allegory in which Dame Scotia calls upon her three sons, the Three Estates, to account for the divisiveness that has racked Scotland, to band together in the face of England's attempts to gain supremacy and to advocate support for the AULD ALLIANCE, the longstanding treaty with France. In that respect *The Complaynt of Scotland* is unashamedly propagandist, but it has a serious nationalistic purpose in advocating pride in national identity. Related to that mood is a defence of Scots as a literary language, and much of the Prologue is taken up with the Complayner's arguments for using Scots and for rejecting the more conventional Latin. The work also displays its author's depth of scriptural learning and his intimate, though frequently biased, knowledge of Scotland's history. A feature that the work shares with the poetry of the period is Wedderburn's aureate style when describing scenery; another element typical of Scottish literature, found in the third part of the work, is the delight in placing learning alongside tomfoolery and lofty ideals alongside low realism. *The Complaynt of Scotland* was first published in 1549 in Paris.

EDITION: A. M. Stewart, ed., *The Complaynt of Scotland*, STS (Edinburgh, 1979)

Conn, Stewart (*b* 1936). Poet and dramatist. He was born on 5 November 1936 in Glasgow and was educated at Kilmarnock Academy and at the University of Glasgow. After completing his National Service in the Royal Air Force, Conn became a producer with BBC Radio and was appointed Senior Drama Producer for BBC Radio Scotland in 1977; in this capacity he has made a signal contribution to Scottish drama through his encouragement of younger writers. His first poems, collected in *Thunder in the Air* (1967) and *Stoats in the Sunlight* (1968), deal with a far from idealized rural past and with man's reactions to the landscape in which he lives. Mankind, as well as nature, can be cruel and indifferent, and in poems such as 'Ayrshire Farm' and 'Todd' a favourite uncle's stern belief in the habits of another age summons up the harsh realities of life on the farm. In *Under the Ice* (1978) Conn's insights have become more private, while still retaining the sharpness of perception that has characterized all his work. He is also a distinguished dramatist and his play *The Burning* (1972) stands comparison with *Jamie the Saxt* by ROBERT MCLELLAN, which it resembles in its treatment of an historical subject – the relationship between JAMES VI and his cousin Francis Bothwell.

WORKS: *Thunder in the Air* (1967); *The Chinese Tower* (1967); *Stoats in the Sunlight* (1968); *The Burning* (1972); *An Ear to the Ground* (1972); *The Aquarium* (1976); *I Didn't Always Live Here* (1976); *The Man in the Green Muffler* (1976); *Under the Ice* (1978)

REFERENCE: D. Abse, ed., *Corgi Modern Poets in Focus 3* (London, 1971)

Constable, Archibald (1774–1827). Publisher. He was born on 24 February 1774 at Carnbee in Fife, where his father was factor to the Earl of Kellie. In February 1788 he was apprenticed to the Edinburgh bookseller Peter

Hill and so began a lifetime's involvement with the book trade in the city. He set up shop on his own account in the High Street in 1795 and made a handsome living by selling antiquarian books. Not content to remain on the retail side, Constable acquired possession of the SCOTS MAGAZINE and GENERAL INTELLIGENCER in 1801 and in 1802 he began to publish the *Edinburgh Review* (see EDINBURGH REVIEW (ii)). In his respect for his editor and the contributors, and his insistence that the magazine be published on a regular basis, Constable was the first modern publisher. His policy paid dividends and he quickly attracted authors to his imprint; Sir WALTER SCOTT joined him in 1803, when the third volume of THE MINSTRELSY OF THE SCOTTISH BORDER was published. To keep Scott, Constable paid him large advances and his firm prospered. In 1811 ROBERT CADELL joined Constable as a partner and his caution became a much-needed balance to Constable's increasingly rash optimism. In 1812 Constable purchased the rights to the ENCYCLOPAEDIA BRITANNICA, and published a number of supplements to it. Following the collapse of its London agents, Hurst Robinson and Company, the firm crashed in 1826 and the bankruptcy and consequent shame led to Constable's early death on 21 July 1827. Despite the ups and downs of his business relationships with Scott and his inability to deal with financial crisis, Constable was a first-class publisher, whom Lord Cockburn described as 'the most spirited bookseller that has ever appeared in Scotland'.

REFERENCE: T. Constable, ed., *Archibald Constable and his Literary Correspondents*, 3 vols. (Edinburgh, 1873)

Corrie, Joe (1894–1968). Dramatist. He was a native of Bowhill in Fife. His early life was spent working as a miner in the Fife coalfields and during that time he began writing. In 1923 the Reform Union awarded him a small weekly wage for his contributions to *The Miner* and that allowance, together with his increasingly weak health, persuaded him to turn to full-time writing. The events of the 1926 General Strike had a profound effect on Corrie and coloured the background to his finest play, *In Time of Strife* (1929). This follows the fortunes of a coalmining family during the strike, and through their eyes we see a community's attitude to the strike, the trade unions, strike breaking and the mine owners. Corrie offered a stout defence of the miners' dignity during the strike and the subsequent lock-outs in the Fife mines; as the play unfolds, a bitter picture emerges of the inevitable poverty and grinding despair caused by the long period of confrontation. In his best work Corrie continued to explore the themes of the exploitation of the working class and the ordinary man's struggle to create a better world for himself; by concentrating on the domestic minutiae he was able to build up a convincing picture of the effects of moral and physical poverty.

Later in life Corrie turned from social reality to mawkish comedies, which were little more than stage equivalents of KAILYARD novels. He wrote most of his work for amateur companies, many of his one-act plays being conceived for his local drama group in Bowhill; had he benefited from an association with the mainstream theatre, his contribution to Scottish drama would undoubtedly have been greater. He also wrote several poems, which were published in *The Miner* and in the socialist magazine *Forward*. The best of these is 'The Image o' God', a noble statement of the hard work and dangers endured by the miners. He spent much of his later life in Alloway in Ayrshire.

WORKS: *Poems* (1926); *The Poacher* (1927); *A Near Thing* (1930); *Three One-Act Plays* (1930); *The Home-Coming* (1931); *The New Gamekeeper* (1931); *The Tally Man* (1931); *The Darkness* (1932); *Glensheugh* (1932); *The Hoose o' the Hill* (1932); *A Man o' War* (1932); *The Miracle* (1932); *Rebel Poems* (1932); *The Shilling a Week Man* (1932); *The Glendarroch Affair* (1933); *Speed up* (1933); *Kye amang the Corn* (1934); *Tullycairn* (1934); *Apron Strings* (1935); *The Incomer* (1935); *Martha* (1935); *The Mistress o' Greenbyres* (1935); *Red Roses* (1935); *Salmon Poachers* (1935); *And so to War* (1936); *Bread and Roses* (1936); *The Dreamer* (1936); *Hikers* (1936); *A Plumber and a Man* (1936); *Cobbler's Luck* (1937); *Horoscope* (1937); *The Image o' God* (1937); *Madame Martini* (1937); *The Rake o' Mauchline* (1938); *The Tinkers' Road* (1938); *Up in the Mornin'* (1938); *Black Earth* (1939); *The Best Laid Schemes* (1940); *First o' the Year* (1941); *Robert Burns* (1943); *When the Mavis Sings* (1943); *There is no Glory* (1944); *Domestic Dictator* (1945); *Green Grow the Rashes* (1945); *Every Inch a King* (1947); *The Failure* (1947); *Litchen Fair* (1947); *At the Fall of the Leaf* (1948); *The Gaberlunzie Man* (1948); *Home ain't so Sweet* (1948); *John Grumbie* (1948); *Murder at the Play* (1948); *Our Tommy* (1948); *The Prince he would a Wooing go* (1948); *A Storm on Parnassus* (1948); *When the Old Cock Crows* (1948); *Queen of the May* (1949); *The Trailer* (1949); *Tell it not in Gath* (1950); *Valhalla* (1950); *What's Good for the Goose* (1950); *When Bachelors Bargain* (1950); *The Witch o' Pitlowrie* (1950); *Crowdie Hill* (1952); *Billy Shaw* (1953); *Colour Bar* (1954); *Love and the Boxer* (1954); *The Theft* (1954); *When the Roses Bloom Again* (1954);

Burnieknowe (1955); *The Favourite Lass* (1955); *The Glory o' it* (1955); *Poems* (1955); *A Jean Tamson's Bairns* (1957); *The Piper o' Kinlowie* (1957); *The Flittin'* (1958); *The Auld Blue Cap* (1959); *Old Verity* (1959); *Golden Wedding* (1960); *Occupation Moonray* (1960); *Remembrance* (1960)

Cotter's Saturday Night, The. A poem by ROBERT BURNS, probably written in the winter of 1785 and published in the KILMARNOCK EDITION of 1786. It is one of the best-known of Burns's poems and was much praised by the Edinburgh *literati*, especially by Henry Mackenzie who called it 'one of the happiest and most affecting scenes to be found in country life'. The poem gives a fairly accurate picture of Scottish agricultural society, but the high rhetorical Augustan tone of Burns's religious moralizing is at odds with the Scots vernacular stanzas whose influence is 'The Farmer's Ingle' by ROBERT FERGUSSON.

Court of Session. The Supreme Court in Scotland for civil matters. The Court of Session was developed during the reign of JAMES IV and came into being officially in 1532, with the foundation of the College of Justice. The senators of the college were, and continue to be, judges of the Court of Session and the court's early procedures followed European legal practices. The earliest systematization of the law in Scotland was made by Viscount Stair (1619–95) with the publication of his *Institutes of the Law of Scotland* (1681); he made the office of Lord President of the Court of Session the paramount Scottish legal post. The corresponding court for criminal matters is the High Court of Justiciary.

Covenant, National. Statement drawn up by Sir Archibald Johnston of Warriston and Alexander Henderson, minister of Leuchars, and revised by leading Presbyterians, which stated the subscribers' adherence to the Presbyterian Church in Scotland and their abomination of all corruptions of it. Although the Covenant was drawn up in opposition to Charles I's attempts to introduce an Episcopalian form of church government in Scotland, the signatories ended by stating their allegiance to 'the defence of our Dreade Soveraigne, the Kings Majesty, his Person and Authority, in the defence and preservation of the foresaid true Religion, Liberties and Lawes of the Kingdome'. The National Covenant was first signed in Greyfriars' Churchyard, Edinburgh, by the nobility and gentry on 28 February 1638 and on subsequent days by the clergy and the people of the city. Later, copies were despatched for signature to other parts of Scotland. Adherents and signatories came to be known as COVENANTERS.

Covenanters. The supporters of the NATIONAL COVENANT, which was signed on 28 February 1638 in Edinburgh. It was drawn up to protect the institution of the Church in Scotland from the English liturgy and from the ultimate control of the Crown. Although the Covenant was defensive in concept its supporters became more aggressive in their demands for free assemblies and independence. The events of the Civil War drew the Covenanters into an uneasy alliance with the English Parliamentarians through the Solemn League and Covenant of 1643. For the Scots this entailed a commitment to preserve the reformed Church, to extirpate Catholicism and to bring the two countries together in religious unity. The Covenanting cause was split by the war, notably because of the English Parliament's lack of enthusiasm for Scottish involvement; by the campaigns of JAMES GRAHAM, Marquis of Montrose in 1644–5; by the Engagement of 1647, in which a section of the nobility attempted a rapprochement with Charles I; and finally by the support for his son Charles II. Adherence to the Covenant implied a strict belief in Presbyterianism and defaulters were punished severely.

Charles II's attempts to reintroduce an Episcopalian form of church government in Scotland saw the Covenanting movement enter its most bitter period, with the savage harassment of the field conventicles – services held in the open air – and the execution of Covenanting leaders. The defeat of the conventiclers at the Battle of Bothwell Brig by JOHN GRAHAM of Claverhouse in 1679 virtually ended their opposition, although a splinter group, the CAMERONIANS, continued to express a more militant form of Covenanting. The Revolution Settlement of 1690 established the Presbyterian Church, which was effectively controlled by the moderates, and the 18th century saw a number of secessions from the Church by ministers who held to the stricter, more puritanical views of the Covenanters.

Despite their internal divisions and their narrow beliefs, the Covenanters remain a powerful cause in Scotland's history through their espousal of individual liberty, their steadfastness in the face of massacre and execution, and their own sense of self-discipline. The novel OLD MORTALITY by Sir WALTER SCOTT tells the story of the Covenanters from Graham's point of view, while maintaining a balanced attitude towards the Covenanters themselves. *Ringan Gilhaize* by JOHN GALT is a realistic description of the suppression of the Covenanters. The movement haunted many other 19th-century writers, including the poet JAMES HOGG, whose *Covenanter's Scaffold Song* captures something of the mood of religious exaltation with which many followers met their deaths.

Craig, Alexander (1567–1627). Poet. He was born at Banff and educated at the University of St Andrews. After the accession of JAMES VI to the throne of England in 1603, Craig wrote a series of complimentary verses to the king in *The Political Essayes of Alexander Craige, Scoto-Britane*, published in 1604. His flattery succeeded in attracting a court pension, which enabled him to buy an estate near Banff from where he continued to write a succession of classical sonnets and odes to those he met on his frequent visits to the court in London. Although his verse is of no value, his *nom de plume* 'Scoto-Britane' is an early indication of the cultural schizophrenia that began to grip Scottish writers after the Union of the Crowns in 1603.

EDITION: D. Laing, ed., *The Works of Alexander Craig* (Glasgow, 1873–4)

Craig, James (*d* 1795). Architect. He was the winner in 1767 of the gold medal presented by the town council of Edinburgh for plans for a new town on the north side of the Nor' Loch. Craig designed the series of parallel streets and exact squares that give the Georgian New Town of Edinburgh its characteristic formality and symmetry. Although the development did not progress precisely in accordance with his intentions, Craig's vision embodied many of the ideals of the SCOTTISH ENLIGHTENMENT. At the head of his plans Craig quoted the poem 'Liberty' by his uncle JAMES THOMSON (i).

August, around, what Public Works I see!
Lo! stately Streets, lo! Squares that court the breeze!
See long canals and deepened Rivers join
Each part with each, and with the circling Main
The whole enlivened Isle.

Craig, Sir **Thomas** (1538–1608). Poet. His chief claim to fame during his lifetime was as an expert in feudal law and his *Jus feudale* (1603) was a standard work for many years. His education took him from St Andrews to Paris, and on his return in 1561 he rose quickly in the legal hierarchy; he later became an adviser to JAMES VI on jurisdictional problems thrown up by the Union of the Crowns in 1603. His poems, written in Latin for state occasions, were published in Sir JOHN SCOTT of Scotstarvit's DELITIAE POETARUM SCOTORUM in 1637.

WORKS: *Henrici illustrissimi Ducis Albanis Comites Rossiae* (1565); *Ad sereniss.* (1603); *Jus feudale* (1603); *Serenissimi et invectissimi principis Iacobi Britanniarum et Galliarum Regis* (1603)

EDITIONS: J. Gatherer, trans., *The Right of Succession to the Kingdom of England* (London, 1703); C. S. Terry, ed., *De unione regnorum Britanniae tractatus* (Edinburgh, 1909)

REFERENCE: P. F. Tytler, *An Account of the Life and Writings of Sir Thomas Craig of Riccarton* (Edinburgh, 1823)

Craigie, Sir **William Alexander** (1867–1957). Lexicographer and philologist. He was born on 13 August 1867 in Dundee and was educated there and at the University of St Andrews. After a year spent at Balliol College, Oxford, Craigie used his time to further his interests in the study of Scandinavian languages: between 1892 and 1893 he studied Icelandic in Copenhagen, and from 1893 to 1897 he assisted the Professor of Latin at St Andrews, during which time he contributed Scandinavian stories to the *Fairy Books* by ANDREW LANG and also produced his own *Scandinavian Folk-Lore* (1897). His work as a lexicographer, for which he is perhaps best remembered, began in 1897 when he joined Sir JAMES A. H. MURRAY in the compilation of the *Oxford English Dictionary*. While at Oxford he became a lecturer in Scandinavian languages and in 1916 he was appointed Professor of Anglo-Saxon. In 1925 he became Professor of English at the University of Chicago and compiled the *Dictionary of American English*, a four-volume work which was published in 1944. On his resignation from the Chicago chair in 1936 he turned to the compilation of the *Dictionary of the Older Scottish Tongue*, which enjoyed his direction until his retirement in 1955. Craigie was knighted in 1925 and enjoyed many British and foreign honours, including the appointment of Knight Commander of the Icelandic

Falcon for his work on Icelandic literature and language. He died on 2 September 1957 at Watlington in the Chiltern Hills.

Recognized as one of the leading language scholars of his day, Craigie had an encyclopaedic knowledge of Scandinavian languages, especially of Icelandic, and complete mastery of the Scottish dialects, ancient and modern, and of Gaelic. For the SCOTTISH TEXT SOCIETY, of which he was president, he edited, among other things, the MAITLAND MANUSCRIPTS (1919–27) and the ASLOAN MANUSCRIPT (1923–5).

Crawford, David, of Drumsoy (1665–1726). Historian. He was educated at the University of Glasgow where he studied law. He was called to the Scottish Bar but never practised, preferring to devote himself to his antiquarian and literary interests. His Tory sympathies led to his appointment by Queen Anne as Historiographer Royal for Scotland and his prestige as a historian was enhanced by the publication in 1706 of the *Memoirs of the Affairs of Scotland*. Crawford's aim was to provide a history that would counter the prejudices of GEORGE BUCHANAN and present a more favourable view of MARY, Queen of Scots. However, part of the 'authentic manuscript', which had come to him from James Baird of Saughtonhall, was discovered by later scholars to have been forged. Crawford's reputation was tarnished by the findings, but he was, nevertheless, one of the first historians to attempt a well-balanced picture of the events of the mid-16th century in Scotland. He also wrote three pieces of fictional prose, laboured attempts at comedies of manners in the Restoration style.

WORKS: *Courtship à la Mode* (1700); *Ovidius britannicus* (1703); *Love at First Sight* (1704); ed., *Memoirs of the Affairs of Scotland, Containing a Full and Impartial Account of the Revolution in that Kingdom before 1567 Faithfully Compiled from an Authentic Manuscript* (1706)

Crawford, Robert (i) (*d* 1733). Poet. Very little is known about his life other than that he was the son of a merchant in Edinburgh and was related to the historian DAVID CRAWFORD of Drumsoy. He is best known for the two songs he contributed, under the signature 'C', to THE TEA-TABLE MISCELLANY by ALLAN RAMSAY. These were 'Tweedside', written in English, to replace the older Scots version composed by Lord Yester (1645–1713), and 'The Bush

Abune Traquair', a lively Scots song which was altered in the 19th century by J. C. SHAIRP.

Crawford, Robert (ii). Pen-name of HUGH C. RAE.

Creech, William (1745–1815). Publisher. He was born on 21 April 1745 at Newbattle, Midlothian, the son of a minister. He attended the University of Edinburgh with the intention of studying for a career in medicine, but his interests were diverted by the art of printing and the intricacies of the book trade. After a Continental tour in the company of JAMES CUNNINGHAM, Earl of Glencairn, he became a partner in a printing firm in 1771 and two years later he became the sole proprietor. His office in Craig's Close, off the High Street, became a centre of literary activity in Edinburgh, and his morning meetings in his breakfast-room became known as 'Creech's Levee'. Creech enjoyed the friendship of the leading *literati* of his day, was a founder of the SPECULATIVE SOCIETY, and for HENRY MACKENZIE printed the periodicals THE MIRROR and THE LOUNGER. He is best remembered for his business connection with the poet ROBERT BURNS, a relationship that was distinctly one-sided. On 17 April 1787 Burns accepted 100 guineas from Creech for the copyright of the 'Edinburgh' edition of his poems, and the book was printed that year by WILLIAM SMELLIE; a second edition was printed in 1793, with a reprint the following year. Because he held the copyright, all the profits went to Creech. In 1811 he was elected Lord Provost of Edinburgh and a selection of his writings, *Edinburgh Fugitive Pieces* (1815), was published posthumously.

Crichton, James, of Cluny (1560–c1585). Poet and scholar. He was born on 19 August 1560 in Cluny, Perthshire. He was educated at the University of St Andrews, where his ability to master the arts and the sciences was a marvel to all his teachers, and where his strength and graciousness made him a favourite with all his fellow students. In 1577 he was in Paris and there a number of legends grew up round his name, which were repeated and embellished later by his most famous biographer, Sir THOMAS URQUHART of Cromartie. Crichton became renowned for his intellectual and physical prowess and, although allowances must be made for the excesses of his later hagiographers, there is little doubt that he was a

remarkable man with great powers of memory and elucidation. The remainder of his life was spent in Italy, in Venice, Padua, and Mantua, where he was killed in a sword fight under mysterious circumstances. Of his poetry in Latin little survived, and although several of his learned disquisitions were printed after his death, his literary fame rests on his title 'THE ADMIRABLE CRICHTON' and on Urquhart's account of his life and times in *The Discoverie of a Most Exquisite Jewel*. Crichton was the subject of an historical novel of the same name by Harrison Ainsworth (1805–82), and he lent his name to the play *The Admirable Crichton* by J. M. BARRIE.

Crochallan Fencibles. A drinking club which met in DAWNEY DOUGLAS'S TAVERN in Anchor Close, Edinburgh. Its title came from Douglas's favourite Gaelic song *Crodh Chailein* ('Colin's Cattle'), which he was in the habit of singing to his customers, and from the voluntary raising of 'fencibles' or armed citizenry during the American War of Independence. Each member of the club was given a pseudo-military title. The printer WILLIAM SMELLIE was a prominent member of the club, to which he introduced ROBERT BURNS in 1787. Burns composed much of the bawdry in THE MERRY MUSES OF CALEDONA for the club, and for its president William Dunbar, an Edinburgh lawyer, he wrote the song *Rattling, roaring Willie*.

Crockett, S(amuel) R(utherford) (1859–1914). Novelist. He was born on 24 September 1859 in the parish of Balmaghie, Kirkcudbrightshire, the son of a tenant farmer. He went to the village school in nearby Laurieston and in 1867 his parents moved to Castle Douglas where he completed his secondary education. In 1876 he won a bursary which took him to the University of Edinburgh and on graduating he worked for six months as a journalist in London, before spending a short period at Oxford. While there he won a travelling scholarship which allowed him to spend a year in Germany and Switzerland. Between 1883 and 1886 he was back in Edinburgh to study for the ministry of the Free Church, and his first charge was in the village of Penicuik, Midlothian. Success as a writer led him to resign his charge in 1895 and he moved to Peebles where he died on 21 April 1914.

Crockett wrote over 40 novels, all of which

were well received in his lifetime. Although work like the sickly sentimental *The Lilac Sunbonnet* (1894) condemns him to membership of the KAILYARD school, some of his fiction is still worthy of note. *Cleg Kelly, Arab of the City* (1896) contains several vivid scenes of urban deprivation, and in novels such as *The Raiders* (1894) and *The Men of the Moss Haggs* (1895) Crockett evoked his native Galloway with a firm sense of realism. His second book (his first was a collection of poems, *Dulce cor*, published in 1886), a collection of sketches, *The Stickit Minister* (1893), was dedicated to ROBERT LOUIS STEVENSON who was prompted to write his moving poem of exile 'Blows the Wind Today' for Crockett. Like the other main Kailyarders, J. M. BARRIE and JOHN WATSON ('Ian Maclaren'), Crockett received considerable encouragement from WILLIAM ROBERTSON NICOLL.

WORKS: *Dulce cor* (1886); *The Stickit Minister* (1893); *In the Matter of Incubus and Co* (1894); *The Lilac Sunbonnet* (1894); *The Playactress* (1894); *The Raiders* (1894); *Bog Myrtle and Peat* (1895); *The Men of the Moss Haggs* (1895); *Sweetheart Travellers* (1895); *Cleg Kelly, Arab of the City* (1896); *The Gray Man* (1896); *Lad's Love* (1897); *Lochinvar* (1897); *The Red Axe* (1898); *The Standard Bearer* (1898); *The Black Douglas* (1899); *Kit Kennedy* (1899); *Lone March* (1899); *Joan of the Sword Hand* (1900); *Little Anna March* (1900); *The Stickit Minister's Wooing* (1900); *Cinderella* (1901); *The Firebrand* (1901); *Love Idylls* (1901); *The Silver Skull* (1901); *The Dark o' the Moon* (1902); *Flower o' the Corn* (1902); *The Adventurer in Spain* (1903); *The Banner of Blue* (1903); *The Loves of Miss Ann* (1903); *Raiderland* (1904); *The Cherry Riband* (1905); *Maid Margaret of Galloway* (1905); *Sir Toady Crusoe* (1905); *Fishers of Men* (1906); *Kid McGhie* (1906); *The White Plumes of Navarre* (1906); *Little Esson* (1907); *Me and Myn* (1907); *Vida* (1907); *The Bloom o' the Heather* (1908); *Deep Moat Grange* (1908); *The Men of the Mountain* (1909); *Rose of the Wilderness* (1909); *The Seven Wise Men* (1909); *The Dew of their Youth* (1910); *Young Nick and Old Nick* (1910); *The Lady of the Hundred Dresses* (1911); *Love in Penicketty Town* (1911); *The Smugglers* (1911); *Anne of the Barricades* (1912); *The Moss Troopers* (1912); *Sweethearts at Home* (1912); *Sandy's Love Affair* (1913); *A Tatter of Scarlet* (1913); *Silver Sand* (1914); *Hal o' the Ironsides* (1916); *The Azure Hand* (1917); *The White Pope* (1920); *Rogue's Island* (1926)

Cronin, A(rchibald) J(oseph) (1896–1981). Novelist. He was born on 19 July 1896 at Cardross in Dunbartonshire. He was educated at Dumbarton Academy and at the University of Glasgow, where he studied medicine. During World War I he served as a surgeon with the Royal Naval Volunteer Reserve before returning to work as a general practitioner in Scotland and later as a medical inspector of mines in South Wales. A breakdown in his health in 1930 forced him to reconsider his future and during a period of recuperation he turned to writing; the result was his first novel *Hatter's Castle* (1931), a thinly disguised autobiographical work, whose success led him to take up writing as a full-time career. There followed at regular intervals over a period of some 40 years a number of novels that were destined to entertain a massive audience throughout the English-speaking world: most have a medical background and are solidly based in skilfully painted settings, whether in Scotland, Switzerland or Spain. Cronin was at his best, though, in his Scottish novels which were drawn from his own experiences. During the 1960s these were made into a successful television series, with the title 'Dr Finlay's Casebook', set in the fictional town of Tannochbrae. Cronin's autobiography *Adventures in Two Worlds* (1952) is a partly fictionalized account of his life and times, but it does give a good indication of the background to the creation of his novels of general medical practice. The latter years of his life were spent in the USA and in Switzerland, where he died on 6 January 1981.

WORKS: *Hatter's Castle* (1931); *Three Loves* (1932); *Grand Canary* (1933); *The Citadel* (1937); *Jupiter Laughs* (1941); *The Stars Look Down* (1941); *The Keys of the Kingdom* (1942); *The Green Years* (1945); *Shannon's Way* (1948); *The Spanish Gardener* (1950); *Adventures in Two Worlds* (1952); *Beyond this Place* (1953); *Crusader's Tomb* (1956); *The Innkeeper's Wife* (1958); *The Northern Light* (1958); *The Judas Tree* (1961); *A Song of Sixpence* (1964); *Adventures of a Black Bag* (1969); *A Pocketful of Rye* (1969); *The Minstrel Boy* (1975); *Lady with Carnations* (1976); *Gracie Lindsay* (1978)

Cruickshank, Helen Burness (1886–1975). Poet. She was born on 15 May 1886 in Hillside, Angus. She was educated at the village school and at Montrose Academy until 1903 when she joined the Civil Service, working for the Post Office in London. In 1912 she returned to live in Edinburgh and worked for the newly established National Health Insurance scheme. Edinburgh remained her home for the rest of her life and it was there that she first started writing poetry, contributing to the *Scottish Chapbook* and *Northern Numbers* produced by CHRISTOPHER MURRAY GRIEVE. Grieve became a close friend, and a year after he had helped to found Scottish PEN in 1927 Helen Cruickshank became its secretary, a post she held until 1934. Through this work she became the friend and confidante of many of the writers connected with the SCOTTISH RENAISSANCE, including JAMES LESLIE MITCHELL ('Lewis Grassic Gibbon'). After World War II she retired from the Civil Service, and from her home in Corstorphine she continued to offer friendship and encouragement to a new generation of writers. Illness and infirmity forced her in 1973 to move to Queensberry Lodge in the Canongate and it was there that she died on 2 March 1975.

Helen Cruickshank's poems were first published in 1934 in *Up the Noran Water* which included her song of unrequited love, 'Shy Geordie'. A feature of all her work is her economy of language and a freshness of observation particularly in her poems of childhood remembrance. In 1971 she was awarded the honorary degree of MA from the University of Edinburgh for her contribution to Scottish letters.

WORKS: *Up the Noran Water* (1934); *Sea Buckthorn* (1954); *The Ponnage Pool* (1968); *Collected Poems* (1971); *Octobiography* (1976); *More Collected Poems* (1978)

Culdees. The name given to a body of religious men which was attached to the medieval church in Ireland and Scotland. It means 'friends, or servants of God' and is derived from the Old Irish 'Céli De'. The Culdees practised abstinence and strict observance of the liturgy; many lived together in small communities or alone as hermits, while others attached themselves to monastic orders as scribes. The main centres in Scotland were at St Andrews and Dunkeld. By the 11th century the order had been brought under the control of canonical rule.

Culloden, Battle of. A battle fought on 16 April 1746 at Culloden Moor near Inverness between the JACOBITE army of Prince CHARLES EDWARD STUART and the government army commanded by the Duke of Cumberland. The choice of the battlefield was made by Colonel John William O'Sullivan, an aide to the Prince, but the open moorland was unsuitable for the Highlanders' usual tactics of charging the enemy, and the Jacobites were decimated by the government army's superior firepower and by its use of cavalry and artillery.

The defeat of the Jacobites marked the end of their uprising of 1745–6 and the beginning of the end of traditional Highland society. In the savage reprisals that followed, supporters of the Jacobite cause were systematically hunted down and killed, and the Duke of Cumberland came to be known in Scotland as 'Butcher'. Charles Edward Stuart eventually fled to France and the Battle of Culloden, the last battle fought on British soil, was the final attempt to regain the throne of Britain for the Stuarts. Among the many Gaelic laments for the dead at Culloden, 'O gúr mor mo chùis mhulaid' by IAIN RUADH STIÙBHART is perhaps the best known.

Cunningham, Allan (1784–1842). Poet and man of letters. He was born on 7 December 1784 in the parish of Dalswinton, Dumfriesshire. Apprenticed as a stonemason, he worked with his brother for a short period, but through his father's friendship with ROBERT BURNS he turned to a literary career, collecting ballads for Robert Cromek's *Remains of Nithsdale and Galloway Song* (1810). Unwisely for his future reputation, Cunningham chose to deceive his publisher by himself creating many of the ballads he was supposed to have collected from oral sources, but his work gave him the friendship of JAMES HOGG and Sir WALTER SCOTT. From 1811 until his death on 30 October 1842 he lived in London, working as a parliamentary reporter and later as superintendent of works to the sculptor Chantrey. At this period he wrote little of value, although his poem 'A wet sheet and a flowing sea' is not without merit and his Jacobite poem 'The wee, wee German lairdie' is an apt summary of the unpopularity of the Hanoverian dynasty in Scotland. Cunningham's interest in art led him to write a biography of the artist Sir DAVID WILKIE and *Lives of the Most Eminent British Painters, Sculptors and Architects* (1829–33). He also edited a collection of Burns's poems and was the author of three undistinguished novels.

EDITION: P. Cunningham, ed., *Poems and Songs* (London, 1847)

REFERENCES: D. Hogg, *Life of Allan Cunningham* (Edinburgh, 1875); J. A. Fairley, *Allan Cunningham* (London, 1907)

Cunningham, James, Earl of Glencairn (1749–91). Politician and patron of ROBERT BURNS, he was responsible for introducing the poet to Edinburgh society during his visit to the city in 1786. He also arranged the subscription list for the 'Edinburgh' edition of Burns's poems, and persuaded the gentlemen of the CALEDONIAN HUNT to subscribe to 100 copies. On his death Burns wrote 'The Lament for James, Earl of Glencairn'.

Currie, James (1756–1805). The first editor and biographer of ROBERT BURNS. He was born on 31 May 1756 at Kirkpatrick Fleming, Dumfriesshire, the son of a minister. He emigrated to Virginia in 1771 and fought in the American War of Independence in the Colonial Army, before returning to Scotland in 1777 to study medicine at the University of Edinburgh. After a short stay in Liverpool he settled in Dumfriesshire in 1792, when he met Robert Burns, briefly, in Dumfries. After Burns's death Currie was chosen to edit the poems and to write the official biography. He took a censorious attitude to Burns's life: it was he who started the legend that Burns was a besotted womanizer and he also took liberties with the documentary evidence available to him. To his credit, however, the four-volume collection of poems, which went through eight editions between 1800 and 1820, helped to raise money for the poet's family. Currie died on 31 August 1805 at Sidmouth.

WORKS: *A Letter Commercial and Political Addressed to the Right Hon, William Pitt* (1793); *Water, Cold and Warm, as a Remedy for Fever* (1797); ed., *The Works of Robert Burns*, 4 vols. (1800)

REFERENCE: R. D. Thornton, *James Currie: the Entire Stranger and Robert Burns* (Edinburgh, 1963)

D

Daft Days. The Twelve Days of Christmas, or the period that begins on Christmas eve and ends on Epiphany or UPHALIEDAY. Until comparatively modern times it was the one recognized public holiday of the year and, traditionally, it was celebrated with gay abandon and communal feasting. There is a good description of the festival in Edinburgh in the poem 'The Daft Days' by ROBERT FERGUSSON, which was published in Ruddiman's THE WEEKLY MAGAZINE, OR EDINBURGH AMUSEMENT of 2 January 1772. NEIL MUNRO also used the phrase as the title for one of his novels.

Daiches, David (*b* 1912). Critic. He was born on 2 September 1912 in Leeds, the son of a rabbi, but his childhood was spent in Edinburgh where he was educated at George Watson's College and at the University. After graduating in 1934 he did research at Balliol College, Oxford, on the English translations of the Hebrew Bible. He became a Fellow there but left in 1937 to teach at the University of Chicago. During the last two years of World War II he was second secretary in the British Embassy in Washington. Between 1947 and 1951 he was professor of English at Cornell University but resigned his post in order to return to Britain, to teach at Cambridge. In 1961 he was appointed Professor of English and American Literature at the new University of Sussex at Brighton, a post he held until 1977, when he retired to live in Edinburgh.

Daiches is one of the world's leading literary scholars and a critic who has helped to break down traditional resistance to contemporary literature in academic circles. In the field of Scottish literary studies his book on ROBERT BURNS, first published in 1950, emphasized the poet's place in the 18th-century intellectual scene, the period of the SCOTTISH ENLIGHTENMENT which he has so ably portrayed in *The Paradox of Scottish Culture* (1964). He has also written on other aspects of Scottish history and on whisky; his autobiographical sketch, *Two Worlds* (1956), is a sympathetic account of a Jewish childhood in Edinburgh and contains a moving portrait of Daiches's father.

WORKS: *The Place of Meaning in Poetry* (1935); *New Literary Values* (1936); *Literature and Society* (1938); *The Novel and the Modern World* (1939); *Poetry and the Modern World* (1949); *The King James Bible: a Study of its Sources and Development* (1941); *Virginia Woolf* (1942); *Robert Louis Stevenson* (1947); *A Study of Literature* (1948); *Robert Burns* (1950, rev. 2/ 1966); *Willa Cather: a Critical Introduction* (1951); *Critical Approaches to Literature* (1956); *Literary Essays* (1956); *Two Worlds* (1956); *John Milton* (1957); *A Critical History of English Literature* (1960); *George Eliot's Middlemarch* (1963); *The Paradox of Scottish Culture* (1964); *English Literature* (1965); *More Literary Essays* (1968); *Scotch Whisky* (1969); *Some Late Victorian Attitudes* (1969); ed., *Companion to Literature: British and Commonwealth* (1971); *Robert Burns and his World* (1971); *Sir Walter Scott and his World* (1971); *A Third World* (1971); *Charles Edward Stuart* (1973); *Robert Louis Stevenson and his World* (1973); *Moses* (1975); *Was* (1975); *James Boswell and his World* (1976); *Glasgow* (1977); *Scotland and the Union* (1977); *Edinburgh* (1978); ed., *Fletcher of Saltoun: Selected Writings* (1979); with John Flower, *Literary Landscapes of the British Isles* (1979); *Selected Poems of Robert Burns* (1979); ed., *A Companion to Scottish Culture* (1981); *Robert Fergusson* (1982)

Daily Courant. The name, from 1860, of the newspaper founded as the EDINBURGH EVENING COURANT.

Dalrymple, Sir David, Lord Hailes (1726–96). Historian and judge. He was born on 20 October 1726 in Edinburgh, the eldest son of Sir James Dalrymple of Hailes; through his father he was related to the notable Scottish statesman Viscount Stair (1648–1707), and his mother was the daughter of the 6th Earl of Haddington, a prominent landowner in East Lothian. Dalrymple was educated at Eton and from there he proceeded to the University of Utrecht to study law, before returning to complete his studies in Edinburgh. He was called to the Scottish Bar on 23 February 1748 and went on to enjoy a successful career as an advocate. In 1766 he was raised to the bench, taking the title 'Lord Hailes'; in an age of considerable barbarity in the courts he gained a reputation for the humanity he showed to the prisoners who appeared before him. However, his father's death and the subsequent possession of the family estate of Hailes allowed him to indulge his literary tastes at the expense of his legal career and he became an ardent member of the SELECT SOCIETY, then Edinburgh's foremost literary debating club. He died on 29 November 1792 at Inveresk and the funeral oration was read by his friend and admirer the Revd ALEXANDER CARLYLE.

Most of Dalrymple's early writings are short but scholarly papers on Christian antiquities and on lesser-known aspects of Scottish history. He is remembered for his *Annals of Scotland from Malcolm Canmore to Robert I* (1776), an admirably clear and unbiased history of the period it covers, and also for his edition of the poems contained in the BANNATYNE MANUSCRIPT which he completed in 1770. Dalrymple was considered one of the most accomplished prose stylists of his day; he was also an excellent Latinist who enjoyed translating fragments of prose into a Latin as elegantly composed as the original.

WORKS: *Sacred Poems from the Holy Scriptures* (1751); *The Wit of Solomon* (1755); *Select Discourses* (1756); *A Discourse on the Vile Conspiracy Attempted by the Earl of Gowrie* (1757); *A Sermon* (1761); *Memorials and Letters Relating to the History of Britain in the Reign of James I* (1762); ed., *The Works of the Ever Memorable John Eaton*, 3 vols. (1765); ed., *A ne Compendious Book of Godly and Spiritual Songs* (1765); *An Account of the Preservation of Charles II after the Battle of Worcester* (1766); *Memorials and Letters Relating to the History of Britain in the Reign of Charles I* (1766); *The Secret Correspondence between Sir Robert Cecil and James VI* (1766); *A Catalogue of the Lords of Session* (1767); *An Examination of Regiam Majestatem* (1769); *Historical Memoirs* (1769); ed., *Ancient Scottish Poems from the Bannatyne Manuscript* (1770); *Annals of Scotland from Malcolm Canmore to Robert I* (1776); *Account of the Martyrs of Smyrna and Lyons* (1776); *Remains of Christian Antiquity*, 3 vols. (1778–80); ed., *Sermons by Jacobus a Vorgine* (1779); *Octavius* (1781); *Antiquities of the Christian Church* (1783); *Sketch of the Life of John Barclay* (1786); *Sketch of the Life of John Hamilton* (1786); *Sketch of the Life of Sir James Ramsay* (1787); *Sketch of the Life of George Lesley* (1787); *Sketch of the Life of Mark Alexander Boyd* (1787).

Darien Scheme. A scheme promoted by William Paterson, the Scottish founder of the Bank of England, to establish a trading colony on the Isthmus of Darien in Panama, which would provide an ideal trading base between the Pacific and Atlantic Oceans. It had its genesis in an act of parliament of 1693 which authorized the establishment of a trading company for Scotland with any country against whom the king was not at war. A company was formed in 1695 with an equal number of Scottish and English directors to subscribe the necessary £600,000 required to finance the scheme, but pressure from the House of Commons (many of whose members were jealous of any attempt to break the monopoly of the East India Company) and the active hostility of William of Orange forced the withdrawal of the English directors. Undeterred, Paterson and his fellow Scots raised £400,000 in Scotland, a sum that was supposed to represent half of the nation's capital, and in July 1698 the first Scottish fleet left Leith bound for Darien. A base called New Edinburgh was established in October but disaster followed hard on its foundation. A combination of dissent amongst the settlers, fever, and lack of English support to drive off Spanish attacks on the colony put the scheme in immediate jeopardy. More ships and men were despatched in 1699 and although some minor gains were made, by 1700 the expedition came to an ignominious end and the Scots were forced to surrender to superior Spanish forces. Scotland lost half of the venture capital, 2000 men and women died, and relations between Scotland and England were badly damaged. Scottish pride had been hurt too: one consequence of the failure of the Darien Scheme was the realization that Scotland could act as a trading nation only in concert with England, a feeling that hastened the ACT OF UNION of 1707.

REFERENCE: J. Prebble, *The Darien Disaster* (London, 1968)

Darling, Sir **Frank Fraser** (1903–70). Naturalist. He was born on 23 June 1903 in Edinburgh. He was educated at the University of Edinburgh and joined the agricultural staff of Buckinghamshire County Council in 1924. He returned to Edinburgh in 1928 and a number of international research fellowships allowed him to resume his interests in ecology, conservation and agricultural improvement. His research findings won him international acclaim and he was knighted in 1970. Much of his later work was carried out in America, where he worked with the Conservation Foundation of New York, and his ecological research took him to the tropics and the polar regions. Although most of his books are specialized studies, he was no pedant, and in all his works his infectious enthusiasm for his subject is the greatest attraction of his literary style. His *Natural History in the Highlands and Islands* (1947) is an unsurpassed survey of a part of the country he had come to love during his period with the West Highland Survey between 1944 and 1950. He died on 22 October 1970 in Forres, Moray.

WORKS: *Biology of the Fleece of the Scottish Mountain Blackfaced Breed of Sheep* (1932); *Animal Breeding in the British Empire* (1934); *Wild Life Conservation* (1934); *A Herd of Red Deer* (1937); *Bird Flocks and the Breeding Cycle* (1938); *Wild Country* (1938); *A Naturalist on Rona* (1939); *The Seasons and the Farmer* (1939); *Island Years* (1940); *The Seasons and the Fisherman* (1941); *The Story of Scotland* (1942); *The Care of Farm Animals* (1943); *Island Farm* (1943); *Wild Life in Britain* (1943); *Crofting Agriculture* (1945); *Natural History in the Highlands and Islands* (1947, rev. 1969, with J. M. Boyd); *Report of the West Highland Survey* (1952); *Alaska: an Ecological Renaissance* (1953); *West Highland Survey* (1955); *Pelican in the Wilderness* (1956); *An Ecological Reconnaissance of the Mora Plains of the Kenya Colony* (1960); *Wild Life in an African Territory* (1960); *The Unity of Ecology* (1963); *The Nature of a Natural Park* (1968); *Impacts of Man on the Biosphere* (1969); *Wilderness and Plenty* (1970)

Davidson, John (i) (1726–1806). Shoemaker at Glenfoot of Ardlochan, Ayrshire. He is supposed to have been the model for Soutar Johnnie in the long poem TAM O'SHANTER by ROBERT BURNS.

Davidson, John (ii) (1857–1909). Poet, novelist, dramatist and journalist. He was born on 11 April 1857 at Barrhead, Renfrewshire, the son of a minister of the Evangelical Union. His early childhood was spent in Glasgow but when he was nine his father accepted the charge of the Nelson Street Church in Greenock; his family remained in Greenock until 1886. After a brief education at the Highlander's Academy, Greenock, he left in 1870 to join the laboratory staff of Walker's sugar company in the same town, but he returned to the Academy between 1872 and 1876 as a pupil-teacher or monitor. He entered the University of Edinburgh in 1876 but he did not complete the course and the next 12 years were spent in a variety of teaching posts in the Glasgow area, Perth and Crieff. The drudgery

of his work forced him to move to London in 1888 where he took up an equally unsatisfying career in journalism, writing for *The Speaker* and the GLASGOW HERALD.

Davidson had started writing before he left Glasgow – four verse dramas, *Bruce* (1886), *Diabolus amans* (1885), *Smith* (1888) and *Scaramouch in Naxos* (1890); two novels, *The North Wall* (1885) and *Perfervid* (1890); and numerous short stories and poems – but it was in London that he began to publish and make a reputation, becoming a member of the Rhymers' Club, contributing to the *Yellow Book* and befriending Max Beerbohm and George Gissing. During the 1890s he published a number of collections of poetry which enjoyed a wide popular success, among them *In a Music-Hall* (1891), *Fleet Street Eclogues* (1893) and *Ballads and Songs* (1894). Like much of the poetry published in that period by the 'decadent poets' Oscar Wilde and Arthur Symons, Davidson's verse is in the minor key, though T. S. Eliot was later to acknowledge his debt to the urban imagery and colloquial flow of 'Thirty Bob a Week'. Davidson's poetic thought during this period is characterized by a series of conflicting tensions both within himself and within his work: between religion and doubt, scientific discovery and the physical unity of nature, the need for wealth and the disgrace of poverty in the industrial world.

Despite that fleeting taste of fame, for the rest of his life Davidson was bedevilled by a lack of money and his distaste for his work as a journalist. His problems were compounded by his own bronchial illnesses and by having to support his own family as well as his mother, sister and insane brother. In 1899 he was awarded a grant from the Royal Literary Fund and his friends obtained for him a Civil List pension in 1906. He lived in Shoreham, Sussex, from 1897 and although he returned, briefly, to live again in London, poverty and literary rejection brought increasing isolation from his friends. In May 1907 he moved to Penzance, Cornwall where he committed suicide on 23 March 1909.

At the turn of the century Davidson moved away from the lyric and turned his attention to a blank verse which incorporated the use of scientific language. Although he had employed blank verse with some success in his verse dramas, the *Testaments – of a Man Forbid* (1901), *of a Vivesector* (1901), *of an Empire-Builder* (1902), *of a Prime Minister* (1904) and *of John Davidson* (1908) – which are his last works, are structurally unbalanced and obscured by the overuse of complicated scientific terminology. Nevertheless, his influence was felt by the young Hugh MacDiarmid (CHRISTOPHER MURRAY GRIEVE), who later paid tribute to Davidson's role as a poet of ideas, especially in his attempts to wed the language of modern science to poetry.

Throughout his life Davidson wrote unsuccessfully for the theatre. He translated four French romantic costume dramas, but most of his own work was unstageable, including his unfinished trilogy *God and Mammon* (1907–8), only two parts of which were completed before his death. Of his novels, *Perfervid* is an ironic glance at Scottish, small-town life, and *Baptist Lake* (1894) contains an attack on the KAILYARD school and the artificiality of contemporary rural fiction. As with much of his poetry, his fiction is flawed by lack of revision and careless editing.

WORKS: *The North Wall* (1885); *Diabolus amans* (1885); *Bruce* (1886); *Smith* (1888); *Plays* (1889); *Perfervid* (1890); *Scaramouch in Naxos* (1890); *The Great Men, and A Practical Novelist* (1891); *In a Music-Hall and Other Poems* (1891); *Persian Letters* (1892); *Laura Ruthven's Widowhood* (1892); *Fleet Street Eclogues* (1893); *Sentences and Paragraphs* (1893); *A Random Itinerary* (1894); *Plays* (1894); *Ballads and Songs* (1894); *Baptist Lake* (1894); *St George's Day* (1895); *The Full and True Account of the Wonderful Mission of the Earl Lavender* (1895); *A Second Series of Fleet Street Eclogues* (1896); *Miss Armstrong's and Other Circumstances* (1896); *For the Crown* (1896); *New Ballads* (1897); *Godfrida* (1898); *The Last Ballad and Other Poems* (1899); *Self's the Man* (1901); *The Testament of a Vivisector* (1901); *The Testament of a Man Forbid* (1901); *The Testament of an Empire-Builder* (1902); *The Knight of the Maypole* (1903); *A Rosary* (1903); *The Testament of a Prime Minister* (1904); *A Queen's Romance* (1908); *The Ballad of a Nun* (1905); *Selected Poems* (1905); *The Theatrocrat* (1905); *Holiday and Other Poems* (1906); *God and Mammon: The Triumph of Mammon* (1907); *God and Mammon: Mammon and his Message* (1908); *The Testament of John Davidson* (1908); *Fleet Street and Other Poems* (1909)

EDITIONS: E. J. O'Brien, ed., *The Man Forbid and Other Essays* (Boston, 1910); R. M. Wenley, ed., *Poems by John Davidson* (New York, 1924); R. D. Macleod, ed., *Poems and Ballads* (London, 1959); M. Lindsay, ed., *John Davidson: a Selection of his Poems*, with a preface by T. S. Eliot and an essay by Hugh MacDiarmid (London, 1961); A. Turnbull, ed., *The Poems of John Davidson*, 2 vols., ASLS (Edinburgh and London, 1973)

REFERENCES: H. Fineman, *John Davidson: a Study of the Relation of his Ideas to his Poetry* (Philadelphia, 1916); R. D. Macleod, *John Davidson: a Study in Personality* (Glasgow, 1957); J. B. Townsend, *John Davidson: Poet of Armageddon* (New Haven, Conn., 1961)

Davie, Elspeth (*b* 1919). Novelist. She was born in Ayrshire and spent her early years in England. After graduating from the University of Edinburgh she attended Edinburgh College of Art and taught for a time in Ireland. Edinburgh has been her home for several years and she is married to the philosopher GEORGE ELDER DAVIE. Her work has received several literary prizes and she was the recipient of the Katherine Mansfield Award for short stories in 1978. An Edinburgh background is rarely far away in Elspeth Davie's fiction, whether it be the grandeur of the historical city or the bleak outposts of its suburbs and modern housing estates. But it is not her chief aim to paint a persuasive portrait of the city: rather it is her characters who fascinate, whether it be Foley the failed art teacher of *Creating a Scene* (1971) or the mélange of suburban ladies in *Climbers on a Stair* (1978). Underpinning all her characters is 'human vulnerability, and her short stories are solemn vignettes of day-to-day experience as she explores life's complexities and their effects on ordinary people. The expressive simplicity of her dialogue and the personal nature of her vision, which allows her to develop her characters fully, make Elspeth Davie one of Scotland's finest post-war writers of fiction. Her short stories, which have appeared in several literary magazines, have been published in *The Spark* (1968), *The High Tide Talker* (1976) and *The Night of the Funny Hats* (1980).

WORKS: *Providings* (1965); *The Spark* (1968); *Creating a Scene* (1971); *The High Tide Talker* (1976); *Climbers on a Stair* (1978); *The Night of the Funny Hats* (1980)

Davie, George Elder (*b* 1912). Philosopher. He was born in Dundee and was educated there at the High School before going on to study classics and philosophy at the University of Edinburgh. After graduating he taught for several years at the Queen's University of Belfast. He is Reader in Philosophy at the University of Edinburgh and is married to the novelist ELSPETH DAVIE. Davie's magnum opus is *The Democratic Intellect* (1961), a magisterial survey of Scottish educational philosophy, which deals in particular with the attempts made during the 19th century to anglicize the four ancient Scottish universities. Central to his thesis is the defence made by Sir WILLIAM

HAMILTON (iii) among others, of the Scottish system of education and his insistence that it should be open to a large number of students and general in its approach to set courses. Their belief that a unified metaphysics could hold together the nation's intellectual culture was challenged by scholars like J. C. SHAIRP and others, who argued for specialization and universality. Other factors, such as the advent of industralized society with its more precise needs, also helped to change the course of the Scottish university system; Davie's defence of it is a passionately argued commitment to education in Scotland, reinforced by an identifiable metaphysical tradition.

REFERENCE: H. MacDiarmid, *The Company I've Kept* (London, 1966)

Dawney Douglas's Tavern. A tavern in Anchor Close, Edinburgh, and meeting-place of the convivial drinking club the CROCHALLAN FENCIBLES, of which ROBERT BURNS and WILLIAM SMELLIE were members.

Death and Dr Hornbook. A poem by ROBERT BURNS; it was omitted from the KILMARNOCK EDITION of 1786. The inspiration for the poem came from Burns's listening to a talk on medical matters given by the Tarbolton schoolmaster John Wilson at a meeting of the BACHELORS' CLUB. In a gentle, mocking satire the poet describes a meeting with Death, who complains that he is being put out of business by Jock Hornbook. (A hornbook was a sheet of paper, containing elementary sums and spelling and The Lord's Prayer, mounted on wood and covered in transparent horn. Burn's use of the name is a direct reference to John Wilson.) As in many of Burns's poems dealing with supernatural figures, Death is genial and uncomplicated and almost human in his country directness.

Debatable Lands. The lands of Liddesdale on the Scottish West March, which were claimed by both Scotland and England before the ACT OF UNION of 1707. Because the area was so remote there could be no enforcement of law, and Liddesdale became the scene of countless cattle raids and feuds between neighbouring Border families. The Debatable Lands were also the source of many Border ballads, and the region was the home of WILLIAM ARMSTRONG whose deeds were recounted in the ballad 'Kinmont Willie'. Sir WALTER SCOTT visited the

region in 1791 during his 'raids' with Robert Shortreed to collect the ballads he published later in THE MINSTRELSY OF THE SCOTTISH BORDER.

Declaration of Arbroath [Declaration of Independence]. *See* ARBROATH, DECLARATION OF.

Delitiae poetarum Scotorum. An anthology of work in Latin by 37 Scottish poets, published in 1637 in Amsterdam as part of a series of *delitiae* for various countries produced by Janus Gruter. Work was started on the anthology by Sir JOHN SCOTT of Scotstarvit in 1617 with the help of his brother-in-law, WILLIAM DRUMMOND of Hawthornden, and it was completed under the editorship of ARTHUR JOHNSTON. Although it omits the poetry of GEORGE BUCHANAN, the Scottish *Delitiae* is the main source for texts of the neo-Latinists, who flourished in Scotland during the post-Renaissance period and who make up Scotland's humanist tradition.

Dempster, Thomas (1579–1625). Poet and scholar. He was born on 23 August 1579 on the estate of Cliftbog in Donside, Aberdeenshire. He was educated in Aberdeen and at the age of ten he was sent to Pembroke Hall, Cambridge. Within a year he had transferred to Paris, but his studies were interrupted by various misfortunes including the loss of all his possessions after a robbery. After a period at Louvain he travelled in Europe in the company of several papal missions and thereafter studied at Douai and then again in Paris. His academic progress was bedevilled by squabbles with his professors, and at one point he came to blows with an opponent over the appointment to a chair at Nîmes. In 1613 he made a fruitless journey to Scotland to attempt the recovery of his father's estate, but finding his own temperament and his Catholic faith disadvantages to any progress he returned to live in Paris, where he began writing the histories on which his fame rests. However, his unruly temper again interfered with his career and he was forced to flee to England after an altercation with his students. His adherence to Catholicism denied him the royal patronage of James I and the last years of Dempster's life were spent in Pisa and Bologna. After further storms and litigation involving his private life and his religious beliefs, Dempster entered a period of comparative calm. He was knighted by Pope Urban VIII a few years before his death on 6 September 1625.

Dempster was a man of contrasts who was very much at one with the times in which he lived: he was a courageous swordsman who was frequently wild and intemperate, yet he was also a widely read scholar, celebrated for his complete mastery over the classics. His principal work was the *Historia ecclesiastica gentis Scotorum* (1627), a bombastic history of Scotland which paid little attention to the requirements of historical truth. It is retrieved to some extent by the inclusion of biographical sketches of many of his contemporaries, but Dempster's own self-portrait is marred by exaggeration and by a tendency to overindulge in fantasy. However, in matters of classical, antiquarian and legal studies he was considered to be an authority and he was also a pleasing poet in Latin. A selection of his work appeared in the DELITIAE POETARUM SCOTORUM of 1637.

EDITION: D. Irving, ed., *Thomae Dempsteri Historia ecclesiastica gentis Scotorum, sive De scriptoribus Scotorum*, 2 vols., Bannatyne Club (Edinburgh, 1829)

Deòrsa Mac Iain Deòrsa. The Gaelic name of GEORGE CAMPBELL HAY.

Disruption, the. A schism within the Church of Scotland which occurred on 18 May 1843 in Edinburgh during the Church's annual General Assembly. Led by Dr David Welsh, some 190 ministers left the Assembly, the Church of Scotland's governing body, to form the Free Church of Scotland with THOMAS CHALMERS as its first Moderator. Their first act was to prepare a deed of demission whereby all signatories resigned their livings and privileges in the established Church; the deed was signed by 451 ministers. In 1847 a Free Church College was founded in Edinburgh to train men for the ministry, by which time the movement had 700 churches of its own and was a recognized force in religious politics. The Disruption, as it came to be known, had its origins in the Patronage Act of 1712 which restored to patrons of ecclesiastical benefices the right of presentation of a minister to a parish, a move that threatened the traditional rights of congregations to elect their own ministers. The arguments continued throughout the 18th century, during which there were several secessions from the Church as congregations refused

to accept ministers chosen for them by patrons. The belief that the Church should not be trammelled by political interference in its governance gained ground in the 19th century, culminating in the Disruption, and the establishment of the Free Church, which relied on its own membership for its support, spiritual and financial; this was a significant move in Scottish church history and one that influenced Scottish cultural life. Many of the leading members of the KAILYARD school owed their spiritual allegiance to the Free Church of Scotland.

Don Manuscript. A collection of letters by ROBERT BURNS, presented to Lady Henrietta Don, the sister of JAMES CUNNINGHAM, Earl of Glencairn. It is now known as the Laing Manuscript and is in the possession of the library of the University of Edinburgh.

Donn, Rob. *See* MACAOIDH, ROB DONN.

Doric. A word used to describe 'a broad or rustic dialect of English, Scotch etc, 1870' (OED). It has its origins in the ancient Greek name 'Doris', a small area of central Greece south of Thessaly, which was the home of the Dorians. In Scotland it is applied in particular to the language of the north-east of the country, where it is also known as 'Buchan Doric'. Poetry has claimed its greatest usage and among the contemporary or near-contemporary poets who have been associated with the Doric are CHARLES MURRAY, FLORA GARRY, VIOLET JACOB, DAVID RORIE, Sir ALEXANDER GRAY and MARION ANGUS, but it has also formed the vocabulary of several dialect novels of which JOHNNY GIBB OF GUSHETNEUK by WILLIAM ALEXANDER (ii) and *Eppie Elrick* (1956) by W. P. Milne (1882–1958) may be counted the most successful.

Douglas. Play in five acts by JOHN HOME, first performed on 14 December 1756 in Edinburgh to an enthusiastic audience. It was produced in London the following year and it became a favourite of Mrs Sarah Siddons who in later life became associated with the role of Lady Randolph. It was first published in 1757. The play centres on Norval, Douglas's son, who has been abandoned in childhood and reared by Old Norval, a shepherd. His mother, Matilda, the daughter of Sir Malcolm, has married Lord

andolph whose life is saved by Norval, and he
s given a commission in the army for his
bravery. However, the hatred of Glenalvon,
Randolph's heir-presumptive, leads to a quar-
el and in a fight precipitated by Glenalvon he
s murdered by Norval who in turn is killed by
Randolph. In despair at the loss of the man she
recognizes as her son Lady Randolph commits
suicide. In a play resounding with pathetic
tragedy and Gothic–Romantic undertones,
Norval stands out as the traditional 18th-
century gallant, with his heroic idealism and
'infelt greatness'. Much of the plot comes from
the ballad 'Gil Morice' which tells the story of
the murder of a youth by his mother's jealous
husband.

Douglas, Archibald, 5th Earl of Angus
(1449–1513). Also known as 'Bell-the-Cat',
Angus was a supporter of Alexander, Duke of
Albany, the brother of JAMES III. He gained his
nickname by telling his supporters 'I will bell
the cat' when they complained of their inability to rid the king of his low-born favourites.
Although he enjoyed a stormy relationship
with JAMES IV, he was chancellor between
1493 and 1497, and two of his sons, including
his heir, died at the BATTLE OF FLODDEN. He
features in *Marmion* by Sir WALTER SCOTT.

Douglas, Gavin (c1474–1522). Poet. He was
the third son of ARCHIBALD DOUGLAS, 5th
Earl of Angus, and was probably born in 1474
at the castle of Tantallon in East Lothian, then
one of the chief seats of the Angus family.
Little is known about his early education but he
was at the University of St Andrews between
1490 and 1494 and there is some evidence to
suggest that he may have studied for a time at
the University of Paris. As he had been born
into a powerful family, influential in Scottish
politics, Douglas enjoyed the benefits of court
patronage throughout his life. His first appointment as a churchman was to the deanery
of Dunkeld in 1497 and he was also styled
Rector of Linton (or Prestonkirk), a small
village between Tantallon and Dunbar in East
Lothian. In 1503 he became Provost of the
Collegiate Church of St Giles in Edinburgh, a
post of spiritual and temporal importance
which he held until 1515 when he became
Bishop of Dunkeld.

After the BATTLE OF FLODDEN in 1513
Douglas's nephew, Angus Douglas, 6th Earl of
Angus, married Margaret Tudor, the widow of

JAMES IV and from that date Douglas's fortunes
were tied to the queen's party. During the
political upheavals of 1515 and 1516, when
Scotland was under the regency of the Duke of
Albany, Douglas was imprisoned in St Andrews and Edinburgh and on his release he had
to fight off the challenge of a rival claimant,
Andrew Stewart brother of the Earl of Atholl,
to the bishopric of Dunkeld. By 1517 Douglas
was again in favour and went on embassy in
France to arrange a marriage between JAMES V
and a daughter of Francis I. On his return to
Scotland he became involved in the tortuous
plotting and counterplotting rife among the
Scottish nobility during Albany's regency. He
was exiled to England in 1521 and he died in
London of plague in September the following
year. Douglas's family background had drawn
him into public affairs but he was also an
ambitious man and even at his death he was
attempting to persuade Cardinal Wolsey to
support his claim to the archbishopric of St
Andrews, a post that had eluded him in 1514.

Apart from 'Conscience', an attack on
cupidity in the Church, Douglas's only surviving poems are *The Palice of Honour* and his
great translation, *The XIII Bukes of Eneados of
the Famous Poete Virgile Translated out of Latyne
Verses into Scottis Meter*, normally referred to as
the ENEADOS. He may also have been the
author of *King Hart*, an allegorical poem about
the control and governance of the heart, the
'king' in the human personality (for a full
discussion see P. Bawcutt, 'Did Gavin Douglas
write *King Hart?*', *Medium Aevum*, 28 (1959),
pp.31–47). All his poetry had been completed
by 1513 and *The Palice of Honour*, which was
written by 1501, was dedicated to James IV. It
opens in the tradition of the *Roman de la rose*
with an allegorical dream sequence in which
the poet falls asleep in a beautiful garden but
awakes in a wilderness, the domain of Fortune.
Three processions pass by him, led in turn by
Minerva, Diana and Venus, for whom he sings
a 'ballat' of love's inconstancy. For his treason
the poet is tried by Venus and only the inter-
cession of Calliope and a court of poets can
save him from the goddess's wrath. In penance
to Venus the poet sings a light-hearted song of
love and he sets out through a fabulous landscape on an imaginatively described journey to
the palace of honour, the dwelling-place of
Venus and the Muses, which is set on top of a
high mountain. The poem ends with a hymn of
praise to honour, which is equated with the

medieval concepts of gallantry and moral perfection. *The Palice of Honour* is in the central, European tradition of courtly allegory and the poem reflects Douglas's knowledge of Latin and Italian poetry and his pre-occupations with the themes of love, poetry and honour.

Douglas's fame as a poet rests ultimately with the *Eneados*, his translation of Virgil's *Aeneid* into Middle Scots, which he dedicated to his cousin, Henry Lord Sinclair, the captain of James IV's warship the Great Michael. The reasons for Douglas's translating the *Aeneid* into Scots are threefold: to widen the usage of Scots, to communicate to a larger audience and to provide a contemporary means of understanding Virgil's poem. Each of the 13 books, including book XIII written by the Italian humanist Maphaeus Vegius, is prefaced by a prologue, and these contain some of Douglas's most original poetry. Although the writing of prologues was a recognized medieval convention used by Chaucer and Boccaccio, Douglas used his prologues both as critical exposition and to emphasize his part in the creative process. Especially arresting are the Prologue to book VII with its description of the miseries of a harsh northern winter, told in coarse onomatopaeic language, and its counterparts in the Prologues to books XII and XIII which depict the corresponding glories of summertime in May and June. The *Eneados* is the most sustained long poem of quality and quantity in Scots, and in writing it Douglas had to broaden the use of his native language by conventional alliteration, aureation, and also the use of folk speech. Douglas is at his best in the scenes of natural and supernatural description and in the sea scenes and descriptions of battles; he is less successful in capturing the resonances of the great individual speeches of Virgil's original.

Douglas was the most learned of the medieval makars; although he has been described as one of the SCOTTISH CHAUCERIANS, along with ROBERT HENRYSON, WILLIAM DUNBAR and others, the influences of Chaucer are slight, and he remains an individual, if at times pedantic, figure, who confronted successfully the possibilities of Middle Scots as a consistent literary language. His social position gave him access to political power, but it also allowed him to follow scholarly pursuits, and among his associates were the influential schoolmen JOHN MAJOR and Robert Cockburn and in later life Polydore Vergil, the Italian author of the *Historia anglica*.

EDITIONS: J. Small, ed., *The Poetical Works of Gavin Douglas*, 4 vols. (Edinburgh, 1974); D. F. C. Caldwell, ed., *Virgil's Aeneid Translated into Scottish Verse by Gavin Douglas*, STS (Edinburgh and London, 1957); D. F. C. Caldwell, ed., *Selections from Gavin Douglas* (Oxford, 1964); P. Bawcutt, ed., *The Shorter Poems of Gavin Douglas* (Edinburgh and London, 1967)

REFERENCES: L. M. Watt, *Douglas's Aeneid* (Cambridge, 1920); P. Bawcutt, *Gavin Douglas: a Critical Study* (Edinburgh, 1976)

Douglas, Gawin. Pen-name of ALLAN RAMSAY.

Douglas, George. Pen-name of GEORGE DOUGLAS BROWN.

Douglas, George Norman (1868–1952). Novelist and essayist. He was born on 8 December 1868 at Tilquhillie on Deeside, the son of a Scottish father and Scottish–German mother. He was educated at Uppingham School and at Karlsruhe in Germany and entered the Foreign Office as a diplomat in 1894. In that capacity he served in St Petersburg before retiring early to settle on the island of Capri. His first book, *Unprofessional Tales* (1901), was written jointly with his wife under the pseudonym 'Normyx' but he received his first critical attention with the publication in 1911 of *Siren Land*, an account of his travels in southern Italy. His reputation as a travel writer was enhanced by *Old Calabria* (1915), a witty and entertaining account of a little-known part of Italy, in which Douglas's erudite knowledge of classical mythology and his manifest love for the country turned a travel book into a minor literary classic. Douglas was not afraid of allowing his personality to intrude on his non-fiction writing, an engaging trait that also pervades his novels so that even the best-known of them, *South Wind* (1917), is perhaps more distinguished for his evocation of Capri and his hedonistic enjoyment of life in the south than for its plot or characterization. Much admired as a literary stylist, Douglas wrote two autobiographical works, *Looking Back* (1933) and *Late Harvest* (1946), which help to explain his fascination for, and love of, Italy. He died on 9 February 1952.

WORKS: as Normyx, *Unprofessional Tales* (1901); *The Forestal Conditions of Capri* (1904); *Three Monographs* (1906); *Some Antiquarian Notes* (1907); *Siren Land* (1911); *Fountains in the Sand* (1912); *Old Calabria* (1915); *London Street Games* (1916); *South Wind* (1917); *They Went* (1920); *Alone* (1921);

Together (1923); *D. H. Lawrence and Maurice Magnus* (1924); *Experiments* (1925); *Birds and Beasts of the Greek Anthology* (1927); *In the Beginning* (1928); *Some Limericks* (1928); *One Day* (1929); *Capri* (1930); *How about Europe?* (1930); *Paneros* (1931); *Summer Islands* (1931); *Looking Back* (1933); *An Almanac* (1945); *Late Harvest* (1946); *Footnote on Capri* (1952); *Venus in the Kitchen* (1952)

REFERENCES: H. M. Tomlinson, *Norman Douglas* (London, 1931); R. M. Dawkins, *Norman Douglas* (London, 1933); N. Cunard, *Grand Man* (London, 1954); I. Greenlees, *Norman Douglas* (London, 1957)

Douglas, O. Pen-name of ANNA BUCHAN.

Doyle, Sir **Arthur Conan** (1859–1930). Novelist, writer of crime fiction and the creator of Sherlock Holmes. He was born on 22 May 1859 in Edinburgh, the son of a clerk of works to the Government Office of Works. His father was of Irish Catholic ancestry and at the age of nine Doyle was sent to Hodder, the preparatory school of Stonyhurst College the Jesuit boarding-school, which he attended until 1876. That year he entered the University of Edinburgh to study medicine, but lack of finance forced him to study for only six months of the year while spending the remainder as a doctor's assistant. In 1880 he spent seven months as a surgeon on a whaling ship in the Arctic, and after graduating in 1881 he went to sea again as a doctor on a passenger ship bound for West Africa. On his return to Britain he set up practice in Southsea near Portsmouth.

To supplement his income Doyle began writing again, his interest in the short story having been fired while he was working as an assistant in Birmingham by the publication of his story *The Mystery of the Sassana Valley* in CHAMBERS'S JOURNAL. His first story to feature Sherlock Holmes, *A Study in Scarlet*, was published in 1887 and introduced to the world the character that was to make Doyle famous. A novel, *The Sign of Four*, appeared in 1890, but it was in the pages of the *Strand Magazine* that Sherlock Holmes reached his most enthusiastic public. Starting with the publication in July 1891 of *A Scandal in Bohemia*, Doyle followed Holmes's adventures until December 1893, when he killed him off along with his arch-enemy Professor Moriarty. The stories were later collected and published in *The Adventures of Sherlock Holmes* (1892), *The Memoirs of Sherlock Holmes* (1894), *The Return of Sherlock Holmes* (1905), *The Last Bow* (1917) and *The Casebook of Sherlock Holmes*

(1927). Such was the public demand for Sherlock Holmes that Doyle had to resurrect him, and he reappeared in the novel *The Hound of the Baskervilles* (1902). Holmes and his colleague Dr Watson had become public property and their success helped to make Doyle one of the most popular and best-known authors of his day.

At Doyle's own admission, one of the models for Holmes was Dr Joseph Bell (1837–1911), one of his Edinburgh teachers and a pioneer of forensic medicine, whose deductive abilities had much impressed his students. The name owed its origins to the American poet Oliver Wendell Holmes (1809–94) who was much admired by Doyle. Sherlock Holmes became, and remains, a cult figure and the concept of his powers of rapid deduction, allied to Watson's slow-thinking empiricism, was an irresistible literary invention. Moreover Doyle developed a simple narrative formula that suited the spirit of the Victorian age and he had the happy ability of suggesting to his readers that they too were part of the story.

Doyle's interest in history and chivalry led to the creation of the Napoleonic soldier Brigadier Gerard whose *Exploits* were published in 1896. Doyle placed a high value on his historical novels, among which are *The White Company* (1891) and *Sir Nigel* (1906). Both manage to maintain historical accuracy while displaying Doyle's easy, flowing narrative, rather in the style of ROBERT LOUIS STEVENSON, a writer and fellow Scot whom Doyle resembled in many ways. An early novel, *The Firm of Girdlestone* (1890), published once he had become famous, presents a telling picture of the Edinburgh of his student days, and several of his early stories are also set in the city of his birth. The other creation who contributed to Doyle's fame was the scientist Professor Challenger, who appears in the novels *The Lost World* (1912) and *The Poison Belt* (1913).

In politics Doyle was a New Imperialist and his sense of adventure took him to the Boer War as a war correspondent. From that experience came two books *The Great Boer War* (1900) and *The War in South Africa: its Causes and Conclusion* (1902), which were both admired for his ability to describe the terrain of the country and the manoeuvres employed by the British generals. For his public services he was knighted in 1902. The death of his son during World War I may have been one of the reasons why his interests turned to spiritualism during the latter part of his life. He died on 7 July 1930.

WORKS: *A Study in Scarlet* (1887); *Micah Clarke* (1889); *Mysteries and Adventures* (1889); *The Mystery of Cloomber* (1889); *The Captain of Polestar* (1890); *The Firm of Girdlestone* (1890); *The Sign of Four* (1890); *The White Company* (1891); *The Adventures of Sherlock Holmes* (1892); *Beyond the City* (1892); *The Doings of Raffles Haw* (1892); *The Great Shadow* (1892); with J. M. Barrie, *Jane Annie* (1893); *The Refugees* (1893); *The Memoirs of Sherlock Holmes* (1894); *The Parasite* (1894); *Round the Red Lamp* (1894); *The Stark Munro Letters* (1895); *The Exploits of Brigadier Gerard* (1896); *Rodney Stone* (1896); *Uncle Bernac* (1897); *Songs of Action* (1898); *The Tragedy of the Korosko* (1898); *A Duet with Occasional Chorus* (1899); *The Great Boer War* (1900); *The Green Flag* (1900); *The Hound of the Baskervilles* (1902); *The War in South Africa: its Causes and Conclusions* (1902); *Adventures of Gerard* (1903); *The Return of Sherlock Holmes* (1905); *Sir Nigel* (1906); *Round the Fire Stories* (1908); *The Crime of the Congo* (1909); *The Last Galley* (1911); *Songs of the Road* (1911); *The Lost World* (1912); *The Poison Belt* (1913); *The German War: Sidelights and Reflections* (1914); *The Valley of Fear* (1915); *The British Campaign in France and Flanders*, 6 vols. (1916–19); *A Visit to Three Fronts* (1916); *The Last Bow* (1917); *Danger and other Stories* (1918); *The New Revelation* (1918); *The Guards Came Through* (1919); *The Vital Message* (1919); *The Wanderings of a Spiritualist* (1921); *The Case for Spirit Photography* (1922); *The Coming of the Fairies* (1922); *Our American Adventure* (1923); *Three of them* (1923); *Memories and Adventures* (1924); *Our Second American Adventure* (1924); *The Spiritualist's Reader* (1924); *The History of Spiritualism* (1926); *The Land of Mist* (1926); *The Casebook of Sherlock Holmes* (1927); *Pheneas Speaks* (1927); *The Maracot Deep and Other Stories* (1929); *Our African Winter* (1929)

EDITIONS: *Collected Poems* (1922); *Historical Romances*, two vols. (1931–2); W. S. Baring-Gould, ed., *The Annotated Sherlock Holmes* (1968)

REFERENCES: H. Pearson, *Conan Doyle: his Life and Art* (London, 1943); O. D. Edwards, *The Quest for Sherlock Holmes* (Edinburgh, 1982)

Drama. Although the earliest extant Scottish play is ANE PLEASANT SATYRE OF THE THRIE ESTAITIS of 1540 by Sir DAVID LYNDSAY, the drama tradition in Scotland, as in other European countries, had its origins in medieval mystery plays such as the Corpus Christi passion play *Haliblude* performed in Aberdeen in the mid-15th century, and in the pageants of the Abbot of Narent and Robin Hood, which took place in the major Scottish towns. There is a good account of those festivities in *The Abbot* by Sir WALTER SCOTT. Associated with the pageants was a stylized play of unknown antiquity, THE GOLOSHAN. But the banning of

public revelries from 1555 onwards meant that the public's interest in dramatic presentations gradually dissipated; as the reformed Church grew in strength so their proclamations became more vehement. But it would be wrong to place the entire blame for the stilted development of drama in Scotland on the Church. Other factors, too, played their part: the lack of a wealthy court as patron, the uneven development of civic society, the climate, and the religious upheavals of the 17th century.

Lyndsay's play, *Ane Pleasant Satyre*, written before dramatic performances acquired a bad name, is a milestone in Scottish literature. Rich with the cadences of spoken Scots, it mixes comedy with moral seriousness and also makes a number of pertinent points about social and spiritual reform. A second play attacking corruption within the Church, *The Beheading of Johne the Baptist* was written in Dundee by JAMES WEDDERBURN; other works of note are the two Latin plays by GEORGE BUCHANAN, *Jepthes sive Votum* (1557) and *Baptistes sive Calumnia* (1578), both of which contain fierce attacks on the Catholic Church.

Drama was popular at the court of JAMES VI; among the CASTALIAN BAND, Sir WILLIAM ALEXANDER (i) attempted four Senecan tragedies which were published under the title *The Monarchicke Tragedies* (1607), but the only play of any note to survive from the period is the anonymous *Philotus* of 1603. The removal of the court to London in that year effectively ended any hope of court patronage, and for the next 300 years Scottish writers interested in the theatre were to write for a London audience. *The Assembly* (1692) by ARCHIBALD PITCAIRNE, a satire on the Presbyterian Church, was first performed in London in 1722 as the nature of its subject matter would have made it unacceptable in Scotland; even the pastoral play THE GENTLE SHEPHERD by ALLAN RAMSAY, published in 1725, had to wait until 1747 for a professional production.

The most popular play of the 18th century was DOUGLAS (1756) by JOHN HOME, which prompted on its opening night the oft-quoted remark from an excited member of the audience, 'Whaur's yer Wullie Shakespeare noo?'. Its performance in Edinburgh challenged the Church's stranglehold on the theatre, and Home, a minister, was forced to resign his charge. By then Edinburgh had become a centre of theatrical activity, despite the earlier closure of Ramsay's Carruber's Close theatre by

Walpole's Licensing Act of 1737. Other 18th-century plays of note written by Scots include *The Prince of Tunis* (1773) by HENRY MACKENZIE, *Runnemede* (1784) by JOHN LOGAN, and *Tancred and Sigismunda* by JAMES THOMSON (i), which enjoyed a degree of success in London.

By the beginning of the 19th century the theatre had grown into a respectable form of public entertainment and travelling stock companies toured the country, often with famous stars like Mrs Siddons and Edmund Kean. Scott's work were dramatized and caught the public's imagination, with the actor Charles MacKay making his name for his portrayal of Bailie Nicol Jarvie in the adaptation of *Rob Roy*. On the same level the historical romance *De Montfort* by JOANNA BAILLIE was well received by the critics when it was produced at Drury Lane Theatre in London in April 1800, though it ran for only eight nights. London continued to be the fulcrum but it was a Scot, WILLIAM ARCHER, who introduced British audiences to the plays of Ibsen. J. M. BARRIE made a name for himself by writing for the London stage but his plays belong properly to the English dramatic tradition. 'Scotch comics', such as Sir Harry Lauder, were popular music-hall comedians and presented to the world a sterotyped picture of Scotland, all kilts, heather, bagpipes, whisky and drunken bonhomie.

Glasgow was the centre of the 20th-century revival of interest in drama. Alfred Waring established the Glasgow Repertory Company in 1908 and after World War I regular visits by the Abbey Theatre of Dublin showed that a national theatre was possible; this prompted the establishment in 1922 of Tyrone Guthrie's Scottish National Players, which survived until 1934 and produced the first plays written by O. H. MAVOR ('James Bridie'). The renaissance was matched by the emergence of several new dramatists, among whom may be mentioned JOHN MACINTYRE ('John Brandane'), ROBERT MCLELLAN, ROBERT KEMP, ALEXANDER REID, JOE CORRIE and ALEXANDER SCOTT (ii). Other developments were the Glasgow Unity Theatre of 1938–47, the establishment of the Glasgow Citizens Theatre in 1943 and the opening of repertory theatres in Dundee and Perth.

After World War II the wartime Council for the Encouragement of Music and the Arts (CEMA) gave way to the Arts Council, which introduced a policy of providing public funds for the theatre. From the 1960s the SCOTTISH ARTS COUNCIL and the local authorities became the theatre's main patrons in Scotland, supporting repertory theatres in the main cities, and travelling stock companies and providing funds for the encouragement of the writing and performance of new plays. Television and radio have also played a significant part in encouraging new drama, and the Scottish Community Drama Association, founded in 1932, has been a driving force in widening the public's interest in drama.

REFERENCES: J. Dibdin, *Annals of the Edinburgh Stage* (Edinburgh, 1888); D. Mackenzie, *Scotland's First National Theatre* (Edinburgh, 1963); T. Tobin, *Plays by Scots, 1660–1800* (Iowa, 1974); D. Hutchison, *The Modern Scottish Theatre* (Glasgow, 1977)

Drinan, Adam. Pen-name of JOSEPH MACLEOD.

Drummond, Henry (1851–97). Divine. He was born on 17 August 1851 at Stirling and was educated there and at Morrison's Academy, Crieff, before matriculating at the University of Edinburgh. In 1870 he left, without taking a degree, to study for the ministry of the Free Church of Scotland, and it was during that period of preparation that he became involved in the Moody and Sankey evangelical revival. Although he became a leading light in the movement, he could not be persuaded to join Moody in New York until 1879, by which time he was a lecturer in natural science at the Free Church College in Glasgow and was engaged in geological research in the Rocky Mountains. As a result of that work he published *Natural Law in the Spiritual World* (1883), the first of his highly successful tracts on the process of natural selection in evolution. After further travels and research in southern Africa, his career culminated in a series of lecture tours in Britain, Australia and America, all of which were marked by his forceful and persuasive rhetoric. Drummond was a leading supporter of the KAILYARD novelists of his day and enjoyed the friendship of WILLIAM ROBERTSON NICOLL and his protégé the novelist JOHN WATSON ('Ian Maclaren'). In his scientific writings he produced little in the way of original thinking, having been overtaken by Charles Darwin (1809–82) and Herbert Spencer (1820–1903), but the attraction of his work to contemporary audiences clearly lay in his ability to deal with old arguments in a clear and uncomplicated way.

WORKS: *Natural Law in the Spiritual World* (1883); *Tropical Africa* (1888); *Baxter's Second Innings* (1892); *The Ascent of Man* (1894); *The New Evangelism* (1899)

REFERENCE: G. A. Smith, *Life of Henry Drummond* (London, 1899)

Drummond, William, of Hawthornden (1585–1649). Poet. He was born on 13 December 1585 in the family house of Hawthornden near Roslin in Midlothian. His father was a gentleman-usher to JAMES VI and during his younger years Drummond enjoyed a close relationship with the court, until it removed itself to London in 1603 on the Union of the Crowns. He was educated at the HIGH SCHOOL OF EDINBURGH and at the newly founded University, where he graduated in July 1605. After a short period in London he studied at Bourges and Paris between 1607 and 1609, when he returned to live in Scotland. Drummond intended to practise law but his father's death in 1610 left him Laird of Hawthornden and free to follow the literary interests he had pursued while studying abroad. From then on he led a retiring life among the books in his substantial library and cultivated the idea of himself as a solitary poet wandering in the valley of the River Esk on which Hawthornden stood.

Widely read in the poets of his day, Drummond was well versed in the poetry of England, France, Italy and Spain, as well as in the classics. Among his friends and literary correspondents were his cousin WILLIAM FOWLER, Sir WILLIAM ALEXANDER (i), ARTHUR JOHNSTON and Sir JOHN SCOTT of Scotstarvit, and the English poet Ben Jonson (1572–1637) who visited him in 1618 and who kept a record of their conversations. Drummond was also associated with the CASTALIAN BAND of poets who surrounded James VI. In 1615 his intended wife, Euphemia Cunningham of Barns, died, thus adding grief to Drummond's solitude and although he took a mistress by whom he had three children, he remained single until 1630, when he married Elizabeth Logan of Restalrig. The latter years of his life were clouded by poverty and litigation for debt and by the struggles within Scotland following the signing of the NATIONAL COVENANT of 1638. Although Drummond signed the Covenant in April 1639 his sympathies lay with the Royalists and he corresponded with JAMES GRAHAM,

Marquis of Montrose. On his death, on 4 December 1649, his library was presented to the University of Edinburgh.

Because most of Drummond's poems were written in the Petrarchan tradition, he was considered to be out of tune with the metaphysical poets of his day, but his verse, mainly madrigals and sonnets, reflects his wide reading and European literary interests. His first poem, 'Teares on the Death of Meliades', a pastoral lament, was published in 1613 on the death of Prince Henry; his collection *Poems, Amorous, Funereall, Divine, Pastorall in Sonnets, Songs, Sextains, Madrigals* was published by ANDRO HART in 1614 and again, with revisions, in 1616. In Petrarchan fashion the poems echo the poet's love for a beautiful, ethereal girl, Auristella, and on her death he laments the impermanency of life: 'But (woe is mee) long count and count may I,/Ere I see Her whose absence makes me die' (sonnet 50). His second collection, *Flowres of Sion*, continues Drummond's reflections on life's transitoriness, but the poet is able to overcome his anxieties by trusting in Christ's redemption of souls. The collection contains his best-known sonnets 'For the Baptiste' and 'Content and Resolute', and to it was appended his great prose essay on death and salvation, 'A Cypress Grove'. Among other works of note are 'The Entertainment' (1633), a poem in honour of Charles I's visit to Edinburgh, *Irene*, a pamphlet attacking the COVENANTERS, and a number of satirical verses including 'A Character of the Anti-Covenanter of Malignant' and 'For a Ladyes Summonds of Nonentree' an attack on sexual excess. Drummond also wrote an indifferent history of Scotland and towards the end of his life he was engaged on the genealogy of his family. In 1627 he patented the invention of 16 wonderful engines of war. Although he wrote several political squibs in the Royalist cause, his isolation effectively cut him off from the main events of his lifetime.

WORKS: *Mausoleum* (1613); *Teares on the Death of Meliades* (1613); *Poems, Amorous, Funereall, Divine, Pastorall in Sonnets, Songs, Sextains, Madrigals* (1614); *Poems* (1616); *Forth Feasting* (1617); *Flowres of Sion* (1623); *The Entertainment* (1633); *The History of Scotland* (1655)

EDITIONS: L. C. Kastner, ed., *The Poetical Works of William Drummond of Hawthornden*, 2 vols., STS (Edinburgh and London, 1913); R. H. Macdonald, ed., *William Drummond of Hawthornden: Poems and Prose*, ASLS (Edinburgh and London, 1976)

Drunk Man Looks at the Thistle, A. A poem of 2685 lines written by CHRISTOPHER MUR-RAY GRIEVE (under his, better-known, pseudonym 'Hugh MacDiarmid') between 1925 and 1926, the year of its first publication. During its creation MacDiarmid bombarded the GLASGOW HERALD with a series of press releases announcing its progress, and one dated 17 December 1925 gives ample notice of the poet's aspiration. 'The matter includes satire, amphigouri, lyrics, parodies of Mr T. S. Eliot and other poets, and translations from the Russian, French and German. The whole poem is in braid Scots, except a few quatrains which are in the nature of a skit on Mr Eliot's "Sweeney" poems, and it has been expressly designed to show that braid Scots can be effectively applied to all manner of subjects and measures.' Those ambitions were justified by the poem itself, which is the finest sustained work in Scots written in the 20th century and by any standards a major work of art.

Its central creation, the drunk man, is found lying in the moonlight in front of a huge thistle which seems to him to be in a constant state of metamorphosis. He reflects on his drunken condition and on the condition of Scotland and all the while the thistle becomes different things to him: bagpipe music, a pair of bellows, a skeleton, a flash of lightning, an octopus, parts of the human anatomy – a brain laid bare, an erect penis, a foetus – a rigged ship and an aspect of the man himself. Although the drunk man's struggle to perceive the nature of the thistle is seen as a facet of his dichotomous attitude towards Scotland, MacDiarmid uses that as a starting-point to investigate the divided nature of all mankind.

There follows a long philosphical sequence, interspersed with an intricately woven address to the Russian writer Dostoyevsky, and by translations, in which the drunk man's mind leads him onwards in a quest to solve the problem of man's existence and of his place in the cosmos. Then the thistle becomes Yggdrasil, the Scandinavian mythological tree of life, and, finally, the ultimate puzzle:

> And still the puzzle stands unsolved.
> Beauty and ugliness alike,
> And life and daith and God and man,
> Are aspects o't but nane can tell
> The secret that I'd fain find oot
> O' this bricht hive, this sorry weed,
> The tree that fills the universe,
> Or like a reistit herrin crines.

Central to the poem's interpretation is Mac-Diarmid's theory of the CALEDONIAN AN-TISYZYGY, the balancing of opposites, which Gregory Smith had described as the dynamic impulse behind Scotland's poetic literature. Thus, as well as examining man's genesis and his place in eternity, MacDiarmid also refuses to lose sight of the matter of Scotland, and the poem is notable for the sudden, and at times bewildering, switches of mood and pace, and for many seeming contradictions of attitude. Also included in the poem, which by the ambition and scope of its achievement defies a brief analysis, are the important symbols of the rose as the motif of man's desire for transcendance, the theme of the divine insights inspired by drink and the all-pervasive deceptions of the moonlit hillside. In the last lines, in another characteristic reversal, MacDiarmid returns the drunk man, now fully sober, to the hillside, far removed from the night's far-ranging philosophical speculations.

Controversy surrounds the role played by MacDiarmid's friend, the composer FRANCIS GEORGE SCOTT in the poem's creation. From the evidence of both men it would seem that Scott did have a hand in the poem's structure and in deleting much extraneous material. In his autobiographical essays, *The Company I've Kept* (1966), MacDiarmid admitted that he 'handed over the whole mass of my manuscript to him [Scott]' and that 'he was not long in seizing on the essentials'. However much, though, Scott was responsible for helping to shape the poem, there is no doubt that it is entirely of MacDiarmid's creation. (In his *History of Scottish Literature* (1977) Maurice Lindsay repeats Scott's story that he was the begetter of the poem's title and the originator of the final two lines, 'And weel ye micht,/Sae Jean'll say, efter sic a nicht!', which end the drunk man's soliloquy.)

Dunbar, William (c1460–c1520). Poet. He belongs to a group of poets, BLIND HARRY, JAMES I, ROBERT HENRYSON, GAVIN DOUG-LAS and others, commonly referred to as the 'SCOTTISH CHAUCERIANS'. Although Dunbar was influenced indirectly by Chaucer, a more accurate term is 'makar', the fashioner of the literary artefact. Very little is known with certainty about Dunbar's life, although there is evidence to suggest that he was born in East Lothian, and that in the period 1477 to 1479 he was a student at the University of St Andrews (a William Dunbar appears on the University's matriculation roll for those years). Much of our knowledge about Dunbar's life comes from his poetry: in 'How Dumbar was desyred to be ane Freir' he tells of his life as a Franciscan novice, of his travels to England and to Picardy and of his decision to leave the order. Between that period and 15 August 1500, when his name appeared on the Privy Seal record as receiving an annual pension of £10, which secured his position as a court poet, Dunbar is thought to have worked on several of the diplomatic missions maintained by JAMES IV with the leading states in Europe.

In 'The Flying of Dunbar and Kennedy' (the titles of Dunbar's poems are from Mackenzie's edition), another poem that contains biographical information (much of it dubious), reference is made to at least two visits abroad, to France and Scandinavia, before 1500. In December 1501 Dunbar was part of the Scottish mission to London to arrange James's marriage to Margaret Tudor, an event he honoured in 1503 in 'The Thrissell and the Rois'. Another praise poem, 'To Aberdein', was composed in 1511 on the occasion of Queen Margaret's visit to the city and includes a vivid description of the celebratory pageants mounted in her honour. At court Dunbar continued to be a favourite of the queen but much of his work was concerned with petitions to the king for increases in his pension, such as 'The Petition of the Gray Horse, Auld Dunbar', 'To the King' and 'Of Discretioun in Asking', and also with his disgust at the king's support of false claimants such as the physician John Damian who is attacked in 'The Fenyeit Freir of Tungland'.

The reign of James IV has been characterized as a 'golden age' in Scottish history, but although James possessed many personal virtues, there was widespread poverty, disease and corruption within his kingdom. Many of Dunbar's comments on the state of contemporary society are complaints or satires, and in 'Of the Warldis Instabilitie' he bemoans the triumph of evil and disorder – 'gude rewle is banist our bordour' – a theme that was taken up later by Sir DAVID LYNDSAY in ANE PLEASANT SATYRE OF THE THRIE ESTAITIS. In 'Remonstrance to the King' his target is the group of flatterers and hangers-on at court who receive the king's patronage in preference to more worthy claimants. In 'To the Merchants of Edinburgh' he castigates the citizens of Edinburgh for their

profiteering and for their idleness in allowing the city to become a stinking slum. In 'Tydingis fra the Sessioun' the object of his moralizing i the gross corruption commonly practised in the law courts. In 'A General Satyre' and 'The Devillis Inquest' he attacks the decadence and lack of spiritual values prevalent in Scotland. The satires are Dunbar's personal view of matters in Scotland, but as a court poet he would have been expected to compose ceremonial poems. In that category are two aureate dream allegories, 'The Dance of the Sevin Deidly Synnis' and 'The Goldyn Targe', in which the poet is overcome by Beauty after a length defence by Reason before the court of Venus. The poem is remarkable for the brilliant pictures created by Dunbar, the harmony of it language and its use of classical allegory in the tradition of the *Roman de la rose*. The lighter side of James IV's court life, and its fashions and foibles, is described in 'Of a Dance in the Quenis Chalmer', 'Of James Dog, Kepar of the Quenis Wardrop', 'Of Sir Thomas Norny' and 'Of ane Blak-moir'.

Dunbar's pension was increased to £20 on 12 November 1507 and to £80 on 26 August 1510, and he spent the rest of his life as a courtier unable to win preferment for the church benefice, 'ane kirk scant coverit with heather', that he desired. After the BATTLE OF FLODDEN in 1513 his name disappeared from the treasurer's accounts, which are missing from August 1513 to June 1515 and from September 1518 to June 1522, the year that is generally considered to have been the year of Dunbar's death. An increasing weariness with court life crept into his work and it lead to the composition of sacred poems which demonstrate the same linguistic virtuosity and rhyming structures as his secular verse. 'The Tabil of Confessioun' is a penitential poem that contrives to be both a statement of the medieval Catholic Church's credo and Dunbar's personal confession of faith. 'Of the Passioun of Christ' is a dream poem of Christ's crucifixion and 'On the Resurrection of Christ' is a nobl hymn of praise for Easter morning in which the dominant imagery is the triumph of light over darkness. 'Ane Ballat of Our Lady' a paean of praise addressed to Mary, the Mother of God is composed in joyful, polychromatic language and the culmination of the poem has a ringing musical intensity.

In contrast to the exuberance of most of Dunbar's work, there is a small number of personal poems which betray his occasional despondency and depression, the best known of which is 'Lament quhen he was seik', or as it is more familiarly known, 'Lament for the Makaris'. Each of its 25 stanzas ends with the refrain from the Office of the Dead, 'Timor mortis conturbat me', and the whole poem is imbued with Dunbar's awesome contemplation of the inevitability of death. Everyone, of whatever rank or station, has to die, but Dunbar's main concern is the roll-call of dead makars of Scotland and England, which unfolds as a memorial of their passing. In 'On his heid-ake' the reader discovers that Dunbar suffered from migraine, and 'Ane his awen enemy' describes the poet's ailments and his consequent mental depression. 'Meditatioun in Wynter' compares the long, cold, dark northern winter with the despair of death and several poems deal with the inconstancy and impermanency of the world's pleasures: 'Of Lyfe', 'Of the wordis vanitie', 'Of the changes of lyfe', 'All erdly joy returns to passe', 'Of manis mortalitie', 'No tressour availis without glaidnes' and 'Elegy on the death of Lord Bernard Stewart, Lord of Aubigny'.

Like other medieval poets Dunbar was influenced by the *Roman de la rose* and its philosophy of courtly love; in that tradition he wrote 'The Goldyn Targe', 'In prais of wemen', 'Bewty and the Presoneir', 'Quhone he list to feyne', 'Of the ladyis solistaris at court', 'The twa cummeris' and 'To a Ladye'. His greatest poem, in which he transcends the tradition and bends it to his own use, is THE TRETIS OF THE TUA MARIIT WEMEN AND THE WEDO. After midnight on Midsummer's Night the poet comes across three high-born ladies drinking wine and discussing their love lives. He hides in the foliage and listens to them gossiping. The first lady is married to a senile old man; the second to a young man who is impotent; the widow has had two husbands, the first a cough-ridden packman, the second a wealthy merchant. Having rid herself of both she can maintain public respectability while attracting numerous lovers in private. Although the relationships related by the three women contain many of the elements of *amour courtois*, the poem is Dunbar's satire on women and marriage, and he ends the work by asking his audience which woman they would take for their wife: 'quhilk wald ye wail to your wife, gif ye suld wed one!'

In 'THE FLYTING OF DUNBAR AND KENNEDY'

Dunbar employed the ancient practice of 'flyting', pursuing a battle of words, usually scurrilous and abusive, between two poets, which has its origins in Scottish Celtic literature. Dunbar's opponent was WALTER KENNEDY with whom he exchanged a succession of highly stylized insults in 69 stanzas that are remarkable for their intricate rhyming structure and use of coarse, alliterative language. Also ascribed to Dunbar by some critics is 'Kynd Kittock', an anonymous ballad which tells of the establishment of an alehouse between heaven and earth.

Dunbar is perhaps the most varied and creative of the Scottish medieval makars. His subject matter is complex and wide-ranging: it includes satirical comment on contemporary church, court and town life, the matter of medieval scholarship and the poet's relationship to spiritual affairs, and there is a spectrum of moods from the pangs of despair to the joy of exultation. Equally important is his technical ability and his mastery of stanza form and rhyming structure, from the unrhymed alliteration of *The Tretis of the Tua Mariit Wemen and the Wedo* to the variety of rhymed lyric verses used in the rest of his work.

The bulk of Dunbar's work exists in the Maitland Folio Manuscript (*see* MAITLAND MANUSCRIPTS), the REIDPATH MANUSCRIPT, the BANNATYNE MANUSCRIPT and the ASLOAN MANUSCRIPT and in the Aberdeen Minute Book of Seisins, volumes 2 and 3. Six poems were printed by WALTER CHAPMAN and Andrew Myllar in 1508, but the first collection was not published until 1834.

EDITIONS: D. Laing, ed., *Poems of William Dunbar*, 2 vols. (Edinburgh, 1834); J. Small, A. J. G. MacKay and W. Gregor, eds., *The Poems of William Dunbar*, 3 vols., STS (Edinburgh and London, 1884–93); J. Schipper, ed., *The Poems of William Dunbar* (Vienna, 1892); W. M. Mackenzie, ed., *The Poems of William Dunbar* (Edinburgh, 1932); J. Kinsley, ed., *William Dunbar: Selected Poems* (Oxford, 1958); J. Kinsley, ed., *The Poems of William Dunbar* (Oxford, 1979)

REFERENCES: J. Schipper, *Dunbar: sein Leben und seine Gedichte* (Berlin, 1884); R. A. Taylor, *Dunbar the Poet and his Period* (London, 1931); J. W. Baxter, *William Dunbar: a Biographical Study* (Edinburgh, 1952); T. Scott, *Dunbar: a Critical Exposition of the Poems* (Edinburgh, 1966)

Duncan, Jane ['Janet Sandison'] (1910–76). Novelist. She was born on 10 March 1910 in Glasgow and was educated there at Lenzie Academy and the University. During World

War II she served with the Women's Auxiliary Air Force and between 1945 and 1958 she lived in Jamaica. Until her death on 20 October 1976 her home was Conon Bridge in Ross-shire. Most of Jane Duncan's novels are set in the fictional village of Reachfar on the Black Isle where she places her heroine, Janet Sandison, in a series of events that plot the break-up of a small Highland community. Written under the composite series title 'My Friends' the novels are a thinly disguised autobiographical account of many of the events of the author's own life and include a Caribbean background in the St Jago of the later novels. The central character and narrator, Janet Sandison, became an elaborate self-projection for Jane Duncan; she even wrote under that name four novels about Jean Robertson, an impoverished girl from the claustrophobic Lowland town of Lochfoot who rises, somewhat improbably, to a position of wealth and authority. Although Lochfoot can be compared with the Barbie of THE HOUSE WITH THE GREEN SHUTTERS, Jane Duncan's novels are concerned more with the interrelationship of character and event than with the dynamism of evil that permeates the world of Brown's creation.

WORKS: *My Friend Muriel* (1959); *My Friends the Miss Boyds* (1959); *My Friend Annie* (1960); *My Friend Monica* (1960); *My Friend Sandy* (1961); *My Friend Martha's Aunt* (1962); *My Friend Flora* (1963); *My Friend Madame Zora* (1963); *My Friend Cousin Emmie* (1964); *My Friend Rose* (1964); *My Friends the Miss Millers* (1965); *My Friends from Cairnton* (1966); *My Friend my Father* (1966); *My Friends the Macleans* (1967); *My Friends the Hungry Generation* (1968); *My Friend the Swallow* (1970); *My Friend Sashie* (1971); *My Friends the Misses Kindness* (1974); *Letter from Reachfar* (1976)
as Janet Sandison: *Jean in the Morning* (1969); *Jean at Noon* (1970); *Jean in the Twilight* (1972); *Jean Towards Another Day* (1975)

Dundas, Henry, 1st Viscount Melville (1742–1811). Statesman and lawyer. He was educated at the HIGH SCHOOL OF EDINBURGH and at the University of Edinburgh where he studied Law. He held several important legal posts, including Solicitor-General in 1766 and Lord Advocate in 1775, and he was a member of the Younger Pitt's Tory administrations of 1784–1801 and 1804–6. During that period he became Pitt's 'manager for Scotland', controlling not only the elections but also the patronage of the main political posts. His absolute power alienated many of his fellow coun-

trymen and he retired from political life in 1806, four years after he had been created a Viscount. Lord Cockburn, in *Memorials of his Time*, remarked of Melville that he was 'well calculated by talent and manner to make despotism popular'.

Dundee. A city in the east of Scotland on the Firth of Tay. In many people's minds Dundee is associated with the production of news- and comic papers by the publishing empire of D. C. Thomson, and with the excruciating rhymes and baneful descriptions of the poetry of WILLIAM MCGONAGALL, who although not a Dundonian by birth is forever linked to the city of his adoption. But Dundee has a longer and more venerable history than that conjured up by its 19th-century promoters. Through its physical position on the estuary of the River Tay it has long enjoyed the position of a trading port and until recently it was one of the world's centres for the spinning of jute, which it imported direct from Bengal. Dundee's claim to be a royal burgh was confirmed in 1327 by ROBERT I, and it prospered to become Scotland's second city, a title it kept until the 17th century when it was racked on several occasions by the opposing Royalist and Parliamentary forces. A century earlier, the city had become a melting-pot for the ideas generated by the Protestant reformers, and three of its sons, the WEDDERBURN brothers, compiled Scotland's first collection of hymns, psalms and secular songs, the GUDE AND GODLIE BALLATIS. The proximity of St Andrews and its university fed the intellectual life of Dundee, and long after the events of the Reformation struggle it remained an ecclesiastical centre of note and authority. The industrialization of the city, which began in the late 18th century and continued throughout the 19th, expanded its size and its population, but unfortunately neither care nor attention was paid to the architectural merit of new buildings, and the planners failed to design the city so as to exploit its relation to the natural beauty of its surroundings.

Dundee, 1st Viscount. *See* GRAHAM, JOHN.

Dunlop, Mrs **Frances Anna,** of Dunlop (1730–1815). She was a friend and confidante of ROBERT BURNS whom she met in 1786 after the publication of the KILMARNOCK EDITION of his poems. Between then and 1794 they were frequent correspondents and, although they were sometimes in disagreement, Burns valued her friendship and her 'patronising me and interesting yourself in my fame and character as a poet' (letter, 15 January 1787). Their friendship came to an end in January 1795 when Burns wrote to Mrs Dunlop praising the French Revolution in a style which offended her – she was a Royalist and two of her daughters were married to French Royalist refugees. The break lasted until shortly before Burns's death when Mrs Dunlop relented, and wrote to him again in fond terms. Mrs Dunlop adopted a maternal attitude towards Burns and despite her censure of his earthier poems she acted as a sounding-board for many of his thoughts especially during his visit to Edinburgh 1786–7. Their correspondence was edited by William Wallace and published as *Robert Burns and Mrs Dunlop* (1898).

Dunlop, William ['Tiger'] (1792–1848). Man of letters. He was born on 19 November 1792 in Greenock. Between 1806 and 1813 he studied medicine at the University of Glasgow and, on graduating, joined the army as a surgeon. He took part in the Canadian–American war of 1814, but within two years he had resigned his commission to work in India, and he did not return to Scotland until 1820. He set up medical practice in Edinburgh and lectured on medical jurisprudence at the University, but in 1824, on becoming a member of the Royal College of Surgeons, he moved to London, where he became involved with JOHN GALT in the establishment of the Canada Company. From 1826 until his death on 29 June 1848 Dunlop lived in Canada and enjoyed a distinguished public life as an army officer and later as a member of parliament. Dunlop had started writing while in India and during his stay in Edinburgh he was closely associated with the newly founded BLACKWOOD'S MAGAZINE. He edited two London-based newspapers, *The British Press* and *The Telescope*, and wrote widely on Canadian affairs, publishing his *Statistical Sketches of Upper Canada* in 1832.

WORKS: *Elements of Medical Jurisprudence* (1825); *Statistical Sketches of Upper Canada* (1832); *Defence of the Canada Company* (1836); A. H. V. Colquhoun, ed., *Recollections of the American War* (1905)

REFERENCE: C. F. Klinck, *William 'Tiger' Dunlop* (Toronto, 1958)

Dunn, Douglas (*b* 1942). Poet. He was born on 23 October 1942 at Inchinnan, Renfrewshire, and was educated at Renfrew High School and the Scottish School of Librarianship. After working in Glasgow he attended the University of Hull between 1966 and 1969 and for a time he worked there as a librarian; he has lived in Hull ever since. Much of his poetry shows the same texture and feel for local life that characterizes the poetry of Philip Larkin (*b* 1922), Dunn's university colleague at Hull. He has also produced a number of anthologies and is an accomplished radio dramatist and critic.

WORKS: *Terry Street* (1969); *Backwaters* (1971); *Night* (1971); *The Happier Life* (1972); ed., *New Poems 1972–1973* (1973); ed., *A Choice of Byron's Verse* (1974); *Love or Nothing* (1974); ed., *Two Decades of Irish Writing* (1974); ed., *Selected Poems of Delmore Schwartz* (1976); *Barbarians* (1979); ed., *The Poetry of Scotland* (1979); *St Kilda's Parliament* (1981)

REFERENCE: D. Abse, ed., *Corgi Modern Poets in Focus 1* (London, 1971)

Dunnett (née Halliday], **Dorothy** (*b* 1923). Novelist. She was born on 25 August 1923 in Dunfermline, Fife. Her early career was in the Civil Service in Edinburgh, where she worked as a press secretary. On 17 September 1946 she married Alistair Dunnett (*b* 1908), the editor of THE SCOTSMAN. As a portrait painter she has exhibited at the ROYAL SCOTTISH ACADEMY and she is a member of the Scottish Society of Women Artists. She has written several successful detective novels under the name 'Dorothy Halliday', but she remains best known for her saga cycle of novels set in the 16th century and centred on the adventures of the fabulous Scots mercenary Francis Crawford of Lymond and Sevigny. Six novels chart his Don Juanish wanderings in Europe – *Game of Kings* (1961), *Queen's Play* (1964), *The Disorderly Knights* (1966), *Pawn in Frankincense* (1969), *The Ringed Castle* (1971) and *Checkmate* (1975) – and in each, romance is the central fictional motif. Crawford is a vexed hero figure, conscious that, however brilliant he may be, disaster overtakes those who are drawn to him. In his manifest awareness of his own destiny we find many of the elements that torment the life of James Durie in Stevenson's THE MASTER OF BALLANTRAE, and Dorothy Dunnett's cycle of novels is central to the tradition of the historical romance in Scottish fiction.

WORKS: *Game of Kings* (1961); *Queen's Play* (1964); *The Disorderly Knights* (1966); *Pawn in Frankincense* (1969); *The Ringed Castle* (1971); *Checkmate* (1975); *King Hereafter* (1982)
as Dorothy Halliday: *Dolly and the Singing Bird* (1968); *Dolly and the Cookie Bird* (1970); *Dolly and the Doctor Bird* (1971); *Dolly and the Starry Bird* (1973); *Dolly and the Nanny Bird* (1976); *Dolly and the Bird of Paradise* (1983)

Duns Scotus, Johannes (*fl* 1280). Philosopher. He was born in Maxton, Roxburghshire and he entered the Franciscan order in Dumfries in 1278. He lectured at Oxford and Paris and is thought to have died in 1308 in Cologne. His philosophy embraced the doctrine that universal matter is the common basis of all existence, which was in direct opposition to St Thomas Aquinas's reconciliation of the truths of Aristotelian philosophy with Christian doctrine. During his lifetime scholars were divided in their support of Scotists or Realists and Thomists or Nominalists, but by the 16th century Duns Scotus's philosophy had been discredited and Dunsmen or Dunses gave their name to 'dunce': 'an adherent of Duns Scotus; a hair-splitting reasoner, a cavilling sophist', hence 'one who shows no capacity for learning; a dullard, blockhead' (*OED*).

E

Eachann Bacach (*fl* 1650). Poet in the service of the Macleans of Duart. Very little is known about his life. Only seven of his poems have survived and all are concerned with praise of the Macleans, especially of the 16th chief, Sir Lachlann, whose death in April 1648 is lamented in 'A' chnò Shamhana' ('The Hallowe'en nut'), and his son, Sir Eachann, who was killed at the Battle of Inverkeithing in 1651. The poems have been collected in *Bàrdachd Chloinn Ghill-Eathain* (1979) edited by Colm O Baoill for the SCOTTISH GAELIC TEXTS SOCIETY.

Easy Club. A social club for debating political and literary matters, founded on 12 May 1712 by ALLAN RAMSAY and a group of his acquaintances. Each of the 12 members was expected to adopt a literary pseudonym, Ramsay's being 'Isaac Bickerstaff', after Jonathan Swift's fictional creation, although it was later changed to the more patriotic 'Gawin Douglas'. The club had sentimental, Jacobite leanings and Ramsay was its 'poet laureate'.

Edina. A poetic name for Edinburgh, first used by GEORGE BUCHANAN in the 16th century and later taken up by countless poets, including ROBERT BURNS in 'Address to Edinburgh' and Lord BYRON in *English Bards and Scotch Reviewers*.

Edinburgh. The capital city of Scotland. Edinburgh was established first as a military base in the 2nd century by the Votadini or Goddodin tribe, who gave it the name 'Din Eidin' ('the fortress on the hill'). During the 7th century it was held for a time by King Edwin of Northumbria but the first mention of the city as a place of importance comes during the reign of MALCOLM III (Malcolm Canmore) in the 11th century. In 1329 the city was granted a royal charter by ROBERT I (Robert the Bruce), and later the STEWART kings made it their capital and the principal centre of law and the church. Edinburgh is dominated by the castle rock and the long sweep of its ridge, which leads to the palace of HOLYROODHOUSE and on which stands its medieval foundations; to the north of this is the 18th- and early 19th-century New Town, planned from a design by JAMES CRAIG.

Printing has been a traditional industry in Edinburgh since the 16th century when the first printing press in Scotland was established by WALTER CHAPMAN in 1507. In 1579 THOMAS BASSENDYNE and ALEXANDER ARBUTHNOT (i) produced the first Bible to be printed in Scotland; the availability of books made an important contribution to the SCOTTISH ENLIGHTENMENT of the 18th century. During that period and in the early 19th century many booksellers such as WILLIAM BLACKWOOD and ADAM BLACK became publishers, and for a few years Edinburgh was an important literary centre, publishing the *Edinburgh Review (see* EDINBURGH REVIEW (ii)), BLACKWOOD'S MAGAZINE and TAIT'S EDINBURGH MAGAZINE among many others. Theatre, too, has been associated with Edinburgh: firstly with the production in August 1554 of Sir David Lyndsay's ANE PLEASANT SATYRE OF THE THRIE ESTAITIS and secondly its promotion in the 18th century by ALLAN RAMSAY. Both the theatre and publishing are enjoying a revival in the last quarter of the 20th century.

A significant number of writers have been associated with the city, among whom may be mentioned WILLIAM DUNBAR, GAVIN DOUGLAS, WILLIAM DRUMMOND of Hawthornden, GEORGE BUCHANAN, Allan Ramsay, ROBERT FERGUSSON, ROBERT BURNS, Sir WALTER SCOTT, HENRY THOMAS Lord COCKBURN, ROBERT LOUIS STEVENSON, SYDNEY GOODSIR SMITH and ROBERT GARIOCH SUTHERLAND.

REFERENCE: T. Royle, *Precipitous City: the Story of Literary Edinburgh* (Edinburgh, 1980)

Edinburgh, High School of. The grammar school of Edinburgh. It was probably founded in the 13th century, though there is no official record of its existence until a town council minute of 11 April 1519. Latin was the central subject in the school's curriculum and during the 18th century its classics classes were taught by the rector, ALEXANDER ADAM, and Luke Fraser, both of whom instructed some of the leading figures of their day. The school was housed in the Yards near the Cowgate until 1829, when it moved to Thomas Hamilton's classical building in Regent Road beneath Calton Hill. Over the centuries the High School has educated many leading scholars and writers, including WILLIAM DRUMMOND of Hawthornden, JAMES BOSWELL, DUGALD STEWART, Sir WALTER SCOTT, FRANCIS JEFFREY and HENRY THOMAS Lord COCKBURN. The title 'Schola regia edimburgensis' was given to the school by JAMES VI. The school is now in modern buildings in the suburb of Barnton.

Edinburgh Evening Courant. A newspaper first published in Edinburgh on 15 December 1718 and printed by William Browne, James Mosman and James McEuan, who had taken over the circulating library founded by ALLAN RAMSAY. Between 1732 and 1783 the *Courant* was owned by Robert Fleming who sold it to David Ramsay. The *Courant* was anti-Jacobite and pro-government and during the early 19th century it enjoyed a pre-eminent reputation for publishing news at the same time as the London press. The first known editor was George Huoy, who was succeeded between 1827 and 1848 by David Buchanan, who had come from the CALEDONIAN MERCURY. The newspaper's other editors were, in turn, JOSEPH ROBERTSON, William Buchanan and JAMES HANNAY, who altered the name to *Daily Courant* in 1860. During the Derby–Disraeli administration of the 1860s the *Courant* was a powerful supporter of the Tory party, and it was bought by an English financier Charles Wescomb to further that cause. The last owner was George Dominy and on 6 February 1886 it was amalgamated with the *Glasgow News* to form a new newspaper, *The Scottish News*. The editors after Hannay were: Francis Espinasse, James

Scot Henderson, James Mure and W. R. Lawson.

Edinburgh Review (i). A magazine published in Edinburgh from January 1755, of which only two numbers appeared, the second in July of the same year. Its intentions were to give 'an account of all the books and pamphlets that have been published in Scotland from the first of January to the first of July 1755. To each number will be added an Appendix, giving an account of the books published in England and other countries that are most worthy of notice.' The magazine contained the first known published work of ADAM SMITH and WILLIAM ROBERTSON.

Edinburgh Review (ii). A literary magazine first published by ARCHIBALD CONSTABLE on 10 October 1802. It was founded by an editorial triumvirate of Sydney Smith (1771–1845), Francis Horner (1778–1817) and FRANCIS JEFFREY for the purpose of providing a forum for the debate of literary and political matters. According to Jeffrey's biographer, Lord Cockburn, the editors' intention was to capture in print 'the irrepressible passion for discussion which succeeded the fall of old systems on the French Revolution'. The first issue quickly sold out its edition of 750 copies and proved to Constable that there was a market for the review article. The *Edinburgh Review* set the standard that later 19th-century literary magazines had to follow: its anonymous reviewers were paid for their essays which ranged over a variety of literary, political and scientific subjects.

In May 1803 Jeffrey was appointed sole editor at a salary of £300 per year, and he gave the post a previously unheard of dignity and power. He remained editor until 1829 and under his rule the *Edinburgh Review* became the most influential magazine and arbiter of literary taste in Britain and Europe. HENRY PETER BROUGHAM became a close adviser and Jeffrey attracted to the magazine most of the leading writers of the period. Nevertheless, he was a tepid reviewer and a supporter of the conventional, who attempted to quash public interest in the Lake school of poets; he is best remembered for his infamous remark on Wordsworth's long poem *The Excursion* in November 1814, 'This will never do!', for his attack on MARMION by Sir WALTER SCOTT; and for publishing the acid review of Byron's early poems that led to the rejoinder *English Bards and Scotch Reviewers*, a satirical poem in heroic couplets, in 1808 (*see* BYRON, GEORGE GORDON NOEL).

After Jeffrey's period the *Edinburgh Review* lost its place of influence and by the time of its demise in 1929 it was a spent force with only its title a reminder of its past glories. The first copies carried a blue and yellow cover to signify its allegiance to the Whig Party and its colours gave the magazine its nickname 'THE BLUE AND YELLOW'.

REFERENCE: J. Clive, *The Scotch Reviewers: the Edinburgh Review, 1802–1815* (London, 1957)

Eglintoun, Sir **Hew** (*d* 1376). Statesman. He is mentioned as a poet in 'Lament for the Makaris' by WILLIAM DUNBAR as 'gude Sir Hew of Eglintoun'. He was a native of Ayrshire and a kinsman of the nephew of David II, Robert the Steward, who succeeded to the throne of Scotland as Robert II in 1371. Under his patronage Sir Hew enjoyed a close relationship to the royal household and was appointed an Auditor of the Exchequer, in which post his colleague was the poet JOHN BARBOUR. Eglintoun's personal wealth, his interest in chivalry and his prestige at court are factors that have associated his name with that of the poet HUCHOWNE OF THE AWLE RYALE (Huchon, or Hugh, of the king's palace), but there is little evidence to support the identification of the two. No poetry by Sir Hew is known to survive.

For references *see* HUCHOWNE OF THE AWLE RYALE.

Eildon Hills. Three hills near the Border town of Melrose, formed by the remnants of plutonic rock from the end of the Devonian system. According to tradition, recounted by, among others, JAMES HOGG in *The Three Perils of Man*, the Eildon Hills were originally one unbroken hill which was twisted into three parts by the astrologer MICHAEL SCOTT (i). The area is rich in literary association and the view of the hills from the road which leads from ABBOTSFORD to Dryburgh Abbey was reputed to be Sir Walter Scott's favourite. THOMAS OF ERCELDOUNE is supposed to have met the Queen of Elfland 'down by the Eildon tree'. In the neighbouring Melrose Abbey, a Cistercian foundation of 1136, lies buried the heart of ROBERT I (Robert the Bruce), and it is

also one of the reputed burial places of Michael Scott.

Elliot, Jean of Minto (1727–1805). Songwriter. She is best remembered for her composition of the moving lament for the dead of the BATTLE OF FLODDEN, THE FLOWERS OF THE FOREST. Other versions of this well-known song were written during her lifetime, including one by ALISON COCKBURN, but the song may well have existed in traditional form before it was reworked by songwriters in the 18th century. Jean Elliot was the daughter of Sir Gilbert Elliot of Minto, the Lord Justice Clerk for Scotland, and she is supposed to have written *The Flowers of the Forest* at her brother's instigation. Her version is generally considered to be the most durable and beautiful, but when it was first published she disowned her part in its composition; none of Jean Elliot's other work has survived. She died on 29 March 1805.

Encyclopaedia Britannica. The *Encyclopaedia Britannica* has its beginnings in the interest created by the appearance in 1751 of the first parts of Denis Diderot's *Encyclopédie*. Originally intended as a translation of the *Cyclopaedia* of 1708 by Ephraim Chambers (*d* 1740), the French *Encyclopédie* became, under Diderot's direction, more than just a repository of general knowledge. Voltaire and Rousseau were among the contributors, and its editorial stance reflected the general aims of the European Enlightenment – to espouse rational thinking and to dismiss faith and superstition. Its publication created a new interest in books of reference that would help to explain the spirit of the age.

Determined to share the newly available market, three Edinburgh printers, Andrew Bell, Colin MacFarquhar and WILLIAM SMELLIE, issued a prospectus in 1768 for an *Encyclopaedia Britannica*, which would contain lengthy essays on the arts and sciences, each subject being listed under its proper denomination. To Smellie fell the task of editing the work, and in the event he wrote most of the articles, which demonstrate that love of plain expression that was a hallmark of the prose style of the *literati* of the SCOTTISH ENLIGHTENMENT. Bell and MacFarquhar were responsible for providing the necessary funds and they achieved this by raising a subscription list of a

'Society of Gentlemen in Scotland'.

The encyclopaedia was published serially from December 1768, with the first bound volume, 'Aa to Bzo', appearing in 1769. 'Caaba to Lythrum' was published in 1770, and 'Macao to Zyglophyllum' in 1771. It ran to 2659 pages, included 160 copper-plate illustrations and the entire set cost £12. Smellie intended that the work should reach as wide a public as possible and his editorial objectives were stated in the Preface: 'Utility ought to be the principal intention of every publication. Wherever this intention does not plainly appear, neither the books nor the authors have the smallest claim to the approbation of mankind.'

A second edition was published in 1777–84 under the editorial control of JAMES TYTLER, a brilliant eccentric, whose radical political views forced him to flee from Edinburgh in 1793. The revised and enlarged edition ran to ten volumes and included historical and biographical essays. Bell, who had assumed full control of the project, then put in hand a third edition. This was published in 15 volumes between 1788 and 1797 and was dedicated to George III. In 1812 ARCHIBALD CONSTABLE purchased the rights to the work and, through his astute dealings, was able to attract as contributors to the encyclopaedia's supplements many of the leading writers and thinkers of the day. On the collapse of his business in 1826 the undertaking was sold to another Edinburgh publisher ADAM BLACK and it remained with his firm until 1898.

In the hands of an alliance between the American publishers James Clark and *The Times* newspaper the encyclopaedia was marketed through mass advertising and by the expedient of payment by instalments. Cambridge University Press published the *Encyclopaedia Britannica* between 1910 and 1922, when an independent publishing house was established to control the work and its future editions. A fourteenth edition appeared in 1929 and since then a system of continuous revision has replaced the publication of complete new editions. Although the work has altered dramatically in size and scope, its editors have not lost sight of William Smellie's intention that knowledge should be presented to the reader in a clear and concise way, and that the authors should then receive 'the approbation of mankind'.

Eneados. The translation of Virgil's *Aeneid* into Middle Scots made by GAVIN DOUGLAS in 1513 and first printed in 1553 by William Copland of London. The prologues to each of the 13 books contain some of Douglas's best original work.

Entail, The. A novel by JOHN GALT, published in three volumes in 1823, with the subtitle 'The Lairds of Grippy'. At the novel's centre is the monstrous creation of Claud Walkinshaw, a character ready to delude others and himself to satisfy his own insatiable greed. Having spent most of his life building up a small fortune in Glasgow, he returns to his native Ayrshire, intent on recovering the lands lost by his grandfather during the time of the DARIEN SCHEME. To achieve his aims he marries the daughter of the estate of Plealands, purchases the lands of Grippy which he entails on his eldest son, Charles, and then arranges for Plealands to be left to his half-witted 'natural' son, Watty. This gross act of disinheritance allows him to combine the estates, but the result of his legal machinations is a series of domestic disasters. Charles makes an ill-advised match, Watty marries but his wife dies in childbirth leaving a daughter, and he himself is declared insane. On the point of death Claud attempts to undo some of the mischief but he is succeeded by an equally ruthless third son. At this, the lowest point in the tale, Leddy Grippy, Claud's widow, comes into her own, asserts her rights and the novel ends with the restoration of the inheritance to Charles's son, the legal heir.

Although *The Entail* relates the bleak downfall of a family, ensnared by the overreaching greed of its head, Galt was also at pains to present the common humanity of characters like Watty with his simple innocence and Leddy Grippy with her shrewd ability to turn her own shortcomings to her own use. In this novel Galt was writing at the height of his powers in describing the transition of West of Scotland society and the basis of their economy; and if he displays an obsession with the past he also examines ruthlessly enduring Scottish character traits. Claud Walkinshaw's acquisitive and overbearing nature stands comparison with that of Adam Weir in WEIR OF HERMISTON by ROBERT LOUIS STEVENSON, or of John Gourlay in THE HOUSE WITH THE GREEN SHUTTERS by GEORGE DOUGLAS BROWN. The novel is also to be admired for Galt's handling of Scots dialogue and for his subtle shifts of emphasis in assigning particular vernaculars to his characters.

Epistles of Robert Burns. ROBERT BURNS wrote 21 verse epistles to various friends and acquaintances which are important for an understanding of his personal philosophy and his poetic art. The earliest, 'Epistle to John Rankin' was written as an earthy account of Burns's affair with Elizabeth Paton. Although Burns used the STANDARD HABBIE form in most of the epistles, the metre used in 'Epistle to Davie, a brother poet' is an adaptation of a traditional Scots stanza used by ALEXANDER MONTGOMERIE in THE CHERRIE AND THE SLAE, which had been reprinted in the CHOICE COLLECTION OF COMIC AND SERIOUS SCOTS POEMS (1706–11) by JAMES WATSON and in THE EVER GREEN (1724) by ALLAN RAMSAY. 'Davie' was DAVID SILLAR, a member of the Tarbolton BACHELORS' CLUB and an early friend. The poem is remarkable both for its atmospheric description of winter in the opening stanzas and for Burns's exposition of a Rousseau-like ideal of freedom and natural poverty.

More representative of Burns's style are his three epistles to JOHN LAPRAIK, two of which were printed in the KILMARNOCK EDITION of the poems in 1786. In these brief conversational poems Burns linked himself with the Scots folk tradition and with Allan Ramsay and ROBERT FERGUSSON: 'O for a spunk o' Allan's glee,/Or Fergusson's the bauld an' slee'. These themes are taken up again in 'Epistle to William Simpson of Ochiltree', which also paints the familiar natural minutiae of Burns's native countryside. Two contrasting poems are 'Epistle to James Smith', in which Burns celebrates the iconoclasm of youth and castigates the worshippers of Mammon, and 'Epistle to a Young Friend' (Andrew, the son of ROBERT AIKEN), a clear statement of Burns's concept of personal honour and virtue.

In all the epistles Burns was able to dramatize his own conflicting feelings about life and his personal philosophy, and to give expression to them in verses which figure amongst his best work. The other epistles are: 'Epistle to William Creech', 'Epistle to Alexander Cunningham', 'Second Epistle to Davie', 'Epistle to Alexander Findlater', 'Epistle to John Goldie', 'Epistle to Capt. Adam Gordon', 'Epistle to Robt. Graham Esq., on the Election', 'Epistle to Captain William Logan', 'Epistle to John

McAdam', 'Epistle to Hugh Parker', 'Epistle to John Renton', 'Epistle to William Stewart' and 'Epistle to Mr. Tytler'.

Erceldoune, Thomas of. *See* THOMAS OF ERCELDOUNE.

Erskine, Ralph (1685–1752). Poet and clergyman. He was born on 15 March 1685 at Monilaws, Northumberland, and was educated at the University of Edinburgh. After working as a tutor for his uncle in Fife he was ordained on 7 August 1711 in Dunfermline. With his brother Ebenezer he was part of the 'Marrow' secession from the Church of Scotland in 1721 and subsequently he became friendly with the English Methodists Wesley and Whitefield. Erskine produced a popular collection of religious verses, *Gospel Sonnets*, a paraphrase of the *Song of Solomon* (1738), a new version of the book of *Lamentations* (1750) and a collection of Job's hymns. His *Scripture Songs*, written for use in public worship, were collected in 1754. He died on 9 November 1752 in Dunfermline.

WORKS: *The Believer's Dowry* (1708); *A Congratulatory Poem on the Coronation of His Majesty King George* (1714); *Gospel Canticles* (1720); *The Best Bond* (1724); *The Harmony of Divine Attributes* (1724); *Law Death, Gospel Life* (1724); *Christ the People's Covenant* (1725); *The Comer's Conflict* (1736); *God's Great Name* (1737); *Gospel Sonnets* (1738); *Song of Songs* (1738); *The Best Match* (1739); *The Gospel Confession* (1739); *The Great Ruin* (1739); *Chambers of Safety in Times of Danger* (1740); *The Fountainhead of All Blessings* (1740); *The Giving Love of Christ* (1740); *The Main Question of Gospel Catechism* (1741); *Faith no Fancy* (1745); *Heaven Pos'd and Prais'd* (1746); *Christ's Treasures Opened by Himself* (1747); *Clean Water* (1747); *The Best Security for the Best Life* (1750); *Book of Lamentations* (1750); *Scripture Songs* (1754); *Preventing Love* (1764); *Redemption by Christ* (1772); *The Gradual Conquest* (1782); *The Rent Veil* (1782); *The Happy Hour of Christ's Quickening Voice* (1789); *The Believer's Principles* (1811); *The World's Verdict on Christ* (1818); *Gospel Catechism* (1826); *Faith's Warrant* (1830); *Hints on the Lord's Supper* (1830); *The Gathering of the People to Shiloh* (1857)

REFERENCE: J. L. Watson, *The Life of Ralph Erskine* (Edinburgh, 1882)

Ettrick Shepherd, the. Pen-name of JAMES HOGG.

Ever Green, The. A two-volume collection of early and Middle Scots poetry made by ALLAN RAMSAY and published in 1724. Its full title is *The Ever Green: a Collection of Scots Poems Wrote by the Ingenious before 1600.* Although

Ramsay was permitted to make use of the BANNATYNE MANUSCRIPT by its owner, Lord Hyndford, he chose to bowdlerize many of the texts, anglicizing where he felt elucidation was necessary, changing lines and stanzas and even adding verses of his own composition. Thus two patriotic songs written by Ramsay are attributed to ALEXANDER SCOTT (i) and many poems by WILLIAM DUNBAR are altered almost beyond recognition. As in the companion volume, THE TEA-TABLE MISCELLANY, Ramsay published a number of ballads, including 'The Battle of Harlaw' and 'Johnny Armstrong'. A paradox in Ramsay's editorial policy is that although the collection was made for patriotic reasons he felt it necessary to anglicize much of the 16th-century Scots, thus making a mockery of his Preface: 'When these good old *Bards* wrote, we had not yet made Use of imported Trimming upon our Cloaths, nor of foreign Embroidery in our writings. Their *Poetry* is the Product of their own Country, not pilfered and spoiled in the Transportation from abroad: Their *Images* are native, and their *Landskips* domestick; copied from those Fields and Meadows we every Day Behold.'

Ewen, John (1741–1821). Songwriter. He was a native of Montrose but most of his life was spent in Aberdeen, where he kept a hardware shop. Through his marriage to the daughter of a wealthy Aberdeen manufacturer he prospered, and on his death he was found to have left money to various charities in Aberdeen and Montrose. A long-drawn-out court case, brought by his daughters who challenged his will, ended with his wishes being rescinded in 1830. Ewen was the author of the fishing song *O weel may the boatie row* which was printed by JAMES JOHNSON in THE SCOTS MUSICAL MUSEUM; it was probably based by Ewen on an older fragment.

F

Fables. The most impressive Scottish animal fables are the 13 written by ROBERT HENRYSON. The recasting of Aesop's fables was an accepted part of the medieval Christian tradition and like many other fabulists of his day Henryson wrote the poems on the lives of birds and beasts as allegories in order to provide a pattern for human behaviour set against a Christian *moralitas*. Thus the fables were supposed to describe a world in which animals and birds assumed human characteristics and behaved in a thoroughly human manner. Humour and witty dialogue were as important to the telling of the story as was the heavy underlining of the moral. Henryson wrote within those accepted forms but the inventiveness of his fables lay in his happy ability to mix social observation with a minute and loving description of animal life. The birds and beasts are themselves first and human beings second, so that in 'The Taill of the Uponlandis Mous and the Burges Mous' the mice remain mice and the moral is worked in terms of the facts of their own existence. In all the fables Henryson demonstrated a generosity of spirit and a concern for the well-being of his animals that is absent from other writers of the fable in the same period and is a hallmark of his poetry. The most able exponent of the fable after Henryson is ALLAN RAMSAY although the fables of WILLIAM WILKIE, published in 1768, are not without their charms.

Animal poems are a recognized part of the Scottish literary tradition. Sir DAVID LYNDSAY used the parrot (*Testament and Complaynt of . . . Papyngo*) and the hound (*Complaynt . . . of . . . Bagsche*) as motifs, and WILLIAM DUNBAR, to gain favour at court, employed the image of himself as the honest horse in 'Petition of the Gray Horse, Auld Dumbar'. Mock elegies and testaments uttered by animals became popular in the 18th century, but the poet who most resembles the Henryson of the fables is ROBERT BURNS, who wrote about animals as if they were true companions. His poem 'The Twa Dogs' is an echo of Henryson with its protagonists Caesar and Luath able to comment on the follies of human life while still retaining their canine qualities.

Falconer, William (1732–69). Poet. He was born in Edinburgh, the son of a barber, and most of his life was spent at sea. His experiences as a sailor stood him in good stead when he came to write his long poem *The Shipwreck* (1762); although its love story is conventionally pathetic, the poem is distinguished for its vividly accurate descriptions of a ship at sea and for Falconer's uncanny ability to blend stark realism with a lyrical passion for the sea in all its different moods. As a result of its publication Falconer gained the patronage of the Duke of York and served as a purser in a number of warships of the Royal Navy. He was drowned when the frigate *Aurora* capsized off Cape Town. Other publications of his include his *Universal Marine Dictionary* (1769) and a political satire *The Demagogue* (1764).

WORKS: *A Poem Sacred to the Memory of His Royal Highness, Frederic, Prince of Wales* (1751); *The Shipwreck* (1762); *The Demagogue* (1764); *Universal Marine Dictionary* (1769); *The Poetical Works of William Falconer* (1796)

Fastern's E'en [Bannock Night]. Shrove Tuesday, the day before Lent, which was a period of fasting in the Catholic Church. Fastern's E'en was marked by games and merry-making and a final indulgence in food and drink. It is also known in the north-east as Bannock Night from the custom of preparing bannocks or pancakes for Lent.

Fasti ecclesiae scoticanae. A biographical dictionary of the succession of ministers of the Church of Scotland, which was begun by the

Revd Hew Scott (1791–1872) in the 1820s and was first published in three volumes between 1866 and 1871. In the preparation of his work Scott visited 760 parishes to investigate the records of the Kirk Sessions, Presbyteries and Synods, and the result is an accurate and illuminating work of scholarship. The original intention was to divide the work into Synods and Presbyteries and to list the ministers from the period of the Reformation to June 1839, but Scott later extended that date to include ministers in charges at the time of his completion of the book. After Scott's death the work of updating the *Fasti ecclesiae scoticanae* was undertaken by a committee of the Church of Scotland, who published a further nine volumes between 1915 and 1961.

Ferguson, Adam (1723–1816). Philosopher. He was born on 20 June 1723 in Logierait, Perthshire, where his father was the parish minister. He was educated at home, at the academy in Perth and, from 1739, at the University of St Andrews, taking his degree in 1742. After a year's study in the Divinity Halls of St Andrews and Edinburgh, he acted as a private secretary to Lord Milton before becoming chaplain to the 42nd Highlanders, the Black Watch. In that capacity he fought at the Battle of Fontenoy in 1745. He espoused firm anti-Jacobite views, becoming a supporter of the government during the JACOBITE rebellion of the same year. In 1757 he forswore the chaplaincy of the regiment, having failed in his bid to find patronage from the 7th Duke of Atholl. Through his earlier friendships with men such as JOHN HOME and WILLIAM ROBERTSON, he succeeded DAVID HUME (ii) as librarian of the Advocates' Library, and two years later he was appointed to the Chair of Natural Philosophy in Edinburgh. In 1764 he gave up the teaching of physics to become Professor of Moral Philosophy, a post he held until 1785 when he was succeeded by one of his students, DUGALD STEWART. Following the publication in 1778 of a pamphlet pleading for conciliation with the American colonies, Ferguson was appointed secretary to the British commission sent to Philadelphia to negotiate the final peace treaty; his tenure of the chair at Edinburgh was also interrupted by a Continental tour with Lord Chesterfield in 1773–5.

Ferguson enjoyed the company of Edinburgh's literary society and it was in his house at Sciennes in 1786 that the famous meeting took place between the young WALTER SCOTT and ROBERT BURNS. Ferguson was a founder-member of the POKER CLUB and he was one of the first members of the ROYAL SOCIETY OF EDINBURGH, founded in 1783. Towards the end of his life he travelled on the Continent to pursue his interest in Roman history. His last years were spent farming, first near Peebles and then near St Andrews, where he died on 22 February 1816.

A Gaelic speaker, Ferguson took the side of JAMES MACPHERSON during the OSSIAN controversy and he maintained a correspondence with Macpherson on the possibility of using the Greek alphabet for the printing of Gaelic literature. Of his own publications, Ferguson was perhaps best known during his own lifetime for his *History of the Progress and Termination of the Roman Republic* (1782), which is remarkable for his firm grasp of Roman military theory and tactics. He also published an attack on the government, in the style of Swift, for its refusal to establish a Scottish militia, and several works of philosophy, the most influential being his *Essay on the History of Civil Society* (1766). Ferguson repudiated the teachings of Rousseau and followed instead Montesquieu, believing that the history of man had to be studied in relation to the society and social institutions created by him. Although he never achieved the intellectual standing of his successor, Dugald Stewart, Ferguson was a clear and analytical thinker, possessed of a polished prose style.

WORKS: *The History of the Proceedings in the Case of Margaret, Commonly called Peg, only Sister to John Bull esq* (1761); *Essay on the History of Civil Society* (1766); *Institutes of Moral Philosophy* (1772); *Remarks on a Pamphlet lately Published by Dr Price Entitled 'Observations on the Nature of Civil Liberty'* (1776); *History of the Progress and Termination of the Roman Republic* (1782); *Principles of Moral and Political Science* (1792); *Minutes of the Life and Character of Joseph Black* (1805); *Biographical Sketch of Lieutenant Patrick Ferguson* (1816)

REFERENCES: J. Small, *Biographical Sketch of Adam Ferguson* (Edinburgh, 1864); H. Huth, *Soziale und individualistische Auffassung im 18. Jahrhundert, vornehmlich bei Adam Smith und Adam Ferguson* (Leipzig, 1907); W. C. Lehman, *Adam Ferguson and the Beginnings of Modern Sociology* (New York, 1930); H. H. Jogland, *Ursprünge und Grundlagen der Soziologie bei Adam Ferguson* (Berlin, 1959); D. Kettler, *The Social and Political Thought of Adam Ferguson* (Columbus, Ohio, 1965)

Fergusson, Robert (1750–74). Poet. He was born on 5 September 1750 in Cap and Feather

Close, Edinburgh. His parents had their roots in Aberdeenshire and in 1748 had come to live in Edinburgh, where his father, William, worked as a solicitor's clerk. Fergusson was educated privately and at the HIGH SCHOOL OF EDINBURGH, and in 1762 he was awarded a bursary to study at the High School of Dundee. He remained there until 1765 when he matriculated at the University of St Andrews. While at St Andrews he started writing poetry and he displayed a gift for satire, the comic 'Elegy on the Death of Mr David Gregory, late Professor of Mathematics in the University of St Andrews' being a good example of his early ability.

Fergusson left the University in May 1768 without taking a degree, and returned to Edinburgh where he was employed in the lowly position of clerk in the Commissary Office. His father's death in 1767 had left him as the only means of financial support for his mother and sister, and for the rest of his short life he remained in the unrewarding occupation of copying legal papers for testamentary and matrimonial cases. He did have time to indulge his interest in the theatre and he became a friend of one of the best-known singers of his day, Giusto Ferdinando Tenducci, who introduced three of Fergusson's songs into his production of Thomas Arnes's opera *Artaxerxes*.

On 7 February 1771 Fergusson's first poems were published by WALTER RUDDIMAN in THE WEEKLY MAGAZINE, OR EDINBURGH AMUSEMENT: 'Morning', 'Noon' and 'Night', three elegiacs in the pastoral style of William Shenstone and Thomas Gray. These were followed by a further set of undistinguished poems in English, but by the beginning of the following year Fergusson had turned from English and was writing in Scots. In January 1772 Ruddiman published 'The Daft Days', a celebration of winter festivities, written in a rigorous, self-confident Scots. It was followed that year by a succession of poems in Scots that attracted attention and praise: 'Elegy on the Death of Scots Music' in March, 'The King's Birthday in Edinburgh' in June, 'Caller Oysters' and 'Braid Claith' in October, and 'To the Tron Kirk Bell' in November. The subject matter of his poems had changed too, from pastoral Arcadia to the matter of the bustling city of Edinburgh.

In Fergusson's lifetime the city of Edinburgh was mainly confined to the tall tenements and narrow wynds of the Royal Mile where the taverns and drinking clubs were the centre of the city's social life. In October 1772 Fergusson became a member of the CAPE CLUB, a convivial debating club which met in a number of taverns in the city. Following the custom of the club, Fergusson took a pseudonym 'Sir Precenter'; among his friends and fellow members were the antiquary DAVID HERD and the artist ALEXANDER RUNCIMAN. Through the Cape Club's activities Fergusson gained encouragement for his poetry and for his vivid pictures of contemporary Edinburgh life. Throughout 1773 he continued to publish with *The Weekly Magazine* and a collection of poems was issued by Ruddiman who continued to be the poet's greatest patron. Fergusson's long poem *Auld Reekie* (*see* AULD REEKIE (ii)), written in praise of Edinburgh was printed independently that same year. The last poem to be printed during Fergusson's lifetime 'Codicile to Rob Fergusson's Last Will' appeared in *The Weekly Magazine* of 23 December 1773.

Illness and acute depression forced Fergusson to leave the Commissary Office in December 1773. Although fellow members of the Cape Club rallied to his support, his condition deteriorated in July 1774 after he fell down a flight of stairs, and he was removed to the Edinburgh Bedlam where he died in conditions of neglect on 17 October 1774.

Fergusson left 33 poems in Scots and some 50 in English. Immediately after his death his reputation was confined to his circle of friends in Edinburgh but later he was considered to be a seminal influence on the poetry of ROBERT BURNS, who raised a gravestone to him in the Canongate Churchyard, addressing him as 'my elder brother in misfortune, by far my elder brother in the muse'. Burns's debt to Fergusson can be seen in a comparison of their festive and domestic poems, comic addresses and nature poems, but more importantly, Fergusson gave Burns the confidence and freedom to write in a colloquial, self-expressive Scots. Fergusson's language is basically the Edinburgh dialect with words and idioms from rural Aberdeenshire. Of his poems in English, most of which are written in imitation of his Augustan contemporaries, only the autobiographical 'The Author's Life' and 'Rob Fergusson's Last Will' are of much interest.

Fergusson's favourite and most effective stanza was STANDARD HABBIE, but he did not allow his verse to fall into comic vernacular parochialism. His 'Elegy on the Death of Scots Music' invites comparison with classical Augustan poetry and in poems such as 'To the Tron Kirk Bell' and 'Hallow Fair' he extended the range of Standard Habbie to more serious subjects. Like his predecessor ALLAN RAMSAY, Fergusson also had a patriotic intention in writing in Scots. His prejudices in favour of Scotland are wittily expressed in the epistle 'To the Principal and Professors of the University of St Andrews on their Superb Treat to Dr Samuel Johnson', where he imagines a feast of Scottish delicacies served to the distinguished Scotophobe, and 'The Ghaists: an Eclogue', in which the ghost of George Heriot and George Watson, two Edinburgh benefactors, bemoan the London government's decision under the Martmain Bill to transfer private trusts to government control.

In his Edinburgh poems Fergusson caught the city in all its different moods and he observed contemporary city life with a sharp and at times satirical eye. 'Caller Oysters' describes the congenial world of tavern life in midwinter, 'Hallow Fair' and 'Leith Races' paint vivid pictures of holiday crowds, and 'The Rising of the Session' is a keen satire on Edinburgh's legal life. 'Auld Reekie', the first part of a planned comedy of Edinburgh life, is his finest Edinburgh poem, offering an evocative panorama of the city, its citizens and its low life.

WORKS: *Poems* (1773); *Auld Reekie: a Poem* (1773); *A Poem to the Memory of John Cunningham* (1773); ed. W. Ruddiman, *Poems on Various Subjects* (1779)

EDITIONS: D. Irving, ed., *The Poetical Works of Robert Fergusson* (Glasgow, 1800); A. B. Grosart, ed., *The Works of Robert Fergusson* (London, 1851); W. E. Gillies, ed., *Unpublished Poems of Robert Fergusson* (Edinburgh, 1855); M. P. McDiarmid, ed., *Poems of Robert Fergusson*, 2 vols., STS (Edinburgh and London, 1947–56)

REFERENCE: S. G. Smith, *Robert Fergusson: Essays by Various Hands to Commemorate the Bicentenary of his Birth* (Edinburgh, 1952); A. H. Maclaine, *Robert Fergusson* (New York, 1965); D. Daiches, *Robert Fergusson* (Edinburgh, 1982)

Ferrier, J(ames) F(rederick) (1808–64). Philosopher. He was born on 16 June 1808 in Edinburgh, the son of a solicitor. His aunt was the novelist SUSAN EDMONSTOUNE FERRIER, and his mother was a sister of JOHN WILSON (iii) the novelist and editor who wrote under the pseudonym of 'Christopher North'. Ferrier was educated at the HIGH SCHOOL OF EDINBURGH, going from there to the University of Edinburgh, Magdalen College, Oxford, and Heidelberg in Germany. He was called to the Scottish Bar but never practised law, preferring instead to devote himself to literature and metaphysics. From 1842 to 1845 he was Professor of Civil History at Edinburgh, and between 1845 and his death on 11 June 1864 he held the Chair of Political Economy at St Andrews. Ferrier maintained that a deity lay at the centre of the universe, an argument put forward in his main work, *Introduction to the Philosophy of Consciousness* (1838–9), and one that he shared with George Berkeley (1685–1753), whose idealist philosophy he interpreted in *Berkeley and Idealism* (1842). Ferrier also edited the collected works of his father-in-law, John Wilson.

WORKS: *Introduction to the Philosophy of Consciousness*, 3 vols. (1838–9); *Berkeley and Idealism* (1842); *Observations on Church and State* (1848); *Institutes of Metaphysics* (1854); ed., *The Works of Professor Wilson*, 12 vols. (1855–8); *Scottish Philosophy Old and New* (1856); *Lectures on Greek Philosophy* (1866)

REFERENCE: E. S. Haldane, *James Frederick Ferrier* (Edinburgh, 1899)

Ferrier, Susan Edmonstoune (1782–1854). Novelist. She was born on 7 September 1782 in Edinburgh. Her Father, James Ferrier, was a WRITER TO THE SIGNET and the legal agent of the Duke of Argyll. Later he was to became a Principal Clerk to the COURT OF SESSION with Sir WALTER SCOTT. James Ferrier's sister was married to the printer and publisher, WILLIAM SMELLIE. As a child Susan Ferrier enjoyed the social background both of the *literati* in Edinburgh and the aristocracy in Inverary, the seat of the Argylls. In 1800 she moved to London to be with her sister, returning to Edinburgh in 1804 where she settled with her father in Canaan Lane, Morningside. In 1811 she began a friendship with Sir Walter Scott that became increasingly close; her links with the *literati* were increased through her friendship with JOHN LEYDEN and her brother's marriage to Margaret Wilson, the sister of JOHN WILSON (iii) ('Christopher North'). She died on 5 November 1854.

Susan Ferrier wrote three novels, *Marriage* (1818), *The Inheritance* (1824) and *Destiny* (1831), all of which enjoyed a wide popularity. The first two were published anonymously by WILLIAM BLACKWOOD, but following Scott's intervention her last novel was published by Cadell and the copyright sold for £1700. Her

novels show an acute observation of contemporary society, combining humorous satire
with moral statement. *Marriage* is a study of
Scottish provincial manners where marriage is
seen as the end result of a successful social
education. *The Inheritance* is in similar vein,
with its racy humour and rich caricatures, but
her observations on vulgar social aspirations
are more cruelly drawn; worldly inheritance is
contrasted with natural piety, and the heroine,
Gertrude, triumphs by abandoning idolatrous
love and accepting true Christian principles.
More successful is *Destiny*, a romance with a
shrewd characterization of Highland society.

WORKS: *The Marriage* (1818); *Inheritance* (1824);
Destiny (1831)

EDITION: M. Sackville, ed., *The Works of Susan
Ferrier*, 4 vols. (London, 1929)

REFERENCES: A. Grant, *Susan Ferrier: a Biography*
(Denver, Colorado, 1957); W. M. Parker, *Susan
Ferrier* (London, 1965)

Findlater, Jane (1866–1946). Novelist. She
was born on 4 November 1866 at Lochearnhead, Perthshire, daughter of a minister of
the Free Church of Scotland. Like her sister
MARY FINDLATER, she was educated at home, and
the two sisters were to remain lifelong
companions and collaborators. Following the
death of her father in 1886 she moved with her
family to Prestonpans, East Lothian, but the
success of her first novel *The Green Graves of
Balgowrie* (1896) offered financial security and
enabled the family to live in Devon and later in
London, Rye and Comrie in Perthshire, where
she died on 20 May 1946.

The accuracy of her backgrounds and her
ability to draw rounded characters are hallmarks of Jane Findlater's fiction and her best
novel, *The Green Graves of Balgowrie,* set in the
18th century, was based on family papers and
stories. Her other novels, which are equally
well told are *A Daughter of Strife* (1897),
Rachel (1899), *The Story of a Mother* (1902)
and *The Ladder to the Stars* (1906). She also
wrote two collections of short stories, *Seven
Scots Stories* (1912) and *A Green Grass Widow*
(1921), and her essays were collected in *Stones
from a Glass House* (1904). She collaborated
with her sister, Kate Douglas Wiggin and
'Allan McAulay' (the pseudonym of the novelist Charlotte Stewart) in the production of two
long, uneven novels. By far the sisters' greatest
achievement was the novel *Crossriggs*, which

they wrote together and published in 1908. A
romance of upper-class manners, the novel is a
light-hearted and frequently humorous examination of village life and is made memorable by
its gallery of well-drawn characters, especially
the heroine Alex Hope. This was followed by
the equally successful collaborations *Penny
Monypenny* (1911) and *Beneath the Visiting
Moon* (1923). By the 1920s the artificial Victorian world – similar to that created by MAR-
GARET OLIPHANT, whose work that of the
sisters resembles – was a thing of the past, and
the Findlaters' novels, rooted in the forgotten
manners of that age, passed with it into obscurity.

WORKS: *The Green Graves of Balgowrie* (1896); *A
Daughter of Strife* (1897); *Rachel* (1899); *The Story of
a Mother* (1902); *Stones from a Glass House* (1904);
All that Happened in a Week (1905); *The Ladder to the
Stars* (1906); *Seven Scots Stories* (1912); *A Green
Grass Widow and Other Stories* (1921)
  with Mary Findlater: *Tales that are Told* (1901);
Crossriggs (1908); *Penny Monypenny* (1911); *Con-
tent with Flies* (1916); *Seen and Heard Before and After
1914* (1916); *Beneath the Visiting Moon* (1923)
  with Mary Findlater, Kate Douglas Wiggin and
Allan McAulay: *The Affair at the Inn* (1904);
Robinetta (1911)

REFERENCE: E. Mackenzie, *The Findlater Sisters: Literature and Friendship* (London, 1964)

Findlater, Mary (1865–1963). Novelist. She
was born on 26 March 1865 at Lochearnhead,
Perthshire, the daughter of a minister of the
Free Church of Scotland. Her sister JANE FIND-
LATER was also a novelist and her lifelong
companion and collaborator. The sisters were
educated at home but on the death of their
father in 1886 they moved to live in Prestonpans, East Lothian. The success of Jane's first
novel *The Green Graves of Balgowrie* (1896)
enabled the family to live in Devon where they
remained until the outbreak of World War I,
when they chose to live in London. After a stay
in Rye, they lived in Comrie, Perthshire,
where Mary died on 22 November 1963.

Although she lacked her sister's ability to
draw realistic characters and to evoke social
backgrounds, Mary's own novels, which are
well-told comedies of manners, are not without their merits. *The Rose of Joy* (1903) debates
the relative values of marriage, and is saved
from over-seriousness by her ability to draw on
life's absurdities. Besides other novels, she
wrote one collection of verse, *Songs and Sonnets* (1895). With Jane she collaborated in the
writing of three novels and two collections of

short stories and they wrote *The Affair at the Inn* (1904) and *Robinetta* (1911) with Kate Douglas Wiggin and 'Allan McAulay' (the pseudonym of the novelist Charlotte Stewart).

WORKS: *Songs and Sonnets* (1895); *Over the Hills* (1897); *Betty Musgrave* (1899); *A Narrow Way* (1901); *The Rose of Joy* (1903); *A Blind Bird's Nest* (1907); *Tents of a Night* (1914)
with Jane Findlater: *Tales that are Told* (1901); *Crossriggs* (1908); *Penny Monypenny* (1911); *Content with Flies* (1916); *Seen and Heard Before and After 1914* (1916); *Beneath the Visiting Moon* (1923)
with Jane Findlater, Kate Douglas Wiggin and Allan McAulay: *The Affair at the Inn* (1904); *Robinetta* (1911)

REFERENCE: E. Mackenzie, *The Findlater Sisters: Literature and Friendship* (London, 1964)

Fingal. The name given by JAMES MACPHERSON in his OSSIAN poems to the principal hero, the son of the giant Comhal, King of Morven (in present-day Argyll). In *Fingal* the hero crosses to Ireland to aid Cuthullin against the invading Norse king Swaran. His adventures were continued in *Temora*, and throughout the cycle (which also includes the *Fragments* published in 1760) Fingal is presented as a defender of the oppressed and the poor. Fingal is based on the Irish hero-warrior Finn Mac Coul but the events of the Ossian poems are different in time and place from those of the Irish Fenian cycle. There are several place names in Scotland connected with Fingal, in particular Fingal's Cave on the Isle of Staffa, which is described by Sir WALTER SCOTT in *Lord of the Isles*, canto iv.

Finlay, Ian Hamilton (*b* 1925). Poet. He was born on 28 October 1925 in Nassau, in the Bahamas, but was brought up in Scotland. Since 1969 he has lived at Dunsyre, Lanarkshire, where the principal holding of his creative work is kept. In the 1960s he became known by the somewhat confining title of 'concrete' poet or artist. His work has a strong visual element and is executed on different materials such as stone or wood. The creations frequently echo man's relationship to nature in the apparent simplicity of an epigram, and Finlay has taken as his themes natural scenery, the sea and fishing, and images derived from World War II. His early collections of poems, *The Dancers Inherit the Party* (1960), *Glasgow Beasts and a Bird* (1961) and *Concertina* (1962), show Finlay's wit and brevity of style and also his movement towards visual involve-

ment and economy of language. A large number of Finlay's poems have been printed as posters or postcards and published under his Wild Hawthorn Press imprint. Between 1961 and 1970 he edited with Sue Finlay *Poor. Old. Tired. Horse.*, a magazine devoted to 'concrete' poetry, and in 1958 he published a collection of short stories, *The Sea-Bed and Other Stories*.

WORKS: *The Sea-Bed and Other Stories* (1958); *The Dancers Inherit the Party* (1960); *Glasgow Beasts and a Bird* (1961); *Concertina* (1962); *Und alles blieb wie es war ...* (1965); *Poems to Hear and See* (1971); *A Sailor's Calendar* (1973); *Honey by the Water* (1973); *Selected Ponds* (1976); *Heroic Emblems* (1977)

First Blast of the Trumpet against the Monstrous Regiment of Women, The. Tract by JOHN KNOX while he was in exile in Dieppe in 1557 and published anonymously in Geneva in the following year. Despite the title, which implied an attack on the unnaturalness of government by women, the main subject of Knox's attack was the rule of Queen Mary Tudor of England (1516–58), whom he condemned as a tyrant and oppressor of the Protestant faith. Knox contended that a woman ruler was a violation of nature and, challenging the Christian doctrine of obedience, he called on the nobility to overthrow their queen, arguing that to obey an idolatrous ruler was an affront to God. Knox brushed aside the example of Deborah, who in the book of *Judges* was called upon to lead the people of Israel, and that usurpation of biblical doctrine, together with his immoderate language, brought censure from his fellow Protestants, even from those who, like Knox, held extreme views. Not unnaturally, the book was condemned in England and Knox was branded as a renegade for advocating revolution against princes, quite apart from his conviction that government by a woman was sinful.

The book is written in a highly coloured, hectoring style, punctuated by abusive adjectives and made memorable by the powerful nature of its rhetoric, of which the following extract is a good example: 'I feare not to say, that the day of vengeance, whiche shall apprehend that horrible monstre Jesabel of England and such as maintein her horrible crueltie, is alredie apointed in the counsell of the Eternall: and I verelie beleve, that it is so nigh, that she shall not reigne so long in tyrannie as hitherto she hath done, when God shall declare him selfe to be her ennemie, when he shall poure furth contempt upon her, according to her crueltie, and shal kindle the hartes of such as sometimes did favor her with deadly hatred against her, that they may execute his judgements.'

By publishing *The First Blast* Knox antagonized Mary's successor, Elizabeth (1533–1603), who came to the throne in 1558 and who, as a Protestant, might have been expected to offer assistance and moral leadership to the Scottish Protestants. Its publication also led to future generations' reviling Knox as a woman-hater, a viewpoint that is belied by his personal relationships and by his known liking for women.

Fisher, William (1737–1809). Farmer in Mauchline, Ayrshire, and an elder of the Church. He was the model for Holy Willie in the poem 'HOLY WILLIE'S PRAYER' by ROBERT BURNS. The incident that fired the poem took place in 1785 when Fisher instigated the Church Session of Mauchline to prosecute Burns's friend GAVIN HAMILTON for Sabbath-breaking. Although Burns, in his head-note to the poem, described Holy Willie as a bachelor, Fisher was married. In 1790 Fisher was arraigned for drunkenness before the minister WILLIAM AULD. He died in a snowdrift in February 1809.

Fleming, Marjory (1803–11). Child author. She was born on 15 January 1803 in Kirkcaldy, Fife. Through her mother's family she was distantly related to Sir WALTER SCOTT and after her death from meningitis on 19 December 1811 Dr JOHN BROWN (who christened her 'Pet Marjorie') and others nurtured the legend that the child author and Scott were intimate friends. Although it is possible that the two might have met during Marjory's stay with relatives in Edinburgh, neither mentions the other in their journals. It is to her three-volume diary that Marjory Fleming owes her place in history. During the last 18 months of her life she kept a journal of events, which also includes a number of poems; the childish simplicity of her writing ensured the success of the work when it was published in 1858 by H. B. Farnie, a London journalist, in 1863 by Dr John Brown, and in 1904 and 1928 by Lachlan Macbean, a family friend. The three editors bowdlerized much of Marjory's text, and a complete edition by Frank Sidgwick, based on the manuscripts, was published in 1935.

EDITIONS: A. Esdaile, ed., *The Journals, Letters and Verses of Marjory Fleming* (London, 1934); F. Sidgwick, ed., *The Complete Marjory Fleming* (London, 1935)

REFERENCE: J. Brown, *Marjorie Fleming* (Edinburgh, 1863)

Fletcher, Andrew, of Saltoun (1653–1716). Politician and patriot. He was the son of Sir Robert Fletcher of Saltoun and Innerpeffer in East Lothian, and Catherine Bruce, the daughter of Sir Henry Bruce of Clackmannan, a lineal descendant of ROBERT I (Robert the Bruce). After his father's death in 1665, Andrew was educated and brought up by GILBERT BURNET, minister of Saltoun and later Bishop of Salisbury. Fletcher completed his education by travelling in Europe, and on his return he was member for Haddington in the Convention of Estates in June 1678, when he opposed the Duke of Lauderdale's policies. Following his refusal to take the Test Oath of 1681, he fled to England, where he was involved in the Rye House Plot and was exiled to Holland. There he joined Monmouth's unsuccessful rebellion of 1685; as punishment he was condemned as a traitor in Edinburgh and his estates were forfeited, but following the Glorious Revolution of 1688 he was allowed to return to Scotland.

In the last Scottish Parliament (1703) Fletcher was a prominent anti-Unionist and introduced a scheme of 'limitations' whereby power of government in Scotland would be transferred from the Crown to Parliament. In *State of the controversy betwixt United and Separate Parliaments* (1706) he proposed a federal union in which England and Scotland could continue to have separate parliaments; this was the last of several pamphlets and published speeches that he wrote during the debates leading to the ACT OF UNION .

Fletcher's most important political works are *Two Discourses Concerning the Affairs of Scotland* (1698), the second of which contained radical proposals to alleviate rural poverty in Scotland, and *An Account of a Conversation Concerning the Right Regulation of Governments for the Common Good of Mankind in A Letter to the Marquis of Montrose, The Earls of Rothes, Roxburgh and Haddington*, which states Fletcher's political beliefs in the form of a Platonic dialogue. Fletcher was a determined, if at times hot-tempered patriot and a passionate idealist, at odds with the times in which he lived. On retiring from public life he devoted the rest of his life to agricultural improvement in East Lothian, His *Political Works* were published in 1732.

WORKS: *A Letter to a Member of the Convention of States in Scotland* (1689); *A Discourse Concerning Militias and Standing Armies* (1697); *Two Discourses Concerning the Affairs of Scotland; A Short and Impartial View of the Manner and Occasion of the Scots Colony Coming Away from Darien* (1699); *Overtures Offered to Parliament* (1700); *Some Thoughts Concerning the Affairs of this Session of Parliament* (1700); *Overture for Limitations on the Succession of Her Majesty Deceasing without Heirs* (1703); *Speeches by a Member of the Parliament which began at Edinburgh on 6th of May 1703* (1703); *An Account of a Conversation Concerning the Right Regulation of Governments* (1704); *Scotland's Interest* (1704); *A Speech without Doors* (1705); *State of the Controversy betwixt United and Separate Parliaments* (1706); *The Political Works of Andrew Fletcher Esq* (1732)

EDITIONS: I. J. Murray, ed., *The Letters of Andrew Fletcher of Saltoun* (Edinburgh, 1893); D. Daiches, ed., *Fletcher of Saltoun: Selected Writings* ASLS (Edinburgh, 1979)

REFERENCES: G. W. T. Omond, *Fletcher of Saltoun* (Edinburgh and London, 1897); W. C. Mackenzie, *Andrew Fletcher of Saltoun: his Life and Times* (Edinburgh, 1935)

Flodden, Battle of. A battle fought on 9 September 1513 between the armies of JAMES IV of Scotland and the Earl of Surrey on behalf of Henry VIII of England. James had been drawn into the war through the AULD ALLIANCE with France, who had, in turn, been threatened by the Holy League of the Pope, Spain, Venice and England. The Scottish army raised by James, and consisting of Highland and Lowland troops, surrendered their better tactical position and were defeated by the superior English force. James was killed in the battle, together with several nobles and members of the royal household and, according to English sources, 12,000 troops. The disaster of Flodden Field has been mourned in the haunting song, THE FLOWERS OF THE FOREST, the best-known version of which is the one by JEAN ELLIOT of Manto, and in the sixth canto of MARMION by Sir WALTER SCOTT.

Flowers of the Forest, The. A song, the melody of which is found in the Skene Manuscript of 1630 but whose words are known only from three 18th-century versions. The best-known was composed by JEAN ELLIOT of Minto and published by DAVID HERD in 1776 in ANCIENT AND MODERN SCOTTISH SONGS; its

inspiration was the tragedy of the BATTLE OF FLODDEN and some of the lines may have belonged to an earlier oral version. In 1764 ALISON COCKBURN produced a version which referred not to the battle but to a local financial disaster in the Borders. A third, lesser-known, song was written by Anne Home (1742–1821) and published by JAMES JOHNSON in THE SCOTS MUSICAL MUSEUM. In Jean Elliot's version the song has taken on the attributes of a national air of lament, with its refrain, 'The Flowers of the Forest are a' wede away.'

Flyting of Dunbar and Kennedy, The. A poem in four parts by WILLIAM DUNBAR and WALTER KENNEDY, in which the two poets exchange a succession of highly stylized insults during the course of 69 stanzas that are remarkable for their intricate rhyming structure and coarse, alliterative language. The ancient practice of 'flyting', carrying on a battle of words, usually scurrilous and abusive, has its origins in Scottish Celtic literature, although it is known elsewhere. 'The Flyting' also provides some accurate background information about the little-known life of William Dunbar: that he travelled on an embassy for JAMES IV and that he was small in stature.

Dunbar opens his sally by appointing a second, 'Schir Johin the Ros' (of whom nothing is known), and delivers a general warning to Kennedy and his second, Quintene, who return the challenge. The preliminaries over, Dunbar accuses Kennedy of a variety of personal shortcomings and misdeeds: he has attempted to poison the king in Paisley, Kennedy's ability as a poet is questionable owing to his Gaelic background, he is syphilitic and poverty-stricken, and when as a leprous beggar he visits Edinburgh from his house in Carrick, the dogs and children drive him from the city's walls. Kennedy's reply is equally outrageous: Dunbar is a member of the treasonable Cospatrick family, whereas Kennedy has sipped the cool waters of Parnassus Dunbar has swallowed frog-spawn, Dunbar has been a beggar throughout Europe and is fit only to be a hangman's assistant, while on embassy he has besmirched the ship with his sea-sickness, he was born in the darkness of an eclipse and has no feeling for the art of poetry, and as such he is unworthy of a benefice from the king. The poem ends with a *crescendo* of abuse that is characteristic of what has gone before: 'Tale tellare, rebellare, induellar wyth the devillis,/Spynk, sink with stynk ad Tertara Termagorum.'

The flyting between the two poets does not necessarily imply personal hostility – there is a generous mention of Kennedy in Dunbar's 'Lament quhen he was seik'. Rather it is an extravagant intellectual game played by two equal poetic adversaries, and the abusive rhetoric is stylized within the bounds of an accepted poetic form. It was probably composed over a number of years, evidence pointing to the years 1500–05 (J. W. Baxter, *William Dunbar: a Biographical Study* (Edinburgh, 1952), pp. 74–84).

Ford, James Allan (*b* 1920). Novelist. He was born on 10 June 1920 in Auchtermuchty, Fife, and was educated at the HIGH SCHOOL OF EDINBURGH and at the University. During World War II he served with the Royal Scots and was interned by the Japanese after the fall of Hong Kong, an experience that provided the background for his first novel, *The Brave White Flag* (1961). Ford worked as a civil servant until his retirement in 1979, rising to the senior positions of Registrar-General for Scotland (1966–9) and Principal Establishment Officer for Scotland (1969–79), service that has interfered with the quantity of his literary output. In all his novels there is an insistence on nicety of background detail and fineness of character delineation, and in no work are these virtues better employed than in his study of Edinburgh legal life, *A Judge of Men* (1968).

WORKS: *The Brave White Flag* (1961); *Season of Escape* (1961); *A Statue for a Public Place* (1965); *A Judge of Men* (1968); *The Mouth of Truth* (1972)

Fordun, John of. *See* JOHN OF FORDUN.

Forty-five, the. The popular name for the JACOBITE rebellion of 1745 undertaken by Prince CHARLES EDWARD STUART to retrieve the throne of Britain for his father, James. Lairds who supported the rebellion were known later to have been 'out during the Forty-five'.

Foulis, Hugh. Pen-name of NEIL MUNRO.

Foulis, Robert (1707–76). Printer. He was educated at the University of Glasgow, where he studied philosophy. With his brother Andrew (1712–75) he visited Oxford and France,

collecting rare books, and on their return they started a bookselling and printing business in Glasgow. In 1741 they became official printers to the University and gained a reputation for immaculate printing. Among their most distinguished publications were editions of the Greek and Latin classics, especially their six-volume edition of Homer (1765–8) and quarto editions of Gray's poems (1768) and *Paradise Lost* (1770). Robert Foulis founded an art academy in Glasgow in 1753 but it was a financial failure. His insistence on printing of the highest quality ran the firm into debt and he died in poverty in 1776.

REFERENCE: J. McLehose, *The Glasgow University Press* (Glasgow, 1931)

Fowler, William (1560–1612). Poet. He was born into a wealthy Edinburgh family and was educated at the University of St Andrews, graduating in 1578. He lived in Paris for a time and worked as a spy for the Protestant cause before returning to Scotland as a minister in Hawick in 1584. During the reign of JAMES VI Fowler enjoyed considerable patronage at court and he was secretary to Queen Anne until his death in 1612 in London. He helped in the preparation of James's BASILICON DORON and he translated a version of Machiavelli's *Il principe*. A visit to Italy increased his interest in Italian poetry: he translated Petrarch's *Trionfi* in 1587 and wrote a sonnet sequence, *The Tarantula of Love*, after the manner of Baldassare Castiglione (1478–1529). Fowler's prose pieces include a description of his arrangements for the baptism of Henry, Prince of Wales, and an attack on John Hamilton, Rector of the University of Paris, which was printed by ROBERT LEKPREVIK.

WORKS: *An Answer to Hammiltoun* (1581); *Epitaphe upon Sir John Seton* (1594); *A True Reportarie of the Baptisme of Prince Henry* (1594); *An Epitaphe upon Robert Bowes* (1597); *A Funeral Sonet* (1597)

EDITION: H. W. Meikle, James Craigie and John Purves, eds., *The Works of William Fowler*, 3 vols., STS (Edinburgh and London, 1914–40)

Fraser, G(eorge) S(utherland) (1915–80). Poet and critic. He was born on 8 November 1915 in Glasgow and was educated in Glasgow and Aberdeen, and at the University of St Andrews, graduating in 1937. After serving in the Middle East during World War II, he worked as a journalist and critic before becoming a lecturer at the University of Leicester

(1959–79). Fraser described himself as an 'occasional' poet who responded to particular scenes and situations, and his best works, 'Home Town Elegy' and 'The Traveller has Regrets', reflect his painful sense of exile from Scotland. His early collections, *The Fatal Landscape and Other Poems* (1941) and *Home Town Elegy* (1944), are associated with the 'New Apocalypse' writers of World War II. In his later works, *Leaves without a Tree* (1953) and *Conditions* (1969), there is an autumnal mood of sorrow for the passing of life and the culmination of human experience. Fraser also wrote a number of books of literary criticism. He died on 3 January 1980.

WORKS: *The Fatal Landscape and Other Poems* (1941); *Home Town Elegy* (1944); *The Traveller has Regrets and Other Poems* (1948); *Vision of Scotland* (1948); *News from South America* (1949); *Leaves without a Tree* (1953); *The Modern Writer and his World* (1953); *W. B. Yeats* (1954); *Scotland* (1955); *Poetry Now* (1956); *Dylan Thomas* (1957); *Vision and Rhetoric* (1959); *Ezra Pound* (1966); *Lawrence Durrell* (1968); *Conditions* (1969); *Metre, Rhyme and Free Verse* (1970); ed., *John Keats: Odes* (1971); *P. H. Newby* (1974); *Essays on Twentieth Century Poets* (1977); *Alexander Pope* (1978)

Fraser Darling, Sir **Frank.** *See* DARLING, FRANK FRASER.

Frazer, Sir **James George** (1854–1941). Anthropologist. He was born on 1 January 1854 in Glasgow and he was educated at Larchfield Academy, Helensburgh, the University of Glasgow, and Trinity College, Cambridge, where he was a Fellow in Classics. After a brief period studying law he was called to the English Bar in 1879, but he never practised as by then he had become involved in his lifelong study of the evolution of religious belief and ritual. His great work is *The Golden Bough*, published between 1890 and 1915 in 12 volumes; an abridged version appeared in 1920 and a supplement, *Aftermath*, in 1936. The starting-point of this monumental work is a discussion of the riddle of the grove of Nemi or Aricia near Rome, whose sacred king held office until he was slain by his successor: from that myth Frazer evolved a universal philosophy of religion, central to which was the killing of a divine king in man's attempt to appease nature. With its encyclopaedic listing of rituals, magical practices, religious beliefs and world mythology, it was a landmark in the study of totemism and taboo and an important influence in the study of archetypal themes in literary texts. As a classical scholar Frazer made translations of Pausanias, Ovid and Sallust; he also prepared an edition of the letters of the poet William Cowper. He received honorary degrees from several British and European universities, was knighted in 1914 and awarded the Order of Merit in 1925. He died on 7 May 1941.

WORKS: *Totemism* (1887); *The Golden Bough*, comprising *The Magic Art and Evolution of Kings, Taboo and the Perils of the Soul, The Dying God, Adonis, Attis and Osiris – Studies in the History of Oriental Religion, Spirits of the Corn and Wild, The Scape-Goat, Balder the Beautiful – Fire Festivals of Europe, The Doctrine of the External Soul* (1890–1915); ed. and trans., *Pausanias and Other Greek Sketches* (1900); *Lectures on the Early History of Kingship* (1905); *Questions on the Customs, Beliefs and Languages of Savages* (1908); *Totemism and Exogamy*, 4 vols. (1910); *The Belief in Immortality and the Worship of the Dead*, 3 vols. (1913–22); *Psyche's Task* (1913); *Jacob and the Mandrakes* (1917); *Folk-Lore in the Old Testament*, 3 vols. (1918); *Sir Roger de Coverley* (1920); *Sir Ernest Renan* (1923); *The Worship of Nature* (1926); *The Gorgon's Head* (1927); *Man, God and Immortality* (1927); *Graecia antiqua* (1930); *The Growth of Plato's Ideal Theory* (1930); *Myths of the Origin of Fire* (1930); *Garnered Sheaves* (1931); *Condorcet on the Progress of the Human Mind* (1933); *The Fear of the Dead in Primitive Religions*, 3 vols. (1933–6); *Creation and Evolution in Primitive Cosmogens* (1935); *Aftermath* (1936); *Anthologia anthropologia* (1938)

REFERENCES: R. A. Downie, *James George Frazer: the Portrait of a Scholar* (London, 1940)

Friel, George (1910–76). Novelist. He was born on 15 July 1910 in Glasgow and was educated there at St Mungo's Academy and at the University of Glasgow. After a period of service in the army he spent the rest of his life working as a teacher in the city of his birth, an experience that culminated in his finest novel, *Mr Alfred M.A.* (1972). The eponymous teacher is a shy, timid man, unable to cope with the demeaning and often squalid realities of day-to-day life and yet made painfully aware of the saving grace of his own poetic sensibility. It is a theme central to Friel's fiction: the striking contrast between the harshness of life and the possibilities of physical and moral regeneration. Friel seems to be saying that we need not create a system that degrades our own and others' lives, a belief that makes itself felt all the more acutely through his own sensitive use of a highly poetic language. A wry humour, though, is never far away, and in *Grace and Miss Partridge* (1969) his descriptions of the horrors of slum life are offset by comic episodes that restore humanity to his vision of a world gone mad.

WORKS: *The Bank of Time* (1959); *The Boy who Wanted Peace* (1964); *Grace and Miss Partridge* (1969); *Mr Alfred M.A.* (1972); *An Empty House* (1974)

Fulton, Robin (*b* 1937). Poet. He was born on 6 May 1937 on the Isle of Arran and was educated at the University of Edinburgh. Since 1973 he has lived and worked in Norway, where he has gained an international reputation for his translations of contemporary Scandinavian poets, including Tomas Tranströmmer, Lars Gustafsson and Gunnar Harding. A detached observer of life and human frailties in his own poetry, Fulton rarely lets his *persona* intrude, and as a result much of his work has a reserved, intellectual quality. *Tree Lines* (1974) represents the best of his published work. He has also been an editor of the poetry magazine LINES REVIEW.

WORKS: *A Matter of Definition* (1963); *Instances* (1967); *Inventories* (1969); *Quarters* (1971); *The Spaces between the Stones* (1971); *The Man with the Surbahar* (1971); *Contemporary Scottish Poetry: Individuals and Contexts* (1974); *Tree Lines* (1974); *Music and Flight* (1975); *Between Flights* (1976); *Places to Stay In* (1978); *Fields of Focus* (1982)

G

Gaberlunzie man. The name given to a professional travelling beggar, 'in later use: a travelling tinker, a beggar in general' (*SND*). It is the title of a popular song in Allan Ramsay's THE TEA-TABLE MISCELLANY and of a play by JOE CORRIE, and the mendicant beggar has long been a potent myth figure in Scotland's oral tradition. It was also one of the names by which JAMES V was known when he travelled anonymously among his people.

Gaelic. Gaelic belongs to the Celtic group of languages which were spoken in large tracts of Europe in prehistoric times. The language group falls into two main sections: Brythonic, or P-Celtic, which includes Welsh, Cornish and Breton, and Goidelic, or Q-Celtic, which includes Scottish and Irish Gaelic. Gaelic probably arrived in Scotland at the time of the first Irish settlements in the third century, by which time there had been widespread occupation of the Forth and Clyde valleys by a Celtic people speaking a Brythonic language. To begin with, the settlement of the Gaelic-speaking people was in present-day Argyll and in the islands of the inner Hebrides. By the tenth century Gaelic had spread to all parts of Scotland and its prestige had increased to the extent that it was used in political, ecclesiastical and legal documents and that it was also employed in personal and state nomenclature. The supremacy of Gaelic implies a decline in the Brythonic languages and also in Pictish, which was to become extinct; but by the 11th century the Anglian influence was in the ascendancy, supported in the following century by the incursion of Anglo-Norman influences. The use of Scots English in political and commercial affairs and its association with success and power placed Gaelic in the beleaguered position it has occupied to this day.

During the 19th century there was an active discrimination against Gaelic-speakers by means of the CLEARANCES, which removed them from their Gaelic homelands in the Islands and the western Highlands, and the Education Act of 1872, which prescribed the use of English for the education of Gaelic-speaking children. Both measures helped to emphasize the schism that had grown between Gaelic-speaking Scotland and the rest of the country, a divide that in many respects has continued until the present day. Although Gaelic survived in isolated pockets of mainland Scotland until the early part of the 20th century, the census of 1971 established that it was strongest in the islands of the inner Hebrides and in the Western Isles.

As a result of the separation of Gaelic speakers most Gaelic literature has existed in isolation and the work of its great masters, poets such as ALASDAIR MAC MHAIGHSTIR ALASDAIR, MÀIRI NIGHEAN ALASDAIR RUAIDH, DONNCHADH BÀN MAC AN T-SAOIR, and ROB DONN MACAOIDH, remains hidden from most non-Gaelic-speaking readers. However, the 20th century has seen a revival of interest in Gaelic, many texts are now available and the work of poets such as DOMHNALL MACAMHLAIGH, SOMHAIRLE MACGILL-EAIN and RUARAIDH MACTHÓMAIS is as well known as that of their contemporaries who write in English or Scots. Much Gaelic literature has existed in the oral tradition and the songs, poetry and tales have been collected in such valuable works as Alexander Cameron's *Reliquiae Celticae*, 2 vols. (1892–4), J. F. Campbell's *Popular Tales of the West Highlands*, 4 vols. (1860–62), Alexander Carmichael's *Carmina gadelica*, 5 vols. (1928–56) and John Lorne Campbell's *Highland Songs of the Forty-five* (1933).

Gaelic Books Council. An agency formed in September 1968 with the twin purpose of funding the publication of books in Gaelic and of promoting their sales within Scotland. It is funded by the Scottish Education Department and the SCOTTISH ARTS COUNCIL, and its mobile bookselling service receives aid from the Highlands and Islands Development Board and from Comhairle nan Eilean. The University of Glasgow provides accommodation and services, and the Council of ten unpaid members meets regularly to decide policy, which is implemented by three full-time members of staff. From the outset the Gaelic Books Council has organized literary competitions and commissioning schemes for new work and its foundation has been a much needed stimulus to contemporary Gaelic literature.

Gairm. First published in 1951, *Gairm* is Scotland's most influential Gaelic magazine. As well as publishing articles on various topics affecting the Gaelic language, and on the Highlands and Islands of Scotland, it has provided much-needed space for work by established and younger writers, both in prose and verse. Its editor and co-founder is the poet RUARAIDH MACTHÓMAIS. The publishers of the magazine have also established a publishing company of the same name which produces a wide variety of books in Gaelic, ranging from poetry and fiction to dictionaries and nonfiction.

Gaitens, Edward (1897–1966). Novelist. He was born in the Gorbals in Glasgow and left school at the age of 14; having no training, he drifted through a number of menial jobs, ending up in London in 1914. During World War I he was imprisoned as a conscientious objector. Through the influence and friendship of O. H. MAVOR ('James Bridie'), Gaitens was persuaded to send his early short stories to publishers, and much of his work was published by J. B. SALMOND in the SCOTS MAGAZINE. A collection, *Growing Up and Other Stories*, was published in 1942 and six of those realistic scenes of slum life in Glasgow became chapters in his novel *Dance of the Apprentices* (1948). With its vividly presented picture of domestic life in the Gorbals, the novel has a good deal of warmth and vitality, especially in Gaitens's treatment of human relationships. There is no attempt to moralize and sentimentality is kept at a safe distance, making this one of the more successful examples of Scottish working-class fiction. Gaitens lived in Dublin and London for several years and also wrote a number of

unpublished stories and sketches set in those cities. He died on 16 December 1966.

WORKS: *Growing Up and Other Stories* (1942); *Dance of the Apprentices* (1948)

Galgacus. *See* CALGACUS.

Galt, John (1779–1839). Novelist. He was born on 2 May 1799 in Irvine, Ayrshire, the son of a sea captain. In 1789 his family moved to Greenock, where he was educated at the town's Grammar School before being apprenticed to the Greenock Custom House and becoming a junior clerk with a local firm of merchants, James Miller and Company, in 1796. As well as building up a solid background in business, Galt contributed essays and stories to a number of local journals – two separate strands which were to dictate the later course of his life. In 1804 he moved to London and set himself up in business in his own right. He met with little success and entered Lincoln's Inn to study law in 1809. For the next two years (1809–11), he travelled extensively in Europe, where he befriended Lord Byron. On his return he published an account of his travels, *Voyages and Travels in the Years 1809, 1810, and 1811; Containing Statistical, Commercial, and Miscellaneous Observations on Gibraltar, Sardinia, Sicily, Malta, Serigo and Turkey* (1812); he followed up the success of his first book with *The Life and Administration of Cardinal Wolsey* (1812).

Galt continued his interest in the mercantile world and in 1813 he attempted to establish a trading company in Gibraltar which would break Napoleon's embargo, imposed in 1807 to prevent the import of British goods into Europe. Wellington's victories in Spain that same year ended those plans and he returned to London and married Elizabeth Tilloch. In 1815 he was appointed Secretary of the Royal Caledonian Asylum, a charity run by the Highland Society of London. Between then and 1820 Galt used his parliamentary connections to act as a consultant to various business concerns; he lived in Glasgow for several months in 1818. He was also a regular contributor to the *Monthly Magazine* and between 1819 and 1820 he wrote a number of school textbooks under the pseudonym of the Rev. T. Clark.

The years between 1820 and 1822 were Galt's most productive: he wrote six novels for WILLIAM BLACKWOOD, which were published serially in BLACKWOOD'S MAGAZINE. In all the novels· Galt examined the changes that were radically altering Scottish country life in his own lifetime; but they are not merely social documentation. His first novel, *The Ayrshire Legatees*, was published in *Blackwood's Magazine* between June 1820 and February 1821. It takes the form of a series of letters written by four characters from an Ayrshire village who describe the impact of a visit to London. The novel's immediate success encouraged Blackwood to follow up its publication with *The Steam-Boat* (1821), which contains a fine account of the coronation of George IV and which reintroduces some of the characters from *The Ayrshire Legatees*. In the same year Galt published the novel for which he is best known, ANNALS OF THE PARISH. Set in the imaginery Ayrshire village of Dalmailing, the *Annals* owe much to Galt's memories of his childhood and are a rich evocation of country life which never fall into the trap of being sentimental or over-nostalgic. The novel has no plot but Galt views the action through the eyes of the elderly minister Micah Balwhidder, and it remains the most authentic and human picture of Scottish village life during the reign of George III. Its publication cemented Galt's reputation as a novelist and he moved briefly from London to Edinburgh to complete his next Blackwood novels, *Sir Andrew Wylie* (1822) and *The Provost* (1822).

Galt was becoming increasingly concerned with Blackwood's editorial interference in his work, and after the publication of THE ENTAIL (1823), which examined the corruption of the human spirit by a harsh economic system, he broke with Blackwood and moved to Oliver and Boyd, another old-established Edinburgh publisher. For them he wrote *Ringan Gilhaize* (1823), one of the few novels which takes a sympathetic view of the COVENANTERS. In 1825 he returned to Blackwood and wrote for him *The Omen*, a story of the supernatural, *The Last of the Lairds* (1826), an earthy comedy which was expurgated by DAVID MACBETH MOIR, and *Lawrie Todd*, a novel which grew out of his Canadian experiences (see below). One of his last novels, *The Member* (1832), was among the first British novels to deal with political corruption in parliamentary elections.

During his years with Blackwood, Galt managed to maintain his many business interests. In 1820 he acted for the settlers in Upper Canada who had been dispossessed during the American War of 1812, and in 1824 he was appointed Secretary to the Canada Company, which had been founded to develop unexplored areas of Canada. He spent three years in Canada before being recalled on a charge of negligence and he was imprisoned for a few months during 1829 in the King's Bench prison for debtors. However, the connection with Canada was strengthened after his death: Galt in Ontario was named after him and one of his sons became a minister of Finance in the Canadian government. Galt's last years were spent in Greenock and he died there on 11 April 1839. He published his *Autobiography* in 1833 and a series of sketches from his life, *Literary Life*, in 1834.

In a sense, Galt wrote too much too quickly and his reputation languished after his death, several critics doubting that his novels, with their photographic realism, were fiction. He remains, though, one of the best novelists of the early 19th century, sensitive to the major social, political and economic issues of his day and a sympathetic interpreter of Scottish CALVINISM.

WORKS: *Cursory Reflections on Political and Commercial Topics* (1812); *The Life and Administration of Cardinal Wolsey* (1812); *The Tragedies of Maddelen, Agamemnon, Lady Macbeth, Antonia and Clytemnestra* (1812); *Voyages and Travels* (1812); *Letters from the Levant* (1813); *The Life and Studies of Benjamin West* (1816); *The Majolo*, 2 vols. (1816); *The Appeal* (1818); *The Earthquake*, 3 vols. (1820); *Glenfell* (1820); *The Life, Studies and Works of Benjamin West* (1820); *Annals of the Parish* (1821); *The Ayrshire Legatees* (1821); *Sir Andrew Wylie*, 3 vols. (1822); *The Provost* (1822); *The Steam-Boat* (1822); *The Entail*, 3 vols. (1823); *The Gathering of the West* (1823); *Ringan Gilhaize*, 3 vols. (1823); *The Spaewife*, 3 vols. (1823); *The Bachelor's Wife* (1824); *Rothelan*, 3 vols. (1824); *The Omen* (1825); *The Last of the Lairds* (1826); *Lawrie Todd* (1830); *The Life of Lord Byron* (1830); *Southennan*, 3 vols. (1830); *Bogle Corbet or The Emigrants*, 3 vols. (1831); *The Lives of the Players* (1831); *The Member* (1832); *The Radical* (1832); *Stanley Buxton*, 3 vols. (1832); ·*Autobiography*, 2 vols. (1833); *Eben Erskine or The Traveller*, 3 vols. (1833); *The Ouranoulogos or The Celestial Volume* (1833); *Poems* (1833); *The Stolen Child* (1833); *Stories of the Study*, 3 vols. (1833); *Literary Life and Miscellanies*, 3 vols. (1834); *A Contribution to the Greenock Calamity Fund* (1834); *Efforts by an Invalid* (1835); *The Demon of Destiny and Other Poems* (1839)

REFERENCES: R. K. Gordon, *John Galt* (Toronto, 1920); J. W. Aberdein, *John Galt* (London, 1936); F. H. Lyell, *A Study of the Novels of John Galt* (Princeton, 1942); I. A. Gordon, *John Galt: the Life of a Writer* (Edinburgh, 1972)

Garioch, Robert. Pen-name of ROBERT GARIOCH SUTHERLAND.

Garry, Flora (*b* 1900). Poet. She was born in the village of New Deer in Aberdeenshire, and was educated at the local school and later at Peterhead Academy and the University of Aberdeen. After graduating she taught at schools in Dumfries, Strichen and Glasgow, where her husband was Professor of Physiology. Her poems were published in *Bennygoak and Other Poems* (1974) and they owe their strength to her memory of the Scots of her childhood and to the rich idioms of the northeast of Scotland.

Gau [Gaw], John (*d* 1533). Divine. He was a native of Perth and was educated at the University of St Andrews, where his name first appeared on the matriculation list of 1509 in the company of Sir DAVID LYNDSAY. On graduating he may have lived in a monastic establishment in St Andrews or in his home town, but of this period in his life nothing is known. In 1533 he was in the Danish seaport of Malmö, which contained a large population of Scottish merchants, and it is possible that he acted as a chaplain to them. He was converted to Lutheranism and ended his days as a minister in Copenhagen. His treatise, *The Richt Vay to the Kingdome of Heuine*, is an analysis of the Scriptures in Scots; it is one of the few instances of a religious work in Scots written by a Protestant during the Reformation period. Although it was considered for many years to have been an original work, later scholarship proved that it had been translated from Danish and German religious texts. The work was first printed in 1533, but only one copy of it has survived; it was edited for the SCOTTISH TEXT SOCIETY by A. F. Mitchell (1883).

Geddes, Alexander (1737–1802). Theologian and poet. He was born at Ruthven in Banffshire and trained for the priesthood in Paris. A first-rate scholar, Geddes translated Horace's *Satires* and also prepared a version of the Bible for Catholics. His textual analyses of Hebrew Scripture led to his suspension from the Church and he lived for a time in London. Geddes wrote a number of poems and lyrics in a vigorous Scots, the best-known of which is his witty 'The Epistle to the President, Vice-Presidents and Members of the Scottish Society of Antiquaries: on Being Chosen a Corres-

pondent Member' (1780). He also wrote *Linton: a Tweedside Pastoral* (1781).

Geddes, Jenny (*fl* 1637). The woman who, by popular repute, is supposed to have thrown a stool at the head of David Lindsay, Bishop of Edinburgh, on 23 July 1637, when he attempted to read Laud's prayerbook in the Church of St Giles in Edinburgh. Although the story may be apocryphal, a riot did take place on that day; one consequence of Charles I's attempts to foist the prayerbook on Scotland and the ensuing riots in Edinburgh and elsewhere was the signing of the NATIONAL COVENANT the following year. The name 'Jenny Geddes' came to be used in Edinburgh to describe any woman who made herself conspicuous in mobs, but she is an important myth figure in the history of the Scottish church. Her story appears in the histories of, among others, ROBERT WODROW and JOHN HILL BURTON.

Geddes, Patrick (1854–1932). Social reformer. He was born on 2 October 1854 at Ballater, Aberdeenshire, and was educated at Perth Academy. In 1871 he joined the National Bank of Scotland and in 1873 he moved to London to study under T. H. Huxley (1825–95). There followed a period of study in Mexico before Geddes returned to Scotland in 1880. In spite of his qualifications, he failed to gain an academic appointment until 1888, when he became Professor of Botany in University College, Dundee, a post he held for 30 years. In Edinburgh Geddes became involved in the work of the Edinburgh Social Union, which attempted to better the abysmal conditions that prevailed in the Royal Mile; he built Ramsay Garden on the site of the house of ALLAN RAMSAY, and he rebuilt the *camera obscura* in Outlook Tower. Geddes's economic philosophy rested on a belief that resources were more important than finance, and he became an early proponent of the need for town planning; on this subject his most durable books are *City Development* (1904) and *Cities in Evolution* (1915). Much of his later life was spent in travelling and lecturing abroad. He was knighted in 1932 and died that same year on 17 April.

WORKS: *John Ruskin* (1884); *An Analysis of the Principles of Economics* (1885); *Every Man his Own Art Critic* (1887); *Industrial Exhibitions* (1887); with J. A. Thomson, *The Evolution of Sex* (1890); *City Development* (1904); *Cities as Applied Sociology* (1905); *The*

World Without and the World Within (1905); with J. A. Thomson, *Evolution* (1911); with J. A. Thomson, *Sex* (1911); *The Masque of Ancient Learning* (1912); *Cities in Evolution* (1915); *On Universities in Europe* (1915); with Victor Branford, *The Making of the Future* (1917); with Gilbert Slater, *Ideas at War* (1917); *The Life and Work of Sir Jagadis C. Bose* (1920); *Town Planning in Colombo* (1921); *Education in Return to Life* (1924); with J. A. Thomson, *Biology* (1925)

REFERENCES: P. Boardman, *Patrick Geddes: Maker of the Future* (London, 1944); P. Mairet, *Pioneer of Sociology: the Life and Letters of Patrick Geddes* (London, 1957); P. Kitchen, *A Most Unsettling Person* (London, 1975)

Gentle Shepherd, The. A verse drama, subtitled 'A Pastoral Comedy', by ALLAN RAMSAY, first published in 1725. The play is set in a rural area near Edinburgh at the time of the Restoration. Sir William Worthy, a landowner who has fought with Montrose, has been forced into exile, leaving his son Patrick in the care of an old shepherd called Symon. Nearby lives another shepherd, Glaud, who has in his care Peggy, cousin to Patrick, who has been saved by her nurse Mause from avaricious relatives anxious to murder her and thus win her estate. Both are unaware of their true identities. The play opens with two herds discussing their love lives and the complications caused by them: Patie loves Peggy who returns his affection, but Roger is scorned by Jenny who seems to prefer Bauldy. There is an added complication in that Bauldy prefers Peggy to his own Neps, who does not appear in the play. Patie's advice to Roger is to ignore Jenny for a time and the first act ends with Patie and Peggy declaring their love for each other.

Meanwhile Sir William has returned in the guise of a fortune-teller and he confides his true identity to Symon. Pleased that Patie – his son Patrick – has grown into such a charming young man, Sir William reveals himself as his father and promises to send his son to complete his education in London and Paris. For a moment it seems as if Patrick will have to forsake Peggy, but all ends well when Mause tells the true story of Peggy and her ancestry. Sir William dispenses justice on all sides and Roger and Jenny are also brought together to be betrothed. The character Bauldy, who returns to his Neps, provides the comic subplot, with his ludicrous belief that Mause is a witch capable of raising ghosts. That interlude, written in a racy Scots which looks forward to the mixture of comedy and the supernatural in TAM O'

SHANTER by ROBERT BURNS is one of the highlights of the play. As befits a drama with a happy ending, *The Gentle Shepherd* concludes with a spirited song of rejoicing sung by Peggy. to the folk-tune 'Corn-riggs are bonny'.

The plot in which the lives of a pair of lovers are complicated by mistaken identities is taken from classical comedy and Ramsay was well aware that he was writing in the tradition of European pastoral drama – his dedication to Lady Eglintoun cites both Tasso and Guarini. But *The Gentle Shepherd* is not Tuscan drama transported to the Pentland Hills outside Edinburgh. Patie and Roger are both recognizably Scottish shepherds and their speech is a reflection of a Scots rural dialect. They and the other rural characters speak with a rare gusto, and Ramsay was obviously at his most relaxed in writing in a version of Scots (albeit watered down), even though he doubted that Scots could ever be a polite form of dramatic expression. Thus he signals Patie's return to respectability by allowing him to drift into a stylized Augustan prose, whose English sounds stilted and naïve after the vigorous and earthy Scots.

The Gentle Shepherd is written in heroic couplets and Ramsay provided 20 ballads to be sung within the body of the play. In 1729 he transformed it into a ballad opera in the style of John Gay's *Beggar's Opera* and it enjoyed a wide popularity with audiences throughout the 18th century and well into the 19th. One reason for its continuing popularity was Ramsay's insistence on presenting country life in as realistic a way as possible; Symon and Glaud are well acquainted with the hardships of work and weather and are definitely not Arcadian shepherds in a Scottish setting. It also supported the philosophy of change and improvement and offered moral sentiments that were entirely in keeping with the ideals of the men of the SCOTTISH ENLIGHTENMENT. On another level *The Gentle Shepherd* is an important landmark in the history of Scottish drama, being the first play of any substance since the 16th-century ANE PLEASANT SATYRE OF THE THRIE ESTAITIS by Sir DAVID LYNDSAY.

Gibbon, Lewis Grassic. Pen-name of JAMES LESLIE MITCHELL.

Gilfillan, George (1813–78). Poet and critic. He was born on 30 January 1813 in Comrie, Perthshire, the son of a Secessionist minister. He was educated in Glasgow and Edinburgh and became a minister in March 1836, taking the charge of the School Wynd Church in Dundee. In addition to several religious tracts, Gilfillan published lives of ROBERT BURNS (1856) and Sir WALTER SCOTT (1870); his three-volume *Gallery of Literary Portraits* (1845, 1849, 1854) was intended to make literature more accessible and was a popular publication in its day. Most of Gilfillan's poetry was of little import, and through his admiration of the 'Spasmodic' poets and his friendships with ALEXANDER SMITH and Sydney Dobell (1824–74) he earned the scorn of WILLIAM EDMONSTOUNE AYTOUN in BLACKWOOD'S MAGAZINE. He died on 13 August 1878 at Arnhalt near Brechin.

WORKS: *A Gallery of Literary Portraits,* 3 vols. (1845–54); *The Christian Bearings of Astronomy* (1848); *The Apocalypse of Jesus Christ* (1851); *The Book of British Poesy* (1851); *The Bards of the Bible* (1852); *The Grand Discovery* (1854); *Life of Robert Burns* (1856, rev. 2/1879); *Christian Missions* (1857); *Alpha and Omega* (1860); *Specimens of the Less Known British Poets* (1866); *Night* (1867); *Remoter Stars in the Church Sky* (1867); *Modern Christian Heroes* (1869); *Life of Sir Walter Scott* (1870, rev. 2/1871); *Comrie and its Environs* (1872); *Life of Rev. W. Anderson* (1873); *Memoir of James Thomson* (1874); *Sketches Literary and Theological* (1881); *Gilfillan Memorial Hymnbook* (1886); *The Martyrs, Heroes and Bards of the Scottish Covenant* (1914)

Gillespie. A novel by JOHN MACDOUGALL HAY, published in 1914. Like THE HOUSE WITH THE GREEN SHUTTERS by GEORGE DOUGLAS BROWN, *Gillespie* deals with a ruthless central character, Gillespie Strang, a self-made man who has risen to prominence in a small town, Brierton, at the expense of his family's happiness. The novel is divided into four books of unequal length which are interrelated in the development of the main theme: 'the growing spirit of materialism in Scotland', which Hay argued, 'needed a Gillespie'. Book 1 sets the scene in Brierton, a mid-19th-century, west coast fishing village, and traces Gillespie's rise to power as a merchant, his grasping nature, and his infamous marriage to Morag; book 2, the longest and the central section of the novel, follows Gillespie's inexorable march towards total control of the village's economy; book 3 is devoted to his sons, Iain and Eoghan, and their awareness of Gillespie's pride and of their mother's slump into alcoholism and prostitution; book 4 is the culmination, the violent end of Gillespie and his family and the symbolic retribution of the Fates. Gillespie Strang

is a monstrous creation, characterized by his cunning and the dark force of his ambition. Morag Strang is a pitiable victim of her husband's greed, and her degradation is the spur for Eoghan's denunciation of the hell that Gillespie has created, for in the final scenes of massive self-destruction Hay underlines God's divine vengeance on man's overreaching ambitions. Although evil is the dominant theme, there are a score of minor characters who, at the end, allow redemption to be visited on the town after the depredations it has suffered at the hands of Gillespie Strang.

When *Gillespie* first appeared its reception was muted by the outbreak of war, and subsequently it suffered from moral coolness towards Hay's explicit treatment of Morag's drunken promiscuity. It was republished in 1963 with an introduction by ROBERT KEMP and again in 1980 with an introduction by Bob Tait and Isobel Murray.

Gillies, John (1747–1836). Historian and classicist. He was born at Little Keithock near Brechin and was educated at the University of Glasgow. Most of his life was spent working as a tutor in Europe, and between 1784 and his death on 15 February 1836 he lived and worked in London. He wrote several histories, including what was for many years a standard authority, *History of Greece* (1786); he was appointed His Majesty's Historiographer for Scotland in 1793.

WORKS: *The Orations of Lysias and Isocrates* (1778); *History of Greece* (1786); *A View of the Reign of Frederick II of Prussia* (1789); *Aristotle's Ethics and Politics* (1797); *History of the World from Alexander the Great to Augustus,* 2 vols. (1807); *Aristotle's Rhetoric* (1823)

Gillies [née Simmons], **Valerie** (*b* 1948). Poet. She was born on 4 June 1948 in Edmonton, Alberta, but her childhood was spent in Edinburgh. She was educated there and graduated from the University of Edinburgh in 1970, and then spent a year at the University of Mysore in India. Several of her best early poems have their origins in that experience, and what gives these works special interest is the relationship between what she chooses to describe and what she witholds or keeps below the surface of meaning. Her later works, collected in *Each Bright Eye* (1977), are more objective and are concerned with material and domestic matters. Animals, too, are a favourite subject but it is her ability to capture the spirit of dog or fish rather than any attempt to give them human qualities, that makes those poems so fresh and entertaining.

WORKS: with Roderick Watson and Paul Mills, *Trio* (1971); *Each Bright Eye* (1977)

Glasgow. Scotland's largest city. The known history of the city goes back to the construction of its cathedral by Bishop John Achaius in the 12th century, though legend claims that the city owed its foundation to an earlier church built by ST KENTIGERN, or St Mungo as he is also known, Glasgow's patron saint. The medieval town was regulated by its flourishing guilds of craftsmen, and it acquired additional status in 1450 with the granting of the papal bull that led to the foundation of its university. In 1492 it became the seat of an archbishopric and began its long involvement in the ec- clesiastical affairs of the country. Develop- ment continued apace throughout the 17th century, and the passing of the ACT OF UNION of 1707 led to increased trade from the city, particularly in tobacco with America and the West Indies. The so-called 'tobacco lords' de- veloped the city to the west, and, as the 18th century progressed, cotton too became a staple trade in the west of Scotland. With the coming of industrialization, the exploitation of the coalfields and the development of shipbuilding on the Clyde the face of the city changed and Glasgow enjoyed great prosperity; it became known as the 'second city of the Empire'. But the new wealth also bred slum conditions, malnutrition and poverty for a large proportion of the work force. Although conditions in the city have improved since World War II, Glas- gow is still bedevilled by many of the social problems thrown up in the wake of its Vic- torian expansion.

The production of newspapers, the vitality of the theatre and the presence of publishers such as WILLIAM COLLINS have helped to pro- vide the city with a literary ambience, and among the 20th-century writers associated with Glasgow may be mentioned O. H. MAVOR, JOHN JOY BELL, NEIL MUNRO, GEORGE BLAKE, CATHARINE CARSWELL, FRE- DERICK NIVEN, HUGH C. RAE and GEORGE FRIEL. The post-war city and its problems have also acted as subject matter for several novels that have charted the changing face of the industrialized west of Scotland.

REFERENCES: M. Lindsay, *Portrait of Glasgow* (Lon- don, 1972); D. Daiches, *Glasgow* (London, 1977)

Glasgow Herald. A newspaper founded in 1783 by John Mennons, an Edinburgh man who had moved to Glasgow after several pub- lishing failures in his native city. Until 1805 it was known as the *Glasgow Advertiser* and with its change of title and its new editor, Samuel Hunter, it adopted a middle-of-the-road at- titude to politics, while its Glasgow rivals kept a strict Tory line. In 1837 George Outram became the editor and his propitiatory at- titudes over THE DISRUPTION and Free Trade were a key factor in maintaining Conservative unity in Scotland. Besides changing the news- paper's political direction, Outram brought a new scholarly attitude to the press and he made it his business to exclude unworthy or crooked advertisements in defiance of contemporary practice. By mid-century the *Glasgow Herald* had become the most influential and financial- ly secure newspaper in the west of Scotland and by 1859 it was a daily publication. It has maintained its pre-eminence and the name of George Outram has been kept alive in the title of the newspaper's managing company.

REFERENCE: A. Phillips, *Glasgow's Herald* (Glasgow, 1982)

Gleig, G(eorge) R(obert) (1796–1888). Novelist and historian. He was born on 20 April 1796 in Stirling, the son of the Bishop of Brechin. He was educated at the University of Glasgow and at Balliol College, Oxford, but his studies were interrupted by military service in the Peninsular War and in North America. In 1816 he returned to Oxford where he took orders, and he then went back to the army as a curate, becoming Chaplain-General of the Forces in 1844. Gleig was a lifelong con- tributor to BLACKWOOD'S MAGAZINE, writing on a wide variety of subjects, but it was on military matters that he made his literary name. His novel *The Subaltern* (1826) was published originally as a serial in *Blackwood's*, and with its entertaining picture of army life it enjoyed a wide measure of popular success. Equally rewarding was his biography of the Duke of Wellington (1862), who became a lifelong friend. On his retirement from the army Gleig lived in the Chelsea Hospital in London and he died on 9 July 1888.

WORKS: *Campaigns of the British Army at Washington and New Orleans* (1820); *The Subaltern* (1826); *The*

Chelsea Pensioners (1829); *Sermons* (1829); *Allan Breck* (1830); *The Country Curate* (1830); *History of the Bible,* 2 vols. (1830–31); *History of India,* 5 vols. (1830–35); *The Life of Sir Thomas Munro,* 3 vols. (1830); *Lives of Military Commanders,* 3 vols. (1831); *Chelsea Hospital and its Traditions,* 3 vols. (1838); *Warren Hastings* (1841); *Sketch of the Military History of Great Britain* (1845); *Sale's Brigade in Afghanistan (1847); The Story of the Battle of Waterloo* (1847); *Lord Clive* (1848); *India and its Army* (1857); *Life of Arthur, First Duke of Wellington* (1862); *The Soldier's Manual of Devotion* (1862)

Glen, Duncan ['Ronald Eadie Munro'] (*b* 1933). Poet. He was born on 11 January 1933 at Cambuslang, Lanarkshire, and was educated at Rutherglen Academy, Heriot Watt College, Edinburgh (1950–53), and Edinburgh College of Art (1953–6). Since completing his National Service in the Royal Air Force he has worked as a lecturer in typography and graphic design in various colleges in England, a career that has helped him to maintain the high standards of design in his private poetry press, Akros Publications, which he founded in 1965. Since that date he has also been the editor of AKROS, one of the leading contemporary magazines devoted to Scottish poetry. In both capacities, as publisher and editor, he has been a driving force behind the promotion of Scottish poetry, and in *Akros* he has not only provided valuable space for new writers but has also introduced new critical standards through his editorial standpoint. As a poet, Glen writes a vigorous, conversational Scots which is firmly rooted in his childhood background in Lanarkshire. Most of his work has appeared in pamphlet form under the pseudonym 'Ronald Eadie Munro'; his collection *In Appearances* (1971) showed him to be a lyrical poet able to transform familiar domestic material into public utterances of great power and subtlety.

WORKS: ed., *Hugh MacDiarmid and the Scottish Renaissance* (1964); ed., *Selected Essays of Hugh MacDiarmid* (1969); ed., *The Akros Anthology of Scottish Poetry 1965–70* (1970); ed., *Whither Scotland?* (1971); *In Appearances* (1971); ed., *Hugh MacDiarmid: a Critical Survey* (1972); *A Bibliography of Scottish Poets from Stevenson to 1974* (1974); *A Cled Score* (1974); *Realities* (1980)

Glen, William (1789–1826). Poet. He was born in Glasgow but spent the greater part of his life in the West Indies, where he was dogged by lack of success in his business enterprises. His one collection of poems and songs, *Poems Chiefly Lyrical,* was published posthum-

ously in 1815 and is remembered for the inclusion of Glen's popular Jacobite lament, 'Wae's me for Charlie'.

EDITION: C. Rodger, ed., *Poetical Remains of William Glen, with a Memoir* (Edinburgh, 1874)

Glencairn, Earl of. *See* CUNNINGHAM, JAMES.

Glencoe, Massacre of. The slaughter of 38 members of the Clan Macdonald in Glencoe, Argyll, by a regiment of soldiers from the Clan Campbell, which took place on the night of 13 February 1692. Ostensibly the massacre had its origins in the failure of Macdonald of Glencoe to sign by the agreed date the oath of allegiance to King William – a snowstorm and misunderstood instructions delayed his journey to Inverary to take the oath – but political and social reasons were also at work. Viscount Stair, Secretary of State for Scotland, was anxious to exert political pressure in the Highlands by punishing the Macdonalds for their cattle raids and their recalcitrant attitude towards the Crown; and the Campbells were the traditional enemies of the Macdonalds. But the massacre was botched. Over 100 Macdonalds managed to escape and public revulsion was increased when it was discovered that the Campbell soldiers had accepted Macdonald hospitality in the fortnight that passed before they fell upon their hosts. The news of the massacre contributed to Stair's political fall, but the accession of Queen Anne saw him recalled to power to help execute the ACT OF UNION. Although the massacre had the desired effect of persuading the remaining clan leaders to sign the oath of allegiance, in the long term it failed to bring them all within the Crown's sphere of influence.

REFERENCE: J. Buchan, *The Massacre of Glencoe* (London, 1933); J. Prebble, *Glencoe: the Story of the Massacre* (London, 1966)

Glenriddell Manuscripts. A collection of manuscripts in two volumes made by ROBERT BURNS for his friend ROBERT RIDDELL of Friar's Carse. The bound volumes contain 53 unpublished poems and 27 letters. On Riddell's death the manuscripts were returned to Burns and they helped to form the basis, together with the poet's other papers, of Burns's collected poems and the biography published by Dr JAMES CURRIE, into whose possession they passed. In 1853 the manuscripts were presented to the Liverpool Athenaeum and they were later sold to an American collector, John Gribbel, who placed them on permanent loan to the NATIONAL LIBRARY OF SCOTLAND in 1914.

Globe Tavern. An inn in Dumfries frequented by ROBERT BURNS. For Anna Park, the niece of its owner, Burns wrote the song 'Yestreen I had a pint of wine'.

Golden age. Traditionally, the dawning of man's existence on earth when, according to classical mythology, he lived in a state of grace. It has since been applied to any age of cultural well-being, political harmony and economic stability. In Scottish history the two so-called 'Golden ages' occurred in the reign of JAMES IV and the first period of the SCOTTISH ENLIGHTENMENT in Edinburgh.

Goloshan, The. A play of great antiquity traditionally performed at Christmas. It falls into three parts, the 'Presentation', the 'Drama' and the 'Quete' (the collection of the reward). The play's title is thought to be derived from CALGACUS, the leader who fought against the Romans in Scotland.

Gordon, James, of Rothiemay (*c*1615– 1686). Cartographer. He was the son of Robert Gordon of Straloch (1580–1661), who was a colleague of the map maker TIMOTHY PONT. James was educated at Aberdeen and in 1641 became minister of Rothiemay. Through the influence of his father and the practical patronage of Sir JOHN SCOTT of Scotstarvit, he became interested in map making himself. His distinction lies in the remarkable three-dimensional maps he made of Edinburgh in 1646 and 1647. In them it is possible to perceive the location of the main buildings in relation to the streets and wynds and to re-create a picture of the narrow, crowded old town of Edinburgh. He also prepared similar maps of Aberdeen, St Andrews and Cupar in Fife. Gordon's commonplace book was published in 1841 by the New Spalding Club.

EDITION: J. Roberston and G. Grub, eds., *History of Scots Affairs, MDXXXVII to MDCXLI*, 3 vols., New Spalding Club (Aberdeen, 1841)

Gordon, Neil. Pen-name of A. G. MACDONELL.

Graham, James, 5th Earl and 1st Marquis of Montrose (1612–50). He was educated at the University of St Andrews. He succeeded to his father's title in 1628 as the 5th Earl, and was created 1st Marquis in 1644. Although he was an early supporter of the NATIONAL COVENANT, he was opposed to the policies of ARCHIBALD CAMPBELL, Earl of Argyll, and was imprisoned in Edinburgh in 1641. During the Civil War he fought on the side of Charles I and raised a Highland and Irish army with ALASDAIR ('Colkitto') MACDONALD. Despite a series of victories Montrose's army was finally defeated at the Battle of Philiphaugh on 13 September 1645. Montrose spent the next five years wandering in Europe, attempting, unsuccessfully, to gain support for the Royalist cause. He returned to Scotland in 1650 but was defeated at the Battle of Carbisdale on 27 April and executed in Edinburgh on 21 May.

Montrose was also a poet and although his work is in the minor key, 'His Metrical Prayer, On the Eve of his Execution' resounds with a calm, religious beauty. As a historical character, Montrose has appeared in work by Sir WALTER SCOTT and WILLIAM EDMONSTOUNE AYTOUN, among others, and he is the subject of a fine biography by JOHN BUCHAN.

Graham, John, of Claverhouse, 1st Viscount Dundee ['Bonnie Dundee'] (1648–89). Soldier and Royalist. He was educated at the University of St Andrews and served in the French and Dutch armies before returning to Scotland in 1677, when he was employed by the Scottish Privy Council to put down the militant COVENANTERS in south-west Scotland. Their rebellion was crushed by Graham at the Battle of Bothwell Brig on 22 June 1679, and between then and 1685 he helped in the suppression of the Covenanting conventicles, earning the name 'Bloody Clavers'; Graham was obeying the letter of the law and his reputation as a sadistic killer is somewhat distorted. When William of Orange took the British throne, Graham supported James VII, and he was created Viscount Dundee on 12 November 1688. He rallied a Highland army for James but was killed in his hour of victory at the Battle of Killiecrankie on 27 July 1689 and the uprising came to nothing. Graham figures in Sir Walter Scott's OLD MORTALITY and there is a spirited song called *Bonnie Dundee* in Scott's play *The Doom of Devorgoil* (1830).

Graham, Robert (*c*1735–97). Songwriter. He was born at Gartmore, Stirlingshire, and spent the greater part of his life in Jamaica, where he held the post of Receiver-General. He was Lord Rector of the University of Glasgow in 1785 and Member of Parliament for Stirlingshire (he had Whig inclinations). The composer of a number of lyrics in Scots, the best known of which, *O tell me how to woo thee*, begins with the line 'If doughty deeds my lady please', Graham was the grandfather of ROBERT BONTINE CUNNINGHAME GRAHAM who wrote a memoir of his life in *Doughty Deeds* (1925).

Graham, Robert Bontine Cunninghame (1852–1936). Politician, travel writer and essayist. He was born on 24 May 1852 in London, the son of a Scottish landowner, William Graham Bontine, and Anne Elizabeth Elphinstone Fleming, the daughter of a Scottish Admiral and a Spanish aristocrat. His grandfather, ROBERT GRAHAM, was a well-kown songwriter, and the family had a claim, through the dormant title of Menteith, to be the legitimate heirs of Robert II (*see* JAMES I). In later years Graham's Spanish aristocratic and Scottish regal ancestry earned him the nicknames 'Don Roberto' and 'the uncrowned King of Scots'. His childhood was divided between London and the family estates at Gartmore, Stirlingshire, and after a preparatory school education at Hill House, Leamington, he entered Harrow School in autumn 1865. Owing to financial problems and his father's mental instability, Graham left Harrow at the age of 15 and was tutored privately in England and Belgium. During that period he improved his childhood knowledge of Spanish and on 13 May 1870 he left Britain for Argentina. For the next seven years he was a frequent visitor to that country and Paraguay, travelling the continent and embarking on several unsuccessful business ventures in cattle ranching and horse droving. He returned to Britain in 1877 and married a Chilean poetess, Gabriela de la Belmondiere, while on a visit to Paris in October 1878. They spent two years (1879–81) travelling and ranching in Texas and Mexico before finally settling in Britain. In 1884 his father died and he succeeded to the Gartmore estates which remained a troublesome financial burden to him until they were sold in 1900. His Scottish base then became the smaller estate of Ardoch on the Clyde.

On 9 September 1887 Graham was adopted as the Liberal candidate for North-West Lanarkshire, a seat he held between 1886 and 1892. In parliament he committed himself to a radical approach and was a promoter of the reduction of the working day for miners. He took part in the Trafalgar Square riots on 13 November 1887 after the government banned a mass demonstration by the unemployed, and he was jailed for six weeks in Pentonville for unlawful assembly. He became a close friend and confidant of KEIR HARDIE, and when the Scottish Labour Party was formed on 19 May 1888 he became its first president. After World War I his interest in nationalism increased when he joined the Scottish Home Rule Association; he was president of the National Party of Scotland in 1928 and on its amalgamation with the Scottish Party in 1934 he became the first president of the Scottish National Party.

After he left parliament much of his time was spent in Spain and Morocco, which he visited in 1897 while attempting to reach the forbidden city of Tarudant. Out of those experiences he wrote *Mogreb-el-Acksa* (1898), an account of his adventures which also contains a compassionate defence of a society under threat from the civilizing forces of the West. He followed this with a history of the Jesuits in Paraguay, *A Vanished Arcadia* (1901). After becoming friendly with the critic Edward Garnett he published a series of sketches, essays and short stories, beginning with *The Ipané* (1899).

During World War I he volunteered for service as a Rough Rider but was turned down as being, at the age of 62, too old. His wife Gabriela died in 1906 and he died on 20 March 1936 in Argentina. He was buried among his ancestors at Inchmahome on the Lake of Menteith. After his death, A. F. Tschiffely wrote a romanticized biography of his friend, *Don Roberto* (1937), and his fellow nationalist Hugh MacDiarmid (CHRISTOPHER MURRAY GRIEVE) contributed a centenary study in 1952 about 'the damned aristo who embraced the cause of the people'.

Although Graham never enjoyed a wide reputation as a writer, he was considered by his contemporaries to be a writer's writer, and the sketches, which are mainly set in Scotland and South America, are characterized by the strength of their realism and the energy of the expression. The short stories are written within

Graham's technical and imaginative limits but their cosmopolitan topics and locations give them an exotic glamour, which is a reflection of the author's own life and interests. The best-known Scottish story is the often anthologized *Beattock for Moffat*, a gently ironic story about a dying Scotsman's last journey home. Graham had a wide circle of literary friends including Conrad, Hudson, James, Shaw and Wilde, and he was used as a model for characters in Shaw's plays *Arms and the Man* and *Captain Brassbound's Conversion*. He also wrote a number of biographies, including *Doughty Deeds* (1925), a study of his grandfather, and seven volumes of a history of the Spanish conquest of South America.

WORKS: *Note on the District of Menteith* (1895); *Father Archangel of Scotland and Other Essays* (1896); *Mogreb-el-Acksa* (1898); *The Ipané* (1899); *Thirteen Stories* (1900); *A Vanished Arcadia* (1901); *Success* (1902); *Hernando de Soto* (1903); *Progress and Other Sketches* (1905); *His People* (1906); *Faith* (1909); *Hope* (1910); *Charity* (1912); *A Hatchment* (1913); *Scottish Stories* (1914); *Bernal Díaz del Castillo* (1915); *Brought Forward* (1916); *A Brazilian Mystic* (1920); *Cartagena and the Banks of the Sinu* (1920); *The Conquest of New Granada* (1922); *The Conquest of the River Plate* (1924); *Doughty Deeds* (1925); *Pedro de Valdivia* (1926); *Redeemed and Other Sketches* (1927); *José Antonio Páez* (1929); *The Horses of the Conquest* (1930); *Writ in Sand* (1932); *Portrait of a Dictator* (1933); *Mirages* (1936)

REFERENCES: H. F. West, *A Modern Conquistador: Robert Bontine Cunninghame Graham, his Life and Works* (London, 1932); A. F. Tschiffely, *Don Roberto* (London, 1937); H. MacDiarmid, *Cunninghame Graham: a Centenary Study* (Glasgow, 1952); R. E. Haymaker, *Prince-Errant and Evocator of Horizons* (Kingsport, Tennessee, 1967); C. Watts and L. Davies, *Cunninghame Graham: a Critical Biography* (London, 1979)

Graham, W(illiam) S(ydney) (*b* 1918). Poet. He was born on 19 November 1918 in Greenock and trained as an engineer. Later he spent a year at Newbattle Abbey College, but most of his life has been spent at Madron and Mevagissey in Cornwall. His first collections of poems, *Cage without Grievance* (1942), *The Seven Journeys* (1944) and *2nd Poems* (1945), placed him in the neo-romantic school of Dylan Thomas (1914–53) and George Barker (*b* 1913), and it was not until the publication of *The White Threshold* (1949) and *The Nightfishing* (1955) that his true voice broke through. Implicit in all of Graham's poetry is the stark imagery of the sea in all its different moods, allied to a personal commitment to an exact, uncompromising use of language. His

later work in *Malcolm Mooney's Land* (1970) and *Implements in their Places* (1977) confirmed Graham's obsession with the imagery of the sea but it also moved towards a new sense of the poet's isolation and of the impermanency of life.

WORKS: *Cage without Grievance* (1942); *The Seven Journeys* (1944); *2nd Poems* (1945); *The Voyages of Alfred Wallis* (1948); *The White Threshold* (1949); *The Nightfishing* (1955); *That ye Inherit* (1968); *Malcolm Mooney's Land* (1970); *Penguin Modern Poets 17* (1970); *Implements in their Places* (1977); *Collected Poems 1942–1977* (1980)

Grahame, James (1765–1811). Poet. He was born on 22 April 1765 in Glasgow and educated at the University of Glasgow. After working in an Edinburgh law firm he was called to the Bar, but he was forced to give up his career owing to ill-health. In 1809 he took orders in the Church of England and became a curate in Shipton, Gloucestershire, and later in Sedgefield, Durham. His verse is in the minor key and written on rural subjects. His long poem *The Sabbath* was published in 1804. His great-grand-nephew was KENNETH GRAHAME.

WORKS: *Poems in English, Scotch and Latin* (1794); *Wallace: a Tragedy* (1799); *Mary Stewart, Queen of Scots* (1801); *The Sabbath: a Poem* (1804); *The Birds of Scotland* (1806); *Thoughts on Trial by Jury in Civil Causes* (1806); *Poems*, 2 vols. (1807); *The Siege of Copenhagen* (1808); *Africa Delivered* (1809); *British Georgics* (1809)

Grahame, Kenneth (1859–1932). Essayist and novelist. He was born on 8 March 1859 in Edinburgh, the son of an advocate. The year after his birth Grahame's father was appointed Sheriff-Substitute of Argyllshire and the family moved to Inverary where they remained until 1864, when Grahame's mother died of scarlet fever. He was brought up by his grandmother at Cookham Dene in Berkshire and between 1868 and 1875 he was educated at St Edward's School, Oxford. After a period working for his uncle in London he entered the Bank of England as a gentleman-clerk in 1879.

Grahame became a contributor to W. E. Henley's *National Observer* and to *The Yellow Book*, and several of his essays were reprinted in *Pagan Papers* (1893), a collection that owes much to *Virginibus puerisque* by ROBERT LOUIS STEVENSON. In 1895 he published a second collection, *The Golden Age*, which was extremely popular and which attracted a favourable critical response from writers such as Sir Arthur Quiller-Couch, who became Grahame's close friend and associate. This was followed by the equally successful *Dream Days* in 1898. In both collections the stories are studies of childhood in idyllic rural settings where the adult world of reality is sharply contrasted with the fantasy world of the child. He wrote nothing more until 1908 when he published his best-known book *The Wind in the Willows*, written for his son Alisdair. In this novel for children, which has given equal pleasure to adults, the arcadian world of the Wild Wood and the River is peopled by an organized society of idealized, peaceful animals: Toad, Rat, Mole, Badger and Otter. Throughout the story runs the timeless symbol of the river, a favourite motif in Grahame's work. It was later made into a popular play, *Toad of Toad Hall*, by A. A. Milne. In 1916 Grahame edited *The Cambridge Book of Poetry for Children*.

Grahame became Secretary to the Bank of England in 1898 and he married Elspeth Thomson in 1899. He died on 6 July 1932. His great-grand-uncle was the poet JAMES GRAHAME and he was the cousin of Anthony Hope (A. H. Hawkins), the author of *The Prisoner of Zenda*.

WORKS: *Pagan Papers* (1893); *The Golden Age* (1895); *Dream Days* (1898); *The Wind in the Willows* (1908); ed., *The Cambridge Book of Poetry for Children* (1916)

REFERENCE: P. Green, *Kenneth Grahame: a Study of his Life, Work and Times* (London, 1959)

Grahame, Simeon (*c* 1570–1614). Poet. Very little is known about the life of Simeon Grahame, who was born in Edinburgh, the son of a merchant. In the dedicatory epistle to the Earl of Montrose in his *Anatomie of Humours* (1609), Grahame stated that he had been at different times a traveller, soldier and courtier, but Sir THOMAS URQUHART remarked in *The . . . Jewel* that Grahame was 'too licentious and given over to all manner of debardings'. He seems to have spent some time in exile, when he became a Franciscan, and to have returned on occasion to Scotland before his death in France in 1614. The *Anatomie*, a curious mixture of prose and verse, is remarkable only for the vehemence of Grahame's attacks on the medical profession. He also wrote two fine elegies on the pain of exile, 'His Passionado,

when He was on a Pilgrimage' and 'From Italy to Scotland his Soyle'.

EDITION: R. Jamesone, ed., *The Anatomie of Humours and the Passionate Sparke of a Relenting Mind* (Edinburgh, 1830)

Grainger, James (*c* 1721–1766). Poet. He was born in Duns, Berwickshire, and educated in North Berwick and at the University of Edinburgh, where he studied medicine. He served as a soldier in the British Army in Europe between 1745 and 1748, when he returned to his studies in Edinburgh. In 1753 he settled in London but, failing to earn a living as a doctor, he turned to editing and reviewing for a living. Through his writing he quarrelled with TOBIAS SMOLLETT and the smallness of his own talent prevented any further advancement. In 1759 he moved to the West Indies, where he married the daughter of a wealthy sugar planter and published *Sugar Cane* (1764), a pretentious long poem which was ridiculed mercilessly by the critics in London. Grainger died on 16 December 1766 at St Christopher.

WORKS: *Historia febris anomalae Batavae annorum* (1753); *Accedunt minita siphylica* (1753); *Essays Physical and Literary* (1756); *Poetical Translation of the Elegies of Tibullus and the Poems of Sulpica*, 2 vols. (1759); *Essay on the more Common West Indian Diseases and the Remedies which that Country itself Produces* (1764); *Sugar Cane* (1764)

EDITION: R. Anderson, ed., *Poetical Works of James Grainger*, 2 vols. (Edinburgh, 1836)

Grant [née MacVicar], **Ann**, of Laggan (1755–1838). Essayist. She was born on 21 February 1755 in Glasgow, the daughter of Duncan MacVicar, an army officer. Part of her childhood was spent in North America but her father returned to Scotland in 1773 and was made barrack-master at Fort Augustus. In 1779 she married the barrack chaplain and minister of the neighbouring parish of Laggan, where she lived until her husband's death in 1801. Left destitute she turned to writing for a living, publishing first a collection of simple poems in 1802 and her best-known book, her reminiscences of Highland life, *Letters from the Mountains*, in 1803. The growing interest in the romance of the Highlands was partly the result of the poetry of Sir WALTER SCOTT, and the public was avid for information and descriptions of the Highlanders' way of life. While the *Letters* provided that, not the least of its qualities is the unfolding of Ann Grant's personality from girlhood to mature womanhood and the care of eight children. In 1808 she published *Memoirs of an American Lady*, which contained her childhood memories, and she wrote another Highland book in 1811, *Essays on the Superstitions of the Highlands of Scotland*. In 1810 Ann Grant moved to Edinburgh, where she became a shrewd, and at times tart, observer of contemporary manners. She died on 7 November 1838.

WORKS: *Poems on Various Subjects* (1802); *Letters from the Mountains* (1803); *The Highlanders* (1808); *Memoirs of an American Lady* (1808); *Essays on the Superstitions of the Highlands of Scotland* (1811); *Eighteen hundred and thirteen* (1814); *The Bluebell of Scotland* (1835); *The Touchstone* (1842)

EDITIONS: J. P. Grant, ed., *Memoir and Correspondence of Mrs Grant* (London, 1844); J. R. N. Macphail, ed., *Letters Concerning Highland Affairs* (Edinburgh, 1896)

Grant, Elizabeth (i) (1745–1814). Songwriter. She was a native of the north-east. Her first husband, a soldier, died in 1790; thereafter she married a doctor and lived in Bath, but very little is known about her life. She owes her reputation to a popular song *Roy's Wife of Aldivalloch*, which tells the story of a jilting in the Aberdeenshire countryside of her childhood.

Grant, Elizabeth (ii), of Rothiemurcus (1797–1885). Diarist. She was born on 7 May 1797 in Edinburgh, the daughter of a lawyer and Highland landowner, Sir John Peter Grant. When she was five the family moved to London to enable her father to practice at the English Bar, but her childhood summers continued to be spent on the family estate of Rothiemurcus. In 1814 her father was persuaded to return to Edinburgh, but the move was not a success and he failed to make any headway at the Scottish Bar. Financial difficulties forced him to sell up in Edinburgh and to move his family to Rothiemurcus, but debt continued to be an ever-present threat. Elizabeth's brother William was imprisoned in Edinburgh in 1826 for failing to meet the demands of his creditors and in the following year Sir John was forced to flee to India to escape the same fate. There he became a judge in Bombay and retrieved his social position; it was in India, too, that Elizabeth met and married Colonel Hay Smith in 1830. On his retirement they settled on his Irish estate of Balliboys and Elizabeth died there on 16 November 1885.

Under her maiden name Elizabeth wrote the memoirs of her life, *Memoirs of a Highland Lady*, published after her death, in 1898, for which she bacame famous. Not only do they present a lively and detailed account of Edinburgh during the early years of the century and of the personalities who lived there, but they also portray vividly the customs and manners of her childhood years. Her style is personal and confiding, almost as if she is treating the reader as a valued friend, and not the least of the book's virtues is the admiration it inspires for the author in the midst of all her family's many misfortunes.

EDITION: Lady Strachey, ed., *Memoirs of a Highland Lady, by Elizabeth Grant of Rothiemurcus* (London, 1898)

Grant, James (1822–87). Novelist and historian. He was born on 1 August 1822 in Edinburgh, the son of an army officer. The greater part of his childhood was spent in North America and Spain, and between 1840 and 1843 he served in the army, before returning to Edinburgh to work as an architectural draughtsman. His first novel, *The Romance of War*, was published in 1845 and it was the first of many light novels from his pen dealing with the army, war and famous events from Scotland's history. It is as a historian that he is best remembered; his three-volume *Old and New Edinburgh* (1880) is a standard, and lovingly researched, history of the city. An early nationalist, Grant founded the National Association for the Vindication of Scottish Rights in 1852. He died on 5 May 1887 in London.

WORKS: *The Romance of War* (1845); *The Phantom Regiment* (1847); *Adventures of an Aide-de-camp* (1848); *Memoirs and Adventures of Sir William Kirkcaldy of Grange* (1849); *Memorials of the Castle of Edinburgh* (1850); *The Scottish Cavalier* (1850); *Memoirs and Adventures of Sir John Hepburn* (1851); *Jane Seton* (1853); *Bothwell* (1854); *Philip Rollo* (1854); *Frank Hilton* (1855); *Henry Ogilvie* (1856); *The Highlanders of Glen Ora* (1857); *Arthur Blane* (1858); *Memoirs of James, Marquis of Montrose* (1858); *The Cavaliers of Fortune* (1859); *Holywood Hotel* (1859); *Legends of the Black Watch* (1859); *Mary of Lorraine* (1860); *Jack Manly* (1861); *Oliver Ellis* (1861); *The Captain of the Guard* (1862); *Dick Rodney* (1863); *Letty Hyde's Lovers* (1863); *Adventures of Rob Roy* (1864); *Second to None* (1864); *The King's own Borderers* (1865); *The Constable of France* (1866); *A Haunted Life* (1866); *First Love and Last Love* (1868); *The Girl he Married* (1869); *The Secret Despatch* (1869); *Lady Wedderburn's Wish* (1870); *The White Cockade* (1879); *Only an Ensign* (1871); *Under the Red Dragon* (1872); *British Battles on Land*

and Sea, 3 vols. (1873–5); *Fairer than a Fairy* (1874); *The Queen's Cadet* (1874); *Shall I Win her?* (1874); *One of the Six Hundred* (1875); *Cassell's Illustrated History of India*, 3 vols. (1876–7); *Did she Love him?* (1876); *Morley Ashton* (1876); *Six Years Ago* (1877); *The Lord Hermitage* (1878); *The Ross-shire Buffs* (1878); *Vere of ours* (1878); *The Royal Regiment* (1879); *Cassell's Old and New Edinburgh* (1880); *The Duke of Albany's own Highlanders* (1880); *The Cameronians* (1881); *Derval Hampton* (1881); *Lady Glendonwyn* (1881); *The Scots Brigade* (1882); *Violet Jermyn* (1882); *The Dead Tryst* (1883); *Jack Chaloner* (1883); *Miss Cheyne of Esslemont* (1883); *The Master of Aberfeldie* (1884); *Cassell's Illustrated History of the War in the Sudan*, 6 vols. (1885–6); *Colville of the Guards* (1885); *The Royal Highlanders* (1885); *Dulcie Carlyon* (1886); *The Tartans and Clans of Scotland* (1886); *Playing with Fire* (1887); *Scottish Soldiers of Fortune* (1888); *The Black Watch* (1892); *Recent British Battles on Land and Sea* (1904)

Grant, James Augustus (1827–92). Explorer. He was born on 11 April 1827 at Nairn, the son of a minister of the Church of Scotland. He studied natural history at Marischal College, Aberdeen, and in 1846 he was commissioned into the 8th Battalion of the Bengal Infantry, taking part in the actions of the Indian Mutiny. Wounded during the relief of Lucknow in 1857, he returned to England in the following year, but by then his friendship with John Hanning Speke (1827–64) had attracted him to African exploration and he took part in Speke's expedition to East Africa in 1860–62. Illness prevented him from accompanying Speke on his journey to discover the source of the Nile, but Grant's botanical notes and his meteorological registers provided the basis of the scientific findings published after the expedition's return to Britain. A more human, anecdotal account was published in his *Walk Across Africa* (1864), the title of which was suggested by Gladstone's remark 'You have had a long walk, Captain Grant' (Preface, p.x). Grant took no further part in African exploration and after serving with Lord Napier's staff in the Abyssinian War of 1868 he retired from the army to live in Nairn where he died on 11 February 1892.

Gray, Sir **Alexander** (1882–1968). Poet. he was born on 6 January 1882 in Dundee and was educated at the High School there and at the universities of Edinburgh, Göttingen and Paris. Between 1905 and 1921 he worked in various departments of the Civil Service before being appointed Professor of Political Economy at the University of Aberdeen, a post he held until 1934, when he took up a similar appointment at the University of Edinburgh; in 1956 he became Emeritus Professor of Political Economy. Gray held a number of posts in public bodies and government commissions, including the Schools Broadcasting Council and the Fullbright Commission. As a poet he is best known for his often anthologized 'Scotland', which is in English, though much of his early work was written in the dialect of Mearns in the north-east. With the poets MARION ANGUS, HELEN BURNESS CRUICKSHANK, WILLIAM JEFFREY and others, he contributed to *Northern Numbers* edited by CHRISTOPHER MURRAY GRIEVE and thereby became associated with the SCOTTISH RENAISSANCE movement. Translation from German and the Scandinavian languages occupied his later years, and the poems in *Arrows* (1932), taken mainly from Heinrich Heine (1797–1856), show both his scrupulous accuracy of language and his ability to match the metres of the original works. He died on 17 February 1968 in Edinburgh.

WORKS: *The Scottish People at Veere* (1909); trans., Richard Grelling, *J'accuse* (1915); *The True Pastime, The Upright Sheaf, The New Leviathan* (1915) [pamphlets on World War I]; trans., Richard Grelling, *Der Verbrechen*, as *The Crime* (1917); trans., Richard Grelling, *Belgische Aktenstücke*, as *Belgian Documents* (1919); *Songs and Ballads Chiefly from Heine* (1920); *Some Aspects of National Health Insurance* (1923); *Any Man's Life* (1924); *Poems* (1925); *Family Endowment* (1927); *Gossip* (1928); *Songs from Heine* (1928); *The Development of Economic Doctrine* (1931); *Arrows* (1932); *Robert Burns: an Address* (1944); *The Socialist Tradition* (1946); *Adam Smith* (1948); M. Lindsay, ed., *Selected Poems* (1948); *Sir Halewyn* (1949); *Four and Forty: a Selection of Danish Ballads* (1954); *Historical Ballads of Denmark* (1958); ed., *Timorous Civility: a Scots Miscellany* (1966)

Gray, David (1838–61). Poet. He was born on 29 January 1838 at Merkland near Kirkintilloch, Dunbartonshire, the son of a handloom weaver. He was educated at the University of Glasgow, where he studied divinity, but his calling to the ministry was diverted by his literary interests. In 1860 he moved to London and gained an entry to literary society through the friendship of Monkton Milnes, and later Lord Houghton (1809–85) and Sydney Dobell (1824–74); but ill health forced him to return to Scotland and he died there on 3 December 1861. His only collection of poems was published posthumously in 1874 and it contains *The Luggie*, a long poem in praise of the stream that flowed past his birthplace. With its vivid descriptions of natural scenes and country pastimes, the poem is similar in vein to THE SEASONS by JAMES THOMSON (i).

EDITIONS: H. G. Bell, ed., *The Poetical Works of David Gray* (Glasgow, 1874); J. Ferguson, ed., *In the Shadows* (London, 1920)

REFERENCE: A. V. Stuart, *David Gray: the Poet of 'The Luggie'* (Kirkintilloch, 1961)

Gray, Simon. Pen-name of ALEXANDER BOSWELL.

Gray Manuscript. A manuscript collection of poems in Scots, made by James Gray, a priest of Dunblane and later secretary to James Stewart (*d* 1504), Archbishop of St Andrews. It is now in the possession of the NATIONAL LIBRARY OF SCOTLAND. With the MAKCULLOCH MANUSCRIPT, it is one of the earliest extant collections of Scots poetry. It includes variant readings of several poems by ROBERT HENRYSON, as well as a collection of prayers, genealogical tables and chronological tables of early Scottish history, all written in Latin. It was published with the Makculloch by the SCOTTISH TEXT SOCIETY in 1918.

Great Unknown, the. A name given to Sir WALTER SCOTT by his publisher and friend JAMES BALLANTYNE while the authorship of his novels remained anonymous. Although his identity as an author had long been an open secret it was revealed only on 23 February 1827 at a theatrical fund dinner held in the Assembly Rooms in Edinburgh.

Greig, Gavin (1856–1914). Folklorist and poet. He was born on 10 February 1856 at Parkhill in the parish of Newmachar, Aberdeenshire. On his mother's side of the family he was distantly related to the poet ROBERT BURNS, and his father claimed kinship with the Norwegian composer Edvard Grieg (1843–1907). He was educated at the village school in Dyce and at Aberdeen Grammar School, and between 1872 and 1876 he was a student at the University of Aberdeen. On graduation, he became a teacher at the village school at Whitehill and he held the post until his death on 31 August 1914.

Greig's first poems were published in the WHISTLE-BINKIE anthologies. He was a clever imitator of north-east folk-song, writing a 'ballad corner' each week for the *Buchan Observer*. It was that attraction to folk-song that spurred

his interest in ballad collecting and inspired him to begin the work on which his fame ultimately rests. In 1904 the New Spalding Club asked him to begin work on a ballad collection with the Revd J. B. Duncan of Lynturk (1848–1917); Greig was to have responsibility for the music and his colleague for the words. By the time of Greig's death the distinction between their respective tasks had become blurred and they had recorded 3050 texts and 3100 different tunes, most of the work having been done by Greig, who had an encyclopaedic knowledge of the lore and traditions of the north-east. Although Greig was unable to add conclusions and notes to all the texts, his collection of ballads remains the most comprehensive and the most illuminating of all the major Scottish collections. Greig's work was edited in 1925 by Alexander Keith and was published in its entirety in two volumes in 1981 and 1982.

EDITIONS: A. Keith, ed., *Last Leaves of Traditional Ballads and Ballad Airs* (Aberdeen, 1925); P. Shuldam-Shaw and E. B. Lyle, eds., *The Greig–Duncan Folk Song Collection*, 2 vols. (Aberdeen, 1981–2)

Grierson, Sir Herbert John Clifford (1866–1960). Critic and scholar. He was born on 16 January 1866 at Quendale in Shetland and was educated at King's College, Aberdeen, and Christ Church, Oxford. His academic career began in Aberdeen, where he was Professor of English from 1894 to 1915, and thereafter he was Professor of Rhetoric and English Literature at Edinburgh until 1935. He died on 19 February 1960 in Cambridge.

The holder of a number of honorary degrees from universities in Britain, Ireland and North America, Grierson, who brought a new professionalism to English studies in the universities, was one of the most respected teachers of his generation. He edited the letters of Sir WALTER SCOTT between 1932 and 1937 and wrote a biography of Scott which was published in 1938. Grierson's edition of the poems of John Donne (1912) helped to reintroduce the work of the metaphysical poets, and his *Metaphysical Poets, from Donne to Butler* (1921) with an important critical introduction is considered to be a classic anthology.

WORKS: *The First Half of the Seventeenth Century* (1906); ed., *The Poems of John Donne* (1912); ed., *Metaphysical Poets, from Donne to Butler* (1921); *Blake's Illustrations to Gray's Poems* (1922); *The Back-*

ground of English Literature (1925); ed., The Poems of John Milton (1925); ed., Lyrical Poetry from Blake to Hardy (1928); Cross Currents in the literature of the Seventeenth Century (1929); ed., Letters of Sir Walter Scott, 12 vols. (1932–7); Carlyle and Hitler (1933); Edinburgh Essays on Scots Literature (1933); Milton and Wordsworth: Prophets and Poets (1937); Sir Walter Scott (1938); Essays and Addresses (1940); The English Bible (1944); with J. C. Smith, Critical History of English Poetry (1945); Rhetoric and English Composition (1945); And the Third Day (1948); Criticism and Creation (1950); Swinburne (1954)

Grierson, John (1898–1972). Documentary film producer. He was born on 26 April 1898 in Kilmadock, Stirlingshire, the son of a schoolmaster. He was educated at Stirling High School (1908–15) and served as a radio operator in the Royal Naval Volunteer Reserve in World War I. After four years (1919–23) at the University of Glasgow he was awarded a Rockefeller Fellowship to study the effects of immigration on the social problems of the United States. While in America he worked as a journalist and developed an interest in film.

In January 1927 Grierson returned to Britain and joined the Empire Marketing Board, which had been established to promote the marketing of the products of the British Empire. For them he made Drifters (1928), a documentary film about the Scottish herring fleet, which was the forerunner of a number of films about British life and work, frequently expressed in heroic terms. Grierson is recognized as the founder in Britain of the documentary film movement, and in his later work with the GPO film unit (1934–8) he worked with, among others, W. H. Auden, William Coldstream and Benjamin Britten. In 1939 he was appointed Commissioner to the newly formed National Film Board of Canada, and in 1946 Director of Mass Communication at UNESCO in Paris. Grierson continued his interests in Canada and Scotland: he was appointed a visiting professor at McGill University, Montreal, and served as a member of the Films of Scotland Committee, which was formed in 1955. His collected writings on film, Grierson on Documentary, edited by Forsyth Hardy, was published in 1946. Grierson died on 19 February 1972 in Bath.

EDITIONS: F. Hardy, ed., Grierson on Documentary (London, 1946); F. Hardy, ed., Grierson on the Movies (London, 1981)

REFERENCE: F. Hardy, John Grierson: a Documentary Biography (London, 1979)

Grieve, Christopher Murray ['Hugh MacDiarmid'] (1892–1978). Poet. Christopher Murray Grieve, who wrote under the pseudonym of 'Hugh MacDiarmid', was born on 11 August 1892 in Langholm, the son of a postman. He was educated at Langholm Academy where one of his teachers in the primary school was the composer FRANCIS GEORGE SCOTT, with whom Grieve later collaborated. Grieve was to claim in later life in Lucky Poet, 'A Self-study in Literature and Political Ideas' (1943), that his early learning was aided by his ready access to the books of the town's Thomas Telford Library. In 1908 he became a pupil-teacher at Broughton Higher Grade School in Edinburgh, where his growing literary interests were encouraged by George Ogilvie, the head of the English Department and an early mentor. Between 1910 and 1915 he worked as a journalist in Edinburgh, Langholm, Ebbw Vale in South Wales, Clydebank, Cupar and Forfar, and during World War I he served as a sergeant in the Royal Army Medical Corps in Salonica and France.

At the end of the war Grieve married Peggy Skinner and they lived for a short time in St Andrews before settling (except for a brief period (1920–21) at Kildermorie, Easter Ross) in Montrose. There he worked as a journalist on The Montrose Review and busied himself in civic duties, becoming a town councillor in 1922 and a Justice of the Peace in 1926. His literary interests increased during this period and he became an editor and publisher, producing three anthologies of contemporary Scottish writing, Northern Numbers (1920–22), and a series of magazines devoted to Scottish arts, letters and politics: the SCOTTISH CHAPBOOK (1922–3), the Scottish Nation (1923) and the Northern Review (1924). It was also at that time that he adopted the literary pseudonym 'Hugh MacDiarmid' (originally 'M'Diarmid' and first used in the Scottish Chapbook, vol. 1, no. 1), which was to remain his poetic name for the rest of his life, although he occasionally used other names such as Isobel Guthrie, A. K. Laidlaw, Arthur Leslie, Gillesbriod Mac a'Ghreidhir and James Maclaren.

Grieve's first poems and short stories, which were written in English, were published in 1923 in Annals of the Five Senses, but by the time of its publication he had turned to writing in Scots. Through his study of Sir James Wilson's Lowland Scotch as Spoken in the Lower Strathearn District of Perthshire (1915) and the

Etymological Dictionary of the Scottish Language by JOHN JAMIESON he began to evolve a literary Scots that was very different from the debased sentimentality of 19th-century usage. The result was a series of exquisite short lyric poems, published in *Sangschaw* (1925) and *Penny Wheep* (1926). MacDiarmid insisted on using a large variety of Scots dialect words outside common currency and these lyrics stand as monuments to his stated aims 'to adapt an essentially rural tongue to the very much more complex requirements of our urban civilisation' (*Scottish Chapbook*, vol. 1, no. 3, October 1922).

Out of his literary efforts of the 1920s MacDiarmid evolved the SCOTTISH RENAISSANCE movement, whose aim was to dissociate Scottish literature from the sentimentality of the 19th century and to bring it into line with contemporary European thinking. It was an attitude that was to influence many of his contemporaries and, later in the century, disciples. In 1926 MacDiarmid published his long poem A DRUNK MAN LOOKS AT THE THISTLE, a work of 2685 lines, which is generally considered to be his finest sustained creation. It was followed by an equally ambitious though less successful long poem sequence, *To Circumjack Cencrastus* (1930), which means 'to enfold the curly snake'.

MacDiarmid's campaign for the revival of Scots letters also had a political aspect: he was one of the founder-members of the Scottish section of PEN, the writers' organization, and he became a member of the National Party of Scotland in 1928. His political and literary activities brought a number of stresses on his personal life and after going to London in 1929, to edit the ill-fated radio magazine *Vox* started by COMPTON MACKENZIE, MacDiarmid entered on a period of intense hardship and marital breakdown, which saw him move to Liverpool as a public relations officer, to Thakeham in Surrey, to Edinburgh to edit *The Free Man*, a nationalist journal, and finally in 1933 into self-imposed exile on Whalsay in Shetland. In 1931 he met his second wife Valda Trevlyn. During this period he was expelled from the National Party for his growing Communism; in 1934 he joined the Communist Party of Great Britain, but he was expelled four years later for his 'nationalist deviation'. 'I'll hae nae hauf-way hoose, but aye be whaur/Extremes meet' he had written in *A Drunk Man Looks at the Thistle*.

Despite the impermanency of his personal life, the 1930s was a period of restless literary activity for MacDiarmid. He published *First Hymn to Lenin* (1931), *Scots Unbound* (1932), *Stony Limits* (1934) and *Second Hymn to Lenin* (1935), and in his poetry he began to turn again to English and to make extensive use of political and scientific vocabulary and imagery. His hymns to Lenin relate poetry directly to politics and these volumes include single poems like 'The Seamless Garment', 'Lo, a child is born', 'John Maclean', 'The Skeleton of the Future' and 'On the Ocean Floor', which among others, outline his socialist credo. He also wrote 'On a Raised Beach', his meditation on the mysteries of the past, 'Lament for the Great Music', a plea for the unity of Scottish culture, several introspective, highly personal poems such as 'At my father's grave', and short lyrics like 'Milk-Whort and Bog-Cotton'. In his later work he pursued his political and philosophical preoccupations by selecting long extracts from relatively obscure scientific and literary works and transmuting them into his poetry. In *In Memoriam James Joyce* (1955) he ponders on the different ways in which the diversity of languages has brought with it divisiveness, and on the poet's duty to create unity. *The Kind of Poetry I Want* (1961) enlarged on the importance of language and the indivisibility of its use for the poet. His other collections are: *A Kist of Whistles* (1947), *Three Hymns to Lenin* (1957), *The Battle Continues* (1957), *Collected Poems* (1962) *A Clyack-Sheaf* (1969), *More Collected Poems* (1970) and the *Complete Poems* (1978). Various collections of 'selected poems' have also appeared (1934, 1944, 1946, 1954 and 1970).

MacDiarmid's prose work is also worthy of note. His *Contemporary Scottish Studies* (1926), a collection of essays originally contributed to the *Scottish Educational Journal*, demonstrates his eagerness to attack the shibboleths of the past and to foster the aims of the Scottish literary renaissance; *Albyn, or Scotland and the Future* (1927) and *At the Sign of the Thistle* (1934) argue the case for Scotland's nationhood; with Lewis Grassic Gibbon (JAMES LESLIE MITCHELL) he wrote *Scottish Scene or the Intelligent Man's Guide to Albyn* (1934). Other works include *The Islands of Scotland* (1939), *Scottish Eccentrics* (1936) and *The Company I've Kept* (1966), and some of his essays were collected in *The Uncanny Scot* (1968) and *Selected Essays* (1969).

After World War II MacDiarmid lived for a short period in Glasgow and Strathaven, before moving to a cottage at Brownsbank nr Biggar, which was to be his home until his death on 9 September 1978. In 1956 he had rejoined the Communist Party after once more being a member of the Scottish National Party between 1942 and 1948. His later years were crowned with various forms of public recognition, extensive overseas travel and the publication of his work in several collections and numerous pamphlets. Although many disagreed with his political stances, Hugh MacDiarmid is recognised as the major Scottish literary figure of the 20th century, a poet whose work ranks with that of WILLIAM DUNBAR and ROBERT BURNS and a writer and thinker of international standing.

WORKS: *Northern Numbers*, 3 vols. (1920–22); *Annals of the Five Senses* (1923); *Sangschaw* (1925); *Penny Wheep* (1926); *Contemporary Scottish Studies* (1926); *A Drunk Man Looks at the Thistle* (1926); ed., *Robert Burns 1759–1796* (1926); *Albyn, or Scotland and the Future* (1927); *The Lucky Bag* (1927); *The Present Position of Scottish Music* (1927); *The Present Position of Scottish Arts and Affairs* (1928); *The Scottish National Association of April Fools* (1928); *Scotland in 1980* (1929); *The Handmaid of the Lord* (1930); *To Circumjack Cencrastus* (1930); ed., *Living Scottish Poets* (1931); *O wha's been here before me Lass* (1931); *First Hymn to Lenin and Other Poems* (1931); *Warning Democracy* (1931); *Scots Unbound and Other Poems* (1932); *Second Hymn to Lenin* (1932); *Tarras* (1932); *At the Sign of the Thistle* (1934); *Five Bits of Miller* (1934); with Lewis Grassic Gibbon, *Scottish Scene or the Intelligent Man's Guide to Albyn* (1934); *Selected Poems* (1934); *Stony Limits and Other Poems* (1934); *The Birlinn of Clanranald* (1935); *Second Hymn to Lenin and Other Poems* (1935); *Charles Doughty and the Need for Modern Poetry* (1936); *Scottish Eccentrics* (1936); *Direadh* (1938); *Scotland and the Question of a Popular Front against Fascism and War* (1938); *The Islands of Scotland: Hebrides, Orkney and Shetlands* (1939); *Speaking for Scotland* (1939); ed., *The Golden Treasury of Scottish Poetry* (1940); *Cornish Heroic Song for Valda Trevlyn* (1943); *Lucky Poet* (1943); R. C. Saunders, ed., *Selected Poems of Hugh MacDiarmid* (1944); *Poems of the East-West Synthesis* (1946); *Speaking for Scotland: Selected Poems of Hugh MacDiarmid* (1946); *A Kist of Whistles* (1947); ed., *William Soutar: Collected Poems* (1948); ed., *Robert Burns: Poems* (1949); *Cunninghame Graham: a Centenary Study* (1952); as Arthur Leslie, *The Politics and Poetry of Hugh MacDiarmid* (1952); ed., *Selections from the Poems of William Dunbar* (1952); O. Brown, ed., *Selected Poems of Hugh MacDiarmid* (1954); *Francis George Scott: an Essay on the Occasion of his Seventy-fifth Birthday* (1955); *In Memoriam James Joyce* (1955); ed., *Selected Poems of William Dunbar* (1955); *Stony Limits and Scots Unbound and Other Poems* (1956); *The Battle Continues* (1957); *Three Hymns to Lenin* (1957); *Burns Today and Tomorrow* (1959); *David*

Hume: Scotland's Greatest Son (1961); *The Kind of Poetry I Want* (1961); *The Blaward and the Skelly* (1962); *Bracken Hills in Autumn* (1962); *Collected Poems of Hugh MacDiarmid* (1962, rev. 2/1967); *The Man of (almost) Independent Mind* (1962); *Poetry Like the Hawthorn* (1962); ed., *Robert Burns: Love Songs* (1962); *When the Rat Race is Over* (1962); *The Ugly Birds Without Wings* (1962); *An Apprentice Angel* (1963); *Harry Martinson: Aniara, a Review of Man in Time and Space* (1963); *Sydney Goodsir Smith* (1963); *The Ministry of Water: Two Poems* (1964); *Six Vituperative Verses* (1964); *Two Poems* (1964); *The Burning Passion* (1965); *Poet and Play and Other Poems* (1965); *The Fire of the Spirit: Two Poems* (1965); *The Company I've Kept* (1966); *Whuchulls* (1966); *On a Raised Beach* (1967); *The Eemis Stane* (1967); *A Lap of Honour* (1967); *An Afternoon with Hugh MacDiarmid* (1968); with Owen Dudley Edwards, Gwynfor Evans and Ioan Rhys, *Celtic Nationalism* (1968); J. K. Annand, ed., *Early Lyrics by Hugh MacDiarmid* (1968); *The Uncanny Scot* (1968); *A Clyack-Sheaf* (1969); D. Glen, ed., *Selected Essays of Hugh MacDiarmid* (1969); *The MacDiarmids: a Conversation* (1970); *More Collected Poems* (1970); D. Craig and J. Manson, eds., *Selected Poems* (1970); M. Grieve and A. Scott, eds., *The Hugh MacDiarmid Anthology* (1972); *A Political Speech* (1972); *Song of the Seraphim* (1973); *Direadh I, II and III* (1974); with Campbell Maclean and Anthony Ross, *John Knox* (1976); *Complete Poems*, 2 vols. (1978)

REFERENCES: K. D. Duval and S. G. Smith, eds., *Hugh MacDiarmid: a Festschrift* (Edinburgh, 1962); K. Buthlay, *Hugh MacDiarmid* (Edinburgh and London, 1964); D. Glen, *Hugh MacDiarmid and the Scottish Renaissance* (Edinburgh and London, 1964); D. Glen, ed., *Hugh MacDiarmid: a Critical Survey* (Edinburgh and London, 1972); E. Morgan, *Hugh MacDiarmid* (London 1976); D. Glen, ed., *MacDiarmid Double Issue of Akros* (Preston, 1977); G. Wright, *MacDiarmid: an Illustrated Biography* (Edinburgh, 1977); P. H. Scott and A. C. Davies, eds., *The Age of MacDiarmid* (Edinburgh 1980); K. Buthlay, *Hugh MacDiarmid* (Edinburgh, 1982)

Grosart, A(lexander) B(alloch) (1827–99). Divine and editor. He was born on 18 June 1827 at Stirling, the son of a building contractor. He entered the University of Edinburgh to read for the ministry of the Church of Scotland and on his ordination he became minister of Kinross in October 1856. There he quickly built a reputation as a committed preacher and the author of several pamphlets which dealt with evangelical themes. In 1865 he moved to Liverpool and between 1868 and 1884 he was minister of Whalley Range in Blackburn, Lancashire. Ill health forced him to retire and he died on 16 March 1899 in Dublin. Grosart's editorial career began while he was still a student with a collection (1851) of the poems of ROBERT FERGUSSON.

He subsequently became well-known as an

editor and printer of rare Elizabethan and Jacobean books, which he published in the *Fuller Worthies Library* (39 volumes between 1868 and 1876), *Occasional Issues of Unique and Very Rare Books* (38 volumes between 1875 and 1881), and the *Huth Library* (33 volumes, 1886). He also produced limited editions of several manuscript holdings including those of the Roxburghe Club and he spared neither time nor money in his search for rare, out-of-print literary material. Later scholars were to complain of a lack of organization in his editing and frequent critical lapses, but his reproduction of so many texts did much to further the study of Tudor and Jacobean literature. In all his business transactions Grosart limited his editions to subscribers who could afford to pay the high prices he demanded for his books.

WORKS: *Jesus Mighty to Save* (1863); *Small Sins* (1863); *The Prince of Light* (1864); *Joining the Church* (1865); *The Lambs All Safe* (1865); ed., *The Works of Michael Bruce* (1865); *Representative Non-Conformists with the Message of their Lifework for Today* (1879); *Hanani* (1874); *Songs of the Day and Night, or Three Centuries of Original Hymns* (1890); *Robert Fergusson* (1898)

Gude and Godlie Ballatis. The familiar name given to the collection of chiefly sacramental work in Scots whose full title is *Ane Compendious Book of Godly and Spirituall Songs collected out of sundrie partes of the Scripture, with sundrie of other Ballates changed out of prophaine sangis for avoyding of sinne and harlotrie with augmentation of sundrie gude and godlie Ballatis.* It was written and compiled by the brothers James, John and Robert WEDDERBURN and published in 1567; it is the earliest known metrical treatise in Scots to reflect the aspirations of the Reformation movement in Scotland.

As in other parts of Europe at that time the Reformation had brought with it a desire among churchmen and laity for the propagation of religious works in the vernacular, and the publication of the *Gude and Godlie Ballatis* was the first attempt at fulfilling that need in Scotland. It was published in two volumes: the first included the Catechism, metrical Psalms and hymns, many translated from German, and a miscellaneous group of carols and ballads; the second added further hymns and Psalms but the Wedderburns also chose to include a number of secular songs and political and religious satires. That mixture of the sacred and the profane no doubt increased the work's popularity but it is also an early indica-

tion of the combination of coarseness and refinement that was to characterize so many of the best collections of Scottish traditional songs. The secular songs and satires were also included to maintain and to leaven the Reformation struggle; as the work's SCOTTISH TEXT SOCIETY editor A. F. Mitchell claims in his introduction of 1897, 'They wrote them to support and cheer those who were contending, even unto bonds, imprisonment and death, for the simplicity and purity which the Christian religion imperatively demands of its professors and especially of its ministers.'

In spite of the clumsiness of the songs and in some cases their unsuitability for singing, the *Gude and Godlie Ballatis* provided the Reformation church in Scotland with a strong vernacular base for its services and it was in constant use throughout the 17th century. In making their translations of the hymns and psalms into Scots for the collection, the Wedderburns owed a great debt to the hymnologists of the German and the Swedish reformed Churches.

EDITION: A. F. Mitchell, ed., *A Compendious Book of Godly and Spiritual Songs* STS (Edinburgh and London, 1897)

Guidman o' Ballengeich, the. One of the names by which JAMES V was known when he chose to travel anonymously among his people. The story is told by Sir WALTER SCOTT in his TALES OF A GRANDFATHER (Chapter 27) that 'when James travelled in disguise, he used a name which was known only to some of his principal nobility and attendants. He was called the Goodman (the tenant that is) of Ballengeich.' Guidman means 'the proprietor or tenant of a small estate or farm'. (*SND*).

Gunn, Neil M(iller) ['Dane McNeill'] (1891–1973). Novelist. He was born on 8 November 1891 in Dunbeath, Caithness, the son of a fisherman. Against a background of crofting and fishing, he was educated at the village school until he was 12, when he was sent to live with his married sister at St John's Town of Dalry in Galloway. There he was educated privately and in 1907 he passed by examination into the Civil Service. He moved to live and work in London, where he remained until 1909 when promotion took him back to Edinburgh. After studying successfully for the Customs and Excise service, he was appointed an officer in December 1911 and was based in Inverness. While working as a distillery officer he met the Irish novelist Maurice Walsh (1874–1964) who became a lifelong friend and literary colleague. Something of that friendship can be seen in Walsh's thinly disguised autobiographical novel *The Key above the Door* (1926). During World War I Gunn remained in the Excise, stationed in Kinlochleven, Argyllshire, and it was there that he started to write, contributing poems and short stories to a small London based literary magazine, *The Apple-Tree*. He married in 1921 and after spending a year in Wigan, Lancashire, he moved to Lybster in Caithness before taking up residence in Inverness as the customs officer at the Glen Mhor distillery in 1924.

Gunn started to write for CHAMBERS' JOURNAL and the *Cornhill Magazine*, and his friendship with 'Hugh MacDiarmid' (CHRISTOPHER MURRAY GRIEVE) led him to write short stories for the *Northern Review*, which was edited by Grieve and later by J. B. SALMOND. His first novel *Grey Coast*, which was based on his knowledge of the fishing villages of the northeast, was published in 1926. He turned, less successfully, to writing for the theatre, winning the friendship of the playwrights O. H. MAYOR ('James Bridie') and JOHN MACINTYRE ('John Brandane'); among his plays were *Back Home* (1932), *Choosing a Play* (1938) and *Old Music* (1939). After his second novel *The Lost Glen* (published in 1932) had been serialized in the *Scots Magazine* in 1928, he published *Morning Tide*, his first financially successful novel in 1930. Drawing on Gunn's memories of childhood and on the subtleties of man's relationship to the sea, *Morning Tide* traces the boy Hugh's burgeoning awareness of the elemental forces of life and death, love and sex as he passes into manhood. Gunn's description of the fishing boats escaping from the storm to the safety of harbour is one of the great descriptive set pieces in the novel. *Sun Circle* (1933) continued his interest in the landscape of the past; in this case in the Viking invasion of Scotland and the resistance of the tribes. It mirrored Gunn's preoccupation with the idea of a Golden Age that he believed existed in Scotland during the Pictish period, an idea that was to remain with him throughout his life. His other successful novel of the period before World War II is *Highland River* (1937) in which he explores, symbolically, the source of delight as Kenn, the boy hunter searches for

salmon in the strath of his boyhood. He also wrote *Butcher's Broom* (1934), *Wild Geese Overhead* (1939), an autobiographical sketch *Off in a Boat* (1938) and *Whisky and Scotland* (1935).

Gunn had become increasingly involved in the politics of the Scottish National Party and in 1937 he resigned from the Customs and Excise to become a full-time writer. Between 1938 and 1949, the most creative part of his life, he lived at Brae between Dingwall and Strathpeffer, where he wrote 11 novels including THE SILVER DARLINGS in 1941. Although the action is concerned, again, with the age-old love–hate relationship of man with the sea, the novel takes on an epic symbolism, both in Finn's voyage through life and, especially, in the vividly told scenes of Finn and his companions' battle with the sea during their first fishing trip in search of herring, the 'silver darlings'. Like *Butcher's Broom*, it is also concerned with the aftermath of the Highland CLEARANCES, and Gunn admitted to spending considerable time on its accurately researched background. His reminiscences of Highland life, which originally appeared under the pseudonym of 'Dane McNeil', were published in *Highland Pack* in 1949.

Gunn's latter years were spent at Kincraig, Kerrow in Glen Cannich, and Dalcraig on the Black Isle near Inverness. His last novels were *The Well at the World's End* (1951), *Bloodhunt* (1952) and *The Other Landscape* (1954); he also published a collection of short stories, *The White Hour* (1950), and *The Atom of Delight* (1956), an autobiographical study that emphasized his growing interest in Zen Buddhism. He wrote for several American and British magazines, as well as scripts for documentary films and BBC Radio. After a short illness he died on 15 January 1973. His ability scrupulously to evoke the landscapes and the people of the Highlands, his blending together of myth and reality and his wide-ranging imagination make Neil Gunn the most important Scottish novelist of the 20th century.

WORKS: *Grey Coast* (1926); *Hidden Doors* (1929); *Poaching at Grianan* (1929–30) [serialized in the *Scots Magazine*]; *Morning Tide* (1930); *The Lost Glen* (1932); *Sun Circle* (1933); *Butcher's Broom* (1934); *Whisky and Scotland* (1935); *Highland River* (1937); *Off in a Boat* (1938); *Wild Geese Overhead* (1939); *Second Sight* (1940); *The Silver Darlings* (1941); *Storm and Precipice* (1942); *Young Art and Old Hector* (1942); *The Serpent* (1943); *The Green Isle of the Great Deep* (1944); *The Key of the Chest* (1945); *The*

Drinking Well (1946); The Shadow (1948); The Silver Bough (1948); Highland Pack (1949); The Lost Chart (1949); The White Hour (1950); The Well at the World's End (1951); Bloodhunt (1952); The Other Landscape (1954); The Atom of Delight (1956)

REFERENCES: A. Scott and D. Gifford, eds., Neil M. Gunn: the Man and the Writer (Edinburgh, 1973); F. R. Hart and J. B. Pick, Neil M. Gunn: a Highland Life (London, 1981)

Guthrie, Isobel. Pen-name of CHRISTOPHER MURRAY GRIEVE.

Guthrie, Thomas (1803–73). Minister and philanthropist. He was born on 12 July 1803 at Brechin. In 1815 he matriculated at the University of Edinburgh and spent ten years there studying in the faculties of arts, divinity and medicine. After graduating he lived in Paris for two years and on being licensed to preach he served as minister of Arbirlot until 1837, and then at Old Greyfriars, and later St John's, in Edinburgh. After THE DISRUPTION of 1843 he seceded to the Free Church of St John's in Castlehill and became a leading member of the disestablished church and an influential raiser of funds for the construction of new church buildings. In 1862 he was appointed Moderator of the Free Church General Assembly and he resigned his charge in 1865. The dreadful housing conditions of the Old Town of Edinburgh and the poverty of its inhabitants spurred him in the direction of social reform: he founded several non-sectarian schools and he was a leading supporter of the temperance movement. He died on 24 February 1873.

Guthrie had a commanding rhetorical style and his fame as a preacher was matched by the practical side of his ministry, in which through his medical studies he was able to offer more than spiritual aid to his charges. Apart from his popular The Gospel in Ezekiel (1855), Guthrie's writing is mainly concerned with his social work, and the uncompromising language of A Plea for Ragged Schools (1847) and The City: its Sins and Sorrows (1857) reflect his own firmly held beliefs.

WORKS: The Present Duty and Prospects of the Church of Scotland (1840); A Plea for Ragged Schools (1847); A Plea on Behalf of Drunkards (1850); A Second Plea for Ragged Schools (1851); A Sufficient Maintenance and an Efficient Ministry (1852); A Happy New Year (1853); The Old Year's Warning (1854); The War (1854); The Gospel in Ezekiel (1855); Popular Innocent Entertainments (1856); The City: its Sins and Sorrows (1857); Christ and the Inheritance of Saints (1858); The Principles of the Free Church of Scotland (1859); Twelfth Thousand (1859); Seed Time and Harvest of Ragged Schools (1860); Lord, what wilt Thou have me do? (1861); Speaking to the Heart (1862); The Way to Life (1862); Fortieth Thousand (1863); Fourth Thousand (1864); Man and the Gospel (1865); The Angel's Song (1866); Early Piety (1867); Our Father's Business (1867); Out of Harness (1867); Studies of Character from the Old Testament (1867); The Unspoken Speech (1867); Saving Knowledge (1870); Sundays Abroad (1871); Autobiography (1874); Parables of Our Lord (1908)

Guy Mannering. A novel by Sir WALTER SCOTT, published in 1815. Its success, and the comparative lack of notice given to his long poem The Lord of the Isles which appeared in the same year, confirmed Scott in his career as novelist. In Guy Mannering Scott was able to draw on his memories of Scottish society at the turn of the century and to counterpoint the characters of an older Scotland with those of a modern disposition who looked forward to the new. The most convincing characters are those who represent older, more traditional Scottish virtues: the gypsy Meg Merrilees; the Liddesdale farmer and breeder of terriers Dandie Dinmont; Dominie Sampson, tutor to Harry Bertram; and Councillor Pleydall, one of Scott's many old-fashioned lawyers. The plot is based on the conventional 'missing heir' theme: Harry Bertram has been captured as a child on the instigation of a lawyer, Glossin, and thus denied the estates of Ellangowan. Unaware of his heritage, he serves with distinction under Colonel Guy Mannering in the army in India and falls in love with Mannering's daughter Julia. But Mannering accuses Bertram of philandering with his wife and the two men fight a duel in which Bertram is wounded and then left for dead. After his recovery Bertram returns to Scotland where Meg Merrilees recognizes him as the heir to Ellangowan; at the cost of her own life, and with the help of Dandie Dinmot, Meg restores Bertram to his estates after foiling the lawyer Glossin and his henchman the smuggler Dick Hatteraick. All ends well and Bertram is free to marry Julia.

H

Hacket, George. *See* HALKET, GEORGE.

Hailes, Lord. *See* DALRYMPLE, DAVID.

Haliburton, Hugh. Pen-name of J. LOGIE ROBERTSON.

Halket [Hacket], **George** (*d* 1756). Poet. He was a schoolmaster in the village of Rathen near Fraserburgh from 1714 to 1725, when he was dismissed by the Kirk Session for dereliction of duty. A Jacobite by persuasion he wrote several vigorous anti-Hanoverian satires, but he is best remembered for *Logie o' Buchan*, a haunting song of lost love.

Hallowe'en. The festival celebrated on All Hallows Day, 31 October, to mark the entry of winter; it was one of the two great fire festivals (the other being BELTANE) of the early Celtic world, where it was called *Samhuinn*. Fires were burned at dusk to combat the powers of darkness and the coming of winter, but *Samhuinn* is traditionally associated with the cult of the dead and was supposed to be the time at which dead souls revisited their old homes. It was also considered to be the period when the spirit world was temporarily upset and when witches and warlocks held their covens. In Edinburgh the festival was celebrated by All Hallows Fair which has been described in poems by ROBERT SEMPILL (ii) of Beltrees and ROBERT FERGUSSON. Customs associated with Hallowe'en are guizing, the making of turnip lanterns and dooking for apples. It was commonly believed that any child born on Hallowe'en would be blessed with second sight.

Hallow Fair. A fair that was celebrated in Edinburgh during the first week of November, the period of Hallowmas. It was renowned for its horse trading and for the markets run by tinkers and country people, and it was recog-

nized as one of the main events in the city's calendar. A vivid picture of the fair and of the people who attended it emerges from the poem of the same name by ROBERT FERGUSSON which was published in THE WEEKLY MAGAZINE OR EDINBURGH AMUSEMENT of 12 November 1772. ROBERT BURNS may have used it as a model and inspiration for his poem 'THE HOLY FAIR.

Hamilton, Elizabeth (1758–1816). Novelist. She was born on 21 July 1758 in Belfast, the daughter of Scottish parents. Their early death forced her and her brother and sister to return to Scotland, where they were brought up by relatives in Stirlingshire. Her early life was plagued by misfortune and a disrupted family life. She spent two years in London between 1788 and 1790, when she began writing essays and sketches on contemporary manners, and works of a philanthropic bent. It was not until her return to Edinburgh in 1806 that she began work on the novel for which she is best remembered, *The Cottagers of Glenburnie* (1808) which is a forerunner of the later KAILYARD novels. What she lacks in background detail in this novel (the older characters remain amusing and antiquated half-witted stereotypes) she compensates for in the creation of characters who personify her theories of social and environmental improvement for the masses—by the end of the novel the narrator, Mrs Mason, has successfully improved the villagers' lot. Her other Scottish work of note was the often anthologized song *My ain Fireside*. Her later years were spent in encouraging good works and in the furtherance of the ideals of universal education.

WORKS: *Hindoo Rajah* (1796); *Memoirs of Modern Philosophers* (1800); *Letters on Education* (1801); *Memoirs of the Life of Agrippina*, 3 vols. (1804); *The Cottagers of Glenburnie* (1808); *Exercises in Religious Knowledge* (1809); *Popular Essays on the Elementary*

135

Principles of the Human Mind (1812); *Hints Addressed to the Patrons and Directors of Public Schools* (1815)

Hamilton, Gavin (1751–1805). Lawyer, active in Mauchline, Ayrshire. He was a friend of ROBERT BURNS, to whom he leased the farm of MOSSGIEL in 1784. Hamilton ran into conflict with the local minister WILLIAM AULD and the Kirk Session over the payment of the parish poor fund with which he was entrusted. The failure of their legal proceedings against him led the Kirk Session, on the instigation of WILLIAM FISHER, to prosecute Hamilton for Sabbath-breaking, an incident that prompted Burns to write the poem 'HOLY WILLIE'S PRAYER'. Hamilton appealed to the Presbytery of Ayr and his appeal was upheld, as it was when the Kirk Session appealed in turn to the Synod of Glasgow and Ayr. The row between Hamilton and the Church helped to form Burns's discontentment with the Calvinist doctrine of predestination. Hamilton was an early patron of Burns, and the KILMARNOCK EDITION is dedicated to him.

Hamilton [née Thomson], **Janet** (1795–1873). Poet. She was born on 12 October 1795 at Carshill in Lanarkshire, the daughter of a shoemaker. Although her childhood was hard and poverty-stricken, and she married at 13 and raised a large family, she received a rudimentary education; through her reading of ALLAN RAMSAY and ROBERT BURNS she was inspired to start writing songs and poems. The bulk of her work is derivative but there is an earthy humour in her comic songs, and her poems dealing with the harsh realities of life in a mining area, reflecting the poverty and hardships encountered by the community in which she lived, have a bitter edge. Her reminiscences also paint a vivid picture of her life and times. In her later years she became blind and she died on 27 October 1873 at Langloan near the place where she was born.

EDITIONS: J. Hamilton, ed., *Poems and Essays by Janet Hamilton* (Glasgow, 1885); J. Young, ed., *Pictures in Prose and Verse, or, Personal Recollections of the late Janet Hamilton* (Glasgow, 1877)

Hamilton, Thomas (1789–1842). Novelist. He was born in Glasgow, the son of the Professor of Anatomy at the University, where he himself was educated. His brother was the philosopher and historian Sir WILLIAM HAMILTON (iii). After leaving university, Hamilton

joined the army, rising to the rank of captain, but he retired to live in Edinburgh when he was 29. There he became associated with the group of writers contributing to the newly founded BLACKWOOD'S MAGAZINE and he became a close friend of its editors JOHN WILSON (iii) and JOHN GIBSON LOCKHART. For *Blackwood's* Hamilton wrote chiefly on military matters and his lucid account of the Peninsular Wars was published in 1829 in *Annals of the Peninsular Campaign;* he also wrote *Men and Manners in America* (1833). Although his dry, thoughtful prose style was suited to his interests in military and political matters, he could also turn his hand to fiction. His one, largely autobiographical, novel, *The Youth and Manhood of Cyril Thornton* (1827), is a shrewdly observed account of life and manners in Glasgow at the turn of the century and is particularly memorable for Hamilton's ability to recreate the undergraduate atmosphere of the city's university. Hamilton died on 7 December 1842.

WORKS: *The Youth and Manhood of Cyril Thornton* (1827); *Annals of the Peninsular Campaign* (1829); *Men and Manners in America* (1833)

Hamilton, William (i), of Gilbertfield (c1665–1751). Poet. He was born at Ladyford, Ayrshire, the son of an army officer, a career he pursued himself in his early years. After retiring to live on his estate of Gilbertfield near Glasgow, he turned to collecting and writing verse, and he contributed a number of pieces to the first volume of the CHOICE COLLECTION OF COMIC AND SERIOUS SCOTS POEMS, published by JAMES WATSON in 1706. The most notable of these was his mock-heroic animal fable, 'The Last Dying Words of Bonny Heck', written in STANDARD HABBIE, which reflects a greyhound's view of life and death. Hamilton also exchanged verse epistles with his friend ALLAN RAMSAY and thereby kept alive that literary genre, which was taken up later by ROBERT FERGUSSON and ROBERT BURNS. In 1722 he published his English translation of WALLACE by BLIND HARRY, which, although it enjoyed a wide popular and patriotic appeal and introduced a new readership to Scots history, was a sign of the decline of Scots as a literary medium during the 18th century. He died on 24 May 1751.

WORKS: *Familiar Epistles between W. H. and A. R.* (1719); *A New Edition of the Life and Heroick Actions of the Renown'd Sir William Wallace* (1722)

Hamilton, William (ii), of Bangour
(1704–54). Poet. He is thought to have been
born on 25 March 1704, in Bangour, West
Lothian, the son of an advocate and landowner. On the death of his father in 1706 his
mother married Sir Hew Dalrymple, the President of the Court of Session, and Hamilton
spent most of his childhood in Edinburgh. He
was educated at the HIGH SCHOOL OF EDIN-
BURGH and between 1716 and 1720 at the
University of Edinburgh. He became acquainted with ALLAN RAMSAY and his early
poems, conventional romantic ballads and
songs of some charm, were published in Ramsay's THE TEA-TABLE MISCELLANY. Many of the
early songs were based on translations of
Horace's *Odes*, and throughout his life Hamilton maintained a workmanlike interest in the
revision of his classical translations. His best-
known poem, the ballad 'The Braes of Yarrow',
was a source of inspiration to Sir WALTER
SCOTT and William Wordsworth.

Hamilton was a favourite in Edinburgh society and enjoyed the friendship of HENRY HOME
Lord Kames and DAVID HUME (ii) the
philosopher. He became involved with the
Jacobite cause and between 1739 and 1741 was
a frequent visitor to Italy where he met Prince
CHARLES EDWARD STUART. During the uprising of 1745–6 he served in the Jacobite army,
and after its defeat he went into exile in Europe
until 1750 when his friends secured his pardon.
During that period he wrote 'Gladsmuir', an
Augustan victory ode for the Battle of Prestonpans, and 'Soliloquy', a lament after the BAT-
TLE OF CULLODEN. He succeeded to the Bangour estates on his return, but ill health forced
him to spend the remainder of his life in
France, and he died on 25 March 1754 in
Lyons. Hamilton was twice married – to Kath-
leen Hall of Dunglass (*d* 1745) in 1743, and to
Elizabeth Dalrymple of Cranstoun in 1752.

WORKS: *The Eighteenth Epistle of the Second Book of
Horace, To Lollus Imitated* (1737); *Three Odes*
(1739); *Poems on Several Occasions* (1748)

EDITION: J. Paterson, ed., *The Poems and Songs of
William Hamilton of Bangour* (Edinburgh, 1850)

REFERENCE: N. S. Bushnell, *William Hamilton of Bangour: Poet and Jacobite* (Aberdeen, 1957)

Hamilton, Sir William (iii) (1788–1856).
Metaphysician. He was born on 8 March 1788
in Glasgow, where his father and grandfather
had been distinguished scientists, having held
successively the Chair of Anatomy and Botany

within the University. He was educated at
Glasgow and Balliol College Oxford and was
later called to the Scottish Bar, although he
never practised. In 1816 he succeeded to a
family baronetcy and settled in Edinburgh,
where he became Professor of History and
Logic at the University in 1821. Between 1829
and 1836 he was a regular contributor to the
Edinburgh Review (*see* EDINBURGH REVIEW
(ii)), his philosophical essays gaining him the
reputation that led to his appointment in 1836
to the Chair of Logic and Metaphysics at
Edinburgh. Hamilton was a follower of the
Common-Sense school of THOMAS REID
(whose works he edited between 1846 and his
death on 6 May 1856), and he was one of the
last in a long line of Scottish scholars who
preferred a wide-ranging and liberal education
to intellectual specialization. His papers were
published in 1852 under the title *Discussions on
Philosophy and Literature, Education and University Reform.*

WORKS: *Correspondence Relative to Phrenology* (1828);
*Discussions on Philosophy and Literature, Education and
University Reform* (1852)

EDITIONS: J. Veitch and H. L. Mansel, eds., *Lectures
on Metaphysics* (Boston, Mass., 1859); J. Veitch,
ed., *Lectures on Logic* (Edinburgh, 1874)

Hanley, Clifford ['Henry Calvin'] (*b* 1922).
Novelist. He was born on 28 October 1922 in
Glasgow and has worked there as a journalist
and broadcaster since 1940. He is best known
for his autobiographical study of a Glasgow
childhood, *Dancing in the Streets* (1958), and
his first novel, *Love from Everybody*, which
appeared a year later, confirmed his ability to
write with wit and humour about people and
places. This was followed by *The Taste of Too
Much* (1960), a sensitive study of adolescence.
Hanley's preoccupations are with the minutiae
of everyday life which he is capable of turning
into dramatic and fantastical incidents, linking stylized farce to grim reality: his other
novels of note are, *Nothing but the Best* (1967),
The Hot Month (1967) and *The Red-haired
Bitch* (1969). He has also written a series of
detective novels under the pseudonym 'Henry
Calvin', and, less successfully, for the stage.

WORKS: *Dancing in the Streets* (1958); *Love from
Everybody* (1959); *The Taste of Too Much* (1960); *A
Skinful of Scotch* (1965); *The Hot Month* (1967);
Nothing but the Best (1967); *The Red-haired Bitch*
(1969); *Burns Country* (1975); *The Unspeakable Scot*
(1977); *Prissy* (1978); *The Biggest Fish in the World*
(1979); *The Scots* (1980)

as Henry Calvin: *Miranda Must Die* (1968); *The Chosen Instrument* (1969); *The DNA Business* (1969); *The Poison Chasers* (1971); *Take Two Popes* (1972)

Hannay, James (1827–73). Journalist and novelist. He was born on 17 February 1827 in Dumfries. He entered the Royal Navy as a midshipman in 1840 and saw service in the eastern Mediterranean, but he was unsuited to the life of a naval officer; after publishing a satirical comic ridiculing his senior officers he was court-martialled and dismissed the service in 1845. He returned to Britain to live first in London and then in Edinburgh, working as a journalist and editor of the EDINBURGH EVENING COURANT between 1860 and 1864. Hannay was a natural journalist with a flair for investigating stories of national importance but his promotion of the Tory party led to arguments with the newspaper's proprietors and by 1865 he was in London again. In 1868 he was appointed British consul in Brest but exchanged the posting for a similar appointment in Barcelona where he died on 9 January 1873. From his naval experiences Hannay wrote two passable novels, *Singleton Fontenoy* (1850) and *Eustace Conyers* (1855) and a collection of stories, *Sketches in Ultramarine* (1853). His other works reflect his interests in heraldry and in English literature, and he was a pioneer of the comic paper.

WORKS: *Singleton Fontenoy* (1850); *Sketches in Ultramarine* (1853); *Eustace Conyers* (1855); *Lectures on Satire and Satirists* (1855); *Three Hundred Years of a Norman House* (1866); *A Course of English Literature* (1866); *Studies on Thackeray* (1869)

Hardie, (James) Keir (1856–1915). Socialist reformer. He was born on 15 August 1856 at Legbrannock, Holytown, Lanarkshire. His childhood was spent in dire poverty and from the age of ten he worked in a coal-mine. He found time, though, to attend evening classes, and at an early age became involved in the trade union movement. His radical opinions cost him several jobs and in 1878 he turned to journalism and began a nation-wide agitation for the formation of a miners' union. After an unsuccessful attempt to organize a strike among the Lanarkshire miners he moved to Cumnock in Ayrshire, which was to become his home until his death on 2 September 1915. Hardie was a founder-member with ROBERT BONTINE CUNNINGHAME GRAHAM of the Scottish Labour Party, which later merged with the Independent Labour Party. In 1892 he became ILP Member of Parliament for South West Ham, and although he was to lose the seat in 1895 by 1900 he was back in parliament as member for Merthyr Burgh. An outspoken socialist, Hardie was a firm supporter of the trade union movement and a promoter of home rule for Scotland and Ireland. Through his journalism and pamphleteering he was able to grasp the mood of the times and as an uncompromising orator he attracted the extremes of odium from his enemies and unanimous praise from his friends.

Hart, Andro (*d* 1621). Printer. He was the foremost tradesman of his craft in the Edinburgh of his lifetime. His example of publishing finely printed literary texts was taken up in later centuries by WILLIAM CREECH and ARCHIBALD CONSTABLE, both of whom were destined to occupy Hart's premises in the High Street. He was renowned particularly for the beauty of his bindings, all of which have a centre-piece and corner-pieces, set off by a design containing a heart and a capital A, thus punning the maker's name. Hart was publisher to WILLIAM DRUMMOND of Hawthornden.

Hay, George Campbell (Deòrsa Mac Iain Deòrsa) (*b* 1915). Poet. George Campbell Hay, who writes poetry in Gaelic under the name of Deòrsa Mac Iain Deòrsa, was born in Argyll, the son of the novelist JOHN MACDOUGALL HAY. He was educated at Oxford, where he studied modern languages; unlike the other poets of the 20th-century revival of Gaelic poetry, Gaelic is not his native tongue. During World War II he served in North Africa and the Middle East, and the experience led to a breakdown in his mental and physical health. He has been a semi-invalid ever since. Hay's first collection, *Fuaran Slibh* (1947), contained poems in Gaelic in which he seemed more concerned with the linguistic and metrical possibilities of the language than with an exploration of his poetic sensibility. His second collection, *O na Ceithir Airdean* (1952), was more assured, and it includes two of his best poems, 'Bisearta', a moving description of the destruction of a city by fire during wartime, and 'Atman', in which the poet takes the side of the down-trodden, whose only 'crime' is poverty. As well as writing in Gaelic, Hay may claim the distinction of using Scots and English, and a collection of his poems in both languages was published as *Wind on Loch Fyne* (1948). Many of his poems in all three languages express his feeelings for nationhood, but he is at his best in describing land- and seascapes and the people that inhabit them. A hallmark of all Hay's poetry is his classical restraint and his allusions to European poetry, much of which he has himself translated into English and Gaelic.

WORKS: *Fuaran Slibh* (1947); *Wind on Loch Fyne* (1948); *O na Ceithir Airdean* (1952); with Sorley MacLean, William Neill and Stuart MacGregor, *Four points of a Saltire* (1970); with Somhairle MacGill-Eain, Ruaraidh MacThómais, Iain Mac a'Ghothainn and Domhnall MacAmhlaigh, *Nuabhàrdachd Ghàidlig* (1976)

Hay, Sir Gilbert (*fl* 1450). Poet and scholar. He was probably related to the Hays of Errol, hereditary constables of Scotland. It may be assumed that he was educated at St Andrews and Paris and thereafter spent time as a courtier or soldier at the French court of Charles VIII. His last years may have been spent as a priest in Scotland under the patronage of the Earl of Orkney. Hay is one of the earliest Scots prose writers and his works were published by the ABBOTSFORD CLUB after they were discovered in the library of Sir WALTER SCOTT. They are translations from French works on chivalry and comprise *The Buke of Batailes*, *The Buke of the Order of Knyghthood* and *The Buke of the Ordnaunce of Princes*. His only poetical work, a long-winded poem of some 20,000 verses, *The Buke of the Conqueror Alexander the Great*, was published by the BANNATYNE CLUB in 1834.

EDITION: J. H. Stevenson, ed., *Gilbert of the Haye's Prose Manuscript*, 2 vols, STS (Edinburgh and London, 1901–14)

Hay, Ian. Pen-name of JOHN HAY BEITH.

Hay, John Macdougall (1881–1919). Novelist. He was born on 23 October 1881 at Tarbert, Loch Fyne, in the county of Argyll. He was educated at the local school and at the University of Glasgow, where he began writing for newspapers and journals, quickly becoming a successful freelance journalist. After graduating he turned to the more secure profession of teaching and took posts in Stornoway and later in Ullapool. While there he became seriously ill with rheumatic fever, and it was during this period that he decided to follow the calling of a minister in the Church of Scotland. In 1905 he returned to Glasgow to study in the Universi-

ty's Divinity Hall, but shortage of funds forced him to turn again to freelance writing to maintain himself and his wife. On his ordination his first parish was in Govan, after which he was translated to Elderslie, the birthplace of the Scottish patriot, Sir WILLIAM WALLACE. The publication of his first, and most successful, novel, GILLESPIE in 1914 enticed him to give up the ministry, but he resisted the temptation and remained in his charge until his death on 10 December 1919. *Gillespie* is one of the great Scottish novels and its central character, Gillespie Strang, a self-made man, is a monstrous creation, characterized by his cunning and the dark driving forces of his own ambition. Brierton, the town which is almost destroyed by Gillespie's depredations, is based on Hay's home town, Tarbert. Hay's son, GEORGE CAMPBELL HAY, is a distinguished poet in Gaelic, Scots and English.

WORKS: *Gillespie* (1914); *Barnacles* (1916); *Their Dead Sons* (1918)

EDITION: R. Kemp, ed., *Gillespie* (London, 1963); B. Taic and I. Murray, eds., *Gillespie* (Edinburgh, 1979)

Heart of Midlothian, The. A novel by Sir WALTER SCOTT, published on 4 June 1818 as the second series of TALES OF MY LANDLORD. The novel takes its name from the Tolbooth in Edinburgh, which acted as a prison. The story opens in 1736 with a vivid description of the PORTEOUS RIOTS, when Captain John Porteous of the City Guard was dragged by the mob from the Tolbooth to the Grassmarket to be hanged, after the reprieval of his death sentence for his part in firing on the Edinburgh crowd at the execution of the smuggler Wilson. Against these real events Scott placed the imaginary story of Jeanie Deans and her sister Effie, who had been imprisoned in the Tolbooth for child murder. Unable to help her sister Jeanie goes to London to plead (successfully) for her sister's life. She marries the Presbyterian minister Reuben Butler and Effie is reunited with her lover George Staunton who, under the name of Robertson, had been Wilson's accomplice. It transpires that Effie's child was sold at birth; in his efforts to reclaim him, Staunton is murdered by a boy who turns out to be his own son.

The novel is notable for its host of minor characters (Bartoline Saddletrees, the Laird of Dumbiedykes, Mrs Howden, the Captain of Knockdunder and James Ratcliffe), and for

Scott's ability to place them effectively in the living tapestry of the Edinburgh of the period. Its strengths are Scott's sure ear for language, the richness of his dialogue and the dramatic tensions he was able to bring to key scenes such as the Porteous Riots and Jeanie's successful pleading with Queen Caroline in London. Jeanie Deans is one of Scott's most enduring characters and the novel also contains one of Scott's best songs, Madge Wildfire's haunting lament *Proud Maisie in the Wood.*

Henderson, Hamish (*b* 1919). Poet and folklorist. He was born on 11 November 1919 in Blairgowrie and was educated at Dulwich College, and Downing College, Cambridge. During World War II he served as an intelligence officer with the Highland Division in North Africa. Since 1951 he has worked as a research fellow in the SCHOOL OF SCOTTISH STUDIES at the University of Edinburgh, where he has been responsible for the collection of traditions, songs and stories from Scotland's oral culture, especially that of the travelling people or tinkers. His one collection of verse, *Elegies for the Dead in Cyrenaica* (1948), has its origins in the desert campaign in North Africa; the poems are remarkable for their poignant but noble declaration of the suffering of the common soldier and of the futility of war. As a translator Henderson has produced versions of poems by the modern Italian poets Eugenio Montale, Salvatore Quasimodo, Alfonso Gatto and Giuseppe Ungaretti, and in 1974 he published *Antonio Gramsci: Letters from Prison.* Henderson has also written a number of popular songs expressing his personal view of man's right to freedom, including *The John Maclean March*, in honour of the Scottish socialist JOHN MACLEAN.

WORKS: *Ballads of World War Two* (1947); *Elegies for the Dead in Cyrenaica* (1948, rev. 2/1977); ed., *Antonio Gramsci: Letters from Prison* (1974)

Hendry, J(ames) F(indlay) (*b* 1912). Poet. He was born on 12 September 1912 in Glasgow. He was educated at Whitehall School and at the University of Glasgow, where he studied modern languages. During World War II he served in the Intelligence Corps and since 1946 he has worked as a translator with several agencies of the United Nations. He was one of the instigators of the 'New Apocalypse' movement in which he was joined by G. S. FRASER and NORMAN MACCAIG. With Henry Treece

(*b* 1911) Hendry edited the movement's three anthologies *The New Apocalypse* (1939), *The White Horseman* (1941) and *Crown and Sickle* (1944). The editorial intention was described by Hendry as a 'first attempt . . . to display the influence and show the progress of the work done by the experimental writers since the advent of the Auden–Spender–Day-Lewis triumvirate'. The movement was born out of a reaction to the politically committed literature of the 1930s, but its vaguely defined policies of individual freedom were destined not to survive the war. During that period Hendry wrote two collections of verse reflecting the mood of the Apocalypse poets, and a novel, *Fernie Brae* (1947), based on his memories of a childhood spent in the west of Scotland. His later poems were collected in *A World Alien* (1980), a work that renews the visionary quality of the Apocalypse poems and introduces a new mood of quiet reflection, especially in his poems about Scotland.

WORKS: ed., with Henry Treece, *The New Apocalypse* (1939); *The White Horseman* (1941), *Crown and Sickle* (1944); *Bombed Happiness* (1942); *The Orchestral Mountain* (1943); ed., *Scottish Short Stories* (1943); *The Blackbird of Ospo* (1945); *Fernie Brae* (1947); ed., *Scottish Short Stories* (1969); *Marimarusa* (1976); *Your Career as a Translator and Interpreter* (1970); *A World Alien* (1980); *The Sacred Threshold: a Life of Rilke* (1982)

REFERENCES: A. Salmon, *The Apocalyptic Poets* (Boston, Mass., 1981)

Henry, Robert (1718–90). Historian. He was born on 18 February 1718 in the parish of St Ninians, Stirlingshire, the son of a farmer. He was educated at the University of Edinburgh and was licensed as a preacher in 1748. After a short time in England he became minister first of New Greyfriars' and later of Old Greyfriars' in Edinburgh, a successful period during which he received the degree of Doctor of Divinity and, in 1774, the appointment of Moderator of the General Assembly of the Church of Scotland. Henry wrote a six-volume *History of England on a New Plan* (1771–93), which owed its popularity to his decision to treat the history under seven subject headings instead of chronologically. Its appearance attracted a series of unprecedented critical attacks by Dr GILBERT STUART, a historian and reviewer who was also the implacable enemy of WILLIAM ROBERTSON, the Principal of the University of Edinburgh. Although Stuart failed to damage the *History's* success in its day, Henry's work has now passed into oblivion.

Henryson, Robert (c1420–c1490). Poet. Very little is known about Robert Henryson's life except that he was a schoolmaster in Dunfermline, an important religious and political centre in the 15th century. In 1508 in his 'Lament for the Makaris' WILLIAM DUNBAR mentioned Henryson's death: 'In Dunfermlyne he [Death] hes done roune, With Maister Robert Henrisoun'. The title 'Maister' suggests that he was a Master of Arts and although he probably received his degree from a European university there is evidence (D. Laing, *Poems and Fables of Robert Henryson* (Edinburgh, 1865), *et al.*) to suggest that he was the 'Magister Robertus Hendisone' who was listed as a teacher of law at the University of Glasgow in 1462. Certainly there are references in the prologue to his fable 'The Taill of the Lyoun and the Mous' to Aesop's having surprisingly studied law in Rome, and many of the other fables demonstrate Henryson's acquaintance both with legal vocabulary and the practice of the law.

As a poet Henryson has been historically connected with the group of poets known as the 'SCOTTISH CHAUCERIANS' which includes among others BLIND HARRY, William Dunbar and GAVIN DOUGLAS. Although Henryson used the Chaucerian stanza and was happy to acknowledge his debt to Chaucer in THE TESTAMENT OF CREISSEID – 'I tuik ane Quair, and left all uther sport,/Writtin be worthie Chaucer glorious,/Of fair Creisseid, and worthie Diomeid,' – it is confusing and historically only half true to bracket Henryson under this convenient title. In *The Testament* he was not content merely to imitate Chaucer; and it is more accurate to use the term 'makar', the fashioner of the literary artifact, to describe Henryson and his fellow Scottish Renaissance poets.

The Testament of Creisseid is Henryson's greatest narrative poem, a work of sustained tragedy which, although it is not strictly a sequel to Chaucer's *Troylus and Cryseyde*, takes up the story when Creisseid, deserted by Diomeid, returns to her father, only to be punished with leprosy for her blasphemy of Venus and Cupid. In that condition she meets Troylus who leaves her a gift because she reminds him of his loved one. In her final 'testament' Creisseid laments her unfaithfulness, and on her death Troylus raises a marble tomb for her. The poem has a seasonal opening which, unlike Chaucer's 'lustie May', is set, characteristically, in late winter, with the poet establishing a bleak mood for the telling of the tragedy. The use of alliteration in Creisseid's speech and the harsh consonantal language give the poem a ballad-like austerity, culminating in Creisseid's final despairing lament of her fate at Fortune's hands. *The Testament* is written in rhyme-royal.

In his *Morall Fabillis of Esope the Phrygian* Henryson turned to a lighter literary genre: the medieval conception of the unity of all natural life, wherein the animal world is used as an allegory of its human counterpart. Although this device allows the poet to mock man's vanity by emphasizing both the similarities and differences between animals and men, Henryson's fables never sink into sentimentality, and one of the strengths is his minute and often loving descriptions of animal life. 'The Taill of the Uponlandis Mous and the Burges Mous' may be a direct reference to the rise of a town-based society in Scotland during Henryson's lifetime, but its particular charm lies in the sympathetic treatment of the two mice and the comparison of their ways of life. Following a visit to her country home by her sister the burges mous, the uponlandis mous visits the city, and although she finds luxurious food and drink, there is also the danger of Gib Hunter 'our Jolie Cat' and the Spencer or butler of the house. The 'moralitas' of the poem is not so much that a country life is superior but that man should be wary of pride and false aspiration. Equally in sympathy with the animal world are the fables in which the fox and the wolf appear: 'The Taill of the Scheip and the Doig', 'The Taill of the Wolf and the Lamb', 'The Taill of Schir Chantecleir and the Foxe', 'The Taill how this foirsaid Tod maid his Confessioun to Freir Wolf Waitskaith', 'The Taill of the Sone and Air of the forsaid Foxe, callit Father wer: Alswa the Parliament of fourfuttit Beistis, haldin be the Lyoun', 'The Taill of the Foxe, that begylit The Wolf, in the schadow of the Mone', 'The Taill of the Wolf that gat the Nekhering throw the wrinkis of the Foxe that begylit the Cadgear' and 'The Taill of the Wolf and the Wedder'. In the last, which tells the story of the wedder (sheep) who assumed a dog's skin to guard the flock, with sorry results, Henryson directs his sympathy not to the obvious sheep but to the deceived wolf; for the morals of the fables are rarely straightforward and do not always reflect the moral of the original story. They are also notable for their colourful descriptions of natural scenery, social and religious satire mixed with gentle humour, and Henryson's knowledge of the legal process. The other fables are: 'The Taill of the Cok and the Jasp', 'The Taill of the Paddok and the Mous' and 'The Preiching of the Swallow'. Henryson had access to the Aesopic tradition of several European poets (for a full discussion of Henryson's sources, *see* the appendices to MacQueen, *Robert Henryson: a Study of the Major Narrative Poems*); the fables are provided with a general prologue in the style of the Latin verse *Romulus* of Gualterus and its derivative the French *Isopet de Lyon* (MacQueen).

In addition to *The Testament of Creisseid* and the fables, Henryson wrote 14 other poems. Of these his *Orpheus and Eurydice* is based on the version by Nicholas Trevet (*c* 1285–1328) of the legend out of Boethius (*fl* 6th century) and is a heavily allegorical interpretation of the story. Eurydice represents appetite, Orpheus intellect and his fateful glance to her at the threshold of hell is the triumph of desire over the will. 'Robene and Makyne' is a pastoral dialogue between two lovers; 'The Bloody Serk' is a ballad-like telling of a traditional story in which a king's beautiful daughter is rescued from a giant's possession by a knight, only for him to die. Four poems reflect on life's impermanence: 'The Thrie Deid Pollis', 'The Reasoning betwix Death and Man', 'The Prais of Aige' and 'The Abbey Walk'. Two satires against corruption foreshadow Sir DAVID LYNDSAY: 'The Want of Wyse Men' and 'Against Haisty Credence of Tytlaris'. And 'Sum Practysis of Medecyne' is a satire on medieval medical practice.

Henryson is the most learned of the makars, a man versed in the knowledge of his day and a humanist in the northern European tradition. His poetry reflects that intellectualism but he was neither pedant nor plagiarist: in all his work his inventive use of language, the range of subject and the subtle shifts of imagery make him one of the most original and accessible poets in Scottish letters.

EDITIONS: G. G. Smith, ed., *The Poems of Robert Henryson*, 4 vols., STS (Edinburgh and London, 1906–14); H. H. Wood, ed., *The Poems and Fables of Robert Henryson* (Edinburgh, 1953); C. Elliott, ed., *Robert Henryson: Poems* (Oxford, 1963); D. Fox, ed., *Testament of Cresseid* (London, 1968); H. MacDiarmid, ed., *Selected Poems of Robert Henryson* (London, 1973); W. R. J. Barron, ed., *Robert Henryson: Selected Poems* (Manchester, 1981)

REFERENCES: M. Y. Stearns, *Robert Henryson* (New York, 1949); J. MacQueen, *Robert Henryson: a Study of the Major Narrative Poems* (Oxford, 1967); M. P. McDiarmid, *Robert Henryson* (Edinburgh, 1982)

Hepburn, James, 4th Earl of Bothwell (*c* 1535–78). Third husband of MARY, Queen of Scots. He was the most powerful nobleman in southern Scotland, holding the posts of Sheriff of Edinburgh and Haddington, Warden of the Marches, Lord High Admiral and master of the castles of Borthwick, Crichton, Hailes, Dunbar and Hermitage. He had been out of favour early in Mary's reign but returned to power in 1565 and took part in the plot to murder the Earl of Darnley, Mary's second husband. After divorcing his wife, Jane Gordon, the sister of the Earl of Huntly, he married Mary on 15 May 1567 but was forced to flee to Norway after the queen's defeat at the Battle of Carberry that same year. He spent the remainder of his life in prison in the castle of Dragsholm in north Zealand, Denmark, and died there in 1578. He is the subject of a long poem by WILLIAM EDMONSTOUNE AYTOUN and a tragedy by Swinburne.

Herd, David (1732–1810). Collector and editor. He was born in Marykirk, Kincardineshire, the son of a farmer, and worked for most of his life as an accountant in Edinburgh. In his spare time he collected songs and ballads and his monument is his collection ANCIENT AND MODERN SCOTTISH SONGS, which appeared in two volumes in 1776 and was reprinted in 1791. Herd's virtue as an editor was that, unlike later collectors, he chose not to change or bowdlerize his texts, and he also printed odd verses and fragments in the hope of finding complete versions of songs. Both ROBERT BURNS and Sir WALTER SCOTT made use of Herd's work, and as a member of the CAPE CLUB (his pseudonym was 'Sir Scrape Greystiel') he would have known ROBERT FERGUSSON. After his death on 25 June 1810 his manuscript collections were divided between the libraries of the British Museum and the University of Edinburgh where they still form a formidable basis of research for the scholar of the ballad and folk literature.

Highland Mary. The name by which MARY CAMPBELL, one of the lovers of ROBERT BURNS, is known. She attracted the sobriquet both from her Highland ancestry and from the song that Burns wrote in her memory: *The Highland Lassie O.*

Hogg, James (1770–1835). Poet and novelist. He was born in 1770 at Ettrickhall Farm in Ettrick Forest, the second of four sons of Robert Hogg and Margaret Laidlaw. In later life he claimed that he was born on 25 January 1772, but the parish records show that he was baptized on 9 December 1770. He was characterized as 'The Ettrick Shepherd' by JOHN WILSON (iii) in the 'NOCTES AMBROSIANAE' published in BLACKWOOD'S MAGAZINE between 1822 and 1835; in fact, his childhood was spent in farm service, and at the age of 20 he became a shepherd with WILLIAM LAIDLAW of Blackhouse in Yarrow who encouraged him in his early writing. His first poem was published in The SCOTS MAGAZINE AND GENERAL INTELLIGENCER in 1794. In 1800 his war-song *Donald Macdonald* became popular throughout Scotland and the following year he published a collection of poems, *Scottish Pastorals*. A turning-point in Hogg's early life came when he met Sir WALTER SCOTT and began a lifelong friendship with him through their mutual interest in the Border BALLAD. Between 1803 and 1810 Hogg made several attempts to set himself up as a farmer but met with little success; he lost all his money due to a legal complication in trying to buy a farm in Harris and his farm in Dumfriesshire was a failure.

In 1810 Hogg moved to Edinburgh, where he published *The Forest Minstrel*, a collection of songs, and became the editor and main contributor of *The Spy*, a weekly literary magazine which ceased publication after a year. In 1813 his fortunes changed overnight with the publication of his series of poems THE QUEEN'S WAKE, and the Duke of Buccleuch presented him with Altrive Farm in Yarrow, rent-free for life. He became associated with the group of writers surrounding the newly established *Blackwood's Magazine* and he claimed responsibility for writing the 'CHALDEE MANUSCRIPT', which was published in the magazine in October 1817. He became a regular contributor to *Blackwood's*, writing stories based on his knowledge of Border history and legend. His first novel, *The Brownie of Bodsbeck*, was published in 1818 and was followed by *The Three Perils of Man* (1822) and THE PRIVATE MEMOIRS AND CONFESSIONS OF A JUSTIFIED SINNER (1824), his most famous work, a macabre novel about an extreme form of CALVINISM according to

which no sin can endanger the hope of salvation. His *Altrive Tales* were published in 1834 and in the same year, despite the hostility of JOHN GIBSON LOCKHART, Scott's son-in-law, he published his *Domestic Manners and Private Life of Sir Walter Scott*.

Although Hogg enjoyed considerable success in Edinburgh, and the friendship of Scott, Lockhart, Blackwood and Wilson, he was somewhat out of place in the city and frequently fell foul of the ever-growing snobbery and the prevailing genteel standards of taste and manners. He returned to Yarrow in 1815 and in 1820 he also took on the neighbouring farm of Mount Benger which he kept until he was bankrupted in 1830. He broke with Blackwood that same year, largely due to contractual problems but also because of his impatience with the attacks made on him in the magazine. He married Margaret Phillips in 1820 when he was 49 and five children were born of their marriage. He died on 21 November 1835 and is buried in Ettrick Churchyard beside his grandfather, Will o' Phaup.

Hogg may have lacked the formal education enjoyed by his literary contemporaries, but he grew up with his imagination richly nourished by the Border ballads, faery lore and legends, and the Old Testament of the Bible. Their influence can be seen in *The Mountain Bard* (1807) and *The Queen's Wake*, which contains his faery poem 'KILMENY', but they also make their presence felt in his prose and short stories. In historical tales like *The Brownie of Bodsbeck* Hogg introduces familiar ballad characteristics: dream and apparition, a timeless atmosphere, the fantastic landscape of the world of faery and an implicit belief in the supernatural. Hogg was steeped in a background of devout Presbyterianism, argument and reading, and those elements from his childhood were to enable him in his later writing to allow belief and scepticism to exist together, leaving the reader to choose between the two. Nowhere is this demonstrated more coherently than in *The Private Memoirs and Confessions of a Justified Sinner*, which most critics consider to be one of the most powerful novels in the Scots tradition. It is a complex work of diabolic possession, theological satire and local legend, with the conception of evil inherent not in the sublimation of the will but in the corruption of theological doctrine. It falls into three parts: the Editor's narrative, the memoirs and confessions of the sinner, and the

Editor's comments at the end; each part is designed so that it forms an overall pattern of rational–objective set against supernatural–subjective experience.

Hogg was a gifted songwriter and his best songs were composed when he wrote to please himself rather than Edinburgh society. His early songs, collected in Songs by the Ettrick Shepherd (1831), make no concessions to gentility but rely heavily on traditional folk-song. In this respect he has been overshadowed by ROBERT BURNS, but in his pastoral songs like The Skylark and When the Kye Comes Hame he shows a delicate and tranquil touch. Like Scott, he was an avid collector of Border ballad and song and his two volumes of THE JACOBITE RELICS OF SCOTLAND (1819–21) are an invaluable source of traditional song material.

WORKS: Scottish Pastorals (1801); The Mountain Bard (1807); The Forest Minstrel (1810); The Queen's Wake (1813); The Pilgrims of the Sun (1815); Mador of the Moor (1816); The Poetic Mirror (1816); The Brownie of Bodsbeck (1818); ed., The Jacobite Relics of Scotland (1819–21); The Poetical Works of James Hogg, 4 vols. (1822); The Three Perils of Man (1822); The Private Memoirs and Confessions of a Justified Sinner (1824); Queen Hynde (1825); Songs by the Ettrick Shepherd (1831); A Queer Book (1832); Altrive Tales (1834); The Domestic Manners and Private Life of Sir Walter Scott (1834)

EDITIONS: The Poetical Works of the Ettrick Shepherd, 5 vols. (Edinburgh and London, 1838–40); T. Thomson, ed., The Works of the Ettrick Shepherd, 2 vols. (London, 1865); D. Mack, ed., James Hogg: Selected Poems (Oxford, 1970)

REFERENCES: G. Douglas, James Hogg (Edinburgh and London, 1899); E. C. Batho, The Ettrick Shepherd (Cambridge, 1927); A. L. Strout, The Life and Letters of James Hogg (Lubbock, Texas, 1946) (vol. 1 only); L. Simpson, James Hogg, a Critical Study (Edinburgh and London, 1962); D. Gifford, James Hogg: a Re-Assessment (Edinburgh, 1976)

Hogmanay. Festival celebrating the last day of the year and the welcoming in of the new year. In Scotland it was once a more important secular festival than Christmas Day, essentially a communal festival when houses were cleaned in preparation for receiving in hospitable fashion the first-foots or first visitors of the new year. The customs of Hogmanay are described vividly in Edinburgh: Picturesque Notes by ROBERT LOUIS STEVENSON.

Holland, Sir Richard (fl 1450). Poet, and the author of the alliterative poem THE BUKE OF THE HOWLAT. He was a member of the Douglas faction at the court of JAMES II, but very little is known about his life. After the fall of the Douglas family in 1455 he may have retired to Shetland to resume his clerical calling. His only extant work, The Buke of the Howlat, is an allegory in which the owl dresses up in the feathers of other birds and meets a sad fate; it is similar in conceit to Chaucer's The Parlement of Foules. Into the poem Holland also interpolated the story of the downfall of the Douglas family. The text existed in the ASLOAN MANUSCRIPT and the BANNATYNE MANUSCRIPT and was first published by the Bannatyne Club in 1823.

EDITION: F. J. Armour, ed., Scottish Alliterative Poems, STS (Edinburgh and London, 1897)

Holy Fair, The. A poem by ROBERT BURNS, first published in the KILMARNOCK EDITION of poems in 1786. A holy fair was, according to Burns in a note to the poem, 'a common phrase in the West of Scotland for a sacramental occasion' which was usually held out of doors at the time of a Communion service. In this gently satirical poem the figure of Fun conducts the poet around the fair to glimpse the absurdities of the event. The celebration of popular occasions is a recurring theme in Scottish literature, and among the models for Burns's poem may be mentioned 'Peblis to the Play', CHRISTIS KIRK ON THE GREEN, and 'HALLOW FAIR' by ROBERT FERGUSSON.

Holyroodhouse. The royal palace of the Kings of Scotland and the principal residence in Scotland of the royal family of the United Kingdom. It is situated at the foot of the Royal Mile, Edinburgh's ancient thoroughfare, beside the volcanic pile of Arthur's Seat and in the old burgh of the Canongate. Beside it stand the ruins of the Abbey of Holyrood, which was founded in 1128 by David I and which stood as a royal place of worship until its destruction in 1544. James IV built a lodging beside the Abbey but it was left to his son James V to construct the first 'fayre Pallais with three towers'. In 1561 Mary, Queen of Scots took up residence in the palace and made many improvements to its interior, but the building fell into disrepair after her son James VI left for London after the Union of the Crowns in 1603. No major work was carried out until 1671–9, when it was rebuilt by the architect Sir William Bruce (1630–1710), who gave the palace its present shape and appearance. A curiosity of the palace grounds was the existence in the nearby Abbey Strand of a building that came to be a debtors' sanctuary; it remained under the heritable jurisdiction of the family of the Dukes of Hamilton from 1646 to 1880.

Holy Willie's Prayer. A satirical poem by ROBERT BURNS, first published in an eight-page pamphlet along with 'quotations from the Presbyterian eloquence'. It was written before the publication of the KILMARNOCK EDITION of poems in 1786, but was omitted due to the topicality of the satire – Burns wrote the poem following the quarrel between his friend the lawyer GAVIN HAMILTON and the Mauchline minister WILLIAM ('Daddy') AULD and the Presbytery of Ayr. The *persona* of Holy Willie is generally held to be based on a local Church elder, WILLIAM FISHER. The poem is a telling indictment both of the Calvinist doctrine of predestination and of the hypocrisy practised as a consequence by those who considered themselves to be among the elect and therefore predestined to salvation. It opens with Holy Willie at prayer in a mood of religious exaltation that moves quickly from humility to self righteousness – Holy Willie's God arranges man's fate without taking into account his moral behaviour. However, Holy Willie is not above the sins of the flesh, which he confesses in the sure knowledge of his salvation. The final six stanzas indict Hamilton as an enemy of the Church, and the poem ends with a complacent plea to 'remember me and mine/wi mercies temporal and divine'. Burns's simple device of allowing the reader to listen in to the bigot at prayer heightens Holy Willie's monstrous beliefs and confessions, which are narrated in a language that is both liturgical and colloquial. 'Holy Willie's Prayer' is one of Burns's most powerful poems and is considered to be one of the greatest satires in European literature.

Home, Henry, Lord Kames (1696–1782). Judge and philosopher. He was born in Berwickshire at Kames, the place from which he was to take his title when he was raised to the bench in 1752. Having trained as an advocate in Edinburgh, he was called to the Scottish Bar in 1723 and he remained involved with the law in Scotland as an advocate and judge until his death on 27 December 1782. He was one of the last of the old school of Scottish judges to use Scots within and without the courts, and his

farewell to his fellow members of the bench is frequently quoted: 'Fare ye weel, ye bitches!' Home was a leading member of the Edinburgh *literati* during the period of the SCOTTISH ENLIGHTENMENT, and among his closest associates were ADAM SMITH, HUGH BLAIR, JAMES BURNETT Lord Monboddo and JAMES BOSWELL. Much of his published work sprang from his legal interests, but he was also interested in philosophy and his *Essays on the Principles of Morality and Natural Religion* (1751), written in opposition to the teaching of DAVID HUME (ii), supported an aesthetic based upon the supposition that man possessed innate ideas of right and wrong. A later book, *Elements of Criticism* (1762), pursued that idea further and emphasized the importance of the workings of human nature in moral philosophy.

A gentleman farmer, Home managed his estate of Blair Drummond himself and introduced modern methods of cultivation and land reclamation. His books on agriculture include *Progress of Flax Husbandry in Scotland* (1765) and *The Gentleman Farmer* (1776).

WORKS: *Remarkable Decisions of the Court of Session from 1716 to 1728* (1728); *Dictionary of Decisions of the Court of Session* (1741); *Essay upon Several Subjects in Scots Law* (1742); *Essays upon Several Subjects Concerning British Antiquities* (1747); *Essays on the Principles of Morality and Natural Religion* (1751); *Historical Law Tracts* (1757); *The Statute Law of Scotland Abridged* (1759); *Principles of Equity* (1760); *Elements of Criticism* (1762); *Progress of Flax Husbandry in Scotland* (1765); *The Gentleman Farmer* (1776); *Elucidations Respecting the Common Law of Scotland* (1777)

REFERENCES: A. F. Tytler, *Memoirs of the Life and Writings of Henry Home of Kames* (Edinburgh, 1807); H. W. Randall, *The Critical Theory of Kames* (Northampton, Mass., 1944); W. C. Lehmann, *Henry Home, Lord Kames* (London, 1971); I. S. Ross, *Lord Kames and the Scotland of his Day* (London, 1972)

Home, John (1722–1808). Dramatist. John Home was born on 21 December 1722 in Leith, the son of the town clerk, and was educated locally and at the University of Edinburgh where he was a friend of ADAM FERGUSON and WILLIAM ROBERTSON. During the Jacobite Rebellion of 1745 he fought on the government side and was held a prisoner in Doune Castle after the Battle of Falkirk. On his release he became minister of Athelstaneford in East Lothian, a post he held until 1757, the year after he had gained notoriety in the eyes of the Church for the production in Edinburgh of his play DOUGLAS. Home had written his first play, *Agis*, in 1749 but it had been rejected in London by David Garrick (1719–79) and it was left to the actor-manager West Digges to stage *Douglas*, his second tragedy, in the Canongate Theatre in Edinburgh. With its Gothic–Romantic imagery and tragic plot, it was an instant success. It tells the pathetic story of Norval, Douglas's son, who has been reared as a shepherd; tragedy occurs when Norval is killed by his stepfather and in despair his mother commits suicide. Its ornate language and stiff rhyming structure preclude its production today but it became a popular favourite with the actress Sarah Siddons after its first production by Garrick in London in 1757. For Garrick Home also wrote a number of lack-lustre dramas: *The Siege of Aquileia* (1760), *The Fatal Discovery* (1769), *Alonzo* (1773) and *Alfred* (1778). Towards the end of his life he wrote his reminiscences of the Jacobite uprising in *History of the Rebellion* (1802).

The production of *Douglas* caused a furore in Edinburgh and Home was forced to give up the ministry of his parish. The Church Session also prosecuted ministers who had attended the performances but their attacks were rebuffed by Home's friend Dr ALEXANDER CARLYLE of Inveresk. Home's play was heralded by others as the beginning of a Scottish national drama, but he chose to write for the London stage following his appointment in 1757 as private secretary to the Earl of Bute. Later he became a tutor to the Prince of Wales who, on his accession as George III, awarded Home the sinecure of Conservator of the Scottish Privileges in Flanders. For this he was granted a pension of £300 a year, which allowed him to return to Edinburgh in 1778. In his latter years he was associated with the *literati* of the SCOTTISH ENLIGHTENMENT in Edinburgh, and he supported HUGH BLAIR in his promotion of the genuineness of the translation of the OSSIAN poems by JAMES MACPHERSON. Home died on 5 September 1808.

WORKS: *Douglas* (1757); *Agis* (1758); *The Siege of Aquileia* (1760); *The Fatal Discovery* (1769); *Alonzo* (1773); *Alfred* (1778); *The History of the Rebellion in the Year 1745* (1802)

EDITION: G. D. Parker, ed., *Douglas* (Edinburgh, 1972)

REFERENCES: E. Wolfe, *Quellenstudien zu John Home's 'Douglas'* (Berlin, 1901); A. E. Gibson, *John Home: a Study of his Life and Works* (Caldwell, Idaho, 1917)

House with the Green Shutters, The. A novel written by GEORGE DOUGLAS BROWN under the pseudonym 'George Douglas' and published in 1901. The principal character, and the object of the author's scorn, is John Gourlay, a man of peasant stock who has risen to prominence as a carrier in the small, claustrophobic town of Barbie. Gourlay's pride in his achievement has attracted the animosity of the 'bodies' of Barbie who act as a chorus in the tragedy of Gourlay's inevitable downfall. Unable to alter course in a rapidly changing world, Gourlay's business is ruined and the fall is made complete by the failure at university of his weak, drink-sodden son. In a moment of confrontation, reminiscent of a similar scene in Stevenson's WEIR OF HERMISTON, Gourlay is murdered by his son who later takes his own life. To complete the tragedy Gourlay's consumptive daughter and sluttish, ill-used wife commit suicide after a final majestic reading from *Corinthians* I, 13 on the theme of charity, a virtue that has been notably absent in the citizens of Barbie. The novel was written in opposition to the KAILYARD school of rural sentimentality, and although it suffers from a confusion of absolutes, it is a tragedy that transcends time and place. Gourlay is a man ruined by his monstrous, self-willed nature and his son is castrated both by the malignancy of his father and the squalid ethics of Barbie. *The House with the Green Shutters* has been reprinted several times, and a memorial edition was published in 1923 with an introduction and memoir by Brown's friend, Andrew Melrose.

Houston, R. B. Pen-name of HUGH C. RAE.

Howie, John (1735–93). Man of letters. He was born on 14 November 1735 at Lochgoin near Kilmarnock in Ayrshire. His father was a farmer and it was to the land that Howie returned in 1760, after spending his early years with his grandparents in neighbouring Blackhill. In his leisure time he built up a substantial library and a collection of antiquities dealing mainly with the Covenanting times. His monument is his *Scots Worthies* (1774), a collection of biographies of the Scots reformers from Patrick Hamilton to James Renwick, which is remarkable for Howie's candid, though at times over-earnest portrayal. The book was revised between 1781 and 1785 and it remained a popular improving work throughout the 19th century. Howie's other work of note is *A Collection of Lectures and Sermons by Covenanting Clergymen* (1779). He died on 5 January 1793.

WORKS: *Scots Worthies* (1774); *A Collection of Lectures and Sermons by Covenanting Clergymen* (1779); ed., Michael Shields, *Faithful Contendings Display'd* (1780)

Huchowne of the Awle Ryale (Huchon, or Hugh, of the King's palace). Poet. He is mentioned in the late 14th-century ORYGYNALE CRONYKIL OF SCOTLAND by ANDREW OF WYNTOUN as the composer of three early alliterative poems *The Pystil of Swete Susan*, *The Awyntyre of Gawane* and *The Gret Gest off Arthure*. He has been identified, on scant evidence, with Sir HEW EGLINTOUN.

EDITION: F. J. Armour, ed., *Scottish Alliterative Poems*, STS (Edinburgh and London, 1897)

REFERENCES: G. Neilson, *Huchowne of the Awle Ryale: the Alliterative Poet* (Glasgow, 1902); W. Geddes, *A Bibliography of Middle Scots Poets*, STS (Edinburgh and London, 1912)

Hume, Alexander (*c*1556–1609). Poet. He was the second son of the 5th Lord Polwarth. He was probably born in 1556 in the family home of Reidbrais on the Polwarth estates in the Borders, and he is thought to have been educated at the University of St Andrews and in France:

Quhen that I had employed my youth and paine,
Foure yeares in France, and was returned againe,
I langed to learne, and curious was to knawe:
The consuetude, the custome and the Lawe.
('Ane Epistle', ll. 135–8)

Much of our knowledge of Hume's early life comes from 'Ane Epistle to Maister Gilbert Moncreif, Mediciner to the Kings Majestie'; Gilbert Moncrieff, a physician to JAMES VI, helped Hume on his return to Scotland when he fell ill with haemorrhaging of the lungs. Hume spent some years at the court of James VI but illness and a growing impatience with the trappings of court life increased his interest in spiritual matters and in 1598 he became minister of Logie in Stirlingshire. He remained a staunch supporter of the Reformed Church until his death on 4 December 1609.

Hume had begun writing poetry while at court and it was during that period that he composed OF THE DAY ESTIVALL, a poem of great beauty, the poet's contemplation of the sights and sounds of a summer's day. With its insistence on the changing light and shadows of the countryside, it takes on the aspect of a painting, with the sun both as its focus and as the symbol of a benign God watching over the unity of life on earth. In the middle of the landscape is man at work and at rest, the silent worshipper of a spirit beyond Nature. The poem appeared in 1599 in Hume's *Hymnes, or Sacred Songs wherein the Right Use of Poesie may be Espied*, a collection that contained seven religious verses, on of which 'The Triumph of the Lord, after the manner of men' celebrates the defeat of the Spanish Armada, the 'Epistle to ... Gilbert Moncreif' and a formal love sonnet.

Hume was a conscientious churchman and a poet who, despite his noble birth, was unafraid of attacking abuses at court; but he is best remembered for *Of the Day Estivall*, a poem that stands in line with the best nature poetry of his predecessors GAVIN DOUGLAS and ROBERT HENRYSON.

WORKS: *Hymnes, or Sacred Songs wherein the Right Use of Poesie may be Espied* (1599)

EDITION: A. Lawson, ed., *The Poems of Alexander Hume*, STS (Edinburgh and London, 1902)

Hume, David (i), of Godscroft (*c*1560–*c*1630). Historian. He was a native of Dunbar, East Lothian, and is best known as the historian of the Douglas family. Very little is known with any certainty about his life, but he is thought to have studied at St Andrews and thereafter in Paris and Geneva, before returning to Scotland to become secretary to the Douglases. Later in life he set himself up as a farmer in Berwickshire on the estate of Gowkscroft, which he renamed The Godscroft. In rural retirement he turned his hand to the composition of pleasing Latin pastoral verses in imitation of Ovid. His history of the House of Douglas, although never dull, is marred by Hume's inability to distinguish between historical accuracy and his own desire to eulogize the part played by the Douglases in Scotland's history. It was arranged for publication after his death by his daughter Anna Hume.

WORKS: *De unione insulae Britanniae* (1605); *History of the House of Wedderburn* (1611); *Apologia basilica* (1626); *History of the House and Race of Douglas and Angus* (1644)

Hume, David (ii) (1711–76). Philosopher and historian. He was born on 26 April 1711 in Edinburgh, the son of a Berwickshire landowner. He was educated at the University of

Edinburgh where he studied law, a subject in which he had little interest, abandoning it after two years for philosophy. Experience as a clerk in a counting-house in Bristol confirmed his lack of commercial aptitude and between 1734 and 1737 he was allowed by his father to follow his literary and philosophical interests at Rheims and La Fleche in France. There he wrote his *Treatise on Human Nature* which was published in 1739, the year of his return to Scotland, where he settled on the family estate of Ninewells in Berwickshire, remaining there until 1745. During that period of calm he wrote his *Essays, Moral and Political* (1741), but his growing reputation as a sceptic, thought to be hostile to religion, cost him the Chair of Moral Philosophy at Edinburgh in 1744 and also the Chair of Logic at Glasgow in 1751. Between 1745 and 1746 he acted as tutor to the insane Marquis of Annandale, and then served for two years as Judge-Advocate to General St Clair during his various missions to European capitals. Further diplomatic appointments followed, as secretary to the British Ambassador in Paris (1763–5), *Chargé d'affaires* (1765) and Secretary of State to the Northern Department in London (1767–8). Between 1751 and 1757 he was resident in Edinburgh, where he was librarian to the FACULTY OF ADVOCATES and it was to that city that he retired in 1768, living there until his death on 25 August 1776. Hume was universally liked and admired, and during his final days he astonished his friends by the equanimity with which he met his death from cancer. It was said that his only genuine enemy was the French philosopher Rousseau who spurned Hume after accepting his assistance in coming to live in England.

Hume's philosophy is contained in his *Philosophical Essays Concerning Human Behaviour* (1748), which became in later editions *An Enquiry Concerning Human Understanding* (1758), and in *An Enquiry Concerning the Principles of Morals* (1751). During the period of their composition he also wrote *Dialogues Concerning Natural Religion* which he forbade to be published during his lifetime. This takes the form of a discussion on the essence of divinity between an orthodox Christian, a deist, and a sceptic whose view – that it is impossible to furnish proof of God's existence – mirrors Hume's. Hume also wrote a five-volume *History of England* which was highly thought of in its day for the scope of his historical investigation and for his comments on the evolution of

society, although later historians have found the first volumes lacking in form and direction. In his *Essays and Treatise on Several Subjects* (1753–6) he wrote about commerce and finance, expounding a political economy based on the theory that the value of money is determined by the balance of trade. Here, as in all his writings, his insights are matched by the clarity of his thought and by his spare, elegantly expressed prose.

As a philosopher, Hume extended the empiricism of John Locke (1632–1704) who held that all genuine knowledge is gained by experience, to evolve a new theory of knowledge which denied that beliefs are based on reason. He stressed that human knowledge is man-made and that our understanding of the facts of the universe is founded on the workings both of human nature and of the imagination, that natural beliefs cannot be based on rationalism. His theory of causation argues that our perception of cause and effect arises from a subjective feeling of certainty that sequences that have taken place in the past will continue to occur in the future.

Hume was resident intermittently in Edinburgh during the period of the SCOTTISH ENLIGHTENMENT, and although his philosophy was diametrically opposed to that held by the *literati*, such as HUGH BLAIR and WILLIAM ROBERTSON, he lived pleasurably enough among his contemporaries and was a founder-member of the SELECT SOCIETY. During his lifetime he was greatly misunderstood and attacked for his scepticism and it was not until the 19th century that his philosophy gained a wider currency. His writings were much admired in Europe and he had a seminal influence on the beliefs of Immanuel Kant (1724–1804) who was the most influential thinker to refute his philosophy. Hume, though, is justly considered to be one of the world's greatest philosophers and an original thinker whose work did much to promote the science of man, the secular and materialist study of human nature and society which underpinned the philosophy of the 18th-century Enlightenment.

WORKS: *A Treatise on Human Nature* (1739); *Essays Moral and Political* (1741); *Philosophical Essays Concerning Human Behaviour* (1748); *The Bellman's Petition* (1751); *An Enquiry Concerning the Principles of Morals* (1751); *Political Discourses* (1752); *Essays and Treatises on Several Subjects*, 4 vols. (1753–6); *Four Dissertations* (1757); *History of England from the Invasion of Julius Caesar to the Revolution of 1688*, 5 vols.

(1763); *Two Essays* (1777); *Dialogues Concerning Natural Religion* (1779)

EDITIONS: T. H. Green and T. H. Grose, eds., *The Philosophical Works of David Hume*, 4 vols. (London, 1874–5); J. Y. T. Greig, ed., *The Letters of David Hume* (Oxford, 1932); R. Klibansky and E. C. Mossner, eds., *New Letters of David Hume* (Oxford, 1954)

REFERENCE: N. K. Smith, *The Philosophy of David Hume* (London, 1941); E. C. Mossner, *The Life of David Hume* (Oxford, 1954)

Hunterian Club. A publishing society founded in Glasgow in 1871 for 'the reproduction of Scottish writers of Elizabethan times'. It was named after the surgeon William Hunter (1718–83), and its one major publication was an 11-part edition of the BANNATYNE MANUSCRIPT which was published between 1873 and 1901. The club ceased publishing in 1902.

I

Innes, Cosmo (1798–1874). Historian. He was born on 9 September 1798 at Durris, Kincardineshire, and was educated at the HIGH SCHOOL OF EDINBURGH, the universities of Aberdeen and Glasgow and at Balliol College, Oxford. He became an advocate in 1822 and during his lifetime held several prominent legal posts: Advocate-Depute between 1833 and 1840, Sheriff of Moray from 1840 until 1852, when he became Principal Clerk of Session, and Professor of Constitutional Law at Edinburgh University from 1846 until his death on 31 July 1874. Innes's most important work was in the field of record scholarship and he assisted THOMAS THOMSON in the preparation for publication of *The Acts of Parliaments of Scotland*, for which he made the index. Among his historical publications are *Scotland in the Middle Ages* (1860), *Sketches of Early Scottish History* (1861) and *Lectures on Scotch Legal Antiquities* (1872), together with a number of scholarly introductions to the publications of the BANNATYNE CLUB, the MAITLAND CLUB and the SPALDING CLUB. A memoir of his life was written shortly after his death by his eldest daughter, who had married the historian JOHN HILL BURTON.

WORKS: *Scotland in the Middle Ages* (1860); *Sketches of Early Scotch History and Social Progress* (1861); *An Account of the Family of Innes* (1864); ed., *Facsimiles of the National Manuscripts of Scotland* (1867); ed., *Ledger of A. Halyburton 1492–1503* (1867); *Ancient Laws and Customs of the Burghs of Scotland* (1872); *Lectures on Scotch Legal Antiquities* (1872); *Memoir of Dean Ramsay* (1874)

Innes, Michael. Pen-name of J. I. M. STEWART.

Innes, Thomas (1622–1744). Historian. He spent most of his life in Paris where his brother was Principal of the Scots College. He returned to Scotland to study in the library of the FACULTY OF ADVOCATES in Edinburgh in 1724 and published his *Critical Essay on the Ancient Inhabitants of ... Scotland* (1729), which denied the existence of the 40 legendary pre-Christian kings of Scotland.

WORKS: *A Critical Essay on the Ancient Inhabitants of the Northern Parts of Britain or Scotland* (1729); *Epistola de veteri apud Scotos Habendi Synodos modo* (1735)

EDITIONS: G. Grub, ed., *The Civil and Ecclesiastical History of Scotland* (Aberdeen, 1853); G. Grub, ed., *A Critical Essay on the Ancient Inhabitants of the Northern Parts of Britain or Scotland, Containing an Account of the Romans, of the Britains betweixt the Walls, of the Caledonians or Picts, and Particularly of the Scots. With an Appendix of Ancient Manuscript Pieces, with a Memoir of the Author* (Edinburgh, 1879)

Irving, David (1778–1860). Biographer. He was born on 5 December 1778 at Langholm and was educated at the University of Edinburgh. Abandoning thoughts of a career in the ministry of the Church of Scotland, Irving turned his hand to literature, and after imperfect attempts to write lives of ROBERT FERGUSSON and WILLIAM FALCONER, he produced his *Lives of the Scottish Poets* (1804), which is still a standard guide to Scottish literary biography. After a period spent tutoring he was appointed librarian to the FACULTY OF ADVOCATES in 1820, a post he held until 1848. He died on 11 May 1860 in Edinburgh. In his later years Irving edited several texts for the MAITLAND CLUB and the BANNATYNE CLUB, and contributed to the seventh edition of the ENCYCLOPAEDIA BRITANNICA. His *History of Scottish Poetry*, published posthumously in 1861, remains a useful introduction especially to the poetry of the medieval period.

WORKS: *Life of Robert Fergusson* (1799); *Three Sketches* (1800); *Elements of English Composition* (1801); *The Lives of the Scottish Poets* (1804); *Life of George Buchanan* (1805); *Lives of Scottish Writers*, 2 vols. (1839); *History of Scottish Poetry* (1861)

Irving, Edward (1792–1834). Divine. He was born on 4 August 1792 at Annan, Dumfriesshire. He was educated at the University of Edinburgh and graduated in 1809 to become a schoolmaster in Haddington, East Lothian. There he taught Jane Welsh who was destined to marry THOMAS CARLYLE whom Irving met in 1816 in Kirkcaldy. Irving was licensed to preach in 1815 and in 1819 he was back in Edinburgh, where his abilities in the pulpit attracted the attention of THOMAS CHALMERS, who invited him to become his assistant in Glasgow that same year. Irving's fame as a preacher began in 1822 when he moved to London to the small parish of Hatton Cross. Through the power and passion of his utterances he transformed the parish and it quickly became one of the most fashionable in London. His apocalyptic vision and his urgent promise of a second coming were strong meat for his followers, but the hysterical 'gift of tongues' that began to affect his congregations helped to brand him as a heretic in official Church circles. In 1833 he was deprived of his ministry by the Church of Scotland and thereafter his health declined and he died on 7 December 1834 in Glasgow. Irving was undoubtedly one of the most striking preachers of an age in which there were many powerful performers in the pulpit, but his ability to create an atmosphere bordering on hysteria was deeply distrusted by his fellow churchmen. A tragedy in his life was his unrequited love for Jane Welsh Carlyle, who later admitted that had she married him 'the tongues would not have been heard'. There is a sympathetic study of him in Carlyle's *Reminiscences*.

REFERENCE: M. Oliphant, *Life of Edward Irving*, 2 vols. (London, 1862)

J

Jacob [née Kennedy-Erskine], **Violet** (1863–1946). Poet and novelist. She was born in Montrose, the daughter of the 18th Laird of Dun whose family had held the lands of Dun since the 15th century. She married an army officer, Arthur Otway Jacob, and spent her early married life in India before returning to her native north-east Scotland. In all her work her intricate knowledge of the lore and language of her native country is made manifest, and she contributed poetry in Scots to Hugh MacDiarmid's *Northern Numbers* (1920–22) and to John Buchan's *The Northern Muse* (1924). Most of her best work, published in several collections, is memorable for her natural use of Scots and the deceptively simple rhyming structure of poems like 'Tam i' the Kirk' and 'The Gowk'. Violet Jacob also wrote fiction, but her short stories, collected in *The Fortune Hunters*, *Stories told by the Miller* and *Tales of my own Country*, seldom rise above the level of rural sentimentality; more rigorous in their execution are her historical novels, *The Sheep-stealers* (1902), *The Interloper* (1904) and *The History of Aythan Waring* (1908). *The Lairds of Dun* (1931) is a loving social history of her family's heritage and also a hymn of praise to the countryside of her birth. She died on 9 September 1946.

WORKS: *The Sheep-stealers* (1902); *The Golden Harp and Other Fairy Stories* (1904); *The Interloper* (1904); *Verses* (1905); *The History of Aythan Waring* (1908); *Irresolute Catherine* (1908); *Stories told by the Miller* (1909); *The Fortune Hunters and Other Stories* (1910); *Flemington* (1911); *Songs of Angus* (1915); *More Songs of Angus and Others* (1918); *Bonnie Joan and Other Poems* (1921); *Tales of my own Country* (1922); *The Northern Lights and Other Poems* (1927); *The Good Child's Yearbook* (1928); *The Lairds of Dun* (1931); *The Scottish Poems of Violet Jacob* (1944)

EDITION: R. Garden, ed., *The Lum Hat and Other Stories: Last Tales of Violet Jacob* (Aberdeen, 1982)

Jacobite. A term, from the Latin *Jacobus* (James), used to describe a supporter of the royal house of Stewart after 1688 when James II of England and VII of Scotland was forced into exile in France. The first Jacobite uprising occurred in 1689 when JOHN GRAHAM of Claverhouse, Viscount Dundee, led a mainly Highland army against the government forces of General Hugh MacKay. Dundee's death at the Battle of Killiecrankie in July ended the revolt, but Jacobites in Scotland continued to keep alive the hope of a Stewart returning to the throne. The discontent aroused by the ACT OF UNION of 1707 and England's engagement in the War of the Spanish Succession quickened Jacobite hopes, but an attempt to land a French force under James VII's son, James Francis, in spring 1708 met with no success. In 1715 James Francis, known as 'the Old Pretender', again tried to force an uprising in Scotland but his forces withdrew after the indecisive Battle of Sheriffmuir. A minor uprising, involving Spanish troops at Glenshiel, was decisively crushed in 1719. The final flowering of Jacobitism in Scotland, also its bitter harvest, came when Prince CHARLES EDWARD STUART, 'the Young Pretender', landed in Scotland in 1745 to claim the throne on his father's behalf. Although successful in the early stages of the campaign, his predominantly Highland army was defeated in April 1746 at the BATTLE OF CULLODEN near Inverness: its defeat meant not only the end of the cause but, for many of the Jacobite supporters, death and ruin.

Jacobitism continued to exercise a strong hold on the Scottish imagination, especially because of its romantic associations, but by the middle of the 18th century, in all reality, most of Scotland had come to accept the Union and the peace provided by the Hanoverian succession. There is a wealth of Gaelic poetry and song associated with the Jacobite uprisings and their aftermath and the events have provided backgrounds for novels by, among others, Sir WALTER SCOTT, ROBERT LOUIS STEVENSON, NEIL MUNRO and NAOMI MITCHISON.

Jacobite Relics of Scotland, The. An anthology of Jacobite songs and ballads collected and edited by JAMES HOGG and published in two volumes in 1819 and 1821. It was undertaken at the suggestion of the Highland Society of London, and in his compilation Hogg went to considerable pains to collect Highland songs of THE FORTY-FIVE, many of which had been translated from Gaelic. However, like many other ballad collectors of his day, Hogg could not resist the temptation of including songs of his own creation and *The Jacobite Relics* is made memorable by two of his best songs, *Donald M'Gillivray* and *Charlie is my Darling*.

James I, King of Scots (1394–1437). He was born in 1394, probably on 25 July, in Dunfermline, the second son of Robert III (1337–1406). On the death of his elder brother David, Duke of Rothesay, in 1402, he became heir to the throne and was created Earl of Carrick in 1404. Shortly before his father's death, James was sent to France for safekeeping in March 1406, but his ship was captured at sea by the English and he remained a prisoner in England for 18 years. During that period James fell in love with Henry V's cousin Lady Joan Beaufort, for whom he wrote THE KINGIS QUAIR, a long poem in Scots, influenced by the poetry of Geoffrey Chaucer. Other poems have been attributed to him, including CHRISTIS KIRK ON THE GREEN and 'The Ballad of Good Counsel'. After the conclusion of the Treaty of London in 1423 James married Lady Joan Beaufort on 2 February 1424 and returned to Scotland two months later.

During James's absence Scotland had been ruled under the regency of his uncle the Duke of Albany (1339–1420), who was succeeded by his incompetent son Murdoch (1362–1425). To secure the throne on his return James executed Murdoch and his sons and banished his near relative the Earl of Menteith. He pursued a ruthless policy to maintain power and alienated the nobility with his efforts to increase the royal revenues. He improved civil and criminal justice in the country and tried to bring lesser landowners into parliament. In the Highlands he exerted his authority in 1428 by imprisoning several clan chiefs including the Earl of Ross who was then Lord of the Isles.

James's policies of checking the nobility and of making Scotland a secure country, where, in his words, 'the key shall keep the castle and the bracken bush the cow', led to his murder on 21 February 1437 in the Dominican Friary in Perth at the hands of Sir Robert Stewart, grandson of the Earl of Atholl and Sir Robert Graham, uncle of the Earl of Menteith. The conspirators were savagely executed and James II succeeded his father on 25 March 1437.

REFERENCE: E. W. M. Balfour, *James I, King of Scots* (London, 1936)

James II, King of Scots (1430–60). He was born on 16 October 1430 in Edinburgh. He was also known as 'James of the Fiery Face' due to a birthmark. His reign is best remembered for his struggle with the Douglases, a powerful Scottish family which also had claims to the throne. James resisted the challenge by gathering together a loyal band of new nobles, and members of the Douglas family were finally defeated at the Battle of Arkinholm in 1455. James was killed on 3 August 1460 when a cannon exploded during the siege of the castle of Roxburgh, held by the English.

James III, King of Scots (1452–88). He was crowned king on 10 August 1460 and during his minority Scotland was ruled by his mother as regent until 1463 and then by a confederation of nobility. He married Margaret of Denmark in 1469. James alienated his supporters, including ARCHIBALD DOUGLAS 5th Earl of Angus, by his policy of fostering low-born favourites, and during the last six years of his reign civil war raged in Scotland. After the Battle of Sauchieburn on 11 June 1488 James was murdered in a cottage following his flight from the field.

James IV, King of Scots (1473–1513). He was born on 17 March 1473 in Stirling and succeeded to the throne in 1488 on the death of his father James III at the Battle of Sauchieburn. During James's reign Scotland enjoyed a period of relative prosperity and cultural advancement. In 1492 an act was passed making it compulsory for substantial landowners to have their sons educated, and under the king's patronage there came into being King's College, Aberdeen (1494), the Royal College of Surgeons (1506) and St Leonard's College, St Andrews (1512).

HOLYROODHOUSE in Edinburgh was begun during his reign and he also improved the Palace of Linlithgow and encouraged the practice of the arts. The poets WILLIAM DUNBAR and GAVIN DOUGLAS enjoyed his patronage, and in 1508 the first Scottish printing press was established in Edinburgh by WALTER CHAPMAN and Andrew Myllar.

A permanent law court, which became the COURT OF SESSION, was established in Edinburgh and James's domestic affairs led him to break up the confederacy of the Lords of the Isles and to secure the friendship of the Highland chiefs. To further his foreign policy James built up Scotland's military strength, especially its navy, causing the largest warship of its day, *The Great Michael*, to be built. He married Margaret Tudor, the daughter of Henry VII of England, on 8 August 1503, but when England joined Pope Julius II's Holy League against France, James renewed the AULD ALLIANCE and went to war with England. He was killed, along with nine earls, thirteen lords, a host of churchmen and lesser nobility, impetuously leading his men at the BATTLE OF FLODDEN on 9 September 1513.

REFERENCE: R. L. Mackie, *King James IV of Scotland* (London, 1958)

James V, King of Scots (1512–42). He was born on 10 April 1512 at Linlithgow and became king on his father's death at the BATTLE OF FLODDEN in 1513. He was married twice – to Madeleine daughter of Frances I of France in 1537, and to Mary of Guise-Lorraine in 1538. James maintained law and order in Scotland and earned a reputation for ruthless severity in the Border BALLAD 'Johnnie Armstrong'. In the folk tradition he was known as the 'Poor Man's King' or 'GABERLUNZIE MAN' because he wandered among his people in beggar's disguise. Both James V and JAMES I have been credited with the composition of the anonymous burlesque poem CHRISTIS KIRK ON THE GREEN. He died on 14 December 1542 in Falkland.

REFERENCE: C. Bingham, *James V* (London, 1971)

James VI, King of Scots (1566–1625). He was born on 19 June 1566 in Edinburgh Castle, the only son of MARY, Queen of Scots and Lord Darnley. He was crowned king on 24 July 1567 after the abdication of his mother, and his early childhood was spent in Stirling under the

tutelage of GEORGE BUCHANAN and Peter Young. James's early learning was influenced by a thorough study of the classics and a grounding in Old Testament history and Calvinistic theology. In 1578 the waning powers at court of the regent Morton, James's second cousin, led James to be proclaimed king, but by then he was under the influence of his French cousin Esme Stewart d'Aubigny, whom he created Earl of Lennox. Fearing that James might lead Scotland back into an alliance with France and restore Catholicism, a group of Protestant nobles captured the king at the Raid of Ruthven in August 1582; they held him captive for a year and banished Esme Stewart. On his escape he relied on the support of the Earl of Arran, who aided him in his policy of bringing the Church under the control of the State. James married Anne, daughter of Frederick II of Denmark, on 24 November 1589.

Although James had to contend with further disruptions and plots during his reign, he proved to be a strong and able monarch, and unlike earlier Stewarts he won the support of the powerful nobility. The law was enforced throughout the country and the Church was brought under the control of an episcopacy appointed by the Crown. As the senior descendant of Henry VII James had the strongest claim to the throne of England, and on the death of Queen Elizabeth on 24 March 1603 he became King of England. The government of Scotland continued through a privy council, but the real power lay in the intelligence that was available to James through agents among the loyal nobility. He visited Scotland only once, in 1617. He died on 27 March 1625 and was succeeded by his son Charles I. James is caricatured in the novel *The Fortunes of Nigel* by Sir WALTER SCOTT and he is the subject of a play, *Jamie the Saxt*, by ROBERT MCLELLAN.

James was the most scholarly of the Scottish monarchs and in his prose works he set down his ideas on literary and political matters. His *Essayes of a Prentise in the Divine Art of Poesie* (1585), commonly known as the REULIS AND CAUTELIS, advocated a revival of interest in Scottish vernacular poetry. The BASILICON DORON (1599) was intended originally as a set of rules for his son Prince Henry but was later expanded and employed as a statement of James's policies. James's other prose works include *A Counterblaste to Tobacco* (1604) and *Daemonologie* (1597), a somewhat turgid study of witchcraft, a lifelong preoccupation of his.

An interest in poetry led him to form a school of court poets, the CASTALIAN BAND, which included ALEXANDER MONTGOMERIE, JOHN STEWART of Baldynneis and WILLIAM FOWLER.

WORKS: *The Essayes of a Prentise in the Divine Art of Poesie* (1585); *His Majesties Poeticall Exercises at Variant Houres* (1591); *Daemonologie* (1597); *The True Lawe of Free Monarchies* (1598); *Basilicon doron* (1599); *A Counterblaste to Tobacco* (1604); *Workes* (1616)

EDITION: J. Craigie, ed., *The Poems of James VI of Scotland*, 2 vols., STS (Edinburgh and London, 1947–52)

REFERENCE: C. Bingham, *James VI* (London, 1979)

Jamieson, John (1759–1839). Philologist and antiquary. He was born in Glasgow where he studied theology and was licensed to preach in 1781. The first 16 years of his ministry were spent in Forfar and in 1797 he was invited to become minister to the Nicolson Street congregation of the Secession Church in Edinburgh, a post he held until his retirement in 1830. Jamieson was an Anti-Burgher, a faction formed within the First Secessionist Church in 1745 after disagreements over the relationship of the Church to secular authority, but he was a party to the moves that led to the reunion of 1820. Several of his earliest published essays and sermons deal with scriptural interpretation, but his duties as a minister did not interfere with his antiquarian pursuits, his *Treatise on the Ancient Culdees of Iona* being particularly admired. Through his studies Jamieson enjoyed the friendship of many of the leading writers and scholars of his day, including Sir WALTER SCOTT.

Jamieson edited THE BRUCE by JOHN BARBOUR and WALLACE by BLIND HARRY, both of which were published in 1820, but his major work, which took 20 years of his life, is his two-volume *Etymological Dictionary of the Scottish Language*, published in 1808 and 1809, with a supplement in 1825. It was originally conceived as a Scots wordbook, but Jamieson was encouraged by the Icelandic scholar Grim Thorkelin to enlarge the work to include as examples the quotations on which he based his definitions. Through his industry and single-minded endeavour, Jamieson collected together from the different cultural traditions in Scotland a wide range of words that might otherwise have been lost, and for many years,

until the publication of the SCOTTISH NATIONAL DICTIONARY in the 20th century, his dictionary was the standard work of reference. It became a useful source book for many writers, including the poet Hugh MacDiarmid (CHRISTOPHER MURRAY GRIEVE), who used it to enrich his own literary Scots.

WORKS: *Socialism Unmasked* (1786); *A Poem on Slavery* (1789); *Congal and Fenella* (1791); *Sermons on the Heart*, 2 vols. (1791); *Vindication of the Doctrine of Scripture*, 2 vols. (1795); *A poem on Eternity* (1798); *Remarks on Rowland Hill's Journal* (1799); *The Use of Sacred History* (1802); *Etymological Dictionary of the Scottish Language*, 2 vols. (1808–9); *A Treatise on the Ancient Culdees of Iona* (1811); *Hermes Scythicus* (1814); *Dissertations on the Reality of the Spirit's Influence* (1844)

Jeffrey, Francis, Lord (1773–1850). Critic and editor. He was born on 23 October 1773 in Charles Street, Edinburgh, the son a Depute-Clerk of the COURT OF SESSION. He was educated at the HIGH SCHOOL OF EDINBURGH between 1781 and 1787, and between 1787 and 1789 at the University of Glasgow, where he read Greek, logic and moral philosophy and was introduced to Whig politics. In 1789 he enrolled at the University of Edinburgh to study law, and in 1791 he spent a year at Queen's College, Oxford, which led him, like many other Scottish intellectuals of his day, to adopt an anglicized accent and to attempt to rid his speech of SCOTICISMS. He returned to Edinburgh in 1792 to study law and history and in 1794 was admitted to the Bar. His career as an advocate was hampered by his Whig politics and he attempted, without success, to supplement his income by writing, a long poem *Dreaming* being suppressed by Jeffrey before it was published.

Jeffrey married Catherine Wilson in 1801 (she died four years later, and in 1813 he married Charlotte Wilkes) and set up house in a third-floor flat at 18 Buccleuch Place, Edinburgh, from which the first number of the *Edinburgh Review* (*see* EDINBURGH REVIEW (ii)) was published on 10 October 1802. The magazine was established by Jeffrey and his friends Sydney Smith (1771–1845) and Francis Horner (1778–1817), and the first edition of 750 copies quickly sold out. The demand took the founders by surprise and in 1803 Jeffrey was appointed editor and paid a salary by the magazine's publisher, ARCHIBALD CONSTABLE. Jeffrey held the post until 1829 when he was appointed Dean of the FACULTY OF

ADVOCATES, but during that period he invested the role of editor with a new public dignity, paying his contributors and extending the scope of the *Edinburgh Review* to cover the arts and the sciences.

With the return of the Whigs to political power, Jeffrey was appointed Lord Advocate in 1830 and was raised to the Bench as Lord Jeffrey in 1834. In 1832 he was elected Member of Parliament for Edinburgh, and in 1843–4 he published his *Contributions to the Edinburgh Review.* Jeffrey died on 26 January 1850 and his biography, *Life of Lord Jeffrey* (1852), was written by his friend HENRY THOMAS Lord COCKBURN. There is a sympathetic study of his work as an editor in Carlyle's *Reminiscences* (1881) and of his powers of legal oratory in PETER'S LETTERS TO HIS KINSFOLK (1819) by JOHN GIBSON LOCKHART.

As a critic Jeffrey was polished and versatile, contributing over 200 articles on subjects as diverse as the composition of water and Augustan poetry. Although he promoted the revival of interest in the Elizabethans, Jeffrey is best remembered for his literary *faux pas* – the statement on Wordsworth's *The Excursion*, 'This will never do!', and for his criticism of Scott's MARMION. His admiration for deliberate design in literature and his opposition to the use of commonplace diction in poetry not only led him to oppose the Lake Poets but also made him praise the artificial and the secondrate. He described himself as an 'official observer' of public taste and it is this middle-of-the-road attitude that has marred his reputation as a critic. During his lifetime Jeffrey was, nevertheless, a powerful literary figure and he used his influence to promote THOMAS CARLYLE and Thomas Macaulay in the *Edinburgh Review.*

REFERENCE: J. A. Greig, *Francis Jeffrey of the Edinburgh Review* (Edinburgh, 1948)

Jeffrey, William (1896–1946). Poet. He was born on 26 September 1896 at Kirk of Shotts, Lanarkshire, the son of a colliery manager. He was educated at Wishaw High School and attended the universities of Glasgow and Edinburgh before his education was interrupted by service with the Royal Artillery during World War I. After being gassed on the Western Front, he turned to journalism in 1920, working for the *Glasgow Evening Times* and later the GLASGOW HERALD as a leader-writer and drama critic. He died on 11 February 1946.

Much of Jeffrey's early work is top-heavy with mystic symbolism and the *gravitas* of his subject matter, but his poetry in Scots shows a deftness of touch and contains a rich vocabulary much influenced by the work of Hugh MacDiarmid (CHRISTOPHER MURRAY GRIEVE). During his lifetime Jeffrey published several volumes of verse, but the best was his posthumous *Sea Glimmer* (1947). He was one of the early members of the SCOTTISH RENAISSANCE of letters.

WORKS: *Prometheus Returns* (1921); *The Wise Men Come to Town* (1923); *The Nymph* (1924); *The Doom of Atlas* (1926); *The Lamb of Lomond* (1926); *Mountain Songs* (1928); *The Golden Stag* (1932); *Eagle of Coruisk* (1933); *Fantasia Written in an Industrial Town* (1933); *Sea Glimmer* (1947)

EDITION: A. Scott, ed., with a memoir, *Selected Poems of William Jeffrey* (Edinburgh, 1951)

Jekyll and Hyde. The names of the two *personae* of the chief character in Robert Louis Stevenson's novel THE STRANGE CASE OF DR JEKYLL AND MR HYDE.

Jenkins, (John) Robin (*b* 1912). Novelist. He was born on 11 September 1912 in Cambuslang, Lanarkshire, and was educated at Hamilton Academy and the University of Glasgow. Between 1936 and his retirement he taught in schools in Scotland, Afghanistan, Spain and Borneo and these countries have provided the backcloths for much of his writing. Jenkins's novels fall into three groups: those dealing with Scotland – *So Gaily Sings the Lark* (1950), *Happy for the Child* (1953), *The Thistle and the Grail* (1954), *The Cone-gatherers* (1955), *Guests of War* (1956), *The Missionaries* (1957), *The Changeling* (1958), *Love is a Fervent Fire* (1961), *A Love of Innocence* (1963), *The Sardana Dancers* (1964), *A Toast to the Lord* (1972), *A Would-be Saint* (1978) and *Fergus Lamont* (1979); those set in 'Nurania', his mythical Afghanistan – *Some Kind of Grace* (1960), *Dust on the Paw* (1961) and *The Tiger of Gold* (1962); and those set in 'Kalamantan', a far eastern sultanate – *The Holy Tree* (1969), *The Expatriates* (1971) and *A Figure of Fun* (1974). His short stories were collected in *A Far Cry from Bowmore* (1973).

In all his work Jenkins's writing is characterized by his probing insights into the paradox that makes human relationships both loving and self-destructive, and by his skilful delineation of character and psychological make-up.

His Scottish novels tend to focus on the sterner aspects of Calvinism; the best of his early novels, *The Cone-gatherers*, set on the patrician country estate of Lady Runcie-Campbell, follows to its bitter conclusion the enmity between Duror the gamekeeper and Calum, a simple-minded hunchback who gathers pine cones for their seeds. The contrast between the Christ-like figure of Calum and the forces of evil ranged against him is pointed up by a symbolism which suffuses the novel with a timeless, poetic quality as the story unfolds like a fable. Loss of innocence is also a central theme of *The Changeling* and *Guests of War*, and is transformed in Jenkins's later novels to a yearning for the level of grace that transcends human frailty. The themes merge in his most mature novel, *Fergus Lamont*, in which Jenkins takes an ultimately depressing view of the self-destructive nature of Scottish society.

His novels set outside Scotland continue many of Jenkins's domestic preoccupations. *Dust on the Paw* contains the ambiguous character of Harold Moffat, torn between his Christian ideals and his intellectual distaste for society in Nurania; the book's other hero, Abdul Wahab, is drawn into a mixed marriage and doubtful social acceptance in a crumbling country. With its skilful characterization and delineation of social niceties, together with Jenkins's own paradoxical views of society's values, *Dust on the Paw* is considered by many critics to be his most convincing novel.

Although Jenkins is capable of ranging easily and fluently over a wide variety of social backgrounds, his vision of the demonic state of the world and of the saving balm of love remain the constant motifs. Anger, sexual disappointments, the betrayal of innocence, are emotions never far removed from the surface, and, like EDWIN MUIR, Jenkins is aware of the fall from grace and the widening gulf between man and Eden.

WORKS: *So Gaily Sings the Lark* (1950); *Happy for the Child* (1953); *The Thistle and the Grail* (1954); *The Cone-gatherers* (1955); *Guests of War* (1956); *The Missionaries* (1957); *The Changeling* (1958); *Some Kind of Grace* (1960); *Love is a Fervent Fire* (1961); *Dust on the Paw* (1961); *The Tiger of Gold* (1962); *A Love of Innocence* (1963); *The Sardana Dancers* (1964); *A very Scotch Affair* (1968); *The Holy Tree* (1969); *The Expatriates* (1971); *A Toast to the Lord* (1972); *A Far Cry from Bowmore* (1973); *A Figure of Fun* (1974); *A Would-be Saint* (1978); *Fergus Lamont* (1979)

Jock Tamson's Bairns. A term commonly used in Scotland to mean 'the sons of Adam', and to imply a sense of common equality among the members of the human race. Its origin is obscure but it has been taken to signify 'the human race, common humanity, also with less sentimental force, a group of people united by a common sentiment or purpose' (*SND*).

John Dowie's Tavern. A tavern in Libberton's Wynd, Edinburgh, owned by John Dowie and patronized by DAVID HERD, ROBERT FERGUSSON and ROBERT BURNS among many others. ROBERT CHAMBERS, in his *Traditions of Edinburgh* (1824), described it as follows: 'A great proportion of this house was literally without light, consisting of a series of windowless chambers decreasing in size till the last was a mere box, of irregular oblong figure, jocularly, but not inappropriately, designated as *the Coffin*.' Dowie's customers were mainly lawyers, writers and men of fashion and the tavern had a reputation for conviviality, selling Younger's Edinburgh Ale, 'a potent fluid which almost glued the lips of the drinker together' (Chambers). It was demolished in 1834.

Johnny Gibb of Gushetneuk. A novel by WILLIAM ALEXANDER (ii), published serially in the *Aberdeen Free Press* between 1869 to 1870. It appeared in book form in 1871. Set in Pyketillim, an imaginary parish in Aberdeenshire, it is a series of 49 scenes of rural life or 'Glimpses of the Parish Politics about A.D.1843', as Alexander chose to subtitle the novel. The background is the events of THE DISRUPTION of 1843, the great schism in the Church of Scotland that brought about the establishment of the Free Church of Scotland and the reverberations of which were felt in every congregation in the country. From a life of seclusion the farmer Johnny Gibb is forced into a position of public prominence to become a supporter of the Free Church and its aims. In so doing he becomes aware of the petty ambitions and deep-seated animosity of those who oppose him – the magnificently realized Mrs Birse of Clinkstyle, whose ambitions are equalled only by the time-serving factor, Dawvid Hadden. Johnny Gibb's triumphant espousal of the new Church is less a vindication of its continued existence than a victory for his own beliefs over the bigotry of his opponents.

Pyketillim is not a rural paradise but a microcosm of the events that blight the larger world.

Sentimentality of vision, the bane of Scottish Victorian novelists who wrote in the debased KAILYARD tradition, is kept at bay, and the novel is a faithful evocation of Scottish village life, with all its contrasting strengths and weaknesses. The central narrative line is carried along in English by an anonymous narrator or observer; in counterpoint with this is the vigorous DORIC dialect of the north-east as uttered by the folk of the parish of Pyketillim.

John of Fordun (c1320–84). Historian. John of Fordun was probably a chantry priest in Aberdeen, but little is known of his life and career. His *Chronica gentis Scotorum* forms the first part of the SCOTICHRONICON, the great source book of Scottish history; John began its compilation by travelling through Britain and Ireland to authenticate his documentation. He brought the history down to 1383, basing much of the work on documents which have since been lost. His work was taken up again in 1440 by WALTER BOWER.

EDITION: W. F. Skene, ed., *Johanis de Fordun, Chronica gentis Scotorum*, 2 vols., The History of Scotland (Edinburgh, 1871)

Johnson, James (c1750–1811). Music publisher. He was probably born in Ettrick, the son of a crofter. He went to Edinburgh as a boy, and after an apprenticeship with a music-seller he set up business in Bell's Wynd where he pioneered a new process for printing sheet music. In 1787 he met ROBERT BURNS and invited him to become involved with volumes ii to v of THE SCOTS MUSICAL MUSEUM (1787–1803), one of the most important collections of traditional Scottish songs and music. The collaboration between the two men gathered together a large number of Scots songs at a time when they were in danger of disappearing from folk memory; and Johnson fired Burns's enthusiasm for song collecting and writing. Despite the importance of *The Scots Musical Museum*, Johnson's work was largely neglected during his lifetime and he died in poverty in 1811.

Johnston, Arthur (1587–1641). Poet and editor. He was a native of Aberdeenshire and was educated at King's College, Aberdeen, before leaving Scotland in 1608 to study in Padua and later at the Protestant University of Sedan. Although he was a frequent visitor to London during his years of absence, he did not

return to Britain until 1632, and five years later he was installed Lord Rector of King's College. He died during a visit to Oxford. Johnston's main work is the anthology of poems in Latin, DELITIAE POETARUM SCOTORUM, which he edited with Sir JOHN SCOTT of Scotstarvit in 1637. It contained the work of 37 Scottish poets who wrote in Latin, but surprisingly omitted that of GEORGE BUCHANAN. The best of Johnston's own poetry is concerned with the sights and sounds of his native Donside and there is a lightness of touch to all his descriptive verse. He also produced Latin translations of the Psalms which, despite the protests of his admirers, are not the equal of Buchanan's.

EDITION: W. Spang, ed., *Arthuri Johnstoni: Poemata Omnia* (Middleburg, 1642); W. D. Geddes, ed., *Musa latina aberdonensis*, 3 vols., New Spalding Club (Aberdeen, 1892–1910)

John Thomson's man. A phrase of uncertain origin, dating from the 16th century, used to describe a hen-pecked husband. 'Some explain John as = *Joan* (Mid. Eng. *Jone*) in which case Joan Thomson might be taken as a generic name for womankind, the feminine equivalent of Jock Tamson.' (*SND.*) Scott uses the phrase to mean 'hen-pecked husband' in OLD MORTALITY (Chapter 38).

Jolly Beggars, The [Love and Liberty]. A 'cantata' by ROBERT BURNS; it was written fairly early in his career, though it was not published in his lifetime. According to ROBERT CHAMBERS, who had the story from Burns's friend John Richmond, Burns wrote the work following a visit to Poosie Nansie's alehouse in Mauchline, where he witnessed 'much jollity amongst a company who by day appeared as beggars'. The 'cantata' is a collection of eight songs by the beggars – a maimed soldier, his doxy, a fool, a female thief, a fiddler, a tinker and a poet – held together by a *recitativo* introducing the characters and an atmospheric description of the warmth inside the inn and the cold winter's night outside. In their songs the beggars extol the pleasures of their lives, the drunkenness and lust as well as the conviviality and independence. W. E. Henley and Thomas Henderson, the editors of the centenary editions of Burns's poems, called the world of the beggars, 'The irresistible presentation of humanity caught in the act and summarised for ever after in terms of art.' Burns may have conceived the idea from the

poem 'Merry Beggars' in THE TEA-TABLE MIS-
CELLANY by ALLAN RAMSAY, but DAVID
DAICHES has pointed to the cantata's belonging to a 'long line of songs and poems in
goliardic vein which goes far back into the
Middle Ages and which includes the legend of
'the Gaberlunzie man' (*Robert Burns* (London,
rev. 2/1966)). Burns omitted *The Jolly Beggars*
from the Edinburgh edition of poems of 1787
and it was first published in Glasgow in 1799.

Journalism. Although the profession of journalism had humble origins in Scotland, many
of the nation's authors have either been news-
papermen or have been frequent contributors
to the Scottish press. Of a career in journalism,
Sir WALTER SCOTT warned his son-in-law
JOHN GIBSON LOCKHART, 'none but a
thorough-going blackguard ought to attempt
the daily press'. Early newspaper production in
Scotland was a chancy business. There was no
daily newspaper until 1847, when the *North
British Daily Mail* first appeared on 14 April;
those publications that were in existence were
little more than advertising sheets, and men of
letters turned to the great reviews, such as the
Edinburgh Review (*see* EDINBURGH REVIEW
(ii)), BLACKWOOD'S MAGAZINE and TAIT'S
EDINBURGH MAGAZINE to publish their essays
and reviews.

Most early newspapers were staffed only by
an editor and his reporter, but by the middle of
the 19th century the growing eminence and
financial security of several weekly and daily
newspapers encouraged men like JOHN
MCDIARMID and HUGH MILLER to turn to
journalism as a full-time occupation. By the
end of the century journalism had become an
accepted and acceptable profession, and Glasgow had become its Scottish centre. NEIL
MUNRO and GEORGE BLAKE both edited the
Glasgow Evening News and WILLIAM POWER
was the literary editor of the GLASGOW
HERALD; other Glasgow writers who have also
been journalists include JOHN BOY BELL, CLIF-
FORD HANLEY, FREDERICK NIVEN and GOR-
DON WILLIAMS. 20th-century Scottish writers
who have made careers as journalists or as
reviewers and leader-writers include J. M. BAR-
RIE, JOHN BUCHAN, JOHN DAVIDSON, CHRIST-
OPHER MURRAY GRIEVE and ERIC LINKLATER.

**Journal of a Tour to the Hebrides with
Samuel Johnson LL.D.** A diary written by
JAMES BOSWELL to record his tour of the Highlands and the Western Isles made in the company of Dr Samuel Johnson (1709–84) between August and November 1773. It was first
published in 1785 and again in 1936 in an
expanded edition following the discovery of
the Boswell papers at Malahide Castle in Ireland. Dr Johnson's account of the same journey
had been published in 1775 in *Journey to the
Western Islands of Scotland*, but it was mainly a
topographical description and a basic record of
the main events of the tour. Boswell's account
is altogether more personal and intimate and
presents a frequently delightful description of
Johnson's attitudes and his reactions to Highland Scotland and its peoples' way of life. It is
also a first-class travel book in which Boswell
presents a racy, almost journalistic account of
the journey, together with a character sketch
of Johnson that is second only to the more
famous *Life*.

EDITION: F. A. Pottle and C. H. Bennett, eds.,
*Boswell's Journal of a Tour to the Hebrides with Samuel
Johnson LL.D. Now First Published from the Original
Manuscript* (New York and London, 1936)

K

Kailyard. A term (meaning 'cabbage patch') first used by the critic J. H. MILLAR in the April 1895 edition of *The New Review* to describe the novelists J. M. BARRIE, S. R. CROCKETT and JOHN WATSON ('Ian Maclaren'). Although it fell to Barrie to be described as '*pars magna*, if not *pars maxima* of the Great Kailyard Movement', particular criticism was reserved for Crockett, and Millar developed the pejorative use of the term in his *Literary History of Scotland* of 1903. 'Kailyard' has been applied to other writers and is a term of adverse criticism for books, newspapers, films and radio and television programmes. Basically, 'Kailyard' describes a school of rural sentimentality with the essential ingredient of characters who represent solid virtues: the minister or the village worthies who voice pastoral morality, the industrious son who rises by dint of hard work and his own endeavour, the honest tenant farmers who give of their best for their families' improvement. Behind them are the stock rapacious landlords, self-satisfied incomers and the ever-present and awesome figures of death and disease. These characters inhabit a well-defined arcadia of village life, far removed from the ills of 19th-century Scotland, its industrial development, poverty and high mortality rate. The city appears only as a distant drum; instead, the virtues of village life are emphasized. The world created by the Kailyard novelists is little more than a projection of 18th-century Romantic views about nature and its beneficial effects on humankind.

Although Millar used the term exclusively for the novels of Maclaren, Barrie and Crockett, it would be wrong to label all their work as Kailyard. Barrie was a distinguished dramatist, many of whose plays eschew the pawky excesses of Thrums and the AULD LICHT IDYLLS. Crockett's *The Raiders* and *The Men of the Moss Haggs* are adventure stories in the best tradi-

tion of ROBERT LOUIS STEVENSON, superior to his cloying tales *The Lilac Sunbonnet* and *The Stickit Minister*, both of which enjoyed great commercial success. In one respect the Kailyard writers were only pandering to the popular taste of a public who preferred the sentimentality of the past to the harsh realities of the present. Foremost among the champions of the Kailyard was the editor of the *British Weekly*, WILLIAM ROBERTSON NICOLL, an influential editor and critic in London who gave unstinted support to Maclaren and Barrie and later to another Kailyard practitioner ANNIE S. SWAN. He was ruled by the principles of publishing economics which determined that a successful story theme be exploited to its utmost; he was also inclined to support his fellow Scots, particularly if they owned to Free Church associations.

Historically, the sentimental school had its origins in the Common-Sense school of Scottish philosophy which emphasized the importance of the emotions. Its literary prophet was HENRY MACKENZIE whose novel THE MAN OF FEELING created a vogue for fiction which dealt with finer human feelings. Sentimentality became a noble virtue, one to be encouraged, and it finds echoes in the early 19th-century novels of JOHN WILSON (iii), ELIZABETH HAMILTON, DAVID MACBETH MOIR and to a lesser extent in some of the work of JOHN GALT and GEORGE MACDONALD. The reaction to the Kailyard came in the 20th century with the publication of the novels GILLESPIE by JOHN MACDOUGALL HAY and THE HOUSE WITH THE GREEN SHUTTERS by GEORGE DOUGLAS BROWN, both of which deploy sensitive realism and carefully delineated characters in place of sentimentality and caricature, while still remaining within the confines of the village.

REFERENCES: G. Blake, *Barrie and the Kailyard School* (London, 1951); I. Campbell, *Kailyard: a New Assessment* (Edinburgh, 1981)

Kames, Lord. *See* HOME, HENRY.

Keddie, Henrietta ['Sarah Tytler']
(1827–1914). Novelist. She was born in
Cupar, Fife, the daughter of a lawyer. Early in
her childhood the family moved to the village
of Elie on the Fife coast in order to be near the
coal-mine in which all their finances were
invested. At the age of 16 she was sent to
Edinburgh to complete her education and it
was while she was there that she met the
essayist JOHN BROWN, who encouraged her
literary aspirations. Her early work appeared in
BLACKWOOD'S MAGAZINE and on her return to
Fife she pursued her literary interests in St
Andrews, where she was an acquaintance of
JAMES FREDERICK FERRIER, A. K. H. BOYD and
JOHN TULLOCH. The death of her father
forced her to earn a living, and with her sisters
she set up a small private school in Cupar,
which they operated between 1848 and 1870.
Eventually the success of her literary career
under her own name and her pseudonym,
'Sarah Tytler', allowed her to give up the
school, and from 1884 she lived first in London
and then in Oxford, where she died on 8 June
1914.

Henrietta Keddie's autobiography *Three
Generations of a Middle-Class Scottish Family*
(1911) is an entertaining account of her girlhood years and literary life and is replete with
fond memories of the people she had known in
the course of a long and busy life. It also
presents her as a modest, yet hard-working and
persevering woman who, against all odds, became one of the most popular and successful
authors of her generation. Much of her work
was written quickly and with the sole object of
making money: biographical sketches, travel
books, advice to young girls and other journalistic pieces; but two novels from her huge
output stand out. *Logie Town* (1887) is a well-
observed portrayal of life in a small Fife town at
the time of the Reform Bill of 1832. Like its
near-contemporary novel JOHNNY GIBB OF
GUSHETNEUK by WILLIAM ALEXANDER (ii), it
records with the minimum of sentimentality
the claustrophobic society and stultifying
bourgeois values of the town of Logie. There is
also a fondness for the town and its people,
balanced against that knowledge of the de-
ficiencies displayed by its society, making *Logie
Town* one of the most satisfying portrayals of
life in a Victorian small town in Scotland. *St
Mungo's City* (1884), which traces the life and

times of a self-made businessman in Glasgow,
is notable for the accurate observation of the
changing industrial society of the west of Scotland. The subtlety with which Henrietta Keddie viewed Scottish society, her ability to delineate aspects of character and to render Scottish speech in these two novels provide a tantalizing glimpse of what she might have
achieved had she not been forced into writing
pulp literature for a living.

WORKS: *Phemie Millar*, 3 vols. (1854); *The Nut Brown
Maids* (1859); *Meg of Elibank* (1860); *Weaving the
Willow* (1860); *My Heart's in the Highlands* (1861); *A
Simple Woman* (1863); *Heroines in Obscurity* (1871);
Lady Bell, 3 vols. (1873); *A Douce Lass* (1877);
French Janet (1889); *Lady Jeans's Vagaries* (1894);
Kincaid's Widow (1895); *Honor Ormthwaite* (1896);
The Machinations of Janet (1903); *Three Generations
of a Middle-Class Scottish Family* (1911)
as Sarah Tytler: *Papers for Thoughtful Girls* (1862);
Citoyenne Jacqueline (1865); *Days of Yore*, 2 vols.
(1866); *The Diamond Rose* (1867); *The Huguenot
Family*, 3 vols. (1867); *Sweet Counsel* (1867); *Girl-
hood and Womanhood* (1868); *Noblesse oblige* (1870);
Sisters and Wives (1871); *The Songstresses of Scotland*
(1871); *Modern Painters and their Work* (1873); *The
Old Masters* (1873); *A Garden of Women* (1875);
Musical Composers and their Work (1875); *By the Elbe*
(1876); *Childhood a Hundred Years Ago* (1877);
Landseer's Dogs and their Stories (1877); *What she
Came Through* (1877); *Scotch Firs* (1878); *Summer
Snows* (1878); ed., *Jane Austen and her Works*
(1880); *Lord Fleur's Champion* (1880); *Oliver Consta-
ble*, 3 vols. (1880); *Footprints* (1881); *A Hero of a
Hundred Fights* (1881); *Beauties and Pageants* (1882);
The Bride's Pass (1882); *Scotch Marriages* (1882);
Marie Antoinette (1883); *Beauty and the Beast*
(1884); *St Mungo's City*, 3 vols. (1884); *The Woman
with Two Wards* (1885); *Buried Diamonds* (1886);
Comrades (1886); *Her Gentle Deeds* (1886); *In the
Fort* (1886); *The Life of Her Majesty the Queen*
(1886); *Disappeared* (1887); *Logie Town* (1887);
Sukie's Boy (1887); *The Blackhall Ghosts* (1888); *Girl
Neighbours* (1888); *Duchess France* (1889); *A House
full of Girls* (1889); *Vashti Savage* (1889); *Heroines in
Obscurity* (1890); *Nobody's Girls* (1890); *Sapphira*
(1890); *A Young Oxford Maid* (1890); *A Morning
Mist* (1892); *A Bubble Fortune* (1893); *A Lonely
Lassie* (1893); *War Times* (1893); *Beneath the Sur-
face* (1894); *Mermaidens* (1885); *The Macdonald's
Lass* (1895); *A Little Lass and Lad* (1896); *Rachel
Langton* (1896); *Tudor Queens and Princesses* (1896);
The American Comes (1897); *Lady Jean's Son* (1897);
The Wild Life (1897); *Miss Carmichael's Goddesses*
(1898); *Six Royal Ladies of the House of Hanover*
(1898); *A Crazy Moment* (1899); *A Honeymoon's
Eclipse* (1899); *Miss Nance* (1899); *Jean Keir of
Craigneil* (1900); *A Loyal Little Maid* (1900); *Many
Daughters* (1900); *A Young Dragon* (1900); *Queen
Charlotte's Maidens* (1901); *Rival Claimants* (1901);
Three Men of Mark (1901); *Atonement by Proxy*
(1902); *The Courtship of Sarah* (1902); *Women Must
Weep* (1902); *At Lathan's Siege* (1903); *Friendly Foes*
(1903); *In Clarinda's Day* (1903); *Sir David's Visitors*
(1903); *Favours from France* (1904); *Four Red Roses*

(1904); *Hearts are Trumps* (1904); *Major Singleton's Daughter* (1904); *The Poet and his Guardian Angel* (1904); *A Daughter of the Manse* (1905); *His Reverence the Rector* (1905); *A Stepmother* (1905); *The Bracebridges* (1906); *The Girls of Innerbarns* (1906); *A Briar Rose* (1907); *The Countess of Huntingdon* (1907); *Innocent Masquerades* (1907); *The Two Lady Lascelles* (1908); *A Banished Lady* (1908)

Keelivine, Christopher. Pen-name of AN-DREW PICKEN.

Kemp, Robert (1908–67). Dramatist. He was born on 25 February 1908 on the island of Hoy, Orkney, the son of a minister of the Church of Scotland. His family had their roots in Edinburgh where they had a long involvement in the weaving trade, and it was in Edinburgh that Kemp was to settle in 1942 and to remain until his death in 1967. In 1914 his father moved to the charge of Birse near Aboyne in Aberdeenshire and Kemp completed his education at the University of Aberdeen. On graduating he took up a career in journalism with the *Manchester Guardian* before becoming a BBC producer in 1937. Through the medium of radio he was able to exploit his lifelong interest in Scots and he produced a number of innovatory radio dramas including a popular adaptation of the fable 'The Taill of the Uponlandis Mous and the Burges Mous' by ROBERT HENRYSON as 'The Country Mouse Comes to Town'.

As well as encouraging the work of other writers Kemp started writing himself, and his first play, *Whuppity Stoorie*, was produced in Edinburgh in 1944. There followed a series of historical dramas, the most popular being *The Other Dear Charmer* (1951), which dealt with the relationship between ROBERT BURNS and AGNES M'LEHOSE. He also wrote Scots translations of Molière's *L'école des femmes* (*Let Wives Tak Tent*, 1948) and *L'avare* (*The Laird o' Grippy*, 1958). His most successful theatrical venture, though, was his adaptation of ANE PLEASANT SATYRE OF THE THRIE ESTAITIS by Sir DAVID LYNDSAY, which was produced by Tyrone Guthrie at the 1948 Edinburgh International Festival. Performed in the round in the Assembly Hall of the Church of Scotland, it introduced new standards of theatre direction and proved that a 16th-century play in Scots, Scotland's first major drama, could be understood and appreciated by contemporary audiences.

Kemp left the BBC in 1948 to concentrate on his own writing and to further his ambition of establishing a professional theatre company in Edinburgh. That was achieved in 1953 with the foundation of the Edinburgh Gateway Theatre, a company set up to encourage the work of Scottish writers and actors, which remained in existence until 1965 when it was incorporated as the Edinburgh Civic Theatre. Kemp lived long enough to see the theatre gain a more certain hold in Scottish cultural life than it had enjoyed earlier in the century, and his contribution must be measured not only in terms of his own commitment to the movement but also in terms of the plays and translations that he wrote, which proved that Scots could be a valid literary language for the stage. He published five novels and was also a prolific journalist, contributing an entertaining editorial diary to the GLASGOW HERALD, the matter of which was based largely on his own life.

WORKS: *The Twa Fiddlers* (1932); *The Saxon Saint* (1950); *The Satire of the Three Estates, Adapted from the play by Sir David Lyndsay* (1951); *The Malacca Cane* (1954); *The Maestro* (1956); *The Other Dear Charmer* (1957); *The Highlander* (1957); *The Campaigns of Captain MacGurk* (1958); *Master John Knox* (1960); *Gretna Green* (1961); *Off a Duck's Back* (1961); *The Heart of the Highlands* (1962)

Kennaway, James (1928–68). Novelist. He was born on 5 June 1928 in Auchterarder, Perthshire, the son of a solicitor and a doctor. He was educated at Trinity College, Glenalmond, and in 1947 was commissioned into the Cameron Highlanders, serving with the Gordon Highlanders in Germany. In 1948 he went up to Trinity College, Oxford, to read philosophy, politics and economics, and on graduating became a publisher in London.

Kennaway began writing as an undergraduate, and his first novel, *Tunes of Glory*, was published in 1956. Set in a Highland regiment, it examines the conflict that arises when two men from different social and military traditions – Jock Sinclair, a hard-drinking Scot who has risen from the ranks, and Basil Barrow a professional with an impeccable military background – vie with one another for the colonelship of the regiment. The mutual antagonism is resolved by Barrow's suicide in the face of Sinclair's stubborn pride and dynamic self-destructiveness, which both repels and attracts his fellow officers. The theme of isolation and mental breakdown is continued in Kennaway's second novel, *Household Ghosts* (1961), also set in Scotland. One of his most memorable characters, 'Pink' (Charles

Henry Arbuthnot Ferguson), lives at second remove from reality in the childhood fantasy and frustrated passion that he shares with his sister Mary. Although the novel is set within the narrow confines of their crumbling aristocratic family, Kennaway centres on the taut, violent relationship that Mary has with the men around her: Pink, her husband Stephen Cameron and her lover David Dow. *Household Ghosts* was later adapted for the stage (1967) and was made into a film (1969), both with the title *Country Dance*.

In 1963 Kennaway published two novels – *The Mind Benders*, a study of brain-washing and interrogation through the use of long periods of isolation, and *The Bells of Shoreditch*, a stark tale of the corrupting nature of the world of international merchant banking and its destruction of human values. There followed two novels which took triangular relationships as their theme. *Some Gorgeous Accident* (1967) traces the affairs of Susie, Fiddes and Link, different yet inextricably related characters, each with the ability to create both love and pain in their personal lives; Link, the central character is a monstrous creation caught in the web of his own self-delusion. In *The Cost of Living Like This* (1969) the relationship between Julian, who is dying of cancer, Christabel his wife, and Sally, a young secretary, is judged by the vivid creation of Mozart Anderson who acts as a puzzled referee over Julian's inevitable slide towards death. As with all Kennaway's novels the action owes more to the strength of the characterization than to the narrative flow of the plot. A posthumous novel, *Silence*, was published in 1972.

Kennaway also wrote a number of short stories, and film scripts including *Violent Playground* (1958), *Tunes of Glory* (1960), *The Mind Benders* (1962) and *Country Dance* (1969). He was killed in a motoring accident on 21 December 1968.

WORKS: *Tunes of Glory* (1956); *Household Ghosts* (1961); *The Bells of Shoreditch* (1963); *The Mind Benders* (1963); *Some Gorgeous Accident* (1967); *The Cost of Living Like This* (1969); *Silence* (1972); T. Royle, ed., *The Dollar Bottom and Taylor's Finest Hour* (1981)

REFERENCES: J. and S. Kennaway, *The Kennaway Papers* (London, 1981); T. Royle, *James Kennaway: a Biography* (Edinburgh, 1983)

Kennedy, Walter (c1460–c1508). Poet. He was the third son of Lord Kennedy of Dunure and through his mother he was related to

Robert III of Scotland. His uncle, James, was Bishop of Dunkeld and St Andrews and the founder of St Salvator's College, St Andrews. He was educated at the University of Glasgow and through his royal connections he became Depute-Bailie of Carrick. Although very little is known about his life and career, some echoes can be heard in 'THE FLYTING OF DUNBAR AND KENNEDY', the great poetic battle of words with his contemporary WILLIAM DUNBAR. Both Dunbar and Sir DAVID LYNDSAY make generous mention of Kennedy's prowess as a poet but very little remains of that output. His extant work was published in SCOTTISH TEXT SOCIETY editions of the MAITLAND MANUSCRIPTS and BANNATYNE MANUSCRIPT.

Kentigern [Mungo], St. Very little is known about St Kentigern's life, though he is the subject of much myth and legend. The story of his life and miracles is told in a 12th-century manuscript by Jocelin of Furness, but this has been found to be a compilation of errors and fiction, involving the stories of other saints. Nevertheless, Kentigern, or 'Mungo' as he was nicknamed, is a potent figure in Scottish hagiology. Legend has it that he was a son of Thenew, or Enoch, daughter of Loth, a Celtic prince whose court was at Traprain Law in East Lothian. His childhood was spent in the tutelage of St Serf (who in reality lived 200 years later), and as a result of his religious training he became a missionary. He is supposed to have founded the religious centre at Cathures or Cleschu, which became the present-day city of Glasgow, and the miracles associated with his name were adopted for the city's coat of arms: the resuscitation of Kentigern's pet robin, the miraculous growth of a tree on the mound on which he preached, and the discovery of the King of Strathclyde's ring in a salmon fished from the Clyde. Kentigern also has associations with Dumfriesshire, Cumbria, and Wales where he is known as Cynderyn. His saint's day is 13 January.

Ker, Robert, Earl of Ancrum (1578–1654). Poet and statesman. He was a Groom to the Bedchamber of Prince Henry, son of JAMES VI, and he accompanied the court to London when it moved in 1603 after the Union of the Crowns. He was banished after fighting a duel in 1620 but returned to London in 1625 on the accession of Charles I. In 1633 he was created Earl of Ancrum and the remainder of his public life was spent in the service of the Crown. During the civil wars he retired to live in Amsterdam and he died there in extreme poverty in 1654. Although he was not one of James's CASTALIAN BAND, Ancrum was a cultivated man who counted among his friends the poet WILLIAM DRUMMOND of Hawthornden, for whom he wrote the sonnet 'In Praise of a Solitary Life'. He also wrote a metrical version of the Psalms which were set to Dutch folk melodies.

EDITION: D. Laing, ed., *Correspondence of Robert Ker, 1st Earl of Ancrum* (Edinburgh, 1875)

Kidnapped. A novel by ROBERT LOUIS STEVENSON, published in 1886. The story is set against the background of the aftermath of the 1745 Jacobite rebellion and the Appin murder in which Colin Campbell of Glenure, the 'Red Fox', was killed following the forfeiture of the Stewart and Cameron lands to the Campbells; the blame for the murder fell on JAMES STEWART of the Glens and his brother ALAN BRECK STEWART, who play an important part in the novel. Stevenson uses the historical facts as the background to the adventure of David Balfour, a Lowland schoolmaster's son, who has been tricked out of his inheritance by his uncle Ebenezer and kidnapped on a ship bound for America. During the voyage the ship rescues Alan Breck Stewart, a Jacobite outlaw who is forced to fight the ship's crew to save his and David's lives. The ship sinks on the coast of Mull and David and Alan journey back to Edinburgh to reclaim David's inheritance. On the journey they meet many adventures: they witness the Appin murder, are pursued by government troops, and meet Robin Oig, a son of ROB ROY MACGREGOR. The novel ends with David's recovery of his inheritance from his rascally uncle and the flight of Alan into exile.

Kidnapped is one of Stevenson's most popular and successful adventure stories: the conflicting characters of David and Alan are finely realized, the historical detail is accurate and there is a splendid evocation of the scenery and atmosphere of the Highlands. Equally important are the contradictions that bind the two men together: the solid Lowlander David and the Highland adventurer Alan and their consequently conflicting loyalties between support of the government and the Jacobite cause, practical Hanoverianism and romantic Jacobitism, the reality of the present and the glamour of the past. At the end of the novel the differences between the two men have served to cement their friendship. A less successful sequel, *Catriona* (1893), deals with David Balfour's love affair with Catriona Drummond and his unsuccessful attempt to secure the release of James Stewart of the Glens.

Kilmarnock edition. The first collection of poems by ROBERT BURNS, entitled *Poems, Chiefly in the Scottish Dialect*, it was published by JOHN WILSON (ii) of Kilmarnock on 31 July 1786 at a cost of three shillings a copy. The first edition of 612 copies sold out within a month of publication and it earned good reviews especially in Edinburgh where HENRY MACKENZIE hailed Burns as the 'heaven-taught ploughman' in the December issue of THE LOUNGER. The edition contained the following poems: 'THE TWA DOGS', 'Scotch Drink', 'The Author's Earnest Cry and Prayer to the Right Honourable and Honourable, the Scotch Representatives in the House of Commons', 'THE HOLY FAIR', 'ADDRESS TO THE DEIL', 'The Death and Dying Words of Poor Mailie', 'Poor Mailie's Elegy', 'Epistle to James Smith', 'A Dream', 'The Vision', 'Halloween', 'THE AULD FARMER'S NEW YEAR MORNING SALUTATION TO HIS AULD MARE MAGGIE', 'THE COTTER'S SATURDAY NIGHT', 'The Lament', 'Despondency, an Ode', 'Man was made to mourn', 'Winter, a Dirge', 'A Prayer in the Prospect of Death', 'The Lament Occasioned by the Unfortunate Loss of a Friend's Amour', 'TO A MOUSE', 'To a Mountain Daisy', 'To Ruin', 'Epistle to a Young Friend', 'Epistle to Davie', two 'Epistles to John Lapraik', 'Epistles to William Simpson of Ochiltree'; 'Epistle to John Rankine', 'On a Scotch Bard gone to the West Indies', 'TO A LOUSE', 'A Bard's Epitaph', and a number of songs. The volume was dedicated to the Mauchline lawyer GAVIN HAMILTON.

Although Burns omitted a number of his most important Scots poems – especially 'The Twa Herds', 'DEATH AND DR HORNBOOK', 'Address to Unco Guid' and 'HOLY WILLIE'S PRAYER' – because they might have given offence, the best poems in the Kilmarnock edition are those written in the language in which Burns excelled, a Scots idiom that combines the literary with the colloquial. Burns deliberately exaggerated his lack of learning in the preface to the collection, presenting himself as: 'Unacquainted with the necessary requisites for commencing Poet by rules, he sings the sentiments and manners he felt and saw in himself and his rustic compeers around him, in his and their native language.' The Edinburgh *literatia* accepted that version of Burns's background with approval, and as a result favoured the minor English neo-classical poems and the sentimental nature poems such as 'THE COTTER'S SATURDAY NIGHT'.

Kilmeny. A poem by JAMES HOGG from THE QUEEN'S WAKE, an idealized description of a festival of poetry held in honour of MARY, Queen of Scots, during which 17 bards take part in a poetic competition. 'Kilmeny' is the 13th bard's song and it tells the story of a young virgin, Kilmeny, who is removed for seven years to another world, where she is bathed in the stream of life before being taken to a green mountain and shown examples of human wickedness in the vision of the lady with the lion and the 'untoward bedeman' (Mary, Queen of Scots, and the Reformation) and the lion and the eagle (the French Revolution). At the end of the poem she asks the spirits to send her back to her own country to tell her tale, but earth cannot hold her and she returns to the spirit world of beauty and tranquillity.

Hogg was influenced in his poetic development by his intimate knowledge of the Border BALLAD, and in the capture of the pure virgin by spirits from another world a link with 'Tam Lin' and 'Thomas the Rhymer' can be seen. However, in 'Kilmeny' the world of faery is not mentioned specifically, and another interpretation of the poem is as an articulation of the Christian view that man lives in a world of sin but beyond it lies a glorious heaven of peace and everlasting joy.

The Queen's Wake was first published in two editions in 1813, reprinted twice in 1814 and again in 1822. In the third edition (1814) Hogg changed some of the mock-antique Scots words in 'Kilmeny' to a more modern form.

King, Kennedy. Pen-name of GEORGE DOUGLAS BROWN.

Kingis Quair, The (The King's Book). A poem in 197 stanzas of rhyme-royal by JAMES I, probably written after his return to Scotland in 1424. James was taken prisoner by the English in 1406 while on a sea journey to France and during his exile he fell in love with Henry V's cousin, Lady Joan Beaufort, whom he married on 2 February 1424. His romance is the basic subject of *The Kingis Quair*, which was ascribed to him in the manuscript copy of the poem held by the Bodleian Library, Oxford (MS Seld. Arch B.24). Other evidence for royal authorship comes from JOHN MAJOR in his *Historia Majoris Britanniae* of 1521 and from GEORGE BANNATYNE in his manuscript of 1568.

The poem itself shows the influence of English poets with whose work James would have been familiar, notably *The Temple of Glass* by John Lydgate (c 1370–c 1451). On one level *The Kingis Quair* is a spiritual autobiography of James's relationship with Joan Beaufort, and on another it is an exegesis of *De consolatione philosophiae* by Boethius (c 480–524), which had been translated into English by King Alfred (849–901) and by Geoffrey Chaucer (c1345–1400). James's story opens with the poet, held prisoner, reflecting on his destiny. The book of Boethius reminds him that even the noblest of men can be wronged by fortune, but that comfort can be found in a reliance on philosophy to control the urges of the will. An autobiographical section follows, with the story of the poet's capture at sea in the image of the poet as a rudderless ship and his glimpse of the loved one from the prison in the tower. The poet falls into a troubled sleep in which he finds himself in the court of Venus, but because Venus realizes that the poet needs 'gude auise' (114, 3) he is passed to Minerva's court. There he learns, in Boethian fashion, that the will must be controlled by wisdom; he turns to Fortune who reminds him of the vagaries of her wheel and at that, with a blow on the ear, the poet wakens at peace with himself and his emotions. The poem ends with a hymn of thanksgiving and James's celebration of happiness in love: 'And thus befell my blissfull auenture/In youth, of lufe that now from day to day/Flourith ay newe.' (193, 5–7)

WILLIAM TYTLER published *The Kingis Quair* in 1783 from a manuscript collection of poems by Chaucer discovered by him; it has since been edited in 1910 by Alexander Lawson, in 1911 by W. W. Skeat for the SCOTTISH TEXT SOCIETY, in 1939 by W. M. Mackenzie, in 1971 by John Norton-Smith, and in 1973 by M. P. McDiarmid.

Kinmont Willie. Nickname of WILLIAM ARMSTRONG.

Kirn. The festival of Harvest Home, held in the middle of October when the crops had been safely gathered in. The centrepiece of the feast was the last sheaf to be cut, which was dressed frequently as the harvest maiden or made into an elaborate dolly or harvest knot.

Knott, Hermann. Pen-name of WALTER CHALMERS SMITH.

Knox [née Craig], **Isa** (1831–1903). Poet. She was born on 17 October 1831 in Edinburgh, the only child of a hosier. She was a regular contributor to THE SCOTSMAN and became a member of its staff in 1853. In 1857 she moved to London to become secretary to the National Association for the Promotion of Social Science, a post she held until May 1866, when she married her cousin John Knox. Although most of her poetry, which was widely published in its day, has been forgotten, she won the centenary ROBERT BURNS poetry competition at the Crystal Palace in 1858. She also wrote a number of successful school textbooks. She died on 23 December 1903 at Brockley in Suffolk.

WORKS: *Poems by Isa* (1856); *The Essence of Slavery* (1863); *Poems* (1863); *Duchess Agnes* (1864); *Esther West* (1870); *The Little Folks History of England* (1872); *Songs of Consolation* (1874); *Deepdale Vicarage* (1881); *The Half Sisters* (1881); *In Duty Bound* (1881); *Hold Fast by your Sundays* (1882); *Easy History for Upper Standards* (1885); *Our Summer Home* (1888)

Knox, John (c1513–72). Divine and reformer. He was born in Haddington, East Lothian, and, although there is no record of his attendance there, he was probably educated at the University of St Andrews under the historian JOHN MAJOR. By 1540 he had left university and had been ordained into the priesthood, becoming a notary public in his home county of East Lothian. During that period he transferred his religious allegiance to the Protestant faith and in 1545 he became a bodyguard to one of the movement's foremost preachers, George Wishart (c1513–46), who was executed in St Andrews. That martyrdom was to have a powerful effect on Knox and, when a group of reformers avenged Wishart's death by murdering his persecutor Cardinal Beaton in the castle of St Andrews, Knox hurried there to join them in April 1547. After the surrender of the rebels to a French force in July, Knox and other members of the garrison

were pressed into service as galley slaves in Rouen. Released early in 1549, Knox moved to England, where Archbishop Thomas Cranmer (1489–1556) was involved in the reformation of the Church in England through the revision of the liturgy and the promulgation of the 42 articles. Knox was sent to preach first in Berwick and then in Newcastle before returning to London, where he became identified with the right wing of the Protestant reformers. In 1552 he was offered two important ecclesiastical posts – the bishopric of Rochester and the rectorship of Allhallows, which would have brought him under the authority of Cranmer's chaplain Nicholas Ridley (c1500–55) – but Knox, fearful for the well-being of Edward VI, turned down both posts. It was a wise move, for when Edward died in the summer of 1553 and Mary Tudor acceded to the throne, Knox missed the Catholic backlash by escaping to Europe. He made his first marriage in 1553 – to Marjory Bowes; after her death he married Margaret Stewart, the 16-year-old daughter of Lord Ochiltree, in 1563.

From January to March 1554 Knox was in Dieppe, where he began the series of letters to 'his afflicted brethren in England' which were intended to encourage those under the persecution of Queen Mary. Later in the year he went to Geneva where he met the reformer John Calvin (1509–64), a meeting that bore fruit in his religious philosophy when he returned to live in Geneva in 1555. Before then he spent some months in Frankfurt-am-Rhein, which had become a centre for the exiled English Protestants, but he quarrelled with them over the use of the *Book of Common Prayer* and was forced to leave the city. From 1556 he was back in Dieppe, where he wrote THE FIRST BLAST OF THE TRUMPET AGAINST THE MONSTROUS REGIMENT OF WOMEN, and in March 1558 he returned to Geneva where he remained until 1559. This 14-month stay was to be the most formative period in his life. In 'the most perfect schole of Christ' he formulated many of the doctrines (mostly adopted from Calvin), such as original sin, predestination and the elect, that formed the basis of Scottish Presbyterianism. *The First Blast of the Trumpet* contended that it was wrong for a woman to rule over a country and was directed principally against the reign of Queen Mary in England. Later letters and pamphlets advocated the removal of a cruel or oppressive monarch by the nobility, acting on behalf of the commonalty; these radical views did not endear him to Elizabeth when she became Queen of England in 1559.

Unable to obtain a passport to return to England, Knox decided that the time was ripe to move back to Scotland, and he landed at Leith on 2 May 1559. There he discovered that the queen regent, Mary of Guise-Lorraine had outlawed the Protestant preachers and that he too had been put to the horn. On 11 May, the day following the queen's declaration, he preached a violent sermon in Perth which led to the destruction of the Catholic churches and monasteries in the surrounding area. This violence sparked off a general Protestant revolt in Scotland, of which Knox become the moral and spiritual leader. Such was his standing that by July he had been invited to become the minister of St Giles's Church in Edinburgh, a post he was to hold until his death on 24 November 1572. With English support, and following the death of Mary of Guise-Lorraine, the Protestant party eventually gained control of Scotland after the conclusion of the Treaty of Leith of 6 July 1560.

When MARY, Queen of Scots, returned to Scotland in August 1561 there were grounds for believing that she wished to restore Catholicism, and a suspicious Knox interviewed her on several occasions with regard to her politics, religion and public behaviour. Knox gave tacit support to the murder of David Riccio, Mary's private secretary, in 1566 because he felt that it would presage the overthrow of the Crown, but when the revolt failed to materialize, he retired to Ayrshire and thence to England to visit his sons. After Mary's abdication, Edinburgh became his home again, apart from the period from May 1571 to August 1572 when Edinburgh Castle was held by Mary's supporters.

History has treated Knox less than kindly. He has been held responsible for promoting a rigorous puritanism in Scotland, yet most of the laws banning public festivities were passed before his time by the Catholic Church or after his death by extreme Protestants. Although he was a radical reformer and a nationalist, Knox favoured closer links with England, and throughout his life he maintained his contacts with English churchmen and politicians. His political influence on the course of the Reformation struggle is debatable, but as a preacher of authority he saw himself as 'God's trumpeter', a prophet in the Old Testament mould. That strength of rhetoric colours his written work, and from the five volumes of the *History of the Reformation of Religion within the Realm of Scotland* (completed 1586), an animated, though biased, picture emerges of the principal events of Knox's lifetime and of the part that he played in them. The work is an authoritative source book for the period, notable, too, for Knox's frequent and immodest personal references to his own part in the struggle. Knox also assisted in the direction of the first *Book of Discipline* of 1561, which, in addition to important changes to church government, advocated the establishment of a national system of education from parish schools to universities.

EDITIONS: D. Laing, ed., *The Works of John Knox*, 6 vols., Bannatyne Club (Edinburgh, 1846–64); W. C. Dickinson, ed., *John Knox's History of the Reformation in Scotland*, 2 vols. (Edinburgh, 1949)

REFERENCES: T. McCrie, *The Life of John Knox*, 2 vols. (Edinburgh, 1812); P. H. Brown, *John Knox*, 2 vols. (London, 1895); A. Lang, *John Knox and the Reformation* (London, 1905); E. Percy, *John Knox* (London, 1937); G. Donaldson, *The Scottish Reformation* (Cambridge, 1960); J. Ridley, *John Knox* (London, 1968); W. Reid, *Trumpeter of God: a Biography of John Knox* (New York, 1974); D. Shaw, ed., *John Knox: a Quatercentenary Reappraisal* (Edinburgh, 1975)

Knox, William (1789–1825). Poet. He was born on 17 August 1789 at Lilliesleaf, Roxburghshire, and was educated at Musselburgh Grammar School. Between 1812 and 1817 he farmed near Langholm, but a financial disaster and his addiction to drink ruined him. Under the patronage of Sir WALTER SCOTT, he became a journalist in Edinburgh where he died on 12 November 1825. He published three collections of minor verse: *The Lonely Hearth and Other Poems* (1818), *The Harp of Zion* (1825), and *The Songs of Israel* (1824), which contains his best-remembered creation, 'Mortality', an epitaph *pro vita sua*.

WORKS: *The Lonely Hearth and Other Poems* (1818); *The Songs of Israel* (1824); *The Harp of Zion* (1825); *The Complete Works of William Knox* (1847)

L

Lady of the Lake, The. A poem in six cantos by Sir WALTER SCOTT, published in 1810. The story is set in the Trossachs around Loch Katrine and the landscape is at once a faithful delineation of the Highlands and a fabulous recreation of Scott's fantasy, with its dream-like battlements and faery-inspired castles. A symbolic framework is provided by the 'Harp of the North' – the symbol of Scottish and Celtic poetry – and throughout the poem Scott introduced figures from romance into a story that he intended to be a 'vivid and exact description' of Highland history. The uneasy relationship between myth and realism in the plot blurs Scott's intentions, but *The Lady of the Lake* was regarded in its day as being the most successful of his ballad-epics.

A knight, Fitz-James, receives hospitality from Roderick Dhu and falls in love with the daughter of the outlawed Douglas, Ellen, who is also courted by Roderick and by Malcolm Graeme. When Roderick is threatened by the king's army he raises his standard, but Douglas, knowing that he is the cause of the trouble, travels to Stirling to surrender himself and to seek a royal pardon. A fight takes place between Roderick, who is mortally wounded, and Fitz-James, who reveals himself to be the king. The story is satisfactorily concluded when Ellen begs for her father's life, using as a boon the ring given to her by Fitz-James, and she marries Malcolm Graeme with the king's blessing. Within the narrative are several songs and poems of great beauty, including Ellen's song 'Soldier rest! thy warfare o'er', the boat song 'Hail to the Chief who in triumph advances', the ballad 'Alice Brand' and the coronach 'He is gone on the mountain'. The publication of *The Lady of the Lake* did much to make the Highlands popular for 19th-century tourists.

Laidlaw, A. K. Pen-name of CHRISTOPHER MURRAY GRIEVE.

Laidlaw, William (1780–1845). Poet. He is best known as the friend, and later the amanuensis, of Sir WALTER SCOTT. He was born on 19 November 1780 at Blackhouse, Selkirkshire, and after an elementary education in Peebles he returned to Blackhouse to farm sheep with his father. Their shepherd for ten years was JAMES HOGG, with whom Laidlaw formed a lasting friendship, and in 1801 the two men helped Scott with the preparation of THE MINSTRELSY OF THE SCOTTISH BORDER. After several unsuccessful attempts at farming on his own account, Laidlaw became factor of Scott's estates at ABBOTSFORD in 1817 and held the post until Scott's bankruptcy of 1826. In later life he became Scott's private secretary and trusted friend, and for him he transcribed THE BRIDE OF LAMMERMOOR, A LEGEND OF MONTROSE and *Ivanhoe*. He wrote several lyrics of his own, including 'Lucy's Flittin'' which was included in Hogg's *Forest Minstrel* (1810). After Scott's death he became a factor in Ross-shire and he died on 18 May 1845 at Dingwall. There are warm descriptions of him in Scott's *Journal* and in the *Memoirs of the Life of Sir Walter Scott* by JOHN GIBSON LOCKHART.

Laing, David (1793–1878). Antiquary. He was born in April 1793 in Edinburgh, the son of a well-established bookseller in the Canongate. In 1805 he entered the University of Edinburgh, but he cut short his studies to go into partnership with his father, with whom he remained as a bookseller until his appointment as librarian to the Signet Library in 1837. The stimulus of working among books and building up an antiquarian library gave Laing an interest in Scotland's early literature, and in February 1823 he was appointed secretary of the newly formed BANNATYNE CLUB. His bibliographical studies, on which his fame as an antiquary rests, took him to Europe several times, frequently on behalf of the British Association, which had been formed in 1831. He also acted as Honorary Professor to the ROYAL SCOTTISH ACADEMY, he was a Fellow of the Society of Antiquaries of Scotland and he was a close friend of many of the leading literary and intellectual figures of his day. He died on 18 October 1878 in Portobello, Edinburgh.

Most of Laing's literary work was concerned with the preparation of editions of early Scottish literature, and as a bookseller between 1821 and 1837 he published editions of the work of ALEXANDER SCOTT (i), ALEXANDER MONTGOMERIE, WILLIAM DUNBAR and Sir DAVID LYNDSAY, as well as the catalogue of the library of WILLIAM DRUMMOND of Hawthornden. For the Bannatyne Club he produced 39 editions and 17 more for the MAITLAND CLUB, the WODROW SOCIETY, the HUNTERIAN CLUB, the Shakespeare Club and the SPALDING CLUB, but his best-known work was probably his edition of *The Works of John Knox* which was published between 1846 and 1864.

WORKS: *Select Remains of Ancient Popular Poetry* (1822); *Various Pieces of Fugitive Scottish Poetry* (1825); *The Miscellany of the Wodrow Society* (1844); ed., *The Works of John Knox*, 6 vols. (1846–64); *Memoir of Thomas Thomson* (1853); *Historical Notices of the Family of James I of Scotland* (1858); *Memoir of Dr Irving* (1861); *Notice of P. A. Munch of Christiana* (1863); *Adversaria* (1867); *An Account of the Scottish Psalter of 1566* (1868); *The Edinburgh School of Design in 1764* (1870); *Ode to the Cuckoo* (1873); *An Historical Account of the Painting of the Altar-Piece in Holyrood* (1875); *Early Scottish Metrical Tales* (1889); *Early Popular Poetry of Scotland* (1895)

REFERENCE: G. Goudie, *David Laing LLD* (Edinburgh, 1913)

Laing, Malcolm (1762–1818). Historian. He was born in Orkney and was educated at the University of Edinburgh, where he studied law. He was called to the Scottish Bar in 1785 but he rarely practised as an advocate and turned instead to historical studies. He published two notable histories: *History of Scotland from the Union of the Crowns, on the Accession of King James VI to the Throne of England, to the Union of the Kingdoms* (1802), which contained an attack on the authenticity of the OSSIAN poems; and *The Life and Histories of James VI* (1804), which threw new light on the Gowrie conspiracy. In 1808 he returned to Orkney and represented Orkney and Shetland in parliament until 1812 when ill health forced him to retire. He died on 6 November 1818.

WORKS: *History of Scotland from the Union of the*

Crowns, on the Accession of King James VI to the Throne of England, to the Union of the Kingdoms (1802); *History of Scotland*, 4 vols. (1804); *The Life and Histories of James VI* (1804)

Laing Manuscript. See DON MANUSCRIPT.

Lallans. The poetic name given to the historic speech of Lowland Scotland which is descended mainly from the northern dialect of Anglo-Saxon (*see also* SCOTS). ROBERT BURNS used it in his 'Epistle to William Simpson of Ochiltree' to describe the language of his poetry.

> In days when mankind were but callans;
> At grammar, logic an sic talents,
> They took nae pains their speech to balance,
> Or rules to gie;
> But spak their thochts in plain braid Lallans,
> Like you or me.

'Since *c* 1946 the name Lallans has been [*specif.*] applied by its exponents to the movement began by Lewis Spence, Hugh McDiarmid and others to recreate and extend the range and vocabulary of Scots in literary usage.' (*SND*) 'Lallans' came to be the generally accepted word for the poetic language employed by the poets of the SCOTTISH RENAISSANCE movement. Their use of the language was not without its opponents, who argued that it was 'synthetic' or 'plastic' Scots, based on archaic words found only in dictionaries and no longer in common currency; in 1948 the use of the word 'Lallans' inspired a lengthy correspondence in the pages of the GLASGOW HERALD. To a certain extent Lallans is an artificial creation but it has provided the poets writing in Scots with a malleable poetic language. *Lallans* is also the title of the magazine of the Scots Language society.

Lammas. A festival celebrating the arrival of the autumn held on 1 August. In the early Celtic world it was named for the god Lugh, in whose honour the great fair of Tailltein in Ireland was also instituted. Similat fairs or markets were held in Scotland at Lammastide and they still survive in St Andrews and Inverkeithing.

Land o' Cakes. A poetic phrase to describe Scotland, from the making of oat-cakes, one of the country's national dishes. It is used by ROBERT FERGUSSON in 'The King's Birthday in Edinburgh' and by ROBERT BURNS in 'On the

Late Captain Grose's Peregrinations Thro' Scotland'.

Land o' the Leal. A song composed by CARO-LINA OLIPHANT, Lady Nairne, in 1798. The Scots adjective 'leal' means 'loyal, faithful, adhering to one's allegiance' and the title of the song refers to 'the land of those who have kept the faith, the country of the blessed dead, Heaven' (*SND*).

Lang, Andrew (1844–1912). Journalist and essayist. He was born in Selkirk on 31 March 1844, the son of the Sheriff-Clerk of Selkirk-shire. He came from an old-established Borders family; his grandfather had been Sheriff-Clerk to Sir WALTER SCOTT and his mother was the daughter of Patrick Sellar, the infamous factor to the Duke of Sutherland. At the age of ten Lang was sent to the Edinburgh Academy and remained there until 1861, when he matriculated at the University of St Andrews. He started writing poetry while at university and retained an affection for the town, which can be felt in his poem 'Almae matres' (1887) and in his history *St Andrews* (1893). In 1863 he spent a year at the University of Glasgow where he won a Snell Exhibition to Balliol College, Oxford; graduating with a first in Greats in 1868, he became a Fellow of Merton College and remained there until 1874, studying myth, ritual and totemism.

During his time at Oxford, Lang became involved with the Rondeliers, a group of poets, encouraged by Swinburne, who were fascinated by intricate stanza forms. He published his best collection, *Ballads and Lyrics of Old France*, in 1872. Although he never lost the urge to be a poet, his later collections, such as *XXII Ballades in Blue China* (1880), *Rhymes à la mode* (1884) and *Grass of Parnassus* (1888), are memorable only for their elegant French rhyming structure. After his death Lang's wife published an incomplete four-volume *Poetical Works* (1923).

In 1875 Lang left Merton for London, where he spent most of his life except in later years, when he wintered in St Andrews. He married Leonore Blanche Alleyne on 17 April 1875. Once settled in London, Lang quickly became one of the most successful and best-known journalists and men of letters of his day. He wrote leaders for the *Daily News* and a column, 'At the Sign of the Ship', for *Longman's Magazine*, and he was an influential reviewer

and publisher's reader. Among his friends were ROBERT LOUIS STEVENSON, Sidney Colvin and W. E. Henley, who called him 'the divine amateur'. Although he enjoyed considerable fame and power, he was an implacable critic of the contemporary novel and attacked the work of Henry James and Thomas Hardy.

Lang's work as an anthropologist deserves attention: his *Myth, Ritual and Religion* (1887) is a thorough examination of primitive mythologies, and he retained an interest in psychical phenomena, putting forward in *The Making of Religion* (1898) the theory of animism as the basis of religion. Out of his studies came the 'coloured' fairy books – blue, red, crimson, lilac – collected in *My own Fairy Book* (1895), which enjoyed a wide popularity. He also wrote a number of fairy stories of some charm, including *The Gold of Fairnilee* (1888) and *Prince Prigio* (1889).

Of Lang's books of scholarship, *Books and Bookmen* and *Letters to Dead Authors* (both 1886) are monuments to the style of *fin de siècle* men of letters, but most of his books are marred by his acceptance of received opinion and lack of research. In 1879 he co-operated in the translation of the *Odyssey* and in 1883 of the *Iliad*. He died on 20 July 1912.

WORKS: *Ballads and Lyrics of Old France* (1872); *Aristotle's Politics* (1877); *Odyssey, Book VI* (1877); *The Folklore of France* (1878); *The Odyssey of Homer* (1879); *Oxford* (1879); *Specimen of a Translation of Theocritus* (1879); *XXII Ballades in Blue China* (1880); *Theocritus, Bion and Moschus* (1880); *XXXII Ballades in Blue China* (1881); *The Library* (1881); *Notes on Pictures by Millais* (1881); *The Black Thief* (1882); *Helen of Troy* (1882); *The Iliad of Homer* (1883); *Ballades and Verses Vain* (1884); *Custom and Myth* (1884); *Much Darker Days* (1884); *The Princess Nobody* (1884); *Rhymes à la Mode* (1884); *That very Mab* (1885); *Letters to Dead Authors* (1886); *Books and Bookmen* (1886); *In the Wrong Paradise* (1886); *Lines on the Shelley Society* (1886); *The Mark of Cain* (1886); *La mythologie* (1886); *Politics of Aristotle* (1886); *Almae matres* (1887); *Aucassin and Nicolette* (1887); *Cupid and Psyche* (1887); *He* (1887); *Johnny Nut and the Golden Goose* (1887); *Myth, Ritual and Religion* (1887); *The Gold of Fairnilee* (1888); *Grass of Parnassus* (1888); *Perrault's Popular Tales* (1888); *Pictures at Play* (1888); ed., *The Blue Fairy Book* (1889); *The Dead Leman* (1889); *Letters on Literature* (1889); *Lost Leaders* (1889); *Ode to Golf* (1889); *Prince Prigio* (1889); *Etudes traditionnists* (1890); *How to Fail in Literature* (1890); *Old Friends* (1890); ed., *The Red Fairy Book* (1890); *Sir Stafford North-cote: Life, Letters and Diaries* (1890); *The World's Desire* (1890), ed., *The Blue Fairy Book* (1891); *Essays in Little* (1891); *On Calais Sands* (1891); *Angling Sketches* (1891); *Grass of Parnassus: First and Last Rhymes* (1892); ed., *The Green Fairy Book* (1892); ed., *The Waverley Novels* (1892); *William*

Young Sellar (1892); *Homer and the Epic* (1893); *Kirk's Secret Commonwealth* (1893); *Prince Ricardo of Pantouflia* (1893); *St Andrews* (1893); *The Tercentenary of Izaak Walton* (1893); ed., *The True Story Book* (1893); *Ban and arrière Ban* (1894); *Cock Lane and Common Sense* (1895); *Memoir of R. F. Murray* (1894); ed., *The Yellow Fairy Book* (1894); *My own Fairy Book* (1895); ed., *The Red True Story Book* (1895); *The Voices of Jeanne D'Arc* (1895); *The Life and Letters of John Gibson Lockhart*, 2 vols. (1896); *A Monk of Fife* (1896); *A Book of Dreams and Ghosts* (1897); *Miracles of Madame Saint Catherine of Fierbois* (1897); *Modern Mythology* (1897); *Pickle the Spy* (1897); ed., *The Pink Fairy Book* (1897); ed., *Arabian Night's Entertainments* (1898); *The Companions of Pickle* (1898); *The Making of Religion* (1898); *Selections from Coleridge* (1898); *Waiting on the Glesca Train* (1898); *Homeric Poems* (1899); *Parson Kelly* (1899); ed., *The Red Book of Animal Stories* (1899); ed., *The Grey Fairy Book* (1900); *A History of Scotland*, vol. 1 (1900); *Notes and Names in Books* (1900); *Prince Charles Edward Stewart* (1900); *Alfred Tennyson* (1901); *Magic and Religion* (1901); *The Mystery of Mary Stuart* (1901); ed., *The Violet Fairy Book* (1901); ed., *The Book of Romance* (1902); *The Disentanglers* (1902); *The Young Ruthvens* (1902); ed., *The Gowrie Conspiracy: the Confessions of Sprott* (1902); *A History of Scotland*, vol. 2 (1902); *James VI and the Gowrie Mystery* (1902); ed., *The Crimson Fairy Book* (1903); *Lyrics* (1903); ed., *Social England Illustrated* (1903); *Social Origins* (1903); *The Story of the Golden Fleece* (1903); *The Valet's Tragedy* (1903); ed., *The Brown Fairy Book* (1904); *Historical Mysteries* (1904); *A History of Scotland*, vol. 3 (1904); *New Collected Rhymes* (1904); *Adventures among Books* (1905); *The Clyde Mystery* (1905); *John Knox and the Reformation* (1905); *The Puzzle of Dickens's Last Plot* (1905); ed., *The Red Book of Romance* (1905); *The Secret of the Totem* (1905); *Homer and his Age* (1906); *Life of Sir Walter Scott* (1906); *The Story of Joan of Arc* (1906); *New and Old Letters to Dead Authors* (1906); ed., *The Orange Fairy Book* (1906); *Portraits and Jewels of Mary Queen of Scots* (1906); *A History of Scotland*, vol. 4 (1907); *The King over the Water* (1907); ed., *The Olive Fairy Book* (1907); *Tales of a Fairy Court* (1907); *Tales of Troy and Greece* (1907); ed., *The Book of Princes and Princesses* (1908); *The Maid of France* (1908); *Origins of Religion* (1908); *Origins of Terms of Human Relationship* (1908); ed., *Select Poems of Joan Ingelow* (1908); *Three Poets of French Bohemia* (1908); *Sir George Mackenzie, King's Advocate, of Rosehaugh: his Life and Times* (1909); ed., *The Red Book of Heroes* (1909); *La vie de Jeanne d'Arc de M. Anatole France* (1909); *Does Ridicule Kill?* (1910); ed., *The Lilac Fairy Book* (1910); *Sir Walter Scott and the Border Minstrelsy* (1910); *The World of Homer* (1910); ed., *All Sorts of Stories Book* (1911); *Ballades and Rhymes* (1911); *Method in the Study of Totemism* (1911); *A Short History of Scotland* (1911); ed., *The Book of Saints and Heroes* (1912); *A History of English Literature* (1912); *In Praise of Frugality* (1912); *Ode on a Distant Memory of Jane Eyre* (1912); *Ode to the Opening Century* (1912); *Shakespeare, Bacon and the Great Unknown* (1912); *Highways and Byways on the Border* (1913); ed., *The Strange Story Book* (1913); *Poetical Works*, 4 vols. (1923)

REFERENCES: J. B. Salmond, ed., *Andrew Lang and St Andrews* (St Andrews, 1944); R. L. Green, *Andrew Lang: a Critical Biography* (London, 1946)

Lapraik, John (1727–1807). Poet and farmer. He lived in the parish of Muirkirk and was an early friend of ROBERT BURNS. To him Burns composed two of his best verse epistles (*see* EPISTLES OF ROBERT BURNS), which were published in the KILMARNOCK EDITION. In the first, dated 1 April 1785, Burns states his poetic ideals, describing himself as a popular poet in the tradition of ALLAN RAMSAY and ROBERT FERGUSSON. The second epistle, dated 21 April 1785, is a confession of Burns's personal faith in his literary ability and the contentment it has brought him. A third, lesser-known, epistle dated 13 September 1785 was published later, in Cromek's *Reliques of Burns, Consisting of Original Letters, Poems and Critical Observations on Scottish Songs* (1808).

Latin. Latin was the accepted medium for the composition of the early Scottish histories, mainly because most scholars finished their studies in European universities, where they came under the influence of the medieval schoolmen. The earliest history is the 14th-century *Chronica gentis Scotorum* by JOHN OF FORDUN, which forms part of the SCOTI-CHRONICON by WALTER BOWER; both are written in Latin. Later scholars have poured scorn on both works for their lack of syntactical grace, but they do provide a first attempt at placing Scotland's earliest history in a chronological order. More successful from a linguistic standpoint, but marred by its inaccuracies and fantastic inventions, is *Scotorum historiae* (1526) by HECTOR BOECE. It was no doubt partly owing to its elegant prose style that JAMES V commissioned the historian JOHN BELLENDEN to translate it into Scots.

Of greater learning and authority than those pioneering historians was JOHN MAJOR, who made his reputation as a Latin scholar while teaching in Paris. His history of 1521, *Historia Majoris Britanniae* (which, with equal justification, may be translated as 'The History of Greater Britain' or 'Major's History of Britain'), is an honest and rigorously thought-out attempt to chart the course of British history. That painstaking care and also his ability to express himself forcefully and candidly are present in the Latin disputations he wrote while he was Provost of St Salvator's College in

St Andrews and fully embroiled in church affairs.

One of Major's pupils in Paris was GEORGE BUCHANAN, the one Scottish Latinist who was acknowledged throughout Europe as a master of scholarship and literary elegance. He composed four plays in Latin, *Medea* and *Alcestis* being translations from Euripedes and *Jepthes* and *Baptistes* being of his own composition. Like his predecessors he wrote a history of Scotland, *Rerum scoticarum historia* (1582) in 20 volumes, and he also wrote *De jure regni apud Scotos* (1579), which was composed to justify the deposition of MARY, Queen of Scots, and was regarded for many years among reformers as the ideal anti-monarchic statement. His rendering of the Psalms into Latin was regarded by his peers as his masterpiece, but that praise has been forgotten by his critics, who prefer to remember him instead only for his persecution of the hapless Queen Mary. Buchanan also wrote in vernacular Scots but it reads today as if it had been translated from Latin, which language continued to be the favoured choice of expression for Buchanan and his fellow humanists. As the 16th century progressed, prose written in Scots became more common, but it tended to be dominated by rhetorical devices borrowed from Latin and was not destined to find a true voice of its own.

Enthusiasm for composing verse in Latin continued throughout the 16th century as is testified by the publication in 1637 of the anthology DELITIAE POETARUM SCOTORUM. Although it failed to include Buchanan, it contained the work of 37 Scottish neo-Latinists who saw in the language the ideal means of expressing the intellectual ideals of the Renaissance. Most of the work is a pale imitation of earlier classical models, but some poets of the period are worthy of further attention. Buchanan was a master of many poetic styles and his influence left its mark on younger poets like JAMES ('the Admirable') CRICHTON and MARK ALEXANDER BOYD, whose well-known sonnet in Scots 'Fra banc to banc' tends to overshadow his Latin verse compositions. ARTHUR JOHNSTON, one of the editors of the *Delitiae* and a poet of a later, 17th-century generation, is considered by AGNES MURE MACKENZIE to be 'second only to Buchanan' (J. Kinsley, ed., *Scottish Poetry: a Critical Survey* (London, 1955), p.89), both on account of his own poetry, which is pleasing for its highly coloured descriptions of rural life, and

for his role in the *Delitiae*. Aberdeen became a centre of enthusiasm for Latin and among the poets included in the three-volume *Musa latina aberdonensis* ((Spalding Club, 1892, 1895, 1910) may be mentioned David Wedderburn (1580–1646), John Leech (*b* 1614) and Alexander Ross (1591–1654).

The final flowering of the Scottish Humanist tradition came in the early 18th century with the classical scholarship of THOMAS RUDDIMAN, who edited, among other Latin texts, the works of GEORGE BUCHANAN, and who also wrote a standard Latin grammar. During the same period, Ruddiman's friend ARCHIBALD PITCAIRNE wrote several diverting Latin odes and epigrams on the events of his life and times. But the movement came to naught. Their belief that Latin could provide a sure base for the nation's literary culture evaporated with the period of the SCOTTISH ENLIGHTENMENT when English became considered, increasingly, to be the only proper means of intellectual communication.

REFERENCE: L. Bradner, *Musae anglicanae: a History of Anglo-Latin Poetry* (London, 1940)

Latto, Thomas Carstairs (*b* 1818). Poet. He was born on 1 December 1818 at Kingsbarns in Fife, the son of the village schoolmaster. He worked as a lawyer's clerk in Edinburgh and as a commission merchant in Glasgow before emigrating to the United States of America in 1858. There he founded the *Scottish American Journal* and worked as a publisher's editor before retiring in 1871 to live in Brooklyn where he ran an estate agency business. Latto was a regular contributor to BLACKWOOD'S MAGAZINE, but his verse rarely rose above the trivial and the sentimental. He remains best known for his lament for days long past, 'When we were at the schule'.

WORKS: *The Minister's Kailyard* (1845); *Memorials of Auld Lang Syne* (1892)

Lauder, Sir **Thomas Dick** (1784–1848). Novelist and man of letters. He was born at Fountainhall, Midlothian, and served for a time as an officer with the Cameron Highlanders. On his marriage he resigned his commission and retired to live near Elgin. Much of his early antiquarian work was concerned with the history of the Moray region, and, as well as a number of topographical articles for the newly founded BLACKWOOD'S MAGAZINE, Lauder also wrote two historical romantic novels, *Lochindhu* (1825) and *The Wolf of Badenoch* (1827); both suffered from Lauder's inability to re-create the past convincingly. The culmination of his studies came in 1830 with the publication of *An Account of the Great Moray Floods*, a work that summarizes his feelings for the landscape of his adopted countryside. In 1832 Lauder returned to Edinburgh where he served as secretary to the Board of the White Fishing Industry and he was a kenspeckle figure in the city until his death on 29 May 1848. Lauder's other books of note are *Highland Rambles and Legends to Shorten the Way* (1837) and *Legends and Tales of the Highlands* (1841).

WORKS: *Lochindhu* (1825); *The Wolf of Badenoch* (1827); *An Account of the Great Moray Floods of 1829* (1830); with Thomas Brown and William Rhind, *The Miscellany of Natural History*, 2 vols. (1833–4); *Highland Rambles and Legends to Shorten the Way*, 3 vols. (1837); *Legends and Tales of the Highlands* (1841); ed., *Essays on the Picturesque* (1842); *A Tour Round the Coast of Scotland* (1842); *Memorial of the Royal Progress in Scotland* (1843)

Lay of the Last Minstrel, The. A poem in six cantos by Sir WALTER SCOTT, published in 1805. It was written at the suggestion of the Countess of Dalkeith and was intended to be another ballad imitation of the kind he had published in THE MINSTRELSY OF THE SCOTTISH BORDER. Based on the legend told in the Border ballad 'Gilpin Horner', *The Lay* tells the story of the feud between two Border families, the Buccleuchs and the Cranstouns, and of the forbidden love of Margaret of Buccleuch for Lord Cranstoun who killed her father. To gain revenge, Lady Buccleuch commissions Sir William Deloraine to recover the lost magic book of the wizard MICHAEL SCOTT (i), but on his return he encounters Lord Cranstoun and is wounded by him in an armed fight. Meanwhile the heir of Buccleuch has been lured away from the family home of Branksome Tower and captured by the English enemy Lord Dacre. Branksome is besieged and a single combat is proposed between the English champion Sir Richard Musgrave and the Buccleuch champion Deloraine who has harried Musgrave's lands. The heir of Buccleuch is to be the prize and the challenge is accepted. At the successful conclusion it is discovered that Cranstoun has taken the place of the injured Deloraine and his service to the house of Buccleuch ends the feud and enables him to marry Margaret. Thus the poem's theme, formulated at the beginning by the Mountain Spirit and the River Spirit, is fulfilled: a mother learns to subjugate her pride when an enemy comes to the aid of her house.

The Lay was Scott's first important piece of original work and in it he employed a variety of rhymes, from the Coleridgean irregular measures used in *Christabel* to a later straight octosyllabic couplet. The poem also contains Scott's passionate statement of nationalism, 'Breathes there the man with soul so dead . . .', in canto vi and the translation of *Dies irae* at the conclusion.

Lays of the Scottish Cavaliers and Other Poems. A collection of historical ballads and romances by WILLIAM EDMONSTOUNE AYTOUN, published in 1849. There are eight 'lays', seven of which appreared originally in BLACKWOOD'S MAGAZINE: 'The Burial March of Dundee' (April 1843), 'Charles Edward at Versailles' (July 1843), 'The Heart of the Bruce' (July 1844), 'The Old Scottish Cavalier' (August 1844), 'The Execution of Montrose' (September 1844), 'The Widow of Glencoe' (December 1847), 'Edinburgh after Flodden' (February 1848) and 'The Island of the Scots'. 'Edinburgh after Flodden' deals with the events of the city of Edinburgh after the disaster of the BATTLE OF FLODDEN, 'The Heart of the Bruce' with the pilgrimage of Sir James Douglas to the Holy Land to bury the heart of ROBERT I (Robert the Bruce); the remainder are concerned with the fluctuating fortunes of the Stewarts and their loyal followers. The main influence on Aytoun was Sir WALTER SCOTT, who had changed the nature of the Scottish ballad by stripping it of coarseness and adding to it a fanciful and romantic version of historical fact, but his immediate model was Thomas Babington Macaulay's *Lays of Ancient Rome* (1842). 'The Island of the Scots', the story of the capture of an island for the French by the exiled remnants of Viscount Dundee's army, is a good example of Aytoun's method and technique.

Learmont, Thomas. *See* THOMAS OF ERCELDOUNE.

Legend of Montrose, A. A novel by Sir WALTER SCOTT, published in 1819 in the third series of TALES OF MY LANDLORD. The novel is set in the wars of 1644 when a number of Highland clans fought for Charles I's cause under the generalship of JAMES GRAHAM, the Marquis of Montrose. Pitted against them are the government armies of Argyle, a Protestant leader whom Scott is at pains to compare unfavourably with the great Marquis. Against this background the principal characters play out their determined roles: Ranald MacEagh, the leader of a mysterious clan called the Children of the Mist; Angus and Allan M'Aulay, who are tied by ancient vows of enmity against the Children, a young gallant, the Earl of Menteith, whose duty and honour lie with Montrose's cause; Annot Lyle, an orphan loved by Allan M'Aulay but who loves Menteith; and Captain Dugald Dalgetty, an opinionated soldier of fortune who throws in his lot with Montrose. The tragedy unfolds with a grim sense of inevitability. MacEagh meets his death at the hands of the M'Aulays who are seen to be disfigured by their brutality and their false pride. Allan attempts to murder Menteith who is forced by the severity of his wounds to leave the army of Montrose, and marries Annot. Although the Highland clans, in their fashion, have been loyal to Montrose, in the final moments of the novel they desert him and revert to savagery.

It may have become a critical touchstone to accuse Scott of excessive sentimentality in his treatment of the Highlands, but in *A Legend of Montrose* his view is moderate and rounded, leaving the reader in little doubt that the clans are incapable of change from within. The character of Dugald Dalgetty stands in line with Scott's other minor pragmatists, notably Bailie Nicol Jarvie in *Rob Roy*.

Lekprevik, Robert (*fl* 1570). Printer. Very little is known about the parentage or the life of Robert Lekprevik other than that he was the principal printer to the reformers during the religious struggles of the late 16th century. His first commission from the reformed Church came in 1564 when he was asked to print an edition of the Psalms; in 1568 he was licensed to print the Geneva Bible. However, it was for the printing of broadsides, pamphlets and proclamations that he was known particularly, and his support of the Church even earned him a spell of imprisonment during the reign of the regent Morton. The control of a printing press was a prerequisite for the leaders of the reformed church and in Lekprevik they had a

zealous supporter, even though his recklessness in printing scurrilous material led to punishment by fine and banishment from the city.

REFERENCE: J. Cranstoun, ed., *Satirical Poems of the Time of the Renaissance*, STS (Edinburgh and London, 1891)

Leonard, Tom (*b* 1944). Poet. He was born on 22 August 1944 in Glasgow. He was educated at Lourdes Secondary School and after working in a bookshop he entered the University of Glasgow in 1967. Since graduating he has worked in a variety of jobs and is now a full-time writer. His reputation was made by his poems in Glasgow dialect, in which he made great use of local words and phrases and their pronunciation. Although at first reading they may seem unintelligible, owing to Leonard's reliance on the idioms of Glasgow speech, their meaning becomes apparent when they are read aloud so that the natural speech rhythms can break through. As his subjects he takes the matter of Glasgow and its people, but his vision is ironic and utterly unsentimental, with a hint of humour never far away. His poem 'The Good Thief' uses the story of the crucifixion of Christ and the two thieves, but turns the setting to Glasgow, with the 'good thief' addressing Christ about two of the city's most potent and enduring myths, football and religion. Much of his work has been written in English and it shows a deft, humorous touch.

WORKS: *Six Glasgow Poems* (1969); *A Priest Came on at Merkland Street* (1970); *Poems* (1973); *If Only Bunty was Here* (1979)

Leslie, Arthur. Pen-name of CHRISTOPHER MURRAY GRIEVE.

Leslie, John (*c*1527–96). Historian. He was the son of a priest and was educated at Aberdeen, Toulouse, Poitiers and Paris. On his return to Scotland he became an official in the diocese of Aberdeen; he was made Doctor of Canon Law at King's College and in 1560 was named by the Lords of the Congregation as one of the two Catholics (the other being Quentin Kennedy) to debate points of belief with JOHN KNOX and John Willock. He became a close confidant of MARY, Queen of Scots, who appointed him a Lord of Session in 1564 and Bishop of Ross in 1566. Although he continued to support Mary's cause after her downfall, under threat of torture he gave evidence in

England against the Norfolk conspiracy and left to live in France and Italy. In 1579 he became Suffragen Bishop of Rouen, and after his estates in Scotland were forfeited he was appointed Bishop of Coustances. He wrote a *Historie of Scotland* (completed 1571), which covered the period from James I to Mary's accession. While in Rome he made extensive additions to the text and composed a Latin version as *De origine moribus et rebus gentis Scotorum*, which was later translated back into Scots by Father James Dalrymple in 1593. Although it is considered to be inaccurate, Leslie's history contains a vivid and intimate picture of the events of the Reformation from the Catholic point of view. His other main publication was the popular *A Defence of the Honour of the Right Highe, Mightye and Noble Princesse Marie, Queen of Scotand and Dowager of France* (1569). Leslie died near Brussels on 31 May 1596.

WORKS: *A Defence of the Honour of Right Highe, Mightye and Noble Princesse Marie, Queene of Scotland and Dowager of France* (1569); *Ad Mariam Scotorum reginam* (1574); *Pro libertate impenetranda oratio* (1574); *De illustrium foemindrum in repub. administranda* (1580); *De origine moribus et rebus gentis Scotorum* (1580); *Congratulatio serenissimo principi* (1596)

EDITIONS: T. Thomson, ed., *The History of Scotland from the Death of King James I in 1436 to the Year 1561*, Bannatyne Club (Edinburgh, 1830); E. G. Cody and W. Murison, eds., *The Historie of Scotland*, trans. J. Dalrymple, 2 vols., STS (Edinburgh and London, 1885–95)

Letters of Malachi Malagrowther, The. Three epistolary essays addressed 'To the Editor of the Edinburgh Weekly Journal from Malachi Malagrowther Esq on the Proposed Change of Currency and Other Late Alterations as they affect, or are intended to affect, the Kingdom of Scotland', published in the *Edinburgh Weekly Journal* of February and March 1826 and subsequently as a pamphlet by WILLIAM BLACKWOOD. Written pseudonymously by Sir WALTER SCOTT, they dealt with an important contemporary topic: the need for Scottish banks to continue the issue of their own notes, which were the main form of currency and credit in Scotland. The publication of the letters caused an immediate sensation and, in the ensuing debate, parliament decided to drop its proposals to include Scotland in its ban on provincial banks' issuing notes beyond the value of £5. As well as being coherently and

passionately argued, the Malachi Malagrowther letters (he was the supposed nephew of Sir Mungo Malagrowther in Scott's novel *The Fortunes of Nigel*) are the clearest statement of Scott's political beliefs, especially of his attitude towards Scottish nationalism. They were republished, with an introduction by Paul Henderson Scott, in 1981.

Leyden, John (1775–1811). Poet and linguist. He was born on 8 September 1775 at Denholm, Roxburghshire, the son of a tenant farmer on the estate of Cavers. He was educated at home until the age of nine when he was sent to the village school at Kirktown where his progress was so exceptional that he was able to matriculate at the University of Edinburgh in 1790. During his holidays he used his time to learn Greek, Hebrew, Arabic and Persian, and on graduating in 1796 he became a private tutor in St Andrews and remained there until 1798 when he was licensed as a preacher. On his return to Edinburgh he was able to give full vent to his literary interests, and his first book, *A Historical and Philosophical Sketch of the Discoveries and Settlements of the Europeans in Northern and Western Africa at the Close of the Eighteenth Century* (1799), was indicative of his eclectic tastes. He was also able to foster his lifelong interest in ballads and, through the antiquary Richard Heber, he met Sir WALTER SCOTT, whom he was able to assist with the preparation of THE MINSTRELSY OF THE SCOTTISH BORDER. Leyden proved to be an indefatigable researcher, and as well as producing five ballads for the first volume he contributed a 'Dissertation on Faery Superstition' to the second. On his own account he wrote 'The Elf King' for the *Tales of Wonder* (1801) by Matthew Gregory Lewis (1775–1818), and he edited *Scottish Descriptive Poems* (1802) after spending some time in the Highlands investigating the authenticity of the OSSIAN poems.

Unable to find a suitable church appointment, Leyden toyed with the idea of African exploration, but in 1803 he was appointed assistant surgeon in Madras in India; from then until his death in Java on 28 August 1811, he lived in India and the Far East. He gained the patronage of Lord Minto, and his facility for learning languages enabled him to master several Indian languages as well as Malay; by the end of his life he could speak 30 languages. Leyden's death was mourned by his fellow countrymen and Lord Cockburn said of this largely self-taught man that there was 'no walk in life depending on ability where Leyden would not have shone'. His death is also mentioned in canto iv of Scott's *The Lord of the Isles*.

WORKS: *A Historical and Philosophical Sketch of the Discoveries and Settlements of the Europeans in Northern and Western Africa at the Close of the Eighteenth Century* (1799); *Journal of a Tour in the Highlands and Western Islands of Scotland* (1800); ed., *Scottish Descriptive Poems* (1802); *Scenes of Infancy* (1808); *A Comparative Vocabulary of the Barma, Malayu and T'hai Languages* (1810); *Poems and Ballads* (1858)

REFERENCE: J. Reith, *Life of Dr John Leyden* (Galashiels, 1908)

EDITION: H. Murray, ed., *The Poetical Works of John Leyden* (Edinburgh and London, 1875)

Lindsay, Sir David (i). *See* LYNDSAY, DAVID.

Lindsay, David (ii) (1878–1945). Novelist. He was born on 3 March 1878 in Blackheath, London, where he was educated, but part of his childhood was spent in Jedburgh with his father's relations. Between 1896 and 1914 he worked as an underwriter at Lloyds and during World War I he served with the Grenadier Guards. On his demobilization he married and lived in Cornwall until 1928, when he moved to Sussex. He died in Brighton in June 1945.

Although Lindsay spent most of his life in England he spent his early summers walking in Scotland and the landscapes of the west Highlands pervade his first novel, *A Voyage to Arcturus* (1920), a work that is an uneasy mixture of science fiction, allegory and mysticism. Maskull, a bearded giant of a man, is transported to the planet of Tormance, whose inhabitants have enhanced physical and intellectual capabilities. Some of the characters represent different facets of human behaviour and one of Lindsay's favourite devices is to create an identity and then to reveal an opposite characteristic: Krag, for example, is represented as a devil figure, Pain, but he is revealed at the novel's end as the real creator of the universe instead of Crystalman or Pleasure. The novel takes on the character of a pilgrimage as Maskull follows various adventures to Arcturus, and it is in the descriptions of the frequently surrealist action that the intensity of Lindsay's imaginative powers is fully realized. *A Voyage to Arcturus* was republished in 1946, 1963 and 1968.

Lindsay's second novel, *The Haunted Woman* (1922), shares many of the fantastic themes of its predecessor: the lovers, Isabel Lamont and Henry Judge, glumpse another world from the window of Judge's ancient, mysterious house, and discover the existence of Crystalman, the creator of pleasure. Judge and his lover are denied happiness but their destruction is only mapped out by Lindsay who shows a reticence about sexual relationships and a tendency to submerge the plot in the other world of fantasy.

Sphinx (1923) has a thinly autobiographical hero, Nicholas Cabot, and *Devil's Tor* (1932) reflects Lindsay's interest in Nietzschean philosophy. He published one light romantic novel, *The Adventures of M. de Mailly*, in 1926. During his lifetime Lindsay's work enjoyed little public success and his last novels, *The Violet Apple* and *The Witch*, were not published.

WORKS: *A Voyage to Arcturus* (1920); *The Haunted Woman* (1922); *Sphinx* (1923); *The Adventures of M. de Mailly* (1926); *Devil's Tor* (1932)

REFERENCE: C. Wilson, E. H. Visiak and J. B. Pick, *The Strange Genius of David Lindsay* (London, 1970)

Lindsay, (John) Maurice (*b* 1918). Poet and critic. He was born on 21 July 1918 in Glasgow and was educated at Glasgow Academy and the Royal Scottish Academy of Music. During World War II he served with the Cameronians, and between 1946 and 1960 he worked as a journalist and critic, before becoming Controller of Border Television in Carlisle. Since 1967 he has been Director of the Scottish Civic Trust. Much of Lindsay's work has been concerned with the understanding and criticism of Scottish literature and culture, and he has been a tireless editor of magazines and collections of contemporary poetry, as well as editing the poetry of Sir ALEXANDER GRAY, Sir DAVID LYNDSAY and JOHN DAVIDSON (ii). His best-known critical work is on ROBERT BURNS in *Robert Burns: the Man, his Work, the Legend* (1954, rev. 2/1971) and *The Burns Encyclopaedia* (1959, rev. 2/1970, rev. 3/1980). He has also written a *History of Scottish Literature* (1977), several topographical books, and critical works on the artist Robin Philipson and the composer FRANCIS GEORGE SCOTT.

Lindsay's first poetry was published in *The Advancing Day* (1940) and he published ten selections of his work before finding his true voice in *This Business of Living* (1969). His *Collected Poems*, which brings together the best of his work from 15 books, was published in 1979. Lindsay's early work was largely derivative: Edward Thomas (1878–1917) was an early influence, he wrote in the style of the New Apocalypse movement, and he has also experimented with Scots. His best work, such as the poems 'Feeling Small', 'This Business of Living' and 'School Prize-Giving' show his acute human observation and a mastery of the well-turned conceit allied to a firm control of language.

WORKS: *The Advancing Day* (1940); *Perhaps Tomorrow* (1941); *Predicament* (1942); *No Crown for Laughter* (1944); ed., *Sailing Tomorrow's Seas* (1944); *The Enemies of Love* (1946); ed., *Modern Scottish Poetry* (1946, rev. 2/1966); *A Pocket Guide to Scottish Culture* (1947); ed., with Fred Urquhart, *No Scottish Twilight* (1947); ed., with Douglas Young, *Saltire Modern Poets Series* (1947); *Selected Poems* (1947); *Hurlygush* (1948); ed., *Selected Poems of Sir Alexander Gray* (1948); ed., *Selected Poems of Sir David Lyndsay* (1948); *The Scottish Renaissance* (1949); *At the Wood's Edge* (1950); ed., *Selected Poems of Marion Angus* (1950); *Ode for St Andrews Night* (1951); *The Lowlands of Scotland: Glasgow and the North* (1953); *Robert Burns: the Man, his Work, the Legend* (1954, rev. 2/1971); *The Lowlands of Scotland Edinburgh and the South* (1956); G. Bruce, ed., *The Exiled Heart* (1957); *Clyde Waters* (1958); *The Burns Encyclopaedia* (1959, rev. 2/1970, rev. 3/1980); *By yon Bonnie Banks* (1961); ed., *John Davidson: a Selection of his Poems* (1961); *Snow Warning* (1962); *The Discovery of Scotland* (1964); *One Later Day* (1964); ed., with George Bruce and Edwin Morgan, *Scottish Poetry 1–6* (1966–72); *This Business of Living* (1969); *The Saving of Georgian Edinburgh* (1970); *Comings and Goings* (1971); *The Eye is Delighted* (1971); *Portrait of Glasgow* (1972); *The Conservation of Georgian Edinburgh* (1972); *Selected Poems* (1973); *Scotland: an Anthology* (1974); ed., with Alexander Scott and Roderick Watson, *Scottish Poetry 7–9* (1974–6); *The Run from Life* (1975); *Robin Philipson* (1976); *History of Scottish Literature* (1977); *Walking without an Overcoat* (1977); ed., *As I Remember* (1979); *Collected Poems* (1979); *Lowland Scottish Villages* (1980); *Francis George Scott and the Scottish Renaissance* (1980); *A Net to Catch the Winds* (1981); with A. F. Kersting, *The Buildings of Edinburgh* (1981)

Lindsay, Robert, of Pitscottie (c1532–80). Historian. He was born on the estate of Pitscottie in the Parish of Ceres near Cupar in Fife. His *Historie and Cronicles of Scotland*, written in Scots, was a continuation of the *Scotorum Historiae* of HECTOR BOECE, which had been translated into Scots by John Bellenden in 1536. The 18th book of Boece's work became Lindsay's first chapter and his history covers the period from 1436 to 1575. Although he has been found to have been inaccurate and credulous, his style is vivid and picturesque, especially in dealing with the events of his own lifetime. The account of the death of James V is especially arresting. The *Historie* was not published until 1728.

WORKS: *The Historie and Cronicles of Scotland* (1728)

EDITION: A. J. G. Mackay, *The Historie and Cronicles of Scotland, Written and Collected by Robert Lindsay of Pitscottie*, 3 vols., STS (Edinburgh and London, 1899–1911)

Lines Review. A literary magazine founded in 1952, printed and published by Callum Macdonald (*b* 1912). It has published most of the main Scottish poets of the period including, especially, ROBERT GARIOCH SUTHERLAND, SYDNEY GOODSIR SMITH and IAIN CRICHTON SMITH, and it has also been a generous starting-point for many younger poets. Amongst its editors have been the poets Alan Riddell, Sydney Goodsir Smith, J. K. ANNAND, TOM SCOTT, ROBIN FULTON and WILLIAM MONTGOMERIE.

Linklater, Eric (1899–1974). Novelist. He was born in Penarth, South Wales, the son of a shipmaster, whose family had ancient roots in the Orkney islands, where he spent most of his childhood and much of his later life. He was educated in Aberdeen at the Grammar School and at the University, where he studied English and, later, medicine. During World War I he served as a private in the Black Watch, an experience he recounted in his autobiography *Fanfare for a Tin Hat* (1970). Between 1925 and 1927 he worked as a journalist for the *Times of India*, but he returned to Aberdeen as assistant to the Professor of English at the University in 1927–8. From 1928 to 1930 he was in the United States of America as a Commonwealth Fellow, and from then until the end of his life his career embraced writing, journalism and broadcasting. He held a variety of posts during World War II, including the command of the Orkney Fortress, and for a time he served in the Directorate of Public Relations. After the war he lived in Orkney, Ross-shire and Aberdeenshire; he died on 7 November 1974 in Aberdeen.

Linklater's first novel, *White Maa's Saga* (1929), was set in Orkney ('White-Maa' is the Orkney word for a seagull), and it is a love-story that owes much to his native knowledge of the islands. *Poet's Pub* (1929) pointed the way to the future Linklater style, which is similar to that of TOBIAS SMOLLETT, with its easy mixture of a comedy of middle-class manners and fantastic farce. It was followed by one of his most successful books, *Juan in America* (1931), a novel of fancy and exploration based on his knowledge of the United States. The eponymous hero, Juan Motley, a descendant of Byron's Don Juan, sets off on a picaresque journey across the America of the Prohibition era, and the book is remarkable both for its acute observation and for Linklater's uncanny ability to use the deflationary power of farce. Its sequel, *Juan in China* (1937), was less successful. *Magnus Merriman* (1934) is a thinly disguised autobiographical story of politics and literary intrigue in the Scotland of the 1930s, and it demonstrates again Linklater's ability to mix grotesque mirth with polite manners, a convention he returned to in *The Merry Muse* (1959), a novel with a similar theme.

After the success of his early novels, Linklater rarely strayed from the north of Scotland, and his interest in the Norse sagas is reflected in *The Men of Ness* (1932) and *The Ultimate Viking* (1955). His best fiction continued in the Rabelaisian vein he had made his own, although in novels such as *Laxdale Hall* (1933), *The House of Gair* (1953), *Position at Noon* (1958) and *A Man over Forty* (1963), which are among his best work, he added the hard edge of tragedy, often disguised as melodrama, to the farcical proceedings. *Private Angelo* (1946), an amusing study of the lot of the private soldier, reflected Linklater's lifelong interest in the armed services and their relationship to civil society. Linklater was also an accomplished short story writer and his work in this form was collected in 1968.

Linklater was one of the most prolific writers of his generation, and his autobiographical sketch *The Man on My Back* (1941) gives a vivid picture of his early career as a writer. He also wrote on history and topography, his *Orkney and Shetland* (1965) being a minor classic. He was, however, on his own admission, less successful in writing for the stage, with the possible exception of *Breakspear in Gascony* (1958).

WORKS: *Rosemount Nights* (1924); *Poobie* (1925); *Poet's Pub* (1929); *White Maa's Saga* (1929); *A Dragon Laughed* (1930); *Ben Jonson and King James* (1931); *Juan in America* (1931); *The Men of Ness* (1932); *The Crusader's King* (1933); *Laxdale Hall* (1933); *Mary Queen of Scots* (1933); *The Devil's in the News* (1934); *Magnus Merriman* (1934); *The Revolution* (1934); *Robert the Bruce* (1934); *God likes them Plain* (1935); *Ripeness is All* (1935); *Juan in China*

(1937); *The Sailor's Holiday* (1937); *The Impregnable Women* (1938); *Judas* (1939); *The Cornerstones* (1941); *The Man on my Back* (1941); *The Raft and Socrates Asks Why* (1942); *The Great Ship* (1944) *The Wind on the Moon* (1944); *Private Angelo* (1946); *The Art of Adventure* (1947); *Sealskin Trousers* (1947); *The Pirates in the Deep Green Sea* (1949) *A Spell for Old Bones* (1949); *Mr Byculla* (1950); ed. *The Thistle and the Pen* (1950); *Two Comedies* (1950); *The Campaign in Italy* (1951); *The Mortimer Touch* (1952); *Our Men in Korea* (1952); *The House of Gair* (1953); *A Year of Space* (1953); *The Faithful Ally* (1954); *The Ultimate Viking* (1955); *The Dark of Summer* (1956); *A Sociable Plover* (1957); *Breakspear in Gascony* (1958); *Karina with Love* (1958); *Position at Noon* (1958); *The Merry Muse* (1959); *My Father and I* (1959); *Edinburgh* (1960); *Roll of Honour* (1961); *Husband of Delilah* (1962); *A Man over Forty* (1963); *Orkney and Shetland* (1965); *The Prince in the Heather* (1965); *The Conquest of England* (1966); *A Terrible Freedom* (1966); *The Stories of Eric Linklater* (1968); *The Survival of Scotland* (1968); *The Secret Leader* (1969); *Fanfare for a Tin Hat* (1970); *The Royal House of Scotland* (1970); *The Corpse on Clapham Common* (1971); *The Voyage of the Challenger* (1972); with Andro Linklater, *The Black Watch* (1977)

Linton, Bernard de. See BERNARD DE LINTON.

Lithgow, William (c1585–1645). Traveller and poet. He was born in Lanark, but his seduction of a girl from an influential family and his subsequent punishment forced him to flee his homeland and to begin a lifetime of wandering. During his 19 years of travel, Lithgow journeyed first to Orkney and Shetland and then across Europe to the Mediterranean countries, the Middle East and north Africa. His anti-Catholic sentiments led to his imprisonment at Malaga in Spain and his torture by the Inquisition. He returned, badly maimed, to Scotland in 1623 and began to write the account of his travels which were published in *The Rare Adventures and Painful Peregrinations: Nineteen Year's Travels* (1632), *The Siege of Breda* (1637) and *The Siege of Newcastle* (1645). Cynics doubted the veracity of many of Lithgow's stories and anecdotes, which are racily told with a good eye for minor detail. His poetical remains, many of which are anti-Catholic propaganda, were published, with a memoir of his life, in 1863. His most moving poem is a song of exile, 'The Pilgrim's Farewell to his Native Countrey of Scotland', which was printed in Edinburgh in 1618 by ANDRO HART.

WORKS: *The Pilgrimes Farewell to his Native Countrey of Scotland* (1618); *Scotland's Teares* (1625); *The Rare Adventures and Painful Peregrinations: Nineteen Year's*

Travels (1632); *Scotland's Welcome to her Native Son and Soveraigne Lord, King Charles* (1633); *The Siege of Breda* (1637); *The Gushing Teares of Godly Sorrow* (1640); *A Brief and Summarie Discourse upon that Lamentable and Dreadful Disaster at Dunglasse* (1640); *The Siege of Newcastle* (1645); *Scotland's Paranesis* (1660)

EDITION: J. Maidment, ed., *The Poetical Remains of William Lithgow* (Edinburgh, 1863)

Livingstone, David (1813–73). Missionary, explorer and travel writer. He was born on 19 March 1813 in Blantyre, Lanarkshire. After an elementary education he was sent at the age of ten to work in the local cotton mill. During his spare time he read voraciously and increased his knowledge through long periods of study, with the result that in 1836 he was admitted as a student at Anderson's College in Glasgow to train as a medical missionary. He entered the service of the London Missionary Society in August 1838 and in 1841 he received his first posting to southern Africa. There, from the Society's outposts at Kuruman and Koloberg, he began the series of explorations into the Kalahari Desert and beyond that led to the discovery of Lake Ngani in 1849 and of the Zambesi River in 1851. Between 1852 and 1856 he made a further exploration of the African interior and his trans-African expedition of some 4000 miles took him across the territories of present-day Angola, Zambia and Mozambique.

Livingstone's exploits caught the Victorian imagination and his accounts of his deeds, published in *Missionary Travels and Researches in South Africa* (1857), helped to make him one of the best-known men of his day. The book is notable for Livingstone's descriptions of the African tribal way of life and of the topography of central Africa, which he described as a paradise on earth. It was deservedly popular, although critics later in the century dismissed many of his findings and attacked it for his exaggerated claims for the region as a place of imperial exploitation. Nevertheless it brought him sufficient fame to attract funds for further explorations, and having resigned from the London Missionary Society in 1858 he returned to Africa. Another journey on the Zambesi resulted in the discovery of Lake Nyassa, but Livingstone's impatience with his colleagues and his growing belief in the divinity of his mission in Africa led to quarrels and unhappiness among his party. He returned to England in 1864 and published the second

account of his explorations in *The Zambesi and its Tributaries*. Between 1867 and his death on 30 April 1873 he was in Africa again, engaged on his efforts to discover the source of the River Nile, an expedition that was doomed to failure owing to its lack of financial backing and Livingstone's debilitating illness. Contact with him was lost, and then found again by the American reporter Henry Morton Stanley (1841–1904) who greeted him with the famous words, 'Dr Livingstone, I presume.'

Livingstone was one of the great African explorers, a man of God and a humanitarian, who attacked the worst excesses of the slave trade. Although his evangelism failed, he believed implicitly in the missionary's role as educator, physician and improver.

WORKS: *Missionary Travels and Researches in South Africa* (1857); *The Zambesi and its Tributaries* (1865); *Last Journals of David Livingstone in Central Africa* (1874)

Lochhead, Liz (*b* 1947). Poet and dramatist. She was born on 26 December 1947 in Motherwell and was educated there and, between 1965 and 1970, at the Glasgow School of Art. She has worked as a teacher and has been a full-time writer since 1978. Much of Liz Lochhead's work has been written for the stage but her collection *Memo for Spring* (1972) shows her to be a plain-speaking poet, interested in the domestic trivia of life, which she views both tenderly and ironically. This careful balance is particularly brought to bear in poems like 'Revelation' and 'Poem for my Sister', with their different viewpoints on childhood experience. Her play *Blood and Ice* (1982) is an examination of the impossibility of combining freedom and responsibility, as portrayed in the life of Mary Shelley (1797–1851).

WORKS: *Memo for Spring* (1972); *The Grimm Sisters* (1981); *Blood and Ice* (1982)

REFERENCE: T. Royle, ed., *Jock Tamson's Bairns: Essays on a Scots Childhood* (London, 1977)

Lochhead, Marion Cleland (*b* 1902). Novelist and biographer. She was born on 19 April 1902 in Wishaw, Lanarkshire, and was educated there and at the University of Glasgow. After graduating she turned away from a career in teaching to become a full-time writer and journalist. Her first novels, particularly *Ann Dalrymple* (1934), reflected her interest in the devotional aspects of Christianity; a similar theme runs through her religious poems, which appeared in her collections *Poems* (1928), *Painted Things* (1929), *Feast of Candlemas* (1937), and *Fiddler's Bidding* (1939). She found a truer voice in her two works for children *On Tintock Tap* (1946) and *St Mungo's Bairns* (1948), both of which retell folk-tales from Scotland's oral tradition. She has also written a sensitive biography of JOHN GIBSON LOCKHART, and her studies of domestic life in the 18th and 19th centuries brought the past alive in an unacademic and entirely pleasing way. Marion Lochhead was a founder-member of the Scottish section of International PEN in 1927 and she was made a Fellow of the Royal Society of Literature in 1955.

WORKS: *Poems* (1928); *Painted Things* (1929); *Anne Dalrymple* (1934); *Cloaked in Scarlet* (1935); *Adrian was a Priest* (1936); *Island Destiny* (1936); *Feast of Candlemas and Other Devotional Poems* (1937); *The Dancing Flower* (1938); *Fiddler's Bidding* (1939); *Highland Scene* (1939); *On Tintock Tap* (1946); *St Mungo's Bairns* (1948); *The Scots Household in the Eighteenth Century* (1948); *A Lamp was Lit* (1949); *John Gibson Lockhart* (1954); *Their First Ten Years* (1956); *Young Victorians* (1959); *Elizabeth Rigby, Lady Eastlake* (1961); *St Columba* (1963); *The Victorian Household* (1964); *Episcopal Scotland in the Nineteenth Century* (1966); *Portrait of the Scott Country* (1968); *The Renaissance of Wonder in Children's Literature* (1977); *The Other Country* (1978); *Scottish Tales of Magic and Mystery* (1978); *Scottish Love Stories* (1979)

Lochlie [Lochlea]. The farm tenanted by WILLIAM BURNES from Whitsun 1777 until his death on 13 February 1784. Burnes had difficulty in paying his rents in 1782 and was forced to fight a legal battle in Edinburgh which he won just before his death. The present farm building has no connection with Burnes or his sons ROBERT BURNS and GILBERT BURNS.

Lockhart, Sir **(Robert Hamilton) Bruce** (1887–1970). Journalist and man of letters. He was born on 2 September 1887 in Anstruther, Fife, and was educated at Fettes College in Edinburgh and in Berlin. Between 1908 and 1910 he worked on a rubber plantation in Malaya, and in 1912 he entered the diplomatic service, taking up an appointment in Moscow. During World War I Lockhart maintained Britain's diplomatic presence in Russia but when Anglo-Soviet relations deteriorated in 1918 he was arrested and sentenced to death, accused of being implicated in a plot to assassinate Lenin. He was saved by being exchanged for the Soviet politician Litvinoff, whom the British had arrested in retaliation, but the experience did not deter Lockhart from pursuing his career in the Foreign Office and he served next in Czechoslovakia. Between 1928 and 1939 he lived in London, working as a journalist and writer, and it was during this period that he wrote the books for which he is best remembered: *Memoirs of a British Agent* (1932), *Retreat from Glory* (1934) and *Return to Malaya* (1936). He returned to serve with the Foreign Office during World War II and was knighted in 1943.

Lockhart never lost the image of himself as a swashbuckling adventurer and something of that style pervades all his work. His ability to win friends in high places and his knowledge of Soviet and central European politics give his work an authority that might otherwise have been lost through his indiscreet and self-centred style. His volumes of memoirs *My Rod, my Comfort* (1949) and *My Scottish Youth* (1937) offer entertaining accounts of some of the byways of his life. He died on 27 February 1970 at Hove in Sussex.

WORKS: *Memoirs of a British Agent* (1932); *Retreat from Glory* (1934); *Return to Malaya* (1936); *My Scottish Youth* (1937); *Guns or Butter* (1938); *Comes the Reckoning* (1947); *My Rod, my Comfort* (1949); *The Marines were There* (1950); *Jan Masaryk* (1951); *Scotch* (1951); *My Europe* (1952); *What Happened to the Czechs* (1953); *Your England* (1955); *The Two Revolutions* (1957)

EDITION: K. Young, ed., *The Diaries of Bruce Lockhart, 1915–1938*, vol. 1 (London, 1973)

Lockhart, John Gibson (1794–1854). Novelist, critic and editor. He was born on 14 June 1794 at Cambusnethan, Lanarkshire, the son of a Church of Scotland minister. Most of his childhood was spent in Glasgow and he entered the University in 1805, where he won a Snell Exhibition to Balliol College, Oxford, in 1808. After five years at Oxford, where he read Greats, he returned to Glasgow, and in 1815 moved to Edinburgh to enter the FACULTY OF ADVOCATES. A keen linguist, he received financial help from WILLIAM BLACKWOOD to travel to Germany in 1817, as a result of which he translated Schlegel's *Lectures on the History of Literature*. His involvement with Blackwood deepened later that year when he and his friend and fellow advocate JOHN WILSON (iii) were invited to become contributing editors to the newly founded BLACKWOOD'S MAGAZINE. Together with JAMES HOGG, they published the

'CHALDEE MANUSCRIPT' in October 1817, and Lockhart also contributed a savage attack on Leigh Hunt and the Cockney school of poetry under the anonymity of 'Z'.

Lockhart's assault on Hunt, together with his cold and reserved manner, brought him a reputation for vicious satire which increased when, in the August 1818 issue of the magazine, he wrote a cruel review of Keats's long poem *Endymion*. It was with good reason that in the 'Chaldee Manuscript' he had styled himself, 'the Scorpion which delighteth to sting the faces of men'. The notoriety of those early reviews were to remain with him throughout his literary career.

In 1819 Blackwood published his PETER'S LETTERS TO HIS KINSFOLK in three volumes, one of the best pictures of contemporary intellectual life in Edinburgh. The letters, from Peter Morris to his Welsh relative the Revd David Williams, purport to be the record of a visit to Edinburgh, where Morris is given an entrée to society through his fellow Oxonian, the high-Tory antiquary William Wastle. Although the letters contain several satirical portraits of the city's leading Whigs, they also contain an accurate, and at times sharply critical portrait of an Edinburgh culture that was dominated by the Whig ascendancy of the *Edinburgh Review* (*see* EDINBURGH REVIEW (ii)) on the one hand and by the renaissance of the folk culture embodied by Sir WALTER SCOTT on the other.

In 1820 Lockhart married Scott's daughter Sophia, and on his father-in-law's advice began to drift away from Wilson and the Blackwood group. He practised as an advocate and continued to write, publishing four novels in the years following his marriage: *Valerius* (1821), *Adam Blair* (1822), *Reginald Dalton* (1823) and *Matthew Wald* (1824). The most interesting of these is *Adam Blair*, the story of the slow and inexorable growth of passion between a Presbyterian minister – a widower – and his house guest Charlotte Campbell. The tragedy of their adulterous love is built up carefully to Adam's ultimate contemplation of suicide in the horror of remorse and to Charlotte's anguished death. In his *Essays in Literary Criticism* George Saintsbury wrote that 'Lockhart had every faculty for writing novels, except the faculty of novel writing.' And that verdict must stand because, although Lockhart's novels are strong in description, they lack positive characterization, and his em-

phasis on melodrama is a flaw which even his emotive use of language cannot disguise.

Though his novels were flawed, Lockhart remained a prolific critic and essayist. In 1825 he moved to London to take up the editorship of John Murray's *Quarterly Review*, cautiously maintaining the magazine's Tory, High Church views and promoting the Irish writer John Wilson Croker, who became a lifelong friend. He also turned his attention to biography, publishing his *Life of Burns* in 1828; in spite of the careful excisions of Burns's sexual exploits, it was regarded by THOMAS CARLYLE as the finest work about the poet's life. It was followed by *Napoleon* in 1829, but Lockhart's reputation as a profound biographer rests on *Memoirs of the Life of Scott*, which was published in seven volumes in 1837–8. Although later scholarship discovered inaccuracies in the text and a tendency to telescope Scott's letters, the biography is Lockhart's crowning achievement and in early biographical literature ranks second only to the *Life of Johnson* by JAMES BOSWELL.

The latter part of Lockhart's life was marred by the early death of his wife Sophia in 1837 and by his estrangement from his son Walter. He continued to edit the *Quarterly Review* until 1853 when ill health forced him to surrender the post. After a visit to Italy he returned to ABBOTSFORD, which his daughter had inherited, and he died there on 25 November 1854. He was buried at Dryburgh Abbey at the feet of Sir Walter Scott. After his death the first biography was published by his friend G. R. GLEIG in the *Quarterly Review* in 1864, and ANDREW LANG produced a two-volume *Life and Letters of John Gibson Lockhart* in 1896.

WORKS: *Lectures on the History of Literature, Ancient and Modern, from the German of Friedrich Schiller*, 2 vols. (1818); *Peter's Letters to his Kinsfolk*, 3 vols. (1819); *Valerius: a Roman Story* (1821); ed., *The History of the Ingenious Gentleman of La Mancha, translated from the Spanish of Cervantes by Motteux*, 5 vols. (1822); *Some Passages in the Life of Mr Adam Blair* (1822); ed., *Ancient Spanish Ballads: Historical and Romantic* (1823); *Reginald Dalton*, 3 vols. (1823); *The History of Matthew Wald* (1824); with John Wilson, *Janus, or the Edinburgh Literary Almanack* (1826); *Life of Robert Burns* (1828); *Life of Napoleon Buonaparte*, 2 vols. (1829); ed., *Poetical Works of Sir Walter Scott*, 12 vols. (1833–4); *The Ballantyne-Humbug Handled in a Letter to Sir Adam Ferguson* (1837); *Memoirs of the Life of Sir Walter Scott Bart.*, 7 vols. (1837–8); *Narrative of the Life of Sir Walter Scott*, 2 vols. (1848); *Theodore Hook* (1852)

REFERENCES: G. Macbeth, *John Gibson Lockhart: a Critical Study* (Urbana, Illinois, 1935); M. Lochhead, *John Gibson Lockhart* (London, 1954); F. R. Hart, *Lockhart as Romantic Biographer* (Edinburgh, 1971)

Logan, John (1748–88). Poet and dramatist. He was born in 1748 in Soutra, Midlothian, and was educated at Musselburgh Grammar School and the University of Edinburgh. He was appointed minister of South Leith in 1773. His play *Runnemede* was performed on 5 May 1784 in Edinburgh; after its success Logan turned to a life of debauchery and was forced to move to London, where he died in obscurity on 25 December 1788. He is best remembered for his plagiarism of several of the poems of MICHAEL BRUCE, including 'Ode to the Cuckoo', in his own edition of poems published in 1781.

WORKS: *Elements of the Philosophy of History* (1781); *Poems* (1781); *Sermons* (1783); *Runnemede* (1784); *The View of Antient History* (1788)

EDITION: T. Park, ed., *The Poetical Works of John Logan* (London, 1807)

Lom, Iain (John Macdonald) (c1624–c1710). Poet. He was a member of a family closely related to the chiefs of the Macdonalds of Keppoch, Clann Dòmhaill a' Bhràighe. Although Iain Lom's poetry is a remarkable record of an important period in Highland history, little is known of his life and career, but it is suggested in early histories of Lochaber that he was sent to the Catholic seminary at Valladolid in Spain to train as a priest. A staunch Catholic and a lifelong supporter of the royal house of Stewart, Iain Lom acted as a propagandist for their cause and at the Restoration was appointed Charles II's poet laureate in Scotland and awarded a pension. Lom reserved his greatest invective for the Campbells, who supported the Covenanting cause; he attacked them most fiercely in his poem 'Là Inbhir Lòchaidh' on the Battle of Inverlochy, which took place on 2 February between the Royalist army raised by JAMES GRAHAM, Marquis of Montrose, and ALASDAIR 'Colkitto' MACDONALD and the army of ARCHIBALD CAMPBELL, Marquis of Argyll. There is little attempt in the poem to document the exact course of the battle, but in a rapid succession of tense scenes Iain Lom gloats over the defeat of the Argyll army and reserves no pity for the anguish felt by their womenfolk. In counterpoint the valour of the Macdonalds is praised, especially that of their leaders.

Lom's other important poems written for the Jacobite cause are: 'Cumha Morair Hunndaidh', a lament for the Marquis of Huntly which unexpectedly transforms itself into a passionate address to Charles II; 'Crùnadh an Dara Rìgh Teàrlach', an exultant poem commemorating the coronation of Charles II; and laments for Montrose and 'Colkitto' Macdonald, 'Cumha Mhontròis' and 'Cumha Alasdair mhic Colla'. In later years he continued to comment on contemporary events in poems lamenting the Battle of Killiecrankie; 'Oran air Rìgh Uilleam agus Banrigh Màiri', a vituperative poem on the accession of William and Mary; and 'Oran an Aghaidh an Aonaidh', a satire on the ACT OF UNION of 1707, full of bawdy invective against the nobles who took bribes from the English government to support the Union.

As a clan poet Lom composed a number of notable elegies and public poems in praise of the Macdonald chiefs. His poems on the Keppoch murder of 1663 are particularly moving, with a fine combination of sentimentality and sincere emotion. In much of his work he relied on the traditional language, metaphors and metrical techniques of earlier classical poets, but his own poetry is remarkable for its intellectual intensity and creative imagery, and his single-minded loyalty to clan and king has left us a unique view of the events of his lifetime, in many of which he was involved personally. Iain Lom is generally considered to have died in the years following the Act of Union and to have been buried in the graveyard of Cill Choiril at Brae Lochaber. His poems and songs, *Orain Iain Luim* were published by the SCOTTISH GAELIC TEXT SOCIETY in 1964 with an editorial introduction by Annie M. Mackenzie.

Lounger, The. A magazine first published by WILLIAM CREECH in Edinburgh on 5 February 1785 as a successor to THE MIRROR. HENRY MACKENZIE gathered together a similar group of writers and his aims were little different from those he had employed in the previous publication. *The Lounger* is best remembered for the review in the issue of 7 December 1786 of the KILMARNOCK EDITION of the poems by ROBERT BURNS, in which Mackenzie hailed Burns as the 'heaven-taught ploughman'. The magazine ceased publication on 6 January 1787.

Lyndsay [Lindsay], Sir David (c1490–1555). Poet and dramatist. He was the eldest son of David Lyndsay of the Mount, an estate in the Howe of Fife near Cupar. His father also possessed land in East Lothian and it is uncertain whether Lyndsay was educated there at the Grammer School of Haddington or at Cupar. Little is known of his early life – he may have attended the University of St Andrews – but by 1511 he was at the court of JAMES IV. On the birth of Prince James in 1512 Lyndsay was appointed a Gentleman-usher, and throughout the young prince's childhood he was in continuous personal attendance on him. Following the accession of JAMES V as King of Scots in 1524, and the supremacy at court of the Douglases, Lyndsay was banished to his estate at Garmylton in East Lothian. At the beginning of James's personal rule in 1529 Lyndsay was restored to favour and knighted; it was probably at this time that he was created Lyon King of Arms and became an emissary for the young king in his relationships with France, Spain and England. When James married Mary of Guise-Lorraine in 1538 Lyndsay was involved with the marriage preparations, and it was for the royal court that his play ANE PLEASANT SATYRE OF THE THRIE ESTAITIS was performed on Twelfth Night 1540 in Linlithgow. James's death in 1542 did not diminish Lyndsay's standing, and in 1548 he was employed on an embassy to the court of Denmark. The last reference to Lyndsay at Court is in January 1555, when he presided over a chapter of heralds in Edinburgh; in April of the same year his death was recorded in the Register of the Privy Seal.

Lyndsay probably started writing during his first stay at court and during his exile in East Lothian. In his earliest work, *The Dreme* (1528), he introduces himself as James V's servant and the teller of stories (of which this is presented as one) to the young king. It is a dream allegory, concerned with Scotland and its proper governance. The poet falls asleep in a cave and in a dream Dame Remembrance leads him to hell and purgatory, and to a glimpse of heaven and the Garden of Eden, before showing him the ruin that Scotland has become despite its apparent prosperity. John the Common-Weill, who later appears in the *Thrie Estaitis*, is introduced and bewails the

laziness, falsehood, pride and greed into which Scotland has fallen. The poem ends with an exhortation to the king to remember the importance of his high office – a recurring motif in Lyndsay's work. *The Complaynt of the King* (1529) deals with similar themes in a work that is also a petition to the king for patronage.

Lyndsay's most adventurous long poem, *The Testament and Complaynt of Our Soverane Lordis Papyngo*, was published in 1538 but had been completed as early as 1530. It is divided into five sections concluding with two stanzas, one addressed to the reader and the other to the book. The poet, having taught the king's 'papyngo', or parrot, to speak, sees it mortally wounded after falling from a tree, but instead of helping the bird, he hides behind a hawthorn tree. After calling for a priest, the papyngo bemoans her misfortune – 'who sitteth most hie, sal find the saite moist slide' – and in so doing reminds the king of his awesome responsibilities to his people. Three birds, the Pie (canon regular), the Raven (black monk) and the Kite (holy friar), arrive to administer the last rites, but they ignore the papyngo's wishes and on her death they tear up the body, the Kite making off with her heart. Another animal poem *The Complaynt and Publict Confessioun of the Kingis Auld Hound callit Bagsche* (1536) allows Bagsche to complain about his fall from grace and to offer a solemn warning about hubris to Bawtie his successor. *The Historie of ane Nobill and Vailyeand Squyer, William Meldrum, umquhyle Laird of Cleische and Bynnis* (1547) shows Lyndsay's skill as a polished raconteur in the tale of the amorous and valiant knight, Squire Meldrum. The poem falls into two parts: 'The Historie', in rhyming octosyllabic couplets, traces Meldrum's career as lover and soldier; and 'The Testament', in Chaucerian *ballat royal* describes Meldrum's funeral and pronounces his recorded wish that the procession should reflect his interests in love and war.

These are Lyndsay's most important poems: the others, all worthy of note, are: *Ane Answer quhilk Schir David Lyndesay maid to the Kingis Flyting* (1536), a ribald riposte to a poem by James that has not been preserved; *The Deploratioun of the Deith of Quene Magdalene* (1537), a lament on the death of James's first queen; *The Justing betuix James Watsoun and Jhone Barbour Servitouris to King James the Fyft* (1538), a mock-heroic account of a jousting match which formed part of the marriage festivities of James to Mary of Guise-Lorraine; *Ane Supplication Directit to the Kingis Grace in Contemplatioun of Syde Taillis* (1538), an amusing plea to the king to enforce the wearing by women of shorter gowns; *Kitteis Confessioun* (*c* 1542), an attack on the clergy's abuse of the privacy of confession; *The Tragedie of the Cardinall* (1547), in which the shade of Cardinal Beaton makes apology for earthly misdeeds; and *Ane Dialog betuix Experience and ane Courteour* (1553), Lyndsay's last and longest poem in seven books which is an amalgam of his philosophy and an *apologia pro vita sua*.

The work on which Lyndsay's literary reputation rests is also the first great play in Scottish drama: *Ane Pleasant Satyre of the Thrie Estaitis in Commendatioun of Vertew and Vituperatioun of Vyce*. The play gathers together in a dramatic unity many of Lyndsay's main public concerns: the abuse of spiritual and temporal power, the role of the king as head of the body politic, greed and lechery within the Church, and the oppression of the Scottish people by the nobility and the burgesses. Rex Humanitas is beguiled by the Vices who also hold in thrall the three estates, the clergy, the nobility and the burgesses. It is left to John the Common-Weill, a powerful manifestation of the levelling power of democracy, to unmask their crimes and to reorder society. Lyndsay's use of allegorical figures and his mixture of comedy and moral seriousness makes the *Thrie Estaitis* not only a powerful piece of drama but also a telling satirical commentary on the vices of spiritual and secular society of Lyndsay's time.

A reformer by inclination but, as far as is known, a Catholic by persuasion, Lyndsay was an early supporter of JOHN KNOX. In his *His-toria* GEORGE BUCHANAN praised Lyndsay for his integrity and truthfulness, traits also noted by the monarchs to whom he was ambassador; and his support of the commons was no empty gesture – his work resounds to his distaste for the corruption of power and to his acknowledgement of the grievances suffered by the ordinary people. He belongs to a strongly democratic tradition in Scottish literature and ALEXANDER PENNECUIK (i), ALLAN RAMSAY and Sir WALTER SCOTT all bear witness in their work to Lyndsay's long-lasting popularity in Scotland.

WORKS: *The Dreme of Sir David Lyndsay* (1528); *The Complaynt of the King* (1529); *Ane Answer quhilk Schir David Lyndesay maid to the Kingis Flyting* (1536); *The Complaynt and Publict Confessioun of the Kingis Auld Hound callit Bagsche* (1536); *The Deploratioun of the Deith of Quene Magdalene* (1537); *The Justing betuix James Watsoun and Jhone Barbour Servitouris to King James the Fyft* (1538); *Ane Supplicatioun Directit to the Kingis Grace in Contemplatioun of Syde Taillis* (1538); *The Testament and Complaynt of Our Soverane Lordis Papyngo* (1538); *Kitteis Confessioun* (c1542); *The Tragedie of the Late Cardinall* (1547); *The Historie of ane Nobill and Vailyeand Squyer, William Meldrum, umquhyle Laird of Cleische and Bynnis* (1547); *Acta sui temporis* (1548); *Ane Dialog betuix Experience and ane Courteour* (1553); *Ane Pleasant Satyre of the Thrie Estaitis* (1602)

EDITIONS: D. Hamer, ed., *The Works of Sir David Lyndsay of the Mount*, 4 vols., STS (Edinburgh and London, 1931–4); R. Kemp, ed., *The Satire of the Three Estates* (London, 1951); J. Kinsley, ed., *Ane Satyre of the Thrie Estaitis* (London, 1954); M. P. McDiarmid, ed., *A Satire of the Three Estates* (London, 1967)

REFERENCES: H. Aschenberg, *Sir David Lyndsay's Leben und Werke* (München Gladbach, 1891); W. Murison, *Sir David Lyndsay: Poet and Satirist of the Old Church in Scotland* (Cambridge, 1938)

M

Mac a'Ghobhainn, Iain. The Gaelic name of IAIN CRICHTON SMITH.

Mac a'Ghreidhir, Gillesbriod. Pen-name of CHRISTOPHER MURRAY GRIEVE.

MacAmhlaigh, Domhnall (Donald MacAulay) (*b* 1930). Poet. A native of Bernera, Lewis, in the Western Isles, he was educated at the Nicolson Institute, Stornoway, and at the universities of Aberdeen and Cambridge. Since graduating he has taught at the University of Edinburgh and at Trinity College, Dublin, and he is Reader in Celtic at the University of Aberdeen. MacAmhlaigh began publishing verse in 1956 and although only one collection has appeared, *Seobhrach ás a'Chloich* (1967), a good selection of his work, with English translations, was pubished in his edition *Nua-bhàrdachd Ghaidlig* in 1976. Central to much of his work is his Lewis background, which appears in many guises as a theme in his poems: in 'Comharra Stiuiridh' ('Landmark') Lewis appears as an iceberg, 'a primary landmark/dangerous, essential, demanding'; and in 'An t-sean Bhean' ('Old woman') the island community is addressed collectively as an old woman striving to eke a living from her croft. That sense of ambiguity in his imagery characterizes most of his poetry and is especially present in his reflections on the strengths and weaknesses of his island background.

WORKS: *Seobhrach ás a'Chloich* (1967); ed., Somhairle MacGill-Eain, Deòrsa MacIain Deòrsa, Ruaraidh MacThómais and Iain Mac a'Ghobhainn, *Nua-bhàrdachd Ghaidhlig* (1976), ed., *Oighreachd agus Gabhaltas* (1981)

Mac an t-Saoir, Donnchadh Bàn (Duncan Ban MacIntyre) (1724–1812). Poet. He was born on 20 March 1724 in Glen Orchy on the Argyll–Perthshire border; there he worked as a gamekeeper and forester, and the experience of being in such close contact with nature was to exert a considerable influence on much of his later poetry. Another influence was the Revd James Stewart of Killin who may have introduced Mac an t-Saoir to the poetry of ALASDAIR MAC MHAIGHSTIR ALASDAIR after it had been published in 1751. When Mac an t-Saoir began to compose his own poetry it was the minister's son, John, who wrote down the works, and edited them and prepared them for press in 1768, for the poet was not able to write himself, even though his linguistic skills and ability to compose were developed to an astonishing degree. Shortly before the publication of his poems he moved to Edinburgh, where he served in the City Guard and later as a soldier in the Breadalbane Fencibles. Although he continued to write in Edinburgh – mainly satires on the manners of the city – he had no contact with its literary society and it is safe to say that his best work had been written in the earlier part of his life.

In all his nature poetry Mac an t-Saoir brought a freshness of observation to his detailed descriptions of the countryside and the birds and animals that populate the high hills of the country of his birth. No single item seems to be too small to excite his curiosity; in 'Orain Coire a cheathaich' ('Song of the misty Corrie'), for example, a complete picture is painted of the sights and sounds of a burn running through a mountain corrie, and the birds and deer that have made it their home. That visual quality is found again in his long poem 'Moladh Beinn Dòbhrainn' ('The praise of Ben Doran'). Although the mountain and its scenery form the centre-point of his praise, Mac an t-Saoir reserves particular approbation for the deer, imbuing them almost with human qualities as they go about their daily business. The poem is also memorable for its intricate rhyming structure which resembles the formal patterns of PIBROCH or *ceol mor*, the classical music of the Highland bagpipe. It has been translated into English by Hugh MàcDiarmid (CHRISTOPHER MURRAY GRIEVE) and IAIN CRICHTON SMITH.

In all Mac an t-Saoir's nature poetry, which is the finest exposition of his art, it is possible to experience the poet's own warmth of feeling for nature and the positive delight that he took in its beauties. His richly evocative language and the brio of his descriptions make Mac an t-Saoir one of the most remarkable celebrants of nature in either Scots or Gaelic.

Praise poems of a different kind were written for the Campbells, and although these are formal, technically correct offerings, Mac an t-Saoir achieves a sense of genuine feeling in the lament for Colin Campbell of Glenure, who was killed in the Appin murder of 1752. Other examples of his poetic style in the 1768 collection include love poems, satires and drinking-songs.

EDITION: A. Macleod, ed., *The Songs of Duncan Ban MacIntyre*, SGTS (Edinburgh, 1952)

MacAoidh, Rob Donn (Robert MacKay) (c1715–78). Poet. He was born in Strathmore in Sutherland on the lands of the Mac-Kay chief, Lord Reay. Very little is known about his childhood and the first reference to him comes on his entering the service of Lord Reay's tacksman Iain Mac Eachainn 'ic Iain (John MacKay) on his farm at Muisel. Rob Donn, as he came to be styled, started composing poetry at an early age and his poems and songs build up a vivid picture of life in an isolated community, and more especially of the relationships that existed between the clan chief, his tacksmen and the people of the clan.

During the 1745 Jacobite rebellion Lord Reay pledged his support for the Hanoverian cause and a contingent of militia raised from the Clan MacKay fought on the government side. Despite his patron's political leanings, Rob Donn, like other Gaelic poets of the period, inclined to the Jacobite cause and wrote several poems in its support, including 'Na casagan dubha', which criticized the government for proscribing Highland dress in 1747. Between 1759 and 1763 Rob Donn served with the Sutherland Fencibles, although he may have acted only in the capacity of regimental or clan bard. The deaths of Iain Mac Eachainn in 1757 and Lord Reay in 1761 prompted two of Rob Donn's greatest elegies; their deaths accelerated the growing disinteg-

ration of clan society in Strathnaver and Strathmore and presaged the breaking up of the crofting communities.

During his lifetime MacAoidh's poetry remained in the oral tradition and it was not until after his death in 1778 that efforts were made by ministers living in the area to collect his work. Among these were the Revd Donald Sage, Revd Aeneas Macleod and the Revd John Thomson, and a first collection of the 200-odd poems and songs ascribed to Mac-Aoidh appeared in 1829.

Although he had enjoyed little formal education MacAoidh's poetry is not the work of an artless recorder of the society in which he lived. Through his friendship with the minister of Durness he may have come into contact with the work of Alexander Pope (1688–1744), the traces of whose style critics such as IAIN CRICHTON SMITH have noted in his elegies. He also wrote several spirited, though at times, bawdy love-songs, including the well-known song of unrequited love, *Is trom leam an airigh*; but throughout his work he maintained a consistent moral stance which he saw as necessary for the protection of a tightly knit community. A sense of humanity and an intellectual acuity are the hallmarks of his poetic style; and from his poems and songs a finely delineated picture emerges of the niceties of everyday life in the Sutherland of his day and of the people who inhabited it. His dispassionate view of life, coupled with his concern for his fellow men, bring to his poetry a humanity and power of observation that marks him as one of the major figures in 18th-century poetry.

EDITIONS: M. MacKay, ed., *Songs and Poems in the Gaelic Language by Robert MacKay* (Inverness, 1829); A. Gunn and M. Macfarlane, eds., *Songs and Poems by Rob Donn MacKay* (Glasgow, 1899); H. Morrison, ed., *Songs and Poems in the Gaelic Language by Rob Donn* (Edinburgh, 1899)

REFERENCE: I. Grimble, *The World of Rob Donn* (Edinburgh, 1979)

MacAulay, Donald. The English name of DOMHNALL MACAMHLAIGH.

Macbeth, King of Scots (c1005–57). He was born in the early 11th century, the son of Finlay, mormaer of Moray, and his wife, a daughter of Malcolm II. On the accession of Macbeth's cousin, Duncan I, who had married a cousin of Siward, Earl of Northumbria, Macbeth pursued his claim to the throne, and after the Battle of Pitgaveny (1040) he ruled the Kingdom of the Scots with Thorfinn, Earl of Orkney. In 1054 Duncan's eldest son, MALCOLM III (Malcolm Canmore), invaded Scotland with Earl Siward and captured the Lothians (the area round present day Edinburgh). Macbeth was defeated by Malcolm and killed at the Battle of Lumphanan in August 1057. His stepson Lulach was crowned king but was killed four months later at the Battle of Essie, leaving the victorious Malcolm King of Scots.

Shakespeare's tragedy, *Macbeth* (1605), is based on the story of Macbeth and Malcolm as related in Holinshed's *Chronicles*, but the events have been telescoped to suit his dramatic purposes. Much of the information about Scotland in Holinshed had been taken from John Bellenden's Scots translation (1536) of the inaccurate and fanciful *Scotorium historiae* by HECTOR BOECE.

MacCaig, Norman (*b* 1910). Poet. He was born on 14 November 1910 in Edinburgh and was educated at the HIGH SCHOOL OF EDINBURGH and, between 1928 and 1932, the University, where he studied classics. From 1934 to 1970 he worked as a schoolteacher and he taught at the University of Stirling between 1970 and 1979, being Reader in Poetry from 1972. He also held the post of Writer in Residence at the University of Edinburgh from 1967 to 1969.

MacCaig's early poetry *Far Cry* (1943) and *The Inward Eye* (1946) belonged to the New Apocalypse movement, whose work was published principally in *The White Horseman*, edited by Henry Treece (*b* 1911) and J. F. HENDRY. In 1955 he moved away from that short-lived movement when he published *Riding Lights*. MacCaig is a great observer of life and many of his best poems reflect his equal interests in his native Edinburgh and the landscapes around Lochinver in Sutherland, where he spends his summers. The richness of his descriptive powers is matched by the metaphysical conceits he is able to bring to poems like 'Climbing Suilven', 'Midnight Lochinver' and 'Walking to Inveruplan', but his major descriptive work, a paean to the north-west of Scotland, is 'A Man in my Position' which was commissioned by the BBC and published in the collection of the same title. His elegant use of language and his sure hand-

ling of rhyming stanza forms make MacCaig the most accomplished Scots poet writing in English this century.

WORKS: *Far Cry* (1943); *The Inward Eye* (1946); *Riding Lights* (1955); *The Sinai Sort* (1957); ed., *Honour'd Shade* (1959); *A Common Grace* (1960); *A Round of Applause* (1962); *Measures* (1965); *Surroundings* (1966); *Rings on a Tree* (1968); *A Man in my Position* (1969); ed., with Alexander Scott, *Contemporary Scottish Verse 1959–1969* (1970); *Selected Poems* (1971); *Penguin Modern Poets 21* (1972); *The White Bird* (1973); *The World's Room* (1974); *Tree of Strings* (1977); *Old Maps and New: Selected Poems* (1978); *The Equal Skies* (1980)

REFERENCE: R. Fulton, *Contemporary Scottish Poetry: Individuals and Contexts* (Loanhead, Midlothian, 1974)

MacCodrum, Iain [John] (1693–1779). Poet. He was born in North Uist, the son of a tacksman to the Macdonalds. Most of his life was spent in the island of his birth where he enjoyed a reputation for the liveliness and originality of his song writing. Many traditions and stories have grown up around him, the best known being the witty rebuff he gave to JAMES MACPHERSON for his use of crude Gaelic when requesting information from MacCodrum about the poems of OSSIAN. In 1763 he was appointed bard to Sir James Macdonald of Sleat; he died on 14 April 1779 at Eaval, North Uist. Most of his work follows a comic or satiric strain as he comments on the foibles of his fellow men, such as the tuneless piper of *'Diomoladh pioba Dhomhnaill Bhain'* ('The dispraise of Donald Ban's pipes'); but MacCodrum was not simply a singer of comic songs. He was a Jacobite and a firm upholder of the values of the clan system; one of his last songs, *'Oran do na fogarraich'* ('Song to the fugitives') is a bitter comment on the emigration from North Uist of the Macdonald tacksmen as a result of the high rents imposed on their lands. Against it may be compared the beautiful song *'Smeorach chlann Domhnaill'* ('The Mavis of Clan Donald'), an elegant song in praise of the land of his birth.

EDITION: W. Matheson, ed., *The Songs of John MacCodrum*, SGTS (Edinburgh, 1938)

MacColl, Ewan (*b* 1915). Dramatist and folklorist. He was born on 25 January 1915 in Auchterarder, Perthshire. He gained his first theatrical experience with the Glasgow Unity Theatre but is best known for his work after World War II with the Theatre Workshop in

London. For them he wrote *Johnny Noble* (1946), a documentary ballad opera in which poetry and traditional folk melodies are used for the linking narration. Set against the background of the Spanish Civil War and World War II, it tells the story of a young unemployed seaman's love for his girl Mary and traces his growing political awareness through his exasperation with the economic situation. With his wife Peggy Seeger (*b* 1935), MacColl has been a tireless promoter of the revival of interest in British folk music by fostering the extension of traditional styles to modern media. For BBC Radio he has produced eight 'radio ballads', documentary programmes using folk-song and the voices of ordinary people to tell the story of their lives and labours. The most successful of these was *Singing the Fishing* (1960), which recorded the history of the East coast herring-fishing industry.

WORKS: Ed., *Scotland Sings* (1953); ed., *The Shuttle and Cage* (1954); ed., with Peggy Seeger, *The Singing Island* (1960); ed., *A Personal Choice of Scottish Folksongs and Ballads* (1963); ed., with Peggy Seeger, *Songbook* (1963); ed., *Folksongs and Ballads of Scotland* (1965); ed., with Peggy Seeger, *I'm a Freedom Man* (1968); ed., with Peggy Seeger, *Travellers Songs from England and Scotland* (1977)

MacColla, Fionn. Pen-name of THOMAS DOUGLAS MACDONALD.

McCrie, Thomas (1772–1835). Divine and historian. He was born at Duns, Berwickshire, and was educated at the University of Edinburgh, which he left without taking a degree. He became a Secessionist minister, first in Kelso and then in Edinburgh in 1796, but his changing attitude to the dogma of church government led to his ejection from his parish in 1806. Out of his deepening interest in ecclesiastical history he wrote a life of JOHN KNOX, which was published in 1812. It demonstrated McCrie's knowledge not only of the history of the Reformation but also of its social and political implications and did much to put Knox's life into a proper perspective. He also wrote a life of another reformer, ANDREW MELVILLE, and through his interests in Scottish church history was appointed Professor of Divinity at Edinburgh in 1816. In 1817, in the *Edinburgh Christian Instructor*, he attacked Sir Walter Scott's representation of the COVENANTERS in OLD MORTALITY, and although Scott was forced to defend his view in the *Quarterly Review* the argument between

the two men was never resolved. McCrie died on 5 August 1835 and was buried in Greyfriars' Churchyard in Edinburgh.

WORKS: *The Life of John Knox*, 2 vols. (1812); *The Life of Andrew Melville*, 2 vols. (1819); ed., *Memoirs of William Veitch and George Brysson* (1825); *History of the Progress and Suppression of the Reformation in Italy* (1827); *History of the Progress and Suppression of the Reformation in Spain* (1829); *Sermons* (1839); *Miscellaneous Writings* (1841)

REFERENCE: T. McCrie the younger, ed., *Life of Thomas McCrie* (Edinburgh, 1840)

MacCrimmon, Patrick. Pen-name of WALTER PERRIE.

McCrone, Guy (1898–1977). Novelist. He was born in Birkenhead of Glaswegian parents and was brought back to the city of their birth to be educated at Glasgow Academy. After leaving school he read modern languages at Pembroke College, Cambridge, and on graduating he studied singing in Vienna. On his return to Glasgow he interested himself in the promotion of opera and was responsible for the first performance in Britain of Berlioz's opera *Les Troyens*, which was staged at the Theatre Royal in Glasgow in 1935. With his cousin O. H. MAVOR ('James Bridie') he helped to found the Glasgow Citizens' Theatre and he served for a time as its manager. In 1968 he retired to live in the Lake District where he died at Windermere on 30 May 1977.

McCrone made his name as a novelist with the publication of *Wax Fruit* (1947), a chronicle in three parts of the Moorhouse family's rise from Ayrshire farming beginnings to wealth and prosperity in the West End of Glasgow. Although his observation of society is shallow and his prose cliché-ridden, McCrone's novel is a warm-hearted evocation of family life in which the snobbish Bel Moorhouse reigns supreme. *Wax Fruit* was followed by two less successful sequels, *Aunt Bel* (1949) and *The Hayburn Family* (1952), and by several other Glasgow novels, but McCrone was never again able to capture the innocent charm of his first study of Glasgow middle-class mores.

WORKS: *The Striped Umbrella* (1937); *Antimacassar City* (1940); *Wax Fruit* (1947); *Aunt Bel* (1949); *The Hayburn Family* (1952); *James and Charlotte* (1955); *An Independent Young Man* (1961)

MacDiarmid, Hugh. Pen-name of CHRISTOPHER MURRAY GRIEVE.

McDiarmid, John (1790–1852). Journalist. He was born in Glasgow, the son of the minister of the Gaelic Church. His early life was spent as a clerk in the Commercial Bank in Edinburgh, but by 1817 his growing interest in publishing led him to join Charles Maclaren and William Ritchie shortly after they had founded THE SCOTSMAN newspaper. Later that year he moved to Dumfries where he established the *Dumfries and Galloway Courier*. A friend of many of the leading writers of his day, McDiarmid acted as a legal adviser to JEAN ARMOUR, the widow of ROBERT BURNS. Politically on the left, he was one of the first campaigning journalists in Scotland to see the use that could be made of the press in public affairs. He edited a collection of poems by William Cowper and wrote on the topography of Dumfries and Galloway.

WORKS: *An Enquiry into the Principles of Civil and Military Subordination* (1806); ed., *Poetical Works of William Cowper* (1818); *The Scrap Book* (1821); *Sketches from Nature* (1830); *Picture of Dumfries* (1832)

Macdonald, Alasdair ['Colkitto'] (*d* 1647). Soldier. He belonged to a sept of the Macdonalds who had emigrated to Antrim in Ireland in 1639. His father was Cholla Chiotach and the name was also applied to him, erroneously, in its anglicized form of 'Colkitto'. Alasdair proved himself as a soldier during the Ulster rising of 1641 by defeating the superior Protestant forces of Archibald Stewart. His ability to fight a fast-moving campaign and to employ guerilla tactics was put to the test again when he joined forces with JAMES GRAHAM, the Marquis of Montrose, in 1644. His Irish forces fought with particular distinction at the Battle of Inverlochy in February 1645 and were singled out for much praise by the Macdonald bard IAIN LOM. At the end of Montrose's summer campaign Macdonald moved north again to harry his traditional enemies the Campbells. He returned to Ireland in 1646 and died on the Catholic side at the Battle of Knocknanus on 13 November 1647, fighting the government forces of Lord Inchiquin.

Macdonald, Alexander. *See* ALASDAIR MAC MHAIGHSTIR ALASDAIR.

Macdonald, Cicely [Giles]. One form of the English name of SILEAS NA CEAPAICH.

Macdonald, Flora (1722–90). She was born on South Uist, the daughter of a tacksman to Macdonald of Clanranald. Her cousin was the poet ALASDAIR MAC MHAIGHSTIR ALASDAIR. While the leading Jacobites were on the run from government troops in 1746, Flora Macdonald was persuaded to help the Jacobite cause by allowing CHARLES EDWARD STUART to be disguised as her maidservant. Taking the name Betty Burke, the prince and a small party, including Flora, made its way from the Outer Hebrides to Skye from where the prince made good his escape to the mainland. For her part in the escapade Flora Macdonald was arrested and taken to London but she was released in 1747 under a general government amnesty for Jacobite supporters. She returned to live in Skye, where she married Allan Macdonald of Kingsburgh in November 1750. In 1774 she emigrated with her family to America but the events of the War of Independence forced them to move to Canada in 1778 and they returned to Scotland in the following year. Flora's last years were spent on Skye, where she died on 4 March 1790. One of the great heroic figures in Scottish history, Flora Macdonald's selfless protection of the prince inspired many poems and songs, including the popular *Skye Boat Song*, composed in 1884 by Sir Harold Boulton.

REFERENCE: E. G. Vining, *Flora Macdonald: her Life in the Highlands and America* (London, 1967)

Macdonald, George (1824–1905). Novelist and poet. He was born on 10 December 1824 at Huntly, Aberdeenshire, the son of a farmer. Family tradition claimed that they were descendants of the Macdonalds who survived the MASSACRE OF GLENCOE in 1692. He was educated at King's College, Aberdeen (1840–45), and at Highbury Theological College, becoming a Congregationalist minister in 1850. However, failing health and a conflict of doctrinal views with his superiors forced him to resign in 1855, and he turned to journalism and lecturing as a means of earning a living. In 1859 he accepted a professorship at Bedford College, London, and he became a successful occasional lecturer on religious matters in the United States.

Macdonald's first published works, a dramatic poem, *Within and Without* (1856), and *Poems* (1857), show a mind finely tuned to the possibilities of escape to other, mystical or faery worlds, through fantasy, a trait he was to exploit in his novels *Phantastes: a Faery Romance for Men and Women* (1858) and, much later, *Lilith* (1895). The latter was to influence DAVID LINDSAY (ii), among others, and its creation of a separate world of wonder into which Vane, the narrator, can escape through the influence of a miraculous librarian called Mr Raven, inspired J. R. R. Tolkien in *The Lord of the Rings* (1954–5) and C. S. Lewis in the *Last Battle* (1956). Similar territory is explored in his fairy-tales for children, *At the Back of the North Wind* (1871), *The Princess and the Goblin* (1872) and *The Princess and Curdie* (1888), all of which indulge the Victorian liking for a mixture of horror and delight with a good moral message.

Of Macdonald's Scottish novels, *David Elginbrod* (1863), *Alec Forbes* (1865) and *Robert Falconer* (1868) are set in the Aberdeenshire countryside of his childhood, and although they are weakened by the severity, and unfairness, of his attacks on Calvinism, and by his KAILYARD tendency to sentimentalize the peasantry, they do show to good effect Macdonald's ability to draw characters and to realize accurate dialogue. Macdonald was a friend of many of the leading literary figures of the day, including Lewis Carroll (1832–98) and F. D. Maurice (1805–72). His later years were spent in Bordigherra, Italy, and he died on 18 September 1905.

WORKS: *Within and Without* (1856); *Poems* (1857); *Phantastes* (1858); *David Elginbrod* (1863); *Adela Cathcart* (1864); *The Portent* (1864); *Alec Forbes of Howglen* (1865); *Annals of a Quiet Neighbourhood* (1867); *Dealings with the Fairies* (1867); *The Disciples* (1867); *Unspoken Sermons* (1867); *Exotics* (1867); *Guild Court* (1868); *Robert Falconer* (1868); *The Seaboard Parish* (1868); *The Wow o' Rivven* (1868); *The Miracles of our Lord* (1870); *At the Back of the North Wind* (1871); *England's Antiphon* (1871); *Ranald Bannerman's Boyhood* (1871); *The Princess and the Goblin* (1872); *The Vicar's Daughter* (1872); *Wilfred Cumbermede* (1872); *Gutta Percha Willie* (1873); *Malcolm* (1875); *The Wise Woman* (1875); *St George and St Michael* (1876); *The Marquis of Lossie* (1877); *Paul Faber* (1879); *Sir Gibbie* (1879); *A Book of Strife* (1880); *Mary Marston* (1881); *Warlock o' Glenwarlock* (1881); *The Gifts of the Child Christ* (1882); *Orts* (1882); *Weighed and Wanting* (1882); *Donal Grant* (1883); *A Threefold Cord* (1883); *The Tragedie of Hamlet* (1885); *What's Mine's Mine* (1886); *Home Again* (1887); *A Song for Christians* (1887); *The Elect Lady* (1888); *The Princess and Curdie* (1888); *Cross Purposes and the Shadows* (1890); *The Flight of the Shadow* (1891); *The Light Princess* (1891); *A Rough Shaking* (1891); *There and Back* (1891); *The Hope of the Gospel* (1892); *Heather and Snow* (1893); *Scotch Songs and Ballads* (1893); *Lilith* (1895); *The Lost Princess* (1895); *Rampoli*

(1897); *Salted with Fire* (1897); *The Day Boy and the Night Girl* (1904); *The Shadows and Little Daylight* (1904)

REFERENCES: R. L. Wolff, *The Golden Key: a Study of the Fiction of George Macdonald* (New Haven, Conn., 1961)

Macdonald, John. The English name of IAIN LOM.

Macdonald, Thomas Douglas ['Fionn MacColla'] (1906–75). Novelist. Thomas Douglas Macdonald, who wrote under the name 'Fionn MacColla', was born on 4 March 1906 in Montrose, Angus. He trained as a teacher in Aberdeen and worked in the Gairloch area of Wester Ross, before teaching for a time in the Scots College in Safed, Palestine. On his return to Scotland in 1929 he studied Gaelic at the University of Glasgow and between 1939 and 1961 he was a headmaster in various schools in the Highlands and Western Isles. His autobiography, *Too Long in this Condition*, was published shortly after his death in 1975 in Edinburgh.

Macdonald's first novel, *The Albannach* (1932), concerns itself with the gradual spiritual renewal of Murdo Anderson, the son of a Wester Ross Free Church elder, and painstakingly traces Murdo's attempts to escape from the strict religious morality of his upbringing. An education in Glasgow is interrupted by his father's death and Murdo is forced to return to his Highland township, there to sink into alcoholism and despair before finding regeneration in the rhythms of country life and the culture of his Gaelic background.

More successful in its delineation of Highland life and more satisfying in its depiction of the stultifying power of Calvinism (Macdonald's lifelong preoccupation), is *And the Cock Crew* (1945), a novel that is firmly rooted in the horrors of the 19th-century Highland CLEARANCES. Against that brutal background the central character, the minister Maighstir Sachari, a man of intense visionary perception, betrays the community three times in his interpretation of the evictions as part of God's plan. At the end of the novel Sachari is unable to understand the clash between the ancient, life-giving culture of the Gael as represented by his adversary, the bard Fearchar, and the greed of the landowners as exemplified by the factor Byars. The theme of the minister who betrays his flock was continued in a posthumous novel, *The Ministers*, which was published in 1979. Macdonald was a tireless critic of the repressive power of extreme Calvinism, but at times his ardour to expose the evils which he saw in the Presbyterian Church's influence over Scotland unbalanced his judgement, and his creation of the ministers Maighstir Sachari and the Revd Ewan MacRury in *The Ministers* is distorted. Macdonald's philosophy is summed up in *At the Sign of the Clenched Fist* (1967). His other publications are two novels of 16th-century Scotland, *Scottish Noel* (1958) and *Ane Tryall of Hereticks* (1962).

WORKS: *The Albannach* (1932); *And the Cock Crew* (1945); *Scottish Noel* (1958); *Ane Tryall of Hereticks* (1962); *At the Sign of the Clenched Fist* (1967); *Too Long in this Condition* (1975); *The Ministers* (1979)

Macdonell, A(rchibald) G(ordon) ['Neil Gordon'] (1895–1941). Novelist. He was born on 3 November 1895 in Aberdeen and was educated at Winchester. During World War I he served with the Royal Field Artillery, and between 1922 and 1927 he worked for the League of Nations. Although Macdonell lived and worked in England for most of his life, he wrote an affectionate memoir of Scotland, *My Scotland* (1937); but he is best known for *England, their England* (1933), a satire on English manners which is memorable for an evocative description of an English country cricket match. He wrote several other humorous novels and a series of detective novels under the pseudonym Neil Gordon.

WORKS: *The Betrothal* (1928); *England, their England* (1933); *How Like an Angel* (1934); *Napoleon and his Marshals* (1934); *A Visit to America* (1935); *Lords and Masters* (1936); *My Scotland* (1937); *Autobiography of a Cad* (1938); *Flight from a Lady* (1939); *The Spanish Pistol* (1939); *What Next, Baby?* (1939) as Neil Gordon: *The Factory on the Cliff* (1928); *The Professor's Poison* (1928); *The Silent Murder* (1929); *The Big Ben Alibi* (1930); *Murder in Earl's Court* (1931)

MacDonnell, Cicely [Giles]. One form of the English name of SÌLEAS NA CEAPAICH.

MacGill-Eain, Somhairle (Sorley MacLean) (*b* 1911). Poet. He was born on 26 October 1911 at Osgaig on the island of Raasay. He was educated at the secondary school in Portree, Skye, and between 1929 and 1933 he attended the University of Edinburgh, where he read English. After graduating with first-class honours he taught in Skye, Mull and Edinburgh

and he also started writing poetry; he became a friend of Hugh MacDiarmid (CHRISTOPHER MURRAY GRIEVE), who was at that time living in Whalsay, Shetland. During World War II MacGill-Eain served with the Signals Corps in North Africa and was seriously wounded at the Battle of El Alamein in 1943. Between then and 1956 he was a schoolmaster in Edinburgh and from then until his retirement in 1972 he was headmaster of Plockton Secondary School in Wester Ross.

MacGill-Eain's first poems were published in 1940, along with those of ROBERT GARIOCH SUTHERLAND, in *17 Poems for 6d*, but his major work is *Dàin do Eimhir agus Dàin Eile* (1943), a selection of love poems and elegies, which was destined to have a far-reaching effect on the course of 20th-century Scottish Gaelic poetry. The substantial centre to the book is a sequence of love poems addressed to 'Eimhir' (the loveliest of the women of the heroes of Ulster), which was inspired by an intense love affair and the subsequent loss of his loved one. To that expression of love and regret he grafted equally passionately held feelings of a political nature as he explored his sense of anger at the triumph of fascism in Spain after the Spanish Civil War. In 'Gaoir na h-Eòrpa' ('The cry of Europe') the poet's sense of personal loss is allied to his despair for the 'poverty, anguish and grief' of the people of Spain, and the poem is typical of MacGill-Eain's largely successful attempts to forge a link between the opposing claims of love and political commitment. Out of his experiences in the war came three poems that reflect not only his sense of futility at the waste caused by destruction and death but also man's heroism in the face of such madness: 'Curaidhean' ('Heroes'), 'Glac a'Bhàis' ('Death valley') and 'Latha Foghair' ('An autumn day').

MacGill-Eain's selected poems were published in 1977 and from them it is possible to see his continuing preoccupations: his fascination with the strengths of his family background and its traditions; Ireland and politics; and his sense of anguish at the desolation of Gaelic Scotland and the threats facing the continued survival of its language and culture. His elegy 'Cumha Chaluim Iain Mhic Gill-Eain' is a noble panegyric for his brother Calum I. MacLean who was a founder-member of the SCHOOL OF SCOTTISH STUDIES in Edinburgh. It is written in the traditional phrases and cadences of Gaelic elegy and is justly regarded as one of his finest poems. MacGill-Eain has confessed to having been influenced by the poetry of UILLEAM ROS and the songs of MÀIRI MHOR NAN ORAN, but his voice is one of the most original in Gaelic literature and his experimental use of language, metre, imagery and subject matter mark him as the major influence in 20th-century Scottish Gaelic poetry.

WORKS: With Robert Garioch, *17 Poems for 6d* (1940); *Dàin do Eimhir agus Dàin Eile* (1943); with George Campbell Hay, William Neill and Stuart MacGregor, *Four Points of a Saltire* (1970); with Deòrsa Mac Iain Deòrsa, Ruaraidh MacThómais, Iain Mac a'Ghobhainn and Domhnall MacAmhlaigh, *Nua-bhàrdachd Ghaidhlig* (1976); *Reothairt is Contraigh: Taghadh de Dhàin 1932–1972* (1977)

MacGillivray, (James) Pittendreigh (1856–1938). Poet and sculptor, associated with the 'Glasgow School' of artists. He was a native of Aberdeenshire who achieved fame for the distinctive style of his statues for public places, such as those of Robert Burns in Irivine and John Knox in St Giles in Edinburgh. During his lifetime he was a member of most of the leading arts institutions, he became a member of the ROYAL SCOTTISH ACADEMY in 1901 and was appointed King's Sculptor in Ordinary in 1921. MacGillivray was a nationalist, and in his poetry he evolved a distinctive language based on the Scots of the 16th-century makars. Together with LEWIS SPENCE and VIOLET JACOB he was an early member of the SCOTTISH RENAISSANCE movement. He died on 29 April 1938.

WORKS: *Pro Patria* (1915); *Bog Myrtle and Peat Reek* (1922)

McGonagall, William (c1825–1902). Poet and tragedian. He was probably born in Edinburgh in 1825, the son of an immigrant Irish cotton weaver. His childhood was spent in the Orkney island of South Ronaldsay until his family settled in Dundee when he was 11. Apart from a short stay in Perth, Dundee was to be his home for the rest of his life; he joined his father as a handloom weaver and on 11 July 1846 he married Jean King. He showed an early interest in the theatre and became an amateur Shakespearean actor with the travelling groups of players who visited Dundee's Theatre Royal. A first collection of poems, which contained the popular 'Railway Bridge of the Silvery Tay', was published in 1878 and he became a well-known figure in central Scotland, selling his poetry in broadsheets and giving public readings. This was to be his way of making a living in the years to come. He visited London in 1880 and New York in 1887 but he soon became a humorous butt for his audiences and a target for several hoaxes.

McGonagall's poetry, with its execrable rhymes and fascination with contemporary disasters, continued to enjoy a bizarre popularity, and the collections *Poetic Gems* (1890) has been republished many times. A further 50 previously undiscovered poems were published in 1962, with 'The Autobiography of Sir William Topaz McGonagall, Poet and Tragedian', in *More Poetic Gems*. Although McGonagall's broadsheet poetry owes something to the Scottish tradition of humorous folk verse, he was exploited by his audiences into believing he was a writer of merit. The editor WILLIAM POWER, who witnessed a performance by McGonagall, described him, aptly, as 'the Ossian of the ineffably absurd'.

WORKS: *Poetic Gems* (1890)

EDITIONS (collections of broadsheet poems; all published in London): *More Poetic Gems* (1962); *Last Poetic Gems* (1968); *McGonagall: a Library Omnibus* (1969); *Further Poetic Gems* (1980); *Still More Poetic Gems* (1980); *Yet More Poetic Gems* (1980)

Macgregor, James [Dean of Lismore] (*d* 1551). Anthologist. He was the son of the hereditary vicar of Fortingall in Perthshire, to which he himself succeeded in 1514. His *Magnum opus* is the anthology of Gaelic verse which has come to be known as the BOOK OF THE DEAN OF LISMORE. It contains Gaelic poems by Scottish authors, work by Irish poets and heroic poems from the Ossianic cycle, and its rediscovery in the 18th century proved the range and catholicity of Scots Gaelic bardic verse. Macgregor compiled the anthology with his brother Duncan and it is one of the most important source books of early Gaelic poetry.

Macgregor, Rob Roy (1671–1734). The younger brother of the chief of the Clan Macgregor, Rob Roy farmed at Balquhidder and was a noted cattle thief and outlaw. He was imprisoned several times before his death in 1734 and is the subject of a novel, ROB ROY, by Sir WALTER SCOTT.

McIlvanney, William Angus (*b* 1936). Novelist. He was born on 25 November 1936 in Kilmarnock. Educated at Kilmarnock Academy and at the University of Glasgow, he became a schoolteacher in 1960. In 1975 he resigned to become a full-time writer. He has held creative writing fellowships at the universities of Strathclyde and Aberdeen and he taught for a year at the University of Grenoble.

McIlvanney's first novel, *Remedy is None*, was published in 1966. It is a violent onslaught on bourgeois values in which a young man, Charlie, comes face to face with the strengths of his own working-class past. It was a theme McIlvanney returned to in *Docherty* (1975), a powerful and moving evocation of Graithnock, an industrial town in the west of Scotland. Loosely based on Kilmarnock as it was in the first quarter of the century, McIlvanney's chosen instrument of interpretation is the young, all-seeing, all-knowing boy, Conn Docherty. Through his eyes we see the strengths and the weaknesses of the small, claustrophobic mining community and become aware of its mores and of its own inner sense of rhythm. Striding through the novel like a colussus is the figure of Tam Docherty, Conn's father, a man possessed of his own sense of virtue and yet alive to a knowledge of the working man's degraded place in society. Although Tam Docherty resembles many other Scottish fictional father figures, with his brooding and frequently violent temperament, unlike John Gourlay in THE HOUSE WITH THE GREEN SHUTTERS or John Guthrie in A SCOTS QUAIR he possesses both a stern, austere morality and a sense of humour. McIlvanney's poetry is published in his collection *The Longships in the Harbour* (1970).

WORKS: *Remedy is None* (1966); *A Gift from Nessus* (1968); *The Longships in the Harbour* (1970); *Docherty* (1975); *Laidlaw* (1978)

MacIntyre, Duncan Ban. The English name of DONNCHADH BÀN MAC AN T-SAOIR.

MacIntyre, John ['John Brandane'] (1869–1947). Dramatist. John MacIntyre, who wrote under the name 'John Brandane', was born in Rothesay on the Isle of Bute. As a boy he worked in a Glasgow cotton mill and between 1883 and 1895 as a clerk in a warehouse, attending evening classes in his spare time. He entered the University of Glasgow where he studied medicine, graduating as a doctor in 1901. While working as a surgeon at Glasgow Royal Infirmary, he began his lifelong friendship with another doctor-turned-dramatist, O. H. MAVOR, better known by his pen-name 'James Bridie'. MacIntyre's career was interrupted by World War I, during which he served on the French sector of the Western Front at Arc-en-Barrois near Verdun. On demobilization he became medical officer at Lochgoilhead in Argyll and later he was a general practitioner on the island of Mull.

MacIntyre's early involvement with the theatre came from his interest in the Abbey Theatre of Dublin, whose company visited Glasgow regularly during the 1920s. In 1922 he became a founder-member of the Scottish National Players, for whom he wrote his most successful play, *The Glen is Mine* (1923). Set, as are most of his plays, in the Highlands, it deals with a problem central to the contemporary Scottish Highland way of life: whether to cling to the old habits and customs of a rural life or to embrace a new set of values dictated by industrial progress. Although MacIntyre balked at providing a solution and allowed the plot to drift off into a mist of sentimentality, the play is memorable for the Gaelic cadences of the dialogue and for the fully realized central character of Angus the crofter. His other plays are *The Lifting, The Inn of Adventure, Heather Gentry*, and *The Treasure Ship*, a comedy centred on the legend of the Tobermory treasure galleons. He also wrote a number of one-act plays, including the much performed *Rory Aforesaid*, and three novels, *My Lady of Aros* (1910), *The Captain More* (1923) and *Strawfeet* (1932). Through his writing and his enthusiastic support for the Scottish National Players, then Scotland's only indigenous theatre company, the name of John Brandane is honoured in the history of drama in Scotland during the 20th century.

WORKS: *My Lady of Aros* (1910); *Glenforsa* (1921); *Change House* (1921); *The Captain More* (1923); *The Glen is Mine and The Lifting* (1925); *Three Plays: The Treasure Ship, Rory Aforesaid, The Happy War* (1928); *Heather Gentry* (1932); *Strawfeet* (1932); *The Spanish Galleon* (1932); *Man of Uz* (1938)

MacKay, Robert [Rob Donn]. The English name of ROB DONN MACAOIDH.

Mackenzie, Agnes (Muriel) Mure (1891–1955). Historian and novelist. Agnes Muriel Mackenzie (she adopted 'Mure' for her books) was brought up in Stornoway on the island of Lewis, where her father was a doctor. After graduating from the University of Aberdeen she lectured in English there during the years of World War I. In 1920 she was appointed to a similar position at Birkbeck College, London, and shortly thereafter become a full-time writer. Her first works were historical novels, but despite their accuracy of detail they possessed neither credible characters nor a strong narrative line. Her study *The Women in Shakespeare's Plays* (1924) arose out of her doctoral thesis but her main historical and literary work was devoted to things Scottish. Until her death on 26 February 1955 in Edinburgh she remained a patriot and a loyal supporter of Scottish culture. Throughout her life she was dogged by bad eyesight and hearing, but she refused to allow these handicaps to hinder her progress and she was a prolific author. Her *Historical Survey of Scottish Literature to 1714* (1933) contains a stimulating study of the MAKARS and is especially revealing about WILLIAM DUNBAR. She also wrote on ROBERT I (Robert the Bruce) and the later Stewart monarchs, and a glance at her publications reveals her range of interests. Particularly rewarding is her anthology of Scottish writing in three volumes, *Scottish Pageant* (1946–9). For her services to Scottish literature she was made a CBE in 1945 and her *alma mater* awarded her an LLD in 1951.

WORKS: *Spilt Ink* (1913); *Without Conditions* (1923); *The Women in Shakespeare's Plays* (1924); *The Half Loaf* (1925); *The Quiet Lady* (1926); *Lost Kinellan* (1927); *The Playgoer's Handbook to English Renaissance Drama* (1927); *The Process of Literature* (1929); *Keith of Kinellan* (1930); *Cypress in Moonlight* (1931); *Between Sun and Moon* (1932); *An Historical Survey of Scottish Literature to 1714* (1933); *Robert Bruce, King of Scots* (1934); *Single Combat* (1934); *The Rise of the Stewarts* (1935); *The Scotland of Queen Mary* (1936); *The Passing of the Stewarts* (1937); *The Foundations of Scotland* (1938); *I was at Bannockburn* (1939); *The Kingdom of Scotland* (1940); *Scotland's Past History* (1941); *The Arts and the Future of Scotland* (1942); *Scotland in Modern Times, 1720-1939* (1942); *The Springing Thistle* (1942); *Scottish Pageant*, 3 vols. (1946–9); ed., *Old Scottish Christmas Hymns* (1947); *A History of Britain and Europe for Scottish Schools*, 3 vols. (1949–51); *Apprentice Majesty* (1950); *What we do in Church* (1951); *Rival Establishments in Scotland 1560-1690* (1952); *David I* (1953); *A Garland of Scottish Prose* (1956); *The Edinburgh of Queen Mary* (1958)

Mackenzie, Sir (Edward Montague) Compton (1883–1974). Novelist and journalist. He was born on 17 January 1883 in West Hartlepool; his name was originally Edward Montague Compton, but he took the family name Mackenzie to emphasise his Scottish heritage. He was educated at St Paul's School and Magdalen

College, Oxford, and studied for the English Bar but gave up his legal studies in 1907 on the production of his first work, a play called *The Gentleman in Grey*. His first novel, *The Passionate Elopement* (1911) was followed by his story of English theatre life, *Carnival* (1912), which enjoyed a huge popular success. His early career was crowned by the publication of another autobiographical and equally successful novel, *Sinister Street* (1913), which attracted the critical acclaim of both Henry James (1843–1916) and Ford Madox Ford (1876–1939). All his early work is characterized by a sensuous lyricism and *Sinister Street* is one of the best examples of the English *Bildungsroman* of the period.

During World War I Mackenzie served in the Dardanelles and later worked for military intelligence in Greece experience that prompted him to write his bestselling book on the secret service, *Extremes Meet* (1928). For a short period after the war, he was associated with George Norman Douglas on Capri, and the Mediterranean influence was to remain strong in much of his work of that period the best novel being *Vestal Fire* (1927), an energetic and extravagant study of two American spinsters' infatuation for a pederastic French count with artistic inclinations. In 1928 Mackenzie settled in Scotland on the Isle of Barra in the Outer Hebrides and became an early member and supporter of the Scottish Nationalist Party. He started the short-lived radio magazine *Vox* in 1929 and he enjoyed much success as a broadcaster: a broadcast lecture he gave in December 1929 inspired his friend the poet Hugh MacDiarmid to write his nationalistic poem, 'The Little White Rose of Scotland'.

Mackenzie's most significant work is the quartet of novels *The Four Winds of Love* (1937–45) in which a philosophy of the social, economic and political development of the modern world emerges through the story of John Ogilvie and his life and travels. Each of the 'winds' offers a different aspect of love and friendship spanning three generations, and the whole work, in its six volumes, runs to 3000 pages. Mackenzie's strengths in this work lie in his ability to master the many characters and their own ideas as he moves Ogilvie from country to country in search of his destiny. A complex structural symbolism holds together this complicated novel – the winds stand for the four ages of man as well as portraying different aspects of erotic love – whose short-comings arise from the lack of character development than from Mackenzie's easy ability to examine the manifold problems caused by the impingement of scientific development on older, more traditional cultural mores.

In his later years, Mackenzie turned to writing a number of finely observed comedies of Scottish life and manners, including *The Monarch of the Glen* (1941 and *Whisky Galore* (1947) which, like its successor *Rockets Galore* (1957), was made into a successful film. As in all his works, his Scottish comic novels – for which he is perhaps best known – are characterized by their farcical plots, racy dialogue and by Mackenzie's insistence on an elegant prose style.

Mackenzie became a Catholic in 1914 and his last years were spent in Edinburgh where he died on 30 November 1972. His autobiography, *My life and Times*, begun in 1963 and completed in 1971, runs to ten volumes and is a remarkable and faithfully recorded account of the life, travels and friendships of one of the best-known Scottish writers writers of the 20th century.

WORKS: *Poems* (1907); *The Passionate Elopement* (1911); *Carnival* (1912); *Kensington Rhymes* (1912); *Sinister Street* (1913); *Guy and Pauline* (1915); *Plashers Mead* (1915); *The Early Life and Adventures of Sylvia Scarlett* (1918); *Poor Relations* (1919); *Sylvia and Michael* (1919); *The Vanity Girl* (1920); *Rich Relations* (1921); *Never Say Die* (1922); *The Parson's Progress* (1923); *The Seven Ages of Women* (1923); *The Heavenly Ladder* (1924); *The Old Men of the Sea* (1924); *Santa Claus in Summer* (1924); *Coral* (1925); *Fairy Gold* (1926); *Mabel in Queer Street* (1927); *Rogues and Vagabonds* (1927); *Vestal Fire* (1927); *Extraordinary Women* (1928); *Extremes Meet* (1928); *The Unpleasant Visitors* (1928); *The Adventures of Two Chairs* (1929); *Gallipoli Memories* (1929); *The Three Couriers* (1929); *April Fools* (1930); *The Enchanted Blanket* (1930); *Buttercups and Daisies* (1931); *The Conceited Doll* (1931); *Our Street* (1931); *The Fairy in the Window Box* (1932); *Greek Memories* (1932); *Prince Charlie* (1932); *The Dining Room Battle* (1933); *Literature in My Time* (1933); *The Lost Cause* (1933); *Reaped and Bound* (1933); *Water on the Brain* (1933); *The Enchanted Island* (1934); *Marathon and Salamis* (1934); *Prince Charlie and His Ladies* (1934); *Catholicism in Scotland* (1936); *Figure of Eight* (1936); *First Athenian Memories* (1936); *The Naughtymobile* (1936); *The Four Winds of Love*, 6 vols. (1937–45); *Pericles* (1937); *The Stairs that Kept Going Down* (1937); *The Window Tapestry* (1938); *A Musical Chair* (1939); *Aegean Memories* (1940); *The Monarch of the Glen* (1941); *The Red Tapeworm* (1941); *Keep the Home Guard Turning* (1943); *Mr Roosevelt* (1943); *Wind of Freedom* (1943); *Brockhouse* (1945); *Dr Benes* (1946); *The Vital Flame* (1947); *Whisky Galore*

(1947); *All Over the Place* (1948); *Hunting the Fairies* (1949); *The Adventures of Sylvia Scarlett* (1950); *Eastern Epic* (1951); *The House of Coalport* (1951); *I Took a Journey* (1951); *The Rival Monster* (1952); *The Queen's House* (1953); *The Savoy of London* (1953); *Ben Nevis Goes East* (1954); *Echoes* (1954); *Realms of Silver* (1954); *My Record of Music* (1955); *The Altar Steps* (1956); *Thin Ice* (1956); *Rockets Galore* (1957); *Sublime Tobacco* (1957); *The Lunatic Republic* (1959); *Cats Company* (1960); *Greece in my Life* (1960); *Catmint* (1961); *Mezzotint* (1961); *On Moral Courage* (1962); *Look at Cats* (1963); *My Life and Times*, 10 vols. (1963–71); *Little Cat Lost* (1965); *The Stolen Sparrow* (1965); *Paper Lives* (1966)

REFERENCE: L. Robertson, *Compton Mackenzie: an Appraisal of his Literary Work* (London, 1954)

Mackenzie, Sir George (i), Viscount Tarbat, Earl of Cromartie (1630–1714). Historian and politician. He was born in Fife and was educated at the universities of St Andrews and Aberdeen, where he studied law. His support for Charles II brought him to prominence in legal circles and he became a Lord of Session in 1661. During the domination of the Earl of Lauderdale (1616–82) Mackenzie fell from grace but by 1681 he was Lord Justice General and a Privy Councillor, and until his death in 1714 he held a number of powerful political positions, including Secretary of State (1702–04). Mackenzie was a founding member of the ROYAL SOCIETY OF EDINBURGH and he published numerous essays on religious and political matters. Given to vacillating in political life, especially in his attitude to the ACT OF UNION, Mackenzie was created Viscount Tarbat in 1685 and Earl of Cromartie in 1703.

WORKS: *A Memorial for His Highness the Prince of Orange* (1689); *The Mistaken Advantages by Raising of Money* (1695); *A Vindication of Robert III of Scotland* (1695); *Parainesis pacifica* (1702); *Trialogus* (1706); *Synopsis apocalyptica* (1708); *Several Proposals conducing to a Farther Union of Britain* (1711); *An Historical Account of the Conspiracy by the Earl of Gowrie* (1713)

Mackenzie, Sir George (ii), of Rosehaugh (1636–91). Essayist and Lord Advocate. He was born in Dundee, the son of the 2nd Earl of Seaforth. He studied at the universities of St Andrews and Aberdeen and completed his education at Bourges, where he read civil law. In 1659 he was called to the Scottish Bar and, following an elegant, though unsuccessful, defence of the Marquis of Argyll in 1661, he rose quickly in the legal hierarchy. He became Member of Parliament for Ross in 1669 and was appointed a Justice-Depute, although he had to wait until 1677 to become Lord Advocate, ahead of his rival Sir George Lockhart. In this position he conducted the prosecutions of the COVENANTERS, a task he set about with considerable zeal, even if his reputation as the 'Bluidy Mackenzie' of Covenanting legend, who appears in Sir Walter Scott's OLD MORTALITY, is something of an exaggeration: Mackenzie upheld the law of the land and the tortures and corruption of witnesses employed in his courts were standard legal practices in his day. During the reign of James II he lost his power for his refusal to accept the king's Catholicism, but he remained a loyal supporter of the Crown at the time of the Glorious Revolution (1688). His last years were spent in England and he died on 8 May 1691.

During his time as Dean of the FACULTY OF ADVOCATES, Mackenzie pressed for the establishment of a scholarly library in Edinburgh and in 1689 he presided over the opening of the Advocates' Library, which was later to form the basis of the NATIONAL LIBRARY OF SCOTLAND. Mackenzie wrote widely on political and legal matters: his *Institutions of the Law of Scotland* (1684) was superseded by Stair's greater work, he advocated despotism in *Jus regium* (1684), and he wrote two historical works which throw much useful light on the affairs of his day, *A Vindication of the Government of Scotland during the Reign of King Charles II* (1683) and *Memoirs of the Affairs of Scotland from the Restoration of King Charles II* which was not published until 1821. A clear, uncomplicated thinker, Mackenzie was also an elegant prose stylist who defended the use of Scots. In 1663 he published his *Religio stoici*, an essay in the style of Sir Thomas Browne (1605–82), in which Mackenzie stated his moral position and added a plea for religious toleration; he later wrote essays entitled *Preferring Solitude* (1665) and *The Moral History of Frugality* (1691). His one poem, *Caelia's Country House and Closet*, appeared in 1667.

To Mackenzie falls the distinction of having written Scotland's first novel, ARETINA (1660). In four books, of which the third is a coded history of the country from the reign of JAMES VI to that of Charles II, the novel is a pastoral romance set in Egypt and Persia; its complicated plot deals basically with the stories of two knights, Megistus and Philarites, their love for Agapeta and Aretina, and their battles against the intrigues of Sophander, the

favourite of the King of Egypt, and later (in book 4) with Ophni, Duke of Iris, who kidnaps Aretina. the novel incorporates many of the traditional elements of early prose romance: an exotic setting, chivalry, love interest and political intrigue; it also includes an 'Apologie for Romance', a dedication 'To all the Ladies of this Nation' and two Royalist poems by Mackenzie. A planned second part was never realized, doubtless because Mackenzie had moved on to a more complicated and busy political life.

WORKS: *Aretina* (1660); *Religio stoici* (1663); *A Moral Essay* (1665); *Preferring Solitude* (1665); *Caelia's Country House and Closet* (1667); *Moral Gallantry* (1667); *A Moral Paradox* (1667); *Pleadings in some Remarkable Cases before the Supreme Court of Scotland* (1672); *The Laws and Customes of Scotland* (1678); *Observations on the Laws and Customs of Nations as to Precedency* (1680); *Idea eloquentiae forensis hodiernae* (1681); *A Vindication of the Government of Scotland during the Reign of King Charles II* (1683); *The Institutions of the Law of Scotland* (1684); *Jus regium* (1684); *A Defence of the Antiquity of the Royal Line of Scotland* (1685); *Oration inauguratis habita edinburgi* (1689); *De humanae rationis imbecilitate* (1690); *Reason* (1690); *The Moral History of Frugality* (1691); *The Spirit of Fanaticism* (1710); *Essays upon Several Moral Subjects* (1713); *A Discourse concerning the Three Unions between England and Scotland* (1714); *Works*, 2 vols. (1716–22); *Memoirs of the Affairs of Scotland from the Restoration of King Charles II* (1821)

REFERENCE: A. Lang, *Sir George Mackenzie, King's Advocate, of Rosehaugh: his Life and Times* (London, 1909)

Mackenzie, Henry (1745–1831). Novelist and essayist. He was born on 26 July 1745 in Edinburgh, the son of a doctor. He was educated at the HIGH SCHOOL OF EDINBURGH from 1751 until 1758, when he entered the University of Edinburgh to study in the humanities class of Professor George Stuart. In 1761 he was articled to George Inglis of Redhall, a King's Attorney in Exchequer, and he remained with him until November 1765, when he was admitted Attorney in the Court of Exchequer in Scotland. That same year he went to London to work in the English Exchequer, where he remained until he set up practice in the Court of Exchequer in Edinburgh in 1769. In 1771 he purchased the Crown practice of his mentor George Inglis and became one of the leading attornies in taxation; because the Court was governed by London he was a frequent visitor there and he became a close friend and confidant of many leading lawyers and politicians. He married Penuel

Grant, the daughter of the Chief of Clan Grant, on 6 January 1776.

During his legal apprenticeship Mackenzie contributed to the SCOTS MAGAZINE AND GENERAL INTELLIGENCER a number of sentimental verses and romantic ballads, including the popular 'Kenneth' and 'Duncan' which were later collected by DAVID HERD in ANCIENT AND MODERN SCOTTISH SONGS (1776). In 1771 he published the novel for which he is best known, THE MAN OF FEELING, a highly wrought sentimental story, whose hero, Harley, is presented as possessing an ideal sensitivity and as being above the ways of the world. The novel enjoyed considerable success in its day and in later years Mackenzie came to be known himself as 'The Man of Feeling'. He published two other novels in the same sentimental vein, *The Man of the World* (1773) and *Julia de Rubigne* (1777). Mackenzie was a supporter of the Edinburgh theatre and also enjoyed the friendship in London of David Garrick, for whom he wrote the tragedy *The Spanish Father* (1773), which was never performed. In March 1773 his play *The Prince of Tunis*, a heroic tragedy set in the time of Frederick Barbarossa, Holy Roman Emperor, was produced in Edinburgh and it remained a popular play in the Scottish dramatic repertoire throughout Mackenzie's lifetime.

Through his standing as a lawyer and his contributions to literary and learned journals, Mackenzie became one of the leading members of Edinburgh's literary society. He became a member of the influential Mirror Club in 1777 and was appointed editor of its journal, THE MIRROR, which was printed by WILLIAM CREECH. The same club later produced a similar journal, THE LOUNGER, between 1785 and 1787; as the editor of both publications Mackenzie attempted to improve the literary climate of Scotland by imitating the tone and manners of Addison and Steele. On 7 December 1786 Mackenzie published in *The Lounger* his famous essay on ROBERT BURNS to mark the publication of the KILMARNOCK EDITION of his poems; he described Burns as 'this heaven-taught ploughman' and his favour assured Burns of success in Edinburgh. Although the review helped to make the poet's reputation, Mackenzie singled out for praise the moral and sentimental poems written in English and largely ignored the poems in Scots.

In 1783 Mackenzie was one of the founders of the ROYAL SOCIETY OF EDINBURGH and a

year later he helped to establish the Highland Society of Scotland, which was established to promote an interest in Gaelic language and culture. For the Highland Society in 1804 he chaired a committee which reported inconclusively on the authenticity of the OSSIAN poems of JAMES MACPHERSON. In his later years Mackenzie became a grand old man of letters and he was the link between the great literary figures of the 18th-century SCOTTISH ENLIGHTENMENT and the age of Sir WALTER SCOTT. His memories and observations of that long period were published after his death in the readable collection *Anecdotes and Egotisms* (1927).

A supporter of the Dundas régime, in 1799 Mackenzie was appointed Comptroller of Taxes for Scotland, a lucrative position which he held until his death on 14 January 1835. There is a sympathetic portrait of him in Lockhart's PETER'S LETTERS TO HIS KINSFOLK and he was a regular contributor to BLACKWOOD'S MAGAZINE. In 1814 Scott dedicated his novel WAVERLEY to Mackenzie, calling him 'our Scottish Addison'.

WORKS: *The Man of Feeling* (1771); *The Pursuits of Happiness* (1771); *The Man of the World* (1773); *The Prince of Tunis* (1773); *Julia de Rubigne* (1777); *Life and Writings of John Home* (1822); *Virginia* (1824)

EDITIONS: H. W. Thompson, ed., *The Anecdotes and Egotisms of Henry Mackenzie* (London 1927); H. W. Drescher, ed., *Letters to Elizabeth Rose of Kilravock 1768–1815* (Edinburgh, 1967)

REFERENCE: H. W. Thompson, *A Scottish Man of Feeling* (London, 1931)

Mackie, A(lbert) D(avid) (*b* 1904). Poet and dramatist. He was born on 18 December 1904 in Edinburgh and was educated there at London Street School and at Broughton School. After graduating from the University of Edinburgh in 1927, he was a schoolmaster for a period, before embarking on a long and distinguished career in journalism. He has worked for several Scottish newspapers: between 1930 and 1935 he was a leader writer for THE SCOTSMAN and he edited the *Edinburgh Evening Dispatch* from 1946 until 1954. Under his pen-name 'Macnib' he has contributed to the press many learned articles on Scotland's cultures and he has also written much on Edinburgh's history and traditions. He was one of the first of the group of poets who took to writing in a revitalized Scots during the period that has come to be known as the SCOTTISH RENAIS-

SANCE, and his *Poems in Two Tongues* (1928) was particularly admired for his easy and colloquial use of Scots. Mackie also wrote a number of plays for the Edinburgh Gateway Theatre, including *The Hogmanay Story, Festival City* and *MacHattie's Hotel*.

WORKS: *Poems in Two Tongues* (1928); *A Call from Warsaw* (1944); *Sing a Sang o' Scotland* (1944); *The Hearts* (1958); *The Book of Macnib* (1960); *Scottish Pageantry* (1967); *Donald's Dive* (1971); *The Scotch Comedians* (1973); *The Scotch Whisky Drinker's Companion* (1973); *Talking Glasgow* (1978); *Speak Scotch or Whistle* (1979)

Mackie, Alastair (*b* 1925). Poet. He was born on 10 August 1925 in Aberdeen and was educated there at Robert Gordon's College and at the University. After graduating in 1950 he taught in Stromness, Orkney, and in Anstruther, Fife, where he has lived since 1959. During World War II he served with the Royal Air Force and the Royal Navy. Like his fellow Aberdonian ALEXANDER SCOTT (ii), Mackie employs to good effect in his poetry the vigorous Scots of his childhood, but he is also not afraid of linguistic innovation, proving that Scots is capable of embracing words that are not in everyday currency. As a result his poems have a richness and virtuosity of vocabulary and, for all their many difficulties of meaning, repay careful reading. His ironic wit and intellectual energy are especially prevalent in 'Hamesucken' and 'Drappit', two of the most satisfying poems from his collection *Clytach* (1972).

WORKS: *Soundings* (1966); *To Duncan Glen* (1971); *Clytach* (1972); *At the Heich Kirk-Yaird* (1974)

Mackintosh, Ewart Alan (1893–1917). Poet. He was born in Brighton of Highland parents and was educated at St Paul's School and Christ Church, Oxford, where he studied classics and also perfected his childhood knowledge of Gaelic. At the outbreak of World War I he was commissioned in the 5th Seaforth Highlanders and was transferred to the Western Front in July 1915. For his bravery during the Battle of the Somme in 1916 he was awarded the Military Cross, but after being gassed at High Wood he was invalided home. The opportunity of a safe promotion, instructing cadets in Cambridge, was offered to him but Mackintosh volunteered for further service in France and he was killed fighting with the 4th Seaforths at the Battle of Cambrai.

Mackintosh started writing poetry at Oxford, but his early verse was merely a limpid imitation of poets such as W. B. Yeats (1865–1939) and he was much influenced by the movement known as the CELTIC TWILIGHT school. Like many other poets of his generation who fought in the war, he found his true voice while serving in France, and with his contemporary C. H. SORLEY he is Scotland's most distinguished war poet. Initially, his poems exulted in the excitement and glory of warfare but this heroic mood quickly gave way to work that reflected his feelings of horror and anguish at the unnecessary shedding of blood on the Western Front. 'In a Wood' gives a vividly horrifying account of a regiment of raw soldiers under bombardment, and of the benison of prayer, an image that runs through much of his later poetry. In his second collection of verse, *War, the Liberator* (1918), he attempted a prose exegesis of his own and other soldiers' feelings in three essays called 'Studies in War Psychology'. Mackintosh was also a songwriter with a gift for parody and a sure ear for the cadences and phrases of folk-song, and many of his compositions enjoyed a wide currency among Scottish troops on the Western Front.

WORKS: *A Highland Regiment* (1917); *War, the Liberator* (1918); *Miserere* (1919)

MacLachlainn, Eoghan (Ewan MacLachlan) (1775–1822). Poet and translator. He was a native of Lochaber. After a rudimentary education in Fort William he became a private tutor, using both the hours of his calling and his spare time to further his study of Greek and Latin. In 1796 he gained admittance to King's College, Aberdeen, and although he later attended the Divinity Hall with a view to being licensed as a preacher, friends, including the philosopher JAMES BEATTIE, encouraged him to aspire to a life of scholarship. He became a master at Aberdeen Grammar School and librarian to King's College, but ill health forced him to leave Aberdeen and he died on 29 March 1822 in Ayrshire. His years of scholarship in Aberdeen led to his involvement in the production of a Gaelic dictionary and he translated into Gaelic seven books and a fragment of the *Iliad*. Much of his verse was written in Latin and is standard praise poetry, but his verse in Gaelic is more memorable. He wrote a sequence of poems on the seasons in the manner of JAMES THOMSON (i) and his work has been compared to that of his contemporaries

ALASDAIR MAC MHAIGHSTIR ALASDAIR and DONNCHADH BÀN MAC AN T-SAOIR.

EDITION: J. Macdonald, ed., *Ewan MacLachlan's Gaelic Verse* (Aberdeen, 1937)

Maclaren, Ian. Pen-name of JOHN WATSON.

Maclaren, James. Pen-name of CHRISTOPHER MURRAY GRIEVE.

Maclean, Alasdair (*b* 1926). Poet. He was born on 16 March 1926 in Glasgow. Since childhood his life has been peripatetic, and after spending time as a mature student at the University of Edinburgh he lived for several years in Ardnamurchan, the inspiration for several of the poems in *From the Wilderness* (1973). A sure eye for natural detail allied to an unsentimental approach to nature imbue his work, which is reminiscent in language and imagery of the poetry of NORMAN MACCAIG.

WORKS: *From the Wilderness* (1973); *Waking the Dead* (1976)

Maclean, John (1879–1923). Socialist and teacher. John Maclean was born on 14 August 1879 in Pollokshaws, Glasgow, the son of a potter. He was educated at Pollok Academy and between 1896 and 1898 as a student teacher, before becoming a part-time student at the University of Glasgow. He graduated in 1904 but by then his early interest in socialism had been strengthened by becoming a member of the Marxist Social Democratic Federation (later the Social Democratic Party). Maclean attached great importance to workers' education and he was partly responsible for the establishment of the Scottish Labour College. During World War I Maclean advocated a termination of hostilities and the ending of capitalism; he was arrested and imprisoned four times between 1916 and 1921 and was finally released on 22 October 1922. Maclean's position as a socialist and a nationalist is unrivalled in Scottish political history and his achievements in workers' education are important, but his health and his political stance were weakened by long periods of imprisonment. His work has been celebrated in poems by Hugh MacDiarmid (CHRISTOPHER MURRAY GRIEVE), SYDNEY GOODSIR SMITH, HAMISH HENDERSON and SOMHAIRLE MACGILL-EAIN.

MacLean, Sorley. The English name of SOMHAIRLE MACGILL-EAIN.

M'Lehose [née Craig] **Agnes** ['Nanay'] (1759–1841). She was born in Glasgow, the daughter of a surgeon and the niece of Lord Craig, an Edinburgh judge. In 1776 she married John M'Lehose, a dissolute lawyer whom she was forced to leave after the birth of their fourth child. She moved to Edinburgh, where she met ROBERT BURNS on 4 December 1787 in the house of a mutual friend, Miss Nimmo. Burns and Agnes M'Lehose were immediately attracted to each other and they entered into a torrid but chaste affair by exchange of letter, in which Burns took the sobriquet 'Sylvander' and she 'Clarinda'. Their highly stylized and courtly relationship petered out after Burns married JEAN ARMOUR, and ended on 27 December 1792. Burns wrote for 'Clarinda' one of his best love lyrics, the haunting song *Ae fond kiss and then we sever*, which was published in THE SCOTS MUSICAL MUSEUM (1792), to be sung to their air 'Rory Dall's Port'. The Sylvander–Clarinda relationship is the subject of the play *The Other Dear Charmer* by ROBERT KEMP.

McLellan, Robert (*b* 1907). Dramatist. He was born on 28 January 1907 at Linmill, Kirkfieldbank, in Lanarkshire, and a childhood spent there on a farm in the Clyde valley provided the inspiration for his *Linmill* stories, a selection of which was published in 1977. With their insistence on a boy's-eye view of the world and their humorous attitude to life, expressed in a rich Scots, the stories appear at first to have a childlike quality. But McLellan is too clever a writer to limit his canvas to a poetic expression of childhood. In *The Donegals* the boy-narrator's story of a battling Irish immigrant couple is stripped, layer by careful layer, to unveil the wide tapestry of the world of the grown-up and its intertwining relationships.

Though his *Linmill* stories may represent the flower of his literary art, it is as a playwright that McLellan made his reputation. His first major play, *Jamie the Saxt*, was produced in Glasgow in 1937 and it marked him as a writer thoroughly versed in the niceties of stagecraft. At the play's centre is JAMES VI and the action covers the troubled years of the 1590s when his throne was under threat from his cousin Francis, Lord Bothwell. McLellan stresses James's statecraft in protecting his position by playing off his nobles against one another, but he also remains true to the paradox in the king's character. The play is firmly rooted in McLellan's own researches into the period, but it is no mere historical pageant; rather it is a drama full of wit and repartee, all spoken in a vigorous earthy Scots. It was revived in 1946, 1953, 1956 and 1982. *Torwatletie* (1946), *The Flouers o' Edinburgh* (1947) and *Young Auchinleck* (1962) also deal with aspects of Scotland's past, and his other plays, with dates of first production, are: *Jeddart Justice* (1933), *Tarfessock* (1934), *The Changeling* (1934), *Cian and Eithne* (1935), *Toom Byres* (1936), *Portrait of an Artist* (1939), *The Carlin Moth* (1947), *The Cailleach* (1948), *The Smuggler* (1949), *Mary Stewart* (1951), *The Road to the Isles* (1954) and *The Hypocrite* (1967). McLellan has also written a long poem for television, *Arran Burn* (1965), which depicts the sights and sounds of the Isle of Arran where he has lived since 1938, and a dramatic poem for seven voices for radio, *Sweet Largie Bay* (1956).

WORKS: *Linmill and Other Stories* (1977); *Sweet Largie Bay and Arran Burn* (1977); *Collected Plays*, with an introduction by Alexander Scott (1981)

Macleod, Fiona. Pen-name of WILLIAM SHARP.

Macleod, Joseph ['Adam Drinan'] (*b* 1903). Poet. He was born on 24 April 1903 in Ealing, Middlesex, of Scottish parents, and was educated at Rugby and at Balliol College, Oxford. He was called to the English Bar in 1928 but never practised, his life being devoted to the theatre, radio and films until he retired to live in Italy. His early work was compared to that of Ezra Pound (1885–1972), but in the 1940s he turned to composing poems on Scottish themes, rich with the cadences of Gaelic speech. These were published under his pseudonym 'Adam Drinan'.

WORKS: *Beauty and the Beast* (1927); *The Ecliptic* (1930); *Foray of Centaurs* (1931); *Why not the Theatre?* (1935); *Overture to Cambridge* (1936); *Ghosts of the Strath* (1943); *The New Soviet Theatre* (1943); *Actors across the Volga* (1946); *A Job at the BBC* (1947); *The Passage of the Torch* (1951); *A Soviet Theatre Sketch Book* (1951); *Scenes in the Old Scottish Theatre* (1952); *Script from Norway* (1953); *People of Florence* (1968); *The Sisters of d'Aranyi* (1969); *An Old Olive Tree* (1971)
as Adam Drinan: *The Cove* (1940); *The Men of the Rocks* (1942); *Women of the Happy Island* (1944)

MacLeod, Mary. The English name of MÀIRI NIGHEAN ALASDAIR RUAIDH.

MacLeod, Norman (i) ['Caraid nan Gaidheal' (Friend of the Highlanders)] (1783–1862). Author. He was a pioneer in the development of short stories and journalism in Gaelic. His sobriquet refers as much to his work as a minister in Glasgow as to his own writing. Macleod edited two Gaelic magazines between 1829 and 1843, both of which provided a Gaelic readership with a wide range of prose works on contemporary matters and homiletic short stories. A collection of his literary work was published in 1867 after his death and it bears as its title the name that he had come to be known by in life.

Macleod, Norman (ii) (1812–72). Divine. He was born on 3 June 1812 at Campbeltown, Argyll, and his childhood was spent there and in Stirlingshire. Between 1827 and 1837 he studied for the ministry of the Church of Scotland, a period that was interrupted by his employment as a tutor to a Yorkshire family. In March 1838 he was ordained minister of the parish of Loudon in Ayrshire and he quickly made a name for himself in church circles as an invigorating and persuasive preacher. During THE DISRUPTION of 1843 Macleod remained with the Church of Scotland and transferred to Dalkeith, where he remained until his translation back to Glasgow in 1851. There he was able to put into effect many of the philanthropic theories he had expressed in his contributions to religious magazines during the 1840s. He favoured total abstinence and was an early supporter of the Church of Scotland's missions in India, which he visited on several occasions. In 1857 he was appointed chaplain to Queen Victoria and in 1869 he was Moderator of the General Assembly of the Church of Scotland. Macleod was a notable preacher and a liberal-minded minister who enjoyed the friendship of many people in Scotland and abroad. From 1860 until his death on 16 June 1872 he was the editor of the religious magazine *Good Words*, and in all his own writing there is a clarity of expression and lightness of touch that made him one of the most sought-after clerical writers of his day.

WORKS: *A Plea for Temperance* (1843); *A Catechism for Children* (1844); *The Home School* (1856); *Deborah* (1857); *An Old Lieutenant and his Son* (1862); *Parish Papers* (1862); *Wee Davie* (1864); *Eastward* (1866); *Simple Truth Spoken to Working People* (1866); *Reminiscences of a Highland Parish* (1867); *The Starling* (1867); *An Address on Missions* (1868);

Peeps at the Far East (1871); *The Temptation of Our Lord* (1872); *Character Sketches* (1872)

REFERENCE: D. Macleod, *Memoir of Norman Macleod*, 2 vols. (London, 1876)

MacMhuirich. The chief bardic family of Scotland (*see* BARD). The MacMhuirichs owed their origins to an equally powerful Irish Bardic family, the O Dalaighs. Like other bardic families in Scotland, they were landowners and enjoyed considerable temporal power. MacMhuirich bards flourished in the Highlands and Western Isles from the 13th to the 18th centuries and a good selection of the poetry of two of the greatest members of the family, Cathal and Niall, appears in the *Red Book of Clanranald*.

Macmillan, Roddy (1923–79). Dramatist and actor. He was born on 23 March 1923 in Glasgow of Highland parents. He trained as an aero-engineer but began his theatrical career in 1948 as an actor with the Glasgow Unity Theatre. He enjoyed a particularly successful career on the stage, but it was for television that he created the part for which he is best remembered, that of Para Handy in a series based on the Para Handy stories by NEIL MUNRO. He wrote two plays for the stage. *All in Good Faith*, which was produced at the Glasgow Citizens' Theatre in April 1954, caused a sensation with its vividly realistic portrayal of Glasgow working-class life. *The Bevellers* (1973) again showed that Macmillan had a sure ear for the cadences of workaday dialogue as well as an ability to pick out fine background detail; set in the bevelling shop of a Glasgow glassworks, it concentrates on the drabness of manual labour as a new apprentice is introduced to the grind of everyday life. Macmillan was a highly respected actor who did much to encourage the post-war revival of the theatre in Scotland. He died on 9 July 1979.

WORKS: *All in Good Faith* (1954); *The Bevellers* (1973)

McNeill, Dane. Pen-name of NEIL M. GUNN.

McNeill, F(lorence) Marian (1885–1973). Folklorist. She was born on 20 March 1885 at St Mary's Holm, Orkney. She was educated there and at the universities of Glasgow and Paris. After spending two years travelling in Europe she moved to London, where she became secretary to the Association for Moral and Social Hygiene. She also became an active suffragette. Following a breakdown in her health she took up private tutoring in Athens before returning to London to become a freelance journalist. In 1926 she went back to Scotland, where she worked for a time as a researcher for the SCOTTISH NATIONAL DICTIONARY in Edinburgh. She died on 22 February 1973 in Edinburgh.

F. Marian McNeill's only novel, *The Road Home* (1932) is a romance based loosely on her own life and it contains evocative scenes of life in Glasgow and London. By the time of its publication, however, her reputation had been made as a folklorist with *The Scots Kitchen* (1929). This pioneering work, which shows a fine regard for the niceties of Scottish social history, has been republished many times and is rightly regarded as a classic of its kind. As well as including many traditional recipes, F. Marian McNeill used her wide knowledge of the Scots language and the country's lore and traditions to illuminate Scotland's culinary history and especially its links with France. *The Scots Kitchen* was followed by two less successful books in similar vein, *The Book of Breakfasts* (1932) and *The Scots Cellar* (1956). Her magnum opus is *The Silver Bough* (1957–68), a four-volume study of the customs and traditions of Scotland. The first volume deals with Scots Folklore, volumes 2 and 3 with the national festivals from CANDLEMAS to HOGMANAY and the final volume with the local festivals of Scotland.

WORKS: *Iona: a History* (1920); *The Scots Kitchen* (1929); *The Book of Breakfasts* (1932); *The Road Home* (1932); *The Camper's Kitchen* (1933); *Recipes from Scotland* (1946); *An Iona Anthology* (1947); *Recommended Recipes* (1948); *The Scots Cellar* (1956); *The Silver Bough*, 4 vols. (1957–68); *Hallowe'en* (1970)

Macneill, Hector (1746–1818). Poet and novelist. He was born on 22 October 1746 at Rosebank, near Roslin in Midlothian, the son of a retired army officer, whose expensive tastes had plunged his family into poverty. As a result, Macneill was trained for a mercantile career and between 1760 and 1780 he occupied a number of posts as a trader in the West Indies before gaining a commission in the Royal Navy. By 1786 he was back in Scotland where he lived near Stirling and attempted to earn a living from his pen. In 1796 he won the financial security of a pension, awarded to him by an admirer, and he settled in Edinburgh, where he became a friend of the novelist and philanthropist ELIZABETH HAMILTON. It was in that city that he died on 15 March 1818.

Macneill's first novel, *The Memoirs of Charles Macpherson* (1800), is a thinly disguised account of his life and career in the West Indies, a theme that he took up again in *The Scottish Adventurers* (1812). As a poet he was influenced by Mrs Hamilton's improving ideals, and his two long poems, *Scotland's Skaith* and *The Waes o' War* berate the Scottish people for their addiction to alcohol. Neither work has any literary merit, although they were deservedly popular in philanthropic circles. He was more successful as a songwriter and his compositions *My Boy Tammy* and *Come under my plaidie* have a simple appeal, with their graceful melodic lines and heartfelt sentiments.

WORKS: *On the Treatment of Negroes in Jamaica* (1788); *The Harp* (1789); *Scotland's Skaith* (1795); *The Links o' War* (1796); *The Waes o' War* (1796); *The Memoirs of Charles Macpherson* (1800); *Poetical Works*, 2 vols. (1801); *The Pastoral or Lyric Muse of Scotland* (1809); *The Scottish Adventurers* (1812)

Macpherson, Ian (1905–44). Novelist. He was born on 5 October 1905 at Forres, Morayshire, but his family moved to the Mearns of Kincardineshire while he was still very young. He was educated at Mackie Academy, Stonehaven, and at the University of Aberdeen, and for much of the rest of his life the north-east of Scotland was his home. He was killed in a motor-bicycle accident in 1944. The pastoral background of his early years gave him the inspiration for his first novel, *Shepherd's Calendar*, published the year before *Sunset Song* by JAMES LESLIE MITCHELL ('Lewis Grassic Gibbon'), which was also set in the Mearns. Like Gibbon's novel, it is about the contrasting strengths and weaknesses of the farming community and it contains a delicate portrait of adolescent awakening. At the end of the story the hero, John Grant, like Chris Guthrie in *Sunset Song* and the other two novels in the trilogy A SCOTS QUAIR, becomes aware that he has escaped from the past into a new and uncertain future. That sense of epiphany is found again in *Land of our Fathers* (1933), which centres on the CLEARANCES of the Spey valley, a theme that is continued in *Pride in the Valley* (1936). Macpherson's last novel, *Wild Harbour* (1936), is a prophetic vision of a world destroyed by man's inhumanity to man, through warfare and the use of monstrous weapons.

WORKS: *Shepherd's Calendar* (1931); *Land of our Fathers* (1933); *Pride in the Valley* (1936); *Wild Harbour* (1936)

Macpherson, James (1736–96). Poet. He was born on 27 October 1736 at Ruthven, Inverness-shire, the son of a farmer. He was educated at both King's College and Marischal College, Aberdeen, and at the University of Edinburgh; he studied for the ministry, but abandoned that intention in 1756, when he became a teacher in his own village. Two years later he was in Edinburgh, where he published his epic work *The Highlander*, an ambitious and wordy poem which looked forward to many of the interests of his later life. Through his friendships with ADAM FERGUSON, HUGH BLAIR and JOHN HOME, Macpherson was encouraged to expand his interest in Gaelic oral poetry, some of which he had collected and translated. The result of their enthusiasm was the publication of *Fragments of Ancient Poetry Collected in the Highlands of Scotland and Translated from the Gallic or Erse Language* (1760), with an introduction by Hugh Blair, who suggested that, as the work only existed in fragments and had been collected from limited sources, great epic poetry relating to Fingal, as told by his son OSSIAN, was still extant in other parts of the Highlands. The book was an instant success and kindled hopes among the Edinburgh *literati* that Scotland possessed a body of classical poetry on a par with that of ancient Greece or Rome.

Macpherson was commissioned to visit the Highlands in August 1760 to search for lost epics, and his travels took him to Perthshire, Argyll, Inverness-shire, and the islands of Skye, the Uists, Benbecula and Mull. Although his field-work was thorough enough for its time, Macpherson was an indifferent Gaelic speaker and he had to rely on the co-operation of scholars such as Alexander Morrison of Skye for most of the translations. By early 1761 he was back in Edinburgh to work on a composition which he claimed had been created by Ossian, the son of the third-century hero Fingal, a Scottish counterpart of the Irish hero, Finn, of the Fenian cycle of legends. Published as *Fingal: an Ancient Epic Poem* (1761), it met with almost hysterical praise and was referred to in reviews as being the equal of anything written by Homer, Virgil or Milton. Its success owed much to the cult of the primitive savage and to the Augustan preference for imagination and the sublime; and it was to have a considerable influence on the Romantic movement in Europe. *Fingal* and the other 'Ossian' poems (*Fragments* and *Temora*) also introduced the Highlands as being a preserve of innocent tribesmen and noble heroes, a concept that foreshadowed later Victorian interest in the romantic view of Scotland and its past.

Edinburgh's literary society received *Fingal* and its successor, *Temora*, with uncritical praise, but as early as 1762 in England and Ireland, voices were raised against Macpherson, claiming that his work was fraudulent. Macpherson was invited to disclose his manuscript sources and his failure to do so only served to fuel the controversy, which was to last many years. The truth of the matter was that although Macpherson did collect material from original sources, he lacked both the sophistication of research procedures and the necessary knowledge of Gaelic to deal with the original fragments; having altered and amended them, he placed the poems together with passages of his own creation. His work was not completely faked – he used up to 15 original pieces – but he changed the themes and atmosphere to suit 18th-century taste.

After his 'Ossian' poems had been published Macpherson moved to London but in 1763 he sailed for Florida to take up the post of secretary to the Governor. But the work did not suit him and he returned to London in 1766, where he became a political writer and pamphleteer. Later he became a wealthy and fashionable man, with interests in the East India Company and tastes very far removed from those of the Edinburgh *literati* who had given him his start in life. He purchased an estate in his native Badenoch towards the end of his life and it was there that he died on 17 February 1796. At his own request and expense he was buried in Westminster Abbey, London.

WORKS: *The Highlander* (1758); *Fragments of Ancient Poetry Collected in the Highlands of Scotland and Translated from the Gallic or Erse Language* (1760); *Fingal: an Ancient Epic Poem* (1761); *Temora: an Ancient Epic Poem* (1763); *The Works of Ossian* (1765); *History of Great Britain from the Restoration till the Accession of George I* (1775)

REFERENCES: E. D. Snyder, *The Celtic Revival in English Literature* (Cambridge, Mass., 1923); D. S. Thomson, *The Gaelic Sources of Macpherson's 'Ossian'* (Edinburgh, 1952)

Macpherson, Mary. The English name of MÀIRI MHOR NAN ORAN.

MacQueen, Robert, Lord Braxfield (1722–99). Judge. He was born on 4 May 1722 in Lanark and was educated there at the Grammar School and at the University of Edinburgh. In 1744 he became an advocate and through his expertise in feudal law he was employed by the Crown in the cases of the forfeiture of Highland estates after the Jacobite rebellion of 1745. Thereafter his promotion was assured: he was appointed a Lord of Session in 1776, taking the name Braxfield from his father's estate, and became Lord Justice Clerk in 1788. In this capacity he earned a reputation as a brutal 'hanging judge' who hectored prisoners and counsel alike and who was given to insulting his victims: he is supposed to have jeered at a man whom he had sentenced to death, saying that 'he would be nane the waur o' a hangin''. He presided at the trial of THOMAS MUIR of Huntershill and the other 'political martyrs' of 1793, and he showed particular scorn for their ideas for social and political reform. MacQueen was uncompromising about using Scots in court and, like many other men of law of the same period, was widely read in Scots law and history. ROBERT LOUIS STEVENSON used him as the model for the overbearing, Scots-speaking Lord Hermiston in his unfinished novel WEIR OF HERMISTON.

MacThómais, Ruaraidh (Derick Thomson) (*b* 1921). Poet. He was born on 5 August 1921 in Stornoway on the Isle of Lewis. He was educated there at the Nicolson Institute and between 1939 and 1950 at the universities of Aberdeen and Cambridge and at the University College of North Wales, Bangor, his education being interrupted by war service in the Royal Air Force. Since graduating MacThómais has led a distinguished academic career at the universities of Aberdeen and Glasgow, where he became Professor of Celtic in 1963; his services to the administration of Gaelic literature and to the preservation of its culture are no less noteworthy; he has been editor of the magazine GAIRM since 1951 and he was one of the founders of the GAELIC BOOKS COUNCIL in 1968.

As a critic MacThómais's work includes *The Gaelic Sources of Macpherson's 'Ossian'* (1952), *Edward Lhuyd in the Scottish Highlands* (1963, with John Lorne Campbell) and *An Introduction to Gaelic Poetry* (1974), and he has also written on the future of the Highlands and of the Gaelic language and way of life. MacThómais's first collection of poems, *An Dealbh Briste*, was published in 1951 and his other collections are *Eadar Samhradh is Foghar* (1967), *An Rathad Cian* (1970) and *Saorsa agus an Iolaire* (1977). Many of his poems have been translated line-for-line by him into English, and his 1970 collection *An Rathad Cian* was published as *The Far Road* in 1971. Implicit in all MacThómais's poetry are two closely related themes: the life of the islands of his childhood, together with his sense of alienation from it, and a deep feeling of tender, though frequently exasperated, nationalism.

WORKS: *An Dealbh Briste* (1951); *The Gaelic Sources of Macpherson's 'Ossian'* (1952); ed., with J. L. Campbell, *Edward Lhuyd in the Scottish Highlands 1699–1700* (1963); *Eadar Samhradh is Foghar* (1967); ed., with Ian Grimble, *The Future of the Highlands* (1968); *An Rathad Cian* (1970); *An Introduction to Gaelic Poetry* (1974); *The New Verse in Scottish Gaelic: a Structural Analysis* (1974); ed., *Gaelic in Scotland* (1976); with Somhairle MacGill-Eain, Deòrsa Mac Iain Deòrsa, Iain Mac a'Ghobhainn and Domhnall MacAmhlaigh, *Nuabhàrdachd Ghaidhlig* (1976); *Saorsa agus an Iolaire* (1977); *Creachadh na Clàrsaich* (1982)

Magnus, St, Earl of Orkney (*fl* 1100). He was joint Earl of Orkney with his cousin Haakon, and a ruler renowned for his pacifism. Haakon's jealousy of his cousin's popularity led to a supposedly conciliatory meeting on the island of Egilsay; but Haakon tricked Magnus and took him prisoner. Although Magnus offered to go on a long pilgrimage, to be imprisoned or mutilated, he was killed by Haakon and his followers and buried at Christ's Church, Birsay. After his death miracles came to be associated with the place, and his nephew Rognvald built the Cathedral of Kirkwall in his memory, to which Magnus's remains were later removed. The story of St Magnus is told vividly in the ORKNEYINGA SAGA and he is the subject of a novel, *Magnus*, by GEORGE MACKAY BROWN.

Màiri Mhor nan Oran [Màiri nic-a-Phearsain (Mary Macpherson)] (1821–98). Poet. She was born on Skye and achieved her nickname, 'Big Mary of the Songs' through her prodigious height and weight and by her larger-than-life personality. Her popularity in Skye, and throughout the Highlands, was enhanced by her identification with the land reform movement and she was a plain-speaking critic of the earlier CLEARANCES. Many of her songs deal directly with the actions of the land reformers and are deliberate incitements, but she also wrote with great feeling about the island and the people of Skye. A good deal of her life was spent in Inverness and Glasgow. During her lifetime (and after her death) she enjoyed an almost legendary reputation for her fierce espousal of the crofters' cause in their struggle against the uncaring landowners. Her political poems also offer an unusual picture of the history and sociology of the people of her period.

WORK: Màiri nic-a-Phearsain, *Dàin agus Orain Ghàidhlig* (1891)

EDITION: D. E. Meek, ed., *Màiri Mhor nan Oran* (Glasgow, 1977)

Màiri nighean Alasdair Ruaidh [Mary MacLeod] (*c*1615–1705). Poet. She was born at Rodel in Harris. She claimed a connection with the MacLeods of Dunvegan in Skye and lived with them for many years, during which time she composed many songs and verses in the family's honour. From one of her surviving 16 works we discover that she was banished from Dunvegan for a time but was restored to favour in 1699 on the accession of Sir Norman, her favourite among the MacLeod chiefs. Other families who were the subjects of her praise poetry were the Mackenzies of Applecross, MacLeod of Raasay and Macdonald of Sleat, and it is for her proud, lyrical statements of the chiefs' grandeur and open-handed generosity that Màiri is best known. Her panegyrics were composed to be sung, and in all her work there is a careful balance of word to well-timed rhyme and metre. She eschewed classical syllabic metres, preferring the strophic metres that made her work so popular. Like IAIN LOM she stands at the watershed between the classical Gaelic poetry of earlier centuries and the flowering of popular versification of the 18th century.

EDITION: J. C. Watson, ed., *Gaelic Songs of Mary MacLeod*, SGTS (Edinburgh, 1965)

Maitland, Sir Richard, of Lethington (1496–1586). Poet and anthologist. He was born in present-day East Lothian. After training as a lawyer in St Andrews and Paris, he entered the service of JAMES V and later of MARY, Queen of Scots, and JAMES VI, becoming a Privy Counsellor, judge and, between 1562 and 1567, Keeper of the Great Seal. Although he became blind in middle life he kept up his political career, and at the age of 60 started writing tart satires on the customs and foibles of an age that was out of tune with his own beliefs and attitudes. 'Aganis the Theivis of Liddesdaill', a sharp comment on the troubled state of the Borders, is his best-known work; other pieces record his distaste for the Reformation period and lament the happier times of his youth. He lived to a grand old age, surviving most of the Reformation turmoil, and died on 20 March 1586.

Maitland owes his fame principally to his compilation of the Maitland Folio Manuscript (*see* MAITLAND MANUSCRIPTS), which includes 41 of his poems as well as 141 pieces by 15th- and early 16th-century makars, special prominence being given to WILLIAM DUNBAR. Second in importance only to the BANNATYNE MANUSCRIPT as a source of texts of the period, the Maitland Folio Manuscript and the Maitland Quarto Manuscript, compiled by his daughter Marie, are held by the Pepysian Library at Magdalene Collage, Cambridge. In 1828 the MAITLAND CLUB, named after Sir Richard, was established in Glasgow, for the publication of literary texts.

Maitland Club. A publishing society founded in Glasgow in 1828 for the purpose of editing and printing works of Scottish historical and literary interest. It was named after the 16th-century poet and editor, Sir RICHARD MAITLAND of Lethington.

Maitland Manuscripts. Two manuscripts held by Magdalene College, Cambridge, in the Pepysian Library. The Folio Manuscript was compiled by Sir RICHARD MAITLAND of Lethington and it opens with a selection of 41 of his own poems. The remaining 141 works reflect Maitland's own tastes and interests and include poems by WILLIAM DUNBAR, ROBERT HENRYSON, WALTER KENNEDY and ALEXANDER SCOTT (i). A vital source of medieval texts, the Folio Manuscript gives particular prominence to Dunbar. The Quarto Manuscript is the work of Maitland's daughter, Marie, and contains poetry of the 16th and 17th centuries, including the work of ALEXANDER ARBUTHNOT (ii), ALEXANDER MONTGOMERIE and JAMES VI.

EDITION: W. A. Craigie, ed., *The Maitland Folio Manuscript*, 2 vols., STS (Edinburgh, 1919–27); W. A. Craigie, ed., *The Maitland Quarto Manuscript*, STS (Edinburgh and London, 1920)

Major [Mair], John (1469–1550). Historian and philosopher. He was born in 1469 at Gleghornie, North Berwick, and was educated at the universities of Cambridge and Paris. He remained in Paris until 1518, when he was appointed Professor of Theology at the University of Glasgow, and in 1522 he moved to the University of St Andrews. Between 1525 and 1533 he was in Paris again, before returning to Scotland to become Provost of St Salvator's College in St Andrews. Major's best known work is his *Historia Majoris Britanniae* (1521), which deals with English and Scottish history and which advances the cause of the union of the two kingdoms. As a historian Major was more prepared than his contemporaries to rely on facts instead of myth and legend and his political philosophy embraced the theory that authority was vested in the people and not in kings. Although he upheld the teachings of Rome, he was an outspoken critic of corruption in the Church, and in his tract *Disputationes de potestate papae et concilii* (1526) he opposed the role of the clergy in lay affairs. In 1519 he published a Latin 'Commentary on the Sentences of Peter Lombard', and his other work of note is a commentary on the four gospels, *In quatuor evangelia expositiones luculentae* (1529).

WORKS: *In premium sententiarum* (1519); *Introductorium in Aristotelica Dialectica* (1521); *Disputationes de potestate papae et concilii* (1526); *Questiones logicales magistri Joannis Majoris* (1528); *In quatuor evangelia expositiones luculentae* (1529); *Sententiae veterum poetarum* (1541)

EDITION: A. Constable, trans. and ed., with a 'Life' by A. J. G. Mackay, *A History of Greater Britain as well England as Scotland, Translated from the Original Latin* (Edinburgh, 1892)

Makar. A Scots word meaning 'maker' or 'poet', which was used to describe the Scots poets of the 15th and 16th centuries. That it was in popular use may be seen in the 'Lament for the Makaris' by WILLIAM DUNBAR, which presents a roll-call of the poets of his age and bewails their untimely deaths. The last of the makars is generally supposed to have been ALEXANDER MONTGOMERIE. The makars wrote in Scots, and a hallmark of their style is the use of highly aureate diction in scenes of natural description. The term 'makars' was revived in the 20th century to describe the poets who wrote in Scots after the SCOTTISH RENAISSANCE begun by Hugh MacDiarmid (CHRISTOPHER MURRAY GRIEVE).

Makculloch Manuscript. A manuscript collection of poems in Scots written in 1477 at Louvain by a Scottish student named Magnus Makculloch, who later in life became a priest in Scotland. It was bought by the antiquary and historian DAVID LAING in 1854 and he bequeathed it subsequently to the library of the University of Edinburgh. With the GRAY MANUSCRIPT, the Makculloch is one of the earliest extant Scottish manuscripts and provides variant readings for three poems by ROBERT HENRYSON, including the prologue to the fables, and for 'Ane Ballat of Our Lady' by WILLIAM DUNBAR. The manuscript was edited and published by the SCOTTISH TEXT SOCIETY in 1918.

Malcolm III [Malcolm Canmore], King of Scots (c1031–93). Malcolm III is more generally known as 'Canmore' ('great head'; that is, chief). He spent most of his early years in England during the reign of MACBETH, whom he overthrew and defeated in 1057. He was married twice: to Ingebjorg, daughter of Thorfinn, Earl of Orkney; and to ST MARGARET, daughter of Edward 'the Exile' of Wessex. Much of his reign was spent in war against England and he was killed at the Battle of Alnwick on 13 November 1093.

Malloch [Mallet], **David** (c1705–65). Poet and man of letters. He was born at the beginning of the 18th century in Perthshire, the son of a schoolmaster, and a member of the outlawed Clan Macgregor. He was educated at the parish school in Crieff and served as a janitor at the HIGH SCHOOL OF EDINBURGH, before acting as tutor to various families between 1720 and 1723. His services as tutor to the children of the Duke of Montrose took him to London and also allowed him to travel in Europe. Through his friendship with JAMES THOMSON (i) he embarked on a literary career, and his ballad 'William and Margaret', based on an infamous seduction in St Andrews, was published in Allan Ramsay's THE TEA-TABLE MISCELLANY. Most of Malloch's work – the most popular being two sycophantic plays addressed to the royal family, *Eurydice* (1931) and *Mustapha* (1739), and a long poem *An Excursion*

(1728) – has been long forgotten, but in his lifetime he earned considerable notoriety for his attacks on Alexander Pope (1688–1744) and for an anonymous indictment by 'A Plain Man' against Admiral Byng (1704–57). In 1724 he changed his name to Mallet after the critic John Dennis (1657–1734) had satirized him as 'Moloch'; and in his dictionary, Samuel Johnson (1709–84), 'an unforgiving enemy' (*DNB*) gave the meaning of 'alias' as: 'otherwise, as Mallet *alias* Malloch, that is, otherwise Malloch'. Malloch died on 21 April in London.

WORKS: *An Excursion* (1728); *Eurydice* (1731); *Of Verbal Criticism* (1733); *Mustapha* (1739); *The Life of Francis Bacon* (1740); *Masque of Alfred* (1740); *Poems on Several Occasions* (1743); *The Works of Mr Mallet Consisting of Plays and Poems* (1743); *Amyntour and Theodora* (1747); *Memoirs of the Life and Ministerial Conduct of the Viscount Bolingbroke* (1752); *Britannia: a Masque* (1755); *Edwin and Emma* (1760); *Elvira* (1763); *William and Margaret* (1766)

EDITION: F. Dynsdale, ed., *Ballads and Songs* (London, 1857)

Man of Feeling, The. A novel by HENRY MACKENZIE, published in 1771, which belongs to the 'Sentimental' school of the late 18th century. 'Sentimentalism' portrayed an innate benevolence in man and novels written under its influence depicted a world where philanthropic action, sympathy and virtuous weeping were laudable facets of a man's character. The central character – 'The Man of Feeling' – Harley is presented as possessing an ideal sensitivity and as being above the ways of the world. There are two strands to the novel: Harley's own experience, where his innocence is contrasted with other people's worldliness, and the stories of the people he meets. A beggar too ill to work, a woman in Bedlam driven mad by love, a father whose son has been press-ganged, a prostitute seduced by a nobleman's son – for each of these Harley has tears and sympathy. In the last sequence he dies of joy when he discovers that his love for the virtuous Miss Walton is not, as he has imagined, unrequited. The narrative in the novel is related through a series of connected fragments or sequences. *The Man of Feeling* enjoyed a great success in its day, echoing as it did popular sentiments, and ROBERT BURNS called it 'a book I prize next to the Bible'. During his lifetime Mackenzie was known as 'The Man of Feeling'.

Margaret, St (c1046–93). Wife of MALCOLM III (Malcolm Canmore) and daughter of Edward 'the Exile' of the English royal house of Wessex. She was canonized in 1249 and the first biography of her was written by her confessor Turgot. During her reign Margaret attempted to civilize the Scottish court and she interfered in church politics to bring the liturgy into closer contact with Rome. She died in Dunfermline on 16 November 1093 after hearing of her husband's death at the Battle of Alnwick.

Marmion. A poem in six cantos, subtitled 'A Tale of Flodden Field', by Sir WALTER SCOTT, published in 1808. The poem is set in 1513, the year of the BATTLE OF FLODDEN, and the best scenes are the descriptions of the battle in canto VI and Marmion's evocative description of Edinburgh. The plot is tortuous and contrived. Lord Marmion, a fictitious knight at the court of Henry VIII, having tired of Constance de Beverley, courts Lady Clare, who is affianced to Sir Ralph de Wilton. Marmion accuses de Wilton of treachery and the forged letters he produces are corroborated by Constance. A duel is fought and de Wilton is left for dead and Lady Clare retires to a convent, while in a stylized Gothic scene Constance is tried and walled up alive for her perfidy. The two men meet again in Edinburgh where de Wilton is disguised as a palmer. From the Abbess of St Hilda he learns of Marmion's treachery and he is reunited with Lady Clare. Both de Wilton and Marmion fight in the English army at the Battle of Flodden, where Marmion is killed. The poem contains two of Scott's best-known songs, 'Where shall the lover rest?' and 'Lochinvar', and Scott prefaced each of the cantos with an introductory verse epistle addressed to his closest friends. These provide a private expression of his personality as well as much useful autobiographical information, and they have been compared to the verse epistles of ALLAN RAMSAY and ROBERT BURNS. Although *Marmion* is no longer considered Scott's greatest narrative poem – the central character is flawed, being at once a gallant knight and a treacherous coward – it is noteworthy for its wealth of description of the costume and architecture of the period.

Marshall, Bruce (b 1899). Novelist. He was born on 24 June 1899 and was educated at the universities of St Andrews and Edinburgh.

During World War I he served with the Royal Irish Fusiliers and he lost a leg in action. On returning to Edinburgh after the war he trained as an accountant, and between 1926 and 1940 he worked in Paris, before retiring to live in the south of France. He served with military intelligence during World War II and *The White Rabbit* (1952) is an account of the French Resistance movement as related to him by F. F. E. Yeo-Thomas (1901–64). Marshall's early novels dealt with religious matters, subjects he returned to in *Father Malachy's Miracle* (1931), *All Glorious Within* (1944), *A Thread of Scarlet* (1959), *The Bishop* (1970), *Urban the Ninth* (1973) and *Marx the First* (1975), all of which grapple with the problems Catholicism faces in the modern world. Farce is the keynote of much of his work and he has tackled the absurdities of international bureaucracy in *The Red Danube* (1947) and *A Girl from Lübeck* (1962). One of his most entertaining and successfully realized novels is *The Black Oxen* (1972), a satirical, but gently humorous account of three generations in an Edinburgh middle-class family.

WORKS: *This Sorry Scheme* (1925); *Teacup Terrace* (1926); *And there were Giants* (1927); *The Other May* (1927); *The Stooping Venus* (1927); *The Little Friend* (1928); *High Brows* (1929); *The Rough House* (1930); *Father Malachy's Miracle* (1931); *Prayer for the Living* (1934); *The Uncertain Glory* (1935); *Canon to the Right of Them* (1936); *Luckypenny* (1937); *Delilah Upside Down* (1941); *Yellow Tapers for Paris* (1943); *All Glorious Within* (1944); *George Brown's Schooldays* (1946); *The Red Danube* (1947); *To Every Man a Penny* (1949); *The White Rabbit* (1952); *Only Fade Away* (1954); *Thoughts of my Cats* (1954); *Girl in May* (1956); *The Bank Audit* (1958); *A Thread of Scarlet* (1959); *The Divided Lady* (1960); *A Girl from Lübeck* (1962); *The Bishop* (1970); *The Black Oxen* (1972); *Urban the Ninth* (1973); *Operation Iscariot* (1974); *Marx the First* (1975); *Peter the Second* (1976); *The Yellow Streak* (1977); *Prayer for a Concubine* (1978)

Martin, Sir Theodore (1816–1909). Man of letters. He was born on 16 September 1816 in Edinburgh. He was educated at the HIGH SCHOOL OF EDINBURGH and between 1830 and 1833 he read law at the University of Edinburgh, where he first met his future friend and literary collaborator WILLIAM EDMONSTOUNE AYTOUN. After graduating he practised as a solicitor in Edinburgh until June 1846, when he moved to London to become a parliamentary solicitor or agent. London remained his home for the rest of his life but he kept open his links with Scotland through his literary activities and he was elected Lord Rector of the University of St Andrews in 1881.

Martin was a frequent contributor to the leading periodicals of his day, and between 1841 and 1844 he wrote a series of poetic parodies with Aytoun for TAIT'S EDINBURGH MAGAZINE and *Fraser's Magazine*, which were collected in 1845 in *The Book of Ballads edited by Bon Gaultier* known popularly as 'THE BON GAULTIER BALLADS'. Martin established his reputation as a fluent translator of German Literature and he published English versions of Goethe's *Prometheus* (1850) and *Faust* (1865) and Heine's *Poems and Ballads* (1878). He also translated the works of Horace in 1882.

In his day Martin was best known for his well-documented, five-volume biography (1875–80) of Prince Albert, the Prince Consort, which discussed the right of the Crown to intervene in political affairs. For his services to literature Martin was knighted in 1880. In 1868 he wrote a sympathetic memior of his friend Aytoun who had died in 1865.

Throughout his life Martin was a devotee of the theatre and he married an actress, Helena Faucit, on 25 August 1857. He was an early advocate of a national theatre and translated a number of German and Danish plays for the stage. A conservative in politics, Martin was a prolific contributor to BLACKWOOD'S MAGAZINE and in later life became one of their main leader-writers. He died on 18 August 1909 on his estate of Bryntysilio in North Wales.

WORKS: *A Disputation between the Body and the Soul* (1838); with William Edmonstoune Aytoun, *The Book of Ballads edited by Bon Gaultier* (1845); ed. and trans., Goethe, *Prometheus* (1850); *Madonna pia* (1855); with William Edmonstoune Aytoun, *Poems and Ballads of Goethe* (1859); *Poems* (1863); ed. and trans., Goethe, *Faust* (1865); *Memoir of William Edmonstoune Aytoun* (1868); *Horace* (1870); *The life of His Royal Highness the Prince Consort*, 5 vols. (1875–80); ed. and trans., Heine, *Poems and Ballads* (1878); *Horace and his Friends* (1881); ed., *The Works of Horace* (1882); *The Life of Lord Lyndhurst* (1883); *Sketch of the Life of Princess Alice* (1885); *Shakespeare or Bacon?* (1888); *Essays on the Drama* (1889); *Helena Faucit* (1900); *Monographs* (1906); *Queen Victoria as I knew her* (1908)

Martinmas. The feast of St Martin of Tours, held on 11 November. In ballads, such as 'Edom o' Gordon' and 'The Wife of Usher's Well', it was traditionally associated with tragic and uncanny events. Martinmas was also a time for feeing farm servants.

Mary, Queen of Scots (1542–87). She was born on 8 December 1542 in Linlithgow, the daughter of JAMES V and Mary of Guise-Lorraine. She succeeded to the Scots throne on the death of her father when she was only six days old; she became a pawn in the struggle between the factions led by her mother and the reformers, who by the Treaty of Greenwich (August 1543) betrothed her to Prince Edward, the son of Henry VIII of England. The agreement was repudiated later on the return to power of her mother as regent (1554), and in August 1558 Mary married Francis, the Dauphin of France, who succeeded to the French throne in July 1559 but who died 18 months later. Mary was free to return to Scotland to claim her kingdom and she landed at Leith on 19 August 1561 as Queen of Scots. Her accession posed problems for her cousin Elizabeth of England because, in Catholic eyes, Mary, as the granddaughter of Margaret Tudor, was the rightful heir to the English throne. In the early days of Mary's reign her advisers pursued a policy of rapprochement towards the English queen to try to allay her fears of a Catholic plot.

Initially Mary pursued a moderate policy towards both Catholics and Protestants, but she lost many of her supporters by her marriage to her cousin Henry, Lord Darnley, on 29 July 1565. Following his murder in February 1567 she married JAMES HEPBURN, 4th Earl of Bothwell, on 15 May 1567. Scotland was shocked by her action and Mary surrendered to a confederacy of the nobility at Carberry Hill on 15 June and was imprisoned in Lochleven Castle. On 24 July she abdicated in favour of her son JAMES VI; she escaped and gathered an army of supporters, but was defeated again at the Battle of Langside. In the summer of 1568 she took refuge in England, but she spent the rest of her life in detention to prevent her becoming a focus for the aspirations of English Catholics. She was nevertheless implicated in the Babington Plot against her cousin Elizabeth and was executed by beheading on 8 February 1587 at Fotheringhay Castle.

One of the great romantic figures of Scottish history, Mary figures in Scott's novel *The Abbot* and is the subject of plays by Schiller and Swinburne.

Massie, Allan (*b* 1938). Novelist. He was born on 16 October 1938 in Singapore and was brought up in Aberdeenshire. He was educated at Glenalmond and at Trinity College, Cambridge, and after graduating he became a schoolmaster. Between 1972 and 1975 he lived in Rome and on his return to Scotland he settled in Edinburgh, where he became a full-time writer and journalist. His first novel, *Change and Decay in All Around I See*, a study of decay in contemporary social and spiritual life, was published in 1978. It was followed by *The Last Peacock* (1980), a sensitive comedy of manners set against the social background of the Scottish landed gentry, and reminiscent in style of the novels of JAMES KENNAWAY. Massie is an accomplished critic, contributing book and television reviews to the main Scottish newspapers. He has also written a study of the novelist Muriel Spark.

WORKS: *Change and Decay in All Around I See* (1978); *Muriel Spark: a New Assessment* (1979); *The Last Peacock* (1980); *Ill Met by Gaslight: Five Edinburgh Murders* (1980); *The Death of Men* (1981)

Masson, David (1822–1907). Historian and critic. He was born on 2 December 1822 in Aberdeen, the son of a stonemason. He was educated at Aberdeen Grammar School and at Marischal College, and he studied divinity at Edinburgh. After graduating he did not enter the ministry but took up a career in publishing and journalism, moving to London in 1847. Between 1853 and 1865 he was Professor of English at University College, London, and at the same time edited *Macmillan's Magazine*. In 1865 he was appointed Professor of Rhetoric and English Literature at the University of Edinburgh, where he instituted an honours degree course in English. As a historian he worked on *The Register of the Privy Council of Scotland*, editing 13 volumes between 1880 and 1899. He was appointed Her Majesty's Historiographer for Scotland in 1893. He died on 6 October 1907.

Masson's best-known work is his six-volume *Life of John Milton* (1859–80), which combines a biography of John Milton with a thorough investigation of the social and political background. Similarly, his other major biography, *Drummond of Hawthornden* (1873) is as much a history of the politics of the day as it is a study of WILLIAM DRUMMOND of Hawthornden and his poetry. Among Masson's other books are studies of Thomas de Quincey and THOMAS CARLYLE. His autobiography, *Memories of Two Cities* (1911) is a lively picture of life in 19th-century Edinburgh and Aberdeen.

WORKS: *The British Museum: Historical and Descriptive* (1850); *History of Greece* (1850); *Agostino Ruffini* (1856); *College Education and Self Education* (1856); *Medieval History* (1856); *Modern Essays Biographical and Critical* (1856); *Modern History* (1856); *British Novelists and their Styles* (1859); *The Life of John Milton*, 6 vols. (1859–80); *Recent British Philosophy* (1865); *The State of Learning in Scotland* (1866); *University Teaching for Women* (1868); *Drummond of Hawthornden* (1873); *Chatterton* (1874); *The Three Devils* (1874); *Wordsworth, Shelley and Keats* (1874); ed., *The Register of the Privy Council of Scotland*, 13 vols. (1880–99); *De Quincey* (1881); *Carlyle Personally and in His Writings* (1885); ed., *Select Essays of Thomas de Quincey* (1888); *Carlyle* (1891); *In the Footsteps of Poets* (1893); *James Melvin* (1895); *Memories of London in the Forties* (1908); *Memories of Two Cities* (1911)

Master of Ballantrae, The. A novel by ROBERT LOUIS STEVENSON, published in 1889. It is written in the first person by one of Stevenson's most original characters, Ephraim Mackellar, with interpolations of evidence from three secondary characters: the Chevalier Burke, an Irish adventurer; Secundra Dass, the Master's Hindu companion; and John Mountain, an American trader. The action is set in the period following the Jacobite rebellion of 1745 and follows the story of bitter enmity between two brothers, the sons of the House of Durrisdeer: James Durie, the Master of Ballantrae, a violent, self-centred, flawed romantic hero; and Henry, his dull, honest, sober brother. The Master fights for the Jacobite cause and is presumed dead, whereupon Henry succeeds to the family property and name, and marries Alison Graeme, the brothers' childhood companion. On his secret return to Durrisdeer, James starts to persecute his brother, who is finally goaded into fighting a duel late at night – a set-piece action grippingly described by Stevenson. James is left for dead, but, although Henry retains the title, he lives in fear of his brother's return, believing that James has assumed Satanic qualities. After several years of adventure in India and America, James comes again, this time in the company of Secundra Dass, and Henry, now Lord Durrisdeer, is forced to flee to America with his family. James follows, to begin his persecution yet again; but he finds that his brother has sunk to the same level of anger and hatred as himself. Both are destined to die in bizarre circumstances in the wilderness, James on a wild hunt for lost treasure during which he is murdered at his brother's instigation, and Henry, on viewing Secundra Dass's attempts to revive his master.

There are, in effect, two 'Masters' of Ballantrae in the novel – James, the rightful holder of
the title, and Henry, the usurper – and Stevenson makes them mirror images of each other
through the subtle shifts of the plot. James is
described, before the duel, as a demonic figure
intent only on evil and his family's destruction,
but thereafter it is Henry, plunged into guilt by
having believed his brother dead, who betrays
the excesses of moral degredation. The conflict between the two brothers and their symbolic opposition makes The Master of Ballantrae
Stevenson's most telling study of a love–hate
relationship and a more subtle exposition of
evil than THE STRANGE CASE OF DR JEKYLL
AND MR HYDE. The novel also contains some
of his best descriptions of the Scottish landscape and the vagaries of Scottish weather.

Mavor, O(sborne) H(enry) ['James Bridie']
(1888–1951). Dramatist. O. H. Mavor, who
wrote under the name 'James Bridie', was born
on 3 January 1888 in Glasgow, the son of an
engineer. He was educated at Glasgow
Academy and studied medicine at the University of Glasgow, graduating in 1913. During
World War I he served as a doctor in France
and Mesopotamia, and in 1919 he bought a
practice in Glasgow and also joined the staff of
the Victoria Infirmary. In 1938, following his
stage successes, he became a full-time writer,
although he served again in the Royal Army
Medical Corps in World War II. Mavor held
several important public posts, including the
chairmanship of both the Glasgow Citizens'
Theatre and the Scottish Committee of the
Arts Council of Great Britain, later the SCOT-
TISH ARTS COUNCIL. The University of Glasgow conferred on him the degree of Doctor of
Laws in 1939 and he was made a CBE in 1946.
Through his writing he became a major force in
Scottish drama and, as well as encouraging
native drama at the Citizens' Theatre, he was a
founder in 1950 of the College of Drama
within the Royal Scottish Academy of Music.
He died on 29 January 1951 in Edinburgh.

Mavor started writing while a student, contributing rhymes and satirical portraits to the
university magazine. His first plays, The Sunlight Sonata (1928), The Switchback (1929) and
What it is to be Young (1929), displayed his
spirited wit and ability to draw convincing
characters. He came to prominence first in
1930 with two plays that were produced in
London: The Anatomist and Tobias and the

Angel. The Anatomist deals with the story of Dr
Robert Knox and Burke and Hare (see BURKE,
WILLIAM), the body-snatchers employed by
him; Mavor was able to weave together historical fact and fantasy around the compelling
figure of Dr Knox, the man of science who has
to go to extreme criminal lengths in his pursuit
of knowledge. 'If it illustrates anything', wrote
Mavor in a head-note to the play, 'it is the
shifts to which men of science are drawn when
they are ahead of their times.' Tobias and the
Angel follows the journey of Tobias and the
angel Raphael, which is itself a symbol of the
transformation of Tobias from a gauche youth
into an experienced, worldly man. A favourite
Mavor motif, that of the conflict between
good and evil, is present in the confrontation
between Raphael and the prepossessing devil
Asmoday. Evil of a different kind is present in
A Sleeping Clergyman (1933), a powerful play
which takes as its theme hereditary wickedness
in a medical family and the ultimate triumph of
the will over genetic evil.

In the 1930s Mavor wrote 11 plays for the
London west-end stage, including Mary Read
(1934), the story of the woman pirate, and
another biblical play, Susannah and the Elders
(1937). In 1943 he returned to the theme of
moral conflict in Mr Bolfry, which introduces
one of his most engaging characters, the devil
in the human shape of Mr Bolfry. There followed a series of notable plays with Scottish
themes: The Forrigan Reel (1944), a Highland
fantasy; Dr Angelus (1947), a melodrama; John
Knox (1947), a single-minded study of Knox
and his effect on the course of Scottish history;
and Gog and Magog (1948), a thinly disguised
portrait of WILLIAM MCGONAGALL. In his last
plays, Daphne Laureola (1949), Mr Gillie
(1950), The Queen's Comedy (1950) and The
Baikie Charivari, or The Seven Prophets (1952),
Mavor turned to contemporary themes and the
familiar juxtapositions of good and evil, righteousness and sin, are questioned against the
immediate problems of the post-war world.

In all, Mavor wrote 42 plays and several
revues and pantomimes. He also published a
witty, but self-effacing, autobiography, One
Way of Living (1939), and two collections of
essays, Mr Bridie's Alphabet for Little Glasgow
Highbrows (1934) and Tedious and Brief
(1944). Many critics have commented on the
similarities between Mavor and George Bernard Shaw but these are surface likenesses
only. Whereas Shaw's plays have a linear di-

rectness, Mavor was more discursive, posing questions which, except in *The Queen's Comedy*, he did not attempt to answer, preferring to give full rein to his characters' absorption with moral ambiguities. There is also in all his work a mixture of the serious with the jocular, the dignified with the ludicrous, patterns of behaviour that matched his own self-mocking view of his art. Mavor's achievement as 'James Bridie' gave a sense of purpose to the Scottish theatre in the 20th century and he was a tireless worker for the repertory theatre movement.

WORKS: *Some Talk of Alexander* (1926); *The Pardoner's Tale* (1930); *The Sunlight Sonata* (1930); *The Switchback* (1930); *The Amazed Evangelist* (1931); *The Anatomist* (1931); *Tobias and the Angel* (1931); *Jonah and the Whale* (1932); *A Sleeping Clergyman* (1933); *Mr Bridie's Alphabet for Little Glasgow Highbrows* (1934); *Colonel Witherspoon and Other Plays* (1934); *A Sleeping Clergyman and Other Plays* (1934); *The Black Eye* (1935); *Mary Read* (1935); *Mrs Waterbury's Millennium* (1935); *Moral Plays* (1936); *Storm in a Teacup* (1936); *The King of Nowhere and Other Plays* (1938); *One Way of Living* (1939); *What say they?* (1939); *Susannah and the Elders and Other Plays* (1940); *Plays for Plain People* (1944); *Tedious and Brief* (1944); *The British Drama* (1945); *It Depends what you Mean* (1948); *Daphne Laureola* (1949); *John Knox and Other Plays* (1949); with Moray McLaren, *A Small Stir* (1949); *Mr Gillie* (1950); *The Queen's Comedy* (1952); *The Baikie Charivari, or The Seven Prophets* (1953); *Meeting at Night* (1956)

REFERENCES: W. Bannister, *James Bridie and his Theatre* (London, 1955); U. Gerber, *James Bridies Dramen* (Zurich, 1961); H. L. Luyben, *James Bridie: Clown and Philosopher* (Philadelphia, 1965); J. T. Low, *Devils, Doctors, Saints and Sinners: a Critical Study of James Bridie's Major Plays* (Edinburgh, 1980)

Maxwell, William (1760–1834). Physician. He was a friend of ROBERT BURNS, whom he met in Dumfries in 1794 on his return from France, where he had been a supporter of the Revolutionary government. He attended Burns in his last illness but diagnosed as gout the rheumatic fever or endocarditis from which the poet suffered. Maxwell became one of the trustees of the fund created to care for the family after Burns's death.

Mayne, John (1759–1836). Poet. He was born on 26 March 1759 in Dumfries and was educated at the local grammar school. Most of his life was spent as a printer and journalist and he began his career in the offices of the *Dumfries Journal* before working in Glasgow in the publishing house established by ROBERT FOULIS from 1782 to 1787, when he moved to London. Mayne then became the editor and proprietor of an evening newspaper, *The Star*, and he remained in London until his death on 14 March 1836. He was borr in the same year as Robert Burns and in several works their styles are similar: in the November 1780 issue of *Ruddiman's Magazine* Mayne published 'Hallowe'en', a poem which encouraged Burns to write on the same theme; and both men wrote moving songs entitled 'Logan Water', though when Burns borrowed two lines from Mayne's version he was under the impression that he was borrowing from a traditional song. Two other works are memorable: 'The Siller Gun', a humorous poem describing a Dumfries wappinschaw, or shooting competition, in the tradition of poems about country events; and 'Glasgow', a vivid picture of the 18th-century city before industrialization.

WORKS: *Two Scots Poems* (1783); *Glasgow* (1803); *The Siller Gun* (1808)

EDITION: J. M. Colles, ed., *The Journal of John Mayne* (London, 1909)

Mealie Monday. A holiday that used to be granted to students in the Scottish universities at the start of the Candlemas term on 2 February. It enabled the poor students to return home to replenish their meal-sacks.

Melville, Andrew (1545–1622). Scholar, regarded as the founder of Scottish Presbyterianism. He was educated at the universities of St Andrews, Paris, Poitiers, and Geneva where he studied under Calvin's successor Theodore de Bèze. He returned to Scotland in 1574 to become Principal of Glasgow University and later, in 1580, of St Mary's College, St Andrews. Melville propagated the theory of the division of Church and State into 'two kingdoms', a policy which was adopted by the General Assembly in 1578 and finally by parliament in 1592. For a time Melville enjoyed the support of JAMES VI who wanted to subdue the Catholic faction in Scotland, but after the Union of the Crowns in 1603 Melville was detained in London and finally exiled in Europe. His nephew was the diarist JAMES MELVILLE (ii), who was also a committed supporter of Presbyterianism.

WORKS: *Principis Scoto-Britannorum natalis* (1594); *Epithalamium* (1619); *Inscriptiones historiae regium Scotorum* (1620); *Pro supplici evangelicorum ministrorum in Anglia* (1620); *De adiapharis* (1622)

EDITION: J. Boyd, ed., *Historical Memoirs of Andrew Melville* (Edinburgh, 1830)

Melville, Sir James (i), of Halhill (1535–1617). Courtier and diarist. He served as a page to MARY, Queen of Scots, at the French court and later acted as her envoy to Queen Elizabeth and to the Elector Palatine. Much of his life was spent at European courts and his *Memoirs* are a lively, if somewhat self-important account of the main events of his time. The manuscript was not discovered until 1660; it was first published in 1683 and became a frequently quoted source book for the period. Melville died on 13 November 1617.

EDITION: T. Thomson, ed., *Memoirs of his own Life by Sir James Melville of Halhill,* Bannatyne Club (Edinburgh, 1827)

Melville, James (ii) (1556–1614). Minister and diarist. He was educated at the University of Glasgow under the tutelage of his uncle Principal ANDREW MELVILLE, the founder of Scottish Presbyterianism. He was appointed Professor of Oriental Languages at the University of St Andrews, but was forced to flee to England in 1584 because of his outspoken reforming views. On his return he became in turn the minister of Anstruther West and Kilrenny, where he wrote his *Autobiography and Diary* which, besides providing useful information on contemporary religious politics, offers a personal picture of life as a parish minister in 16th-century Scotland. Melville was exiled in England again in 1606 and returned to Scotland in 1613, the year before his death.

WORKS: *A Spirituall Propine of a Pastour to his People* (1589); *Ane Fruitful and Comfortable Exhortatioun anent Death* (1597); *The Black Bastel* (1634); *A Short Relation of the State of the Kirk of Scotland since the Reformation* (1638); *Ad serenissimum Jacobum primum Britanniarum monarcham* (1645).

EDITION: R. Pitcairn, ed., *The Autobiography and Diary of Mr James Melville,* Bannatyne Club (Edinburgh, 1842)

Melville, 1st Viscount. *See* DUNDAS, HENRY.

Memoirs. Memoirs and diaries form an important substructure in Scottish letters and tend to fall into two main groupings: intimate observations of a passing age, reflecting the writer's own personality; and accurate, though frequently biased, accounts of national or local events. Naturally, given the very private nature of the memoir or the diary, there is, in such a division, overlapping in content, style and the writer's own interests. Among the earliest diaries are those by Sir James Melville

of Halhill (*see* MELVILLE, JAMES (ii)), whose account of life at the court of MARY, Queen of Scots, has all the freshness and wit of firsthand observation intelligently expressed, and the Revd James Melville (*see* MELVILLE, JAMES (ii)), a Protestant reformer, who left a highly personal and frequently tendentious account of many of the main events of the post-Reformation struggles during the reign of JAMES VI.

17th-century prose writers tended to dwell on the turmoil caused by religious disruption and, although several histories, both clerical and temporal, were written about the events of the time, it was not until the 18th century that the personal observation that characterizes memoirs and diaries came back into fashion. The greatest of the 18th-century records is provided by the recently discovered private papers of JAMES BOSWELL, which not only offer candid disclosures about his sex life, but, more importantly, a fully realized picture of his life and times. In particular they record his lifelong sense of insecurity, his constant self-analysis and his lack of self-awareness, in language that is always engaging and colourful. No less interesting is the *Autobiography* of ALEXANDER CARLYLE, which offers a shrewd and entertaining account of life in the Edinburgh of the SCOTTISH ENLIGHTENMENT. *Anecdotes and Egotisms* by HENRY MACKENZIE is a readable and individual account of the same period, and other works of note are the *Memoirs of a Highland Lady* by ELIZABETH GRANT (ii) of Rothiemurcus, and ANN GRANT of Laggan's *Letters from the Mountains.*

The *Journal* of Sir WALTER SCOTT is, after Boswell's, the most intimate record of a writer's life and innermost thoughts. It was begun six months before the financial disaster of 1826, when Scott abandoned reticence for the frequently painful exposure of his private reflections; a remarkably uninhibited picture emerges of a man who generally eschewed any display of emotion. The *Journal* is also a faithful record of his brave, and finally successful, attempt to pay off his debts. These very personal writings were to form the basis of the life of his father-in-law by JOHN GIBSON LOCKHART. Scott's contemporary HENRY THOMAS Lord COCKBURN wrote three delightful autobiographical works: *Journal, Circuit Journeys,* and *Memorials of his Time* which gives a pertinent rendering of the manners and personalities, not only of his adult years, but also of his childhood at the end of the 18th century. Likewise, *Reminiscences* by THOMAS CARLYLE, a collection of autobiographical essays, looks back at a past age and presents an honest history of the many vicissitudes he had to face; especially revealing is the account of his relationship with his father. *Reminiscences of Scottish Life and Character* by EDWARD BANNERMAN RAMSAY enjoyed great commercial success and inspired numerous imitations, many of which were autobiographical counterparts of much Victorian KAILYARD fiction.

In the 20th century the encyclopaedic ten-part autobiography by Sir COMPTON MACKENZIE, *My Life and Times* (1963–71), is a remarkable reflection of the author's many interests, friendships and travels over a long and eventful life. Other novelists such as ERIC LINKLATER and EDWIN MUIR have written with varying degrees of frankness about their lives and careers. Most moving of all Scottish memoirs are perhaps the private diaries of WILLIAM SOUTAR, which were published after his death under the title, *Diaries of a Dying Man*; not only do they present a personal account of the poet's friendships with Hugh MacDiarmid (CHRISTOPHER MURRAY GRIEVE) and other poets of the SCOTTISH RENAISSANCE, but they are also an indomitable statement of one man's courage in the face of terminal illness.

Private writing has played a vital part in our understanding of the manners and events of the past and of several writers' literary development; despite the advent of modern technology and the artefacts of mass culture it is doubtful that this very personal literary form will disappear altogether.

Merry Muses of Caledonia, The. A collection of bawdy songs and poems collected by ROBERT BURNS and circulated privately among his friends. The manuscript disappeared after his death and a version was issued in 1800 for the Edinburgh drinking club, the CROCHALLAN FENCIBLES, from which numerous fake copies with unauthorized additions were published throughout the 19th century. The definitive version was published by the Auk Society edited by SYDNEY GOODSIR SMITH and JAMES BARKE. Numerous Burns critics and apologists have suggested that Burns had only a minimal role in collecting *The Merry Muses* but many of the compositions are by his hand. Burns's bawdry celebrates sex and erotic love and laughs at the general human situation, and it should be read in conjunction with the best of his poems and songs.

Meston, William (*c*1688–1745). Poet. He was born in Aberdeen and educated locally at Marischal College. After graduating he became a tutor to the family of George Keith, 10th Earl Marischal, through whose influence he became Regent of Marischal College, a position he lost in 1715 for his support of the Jacobite rising. Unable to establish himself again, Meston relied on patronage from Jacobite sympathizers and he died in poverty in Aberdeen in 1745. Many of his poems were burlesques in the style of Samuel 'Hudibras' Butler (1612–80) whom he admired greatly, and the best of these is 'The Knight of the Kirk', a satire on the Presbyterian Church.

WORKS: *Phaethon* (1720); *The Knight of the Kirk* (1723); *Mob contra Mob* (1731); *Old Mother Grimm's Tales* (1737); *Decadam alteram* (1738); *Poems of William Meston* (1767)

Michaelmas. The Feast of St Michael, held on 29 September. In north-west Scotland and the Hebrides, Michaelmas was one of the great community festivals, celebrating Michael nam Buadh, Michael the patron saint of boats and boatmen, horses and horsemen. It was marked by horse races and feasting, and by the baking of the *struan*, a cake made from all the cereal crops of the farm. In other parts of Scotland it was the day for renewal of leases and the hiring of farm servants.

Mickle, William Julius (1735–88). Poet. He was born on 28 September 1735 in Langholm and was educated at the local grammar school. Between 1750 and 1763 he worked in, and later manged, a brewery in Edinburgh. Business difficulties forced him to leave Scotland and he lived in London in conditions of some financial distress until 1781, when he spent a year as a naval secretary in Portugal. His rewards from the disposal of prize money allowed him to settle near Oxford, where he died on 28 Octboer 1788 at Forest Hill. Mickle started writing poetry while in Edinburgh and his ballad 'Cumnor Hall' was later admired by Sir Walter Scott. During Mickle's lifetime his reputation rested on his translation from the Portuguese of the epic *Os Lusiadas* by Luis de Camoes (*c*1525–1580) as the *Lusiad*; it remained a standard work for many years. He also wrote a large number of minor poems and songs and to him has been ascribed, on little evidence, the song, 'There's nae luck aboot the hoose' (also attributed to JEAN ADAM).

WORKS: The Concubine (1767); Letter to Mr Harwood (1769); Voltaire in the Shades (1770); trans. Luis de Camoes, Os Lusiados as Lusiad (1775); Almada Hill: an Epistle from Lisbon (1781); Prophecy of Queen Emma (1782)

EDITION: J. Sim, ed., Poetical Works of William Julius Mickle (London, 1807)

Mill, James (1773–1836). Philosopher and historian. He was born on 6 April 1773 at Northwater Bridge in Angus, the son of a poor shoemaker. His early education took him to Montrose and through the patronage of a local landowner, Sir John Stuart of Fettercairn, he studied for the ministry of the Church of Scotland in Edinburgh. However, finding himself unsuited to that calling, he moved to London in 1802 and became a man of letters. He edited the London Journal and the St James's Chronicle and was a regular contributor to the Edinburgh Review (see EDINBURGH REVIEW (ii)). His History of British India, begun in 1818, won him a position in the India Office and he eventually became the influential head of the Department of Examination of Correspondence. In London he also met and and became a close friend of Jeremy Bentham (1748–1832) and helped him to develop the theory of Utilitarianism, the belief that the basis of morals is the greatest happiness of the greatest number. Mill's son, John Stuart Mill (1806–73), took the philosophy further in his own writings but departed from it by maintaining that pleasures can differ in quality as well as quantity and that happiness also lies in man's desire for social unity. James Mill was an austere father who believed in educating his children according to his own principles, and a vivid picture of his grim personality emerges from his son's Autobiography (1873). He was also a co-founder of the Westminster Gazette and of the University of London, and was a well-known figure in radical political circles until his death on 23 June 1836.

Millar, J(ohn) H(epburn) (1864–1929). Literary and legal historian. He was the son of Lord Craighall, a senator of the College of Justice, and was educated at Edinburgh Academy and Balliol College, Oxford. He was called to the Scottish Bar in 1889 and after lecturing in law at Edinburgh University he was appointed Professor of Constitutional Law and Constitutional History in 1909, a post he held until his retirement in 1925. Millar's scholarly A Literary History of Scotland (1903) was for many years the standard work on Scottish literature and remains a useful work of reference. In it he maintained his attack on the then fashionable KAILYARD writers, whom he had first criticized in the April 1895 issue of The New Review.

WORKS: Handbook of Prescription According to the Law of Scotland (1893); The Mid-Eighteenth Century (1902); A Literary History of Scotland (1903); Scottish Prose of the Seventeenth and Eighteenth Centuries (1912)

Miller, Hugh (1802–56). Geologist and journalist. He was born on 10 October 1802 in Cromarty, the son of a sea captain who died in 1807. He was educated at the village school but, as he was to confess in his childhood memories, My Schools and Schoolmasters (1854), he was largely self-taught and owed much of the impetus for his early learning to his maternal uncles James and Sandy Wright. Between 1820 and 1822 he served an apprenticeship as a stonemason and began his lifelong interest in geology and the formation of rocks, which resulted, later, in the publication of The Old Red Sandstone (1841), his most influential book, and also Footprints of the Creator (1849) and The Testimony of the Rocks (1857). These were not only among the earliest available geological studies but they also show to good advantage the sparse elegance of Miller's prose style.

In 1823 Miller moved to Edinburgh, but illness (emphysema) forced him to return north, where he took to writing; his first verses were published in the Inverness Courier by ROBERT CARRUTHERS, who was to become a lifelong friend, and through the influence of Sir THOMAS DICK LAUDER his Scenes and Legends of the North of Scotland appeared in 1835. Miller became an accountant in the Commercial Bank of Scotland and moved back to Edinburgh in 1834. There he was active in church affairs: between 1840 and his death he edited the evangelical weekly newspaper The Witness, and he was a firm supporter of the Free Church after THE DISRUPTION of 1843. Miller wrote many essays, some of which were published in book form after his death – The Cruise of the Betsey (1858), Essays (1862), Edinburgh and its Neighbourhood (1864) and Leading Arti-

cles (1890) – but, increasingly, his geological findings clashed with the rigid simplicity of his Church's teachings about the Creation.

Miller was a prodigious worker, and in a fit of depression, which may have been caused by overwork, he committed suicide on 24 December 1856 in his house in Portobello, Edinburgh. Although Miller's religious beliefs brooked no opposition, and in much of his journalism there is an air of sanctimoniousness, his work is memorable for its polished prose and his vivid powers of description.

WORKS AND EDITIONS: *Poems Written in the Leisure Hours of a Journeyman Mason* (1829); *Letters on the Herring Industry* (1829); *Scenes and Legends of the North of Scotland* (1835); *Letter from one of the Scotch People to the Right Honourable Brougham and Vaux* (1839); *Memoir of William Forsyth* (1839); *The Whiggism of the Old School* (1839); *The Old Red Sandstone, Or New Walks in an Old Field* (1841); *First Impressions of England and its People* (1847); *The Geology of the Bass Rock* (1848); *The Sites Bill and the Toleration Laws* (1848); *Footprints of the Creator, or the Asterolepsis of Stromness* (1849); *Thoughts on Education* (1850); *The Fossiliferous Deposits of Scotland* (1854); *My Schools and Schoolmasters, or The Story of my Education* (1854); *Geology versus Astronomy, or the Conditions and the Periods; being a view of the Modifying Effects of Geological Discoverey on the Old Astronomic Inferences respecting the Plurality of Inhabited Worlds* (1855); *The Testimony of the Rocks or Geology in its Bearing on the Two Theologies, Natural and Revealed* (1857); *The Cruise of the Betsey, or a Summer Ramble among the Fossiliferous Deposits of the Highlands; with Rambles of a Geologist, or Ten Thousand Miles over the Fossiliferous Deposits of Scotland* (1858); *Sketch Book of Popular Geology* (1859); P. Baynes, ed., *Essays* (1862); L. Miller, ed., *Edinburgh and its Neighbourhood* (1864); L. Miller, ed., *Tales and Sketches* (1864); *Complete Works of Hugh Miller* (1871–6); *The Headship of Christ and the Rights of the Christian People* (1889); *Leading Articles* (1890)

REFERENCES: W. Bingham, *The Life and Writings of Hugh Miller* (New York, 1858); T. N. Brown, *Labour and Triumph: the Life and Times of Hugh Miller* (London and Glasgow, 1859); P. Bayne, *The Life and Letters of Hugh Miller*, 2 vols. (Edinburgh and London, 1871); W. K. Leask, *Hugh Miller* (Edinburgh and London, 1896); A. Geikie and others, *The Centenary of Hugh Miller* (Glasgow, 1902); W. M. Mackenzie, *Hugh Miller: a Critical Study* (London, 1905); C. D. Waterston, *Hugh Miller, the Cromarty Stonemason* (Edinburgh, 1966); G. Rosie, *Hugh Miller: Outrage and Order* (Edinburgh, 1981)

Minstrelsy of the Scottish Border, The. A collection of Border ballads made by Sir WALTER SCOTT, the first two volumes of which were published by JAMES BALLANTYNE in February 1802 in Kelso. A third volume was published in the following year. During the compilation of the volumes Scott was assisted by the

remarkable scholar JOHN LEYDEN and during his excursions into the Border lands in search of ballad materials he began his lifelong friendships with WILLIAM LAIDLAW and the poet JAMES HOGG. Among the versions of ballads that Scott collected and printed were such great Border ballads as 'Kinmont Willie', 'The Twa Corbies' and 'The Wife of Usher's Well'; at the *Minstrelsy*'s completion he had published 72 ballads, 38 of which had not appeared before in print. Like other collectors of his day, Scott employed editorial principles that suited his own needs. He changed words to elucidate meaning, he transposed lines and stanzes from one ballad to another and in some instances he added verses of his own creation. Nevertheless, the *Minstrelsy* did introduce ballads to a wider audience and Scott's introductions and notes reflect his enthusiasm for, and his love of, Border legend and history. Equally importantly, the compilation of the volumes encouraged Scott to embark on the composition of his first great poem, THE LAY OF THE LAST MINSTREL, which is redolent of the ballad style of writing.

Minto, William (1845–93). Critic and novelist. He was born on 10 October 1845 in Alford, Aberdeenshire , and was educated at the University of Aberdeen, where he achieved distinction by winning the leading prizes in mathematics, classics and philosophy. In 1866 he moved to Merton College, Oxford, but returned to teach in Aberdeen until 1873, when he settled in London. There, much of his time was taken up with journalism and he was considered to be an able and pungent critic and observer of Lord Beaconsfield's imperial policies. It was as a critic, especially on textual matters, that Minto made his reputation, and his three books of literary criticism, *Manual of English Prose Literature, Biographical and Critical* (1872), *Characteristics of English Poets from Chaucer to Shirley* (1874) and *English Literature under the Georges* (1894), were based on solid scholarship and a wide analytic reading of English literature. Minto also wrote a monograph on Defoe and three sentimental novels, *The Crack of Doom* (1886), *The Mediation of Ralph Hardelot* (1886) and *Was she Good or Bad?* (1889). In 1880 he was appointed Professor of English at Aberdeen University, a post he held until his death on 1 March 1893.

WORKS: *Manual of English Prose Literature, Biographical and Critical* (1872); *Characteristics of English Poets from Chaucer to Shirley* (1874); *Life of Defoe* (1879); *The Crack of Doom* (1886); ed., *Poetical Works of Sir Walter Scott* (1887); *The Mediation of Ralph Hardelot* (1886); *Was she Good or Bad?* (1889); *Autobiographical Notes of the Life of William Bell Scott* (1892); *Plain Principles of Prose Composition* (1893); *Universal Extension Manual on Logic* (1893); *English Literature under the Georges* (1894)

Mirror, The. A magazine first published by WILLIAM CREECH in Edinburgh on 23 January 1779, which ceased publication on 7 December the same year. Its editor was HENRY MACKENZIE, who gathered around him a select coterie of the Edinburgh *literati*, such as DAVID DALRYMPLE Lord Hailes, ALEXANDER FRASER TYTLER Lord Woodhouselee and DAVID HUME (ii). The magazine was based on the London *Spectator* and in later life Mackenzie was called 'our Scottish Addison' by Sir Walter Scott. In *The Mirror* Mackenzie tried to improve the literary climate of Scotland by imitating the tone of Augustan London, and when the magazine failed he blamed 'the fastidiousness with which in a place so narrow as Edinburgh, home productions are commonly received'.

Mitchell, James Leslie ['Lewis Grassic Gibbon'] (1901–35). Novelist. He was born on 13 February 1901 on the croft of Hillhead of Segget in Auchterless, Aberdeenshire. His father was a farmer and when Mitchell was eight the family moved to the Howe of the Mearns, which became the setting for his trilogy, A SCOTS QUAIR. He was educated at Arbuthnott Village School where he started writing, and his early essays were collected by the schoolmaster Alexander Gray. They appear in the collection *A Scots Hairst* (1969). In 1916 he went to Mackie Academy in Stonehaven, Kincardineshire, but after a year he left to become a junior reporter in Aberdeen. After two years, in 1919, he moved to Glasgow, where he was employed as a journalist with the *Scottish Farmer*. It was during this period that he became a convert to socialism and for a time he was a member of the Communist Party. After being dismissed from his job, he joined the Royal Army Service Corps in August 1919, and between then and 1923 he served in the Middle East, Mesopotamia, Palestine and Egypt. On his discharge from the army he returned to Scotland but, unable to settle down, he enlisted in the Royal Air Force in which he served until 1929. After leaving the RAF, Mitchell lived in Welwyn Garden City, where he died in 1935.

Mitchell's first book, *Hanno, or The Future of Exploration*, was published in 1928 and in it enthusiastic reference was made to the Diffusionist theory which was to influence much of his writing. The Diffusionist theory was evolved by an Australian, Grafton Elliot Smith, Professor of Anatomy at University College, London, and its adherents believed that primitive man lived in a golden age which had disappeared with the coming of civilization. Mitchell's theory of Scottish history was that Scotland had been peopled by tribes of happy primitive hunters whose descendants were the Picts. Although Scotland had been overrun by a succession of invaders, Mitchell claimed that the last remnants of this tribe in his native north-east were still recognizable until the outbreak of World War I. Diffusionism was an important element in his intellectual background and he returned to it in later books – *Niger: the Life of Mungo Park* (1934), a study of the explorer MUNGO PARK, and *The Conquest of the Maya* (1934), his most scholarly anthropological work.

Mitchell published seven English novels under his own name, the first, *Stained Radiance*, in 1930, which in its Scottish scenes foreshadows the background of *A Scots Quair*. This was followed by an autobiographical novel, *The Thirteenth Disciple* (1931), which follows his own spiritual and intellectual development through the central character Malcom Maudslay; at the end of the novel Maudslay sets off on a symbolic quest for the Lost City in Yucatan and, near to death in a tropical rain forest, he experiences a momentary vision of the Lost City of the Sun. Mitchell's other novels are: *Three Go Back* (1932), a scientific romance, *The Lost Trumpet* (1932), which is set in Egypt; *Image and Superscription* (1933); *Spartacus* (1933), the story of a slave revolt in Rome in 73 BC and of its legendary leader; and *Gay Hunter* (1934), a story of time travel.

In 1932 *Sunset Song* was published, the first of the trilogy *A Scots Quair*, written under the pseudonym he used for his Scottish fiction, 'Lewis Grassic Gibbon'. Mitchell was aware of his divided attitude towards language. The theory of a world language as propounded by H. G. Wells had been an early influence, but he began to accept the importance of his childhood knowledge of Scots. The language he uses in *A Scots Quair* is not a faithful representation of the north-east dialect but a stylized attempt to reproduce its rhythms and cadences. In this he was influenced by the conversational style of the Scots employed in the novels of JOHN GALT, and also by the translation of a German novel, *Jorn Uhl* by Gustav Frenssen, which recreates a stylized language for the Low German of the Holstein peasants. The clash between the languages and cultures of England and Scotland is found in the central character of the trilogy, Chris Guthrie. She has a similarly ambivalent attitude towards the land, loving it for its ancient beauty but also hating it for the work and human degradation that husbandry entails. In the second novel *Cloud Howe* (1933) Chris moves to a small rural town and to a second marriage, and in the final novel *Grey Granite* (1934) to the squalor and poverty of an industrial city. At the end Chris turns again to the country and the final triumphant message of the novels is of the enduring nature of the land.

Mitchell was a friend of the poet Hugh MacDiarmid (CHRISTOPHER MURRAY GRIEVE) and collaborated with him in *Scottish Scene* (1934), a survey of contemporary Scotland, which contains his three best stories, *Smeddum, Clay* and *Greenden*.

WORKS: *Hanno, or The Future of Exploration* (1928); *Stained Radiance* (1930); *The Thirteenth Disciple* (1931); *The Calends of Cairo* (1931); *Three Go Back* (1932); *The Lost Trumpet* (1932); *Persian Dawns, Egyptian Nights* (1932); *Image and Superscription* (1933); *Spartacus* (1933); *Niger: the Life of Mungo Park* (1934); *The Conquest of the Maya* (1934); *Nine against the Unknown* (1934); *Gay Hunter* (1934) as Lewis Grassic Gibbon: *Sunset Song* (1932), *Cloud Howe* (1933), *Grey Granite* (1934), published together as *A Scots Quair* (1946); with Hugh MacDiarmid, *Scottish Scene or the Intelligent Man's Guide to Albyn* (1934)

REFERENCES: I. S. Munro, *Leslie Mitchell: Lewis Grassic Gibbon* (Edinburgh, 1966); D. F. Young, *Beyond the Sunset: a Study of James Leslie Mitchell* (Aberdeen, 1973)

Mitchison [née Haldane], **Naomi** (*b* 1897). Novelist and poet. She was born on 1 November 1897 in Edinburgh and was educated at the Dragon School, Oxford. Her brother was the scientist J. B. S. Haldane, and an evocative picture of their childhood in Scotland and Oxford exists in her volumes of memoirs, *Small Talk* (1973) and *All Change Here* (1975). In 1916 she married the barrister and Labour politician G. Richard Mitchison, later Baron Mitchison, and since 1937 she has lived at Carradale in Kintyre, where she has been deeply involved in Highland local poli-

tics. Travel has always been one of her interests and her long friendship with the Bakgatha tribe of Botswana led to her being adopted as its adviser and Mmarona (mother) during the 1960s.

Naomi Mitchison's first novels came out of her interest in classical mythology and history; the best of these is *The Corn King and the Spring Queen* (1931), which is set partly in the mythical land of Marob in archaic Scythia and partly in ancient Greece and Egypt. The central theme, that of the fertility rites that prolong the life of the tribe and ensure the succession of divinity, is taken from *The Golden Bough* by Sir JAMES GEORGE FRAZER, and the central characters, Tarrik, the Corn King, and Erif Der, the Spring Queen, struggle to find a way out of their barbarian past towards an uncertain future. More accessible is the historical novel, *The Bull Calves* (1947), which is set firmly in her own Haldane family history in Perthshire in the years following the Jacobite rebellion of 1745. The two central characters, the lovers, Kirsty Haldane and William Macintosh of Berlum, are fictional but the events and background are real enough and the mixture of the three provide a solid basis to a lively picture of rural life in 18th-century Scotland.

Naomi Mitchison has written over 70 books, including novels for children, science fiction, two biographies, *Anna Comnena* (1928) and *Socrates* (1937, with R. H. S. Crossman), a volume of poems, *The Cleansing of the Knife* (1978) and a number of Scottish short stories, collected as *What do you Think Yourself?* (1982).

WORKS: *The Conquered* (1923); *When the Bough Breaks* (1924); *Cloud Cuckoo Land* (1925); *The Laburnam Branch* (1926); *The Fairy who Couldn't Tell a Lie* (1927); *Anna Comnena* (1928); *Black Sparta* (1928); *Nix-Nought-Nothing* (1928); *Barbarian Stories* (1929); *Comments on Birth Control* (1930); *The Hostages* (1930); *Boys and Girls and Gods* (1931); *The Corn King and the Spring Queen* (1931); *The Prince of Freedom* (1931); *An Outline for Boys and Girls and their Parents* (1932); *Powers of Light* (1932); *The Delicate Fire* (1933); *The Home and a Changing Civilisation* (1934); *Vienna Diary* (1934); *Beyond this Limit* (1935); *We have Been Warned* (1935); *The Fourth Pig* (1936); *An End and a Beginning* (1937); with R. H. S. Crossman, *Socrates* (1937); *The Moral Basis of Politics* (1938); *The Alban Goes Out* (1939); *As it Was in the Beginning* (1939); *The Blood of the Martyrs* (1939); *Historical Plays for School* (1939); *The Kingdom of Heaven* (1939); *The Bull Calves* (1947); *Men and Herring* (1949); *A Big House* (1950); *Spindrift* (1951); *Travel Light* (1952); *Lobsters on the Agenda* (1952); *Graeme and the Dragon* (1954); *The Swans' Road* (1954); *The Land the Ra-*

vens Found (1955); *To the Chapel Perilous* (1955); *Highlands and Islands* (1956); *Little Boxes* (1956); *Behold your King* (1957); *The Far Harbour* (1957); *Five Men and a Swan* (1957); *Other Peoples' Worlds* (1958); *Judy and Lakshmi* (1959); *The Rib of the Green Umbrella* (1960); *The Young Alexander the Great* (1960); *A Fishing Village on the Clyde* (1961); *Karensgaard* (1961); *Presenting Other People's Children* (1961); *Memoirs of a Spacewoman* (1962); *What the Human Race is up to* (1962); *Young Alfred the Great* (1962); *Ketse and the Chief* (1965); *When we Become Men* (1965); *Friends and Enemies* (1966); *Return to the Fairy Hill* (1966); *The Big Surprise* (1967); *African Heroes* (1968); *Don't Look Back* (1969); *The Family at Ditlaberg* (1969); *The Africans* (1970); *The Big House* (1970); *Sun and Moon* (1970); *Cleopatra's People* (1972); *The Danish Teapot* (1973); *A Life for Africa* (1973); *Small Talk* (1973); *Sunrise Tomorrow* (1973); *Oil for the Highlands?* (1974); *All Change Here* (1975); *Sittlichkeit* (1975); *Solution Three* (1975); *The Cleansing of the Knife* (1978); *What do you Think Yourself?* (1982)

Moir, David Macbeth (1798–1851). Poet and novelist who wrote under the pseudonym 'Δ'. He was born on 5 January 1798 at Musselburgh, East Lothian. He studied medicine at Edinburgh but returned to practise in his home town, where he was to remain until his death on 6 July 1851. Moir became a regular contributor to BLACKWOOD'S MAGAZINE, writing verse under his pseudonym, but gradually assuming the editorial responsibilities that had been held by JOHN WILSON (iii). Among his earliest works for the firm was an edition of the poems of Mrs Hemans (Felicia Dorothea Browne, 1793–1835), but his first original work, *The Life of Mansie Wauch, Tailor of Dalkeith*, appeared as a serial in the magazine from 1824 onwards and in book form in 1828. With its humorous caricatures of life in small-town Scotland, it looks forward to the novels of the KAILYARD school later in the century; it was popular in its day, especially in England where readers were delighted to read about Scottish rural manners as seen through the carefully anglicized Scots of the pawky central character, Mansie Wauch. Moir also wrote some minor verse, collected in *Domestic Verses* (1843), and he was thought by many to have been the author of the 'Canadian Boat Song' which appeared anonymously in *Blackwood's* in 1829. An admirer of JOHN GALT, to whom he dedicated *Mansie Wauch*, Moir wrote a biography of him in 1843. His *Poetical Works*, with a memoir by THOMAS AIRD, appeared in 1852.

WORKS: *Mansie Wauch* (1828); *Outlines of the Ancient History of Medicine* (1831); *The Bridal of Bothwell* (1841); *Biographical Memoir of John Galt* (1843); *Domestic Verses* (1843); *Poetical Works* (1852); *The Roman Antiquities of Inveresk* (1860)

Monboddo, Lord. *See* BURNETT, JAMES.

Mons Meg. A piece of 15th-century ordnance, on show in Edinburgh Castle, which is thought to have been cast in Flanders before finding its way to Scotland. It may have had connections with Dumfries and Galloway and its history is a matter for much speculation. After the Jacobite rebellion of 1745 it was removed to London where it remained in the Tower of London until 1822 when Sir Walter Scott was instrumental in having it returned to Scotland to become part of the country's historical heritage.

Montgomerie, Alexander (*c*1545–98). Poet, and a leading member of the CASTALIAN BAND of poets at the court of JAMES VI. He came from the Ayrshire Montgomeries, who were related to the Earl of Eglintoun, and through his mother, Lady Margaret Fraser, he enjoyed a distant relationship to the king. Very little is known about the facts of his life, but he would have received a liberal education before entering the service of the regent Morton during James's minority. Although he continued to serve James after his accession and was styled 'Captain', his adherence to Catholicism led to unwise associations in Spain and he was banished as a traitor from Scotland, a fate bemoaned in 'Ane Invectione against Fortun'. From other poems it would appear that Montgomerie's behaviour had been reckless and irresponsible from an early age and that he suffered from other misfortunes such as the withdrawal of his pension. Exile claimed him and he died abroad, probably before the turn of the century, after spending a short period in an English prison.

During his period of ascendancy at court Montgomerie was regarded as the leading member of the Castalians, and his work was the embodiment of James's REULIS AND CAUTELIS, which laid the ground rules for the court poets. To some extent he was influenced by Guillaume du Bartas (1544–90), the French poet who was ambassador at the Scottish court, and in particular by the didactic nature of much of his work. In THE CHERRIE AND THE SLAE, for instance, there is a clever allegory of the triumph of reason over emotion which is a thinly veiled hint that James is wrong not to support Catholicism; but this poem, with its complex rhyming stanzas which may have been set to music, is also a beautiful ornament. It was worked at over many years and was first published in 1597.

Many of Montgomerie's sonnets and occasional verses were set to 'musik fyne', the compositions of the period, as opposed to older folk melodies. He also wrote a spirited 'flyting' against his poetic opponent Polwarth and several love lyrics, including his much-admired sonnet, 'To his Mistress'. In all his considerable output he showed himself to be an adept master of metrical forms.

EDITIONS: J. Cranstoun, ed., *Poems of Alexander Montgomerie*, STS (Edinburgh, 1887), *Supplement*, ed. J. Stevenson (1910)

REFERENCES: H. M. Shire, *Song, Dance and Poetry at the Court of Scotland under James VI* (Cambridge, 1969)

Montgomerie, William (*b* 1904). Poet. He was born in Glasgow on 30 May 1904 and was educated there at Newlands Public School, Whitehill Secondary School and the University of Glasgow. After a period spent teaching in Dundee and collecting ballad material for the SCHOOL OF SCOTTISH STUDIES, he did research in Edinburgh into Scottish ballads and folk-song. A good part of his life has been spent abroad and he has lived in Berlin, Provence and Andalusia. With his wife Norah Montgomerie, he has edited four collections of folklore, verse and rhymes for children, all of which offer tantalizing introductions to the Scottish oral tradition. Between 1978 and 1982 he was editor of LINES REVIEW.

WORKS: *Via* (1933); *Squared Circle* (1934); ed., *New Judgements: Robert Burns* (1947)
With Norah Montgomerie, *Scottish Nursery Rhymes* (1946); *Sandy Candy* (1948); *The Well at the World's End* (1956); *The Hogarth Book of Scottish Nursery Rhymes* (1964)

Montrose, Marquis of. *See* GRAHAM, JAMES.

Moore, Edward. Pen-name of EDWIN MUIR.

Moore, John (1729–1802). Novelist and travel writer. He was born in Stirling, the son of a minister. He was educated at the University of Glasgow, where he studied medicine, and between 1747 and 1778 he worked in Europe as an army doctor and as private surgeon to the Duke of Albemarle. He was the author of several travel books, including *A View of Society and Manners in France, Switzerland and Germany* (1779), and he wrote a number of novels including *Zeluco* (1789), which was praised by Byron. Moore became a friend and correspondent of ROBERT BURNS, and Burns's letters to him of 2 August 1787 and 4 January 1789 are important for their autobiographical content. The correspondence ceased in 1795 when Moore published *A View of the Causes and Progress of the French Revolution*, which advertised his Royalist views. He died on 21 January 1802 in London. His eldest son was Sir John Moore, the hero of Corunna.

WORKS: *A View of Society and Manners in France, Switzerland and Germany* (1779); *A View of Society and Manners in Italy* (1781); *Medical Sketches* (1786); *Zeluco* (1789); *A Journal during a Residence in France* (1793); *A View of the Causes and Progress of the French Revolution* (1795); *Edward* (1796); *Sketches of Life, Character and Manners in Various Countries* (1800)

EDITION: R. Anderson, ed., *The Works of John Moore, with Memoirs of his Life and Writings*, 7 vols. (Edinburgh, 1820)

Morgan, Edwin (*b* 1920). Poet and critic. He was born on 27 April 1920 in Glasgow and was educated there at Rutherglen Academy, Glasgow High School and the University. Between 1947 and 1980 he lectured at the University and from 1975 was titular Professor of English. During World War II he served with the Royal Army Medical Corps in the Middle East. His first collection of poems, *The Vision of Cathkin Braes* (1952), gave a clue to many of his future poetic interests – the middle east, science fiction, the cinema and Glasgow – and these strands have run through his subsequent collections. Writing in 1974 (in *Worlds: Seven Modern Poets*, ed. G. Summerfield, p.229), Morgan interpreted his poetry 'as partly an instrument of exploration, like a spaceship, into new fields of feeling or experience . . . and partly a special way of recording moments and events'; thus much of his work is a response to the rapidly changing life of the modern world and he has also made great use of scientific imagery and a technological vocabulary. His native city of Glasgow has been a major source of inspiration both as a celebration, as in 'Trio' and for its history of violence as in 'King Billy' and 'Glasgow Green'.

Like IAN HAMILTON FINLAY, Morgan has written several examples of 'concrete' poems, epigrammatic works which frequently break down words to basic components and rebuild them to give different shades of meaning.

A prodigious translator, Morgan's reworkings of the poetry of 27 Russian, European and English writers, including Boris Pasternak (1890–1960), Eugenio Montale (*b* 1896) and Federico Garcia Lorca (1898–1936), were published in *Rites of Passage* (1976), and his translations into Scots of the poetry of Vladimir Mayakovsky (1893–1930), *Wi' the Haill Voice*, was published in 1972. Other translations include *Beowulf* (1952), *Poems from Eugenio Montale* (1959) and *Selected Poems, Sando Weores* (1970). Morgan has also written on Hugh MacDiarmid (CHRISTOPHER MURRAY GRIEVE) and his collected *Essays* appeared in 1974.

WORKS: *Beowulf* (1952); *The Vision of Cathkin Braes* (1952); *The Cape of Good Hope* (1955); *Poems from Eugenio Montale* (1959); *Sovpoems* (1961); ed., *Collins Albatross Book of Longer Poems* (1963); *Scotch Mist* (1965); *Starryveldt* (1965); *Sealware* (1966); ed., with Maurice Lindsay and George Bruce, *Scottish Poetry 1-6* (1966–72); *Emergent Poems* (1967); *The Second Life* (1968); *Gnomes* (1968); *Penguin Modern Poets 15* (1969); *Proverbfolder* (1969); *The Horseman's Word* (1970); ed., *Penguin New English Dramatists 14* (1970); *Selected Poems, Sando Weores* (1970); *Twelve Songs* (1970); *The Dolphin's Song* (1971); *Glasgow Sonnets* (1972); *Instamatic Poems* (1972); *Wi' the Haill Voice: 25 Poems by Vladimir Mayakovsky* (1972); *From Glasgow to Saturn* (1973); *The Whittrick* (1973); *Essays* (1974); *Rites of Passage: Selected Translations* (1976); *The New Divan* (1977); *Star Gate Science Fiction Poems* (1979); *Poems of Thirty Years* (1982)

Mossgiel [Mossgaville). The farm tenanted by ROBERT BURNS and his brother GILBERT BURNS between 1784 and 1786. It was during this period that Burns wrote most of the poems which appeared in the KILMARNOCK EDITION of 1786. The farm ran to 118 acres and the present farmhouse has replaced Burn's single-storey 'but and ben' cottage.

Motherwell, William ['Isaac Brown'] (1797–1835). Poet. He was born on 13 October 1797 in Glasgow, the son of an ironmonger. His childhood was spent in Edinburgh and Paisley and he was educated at the University of Glasgow. On completing his education he worked for the Sheriff-Clerk of Paisley, and between 1819 and 1829 he was Sheriff-Clerk Depute of Renfrewshire. For a time Motherwell was associated with the WHISTLE-BINKIE poets, and even his best-known ballad, 'Jeannie Robertson', betrays the heavy sentimentality of their verse writing. In the field of ballad and song

collecting he had a surer ear, and his anthology *The Harp of Renfrewshire* (1819) is a good example of a worthwhile collection of local songs and verse. The publication of his *Minstrelsy, Ancient and Modern* (1827) brought him the friendship of Sir WALTER SCOTT, and of JAMES HOGG with whom he was to collaborate in an edition of the poems of ROBERT BURNS in 1835. By then the mental instability, already present in his earlier years, had taken a grip on his life and he died of apoplexy on 1 November 1835. Between 1828 and 1832 he edited a number of newspapers including the *Glasgow Courier* and the *Paisley Magazine*.

WORKS: *The Harp of Renfrewshire* (1819); as Isaac Brown, *Renfrewshire Characters and Scenery* (1824); *Minstrelsy, Ancient and Modern* (1827); *Poems Narrative and Lyrical* (1832); *The Works of Robert Burns* (1835)

EDITION: J. McConechy, ed., *The Poetical Works of William Motherwell*, with a memoir (Glasgow, 1847)

REFERENCE: W. Montgomerie, *William Motherwell and Robert A. Smith* (Oxford, 1958)

Mount Oliphant. The farm tenanted by WILLIAM BURNES between Martinmas 1765 and Whitsun 1777. The poor soil made cultivation difficult and the family's problems were added to when their landlord died and the estate passed into the control of a factor. According to ROBERT BURNS, Burnes's oldest son, 'the farm proved a ruinous bargain', but it was there that he wrote his first song *O, once I lov'd a bonnie lass.*

Muir, Edwin ['Edward Moore'] (1887–1959). Poet and critic. He was born on 15 May 1887 at Deerness on the west of the Orkney mainland. His early childhood was spent on the island of Wyre and at Garth near Kirkwall, where he was educated at the local grammar school. When Muir was 14 his family left Orkney and settled in Glasgow, where Muir worked in a number of menial jobs. After the death of his parents he began to involve himself in socialist politics, becoming a member of the Independent Labour Party. During World War I he worked in Greenock and started writing for A. R. Orage's magazine *The New Age*. On 7 June 1919 he married the novelist WILLA ANDERSON and they settled in London, where he took up a career as a literary journalist.

Muir's first book, *We Moderns*, a collection of aphorisms, was published in 1918 under the pseudonym 'Edward Moore'. Its publication in the United States gave the Muirs the necessary finance to travel in Europe, and between 1921 and 1924 they lived in Germany, Czechoslovakia, Italy and Austria. On his return Muir published a verse collection, *First Poems* (1925), many of which had their origin in an earlier period of psycho-analysis in London. This was followed by a long poem, *Chorus of the Newly Dead* (1926), which shows a group of misfits looking back at their life on earth.

During a period in France in 1926 Muir wrote the best of his three novels, *The Marionette* (1927), which centres on a recurring theme in Muir's work, the value of early memories and the danger inherent in a search for the lost Eden of childhood. In the novel the boy Hans confuses the reality of his own life with the make-believe world of his dolls and of a puppet theatre which portrays Faust's love for Gretchen. Muir's other novels are *The Three Brothers* (1931), an examination of dualism in the soul, and *Poor Tom* (1932), a thinly disguised account of his childhood experiences. More rewarding for him financially was his translation of Lion Feuchtwanger's novel *Jew Süss* (1926) and he became a regular translator of contemporary European literature, including the work of Franz Kafka. In 1927 Muir settled with his family in Sussex; he later lived for a time in London before moving to St Andrews in 1935, where he became friendly with the composer FRANCIS GEORGE SCOTT. He became a prominent member of PEN, the writers' organization, and after a conference in Edinburgh in 1934 he wrote *Scottish Journey* (1935), a sensitive study of contemporary Scotland.

In his poetry Muir used symbolism to formulate a highly personal vision of existence, which included not only the fall from Eden and the impossible yearning for childhood but also the penetration of time to a higher world of eternity. *Variations on a Time Theme*, a complex series of poems which balance eternity with faith in survival, was published in 1934, and *Journeys and Places*, a symbolic journey through time, where mythical figures interpret man's place, was published in 1937. War and pessimism about the past dominate *The Narrow Place* (1943), which contains 'Scotland 1941' and 'Robert the Bruce', two poems that contrast the ancient nobility of Scotland with its destruction as a nation by internal divisiveness and perverse religious dogma. *The Voyage*

(1946), based on a story told to Muir by the novelist ERIC LINKLATER, returns to the theme of man's symbolic journey through life. Muir's reputation as a major poet was established by *The Labyrinth* (1949), which includes some of his best work: 'The Transfiguration', a radiant perception of the state of being, and the poems reflecting Muir's hatred of oppression – 'The Good Town', 'The Interrogation', 'The Usurpers' and 'The Combat'.

In 1942 Muir began working with the British Council in Edinburgh and in 1946 he became director of its Prague office, an unhappy period which ended in 1949 when he moved to Rome. The following year he was appointed Warden of Newbattle Abbey College, a residential adult education college near Edinburgh; during his period of tenure he was able to encourage writers such as GEORGE MACKAY BROWN and TOM SCOTT who were students there. Muir moved to the United States in 1955 as Norton Professor of English at Harvard; he returned in 1956 to live at Swaffham Prior near Cambridge which remained his home until his death on 3 January 1959. He published *One Foot in Eden* in 1956, a final collection which contains 'The Horses', his apocalyptic vision of war and destruction and of the primal grace and endurance of horses and their necessary relationship to man. His *Collected Poems* appeared in 1960 (revised 1963) and *Selected Poems*, edited by T. S. Eliot, in 1965.

As a critic Muir wrote a number of notable books including *The Structure of the Novel* (1928), *John Knox: Portrait of a Calvinist* (1929), *The Story and the Fable* (1940), *Essays on Literature and Society* (1949) and *The Estate of Poetry* (1962). His controversial study *Scott and Scotland* (1936) reached the conclusion that 'Scotland can only create a national literature by writing in English'. His denial of the literary power of Scots led to a breach in his friendship with the poet Hugh MacDiarmid (CHRISTOPHER MURRAY GRIEVE). Muir's *Autobiography* appeared in 1954 (revised 1965), and his wife Willa's memoir *Belonging* in 1968.

WORKS: *We Moderns* (1918); *Latitudes* (1924); *First Poems* (1925); *Chorus of the Newly Dead* (1926); *Transition* (1926); *The Marionette* (1927); *The Structure of the Novel* (1928); *John Knox: Portrait of a Calvinist* (1929); *The Three Brothers* (1931); *Poor Tom* (1932); *Variations on a Time Theme* (1934); *Scottish Journey* (1935); *Scott and Scotland* (1936); *Journeys and Places* (1937); *The Present Age, from 1914* (1939); *The Story and the Fable* (1940); *The Narrow Place* (1943); *The Voyage* (1946); *The*

Labyrinth (1949); *Essays on Literature and Society* (1949); *Collected Poems* (1952); *An Autobiography* (1954); *One Foot in Eden* (1956); *The Estate of Poetry* (1962); *Collected Poems, 1921–1958* (1960); ed. T. S. Eliot, *Selected Poems* (1965)

EDITIONS: P. H. Butter, ed., *Selected Letters of Edwin Muir* (London, 1974); A. Noble, ed., *Edwin Muir: Uncollected Scottish Criticism* (London, 1982)

REFERENCES: J. C. Hall, *Edwin Muir* (London, 1956); P. H. Butter, *Edwin Muir* (Edinburgh, 1962); P. H. Butter, *Edwin Muir: Man and Poet* (Edinburgh, 1966); W. Muir, *Belonging: a Memoir* (London, 1968); E. Huberman, *The Poetry of Edwin Muir* (New York, 1971); C. Wiseman, *Beyond the Labyrinth: a Study of Edwin Muir's Poetry* (Victoria, British Columbia, 1978)

Muir, James Hamilton. Collective pseudonym of DAVID WILLIAM BONE, Muirhead Bone and Archibald H. Charteris.

Muir, Thomas of Huntershill (1765–98). Parliamentary reformer. Thomas Muir, the Laird of Huntershill near Glasgow, was a leading member of the Convention of Delegates of Friends of the People, which met in Edinburgh to promote parliamentary franchise for every man over 21. He also maintained close links with the revolutionaries in France and these associations, together with his political radicalism, led to his arrest in 1793. Released on bail, he escaped to France and was outlawed, but he was persuaded to return to Edinburgh in the following year to stand trial. In 1794 he was tried for sedition under the notorious Lord Braxfield (*see* ROBERT MACQUEEN).

In 1796 Muir, a middle-class advocate, was sentenced to deportation to Australia at a hearing in which the interpretation of sedition was left to the judge's conservative prejudices; the harsh punishments meted out to him and other Friends of the People reflected the government's fears of any repercussions in Britain of the French Revolution. Muir escaped from Australia and after a succession of adventures found his way to France on a Spanish frigate, which was attacked by ships of the Royal Navy. He died in France from wounds he received in the battle.

Munro, Neil ['Hugh Foulis'] (1864–1930). Novelist. He was born on 2 June 1864 at Inverary, Argyllshire, where his father was a farmer. He came from a Gaelic-speaking background and many of his novels are redolent of his love for the history, both real and legendary, of his native Argyll. After a five-year period working in a law office, he turned to journalism in Glaegow, and after working for several newspapers he became the editor of the *Glasgow Evening News*, a post he held from 1918 to 1927. His last years, before his death on 22 December 1930, were spent at Craigendorran near Helensburgh on the Firth of Clyde.

Two of Munro's earliest works, *The Lost Pibroch* (1896), a collection of Celtic tales, and *Gilian the Dreamer* (1899), are romantic pictures of the Highlands, written in the CELTIC TWILIGHT style that had been made fashionable by, among others, W. B. Yeats (1865–1939) and WILLIAM SHARP. Although the past continued to lure Munro's imagination, he turned to writing historical adventures in the style of Sir WALTER SCOTT and ROBERT LOUIS STEVENSON. *Doom Castle* (1901) is set in the years following the Jacobite rebellion of 1745; although the atmosphere of the decaying, mysterious castle pervades the book, it is saved from sentimentality by Munro's firm characterization, especially of the central figure, Count Victor of Montaiglon, an anti-hero who can see through the false allure of Jacobitism. *John Splendid* (1898) has an elegaic, poetic quality, its theme being life's brevity and the futility of human aspiration. The novel is set against the background of Montrose's devastation of the Argyll heartlands in 1644, and the action is seen through the eyes of Elrigmore, a melancholy dreamer who has fallen in with the contrasting character, John Splendid, an adventurer in the style of Stevenson's ALAN BRECK STEWART. The theme of close but contrasting friends is taken up again in *The New Road* (1914); here the friendship is between Norman Campbell, the agent of Argyll, and Aeneas, who sees in the Highlands the false romance of history. Realization comes to Aeneas that civilization is only a thin crust and that below it lie the forces of savagery and greed. The 'new' roads are those built by General Wade in the Highlands after the Jacobite rebellion of 1715, and although they are hated, Aeneas and Norman finally recognize that their construction is only a passing symbol in the march of history: the new road will become, eventually, the old road.

In later life Munro gave up writing historical romances and produced several (mostly unsuccessful) novels of contemporary life; as a result, most of his work is, somewhat unjustly, ignored today. Paradoxically, his most successful and enduring work was the collection of quaint, humorous stories about the adventures of a Clyde puffer, published together as *The Vital Spark* (1906) and still popular as *Para Handy and Other Tales* (1931). Munro's collection of memoirs, *The Brave Days* (1931), contains recollections of his childhood and life as a journalist, and includes two thoughtful essays on the poets WILLIAM MCGONAGALL and JOHN DAVIDSON (ii).

WORKS: *The Lost Pibroch* (1896); *John Splendid* (1898); *Gilian the Dreamer* (1899); *Doom Castle* (1901); *The Shoes of Fortune* (1901); *Children of Tempest* (1903); *Erchie, my Droll Friend* (1904); *The Vital Spark* (1906); *The Clyde, River and Firth* (1907); *The Daft Days* (1907); *Fancy Farm* (1910); *In Highland Harbours with Para Handy* (1911); *Ayrshire Idylls* (1912); *The New Road* (1914); *Jimmy Swan, the Joy Traveller* (1917); *Jaunty Jock* (1918); *The 51st Highland Division* (1920); *Hurricane Jack* (1923); *History of the Royal Bank of Scotland* (1928); *The Brave Boys* (1931); *Para Handy and Other Tales* (1931); J. Buchan, ed., *Poetry* (1931); *The Pirate Ship* (1933); *The Looker-On* (1933)

REFERENCE: H. Wernitz, *Neil Munro und die nationale Kulturbewegung im modernen Schottland* (Berlin, 1937)

Munro, Ronald Eadie. Pen-name of DUNCAN GLEN.

Mure, Sir **William,** of Rowallan (1594–1657). Poet. He was born in 1594 on the family estate of Rowallan in Ayrshire. He was probably educated locally and at the University of Glasgow. In 1639 he succeeded to the family estates becoming a member of Parliament in 1645. A staunch Protestant, Mure fought in the Scots army at the Battle of Marston Moor (1644), but his heart was never in soldiering as we learn from the family *Historie*, which he himself began: 'This Sr Wm was pios & learned & had ane excellent vaine in poyesie; he delighted much in building and plantin.'

Mure's delight in 'poyesie' had begun as early as 1611, and through his mother's family relationship to ALEXANDER MONTGOMERIE he looked on himself as being an hereditary poet. A considerable portion of his poetry was written as propaganda for the COVENANTERS, including *The Cry of Blood and of a Broken Covenant* (1650), and his *Counterbuff* (1640) to those who compared the Covenanters to the Jesuits. His longest religious poem, *The True Crucifixe of True Catholicks* was published in 1629 and he also wrote versions of the Psalms

which were commended for use by the General Assembly of the Church of Scotland. Among his juvenilia are several love poems and courtly addresses which are imitative of the Elizabethans. Mure wrote a number of scholarly translations and his reputation as a poet rests on his skilful rendering into English of the story of Dido asnd Aeneas from the *Aeneid*.

WORKS: *The Muse's Welcome* (1618); *Dommesday* (1628); *Fancie's Farewell* (1628); *A Spirituall Hymne* (1628); *The True Crucifixe of True Catholicks* (1629); *Psalms* (1630); *The Counterbuff to Lysimachus Nicanor* (1640); *Caledon's Complaint* (1641); *The Cry of Blood and of a Broken Covenant* (1650)

EDITION: W. Tough, ed., *The Works of Sir William Mure of Rowallan*, 2 vols., STS (Edinburgh and London, 1897–8)

Murray, Charles (1864–1941). Poet. He was born on 28 September 1864 in Alford, Aberdeenshire. After an apprenticeship with an Aberdeen engineering firm, he emigrated to South Africa in 1888 and worked as an engineer with a gold-mining company. During the Boer War he served as a lieutenant with the Railway Pioneer Regiment and then entered the service of the Government of the Union of South Africa, becoming its Secretary of Public Works in 1912. He was made an Honorary LLD. of the University of Aberdeen in 1920 and was created a CMG in 1922, two years before his retirement and final return to Scotland. He died in Banchory, Kincardineshire, on 12 April 1941.

During his years in South Africa Murray started writing poetry in the dialect of the north-east of Scotland, tinged with nostaglia for his native land. A limited edition of early poems, *A Handful of Heather*, was published in 1893 but subsequently withdrawn, and his reputation rests on his collection, *Hamewith*, which was first published in Aberdeen in 1900. It was revised with an introduction by ANDREW LANG in 1909, and subsequent editions in 1917, 1927 and 1944 contained additional poems from his collections *A Sough o' War* (1917) and *In the Country Places* (1920).

Although Murray's early poetry was characterized by his celebration of the rural past of his childhood, he was no tear-jerking sentimentalist. In his often anthologized poem, 'The Whistle', he shows a lively feeling for the language and cadences of the Aberdeenshire farming countryside, and he was to say in later life that it was 'simply inevitable' that he chose to write in his native dialect. His later poems demonstrate a more controlled and compressed use of language, especially his war poem 'Dockens Afore his Peers', a masterly evocation of the garrulous and insensitive farmer who uses his own standing in the community to gain exemption from war service for his youngest son. After Murray's retirement his popularity and standing in north-east Scotland were such that when his poem 'There's Aye a Something' appeared in the *Aberdeen Press and Journal* in spring 1933 the first edition sold out by 9.00 a.m. and two extra editions had to be printed.

Although Hugh MacDiarmid (CHRISTOPHER MURRAY GRIEVE) criticized Murray's early poems for displaying KAILYARD sentimentality, Murray's vigorous use of language springs directly from his roots in the Scottish countryside and, beyond that, the oral tradition which has been kept alive in the great ballads and folk-songs of the north-east. His *Complete Poems* were published in 1979 with an introduction by Nan Shepherd.

WORKS: *A Handful of Heather* (1893); *Hamewith* (1900, rev. 2/1909, 3/1917); *A Sough o' War* (1917); *In the Country Places* (1920); *Hamewith and Other Poems: Collected Edition* (1927); *The Last Poems* (1969)

EDITION: N. Shepherd, ed., *Hamewith: the Complete Poems of Charles Murray* (Aberdeen, 1979)

Murray, Sir **David,** of Gorthy (1567–1629). Poet. He was born in 1567 in Abercairney, Perthshire. Little is known about his early life and he is first mentioned in a record of 1600, when he was appointed Comptroller of the Royal Household and a Gentleman of the Bedchamber to Prince Henry, the son of JAMES VI. For his services to the Crown he was awarded a state pension, and during the reign of Charles I he acquired the lands of Gorthy in Perthshire, where he died without an heir in 1629. Among his best work are two sonnets to Prince Henry and a metrical version of Psalm 104, 'Bless the Lord o my soul'. His long poem in irregular verse, *The Tragicall Death of Sophonisba*, was praised by his contemporary SIMEON GRAHAME, although it will find few admirers today. Murray's poems were published by the BANNATYNE CLUB in 1823.

WORKS: *The Tragicall Death of Sophonisba* (1611); *Psalm CIV* (1615); *The Complaint of the Shepherd Harpatus* (1620)

Murray, Sir **James A(ugustus) H(enry)** (1837–1915). Lexicographer. He was born on 7 February 1837 in the village of Denholm near Hawick, the son of a tailor. He was educated locally at Minto school until 1854, when he was appointed an assistant master at Hawick United School; he became a prominent citizen of the town, with a wide range of literary and scientific interests. In 1857 he became headmaster of Hawick Academy, but after his first marriage in 1862 his wife's illness forced him to move to London, where he was employed by the Chartered Bank of India. He became a master at Mill Hill School in 1870 and he also studied for an external degree at University College, London. It was at that time that Murray's interest in languages involved him in the work of the Philological Society and in editing texts for the Early English Text Society, founded by Frederick Furnivall (1825–1910). Murray's study of the language of the Borders, *The Dialect of the Southern Counties of Scotland*, was published in 1873.

The culmination of Murray's interest in languages came in 1879 when he was appointed editor of the Philological Society's dictionary, which was later to become the *Oxford English Dictionary*. It was proposed, originally, to complete the compilation in ten years but it was not until 1885 that Murray was able to work full-time as editor, and by his death on 26 July 1915 only half the dictionary had been published. The first part was published in 1884 and the final part in 1928: the entire work includes 414,825 words with 1,827,306 illustrative quotations. The dictionary marked an important step forward in the science of lexicography, and Murray's historical principles, which decreed that a word be traced from its earliest appearance, have been adopted as the model for succeeding dictionaries. James Murray was knighted in 1908 for his work on the dictionary and he received honorary degrees from nine universities.

REFERENCE: K. M. E. Murray, *Caught in the Web of Words: James A. H. Murray and the Oxford English Dictionary* (New Haven, Conn., and London, 1977)

N

Nairne, Lady. *See* OLIPHANT, CAROLINA.

Napier, John, of Merchiston (1550–1617). Mathematician and poet. He is best known for his invention of logarithms, described in his *Mirifici logarithmorum canonis constructio* which was published in 1619. He was born on the family estate of Merchiston in Edinburgh and was educated at the University of St Andrews between 1563 and 1566; on graduating he probably studied in Europe before returning to Scotland in 1571. On his father's death in 1608 he succeeded to the family estates and interested himself in agricultural improvement by experimenting with the use of fertilizers. Military matters also began to concern him and he patented the invention of a number of curious engines of war, including burning mirrors, bullet-proof clothing and advanced artillery. The remainder of his life was spent working on the mathematical calculations that resulted in the invention of logarithms and the construction of a basic calculator, known as 'Napier's Bones' because it employed ivory rods. Napier's scientific studies and his reclusive nature earned him the reputation of a necromancer, and a jet-black cockerel was supposed to be his familiar. His only poem, 'A Plaine Discovery of the Whole Revelation of St John' (1593), is a turgid rhyming attack on the Catholic church. Napier died on 4 April 1617 and is buried in Greyfriars' Churchyard in Edinburgh.

WORKS: *A Plaine Discovery of the Whole Revelation of St John* (1593); *Rabdologiae seu Numerationes per vigulas libri duo* (1617); *Mirifici logarithmorum canonis constructio* (1619); *Logarithmorum canonis constructio* (1620)

REFERENCES: M. Napier, *Memoirs of Merchiston* (1834); E. W. Hobson, *John Napier and the Invention of Logarithms* (London 1914); P. Napier, *A Difficult Country: the Napiers in Scotland* (London, 1972)

Nasmyth, Alexander (1758–1840). Artist. He was born on 9 September 1758 in Edinburgh, the son of an architect. He was educated at the HIGH SCHOOL OF EDINBURGH and at the Trustees Academy of Art under ALEXANDER RUNCIMAN. In 1775 he went to London to study art under the younger Allan Ramsay (1713–84; son of ALLAN RAMSAY), and subsequently spent several years in Italy. On his return to Edinburgh he turned to portrait painting; he became friendly with the publisher WILLIAM CREECH who invited him to paint a portrait of ROBERT BURNS for the first Edinburgh edition of his poems. The portrait became the model for many future engravings of the poet and Nasmyth became a close friend of Burns while he was in Edinburgh. After Burns's death Nasmyth painted the famous full-length portrait for the *Life of Burns* by JOHN GIBSON LOCKHART. In later life Nasmyth returned to his first love, landscape painting, and also to architecture and landscape gardening – he designed the Temple of Hygeia at St Bernard's Well in Edinburgh. In 1820 he designed sets for the theatrical production of *The Heart of Midlothian* in Edinburgh's Theatre Royal. He died on 10 April 1840.

National Covenant. *See* COVENANT, NATIONAL.

Neaves, Charles, Lord (1800–76). Judge and man of letters. He was born on 14 October 1800 in Edinburgh. He was educated at the HIGH SCHOOL OF EDINBURGH and the University, and was called to the Scottish Bar in 1822. His legal career was successful and he steadily advanced to high honours: in 1841 he was appointed Advocate-Depute, and he was Sheriff of Orkney and Shetland from 1845 to 1852, the year in which he became Solicitor-General for Scotland. His career was crowned in 1854 with his appointment as a judge in the COURT OF SESSION, taking the title 'Lord

Neaves'. As a legal man, Neaves was highly respected but he enjoyed almost as high a reputation as a man of letters. He was a lifelong contributor to BLACKWOOD'S MAGAZINE, writing on philology, and the classics, as well as penning a number of witty and entertaining satirical poems and squibs, including a highly regarded parody of the song *Roy's Wife of Aldivalloch* by ELIZABETH GRANT (i).

WORKS: *On Fiction as a Means of Popular Teaching* (1869); *A Glance at Some of the Principles of Comparative Philology* (1870); ed., *The Greek Anthology* (1870); *Lecture on Cheap and Accessible Pleasures* (1872); *Songs and Verses: Social and Scientific* (1872)

Nicholson, William (1782–1849). Poet. He was born on 15 August 1782 in Dumfries. His bad eyesight and poor health prevented him from taking up any strenuous work, and so he became a travelling packman. He became known as 'Wandering Wull' and was a well-liked visitor to the rural areas, where he would sing songs of his own composition, usually to older folk melodies. In later life, drink took its toll of his already weakened health and he died in poverty on 16 May 1849. His work was published by his friend JOHN MCDIARMID in the *Dumfries and Galloway Courier* and enjoyed a wide currency during Nicholson's lifetime. His humorous ballad 'Aiken Drum' is still a popular anth `logy piece and in his long poem *The Brownie of Bludnock* Nicholson showed a sensitive regard for the cadences of rural dialects.

EDITION: M. M. Harper, ed., *Poetical Works of William Nicholson* (Castle Douglas, 1878)

Nicol, William (1744–97). Classical scholar and teacher. He was a master at the HIGH SCHOOL OF EDINBURGH, but his fiery temper led to his dismissal after a quarrel with the rector, Dr ALEXANDER ADAM, in 1795. He accompanied ROBERT BURNS on his Highland tour of 1787, but his vanity was piqued when Burns was invited to dine alone with the Duke of Gordon at Castle Gordon. Burns was forced into leaving with his friend Nicol and losing the opportunity of meeting Robert Graham of Fintry, a fellow guest and Commissioner of Excise who could have furthered Burns's career. Burns wrote 'Elegy on Willie Nicol's Mare' for Nicol.

Nicoll, William Robertson ['Claudius Clear'] (1851–1923). Editor. He was born on 10 October 1857 at Lumsden, Aberdeenshire, the son of a Secessionist minister. He was educated in Aberdeen at the Grammar School and the University, graduating in 1870, when he trained for the ministry of the Free Church. Between 1874 and 1885 he was minister in Dufftown and then in Kelso, but ill health forced him to move south to live in London. There he formed a lifelong link with the publishing house of Hodder and Stoughton who published religious books, and for them he edited *The Expositor* and *The British Weekly*, both of which achieved eminence in evangelical circles. Nicoll proved to be a skilled editor and to *The British Weekly* he attracted writers such as J. M. BARRIE, S. R. CROCKETT and JOHN WATSON ('Ian Maclaren'), whose sentimental novels formed the basis of the KAILYARD school. In 1891 Nicoll founded *The Bookman* and two years later he added to his empire *The Woman at Home*, an illustrated magazine for women whose principal contributor was ANNIE S. SWAN. Under his pseudonym 'Claudius Clear', Nicoll contributed many articles to his own publications and these were collected in *The Daybook of Claudius Clear* (1905) and *A Bookman's Letters* (1915). He was knighted in 1909 and he died on 4 May 1923.

WORKS: *Calls to Christ* (1877); *The Incarnate Saviour* (1881); ed., *The Expositor's Bible*, 50 vols. (1888–1905); *James Macdonnell: Journalist* (1890); *The Lamb of God* (1893); *The Key of the Grave* (1894); *Ten Minute Sermons* (1894); with T. J. Wise, *Literary Anecdotes of the Nineteenth Century* (1895); *The Seven Words from the Cross* (1895); *When the Worst comes to the Worst* (1896); *The Return to the Cross* (1897); ed., *Songs of Rest* (1897); ed., *Sunday Afternoon Verses* (1897); *The Ascent of the Soul* (1899); *A Book of Family Worship* (1899); *The Churchman's One Foundation* (1901); *The Daybook of Claudius Clear* (1905); *The Garden of the Nuts* (1905); with Thomas Seccombe, *The Bookman's Illustrated History of English Literature* (1906); with J. T. Stodart, *The Expositor's Discovery of Texts* (1906); *The Lamb of Sacrifice* (1906); *Ian Maclaren* (1908); *My Faith* (1908); ed., *The Complete Works of Emily Bronte* (1910); *The Round of the Cloth* (1910); *Sunday Evening* (1910); with J. T. Stodart, *The Expositor's Treasury of Children's Sermons* (1912); *The Problem of 'Edwin Drood'* (1912); *Professor Elmslie* (1912); with J. W. Butcher, *The Children for the Church* (1913); *The Lord's Servant Deaf and Blind* (1914); *A Bookman's Letters* (1915); *Prayer in War Time* (1916); *Reunion in Eternity* (1918); *Princes of the Church* (1921); *Dickens' Own Story* (1923); *Memories of Mark Rutherford* (1924); *People and Books* (1926); *The Seen and the Unseen* (1926)

EDITIONS: H. Escott, ed., *God Signs His Name: Gleanings from the Devotional Writings of William Robertson Nicoll* (London, 1940)

REFERENCES: J. T. Stodart, *William Robertson Nicoll: Editor and Preacher* (London, 1903); T. H. Darlow, *William Robertson Nicoll: Life and Letters* (London, 1925)

Nicolson, Alexander (1827–93). Gaelic scholar. He was born on 27 September 1827 at Usabost in Skye. He was educated at the University of Edinburgh where he became assistant to Sir WILLIAM HAMILTON (iii), and he abandoned his calling to the ministry of the Free Church. For a time he worked as a journalist but he turned instead to law and was called to the Scottish Bar in 1860. He continued his interest in literature by editing the *Scottish Jurist*, and in 1872 he was appointed Sheriff-Substitute of Kirkcudbright. Later he took up a similar position in Greenock and he acted as a commissioner in the Crofting Commission of 1883. He died on 13 January 1893 in Edinburgh. Nicolson was a prolific writer and contributed to most of the leading magazines and newspapers of his day but his work in Gaelic studies is notable for his collection of proverbs, *A Collection of Gaelic Proverbs and Familiar Phrases* (1881) and for his revision of the Gaelic Bible. He also wrote a number of sentimental pastiches of Gaelic verse.

WORKS: *The Lady of Beanmhor* (1867); *Facal Earail Mu'n 'Bhallot'* (1880); *A Collection of Gaelic Proverbs and Familiar Phrases* (1881); ed., *Memoirs of Adam Black* (1885); *Song* (1893); *Verses* (1893)

Nisbet, Murdoch (*fl* 1520). Religious reformer. What little we know about Murdoch Nisbet's life comes from a letter written by his descendant Sergeant James Nisbet to Lady Betty Boswell in 1725. It was attached to the version of the New Testament that Murdoch Nisbet had made in Scots from Wycliff's translation of the Bible during the reign of JAMES V. Nisbet was a native of Ayrshire who was forced to flee the country on account of his Lollardry, and it was probably during his period in exile that he completed his work on the Bible. He returned later to Scotland but was forced to hide in a vault in his house of Hardhill in Ayrshire. After his death Nisbet's Bible was passed on by successive generations, from father to son, until it came into the possession of Sir ALEXANDER BOSWELL of Auchinleck. Nisbet used John Purvey's 1388 edition of Wycliff's translation and contented himself with keeping many of the English words and phrases that had a common currency in Scot-land instead of using Scots alternatives. Nevertheless, Nisbet's Bible is one of the few attempts, together with the treatise of JOHN GAU, *The Richt Vay into the Kingdome of Heuine*, to provide Scotland with versions of the Scriptures translated into Scots. That failure by the reformers was one of the factors that led to the gradual anglicization of the SCOTS language during the 17th century, which saw the ascendancy of the King James Bible.

EDITION: T. G. Law, ed., *The New Testament in Scots*, 3 vols., STS (Edinburgh and London, 1901–3)

Niven, Frederick (1878–1944). Novelist. He was born on 31 March 1878 in Chile, of Scots parents, but returned to Scotland and was educated at Hutchesons' Grammar School and Glasgow School of Art. Between 1898 and 1914 he spent most of his time travelling in North America and as a journalist in London and Scotland. During World War I he worked in the Ministry of Information, but illness and disenchantment led him to emigrate to Canada, where he died on 30 January 1944 in British Columbia. His first novel, *The Lost Cabin Mine* was published in 1908 and in all he wrote 30 works of fiction, which are set either in the Glasgow of his childhood or the Canada that he came to know in later years. Despite his long absences from Scotland, he remained an acute observer of Glasgow life and manners, and in *The Justice of the Peace* (1914) and *The Staff at Simsons* (1937) he also showed himself to be a tart and critical commentator on social differences. His Canadian novels frequently deal with the problems facing immigrants, and in *The Transplanted* (1944) there is a telling comparison between the wide open spaces of the Canadian west and the cramped slums which one of the main characters Jock Galbraith has left behind him in Glasgow. Niven's autobiography, *Coloured Spectacles*, was published in 1938.

WORKS: *The Lost Cabin Mine* (1908); *The Island Providence* (1910); *A Wilderness of Monkeys* (1911); *Above your Heads* (1912); *Dead Men's Bells* (1912); *Ellen Adair* (1913); *Hands Up* (1913); *The Porcelain Lady* (1913); *The Justice of the Peace* (1914); *The S.S. Glory* (1915); *Cinderella of Skokum Creek* (1916); *Two Generations* (1916); *Maple Leaf Songs* (1917); *Sage Bush Stories* (1917); *Penny Scots Treasures* (1918); *The Lady of the Crossing* (1919); *A Tale that is Told* (1920); *Treasure Trail* (1923); *Queer Fellows* (1927); *Canada West* (1930); *The Story of Alexander Selkirk* (1930); *The Three Marys* (1930); *The Paisley Shawl* (1931); *The Rich Wife* (1932); *Miss Barry* (1933); *Trumps* (1934); *The Flying Years* (1935); *Old*

Soldier (1936); *Colour in the Canadian Rockies* (1937); *The Staff at Simsons* (1937); *Coloured Spectacles* (1938); *The Story of their Days* (1939); *Mine Inheritance* (1940); *Brothers in Arms* (1942); *Under which King* (1943); *The Transplanted* (1944).

Noctes Ambrosianae. A series of articles published in BLACKWOOD'S MAGAZINE between 1822 and 1835. They took the form of imaginary conversations, usually over gargantuan suppers, in Ambrose's Tavern at 15 Picardy Place, Edinburgh. Some of the participants were fictitious but most of them were real: JOHN WILSON (iii) as 'Christopher North', JAMES HOGG as 'The Ettrick Shepherd', ROBERT SYM as 'Timothy Tickler', Thomas De Quincey as 'The Opium Eater' and William Maginn as 'Ensign O'Doherty'. To begin with, they were the work of many hands but those that appeared after 1825 have been credited to John Wilson who wrote 41 of the 71 pieces published in the magazine. The learned wit and tomfoolery which abounded at the evenings delighted the readers of *Blackwood's Magazine* and added greatly to its popularity. But Wilson was unable to forget the early Blackwood tradition of satire and literary highjinks; Hogg, in particular, became a target, for although in many respects his 'Ettrick Shepherd' is a delightful creation in the *'Noctes'*, Wilson frequently took the opportunity of savaging him in print and of ascribing to him opinions that were not his own. The *'Noctes Ambrosianae'* were published in a four-volume edition in 1885 with an introduction by Wilson's nephew JAMES FREDERICK FERRIER.

North, Christopher. Pen-name of JOHN WILSON (iii).

O

Of the Day Estivall. A poem by ALEXANDER HUME. Literally 'Of a summer's day', it is perhaps one of the most sensuous poems in the Scots tradition of painting word pictures of nature in all its glory. The poem describes the course of a long, hot, sunny day from dawn to dusk, and, in minute detail, observes the country people and the countryside in which they work. Preciseness of decoration in his natural descriptions and an eye for the constantly changing patterns of light allowed Hume to give his poem the qualities of a painting, resplendent with all the colours of many-hued nature.

Ogilvie, Will(iam) H(enry) (1869–1963). Poet. He was born on 21 August 1869 at Holmfield, Kelso, and was educated at Fettes College, Edinburgh. Between 1889 and 1900 he worked on a sheep farm in Australia and it was there that he began writing the simple, unaffected verses about country matters that constitute so much of his work. He was Professor of Agricultural Journalism at Iowa State College from 1905 to 1907 and he served with the Remount Department of the War Office during World War I. He retired to Scotland and lived the life of a Border laird until his death on 30 January 1963. His verse in Scots owes much to the form and imagery of the Border ballads but rarely rises above the level of pastiche, albeit robust.

WORKS: *Fair Girls and Grey Horses* (1899); *Hearts of Gold* (1901); *Rainbows and Witches* (1907); *My Life in the Open* (1908); *Whaup o' the Rede* (1909); *The Land we Love* (1910); *The Overlander* (1913); *The Honour of the Station* (1914); *The Australian and Other Verses* (1916); *Galloping Shoes* (1922); *Scattered Scarlett* (1923); *Over the Grass* (1925); *A Handful of Leather* (1928); *A Clear Wind Blowing* (1930); *Collected Sporting Verse* (1935); *Saddles Again* (1937); *From Sunset to Dawn* (1947); *Saddle for a Throne* (1953); *Border Poems* (1959)

Ogilvy, Gavin. Pen-name of J. M. BARRIE.

Oisin. *See* OSSIAN.

Old Mortality. A novel by Sir WALTER SCOTT, published in 1816 in the first series of TALES OF MY LANDLORD. As in so many of his novels, Scott used the real events of Scotland's past as a backdrop to his story; in the case of *Old Mortality* the setting is the period of the Covenanting wars between 1679 and the Glorious Revolution of 1688. 'Old Mortality' was the nickname of Robert Paterson, an 18th-century religious eccentric, who spent much of his life cleaning and repairing Covenanters' tombs, and who supposedly left a number of anecdotes which Scott was able to use. The opposition of the COVENANTERS to the Government aroused conflicting passions of equal extremity among those who supported the movement and those who were opposed to it. Scott's view is unclouded by the fanaticism of either side and his picture of those troubled times is a moderate, fair one, embodied in the novel's principal character, Henry Morton of Milnwood. Unable to distance himself from the conflict, Morton is drawn into the Covenanters' side after a skirmish with the dragoons of JOHN GRAHAM of Claverhouse. This action brings him into conflict with the Royalist Lady Margaret of Bellenden, the grandmother of his loved one, Edith, whose hand is also sought by Lord Evandale, one of Claverhouse's officers. Their destinies are tied up in the actions that follow: Morton is saved from immediate execution by the intervention of Evandale and this generosity is repaid at the Battle of Drumclog and later, when the fanatical Covenanting leader is about to raze the Bellenden castle of Tillietudlem. After the defeat of the Covenanters at the Battle of Bothwell Brig, Morton is banished, but because of his moderation and generosity to her family Edith remains in love with him and refuses Evandale's persistent advances. The accession of William and Mary allows Morton to return and he marries Edith after the unfortunate Evandale is killed by a group of extremists.

Old Mortality contains a sincere character sketch of Graham of Claverhouse and Scott shows a nice regard for the complexities of the period and for the passions aroused by them. In the Covenanting opposition are the committed religious extremist John Balfour of Burley and a number of minor characters such as Habakkuk Mucklewrath, Peter Poundtext and Mause Headrigg, who mirror Burley's aims. Morton and Evandale stand for moderation in the midst of fanaticism, and one of the novel's great set scenes is Morton's attempt to persuade the Covenanting leaders to accept the government's terms. In *Old Mortality* Scott displayed a remarkable ability to come to terms with the tortured religious and political events of the late 17th century and to place them in an assured historical perspective.

Oliphant, Carolina, Lady Nairne ['Mrs Bogan of Bogan'] (1766–1845). Ballad writer. She was born on 17 August 1766 at Gask, Perthshire, the daughter of Laurence Oliphant, an ardent supporter of the Jacobite cause. She married her cousin, Major William Murray Nairne, on 2 June 1806 and in 1824 he was restored to his forfeited estates and to the peerage that accompanied them. They lived in Edinburgh until Nairne's death in 1830, when Carolina moved to Bristol with her only son; thereafter she travelled widely in Ireland and Europe before returning to the family seat of Gask, where she died on 26 October 1845.

Early in her life Caroline Oliphant interested herself in songwriting, particularly in the work of ROBERT BURNS for THE SCOTS MUSICAL MUSEUM; and she too, under the pseudonym 'Mrs Bogan of Bogan', became a prolific writer of songs to traditional airs. Much of her output was concerned with a sentimental attachment to Jacobitism and her song *Will ye no' come back again* is a heartfelt lament for Prince CHARLES EDWARD STUART. Other memorable songs are her spirited martial setting of *The Hundred Pipers*, a graceful interpretation of contemporary street-cries CALLER HERRIN', and songs of patriotic pride such as THE LAND OF THE LEAL and *The Rowan Tree.* Her *Life and Works*, written and edited by Charles Rogers, was published in 1869.

Oliphant [née Wilson], **Margaret** (1828–97). Novelist, critic and essayist. She was born on 4 April 1828 at Wallyford, East Lothian. Her father, James Wilson, was a businessman, and her early years were spent in Glasgow and Liverpool, and in London, where she published her first novel, *Margaret Maitland*, in 1849. Encouraged by her success, and particularly by a kind review written by FRANCIS JEFFREY, she spent the greater part of 1851 in Edinburgh, where she began a lifelong association with the publishing house of WILLIAM BLACKWOOD, becoming a regular contributor to BLACKWOOD'S MAGAZINE. Although she was in Edinburgh again in 1860–61 most of her life was spent in Europe and in London. She married her cousin, an artist, Frank Wilson Oliphant, in 1857 but he died of tuberculosis two years later leaving her with three children.

Between 1861 and 1876 Margaret Oliphant wrote a series of novels of English provincial life and manners, *The Chronicles of Carlingford*, which were first published in serial form in *Blackwood's*. The best of these are *Salem Chapel* (1863), *The Perpetual Curate* (1864), *Miss Marjoribanks* (1866) and *Phoebe Junior* (1876). They were admired for their insights into English social and religious institutions and although they were written in the style of similarly popular series such as Anthony Trollope's Barsetshire novels, Margaret Oliphant was no mere plagiarist; her critical analysis of life in a Dissenting community in *Salem Chapel* is a masterly evocation of provincial Nonconformism.

Margaret Oliphant also wrote novels of Scottish life, among them *The Minister's Wife* (1869), *Effie Ogilvie* (1886) and *Kirsteen* (1890), which, although marked by the popular sentimentality of the period, are realistic pictures of a closed society and rich with a strongly delineated characterization of Scottish middle-class life. In *Effie Ogilvie* she criticized, in a Scottish setting, the Victorian ideals of justification by work, vindication by making money and the inferior role of women in society; she returned to these themes in *The Railway Man and his Children* (1891), a remarkable novel which examines the social relationships between women and their work. Her other fictional interest was in the supernatural and she wrote two collections of tales, *A Beleaguered City* (1880) and *A Little Pilgrim in the Unseen* (1882), which are little more than literary curiosities.

Despite writing over 100 best-selling novels, Margaret Oliphant's uncompromising attitude towards her work meant that she did not make a fortune. Her unflinching realism and contempt for the 'happy ending' made her novels difficult to market and she was forced into hack work, writing 28 non-fiction books between 1862 and her death. Among these were histories and critical work, the best known being *Francis of Assisi* (1868), *Historical Sketches of the Reign of George II* (1869), *Literary History of England in the End of the Eighteenth and Beginning of the Nineteenth Century* (1882), and biographical sketches of EDWARD IRVING (1862), JOHN TULLOCH (1888) and her cousin Laurence Oliphant (1891), the travel writer and travel correspondent of *The Times*. Her industry paid for the education at Eton College of her two sons who predeceased her, and of her nephew Frank, with whom she wrote *The Victorian Age of English Literature* in 1892.

Margaret Oliphant wrote over 200 articles for *Blackwood's Magazine*, including a series of critical essays called 'The Old Saloon'; she described herself in 1856 in a letter to the editor as 'a sort of general utility woman in the Magazine'. The need to maintain her family from her literary work inevitably distracted her from the novels, but in all her writing there is an ease, vitality and good humour which makes her never dull or unreadable. The last years of her life were spent in writing the first two volumes of Blackwood's, *Annals of a Publishing House: William Blackwood and his Sons, their Magazine and Friends* (1897), which remains one of the best repositories of 19th-century literary gossip as well as being a unique record of her own association with the Blackwood family. She died in London on 25 June 1897 having corrected the proofs of the second volume of the *Annals*. The final volume was written by Mary Porter, the daughter of John Blackwood.

WORKS: *Margaret Maitland* (1849); *Caleb Field* (1851); *Merkland* (1851); *Adam Graeme of Mossgray* (1852); *Harry Muir* (1853); *Katie Stewart* (1853); *Magdalen Hepburn* (1854); *Quiet Heart* (1854); *Zaidee* (1856); *The Athelings* (1857); *The Days of My Life* (1857); *The Laird of Nordlaw* (1858); *Orphans: a Chapter in Life* (1858); *Sundays* (1858); *Agnes Hopetoun's Schools and Holidays* (1859); *Lilliesleaf* (1859); *Lucy Crofton* (1860); *The House on the Moor* (1861); *The Last of the Mortimers* (1862); *Life of Edward Irving*, 2 vols. (1862); *Heart and Cross* (1863); *The Rector and the Doctor's Family*, 3 vols. (1863); *Salem Chapel*, 2 vols. (1863); *The Perpetual Curate* (1864); *Agnes*, 3 vols. (1866); *Miss Marjoribanks* (1866); *A Son of the Soil* (1866); *Madonna Mary*, 3 vols. (1867); *The Brownlows*, 3 vols. (1868); *Francis of Assisi* (1868); *Historical Sketches of the Reign of George II*, 2 vols. (1869); *The Minister's Wife* (1869); *John: a Love Story*, 2 vols. (1870); *The Three Brothers*, 3 vols. (1870); *Squire Arden*, 3 vols. (1871); *At His Gates*, 3 vols. (1872); *Memoirs of the Count de Montalembert* (1872); *Ombra*, 3 vols. (1872); *Innocent: a Tale of Modern Life* (1873); *May*, 3 vols. (1873); *For Love and Life*, 3 vols. (1874); *A Rose in June*, 2 vols. (1874); *The Story of Valentine and his Brother*, 3 vols. (1875); *Whiteladies*, 3 vols. (1875); *The Curate in Charge*, 2 vols. (1876); *Dress* (1876); *The Makers of Florence* (1876); *Phoebe Junior*, 3 vols. (1876); *Carita*, 3 vols. (1877); *Mrs Arthur*, 3 vols. (1877); *Young Musgrave* 3 vols. (1877); *The Primrose Path*, 3 vols. (1878); *The Greatest Heiress in England*, 3 vols. (1879); *The Two Mrs Scudamores* (1879); *Within the Precincts*, 3 vols. (1879); *A Beleaguered City* (1880); *He that Will Not when he May*, 3 vols. (1880); *Harry Joscelyn*, 3 vols. (1881); *In Trust: a Story of a Lady and Her Lover*, 3 vols. (1882); *Literary History of England in the End of the Eighteenth and Beginning of the Nineteenth Century*, 3 vols. (1882); *A Little Pilgrim in the Unseen* (1882); *Hester: A story of Contemporary Life* (1883); *It was a lover and his lass*, 3 vols. (1883); *The Ladies Lindores*, 3 vols (1883); *Sheridan* (1883); *Sir Tom*, 3 vols. (1884); *The Wizard's Son*, 3 vols. (1884); *Madam*, 3 vols. (1885); *Two Stories of the Seen and Unseen* (1885); *A Country Gentleman and his Family*, 3 vols. (1886); *Effie Ogilvie*, 2 vols. (1886); *A House Divided Against Itself*, 3 vols. (1886); *Oliver's Bride* (1886); *The Makers of Venice* (1887); *The Son of his Father*, 3 vols. (1887); *Cousin Mary* (1888); *Lady Car* (1889); *Joyce*, 3 vols. (1888); *The Land of Darkness* (1888); *Memoir of the Life of John Tulloch* (1888); *The Second Son*, 3 vols. (1888); *Neighbours on the Green* (1889); *A Poor Gentleman*, 3 vols. (1889); *The Duke's Daughter*, 3 vols. (1890); *Kirsteen* (1890); *The mystery of Mrs Blencarrow* (1890); *Royal Edinburgh* (1890); *Sons and Daughters* (1890); *Janet*, 3 vols. (1891); *Jerusalem: its History and Hope* (1891); *Memoirs of the Life of Laurence Oliphant and Alice Oliphant his Wife* (1891); *The Railway Man and his Children*, 3 vols. (1891); *The Cuckoo in the Nest*, 3 vols. (1892); *Diana Trelawny*, 2 vols. (1892); *The Heir Presumptive and the Heir Apparent*, 3 vols. (1892); *The Marriage of Elinor*, 3 vols. (1892); with F. R. Oliphant, *The Victorian Age of English Literature*, 2 vols. (1892); *Lady William*, 3 vols. (1893); *The Sorceress*, 3 vols. (1893); *Thomas Chalmers, Preacher, Philosopher and Statesman* (1893); *Historical Sketches of the Reign of Queen Anne* (1894); *A House in Bloomsbury*, 2 vols. (1894); *The Prodigals and their Inheritance*, 2 vols. (1894); *Who was Lost and is Found* (1894); *A Child's History of Scotland* (1895); *The Makers of Modern Rome* (1895); *Sir Robert's Fortune* (1895); *Two Strangers* (1895); *Jeanne d'Arc* (1896); *Old Mr Tredgold* (1896); *The Two Marys* (1896); *The Unjust Steward* (1896); *Annals of a Publishing House: William Blackwood and his Sons*, 2 vols. (1897); *The Lady's Walk* (1897); *The Sisters Brontë* (1897); *The Ways of Life* (1897); *That Little Cutty* (1898); *A Widow's Tale* (1898)

EDITION: Mrs H. Coghill, ed., *Autobiography and Letters of Mrs Margaret Oliphant*, with an introduction by Q. D. Leavis (Leicester, 1974)

Orkneyinga Saga. A medieval chronicle of the Earls of Orkney, which provides a unique account of the history of Orkney and Caithness between the ninth and the 13th centuries. The saga was written early in the 13th century by an unknown Icelandic scribe at a time when Icelandic writers were trying to record the oral traditions of the world as they knew it and to make sense of their knowledge. Thus the history of Orkney as contained in the saga is contemporaneous with other sagas that record the histories of the Scandinavian countries.

To give the *Orkneyinga Saga* a sense of time and place the scribe began his narrative with tales of the legendary gods and heroes and took it rapidly to the conquest of Orkney by the Norse jarl (earl) Harald Harfagri who presented it to Rögnvald, Earl of Moeri (*d* 890). The story of the foundation of the line of the Earls of Orkney is the starting-point for the retelling of a series of stories about heroic fights and adventures, but the saga is not all about warfare. Domestic details of life in the great halls are lovingly described and the cycle of the changing seasons from springtime to harvest home marks the passing of the years. Fact and fiction mix easily together and although some of the stories are ornamented versions of the truth, the saga does provide a framework for an understanding of Orkney's early history and of its Viking heritage. Worked into the narrative are a number of skaldic or bardic songs which both add to the atmosphere of the chronicle and also allow the scribe to tell the story from a different angle.

EDITIONS: J. Anderson, ed., *The Orkneyinga Saga*, trans. J. A. Hjaltalin and G. Goudie (Edinburgh, 1873); G. W. Darsent, ed., *The Orkneyinga Saga* (London, 1894); A. B. Taylor, ed., *The Orkneyinga Saga* (Edinburgh, 1938); H. Palsson and P. Edwards, eds., *The Orkneyinga Saga* (London, 1978)

Orwell. Pen-name of WALTER CHALMERS SMITH.

Orygynale Cronykil of Scotland. A verse history of Scotland from the earliest times to the reign of ROBERT I (Robert the Bruce), written by ANDREW OF WYNTOUN at the end of the 14th century. It survived in several manuscript forms and was first published in two volumes in 1795 in London by David Macpherson. DAVID LAING edited an incomplete version in three volumes between 1872 and 1879, and the definitive edition was published by the SCOTTISH TEXT SOCIETY in six volumes between 1903 and 1914. The first five of the nine books of Andrew's chronicle were taken from Latin sources, available to him but now lost, and deal exclusively with the Creation, the world's early history and genealogies of the British people. In the latter four books he turned to the more recognizable events of Scotland's recent past from the reign of MALCOLM III (Malcolm Canmore). Although many of the facts are inaccurate and Andrew's suppositions debatable, the chronicle is a precursor of the verse histories of Sir WILLIAM WALLACE and Robert the Bruce written later by, respectively, BLIND HARRY and JOHN BARBOUR. At the end of book 7 Wyntoun published a song bemoaning the evil times on which the country had fallen after the death of Alexander III. The Chronicle is generally regarded as the earliest extant specimen of Scottish poetry:

> Quhen Alexander our kynge was dede,
> That Scotlande lede in lauche and le,
> Away was sons of alle and brede,
> Off wyne and wax, of gamyn and gle.
> Our golde was changit in to lede.
> Crist, borne in virgynyte,
> Succoure Scotland, and ramede,
> That is stade in perplexite.

Osbourne [née Vandegrift], **Fanny** (1840–1914). Wife of ROBERT LOUIS STEVENSON. She was born on 10 March 1840 in Indianapolis, Indiana. In 1857 she married a wealthy Kentucky lawyer called Sam Osbourne, but within 15 years his marital indiscretions forced her to leave him. She sailed for Europe with her three children in 1875 and settled in Paris. The following year she met Stevenson at Grez but she returned to her husband in 1878 in an attempt to save her marriage. Undeterred, Stevenson followed her to America aboard an emigrant ship, an experience that gave rise to two of his best travel books, *The Amateur Emigrant* and *Across the Plains*. The couple were reunited in Monterey and following hard on Fanny's divorce they were married on 19 May 1880 in San Francisco.

Fanny remained with Stevenson until the end of his life and nursed him faithfully through the illnesses of his lungs that so plagued his health. After his death in Samoa she oversaw her husband's literary estate, and it was her determination that his memory should be respected that led to unfortunate quarrels with Stevenson's friend and biographer Sidney Colvin (1845–1927). In the event the official biography was written by Stevenson's cousin Graham Balfour. Although friends were to criticize Fanny's possessive attitude towards the memory of her dead husband, during his lifetime she was a stalwart pillar of support to him in all their many wanderings. Her son Lloyd collaborated with his stepfather in two books, and her own diary, *The Cruise of the Janet Nichol Amongst the South Sea Islands* (1915) was completed a few weeks before her death on 17 February 1914.

REFERENCE: M. Mackay, *The Violent Friend: the Story of Mrs Robert Louis Stevenson* (1968)

Ossian [Oisin]. A third-century Gaelic warrior poet, son of Fingal, or Finn, whose legends formed the basis of the poems 'translated' by JAMES MACPHERSON. The 'Ossian' poems became a *cause célèbre* in Scotland in 1760 after Macpherson published his *Fragments of Ancient Poetry Collected in the Highlands of Scotland and Translated from the Gallic or Erse Language*, with an introduction by HUGH BLAIR, who suggested that the fragments belonged to a cycle of uncollected Gaelic oral poetry still extant in the Highlands of Scotland. Money was raised for Macpherson to travel to the Highlands, and on his tour he undoubtedly collected some fragments of Ossianic verse, but, being an indifferent Gaelic speaker, he had to rely on translations by other scholars and lacked the sophistication to make intelligent use of the material he collected.

In 1761 Macpherson published *Fingal: an Ancient Epic Poem*, in which Fingal, the son of the giant Comhal, crosses to Ireland to aid the Irish hero Cuthullin against the Norse king Swaran – a legend which is different in time, place and content from the later Fenian cycle of legends concerning Finn Mac Coul and his warrior band, the Fianna. Macpherson claimed that this was a translation of a Gaelic epic, and it was followed in 1763 by *Temora*. All the 'Ossian' works met with uncritical praise from the Edinburgh *literati*: in their nationalistic fervour they argued that Scotland could boast a poetry to equal the classical epics of ancient Greece and Rome. However, English critics, notably Dr Samuel Johnson, were less sanguine and the 'Ossian' poems became the subject of much controversy, with critics in London and Dublin declaring them to be fraudulent. Macpherson remained aloof from the arguments and refused to declare the origins of his manuscript sources.

It was only after Macpherson's death in 1796, when HENRY MACKENZIE chaired an investigation for the Highland Society into the 'Ossian' sources, that the facts became known. Mackenzie's report, published in 1805, asserted that the legend of Fingal as told by Ossian was extant in the Scottish Highlands and was different from the Irish Fenian cycle; that no single poem was found by Macpherson; that Macpherson produced a free translation of Ossian by filling out the fragments with episodes of his own creation and by amending and altering the originals. Mackenzie's findings do not differ significantly from modern opinion, which acknowledges that Macpherson pieced *Fingal* together from up to 15 original Gaelic pieces with passages of his own creation and that he changed the themes and atmosphere to suit 18th-century taste.

Despite the contemporary blasts and counterblasts about the poems' authenticity, Macpherson's 'Ossian' was to exert a great influence on European thought. The poems fed the cult of the primitive savage, and in their imaginative re-creation of wild lonely places and the manifest power of nature, they looked forward to the later Romantic movement. They were translated into several languages, Goethe and Napoleon declared their debt to 'Ossian', and the pseudo-Celtic mysticism emanating from the works found its way into much music and visual art. In Scotland, 'Ossian' paved the way for the 19th-century interest in the romance of the Highlands and its people, which was taken a stage further in the works of Sir WALTER SCOTT. It is ironic that the desire of the *literati* to claim the heritage of an ancient civilization and a classical poetry should have been satisfied by Macpherson's work, while one of the finest Gaelic poets of the 18th century, DONNCHADH BÀN MAC AN T-SAOIR, was living in obscurity in Edinburgh as a member of the City Guard.

P

Park, Mungo (1771–1806). Explorer and travel writer. He was born on 10 September 1771 at Foulshiels near Selkirk, the son of a farmer. He was educated at Selkirk Grammar School and at the age of 14 was apprenticed to a local doctor, Dr Thomas Anderson. In 1788 he went to the University of Edinburgh to study medicine and he remained there until 1792, when he completed his surgical training without the formality of taking a degree. After a rapid course at the Company of Surgeons in London, he became a ship's surgeon on a voyage to the Far East, an experience that awakened his interest in travel and exploration with a scientific purpose. On his return he offered his services to the African Association which had been established in 1788 to promote African exploration for commercial and scientific reasons.

In July 1793 Park was appointed to lead an expedition to the Gambia and Niger regions of West Africa. The expedition began in May 1795 and Park did not return to London until December 1797. During his two-and-a-half year journey he reached the upper regions of the River Niger, discovering that it flowed eastwards. His account of the journey, *Travels in the Interior Districts of Africa, Performed in the Years 1795, 1796 and 1797* was published in 1799, and its modest and straightforward account made it at once one of the classics of travel literature. He returned to Selkirk where he married Allison Anderson on 2 August 1799; after a period of indecision he became a doctor in Peebles in October 1801 and remained in that post until October 1804. During this period he enjoyed the friendship of a number of his contemporaries including Sir WALTER SCOTT, ADAM FERGUSON and ROBERT CHAMBERS.

In January 1805 Park set off on an expedition sponsored by the government to trace the course of the River Niger and its ultimate source. The expedition was a failure and Park and his party were killed in an ambush at rapids near Bussa on the Niger early in 1806. His *Journal of a Mission to the Interior of Africa in the Year 1805* was published in 1815.

REFERENCES: T. B. Maclachlan, *Mungo Park* (Edinburgh, 1898); W. H. Hewitt, *Mungo Park* (London, 1923); S. Gwynn, *Mungo Park and the Quest for the Niger* (Bristol, 1934); J. L. Mitchell, *Niger: the Life of Mungo Park* (Edinburgh, 1934); P. Brent, *Black Nile* (London, 1977); K. Lupton, *Mungo Park: the African Traveller* (Oxford, 1979)

Paterson, (James Edmund) Neil (*b* 1915). Novelist and film script-writer. He was born on 31 December 1915 in Banff. He was educated at the University of Edinburgh and served as a lieutenant in the Royal Naval Volunteer Reserve during World War II. Most of Paterson's best work has been done for the cinema as a script-writer, but he has written three novels: *The China Run* (1948), based on a family history; *Behold thy Daughter* (1950), a romance of the Moray Firth herring industry; and *Man on a Tightrope* (1953), a thriller. His only collection of short stories, *And Delilah* (1951), contains *Scotch Settlement*, a story of emigration and childhood, which was made into a memorable film, *The Kidnappers*.

WORKS: *The China Run* (1948); *Behold thy Daughter* (1950); *And Delilah* (1951); *Man on a Tightrope* (1953)

Pennecuik, Alexander (i) (1652–1722). Poet. He was a native of Newhall by the River Esk in Midlothian and was educated at the University of Edinburgh, where he studied medicine. His marriage to Margaret Murray brought him an estate near Romano Bridge in the upper reaches of the Tweed valley in Peeblesshire, where most of his life was spent as a country doctor. In the country he pursued his botanical interests, corresponded with the administrators of the newly established botanical garden in Edinburgh and, at the instigation of the physician and naturalist Sir ROBERT SIB-BALD, wrote a short geographical and natural history of Tweeddale in 1715. His occasional verse was written in archaic Scots, in a style reminiscent of the medieval makrs, which was doubtless influenced by the publication by JAMES WATSON of the CHOICE COLLECTION OF COMIC AND SERIOUS SCOTS POEMS.

EDITION: R. Brown, ed., *The Works in Prose and Verse of Alexander Pennecuik*, 2 vols. (Leith, 1814)

Pennecuik, Alexander (ii) (*d* 1730). Poet. He is supposed to have been a relative of his older namesake ALEXANDER PENNECUIK (i), and was a native of Edinburgh. He was an acquaintance of ALLAN RAMSAY and much of his work is little more than a crude pastiche of Ramsay's verse. Nevertheless, there is an earthy, though frequently obscene, wit at play in Pennecuik's poetry and his social observation is sharp and entertaining. Two of his best works are 'A Pil for Pork Eaters', a diatribe against the English, and 'Groans from the Grave', a satire upon resurrectionists in Edinburgh.

EDITION: *A Compleat Collection of all the Poems Wrote by Alexander Pennecuik* (Edinburgh, 1750)

Perrie, Walter ['Patrick MacCrimmon'] (*b* 1949). Poet. He was born on 5 June 1949 in the village of Quarter, Lanarkshire. He was educated at Hamilton Academy and thereafter worked in a variety of jobs before going to the University of Edinburgh to study philosophy. In 1970 he founded with George Hardie (*b* 1933) the literary magazine *Chapman*. Perrie's first verse was written in Scots under the pseudonym 'Patrick MacCrimmon'. After feeling his way through the poetic influences of W. B. Yeats (1865–1939) and Ezra Pound (1885–1972), he found his true voice in his long poem *A Lamentation for the Children* (1977), which takes its title from the great MacCrimmon pibroch *Cumha na Chloinne*; its theme is the exploitation of the Lanarkshire coal-mining communities, which becomes within the poem a metaphor for the general human condition. In 1975 Perrie published the text of a long discussion on philosophy with Hugh MacDiarmid (CHRISTOPHER MURRAY GRIEVE) in *Metaphysics and Poetry*, and his own essays on literature and philosophy were published in *Out of Conflict* (1982).

WORKS: As Patrick MacCrimmon, *Deidre* (1971); *Ulysses* (1971); *Metaphysics and Poetry* (1975); *Surge aquilo* (1975); *Poem on a Winter's Night* (1976); *A Lamentation for the Children* (1977); *By Moon and Sun* (1980); *Out of Conflict* (1982)

Peter's Letters to his Kinsfolk. A series of social and biographical sketches of Edinburgh and Glasgow by JOHN GIBSON LOCKHART, published by WILLIAM BLACKWOOD in three volumes in 1819. They take the form of a group of letters from Peter Morris to his Welsh relative the Revd David Williams, which purport to be the record of a visit to Edinburgh, where Morris is given an entrée to the city's society through his fellow Oxonian the high-Tory antiquary, William Wastle. Volumes 1 and 2 deal with Edinburgh, culminating in a visit to ABBOTSFORD, and volume 3, written with the help of JOHN WILSON (iii) contains descriptions of Glasgow and an account of the preaching of Dr THOMAS CHALMERS.

Although *Peter's Letters to his Kinsfolk* contains several satirical protraits of Edinburgh's leading Whigs, and its publication caused a scandal similar to the uproar created by the 'Chaldee Manuscript', it does paint an accurate and at times sharply critical picture of the Edinburgh of Lockhart's day. There are excellent character sketches of HENRY THOMAS COCKBURN, FRANCIS JEFFREY, HENRY MACK-ENZIE and WALTER SCOTT, and the manners and fashions of their age are sharply delineated. But Lockhart's underlying seriousness of purpose can be seen in his balanced view of the opposing values in Scottish culture: the post-Humean rationalism of the SCOTTISH EN-LIGHTENMENT and the self-renewing traditions of the folk culture embodied by Sir Walter Scott.

When it was published the first edition of *Peter's Letters to his Kinsfolk* was labelled the second edition. Owing to its contentious topicality, the book was dropped from Blackwood's list in 1820. A selection from the letters was published in 1977 by the ASSOCIATION FOR SCOTTISH LITERARY STUDIES, with a critical introduction by William Ruddick.

Pibroch. A Scots word, borrowed from Gaelic *piobaireachd*, meaning bagpipe music or the playing of the bagpipes. It has come to mean two distinct kinds of classical Scottish Highland music for the bagpipe: *ceol mor*, or 'big music', and *ceol beag*, or 'little music'; the latter is usually applied to slow airs and dance music.

In both forms pibroch music was developed by hereditary pipers, and handed on from one generation to the next; it consists of a unique set of formalized compositions with characteristic harmonic progressions. *Ceol mor* finds its greatest expression in the heroic laments, but it also comprises salutes, marches and music for clan gatherings.

Picken, Andrew ['Christopher Keelivine'] (1788–1833). Novelist. He was born in 1788 in Paisley, the son of a wealthy clothing manufacturer. He worked for a time in a bank in Dublin, as a mercantile representative in the West Indies, in a dye works in Glasgow and as a bookseller in Liverpool, before settling in Glasgow in 1826. Robert Chambers called him 'an amiable and agreeable writer in miscellaneous literature' (*A Biographical Dictionary of Eminent Scotsmen* (Edinburgh, 1832–4) vol. 3); the variegated nature of his writing owes much to his need to earn a living from his pen. His most popular book was *Tales and Sketches of the West of Scotland* (1824), a collection of satirical social sketches, written under the pseudonym 'Christopher Keelivine'. His novels have been compared to those of JOHN GALT, with their mixture of social observation and stern realism: *The Sectarian* (1829), a study of religious fanaticism; *The Dominie's Legacy* (1830), an autobiographical novel set in Paisley; *Waltham* (1833); and *The Black Watch* (1834), a novel about the Battle of Fontenoy. At his death on 23 November 1833 Picken was working on a series of family histories.

WORKS: *Tales and Sketches of the West of Scotland* (1824); *The Sectarian* (1829); *The Dominie's Legacy* (1830); *Travels and Researches of Eminent English Missionaries* (1830); *The Club-Book* (1831); *The Canadas* (1832); *Traditional Stories of Old Families* (1833); *Waltham* (1833); *The Black Watch* (1834)

Pinkerton, John (1758–1826). Historian. He was born on 17 February 1758 in Edinburgh, was educated at the Grammar School in Lanark and later apprenticed to an Edinburgh lawyer. In 1781 he moved to London, where he remained until shortly before his death, in Paris on 10 March 1826. Pinkerton's best work was as a historian. He published an early work on numismatics, *Essay on Medals* (1784), which was followed by several histories, including two of Scotland. In the first of these, *An Inquiry into the History of Scotland Preceding the Reign of Malcolm III, or 1056, Including the*

Authentic History of that Period (1789), he expanded on his theory, stated in the *Origins and Progress of the Scythians and the Goths* (1787), that the Celts were a Gothic, aboriginal race vastly inferior to the Scots: 'The Lowlanders are acute, industrious, sensible, erect, free: the Highlanders indolent, slavish, strangers to industry.' More moderate in its opinions and better researched was his *History of Scotland from the Accession of the House of Stuart to that of Mary, with Appendices of Original Documents* (1797), which contains valuable source material especially for the reign of JAMES V.

Pinkerton's irascibility made him several enemies and his work as an editor also provoked considerable hostility for his plagiarism. In *Select Scottish Ballads* (1783) he passed off his own work as traditional Scottish ballads but was forced to admit the error in the introduction to his edition of the MAITLAND MANUSCRIPTS, *Ancient Scottish Poems, never before in Print, but now Published from the Manuscript Collections of Sir Richard Maitland of Lethington, Knight, Lord Privy Seal of Scotland* (1786). His *Literary Correspondence* was published anonymously in 1830.

WORKS: *Craigmillar Castle* (1776); *Rimes* (1781); *Scottish Tragic Ballads* (1781); *Select Scottish Ballads* (1783); *An Essay on Medals* (1784); ed., *Ancient Scottish Poems, never before in Print, but now Published from the Manuscript Collections of Sir Richard Maitland of Lethington, Knight, Lord Privy Seal of Scotland* (1786); *Dissertations on the Origins and Progress of the Scythians and the Goths* (1787); *An Inquiry into the History of Scotland Preceding the Reign of Malcolm III, or 1056, Including the Authentic History of that Period* (1789); *Vitae antiquae sanctorum* (1789); ed., John Barbour, *The Bruce* (1790); ed., *Scottish Poems* (1792); *Iconographia scotica* (1795); *Bothwell Bank* (1796); *The History of Scotland from the Accession of the House of Stuart to that of Mary, with Appendices of Original Documents*, 2 vols. (1797); *The Scottish Gallery* (1799); *An Historical Dissertation on the Gowrie Conspiracy* (1800); *Recollections of Paris in the Years 1802–1805* (1806); *Modern Geography* (1807); *A General Collection of the Best and Most Interesting Voyages and Travels in all Parts of the World*, 17 vols. (1808–14); *The Literary Correspondence of John Pinkerton* (1830); *Early Australian Voyages* (1886)

Pitcairne, Archibald (1652–1713). Poet and dramatist. He was born on Christmas Day 1652 in Edinburgh, the son of a merchant. He graduated from the University of Edinburgh in 1671 and, having foresworn a calling for the Church, he turned to law, which he studied in Edinburgh and Paris. However his interests turned again, to medicine, and he qualified as a doctor in Rheims in 1681. Pitcairne was a founder-member of the College of Physicians in Edinburgh, where he taught medicine, but his career began to be disrupted by his Jacobite sympathies. Controversy surrounded much of his life and this was exacerbated by his publicly pronounced atheism. The composition of his play *The Assembly* in 1692 (it was not performed until 1722) caused a fresh furore on account of its satirical, and frequently ribald view of the ministry of the Church of Scotland. Another, less successful, play, *Tollerators and Contollerators*, is a further satire on the Church, and *Babell* is a long, Hudibrastic satire on his favourite butt, the General Assembly of the Church of Scotland. He wrote a number of conventional classical poems in Latin which were published after his death by THOMAS RUDDIMAN, whom Pitcairne had encouraged during his early days in Edinburgh. For all his courting of public scandal and his liking for bawdy prose, Pitcairne was one of the most respected physicians of his day and a pioneer in the study of the circulation and diseases of the blood.

EDITION: G. Sewell and J. T. Desagulier, eds., *The Whole Works of Dr Archibald Pitcairne Wherein are Discovered the True Foundations and Principles of the Art of Physic* (London, 1727)

REFERENCE: L. J. Jolley, *Archibald Pitcairne* (London, 1953)

Pleasant Satyre of the Thrie Estaitis, Ane. A play in two acts, *Ane Pleasant Satyre of the Thrie Estaitis in Commendatioun of Vertew and Vituperatioun of Vyce*, written by Sir DAVID LYNDSAY and first produced on Twelfth Night 1540 at the royal court at Linlithgow. It was produced subsequently on 7 June 1552 at Cupar, Fife, and again on 12 August 1554 at Greenside, Edinburgh, and the text was published in 1602. For four centuries it lay unperformed until 1948, when a revised version by ROBERT KEMP was produced by Tyrone Guthrie at the Edinburgh International Festival; it was again performed at the Festival in 1973 in a version by TOM WRIGHT. The complete text of the play was published in 1954 with an introductory essay by AGNES MURE MACKENZIE.

The play opens with Diligence announcing the approach of Rex Humanitas with his three estates: Spiritualitie, the first estate or the clergy; Temporalitie, the second estate or the secular lords; and Merchand, the third estate or the burgesses. Rex Humanitas prays to be a

diligent king but his courtiers Wantonnes and Placebo are joined by Sandie Solace who summons up Sensualitie to comfort and seduce the king. The court retires and Gude Counsall, having returned from banishment, takes the stage, but he is quickly thrust aside by Flatterie, Falset and Dissait, who disguise themselves as Devotioun, Sapience and Discretioun. Rex Humanitas, having been beguiled by Sensualitie, falls into the Vices' thrall, and despite their good sense, Veritie and Chastitie are clapped in the stocks. The first act ends with the entrance of Divyne Correctioun who cleanses the court and summons up the three estates.

During an interlude a pauper appears to complain of his treatment at the hands of the Church and the nobility, and this is followed by a richly comic scene between a pardoner selling relics and a soutar and his wife applying to him for a divorce. Diligence reappears to chase them from the stage and to open the second act with the entrance of Rex Humanitas; led by the disguised Vices (Coventice and Sensualitie with the clergy, Oppressioun with the secular lords, and Falset and Dissait with the burgesses), the three estates walk in backwards, symbolically demonstrating their moral and political recidivation. Rex Humanitas then announces his desire to reform the nation, reminding his estates of his position as head of the body politic: 'ye are my members, suppois I be your head'. In a moment of great dramatic solemnity, John the Common-Weill, who represents the welfare of the nation, unmasks the Vices and champions the pauper in the trial of the estates. The secular lords and the burgesses promise to reform themselves and, following John's attack on the spiritual lords for their greed, lechery and incompetence, the first estate is publicly humiliated. Falset and Dissait are executed with comic gusto, but Flatterie escapes, boasting that he of all the Vices, 'begylde all the thrie estaits/With my hypocrisie'. The play ends with a final sermon on folly.

Ane Pleasant Satyre of the Thrie Estaitis is the first great play in Scottish drama. Lyndsay mixes comedy with moral seriousness and colourful colloquial dialogue with the language of the court, in a variety of metres, to underline his concern with the social and spiritual reforms designed to promote the good of the 'common-weill'. The allegorical characters enable Lindsay to express abstract political ideas without descending into rhetoric, and the figure of John the Common-Weill is one of the great levelling democrats in Scottish literature.

Poker Club. A patriotic club, with Jacobite inclinations, formed in Edinburgh in 1762 for the purpose of debate in convivial surroundings. Its membership was made up of the leading *literati* of the SCOTTISH ENLIGHTENMENT period, and there is an account of the club's proceedings in the *Autobiography* of ALEXANDER CARLYLE. The Poker Club was a good reflection of the intellectual vigour that characterized 18th-century Edinburgh, but it could not outlive its members' mortality and by 1787 it had fallen into abeyance. It was the club's custom to meet in a tavern, first at Nicolson's by the Cross and later at Fortune's.

Pollok, Robert (1798–1827). Poet. He was born on 19 October 1798 in the parish of Eaglesham, Renfrewshire. After working as a cabinet maker and farm labourer, he studied for admission to the United Secession Church, and between 1817 and 1822 he was a student at the University of Glasgow. Ill health prevented him from following the ministry and he died on 15 September 1827 in London *en route* for Italy. His one work of note, a long poem called *The Course of Time*, was published in 1827 by WILLIAM BLACKWOOD on the recommendation of JOHN WILSON (iii). Written in blank verse, the poem is on a Miltonic scale, extending to ten books, and its concern is with man's destiny. Pollok also wrote three little-known but entertaining Covenanting stories: *Helen of the Glen*, *Ralph Gemmell* and *The Persecuted Family*.

WORKS: *Helen of the Glen* (1824); *The Course of Time* (1827); *The Persecuted Family* (1828); *Ralph Gemmell* (1829); *Tales of the Covenanters* (1836)

REFERENCE: D. Pollok, *The Life of Robert Pollok* (Edinburgh, 1843)

Pont, Timothy (c1565–1614). Cartographer. He was born in Edinburgh, the son of the minister of the Church of St Cuthbert. He was educated at the University of St Andrews between 1579 and 1583 and in 1601 he was appointed minister of Dunnet in Caithness. After leaving St Andrews, he embarked on the first cartographical survey of Scotland and he received the patronage of JAMES VI for the compilation and completion of a series of maps of the country. These were later added to by

Robert Gordon of Straloch (1580–1661) and his son JAMES GORDON of Rothiemay, and the revised work of three general maps and 46 county maps was published by Johan Blaeu of Amsterdam in 1654. In compiling his work Pont travelled to every part of Scotland and his maps show a careful and accurate delineation of the natural and physical features of the country's landscape.

Porteous Riots. Following a riot in Edinburgh at the executions of two smugglers, Captain John Porteous of the City Guard ordered his men to fire on an angry crowd, killing eight people. Porteous was sentenced to be hanged, but owing to his influence at Queen Caroline's court, he was reprieved. On 7 September 1736 the Edinburgh mob burned down the door of the Tolbooth and dragged Porteous down to the Grassmarket where he was hanged on a dyer's pole. The conspirators were never apprehended and the city council was fined £2000 by the government in the following year. There is a graphic description of the riot, and the events leading to it, in Scott's novel THE HEART OF MIDLOTHIAN.

Porter, Jane (1776–1850). Novelist. She was born in 1776 in Durham but spent most of her childhood in Edinburgh, where her mother was a friend of Sir WALTER SCOTT. In 1803 she moved to London and lived there until her death on 24 May 1850. Although her work stands outside the Scottish tradition, her novel *The Scottish Chiefs* (1810) is a knowledgeable history of Sir WILLIAM WALLACE; it was one of the few novels in its day that rivalled Scott's historical novels in popularity.

Power, William (1873–1951). Author and journalist. He was born on 30 August 1875 in Glasgow, the son of a shipmaster. He was educated in Glasgow and became a bank clerk in 1907, a post he held for only a short time; he then became a journalist with the GLASGOW HERALD, where he remained until 1926, latterly as its literary editor. From then until his death on 13 June 1951, Power worked as an author and freelance journalist. Between 1935 and 1938 he was President of the Scottish PEN Club. He contested the Argyll parliamentary constituency unsuccessfully in 1940 as a Scottish Nationalist. Power's knowledge of Scotland and his fascination with its topography and history are reflected in his principal publications: *Robert Burns and Other Essays and Sketches* (1926), *Scotland and the Scots* (1935), *Literature and Oatmeal* (1935) and *Should Auld Acquaintance* (1937). He was an early supporter of Hugh MacDiarmid (CHRISTOPHER MURRAY GRIEVE) who dedicated to him his collection, *First Hymn to Lenin and Other Poems.* (1931).

WORKS: *Prince Charlie* (1912); *The World Unvisited* (1922); *Robert Burns and Other Essays and Sketches* (1926); *My Scotland* (1934); *Literature and Oatmeal* (1935); *Scotland and the Scots* (1935); *Should Auld Acquaintance* (1937); *The Face of Glasgow* (1938); *The face of Edinburgh* (1939); *A Kelvingrove Jubilee* (1952)

Primrose, Archibald Philip, 5th Earl of Rosebery (1847–1929). Statesman and man of letters. He was born on 7 May 1847 in London and was educated at Eton and Christ Church, Oxford. In March 1868 he succeeded to the family title and embarked on the long political career that was to see him become Foreign Secretary in Gladstone's governments of 1886 and 1892 and Prime Minister in the Liberal administration of 1894–5. One of the great political speakers and thinkers of his day, Rosebery was a supporter of Irish home rule, a promoter of parliamentary devolution for Scotland and a believer in reform of the House of Lords, although in later years he espoused a more conservative point of view. He was a gifted political writer and his studies of English statesmen are shrewd expositions of their parliamentary careers. Much of his personal popularity among the people came from his interest in horse-racing and three of his horses were Derby winners: Ladas in 1894, Sir Visto in 1895 and Cicero in 1905.

WORKS: *The Union of England and Scotland* (1871); *William Pitt* (1891); *Sir Robert Peel* (1899); *Napoleon: the Last Phase* (1900); *Oliver Cromwell* (1900); *Questions of Experience* (1900); *Lord Randolph Churchill* (1906); *Chatham: his Life and Connections* (1910); *Miscellanies*, 2 vols. (1921); A. R. C. Grant and C. Comb, eds., *Lord Rosebery's North American Journal* (1967)

Pringle, Thomas (1789–1834). Poet and editor. He was born on 5 January 1789 in Teviotdale, Roxburghshire, the son of a farmer. He was educated at Kelso Grammar School and the University of Edinburgh and in 1811 he entered the Register Office as a copyist of records. Through his friendship with Sir WALTER SCOTT Pringle was appointed in 1817 editor with JAMES CLEGHORN of the *Edinburgh*

Monthly Magazine, later BLACKWOOD'S MAGAZINE, but after six numbers had appeared he was dismissed by the publisher WILLIAM BLACKWOOD. After a period of poverty in Edinburgh he emigrated in February 1820 to South Africa, where he became an influential public figure in opposition to the slave trade. According to Scott, 'Pringle might have done well there, could he have scoured his brain of politics' (*Journal*, vol. 1, p. 282), and Pringle's involvement in anti-slave trade activities forced him to leave the country in October 1826. Throughout his life Pringle suffered from lameness and he died on 5 December 1834 (shortly after the slave trade was abolished by parliament).

Pringle's first collection of romantic poems, *The Autumnal Excursion, or Sketches in Teviotdale,* was published in 1817 but his best work appears in *African Sketches, Narrative of a Residence in South Africa* (1834), which contains a moving ballad of exile, 'The Emigrants' and a splendid evocation of pioneer life in South Africa 'Afar in the Desert'. A collection of lyrics, *Ephemerides, or Occasional Poems Written in Scotland and South Africa* appeared in 1828.

WORKS: *The Autumnal Excursion, or Sketches in Teviotdale* (1817); *Some Account of the Present State of the English Settlers in Albany South Africa* (1824); *Ephemerides, or Occasional Poems Written in Scotland and South Africa* (1828); *African Sketches, Narrative of a Residence in South Africa* (1834)

EDITIONS: L. Ritchie, ed., *Poetical Works of Thomas Pringle* (London, 1839); W. Hay, ed., *Thomas Pringle: my Life and Times* (Cape Town, 1912)

REFERENCE: D. H. Thomson, *The Life and Work of Thomas Pringle* (Adelaide, 1961)

Private Memoirs and Confessions of a Justified Sinner, The. A novel by JAMES HOGG, first published in 1824. It is a complex work of diabolic possession, theological satire and local legend, in which evil is portrayed as inherent not in the sublimation of the will but in the corruption of religious doctrine. The story, which is set in the years immediately prior to the ACT OF UNION of 1707, is told in three parts, the 'Editor's Narrative', the 'Private Memoirs and Confessions of the Sinner' and the 'Editor's Comments' at the end. Each part is designed so that it forms an overall pattern of objective set against subjective experience.

The 'Editor's Narrative' concerns two brothers, George Colwan, the son of a laird, and Robert, who is supposed to be the illegitimate son of his mother's spiritual adviser, the

Revd Robert Wringhim. The brothers, who grow up apart, are always in conflict when they meet, and when George is murdered Robert is suspected of fratricide and disappears. In the 'Private Memoirs and Confessions' the same story is told from Robert's point of view. This section is also an account of the antinomian obsession that sins committed by an 'elect and justified person' cannot imperil the hope of salvation. Robert has reached this conclusion from the narrowly Calvinistic teachings of the Revd Wringhim and, aided and abetted by Gil-Martin, a shadowy figure of evil who is the personification of the Devil, he commits a number of crimes including the murder of his brother George. At the end of the book, still believing himself to be justified in his actions, but haunted by the diabolic Gil-Martin, he takes his own life. Finally, the 'Editor' tells the reader how he came into the possession of the manuscript and he describes Robert's death.

The figure of Gil-Martin exists on two levels. He is the living impersonation of the Devil in the folk tradition and therefore a figure to be feared: he is also the agent of evil capable of taking possession of Robert's mind and causing him to turn to evil. This dualism between inner and outer reality leads Robert to believe himself to be two people, and the concept of a split personality is the dominant theme of the novel; this theme was taken up by other novelists such as ROBERT LOUIS STEVENSON in THE STRANGE CASE OF DR JEKYLL AND MR HYDE.

Although *The Private Memoirs and Confessions of a Justified Sinner*, which Hogg published anonymously, was not a success in its day, it remains a seminal piece of 19th-century Scottish literature. It was republished in 1947 with an introduction by André Gide.

Psalms. The use of The Metrical Psalms of David as the Church of Scotland's basic form of praise has its origins in the period of the 16th-century Reformation. The early reformers were much influenced by events in Germany, in particular by the teachings of Martin Luther, who had included the use of spiritual songs in his order of praise. Although Scotland was to come under the more austere influence of the Swiss reformer John Calvin, the enthusiasm for the use of song in church services was not lost and the GUDE AND GODLIE BALLATIS, a collection of Psalms and hymns, many translated from German into Scots by the

WEDDERBURN brothers and printed with popular songs and ballads, enjoyed a wide currency in post-Reformation Scotland.

A *Scottish Psalter* was added to the *Book of Common Order* which was printed in Edinburgh in 1564 by ROBERT LEKPREVIK at the command of the reformed Church. It contained versions of the Psalms of differing quality by eight hands, and these were composed for singing in churches. Tunes to many of them were adapted from the material used by the song-schools attached to many of the pre-Reformation churches, so that there was a continuation of the Scottish tradition of part-singing. However, the metrical clumsiness of many of the versions made them unsuitable for singing and there was considerable dissatisfaction with the new psalter, so much so that James VI made it one of his tasks to provide new versions of the Psalms. He was joined in his labours by two of the poets associated with the CASTALIAN BAND, ALEXANDER MONTGOMERIE and WILLIAM DRUMMOND of Hawthornden; but James's psalter never gained public acceptance despite the exhortations made on the work's behalf after his death by his son Charles I.

WILLIAM MURE of Rowallan and ZACHARY BOYD also produced versions of the Psalms for the Church's use but in 1646 the Church of Scotland chose a psalter revised by an Englishman, Francis Rous, Provost of Eton. This was reworked by a Commission of the General Assembly of the Church and it came into use on 1 May 1650 as *The Psalms of David in Meeter: Newly Translated, and Diligently Compared with the Originall Text and Former Translations: More Plaine, Smooth and Agreeable to the Text than any heretofore.* The psalter remained in general use until the 19th century and, despite its lack of tunes, it was the staple of Presbyterian church worship in Scotland. Its demise owed less to its inherent lack of literary or spiritual merit, although those were the reasons put forward for its replacement, than to its use of Scots words and phrases. In the late 18th and early 19th century many Scottish men of learning began to be ashamed of their Scots speech, and as that feeling began to grow within the Church a movement arose to revise the psalter. The Church of Scotland produced its *Scottish Hymnal* in 1870 and the Free Church of Scotland followed suit in 1873 with *Psalm-Versions, Paraphrases and Hymns*, which was followed by the *Free Church Hymnbook* in 1882.

Until the publication of these psalters with tunes, the singing of psalms in church was led by the 'up-taker of the psalm' or the 'precentor' as he was later known; he would sing the first lines of the psalm and once the tune had been recognized the rest of the congregation would join in. This practice began at a time when many members of the congregation were unable to read, but it became an important part of the dignity of the church service in Scotland and remains in common use in many Gaelic-speaking congregations, where it is considered to be a vital part of the culture of the language.

The first translation of the Psalms into Gaelic was made in 1659 when 50 were published by the Synod of Argyll; the task was completed in 1694. The 19th century saw the introduction of the great tunes associated with the singing of psalms, among which may be mentioned 'The Old Hundredth', 'Crimond', 'Martyrdom', 'Kilmarnock' and 'Bangor'.

No essay on the place of the Psalm in the Scottish literary tradition would be complete without mention of the translations of the Psalms into Latin by GEORGE BUCHANAN. In their day they were acknowledged as the finest of their kind in Europe and added to his reputation as a great Latinist.

REFERENCE: M. Patrick, *Four Centuries of Scottish Psalmody* (Oxford, 1949)

Q

Queen's Maries, the. The name given to the ladies-in-waiting who accompanied MARY, Queen of Scots, to France in 1548. The 'Maries' (Icelandic *maer*, a maid, virgin) or maids who looked after the bedchamber of the queens of Scotland came from the families of the nobility. In Mary's case her maids all shared her Christian name—Mary Fleming, Mary Seton, Mary Beaton and Mary Livingstone—and each came from a family that had close associations with the Scottish court. The romance of their queen's life rubbed off on the ladies-in-waiting for the Queen's Maries became an essential part of the legends surrounding Mary. They gave their collective name, though not their actions, to the ballad 'The Queen's Maries'.

Queen's Wake, The. A collection of poems by JAMES HOGG, held together by the narrative framework of a festival of poetry held in honour of MARY, Queen of Scots, in which 17 poets are bidden to compete for her favour. It was published in 1813 and established Hogg's reputation. Although the work includes several undistinguished poems in a mixture of English and archaic Scots, written in a style calculated to win favour with the Edinburgh *literati*, it also contains two of Hogg's best poems: 'The Witch of Fife' and 'KILMENY'. Both deal, in different ways, with supernatural occurrences: 'Kilmeny' tells the story of the other-worldly disappearance of a beautiful girl; and 'The Witch of Fife' is a grotesque, ballad-like story of the goings-on of a group of witches. At the centre of the poem is an exuberant set piece between the drunken husband of one of the witches and her coven; his incoherent interpolations contrast vividly and effectively with the awe-inspiring sense of diablerie conjured by Hogg in his treatment of the witches.

R

Rae, Hugh C(rauford) ['James Albany', 'Robert Crawford', 'R. B. Houston'] (*b* 1935). Novelist. He was born on 22 November 1935 in Glasgow. He was educated there at Knightswood School and worked as an antiquarian bookseller between 1952 and 1966, a period that was interrupted by National Service in the Royal Air Force. Since 1966 he has been a full-time writer and he is one of Scotland's most prolific novelists, writing under his own name and several others, including 'R. B. Houston' and 'James Albany', and 'Jessica Stirling' in his collaboration with Peggie Coghlan (*b* 1920). His early novels deal with the criminal underworld of Glasgow and the west of Scotland, and with the petty acts of unthinking violence that disfigure mankind. The dialogue is taut and well-paced in the tradition of American crime writers such as Raymond Chandler (1888–1959), the backgrounds are vividly and authentically portrayed, and the two detective protagonists, McCaig and Ryan, remain unsentimentally aware of their own shortcomings in coping with the organized world of crime and its origins in human deprivation. Many of the novels were based on real-life crimes and murders in Glasgow. Later Rae turned to writing historical novels and he collaborated in the production of the Jessica Stirling romantic sagas.

WORKS: *Skinner* (1966); *Night Pillow* (1967); *A Few Small Bones* (1968); *The Interview* (1969); *The Marksman* (1971); *The Shooting Gallery* (1972); *The Rock Harvest* (1973); *The Rookery* (1974); *Harkfast* (1976); *Sullivan* (1978); *The Travelling Soul* (1978); *The Haunting of Waverley Falls* (1980); *Privileged Strangers* (1982)
as James Albany: *Warrior Caste* (1982); *Mailed Fist* (1982); *Deacon's Dagger* (1982)
as Robert Crawford: *The Shroud Society* (1969); *Cockleburr* (1969); *Kiss the Boss Goodbye* (1970); *The Badger's Daughter* (1971); *Whiphand* (1972)
as R. B. Houston: *Two for the Grave* (1972)
as Stuart Stern: *The Minotaur Factor* (1977); *The Poison Tree* (1978)

as Jessica Stirling with Peggie Coghlan: *The Spoiled Earth* (1974); *The Dresden Finch* (1976); *The Hiring Fair* (1976); *The Dark Pasture* (1977); *The Deep Well at Noon* (1979); *The Blue Evening Gone* (1981)

Raeburn, Sir Henry (1756–1823). Portrait painter. He was born on 7 March 1756 in Stockbridge, Edinburgh, and his early artistic training was gained as a goldsmith's apprentice. He became a pupil of the fashionable portrait painter David Martin and executed several portraits himself, but it was not until his marriage to a wealthy widow in 1778 that he was able to afford a proper training. The English artist Sir Joshua Reynolds (1723–92) gave him much practical advice and encouraged him to spend some time in Italy. In 1787 he returned to Edinburgh, which remained his home until his death on 8 July 1823. Raeburn was knighted in 1822 and was appointed King's Limner and Painter for Scotland in the year of his death. During his lifetime he painted most of the leading men of his generation, capturing in them something of the personality and wit that characterized the intellectual society of his day; he is justly regarded as one of Scotland's greatest artists and a portrait painter of great verve and individual style. Among his sitters were: HENRY MACKENZIE, ALEXANDER ADAM, ROBERT MACQUEEN, Lord Braxfield, DAVID HUME (ii), JAMES BOSWELL, WILLIAM CREECH and Sir WALTER SCOTT.

Ramsay, Allan ['Isaac Bickerstaff'; Gawin Douglas'] (1684–1758). Poet. He was born on 15 October 1684 in Leadhills, Lanarkshire, the son of John Ramsay, factor to the Earl of Hopeton. Shortly after his birth his father died, and after his mother's remarriage Ramsay was brought up by his stepfather, a farmer. He was educated at the local school until he was 15 and in 1700 he was apprenticed to a periwig maker in Edinburgh. On 19 July 1710 he became a burgess of the city of Edinburgh and tradition claims that he opened his first shop in the Grassmarket. He was a founding member of THE EASY CLUB, which met to discuss political and literary matters, and he adopted two pseudonyms, 'Isaac Bickerstaff' after Jonathan Swift's fictional creation, and later the more patriotic 'Gawin Douglas'.

Ramsay abandoned wig making for bookselling, taking a shop in Niddry's Wynd, before moving to the east end of the Luckenbooths 'at Hawthornden's and Ben Johnson's [sic] Heads' (1727 edition of the Poems). There he established in 1725 what is generally held to be the first circulating library in Britain. In 1736 he turned his attention to the theatre, opening a playhouse in Carruber's Close, which was eventually closed because of Edinburgh's traditional disapproval of the theatre and because the Licensing Act of 1737 banned theatrical performances in Britain except in the City of Westminster, and then only when the monarch was in residence. For the opening of his theatre Ramsay composed a prologue which contained an articulate plea for the need to establish a theatre in Edinburgh. His labours on behalf of his playhouse virtually ended his interest in public affairs, and in 1738 he retired to his house on Castle Hill which was known locally as the 'Goose Pie' because of its octagonal shape.

Ramsay's fiercely stated nationalism and Jacobite preferences grew milder as the century progressed; he took no part in the 1715 rebellion and was prudently absent from Edinburgh when the city was occupied by the Jacobite army of Prince CHARLES EDWARD STUART in September and October 1745. Ramsay was a successful and reasonably prosperous businessman and to the end of his life he remained active in business affairs in Edinburgh. The exact date of his death is unknown but he was buried in Greyfriars' Churchyard on 9 January 1758.

Ramsay probably wrote his earliest poems for the members of the Easy Club and his first collection was published in 1721 and printed by THOMAS RUDDIMAN. Of the 80 poems, half were in English in the florid Augustan style of his contemporaries and the rest were in a mixture of Scots and English, and these are by far his most successful creations. He was at pains to stress the importance of using Scots in his poetry and even claimed of his English poems in the Preface that 'the Idiom and Phraseology is still Scots'. The best of his vernacular poems are those dealing with the personalities and events he encountered in Edinburgh. These are told with a racy originality and are full of wit and humour, expressed in a sharply observed demotic Scots. Ramsay coined the phrase 'STANDARD HABBIE' (after 'The Life and Death of Habbie Simpson, the Piper of Kilbarchan' by ROBERT SEMPILL (ii) of Beltrees) for the metrical form he employed in his mock elegies to Maggy Johnston, a tavern keeper, John Cowper, a church treasurer and informant on sexual matters, and Lucky Wood, the owner of a defunct Canongate tavern. Equally rewarding was his use of the verse epistle in his 'Familiar Epistles between Lieutenant William Hamilton and Allan Ramsay' which he composed for WILLIAM HAMILTON (i) of Gilbertfield. His imitations of Horace's Odes in Scots were less successful and although he attempted consciously, to show the ability of the Scots language to provide literary translations, he lacked a knowledge of Latin, and the resulting creations sit uneasily in comparison with his best work.

Ramsay's commitment to the Scots literary heritage manifested itself also in his work as an editor. In his poems of 1721 he defended his own use of Scots and in 1724 in his two-volume anthology of early Scottish poetry, THE EVER GREEN, he stressed the importance of a thorough understanding of Scots. 'There is nothing can be heard more silly than one's expressing his Ignorance of his native language', he wrote in the Preface. Most of the poems were taken from the BANNATYNE MANUSCRIPT of 1568, and although Ramsay employed a cavalier attitude in his editorial standards he did succeed in gaining a wider audience for early Scots poetry. More popular was the publication in the same year of the first of five volumes of THE TEA-TABLE MISCELLANY. Subsequent volumes appeared in 1725, 1727, 1732 and 1737. This mixture of traditional songs and ballads enjoyed a wide success in Scotland, but Ramsay tended to take liberties with the texts and he frequently altered songs to suit the standards of taste of his own day. Like its companion volumes of poems, The Tea-Table Miscellany was important both for Ramsay's commitment to Scotland's cultural heritage and for his ability to direct the work to a wider audience. Ramsay wrote a number of songs himself, including a spirited drinking song Up in the Air, a love-song, I'll never leave *thee* and a somewhat vapid version of AULD LANG SYNE. His other published work includes his *Fables and Tales* of 1722 and *A Collection of Scots Proverbs* (1737).

Ramsay's one play, THE GENTLE SHEPHERD, a verse drama, is little more than a theatrical oddity but it is memorable for its scenes of country life and for the raw, living language Ramsay accorded to the genuinely rustic characters of Bauldy and Mause. It first appeared in 1725 and was made into a ballad opera for the boys of Haddington Grammar School in 1729. The plot is little more than a pastoral romance and it centres on the story of the shepherds, Patie and Roger, who are in love with Peggy and Jenny; the subplot is the discovery of Patie's noble birth and the restitution of Sir William Worthy to his estate. Although the writing is uneven and Ramsay showed himself to be uncomfortable in his handling of English and a quaint mixture of Scots and English, *The Gentle Shepherd* offers a pointer to Ramsay's own literary position, caught as he was between the conflicting claims of polite English and his own use of Scots. In his one drama Ramsay showed himself to be more at home in the language of the peasantry, and his muse disappeared when he was forced to write in English or his Scots had to be modified to suit the needs of a polite audience.

Ramsay was certainly at his best in his richly comic Scots poems, the mock elegies and the verse epistles and in his long poem *The Monk and the Miller's Wife*. He also added verses to the poem, attributed to both JAMES I and JAMES V, CHRISTIS KIRK ON THE GREEN, and there is little doubt that his work in Scots paved the way for the poetry composed later in the century by ROBERT FERGUSSON and ROBERT BURNS.

WORKS: *A poem to the Memory of the Famous Archibald Pitcairne* (1713); *The Battel* (1716); *Christ's Kirk in the Green in Two Cantos* (1718); *Elegies on Maggy Johnston, John Cowper and Lucky Wood* (1718); *Edinburgh's Address to the County* (1718); *Lucky Spence's Last Advice* (1718); *Scots Songs* (1718); *The Scriblers Lash'd* (1718); *Tartana or the Plaid* (1718); *Content* (1719); *An Epistle to W. H.* (1719); *Familiar Epistles between W. H. and A. R.* (1719); *Richy and Sandy* (1719); *Edinburgh's Salutation to the Most Honourable My Lord Marquis of Carnarvon* (1720); *Grubstreet ane Satyre* (1720); *An Ode on the Marriage of the Right Honourable James Earl of Wemyss and Mrs Janet Charteris* (1720); *Patie and Roger* (1720); *A Poem on the South Sea* (1720); *The Prospect of Plenty* (1720); *The Young Caird and Edinburgh Katie* (1720); *An Elegie on Patie Birnie* (1721); *An Epistle to my Lord*

Ramsay (1721); *Poems* (1721); *Robert, Richie and Sandy* (1721); *Fables and Tales* (1722); *A Tale of Three Bonnets* (1722); *The Fair Assembly* (1723); *Jenny and Maggy* (1723); *The Nuptials* (1723); ed., *The Ever Green*, 2 vols. (1724); *Health* (1724); *The Monk and the Miller's Wife* (1724); *Mouldy-Mowdiewart* (1724); *On Pride* (1724); *On Seeing the Archers Diverting themselves at the Butts and Rovers* (1724); *The Poetick Sermon* (1724); ed., *The Tea-Table Miscellany*, 5 vols. (1724–37); *The Gentle Shepherd* (1725); *A Scots Ode to the British Antiquarians* (1726); *Some Hints in Defence of Dramatic Entertainment* (1727); *An Address of Thanks from the Society of Rakes* (1735); ed., *A Collection of Scots Proverbs* (1737); *To the Honourable Duncan Forbes of Culloden* (1737)

EDITION: B. Martin, J. W. Oliver, eds., *The Works of Allan Ramsay*, vols. 1 and 2 (Edinburgh and London, 1945–6; A. M. Kinghorn and A. Law, eds., *The Works of Allan Ramsay*, vols. 3–6, STS (Edinburgh and London, 1955–74)

REFERENCES: J. B. Martin, *Allan Ramsay: a Study of his Life and Works* (Cambridge, Mass., 1931); A. Smart, *The Life and Art of Allan Ramsay* (London, 1952)

Ramsay, Edward Bannerman (1793–1872). Essayist. He was born on 31 January 1793 in Aberdeen, the son of the Sheriff of Kincardineshire. Most of his childhood was spent on his uncle's Yorkshire estate and he was educated at Durham Cathedral School and later at St John's College, Cambridge, where he graduated in 1816. Between then and 1824 he was a curate in two west country parishes, but he then returned to Edinburgh to work as an assistant to the Bishop of Edinburgh, and he was appointed dean in 1841. Until his death on 27 December 1872 Dean Ramsay was one of Edinburgh's best-known and best-loved figures and through his ecumenical beliefs he enjoyed friendships with many clergymen of other communions. He wrote copiously on religious matters but his abiding monument is his *Reminiscences of Scottish Life* (1858), which went through 21 editions in his lifetime. Composed largely of stories and anecdotes given to him by his friends and family the *Reminiscences* paint a warm-hearted picture of Scottish rural life that gained its charm by avoiding the trap of sentimentality.

WORKS: *A Catechism Compiled and Arranged for the use of Young Persons* (1835); *The Christian's Almoner* (1840); *Manual of Catechitical Instruction* (1851); *Diversities of Christian Character* (1858); *Reminiscences of Scottish Life and Character* (1858); *Pastoral Letters* (1861); *The Christian Life in its Origins, Progress and Perfection* (1862); *The Present Position of the Episcopal Church in Scotland* (1862); *An Earnest Appeal to Members of the Scottish Episcopal Church* (1863); *Christian Responsibility* (1864); *The Great*

Work of the Church Today (1866); Preaching the Gospel to the Poor (1867); Pulpit Table Talk (1868); Thomas Chalmers D.D. (1868); The Art of Reading and Preaching Distinctly (1868); Reminiscences of a Scottish Episcopal Ministry (1892)

REFERENCE: C. Rogers, Memorials and Recollections of the Very Rev. Edward Bannerman Ramsay (London, 1873)

Ramsay, John, of Ochtertyre (1736–1814). Diarist. He was born on 26 August 1736 in Edinburgh, the son of a lawyer, and succeeded to the family estates of Ochtertyre in 1760. He was educated at the University of Edinburgh and was called to the Scottish Bar, but his landowning interests prevented him from ever practising. Like his neighbour HENRY HOME, Lord Kames, Ramsay was an agrarian improver, but he is remembered for his journal of his life and times, which has earned him a minor, though not insignificant place in Scottish literature. His manuscript, which runs to ten bulky volumes, contains not only his observations of the leading men of his day but also his thought on such diverse subjects as church politics, the law, agriculture and the advisability of education for women. The journal is eminently readable and through his eyes as a visitor a vivid picture emerges of the Edinburgh of the SCOTTISH ENLIGHTENMENT, its leading personalities, and the world of tavern and club. ROBERT BURNS visited Ochtertyre in 1787 and the two men remained friendly correspondents, in spite of Ramsay's exasperation over Burns's refusal to take his advice to write poetry in English instead of 'coarse' Scots. Another eminent literary visitor was Sir WALTER SCOTT in 1793, through whom Ramsay achieved another kind of literary immortality by providing Scott with his model for Jonathan Oldbuck in THE ANTIQUARY.

EDITION: A. Allardyce, ed., Scotland and Scotsmen in the Eighteenth Century, 2 vols. (Edinburgh and London, 1888)

Rauf Coilzear. An anonymous Middle Scots alliterative poem, printed by ROBERT LEKPREVIK in St Andrews in 1572, though it has its origins in the late 15th century. It tells the story of a commoner, Rauf, a charcoal burner, entertaining his monarch, Charlemagne, while remaining ignorant of his guest's identity. Charlemagne, or Charles as he is called in the poem, takes shelter in Rauf's hut, is regally entertained and is also given a lesson in good manners. The king pretends to be a mere court official and invites Rauf to the palace whereupon all is revealed. Instead of being punished, Rauf is knighted and enters the king's service. He fights the Saracen knight Magog, is made a Marshal of France and sets up a hostelry for travellers at the spot where he first met the king. Although the poem has a European setting, its best features are essentially Scottish: the homely description of the rude, but welcoming hut, and the evocation of the storm on the moor that drives Charles to seek shelter with Rauf. The theme of the poem, common to much 15th-century European poetry, was popular in Scotland and may be said to look forward to the levelling tradition of the king being the equal of his subjects, which reached its peak in the legends surrounding JAMES V as the GUIDMAN O' BALLENGEICH.

Reid, Alexander (1914–82). Dramatist and poet. He was born on 19 August 1914 in Edinburgh and was educated there at George Heriot's School. Between 1929 and 1936 he was a journalist with the Edinburgh Evening News, followed by a period with the SMT Magazine for which he wrote a series of articles on Scotland's history and literature. During World War II he was a conscientious objector and afterwards worked as a bookseller and accountant until he became a full-time writer and broadcaster in 1948. His most successful play, The Lass wi' the Muckle Mou, an intertwining of the border ballads of THOMAS OF ERCELDOUNE and Muckle-moued Meg Murray's forced marriage to the reiver Willie Scott of Harden, was first performed at the Glasgow Citizens' Theatre in November 1950 and has since been translated into several languages. His other plays are Worlds Without End, The Warld's Wonder, Diana and Voyage Ashore. Although he is one of the neglected dramatists of the 20th-century SCOTTISH RENAISSANCE all his work has a sound philosophical basis, The Warld's Wonder showing a preoccupation with the balance of free will and determinism. Reid also wrote on France, where he lived in 1949, and published two collections of verse. He died on 1 July 1982 in Edinburgh.

WORKS: Steps to a Viewpoint (1947); The Milky Way (1956); The Lass wi' the Muckle Mou (1958); Two Scots Plays (1958); The Warld's Wonder (1958); Zoo-illogical Rhymes (1960); The Young Traveller in France (1963)

Reid, John Macnair (1895–1954). Poet and

novelist. He was born on 14 December 1895 in Glasgow. After leaving school he joined the staff of the GLASGOW HERALD, and, after a short period in Inverness, most of the rest of his working life was spent as a journalist in Glasgow. From 1936 to the outbreak of World War II he lived on the island of Eigg, and the last years of his life were spent in Torridon in Wester Ross. He died as the result of a motoring accident on 17 December 1954.

Reid began writing poetry and short stories in 1929 but very little of his work was published during his lifetime. He used his position as a reviewer with the *Glasgow Herald* and the *Evening Times* to propagate the work of the writers associated with the aims of the SCOTTISH RENAISSANCE movement. He wrote two sensitive novels of Glasgow life both of which are remarkable for their sympathetic treatment of the misery caused by the existence of rigid class boundaries: *Homeward Journey* (1934) and *Judy from Crown Street* which was published posthumously in 1970. Reid also did sterling work as an editor, and his collection of Scottish one-act plays is a valuable record of the drama of the period, especially the work created specifically for the amateur dramatic movement.

WORKS: *The Gleam on the Road* (1928); ed. *Scottish One-Act Plays* (1933); *Symbols and Other Poems* (1933); *Homeward Journey* (1934); *Tobias the Rod* (1968); *Judy from Crown Street* (1970)

Reid, Thomas (1710–96). Philosopher. He was born on 26 April 1710 at Strachan, Kincardineshire, the son of the parish minister, whose family had been Presbyterian ministers in the Banchory area since the Reformation. Through his mother he was related to the mathematicians and scientists James Gregory (1638–75) and David Gregory (1661–1708). He was educated at Marischal College, Aberdeen, and after graduating in 1726 he became minister of Kincardine O'Neil until 1733; he was then appointed librarian of Marischal College, a post he held until 1737, when he again took up the ministry, at New Machar. In 1751 he became Professor of Philosophy at King's College, Aberdeen, and in May 1764 he succeeded to the Chair of Moral Philosophy in Glasgow on the resignation of ADAM SMITH. He retired from public life in 1780 but continued to maintain his many friendships in Glasgow and Edinburgh: among his closest adherents were his pupil, the philosopher

DUGALD STEWART, and Sir WILLIAM HAMILTON (iii) later Professor of History and Logic at Edinburgh, who edited his works. Reid, with them, belonged to the 'Common-Sense' school of Scottish philosophy, which held 'beliefs common to all rational beings as such' and which agreed that philosophy could be treated as a natural science. His most lasting work, *An Inquiry into the Human Mind on the Principles of Common Sense* (1764), put forward the theory that our perception of the external world is intuitive and that the objects of perception are real and not images; it was long considered to be a standard refutation of the scepticism of DAVID HUME (ii).

EDITION: W. Hamilton, ed., *The Works of Thomas Reid*, 2 vols. (Edinburgh, 1846–63) [completed by H. L. Mansell]

REFERENCE: D. Stewart, *The Life of Thomas Reid* (Edinburgh, 1803)

Reidpath Manuscript. A manuscript collection of Middle Scots poems held by the University Library in Cambridge (Moore LL.v.10). It was put together for a John Reidpath in 1622 or 1623 and was based on the writings found in the MAITLAND MANUSCRIPTS. Reidpath's manuscript is notable for its 47 poems by William Dunbar, eight of which are not included in any other manuscript source: 'To the King', 'The Magryme', 'Elegy on the death of Lord Bernard Stewart, Lord of Aubigny', 'To the Lordis of Chalker', 'To the Lord Thesaurair', 'To Aberdein', 'Ane Dreme' and 'To the Merchantis of Edinburgh'.

Reith, John Charles Walsham, Lord (1889–1971). First Director-General of the British Broadcasting Corporation. He was born on 20 July 1889 in Stonehaven and educated at Glasgow Academy and Gresham's School in Norfolk. During World War I he served as an engineer, a career he pursued until 1923, when he was appointed General Manager (later Director-General) of the BBC, a post he held until 1938. Throughout his life Reith held several influential public and political appointments, but he is best remembered for his work in bringing the BBC into being and for preserving its independence from government interference. His autobiography *Into the Wind* was published in 1948.

Reulis and Cautelis. The familiar name given to an influential essay written by JAMES VI and published in *The Essayes of a Prentise in the Divine Art of Poesie* (1585). Its full title is 'Schort Treatise conteining some Reulis and Cautelis to be obseruit and eschewit in Scottis Poesie', and basically it is a handbook of poetic techniques to be employed by the aspiring poet. The king's rules regarding rhyme, metre and prosody were laid down for the special interest and use of the CASTALIAN BAND of poets at his court, and it was the first formal study of that kind in the Scottish tradition. Its major drawback as a textbook was James's insistence on formal poetic rules without making allowance for the poet's own skill or inspiration. Nevertheless, it is a virtuoso performance by a relatively young man, who was convinced that the rules he was proposing could bring about a revival of Scots verse, based on the best precepts of Renaissance Europe.

Riddell (née Woodley), **Maria Banks** (1772–1808). Friend of ROBERT BURNS. She was married to Walter Riddell, the younger brother of ROBERT RIDDELL of Friar's Carse. She enjoyed a close relationship with Burns to whom she wrote several letters and sent her poems for criticism, but their friendship was interrupted when Burns was banished from her sister-in-law's house, Friar's Carse, following a drunken revel in 1793. Although Burns wrote several satires on Maria and her husband, he again became friendly with her in 1795. After his death Maria Riddell wrote a generous *Memoir Concerning Burns* in the *Dumfries Weekly Journal* in August 1796.

Riddell, Robert (1755–94). Soldier and owner of the estate of Glenriddell on which stood his house of Friar's Carse. He was a friend of ROBERT BURNS and shared with him an enthusiasm for collecting songs. For him Burns wrote the GLENRIDDELL MANUSCRIPTS. Their friendship ended following a drunken revel in Friar's Carse in late 1793. Riddell composed a number of fiddle tunes and published a collection of Border and Galloway airs in 1794.

Riding the Marches. *See* COMMON RIDINGS.

Robert I, [Robert the Bruce], King of Scots (1274–1329). He was born in July 1274 at Turnberry, Ayrshire, the son of Robert Bruce and Marjory Countess of Carrick. As the grandson of Robert 'the Claimant' Bruce, who contested the Scottish throne with John Bal-

liol in 1291, Bruce was associated with Edward I of England though he took part in the campaign of 1297 led by WILLIAM WALLACE. After quarrelling with and murdering John Comyn, Balliol's grandson, Robert was crowned King of Scots on 27 March 1306 at Scone. A series of defeats forced him to flee to Ireland and then to Orkney, but he returned to fight a guerilla war against Edward in 1307. The support of the nobility and the clergy and the great victory at the BATTLE OF BANNOCKBURN in 1314 added to his cause, which was confirmed in the resounding tones of the DECLARATION OF ARBROATH in 1320. At the Treaty of Northampton on 4 May 1328 Bruce was recognized as King of Scots and the following year the Pope despatched a papal bull permitting the coronation, which arrived only some days after Robert's death on 7 June 1329 at Cardross.

Robert I occupies a high position in Scottish history as the liberator of his country and as a symbol of national independence; he was also a sound ruler. He concluded a treaty with France at Corbeuil in 1326 and granted royal charters to the principal cities, which allowed them to make single payments to the Crown in lieu of the old dues and customs. Many of the facts of Bruce's life are known from the heroic long poem THE BRUCE by JOHN BARBOUR.

Robertson, J(ames) Logie ['Hugh Haliburton'] (1846–1922). Poet. He was born on 18 September 1846 at Milnathort, Kinross. In 1859 he became a pupil-teacher in Haddington, before enrolling at the University of Edinburgh. He taught at various Edinburgh schools and, between 1876 and his retirement in 1913, at the Edinburgh Ladies College, later Mary Erskine's School. He died on 13 June 1922.

Most of Robertson's early poems, country idylls, were published in THE SCOTSMAN and collected in volumes published on 1878 and 1881. It was not until 1882 that he launched the poetry of 'Hugh Haliburton' in *Horace in Homespun: a Series of Scottish Pastorals*. Although many of these odes to nature, written in Scots, have a simple charm, with their carefully observed descriptions of the Ochil Hills, they rarely rise above the level of pastiche. Further volumes, equally popular, were published in 1891 and 1894, by which time the author's pseudonym had become a household name in Scotland. He also wrote a series of essays on various aspects of Scottish history and literature using the same *nom de plume*.

Despite its artificiality, 'Hugh Haliburton's' work in Scots looked forward to the 20th-century renaissance of Scottish literature. Robertson was a respected teacher, and for schools he produced useful editions of the poetry of WILLIAM DUNBAR, ALLAN RAMSAY, ROBERT BURNS, THOMAS CAMPBELL and ALLAN CUNNINGHAM.

WORKS: *Poems* (1878); *Ordlana and Other Poems* (1881); with Janet Robertson, *Our Holiday Among the Hills* (1882); *The White Angel of the Polly Ann* (1886); ed., *Selected Poems of Allan Ramsay* (1887); ed., *Complete Poetical Works of Sir Walter Scott* (1894); ed., *Complete Works of Robert Burns* (1896); ed., *Complete Works of Thomas Campbell* (1907); ed., *The Complete Poetical Works of James Thomson* (1908) as Hugh Haliburton: *Horace in Homespun: a Series of Scottish Pastorals* (1882); *For Puir Auld Scotland's Sake* (1887); *In Scottish Fields* (1890); *Ochil Idylls* (1891); *Furth in Field* (1894); *Dunbar: being a Selection from the Poems* (1895); *Executions in Prose and Verse* (1905)

Robertson, Joseph (1810–66). Historian and record scholar. He was born on 17 May 1810 in Aberdeen. He was educated at Aberdeen Grammar School and Marischal College, Aberdeen, where he met the historian JOHN HILL BURTON, who became his lifelong friend and colleague. Apprenticed as a lawyer, Robertson turned instead to literature, and his first collection of essays, *Deliciae literariae* (1839), showed his interests to lie in the field of antiquarian studies. He was a founder-member of the SPALDING CLUB, the society formed in Aberdeen to publish works of Scottish historical interest, and he became one of its principal editors. To support himself financially he became a journalist and was appointed editor of the EDINBURGH EVENING COURANT in 1848, a post he held until 1853, when he became Curator of the Historical Records in Register House, Edinburgh. There he continued the work of organizing Scotland's historical records which had been begun earlier by THOMAS THOMSON. Robertson proved to be a thorough and painstaking scholar whose main interest lay in the nation's ecclesiastical records, this interest inspired his best work, an edition of Scots ecclesiastical laws, *Concilia ecclesiae scoticanae* (1866). He died on 13 December 1866.

WORKS: *Guide to Deeside* (1835); *The Book of Bon Accord* (1838); *Deliciae literariae* (1839); *Collections for a History of the Shires of Aberdeen and Banff* (1842); ed., with George Grub, *History of Scots Affairs from MDCXXXVII to MDCXLI*, 3 vols.

(1841), ed., *Liber Colegii Nostre Domini* (1846); *On Scholastic Offices in the Scottish Church in the Twelfth and Thirteenth Centuries* (1853); ed., *Diary of General Patrick Gordon* (1862); ed., *Inventories of Jewels, Dresses, Furniture, Books and Paintings Belonging to Queen Mary* (1863); ed., *Concilia ecclesiae scoticanae* (1866); *History of the Reformation in Aberdeen* (1877)

Robertson, William (1721–93). Historian. He was born on 19 September 1721 in Borthwick, Midlothian, the son of a minister. He was educated at the University of Edinburgh, where he studied divinity; he was minister in Dalkeith (1741–3), Gladsmuir near Haddington (1743–56) and Edinburgh (1758–62), where he had charge of Lady Yester's and Old Greyfriars. In 1762 he was appointed Principal of the University of Edinburgh, and in the following year he was elected Moderator of the General Assembly of the Church of Scotland, and also His Majesty's Historiographer for Scotland.

Robertson had a wide knowledge of religious and historical matters and was one of the most attractive figures of the period of the SCOTTISH ENLIGHTENMENT; contemporary accounts testify both to his academic diligence and to the good humour of his personality. He was an original member of the SELECT SOCIETY, founded by Allan Ramsay, and within that fellowship he became a close friend and confidant of the philosopher DAVID HUME (ii). During the Jacobite rebellion of 1745 Robertson was an ardent supporter of the government and it was in England, during a visit in 1758, that he first enjoyed popular acclaim for his writing.

During his lifetime Robertson was considered one of the most able British historians and although none of his work achieved the standards of his contemporary Edward Gibbon (1737–94) and his studies have been succeeded by those of later historians, his *History of Scotland* (1759), *History of the Reign of the Emperor Charles V* (1769) and *History of America* (1777) were standard works, demonstrating an admirable clarity and lack of prejudice in religious matters. Robertson was a skilled administrator and an eloquent speaker who brought great authority to his leadership of the Church and University. After his death his works were edited in 1817 with a lively biography by his friend of latter years DUGALD STEWART.

WORKS: *The History of Scotland during the Reigns of Queen Mary and James VI till his Accession to the*

Crown of England, 2 vols. (1759); *The History of the Reign of the Emperor Charles V*, 3 vols. (1769); *The History of America*, 2 vols. (1777); *An historical Disquisition Concerning the Knowledge which the Ancients had of India* (1791)

EDITION: D. Stewart, ed., *Collected Works of William Robertson*, 12 vols. (Edinburgh, 1817)

Robert the Bruce. *See* ROBERT I.

Rob Roy. A novel by Sir WALTER SCOTT, published in 1817, which takes its name from the real-life outlaw and drover, ROB ROY MACGREGOR. The work deals with some of the preoccupations Scott had already aired in his first novel, WAVERLEY: the clash between Highland and Lowland culture, and the conflicting values of romantic Jacobitism and Hanoverian Unionism.

Set in the period following the Jacobite rebellion of 1715, the book has as its central character the moderate Francis Osbaldistone, who has been banished to the family seat in the north of England for refusing to follow his father's profession in the City. There Francis becomes the victim of the machinations of his cousin Rashleigh, who threatens to destroy him and to foil his love for Diana Vernon. Francis takes to the Highlands to enlist the support of Rob Roy, and he is accompanied by the Glasgow merchant, Bailie Nicol Jarvie (an inspired creation). One of the novel's highlights is Rob Roy's dramatic fight with and escape from the government troops. Scott brings the action to a triumphant conclusion with the downfall and death of Rashleigh at the hands of Rob Roy for his betrayal of the Jacobite cause, and the reconciliation of Francis with his father and his marriage to Diana. Osbaldistone, faced with the romance of the Highlands, turns instead to a life of security and well-being, ideals that have been constantly praised by the pragmatic, pro-Unionist Bailie Nicol Jarvie. Rob Roy also contains the rascally, double-dealing character of Andrew Fairservice, gardener at Osbaldistone Hall, and a sympathetic portrayal of Helen, wife to Rob Roy Macgregor.

Rodger, Alexander (1784–1846). Poet. He was born on 16 July 1784 in Midcalder, Midlothian, the son of a farmer. He was apprenticed to a silversmith in Edinburgh as a young man, but moved later to Glasgow, where he spent the rest of his life, working variously as a weaver, cloth inspector, music teacher and journalist. Although his reputation was for long dimmed by his involvement as the co-editor of the sentimental WHISTLE-BINKIE anthologies, Rodger was a satirical poet with a fine eye for exposing the ridiculous in public life. His best-known poem, 'Sawney, now the king's come', is a spirited pastiche of Sir Walter Scott's poem of welcome to George IV on his visit to Edinburgh of August 1822. Like most of his satirical poems commenting on the public events of his lifetime, it is written in a vigorous, earthy Scots. While working for a radical newspaper, *The Spirit of the Union*, Rodger was imprisoned briefly for sedition, but this did not dampen his political ardour and his last years were spent as editor of *The Reformers' Gazette*. Of his humorous, sentimental poems and songs, all of which enjoyed great popularity in their day, 'Robin Tamson's Smiddy' is perhaps the most accomplished. He died on 26 September 1846 in Glasgow.

EDITION: R. Ford, ed., *Poems and Songs, Humourous, Serious and Satirical* (Paisley, 1897; rev. 2/1901)

Rolland, John (*fl* 1560). Poet. Very little is known about the life of John Rolland. From contemporary records it can be deduced that he was a presbyter of the diocese of Glasgow and that in 1555 he was a notary in Dalkeith. He may also have had courtly connections, and from his poetic works it can be seen that he had studied law. His major poem, *The Court of Venus*, an allegory written in the style of *The Palice of Honour* by GAVIN DOUGLAS, was published in Edinburgh in 1575 by Johne Ros under the title *Ane Treatis callit The Court of Venus deudit into Four Buikis*. The poet overhears an argument between Esperance, who defends love, and Desperance, who denies it. Venus is called to adjudicate. After many learned discussions, Desperance is sentenced to death but is then reprieved by Venus who takes him into her service under the name 'Dalliance'. Rolland's other work is *The Sevin Sagis translatit out of prois in Scottish meter be Jone Rolland in Dalkeith with Ane Moralitie eftir everie Doctours tale eftir his awin tale and ane exclamatioun and outcrying upon the emperours wife eftir her fals contriuit tale*, which was published in Edinburgh in 1578.

WORKS: *Ane Treatis callit The Court of Venus deudit into Four Buikis* (1575); *The Sevin Sagis translatit out of prois in Scottish meter be Jone Rolland in Dalkeith with Ane Moralitie eftir everie Doctours tale eftir his awin tale and ane exclamatioun and outcrying upon the emperours wife eftir her fals contriuit tale* (1578)

EDITION: W. Gregor, ed., *The Court of Venus*, STS (Edinburgh and London, 1889)

Rorie, David (1867–1946). Poet. He was born on 17 March 1867 in Edinburgh, but his childhood and most of his subsequent life were spent in Aberdeen. He studied medicine there and in Edinburgh, and his early career was spent as a colliery doctor in Fife, an experience that led to his first publication, the essay 'The Folk Lore of the Mining Folk of Fife'. Between 1905 and 1933 he was a general practitioner in Cults near Aberdeen, his career being interrupted by World War I, during which he served with the 51st Highland Division in France. He was awarded the DSO in 1917 and the Légion d'Honneur in 1918 for his war work with the Royal Army Medical Corps. He died on 18 February 1946. Rorie was a lifelong student of the folklore and folk-song of the north-east, and the poem for which he is best known, 'The Lum hat wantin' the Croon', has long enjoyed the status of a folk-song.

WORKS: 'The Folk Lore of the Mining Folk of Fife', *Country Folklore*, vol.7, ed. J. E. Simkins (London, 1914); *The Auld Doctor* (1920); *The Medico's Luck in the War* (1929); *The Lum Hat Wantin' the Croon* (1935); *A Bedfast Prophet* (1937)

Ros, Uilleam [William Ross] (1762–90). Poet. He was born in Strath on the Isle of Skye and was sent to Forres in Moray to be educated. On his return the family settled in Gairloch in Wester Ross, and the young Ros joined his father as a travelling packman, a trade that took him all over Scotland. While visiting Stornoway he fell in love with Marion Ross and his unrequited love for her is one of the major themes in his poetry. In 1786 he was appointed parish schoolmaster in Gairloch but his health, never of the best, deserted him and he died, probably of tuberculosis, in 1790.

After his death, local legend had it that Ros had died of love for Marion, a story that was lent support by his composition of several earthy courting songs such as 'Oran do Chailin àraidh'. His poems to Marion, 'Feasgar Luain' and 'Oran Cumhaidh', are carefully constructed, traditional love-songs but his 'Oran Eile' strikes a harsher note with its bare imagery of the maggot in the breast eating at the heart of love. Ros also wrote a conventional poem on Prince CHARLES EDWARD STUART and the fail-

ure of the Jacobite cause, a number of clan praise poems, two poems on the delights of whisky, and songs illustrating the passing of the seasons; but it is for the elegiac note struck by his many love-songs that he is best remembered. His poems were collected and edited by John Mackenzie in 1830, who published a further selection in his anthology, *Sar-Obair nam Bard Gaelach*, in 1841. His work has been translated by several poets, notably by IAIN CRICHTON SMITH, and he had a marked influence on the early love poems of the 20th-century poet SOMHAIRLE MACGILL-EAIN.

EDITION: G. Calder, ed., *Gaelic Songs by William Ross* (Edinburgh, 1937)

Rosebery, 5th Earl of. *See* PRIMROSE, ARCHIBALD PHILIP.

Ross, Alexander (1699–1784). Poet. He was born on 13 April 1699 at Kincardine O'Neil and was educated at Marischal College, Aberdeen. After graduating, Ross became a schoolmaster at Aboyne, then at Laurencekirk, and finally at Lochlee, a remote Angus village at the head of Glenesk. In 1768 he published *Helenore, or the Fortunate Shepherdess*, a sentimental pastoral drama in which Lindy is abducted by Highland brigands and saved by the shepherdess Nory. Like the rest of his work it is written in the vigorous Scots of the north-east and, with its vivid scenic descriptions, it was compared with THE GENTLE SHEPHERD by ALLAN RAMSAY. Ross also enjoyed a reputation as a skilful songwriter and his wry evocation of a bad match in a country marriage, *Woo'd and married and a'* is perhaps his best-known creation. He died on 20 May 1784.

EDITION: M. Wattie, ed., *The Scottish Works of Alexander Ross* (Edinburgh, 1938)

Ross, William. The English name of UILLEAM ROS.

Row, John (1569–1646). Divine. He was born in Perth and was educated at the University of Edinburgh, where he studied law. He became minister of the village of Carnock in Fife and was a leading opponent of Episcopacy. His *History of the Kirk of Scotland from 1558 to 1637* contains much useful information about the beginnings of the Covenanting movement; it was published in 1842 under the auspices of the WODROW SOCIETY. Row died on 26 June

1646. His son, James Row, an early supporter of the NATIONAL COVENANT, followed his steps in the ministry. He preached the famous 'Red Shankes' sermon in the Church of St Giles, Edinburgh, in April 1638, encouraging those in high office to sign the Covenant.

EDITION: D. Laing, ed., *The History of the Kirk of Scotland from 1558 to 1637 by John Row*, 2 vols., Maitland Club (Edinburgh, 1842)

Royal Scottish Academy. A society of artists, sculptors and architects formed in Edinburgh on 27 May 1826, for the purpose of protecting their own interests, and holding an annual exhibition of members' work. It had its origins in a dissatisfaction felt by many artists at the restrictions placed on public exhibition by the two existing organizations: the Honourable Board of Trustees for Manufactures in Scotland (1727) and the Institution for the Encouragement of the Fine Arts (1819). Having challenged the authority of the establishment, the 15 original academicians arranged a first exhibition in February 1827, and thereafter the exhibition became an annual event. In 1835 the Academy moved into the headquarters of the Board of Trustees in Princes Street, by the Mound, a building designed by William Playfair (1789–1857). The Academy received its royal warrant and charter of incorporation on 13 August 1838. After securing its national status the Academy began pressing for the foundation of a national gallery, to be housed behind its headquarters on the Mound. Building began in 1850, to a design by Playfair, and the National Gallery of Scotland opened its doors to the public in 1857. The royal Scottish Academy continues to hold annual art exhibitions and is regarded as the country's senior art establishment.

Royal Society of Edinburgh. A society founded in 1783 for the purpose of 'promoting natural knowledge'. It was based on the Royal Society of London (1662) and originally had two classes, Physical and Literary. This distinction was abandoned at the beginning of the 19th century as the Society's interests turned increasingly to scientific subjects only. The driving force behind the formation of the Royal Society of Edinburgh was the historian and Principal of the University of Edinburgh, WILLIAM ROBERTSON, who brought it into being through the amalgamation of two earlier

learned societies, the Society for the Improvement of Medical Knowledge (1731) and the Philosophical Society (1739). Each year the Society elects 25 Fellows and there is also a class of Honorary Fellows, two-thirds of whom are from other countries and who have included Goethe and Benjamin Franklin. Since 1909 the Society's offices have been at 22 George Street, Edinburgh, the previous headquarters, on the Mound, having been shared with the ROYAL SCOTTISH ACADEMY. A prominent feature of the Society's work has been the award of prizes for scientific achievement and the administration of bequests for research in the Scottish universities.

Ruddiman, Thomas (1674–1757). Grammarian and literary scholar. He was born in October 1674 in the parish of Boyndie, Banff, the son of a crofter. He was educated at the parish school and between 1690 and 1694 at King's College, Aberdeen, where he studied classics. After leaving Aberdeen he spent a year tutoring before being appointed schoolmaster in Laurencekirk, Kincardineshire, in April 1695. As a result of meeting Dr ARCHIBALD PITCAIRNE, an eminent physician and classical scholar, in 1699 he was invited to move to Edinburgh, and in 1700 he was appointed a copyist in the library of the FACULTY OF ADVOCATES. In 1706 he was employed by the printer Robert Freebairn, who also accepted Ruddiman's younger brother Walter as an apprentice. For Freebairn, Thomas edited the translation by GAVIN DOUGLAS of Virgil's *Aeneid* (1710), adding to it a glossary of Scots words, which, although it contained many errors, was the first of its kind and helped to encourage the growing interest in Scots poetry and song. He also produced editions of the work of WILLIAM DRUMMOND of Hawthornden (1711) and the *Opera omnia* of GEORGE BUCHANAN (1715).

In 1712 Ruddiman established his own printing house and he took his brother into partnership in 1719. They published the work of ALLAN RAMSAY and most of the important scholarly and legal writings of their day, including James Anderson's *Selectus diplomatum et numismatum Scotiae thesaurus* (1739), a study of Scottish coinage, writs and seals, and the first volume of the catalogue of the library of the Faculty of Advocates in 1742. In 1724 the Ruddimans took over the printing of the CALEDONIAN MERCURY and in 1728 they were appointed joint printers to the University of Edinburgh. Their output was prolific but their books were known more for the accuracy of the printing than for the elegance of their design.

Ruddiman's fame as a classical scholar rests on his *Rudiments of the Latin Tongue* (1714), which went through 15 editions in his lifetime and remained a standard Latin grammar until the 19th century. He also wrote the more advanced *Grammaticae latinae institutiones*. Although the *Rudiments* was written in English and became as much a guide to learning correct English as grammatical Latin, Ruddiman defended the practice of speaking Latin, and in the *Institutiones* he was uncompromising in his use of Latin as a means of teaching the language. His adherence to the classical humanism of the 16th century and his belief in Latin as the basis of Scottish culture dissociated him in old age both from the scholars of the SCOTTISH ENLIGHTENMENT and from poets such as Ramsay who chose to write in Scots.

A Jacobite and Episcopalian, Ruddiman allowed his political and religious beliefs to intrude on his work as an antiquarian and for several years he was involved in lengthy disputes on historical matters such as the Scottish royal succession; he published an edition of the letters of JAMES IV, JAMES V and MARY, Queen of Scots. Ruddiman was appointed Keeper of the Library of the Faculty of Advocates on 6 January 1730, and held the post until 7 January 1751, when he resigned it to DAVID HUME (ii). He died on 19 January 1757 and was buried in Greyfriars' Churchyard, Edinburgh.

WORKS: *Latin-English Vocabulary* (1713); *Rudiments of the Latin Tongue* (1714); ed., *Opera omnia* [of George Buchanan], 2 vols. (1715); ed., *Epistolae Jacobi Quarti, Jacobi Quinti et Maria regum Scotorum*, 2 vols. (1722–4); *Grammaticae latinae institutiones pars prima* (1725); *Grammaticae latinae institutiones pars secunda* (1731); *A Vindication of Mr George Buchanan's Paraphrase of the Book of Psalms from the Objections Raised against it by William Benson* (1745); *An Answer to the Reverend Mr George Logan's Treatise on Government* (1747); *A Dissertation Concerning the Competition for the Crown of Scotland, betwixt Lord Robert Bruce and Lord John Baliol in the year 1291* (1748); *Animadversions on a Late Pamphlet, Intituled A Vindication of Mr George Buchanan* (1749); *Anti-crisis, or A Discussion of a Scurrilous and Malicious Libel Published by one Mr James Man of Aberdeen* (1754); *Audi alteram partem, or A Further Vindication of Mr Thomas Ruddiman's Edition of the Great Buchanan's Works* (1755)

REFERENCE: D. Duncan, *Thomas Ruddiman: a Study of Scottish Scholarship in the Early Eighteenth Century* (Edinburgh, 1965)

Ruddiman, Walter (1719–81). Publisher. He was born in Edinburgh in 1719, the nephew of the grammarian THOMAS RUDDIMAN. On 11 September 1754 he was admitted a Burgess of the City of Edinburgh and set up business as a printer in Morocco's Court, off the Lawnmarket. He tried his hand at periodical publishing in 1757 with his short-lived *Edinburgh Magazine*; undeterred by its failure, he returned to the market with the publication of THE WEEKLY MAGAZINE, OR EDINBURGH AMUSEMENT on 7 July 1768. This weekly news digest and compilation of serious articles and poetry became the most popular journal of its kind in Scotland and it made Ruddiman's reputation. In it he published the poetry of ROBERT FERGUSSON, of which he also produced collections in 1773 and 1779, thus ensuring that his friend's work would not be lost to posterity after his death at the early age of 24. In 1777, to avoid the payment of stamp duty, which was levied on newspapers, he separated the news digest from his magazine and published it as *Ruddiman's Weekly Mercury*. Ruddiman was a hard-headed businessman and a forerunner of the entrepreneurial publishers of the early 19th century who were to make Edinburgh a publishing centre of note. He died on 16 June 1781 and lies buried in Greyfriars' Churchyard in Edinburgh.

REFERENCE: G. H. Johnston, *The Ruddimans in Scotland* (Edinburgh, 1901)

Runciman, Alexander (1736–85). Artist. He was the son of an Edinburgh builder, and after a rudimentary education was apprenticed to a firm of decorators which provided landscape painting for the wooden panels above fireplaces. After a period of study in Glasgow, he travelled in Italy, and on his return to Scotland became a painting master at the Trustees' Academy in Edinburgh. For James Clerk, son of Sir JOHN CLERK of Penicuik, Runciman executed at his residence a work entitled *Ossian's Hall*, depicting all the false Romanticism of the then popular OSSIAN poems. In the same house and for the same patron he depicted four scenes from the life of ST MARGARET, in the style of the murals in the Sistine Chapel in Rome. Runciman was a member of the CAPE CLUB taking the name 'Sir Brimstone', and a friend of the leading *literati* of the day. One of his better, more intimate paintings is his thumbnail sketch of the poet ROBERT FERGUSSON.

Russell, William (1741–93). Historian. He was born in Selkirkshire, the son of a farmer, and was educated at the village school of Innerleithen near Peebles. Between 1756 and 1763 he worked in Edinburgh as an apprentice bookseller and printer, but having gained the patronage of Lord Elibank in 1765 he moved to London to work as a printer. There he enjoyed a reputation as a man of letters, writing histories of America and Europe, both of which were later superseded by more authoritative works. Russell also wrote two verse tragedies, neither of which was staged, and among his numerous poems, only his long romance, *Julia* (1774), has any merit. In 1787 he returned to live in Scotland, near Langholm, where he died on 25 December 1793.

WORKS: *Collection of Modern Poems* (1756); *Ode to Fortitude* (1769); *Sentimental Tales* (1770); *Essays on the Character, Manners and Genius of Women* (1772); *Fables, Moral and Sentimental* (1772); *Julia: a Poetical Romance* (1774); *The History of America* (1779); *History of Modern Europe in a Series of Letters from a Nobleman to his Son*, 5 vols. (1779–86); *Tragic Muse* (1783); *History of Ancient Europe* (1793)

Rutherford, Samuel (*c*1600–61). Divine. He was born at Nisbet in Renfrewshire and was educated at the Grammar School at Jedburgh and at the University of Glasgow, graduating in 1621. Between 1623 and 1625 he was Regent of Humanity at the University, but he was forced to resign his post, and he then became minister of Anworth in Kirkcudbrightshire, where his opposition to Episcopacy led to his banishment to Aberdeen. In 1638 he became Professor of Divinity at St Andrews University and he was made Principal of St Mary's College in 1651; he also acted as a commissioner to the Westminster Assembly during this period. The publication of his tract, *Lex rex*, in which he advocated the selection of monarchs by the people, led to his suspension from public office and he was condemned as a heretic. Before further action against him could be taken he died, on 29 March 1661. Rutherford wrote a number of polemical works but he is best remembered for the austere charm of his letters, written from Aberdeen and published in *Joshua redivivus* in 1664.

WORKS: *A Peaceable and Temperate Plea for Paul's Presbytery in Scotland* (1642); *The Due Right of Presbyteries* (1644); *Lex rex* (1644); *The Divine Right of Church Government and Excommunication* (1646); *Christ Dying and Drawing Sinners to Himself* (1647); *Survey of the Spiritual Antichrist* (1648); *Disputatio scholastica de divina providentia, A Free Disputation Against Pretended Liberty of Conscience* (1649); *Exercitationes apologeticae pro divina gratia* (1651); *The Tryal and Triumph of Faith* (1654); *The Covenant of Life Opened* (1655); *Survey of the Survey Penned by Mr Hooker* (1654); *Joshua redivivus* (1664); *Examen armenianisimi* (1668)

EDITIONS: A. A. Bonar, ed., *Fourteen Sermons* (Glasgow, 1878); A. A. Bonar, ed., *Letters of Samuel Rutherford* (Edinburgh, 1891); J. Stephen ed., *Samuel Rutherford's Letters* (London, 1920); C. Downes, ed., *The King in his Beauty* (London, 1955)

S

St Andrew. *See* ANDREW, ST.

St Andrew's Day. *See* ANERMAS.

St Bride. *See* BRIDE, ST.

St Columba. *See* COLUMBA, ST.

St Kentigern. *See* KENTIGERN, ST.

St Magnus. *See* MAGNUS, ST.

St Margaret. *See* MARGARET, ST.

Salmond, J(ames) B(ell) ['Wayfarer'] (1891–1958). Novelist and editor. He was a native of Arbroath. After graduating from the University of St Andrews he served as an officer with the Black Watch during World War I, fighting on the Western Front. Although his original intention had been to read law, he turned to journalism for a living, and in 1927 he became editor of the Dundee *Scots Magazine*, which that year had moved from Glasgow to Dundee. Under his tutelage writers such as JAMES LESLIE MITCHELL, ('Lewis Grassic Gibbon'), LEWIS SPENCE and NEIL M. GUNN received great encouragement; he was a particular source of financial support to Gunn when he became a full-time writer, and he also provided him with the pseudonym 'Dane McNeill'. Salmond wrote articles, stories and poetry for the magazine, using the pen-name 'Wayfarer', and a selection of his verse was published in *The Old Stalker* (1936). In 1948 he retired to live in St Andrews, where he wrote a history of the Royal and Ancient Golf Club and an account of the 51st Highland Division during World War II. He also devoted much time and energy to the affairs of his *alma mater*, editing a selection of the writings of ANDREW LANG at the behest of the Senatus of the University. *Wade in Scotland* (1934) is the standard work on the construction of lines of communication in the Highlands by General Wade (1673–1748), following the 1715 Jacobite rebellion. Salmond was a founder-member of the Scottish Youth Hostel Association and he was also connected with the Arbroath Abbey Pageant Society, which presents plays relating to the abbey's part in the DECLARATION OF ARBROATH. He died on 2 February 1958 in St Andrews.

WORKS: *Bawbee Bowden* (1922); *Wade in Scotland* (1934); *The Old Stalker* (1936); ed., *Andrew Lang and St Andrews* (1944); *Flower of the Flax* (1944); *The Toby Jug* (1947); *Veterum laudes* (1950); *Recording Scotland* (1952); *The History of the 51st Highland Division, 1939–1945* (1953); *The Story of the R and A* (1956)

Sandison, Janet. Pen-name of JANE DUNCAN.

Sassenach. The anglicized form of the Gaelic adjective *sasunnach*, meaning an inhabitant of England. The term is used, often pejoratively, to describe the English or things English.

Satyre of the Thrie Estaitis, Ane Pleasant. *See* PLEASANT SATYRE OF THE THRIE ESTAITIS, ANE.

Saunders, R(obert) Crombie (*b* 1914). Poet. He was born on 23 April 1914 in Glasgow and was educated at the University of Glasgow, since when he has spent much of his life working as a schoolmaster. Most of his literary work has been published in magazines and he has written on many aspects of Scotland's life and culture; among the magazines he has edited are *Scottish Art and Letters* (1944–8) and *Forward* (1951–6). In 1944 he edited a selection of the poems of Hugh MacDiarmid (CHRISTOPHER MURRAY GRIEVE), a publication that did much to resurrect MacDiarmid's reputation during World War II. His own poem about the effects of the CLEARANCES, which has been anthologized frequently, is a reminder of the care and attention devoted to language and metre by this poet, who has published all too little of his work in book form over the years.

WORKS: ed., *Selected Poems of Hugh MacDiarmid* (1944); *A Guide to the Fishing Inns of Scotland* (1951); *XXI Poems* (1955); *The Year's Green Edge* (1955)

Scot, Sir John, of Scotstarvit. *See* SCOTT, JOHN.

Scotichronicon. The name given to the Latin history of Scotland completed by WALTER BOWER between 1440 and his death in 1449. It was based on the *Chronica gentis Scotorum* written by JOHN OF FORDUN some time between 1384 and 1387, which provided a history of Scotland from earliest times to the year 1383. Bower continued John's work to the end of the reign of JAMES I and amplified some of the earlier passages dealing with the mythical tales about the beginnings of Scottish history. The *Scotichronicon*, which comprises the work of both historians, provides a vital source of information about Scotland's pre- and early history, especially as John and Bower both had access to manuscripts that have since been lost. The history survives in 21 different manuscripts but it has not been published as a whole since 1759 (edited in two volumes by Walter Goodall). A two-volume edition of John's work alone was edited by WILLIAM FORBES SKENE in 1871.

Scoticisms. During the middle and the second part of the 18th century, the period generally considered to have been the high-water mark of the SCOTTISH ENLIGHTENMENT, a conscious attempt was made by many of the *literati* to rid their speech and their writings of 'Scoticisms', or Scots words and phrases. There were two principal reasons for this desire. Firstly, increased communication with London, following the ACT OF UNION of 1707 made many Scots who visited the nation's capital, ashamed of their Scots speech; and secondly, the Enlightenment espoused a preference for cultivation in place of rudeness and a general admiration for Augustan standards of constraint and excellence. Thus in 1761, the SELECT SOCIETY, then Edinburgh's foremost literary and debating club, hired an Irish actor, Thomas Sheridan, to give its members elocution lessons so that they could 'avoid any gross improprieties of speech'; and in his short-lived

magazines, which reflected the ideals of the age, THE LOUNGER and THE MIRROR, HENRY MACKENZIE advocated an attention to style that would rid prose of all vulgarities, that is, Scots idiom. The anxiety of the *literati* about accidentally allowing Scots to creep into their speech or writings encouraged the Aberdeen poet JAMES BEATTIE to compile his successful and widely read volume *Scoticisms, Arranged in Alphabetical Order, Designed to Correct Improprieties of Speech and Writing*, which listed 200 words that might be employed by those who had 'no opportunity of learning English from the company they kept'. DAVID HUME (ii), HUGH BLAIR and WILLIAM ROBERTSON, three leading intellectuals of the Scottish Enlightenment, all took Beattie's and others' advice very seriously and worked hard to expunge any hint of Scots from their work.

At the same time Scots was considered an attractive language for songs, proverbs and folk-tales, and those same *literati* who scorned the language took a sentimental delight in the Scots song tradition. It was symptomatic of that paradox that when Burns published his *Poems* in 1786 Mackenzie's review in *The Lounger* referred to the poet as the 'heaven-taught ploughman', almost as if poetry could be the preserve only of the educated, and that poetry in Scots was merely the product of an untutored sensibility. The work of ROBERT FERGUSSON was ignored by the *literati* and yet the pale Augustan imitations of the blind poet THOMAS BLACKLOCK, who was revered by his contemporaries, are now read not at all. The novels of JOHN GALT and Sir WALTER SCOTT and their many imitators used Scots only as a medium for the uneducated or rural classes, and throughout the 19th century it was denigrated both in society and as a literary language.

Despite the efforts of Hugh MacDiarmid (CHRISTOPHER MURRAY GRIEVE) and others associated with the 20th-century SCOTTISH RENAISSANCE to revive the language in the 1920s, the dilemma which faced the 18th-century *literati* has continued to have a profound effect on the culture of the country and its echoes are still felt to this day.

Scotland, National Library of. The successor to the library of the FACULTY OF ADVOCATES, which was founded in the north-east corner of Parliament Close, Edinburgh, in 1689 by Sir GEORGE MACKENZIE (ii) of Rosehaugh. Although this was intended to be a legal library, it also concentrated on works of history, criticism and rhetoric and initiated a policy of collecting books of European scholarship. The library published its first catalogue in 1692, and in 1710 it obtained by Act of Parliament the right of copyright deposit. THOMAS RUDDIMAN and DAVID HUME (ii) were early Keepers, and by the 19th century the library had established itself as the principal library in Scotland. It had become evident by then that it was too large to remain in the control of the Faculty of Advocates and attempts were made to obtain financial aid from the government. In 1925 the library was transferred to the state under the National Library of Scotland Act, after Sir Alexander Grant of Forres had made a permanent endowment for a national library in Scotland.

The library has occupied its premises on George IV Bridge since 1956 and in 1974 it merged with the Scottish Central Library which is responsible for inter-library loans. The National Library holds over 3,000,000 books, including nine tracts printed by WALTER CHAPMAN and Andrew Myllar in 1508 and an illuminated copy of the Gutenburg Bible (c1455). It also maintains the major Scottish historical and literary manuscripts.

Scots. The historic speech of Lowland Scotland (also known as LALLANS), derived principally from the northern dialect of Anglo-Saxon. Following the 5th-century departure of the Romans from Britain, tribes from Germany exploited the power vacuum, with Saxon tribes taking over the south and west of Britain and the Angles the north and the east. In 638 the Angles moved into southern Scotland, capturing the fortress of Din Eiden (Edinburgh), and the tongue spoken by the invaders became the basis of the Scots language. To the west, from the 3rd century onwards, the incoming Scots from Ireland introduced Q-Celtic or Gaelic and by the 10th century Scotland was effectively a bilingual country, with Gaelic enjoying the ascendancy of usage for most legal and administrative purposes. Gaelic influenced the development of Scots, as did the 9th-century Viking invasions, which affected the phonological development of the language. The Anglo-Norman incursions from the 13th century drove Gaelic out of the Lowlands, and for a time French came to be used at court, with Latin as the language of statecraft. However, by the middle of the 14th century, Scots (the residue of the northern dialect with its various influences) was the official language of a Scotland that had become independent in 1328.

The language came to be known as 'Scottis' as opposed to its earlier form of 'Inglis' and its literature flourished. THE BRUCE by JOHN BARBOUR, the verse history of ANDREW OF WYNTOUN, and WALLACE by BLIND HARRY display the range and authority of Scots at this period; and the makars ROBERT HENRYSON, WILLIAM DUNBAR and GAVIN DOUGLAS developed its distinctive courtly 'aureate' style in their poetry. At the same time the language remained colloquial and earthy and the 16th-century play ANE PLEASANT SATYRE OF THE THRIE ESTAITIS by Sir DAVID LYNDSAY is an early example of the shifts of sensibility – from fantasy to reality and from lofty ideals to coarse humour – that became a recognizable feature of later Scottish literature. The coming of the Reformation in 1560 was the first blow to that healthy development of the language: no satisfactory Bible in Scots was ever printed, and the many English Bibles in circulation reinforced the idea that English, being the language of God, must also be the language of solemnity, improvement and intellectual vigour. The second blow was the removal of the Scottish court to London after the Union of the Crowns in 1603. In order to retain royal patronage, the CASTALIAN BAND of poets moved with JAMES VI to London, and English increasingly became the language of polite society, while Scots was considered to be couthy, fit only for domestic, sentimental or humorous subjects.

In 1707 the ACT OF UNION made English the official language of Scotland, and the *literati* of the SCOTTISH ENLIGHTENMENT looked forward to a future in which progress would be measured in terms of correct grammatical English. The reaction to that third blow was a patriotic revival of interest in earlier Scots poetry and song through the 18th-century anthologies of JAMES WATSON, DAVID HERD, and ALLAN RAMSAY who also wrote original poetry in Scots. By far the most influential poets writing in Scots during the 18th-century were ROBERT FERGUSSON and ROBERT BURNS, both of whom showed an awareness of the possibility of revitalizing Scots instead of merely employing a debased and narrow vernacular. But their efforts were not improved upon and throughout the 19th century Scots was little more than an artifical, sentimental and homely means of literary expression, much employed by the later writers of the KAILYARD school. In the novels of Sir WALTER SCOTT, JOHN GALT, SUSAN EDMONS-TOUNE FERRIER, GEORGE MACDONALD, ROBERT LOUIS STEVENSON and others, Scots became the speech of the lesser, more humble characters, while correct English was the preserve of the principal, usually middle-to upper-class and aristocratic characters.

The coming of the modern means of communication in the 20th century was a fourth blow and by the 1950s Scots had become little more than a series of local dialects, each under constant threat from the uniformity imposed by a national use of standard English. Nevertheless, it survives still as a literary language. Many writers, especially poets, use Scots, or Scots words and phrases, and the SCOTTISH RENAISSANCE movement of the 1920s, begun by CHRISTOPHER MURRAY GRIEVE, was a conscious attempt to revive the use of Scots in Scotland. However much it may have failed in achieving that objective, it nevertheless did help to bring about a new and continuing interest in Scotland's literature and to create a fresh concern for the well-being of Scotland's three languages: Scots, Gaelic and English.

REFERENCES: J. Y. Mather and H. H. Speitel, eds., *The Linguistic Atlas of Scotland*, 2 vols. (Edinburgh, 1975–7); W. Graham, *The Scots Word Book* (Edinburgh, 1977); D. Murison, *The Guid Scots Tongue* (Edinburgh, 1977)

Scots Magazine and General Intelligencer. The *Scots Magazine*, as it was more commonly known, was first published in January 1739 as a rival to the London-based *Gentleman's Magazine*, in order that 'our countrymen might have the production of every month sooner, cheaper and better collected than before'. The title-page of the first volume ran '*The Scots Magazine*, containing a general view of the Religion, Politicks, Entertainment &c., in Great Britain, and a succinct account of Publick Affairs, foreign and domestick, for the Year MDCCXXXIX.' The first issue cost 6d. and was printed in a blue cover with the motto, '*Ne quid falsi dicere audeat, ne quid veri non audeat*'. Its intention was patriotic – to publish news and reviews specifically for a Scottish audience – and it enjoyed considerable popularity during the 18th century, one of its innovations being the publication of a register of births, marriages and deaths, a practice which

other journals were forced into following. Between 1759 and 1765 it was edited by WILLIAM SMELLIE, and in 1801 it was purchased by ARCHIBALD CONSTABLE, who amalgamated it three years later with another of his publications, the *Edinburgh Magazine and Literary Miscellany*. It appeared under that title in 1817 'being a new series of the *Scots Magazine*', but by then its popularity had been eroded by the appearance of the more serious literary journals such as the *Edinburgh Review* (*see* EDINBURGH REVIEW (ii)) and BLACKWOOD'S MAGAZINE. The magazine's last editor was THOMAS PRINGLE, who had edited William Blackwood's ill-starred first attempt to publish a monthly magazine. The end came in June 1826 when Constable's business crashed.

The copyright to the magazine was purchased by WILLIAM BLACKWOOD for £25, but he chose not to use the title in any of his publications. Subsequent attempts to revive the name came in 1828 with appearance of the *New Scots Magazine* and again in 1832 with the *Scots Weekly Magazine*. Both publications were short-lived, but the magazine's title lives on in a contemporary publication, The *Scots Magazine*, which is published by the Dundee firm of D. C. Thomson.

Scotsman, The. A newspaper first published on 25 January 1817 in Edinburgh. It had been founded the previous year by Charles Maclaren, a Customs House official, and William Ritchie, a lawyer. They were joined later by John Ramsay McCulloch, an economist, who was to become Professor of Political Economy at the University of London. The newspaper espoused the Whig political cause and was an enthusiastic supporter of the Reform Bill of 1832 and of Catholic emancipation. *The Scotsman* has been owned by several proprietors and in 1953 it was purchased by a Canadian, Roy Thomson (later Lord Thomson of Fleet). Its original office was in 257 High Street and in 1905 it moved to its present headquarters on the North Bridge.

Scots Musical Museum, The. A six-volume collection of Scots songs, published between 1787 and 1803 by JAMES JOHNSON. ROBERT BURNS was responsible for most of the collecting and compilation, and the work is a treasure store of traditional poems and songs and of the airs and melodies attached to them.

Scots Quair, A. A trilogy of novels by JAMES LESLIE MITCHELL, published under the pseudonym 'Lewis Grassic Gibbon', it comprises *Sunset Song* (1932), *Cloud Howe* (1933) and *Grey Granite* (1934). Each novel was published separately, and the volume *A Scots Quair* was published in 1946; it was reset and reprinted with an introduction by Ivor Brown in 1950.

The novels are set in Mitchell's native north-east Scotland in the thinly disguised landscapes and townships of the Howe of the Mearns. The background is the Great War, the effect of which was to break up for ever the already declining crofting communities; this led to the disintegration of small-town life and the turmoil of the strike-ridden cities of the 1920s. The unifying character in each of the novels is Chris Guthrie, a farmer's daughter, who is torn by the inherent conflicts of her character, which pull her between love and hate of the land and lead her to an ambivalent attitude to Scottish and English culture. Chris Guthrie's awareness centres on the rhythms of nature, but her growing sexual longing is stultified by the circumscribed condition of the society in which she lives where women must take second place to men.

Through her three marriages and their break-up owing to death and discontent, she becomes conscious of the land as the only continuing reality and of the lonely permanence of woman's place on it. Critics such as Kurt Wittig have attempted to place Chris Guthrie in the role of 'Chris Caledonia', a women with a wholeness of personality capable of embracing all Scotland; but Mitchell's trilogy subordinates the national myth to Chris Guthrie's final understanding that woman alone is able to live without believing in anything but herself, the inevitability of change and the endurance of the land.

Scots Wha Hae. A song, known properly as 'Bruce's Address to his Troops at Bannockburn', written by ROBERT BURNS in honour of the victory of ROBERT I at the BATTLE OF BANNOCKBURN in 1314. Burns sent it originally to GEORGE THOMSON in August 1793 for inclusion in the *Select Collection of Original Scotish Airs* but because of a disagreement over the words and the tune it was not published during the poet's lifetime. It was published by Thomson in 1799 to the tune 'Lewie Gordon' and in Johnson's THE SCOTS MUSICAL

MUSEUM of 1803 to an air by William Clarke. Following the publication of the edition of Burns's works and the biography by JAMES CURRIE, in which the story of the disagreement was told, Thomson published *Scots Wha Hae* to the tune 'Hey tuttie tatie' as Burns had originally intended. In his letter to Thomson, Burns referred to the trial of the Friends of the People and to THOMAS MUIR of Hunters Hill, adding that the final two stanzas were inspired by contemporary events: 'So may God defend the cause of Trust and Liberty as he did that day! – Amen.' *Scots Wha Hae* has been adopted subsequently as a national song.

Scott, Lady. *See* SPOTTISWOOD, ALICIA ANN.

Scott, Agnes N. Pen-name of WILLA ANDERSON.

Scott, Alexander (i) (*c*1515–83). Poet. He was probably born in 1515 and was presumably trained as a musician since there is evidence that he played the fife in June 1540 in tableaux performed by the Knights of the Round Table of the King of the Basoche, an association of law students in Paris. Little is known of his early life and career: he was presented with the prebend of the Chapel Royal at Stirling in 1539, and on 12 July 1548 he was appointed to a canon's position as musician and organist at the Augustinian Priory of Inchmahome under the patronage of its commendator, Robert Erskine. After Erskine's death at the Battle of Pinkie in 1547 Scott wrote 'The Lament of the Master of Erskine' in his memory.

Scott's connections with the Erskine family took him to France and brought him into contact with the court of MARY, Queen of Scots. During the Reformation Scott may have become a Protestant and his poem 'Ane New Yeir Gift to the Quene Mary, quhen scho come first hame' (1562) contains a severe attack on sexual licence in the Catholic Church. By 1565 he was a canon of Inchaffray in Perthshire and on 2 January 1567 he purchased the estate of Nether Petledie in Fife, becoming a substantial landowner; he acquired further estates in the vicinity of Perth and Edinburgh. He died in the early months of 1583.

36 of Scott's poems survived in the BANNATYNE MANUSCRIPT, and apart from his 'The Justing and Debait up at the drum betwix William Adamsone and John Sym', an earthy pastiche in the central Scottish tradition of

humorous country verse, his work can be said to fall into two groups: his courtly love lyrics and poems about lovers, their joys and sorrows, and his later poems of moral advice and rectitude. Many of the works in the first group deal with the pangs of unrequited love, and GEORGE BANNATYNE added a footnote to the lyric 'To luve unluvit' that it was written, 'Quod Scott, quhen his wife left him'. Unhappiness in love may have led Scott to the cynical detachment which is felt in 'Returne thee, hairt, hamewart again' and in 'Quha is perfyte'. He was capable, though, of extolling the sensual power of love, and 'Up hailsum hairt' is a happy celebration of consummated love. In his later lyrics cynicism gives way to the power of reason over the will, and in 'Quha lykis to luve' triumphant reason turns to the love of God, 'the Lord that maid us'.

The intricate metrical and stanza forms of his lyrics give Scott's poetry a melodic freshness that makes them suitable for singing, and Scott seems to have devised many for music. The concentrated imagery of his love poems and their settings as songs make Scott – 'Scott, sweet-tung'd Scott' as ALLAN RAMSAY called him – the most potent of Scottish love poets before ROBERT BURNS.

EDITION: J. Cranstoun, ed., *The Poems of Alexander Scott*, STS (Edinburgh and London, 1896)

REFERENCE: J. MacQueen *Ballatis of Luve* (Edinburgh, 1970)

Scott, Alexander (ii) (*b* 1920). Poet and dramatist. He was born on 28 November 1920 and was educated at the University of Aberdeen between 1939 and 1941 and 1945 and 1947, his education being interrupted by World War II, during which he served with the Gordon Highlanders. After graduating he taught at the universities of Edinburgh and Glasgow, where he has been Reader in Scottish Literature since 1976 and also head of the Department of Scottish Literature. Scott has edited a number of literary magazines and anthologies of Scottish writing; a founding member of the ASSOCIATION FOR SCOTTISH LITERARY STUDIES, he has been a vigorous worker in its cause in the Scottish universities.

Most of Scott's work has been written in the native Scots of his childhood, and his poetry is remarkable for the breadth and colourfulness of the vocabulary that he has at his command. His first collection, *The Latest in Elegies* (1949), was followed by a brief *Selected Poems*

(1950) and *Mouth Music* (1954), but much of his best work comes from *Cantrips* (1968), which includes 'Heart of Stone', his hymn of praise for Aberdeen. Like all of Scott's work, 'Heart of Stone' is couched in a spare, dramatic language, almost cinematic in its ability to draw out the cold, square lines of 'a teuch toun, whaur even the strand maks siller'. A harsh critic of the foibles of his fellow countrymen in such poems as his series of satirical epigrams *Scotched*, Scott attains a universality in the wry observations of his sonnets 'Dear Deid Dancer' (for the dancer Isadora Duncan), 'Marilyn Monroe Still, 1968' and 'To Mourn Jayne Mansfield'. His *Selected Poems, 1943–1974* was published in 1975. Scott has also written equally succinctly in English, and his work for the stage includes *Right Royal* (1950), *Untrue Thomas* (1952) and *Shetland Yarn* (1954). His best-known critical work is on the poet WILLIAM SOUTAR: *Still Life: William Soutar, 1898–1943* (1958), a biography; and *Diaries of a Dying Man* (1954), an edition of Soutar's private diary.

WORKS: *Prometheus 48* (1948); *The Latest in Elegies* (1949); *Selected Poems* (1950); ed., *Selected Poems of William Jeffrey* (1951); ed., *The Poems of Alexander Scott*, c.*1530–c.1584* (1952); *Untrue Thomas* (1952); *Mouth Music* (1954); *Shetland Yarn* (1954); ed., *Diaries of a Dying Man by William Soutar* (1954); *Still Life: William Soutar, 1898–1943* (1958); *Cantrips* (1968); ed., with Norman MacCaig, *Contemporary Scottish Verse 1959–1969* (1970); *Greek Fire* (1971); *Double Agent* (1972); ed., with Michael Grieve, *The Hugh MacDiarmid Anthology* (1972); ed., with Douglas Gifford, *Neil M. Gunn: the Man and the Writer* (1973); ed., with Maurice Lindsay and Roderick Watson, *Scottish Poetry 7–9* (1974–6); *Selected Poems 1943–1974* (1975)

Scott, Francis George (1880–1958). Composer. He was born on 25 January 1880 in Hawick, the son of a mill furnisher. He was educated at Hawick Academy and privately at Brand's Teviot Grove Academy, before matriculating at the University of Edinburgh and as a student-teacher at Moray House College of Education in 1897. Although he chose not to graduate, Scott became a teacher in 1898 and remained in various posts until 1925, when he was appointed a lecturer at Jordanhill College of Education. He received an external degree in music from Durham University in 1909.

While working in Langholm (1903–12), Scott taught the future poet Hugh MacDiarmid (CHRISTOPHER MURRAY GRIEVE), with whom he was later to enjoy a long friendship and collaboration. Between 1923 and 1933

Scott set several of MacDiarmid's early lyrics to music, including 'Wheesht, wheesht, foolish hert' (1924), 'The Eeemis Stane' (1924), 'The Watergaw' (1927), 'Moonstruck' (1929), 'Milk Whort and Bog Cotton' (1932) and 'An Apprentice Angel' (1933). In 1926 he collaborated in the construction of MacDiarmid's long poem A DRUNK MAN LOOKS AT THE THISTLE, a poetic sequence examining Scotland from the widest possible world viewpoint. Scott also set the work of other Scots poets to music, including poems by WILLIAM DUNBAR, ROBERT BURNS, WILLIAM SOUTAR and GEORGE CAMPBELL HAY. A centenary album of his songs was published in 1980.

Scott was connected with the SCOTTISH RENAISSANCE movement of the 1920s and 1930s and enjoyed the friendship of many of its leading writers. He was the cousin of William Johnstone (1897–1981) the painter and friend of Hugh MacDiarmid. Scott died on 6 November 1958.

WORKS: *Three Short Songs* (1920); *Scottish Lyrics Set to Music*, 5 vols. (1922–39); *Seven Songs for Baritone Voice* (1946); *Songs: Thirty-five Scottish Lyrics and Other Poems Set To Music* (1949); *Songs of Francis George Scott: Centenary Album* (1980)

REFERENCE: M. Lindsay: *Francis George Scott and the Scottish Renaissance* (Edinburgh, 1980)

Scott [Scot], Sir **John,** of Scotstarvit (1585–1670). Statesman and editor. He was born in 1585, the son of Robert Scott of Knightspottie in Perthshire, a Director of Chancery. In 1611 he acquired the estate of Scotstarvit near Cupar in Fife and was knighted in 1617. Scott acted in various legal capacities: Privy Councillor, Lord of Session and circuit judge, posts he lost in 1652 during Cromwell's occupation of Scotland. He was a patron of the cartographer TIMOTHY PONT and provided funds and Pont's maps for Johan Blaeu's *Atlas* (1654). As an editor his work with ARTHUR JOHNSTON in collecting together the principal Scottish Latin poets of the period for the DELITIAE POETARUM SCOTORUM (1637) is noteworthy. His *The Staggering State of the Scots Statesmen*, written between 1650 and 1663 (but not published until 1754), is a powerful indictment of the acquisitive nature of the Scottish nobility.

WORKS: ed., with Arthur Johnston, *Delitiae poetarum Scotorum* (1637); *The Staggering State of the Scots Statesmen from One Hundred Years, from 1550 to 1650* (1754)

Scott, Michael (i) (c1160–c1235). Philosopher and astrologer. He is thought to have been born in Durham, of Scottish Border ancestry. He was educated at the universities of Oxford, Paris, and Padua, where there was a thriving school of magic. He spent much of his life in Europe and enjoyed the patronage of the Emperor Frederick II for whom he translated Aristotle's *De animalibus* (1220) and *De coelo*, both of which survive in manuscripts in several British and European libraries. His own writings include learned works on astrology, alchemy and medicine, including *Quaestio curiosa de natura solis et lunae*, published in 1622. His later life was spent in England and Scotland, and Melrose is one of his reputed burial places. His studies in alchemy and astrology earned him a reputation as a magician and sorcerer and he appears in those guises in several literary works including Dante's *Inferno*, THE LAY OF THE LAST MINSTREL by Sir WALTER SCOTT and *The Three Perils of Man* by JAMES HOGG.

WORKS: *Liber physiognomiae et hominis procreationis* (1477); *De animalibus* (1493); *Super auctorem spherae* (1495); *Mensa philosophia* (1602); *Quaestio curiosa de natura solis et lunae* (1622)

Scott, Michael (ii) (1789–1835). Novelist. He was born on 30 October 1789 at Cowlairs, Glasgow, the son of a merchant. He was educated at Glasgow High School and at the University of Glasgow (1801–5). After graduating he emigrated to Jamaica to set himself up in business and he remained there until 1822, when he returned to work in Glasgow. Out of his West Indian experiences he wrote the novel *Tom Cringle's Log*, which appeared serially in BLACKWOOD'S MAGAZINE between September 1829 and June 1831. With its vivid descriptions of the West Indies and of life at sea, it enjoys comparison with the best of the novels by Captain Frederick Marryat and was deservedly popular in its day. A second novel, *The Cruise of the Midge*, was published in *Blackwood's* between March 1834 and June 1835. Both books appeared anonymously and they were published in 1834 and 1836 respectively. Scott died on 7 November 1835 in Glasgow.

Scott, Tom (b 1918). Poet. He was born on 6 June 1918 in Glasgow and was educated there and in St Andrews. After attending Newbattle Abbey College in 1952, he was a mature student at the University of Edinburgh, where he did research on the poetry of WILLIAM DUN-

BAR. Scott has edited two collections of Scottish poetry and in 1966 he published a critical study of Dunbar's poems. His first published verses were translations – *Seevin Poems o Maister Francis Villon* (1953) – in which his 'Ay, whaur are the snaws o langsyne' is a firm yet harmonious rendering in Scots of '*Mais ou sont les neiges d'antan?*'. In later poems Scott employed a language imbued with the measured cadences of Middle Scots, a language that he felt could create a living contemporary verse. Scott's vision of the good society and his warnings of the evils of the class structure find their expression in *The Ship and Ither Poems* (1963), in which the sinking of the giant steamship *Titanic* is taken as an allegory for society and its ills. In similar vein is *At the Shrine o' the Unkent Sodger: a Poem for Recitation* (1968). His greatest achievement as a poet in Scots is the often anthologized 'Brand the Builder', in which the solid character and warm humanity of Brand springs to life through the controlled emotion of Scott's language. The poem stands in the tradition of ROBERT FERGUSSON and ROBERT BURNS and it was published, together with other pieces from the St Andrews period, in 1975. His work in English includes *The Tree* (1977), a 'symphonic verse' that examines man's evolution and the great chain of being.

WORKS: *Seevin Poems o Maister Francis Villon* (1953); *An Ode til New Jerusalem* (1956); *The Ship and Ither Poems* (1963); *Dunbar: a Critical Exposition of the Poems* (1966); ed., with John MacQueen, *The Oxford Book of Scottish Verse* (1966); ed., *Late Medieval Scots Poets* (1967); *At the Shrine o' the Unkent Sodger: a Poem for Recitation* (1968); *Tales of King Robert the Bruce* (1969); ed., *The Penguin Book of Scottish Verse* (1970); *True Thomas* (1971); *Brand the Builder* (1975); *The Tree* (1977); *Tales of Sir William Wallace* (1980)

Scott, Sir Walter (1771–1832). Poet and novelist. He was born on 15 August 1771 in Edinburgh, the son of Walter Scott, a WRITER TO THE SIGNET, and Anne Rutherford, the eldest daughter of Dr John Rutherford, Professor of Medicine in the University of Edinburgh between 1726 and 1765 and a pioneer of modern methods of clinical instruction. There is some evidence to suggest (Clark, *Sir Walter Scott: the Formative Years*) that the year of Scott's birth was 1770, but it is far from conclusive. At the age of 18 months the young Scott was stricken with infantile paralysis, an illness that left him permanently lame in his right leg; to recuperate he was sent to his grandfather Robert Scott's farm at Sandyknowe in Tweed-

dale in the Borders. There he gained an early grounding in his family's history and Border lore and legend, and began a fascination with the JACOBITE cause. Among his earliest reading was the ballad 'Hardyknute' and ALLAN RAMSAY'S THE TEA-TABLE MISCELLANY.

After the death of his grandfather, his lameness having improved, Scott at the age of four returned to Edinburgh, where his family had moved to a more spacious house in 25 George Square. He spent a year in Bath (1775–6) taking the waters in a further attempt to cure his disability and on his return to Scotland he was sent again to Sandyknowe. In 1778 he went back to Edinburgh, where he was educated privately for admission to the HIGH SCHOOL OF EDINBURGH, which he entered in October 1779 in the class of Luke Fraser. Three years later he graduated to the class of the rector, Dr ALEXANDER ADAM, a distinguished classical scholar, and from a private tutor, James Mitchell, he learned French and gained some knowledge of Scottish church history. Although he never became a great Latinist, Scott won second prize in 1782 for a translation from the *Aeneid*, his first known verses. Before matriculating at the University of Edinburgh in November 1783 he spent the summer in Kelso, where he attended Kelso Grammar School and was influenced by reading Bishop Percy's *Reliques of Ancient English Poetry*, a collection of ballads and folk-songs first published in 1765.

Scott's studies at Edinburgh were interrupted by illness, but on their completion he was indentured in his father's legal practice on 31 March 1786. Through his legal apprenticeship he came into contact with the *literati* of Edinburgh, many of whom were lawyers, judges and politicians, and friends of his later years. Further illness forced him to recuperate again in the Borders. On his family's agreeing that he should become an advocate, he attended (1789–90) the university classes of Professors DUGALD STEWART and ALEXANDER FRASER TYTLER to prepare for his Bar examinations. During this period he became a member of the SPECULATIVE SOCIETY, a select debating society as well as a boisterous drinking club. He was called to the Bar on 11 July 1792. During that summer he spent more time in the Borders and was befriended by the Sheriff-Substitute of Roxburghshire, Robert Shortreed, with whom he made the 'raids' into Liddesdale, collecting the ballads that were to form the basis of THE

MINSTRELSY OF THE SCOTTISH BORDER (1802–3).

Scott became interested in German literature; in 1796 he published *The Chase, and William and Helen, Two Ballads from the German of Gottfried Augustus Bürger*, and in 1799 a translation of Goethe's *Götz von Berlichingen*. On 24 December 1797 he married Charlotte Carpenter and they settled in Edinburgh and later in Lasswade, a village to the south of the city. Through the political influence of the Duke of Buccleuch, Scott was appointed Sheriff-Depute of Selkirkshire on 16 December 1799 and returned to the Borders to live at Ashestiel. Assisted by the self-educated scholar JOHN LEYDEN and the antiquary Richard Heber, he completed *The Minstrelsy of the Scottish Border*, a collection of the finest Border ballads largely gained from the oral tradition. Although Scott edited or 'improved' some of the ballads, printing them in inaccurate versions, his preface and notes demonstrate his wide knowledge of Border history and legend. The first two volumes of *The Minstrelsy* were printed by his old Kelso schoolfriend JAMES BALLANTYNE whom Scott encouraged, with financial assistance, to set up business in Edinburgh.

At the suggestion of the Countess of Dalkeith, Scott agreed to compose a ballad of the Border story of Gilpin Horner for the third volume of *The Minstrelsy*. This grew into THE LAY OF THE LAST MINSTREL which was published in January 1805 and was an immediate critical and financial success. Like all his ballad-epics, the main emphasis in *The Lay* is the telling of a romantic story, set against the backcloth of Scottish history. Scott followed its publication with MARMION, subtitled 'A Tale of Flodden Field', in February 1808, and in 1810 with his most successful historical ballad-epic THE LADY OF THE LAKE. Set in the Trossachs, this tells the story of the love of three men – James Fitz-James (James V *incognito*), an English knight; Roderick Dhu, a Highland chief; and Malcolm Graeme – for Ellen, the daughter of the outlawed Lord James Douglas. The poem is memorable for its set descriptive pieces such as the stag hunt and for its scenes of dramatic action. Scott also wrote six other less successful ballads: *Rokeby* (1813), *The Vision of Don Roderick* (1811), *The Bridal of Triermain* (1813), *The Field of Waterloo* (1815), *The Lord of the Isles* (1815) and *Harold the Dauntless* (1817). The publication

of *Marmion* had brought Scott and Ballantyne into closer business relations with ARCHIBALD CONSTABLE, who was to become Scott's principal publisher.

In 1806 Scott became substantive Clerk of the Court of Session to George Hume, a post that he held without salary until 1812, when Hume died. He divided his time between Edinburgh and the Borders, where he built his country seat, ABBOTSFORD, near Galashiels, in 1811, to which he added over the years. In 1814 Constable published Scott's novel WAVERLEY or ''Tis Sixty Years Since', begun as early as 1805; this was the first of his Scottish historical novels, the most important of which are: GUY MANNERING (1815), THE ANTIQUARY (1816), OLD MORTALITY (1816), ROB ROY (1818), THE HEART OF MIDLOTHIAN (1818), THE BRIDE OF LAMMERMOOR (1819), A LEGEND OF MONTROSE (1819) and *Redgauntlet* (1824).

Scott's attitude to the history of his country was mixed: on the one hand he regretted the turbulent days of its recent independent past, and on the other he admired the peace and prosperity of his time, brought by the Union with England (1707) and the strength of the Hanoverian succession (*see* E. Muir, *Scott and Scotland* (London, 1936)). This ambivalence led to a conflict in his historical writing which usually resulted in the triumph of order and of the will over the emotions. Edward Waverley in *Waverley* turns away from his Jacobite associations and Frank Osbaldistone in *Rob Roy* returns to his life of commerce. However, Scott's knowledge of history and his ability to see both sides of a problem gave great strength of insight to his writing. The characters on the Covenanting and government sides in *Old Mortality* are sketched with care and balance; and in *The Heart of Midlothian*, dealing with the PORTEOUS RIOTS of 1736, Scott examined the theme of justice through a wide range of opposites, building up a vivid picture of the religious and political tensions in Edinburgh during the reign of Queen Anne. No less successful is his handling of Scots speech, and in all his novels there is a splendid gallery of minor characters such as Jeanie Deans, Andrew Fairservice, Dugald Dalgitty, Saunders Fairford, Bailie Nicol Jarvie, Caleb Balderstone, Baron Bradwardine, Edie Ochiltree, Meg Merrilees and Dandie Dinmont, among many others.

Scott published his novels anonymously. Some were issued with 'by the author of

Waverley' on the title-page: *Guy Mannering,
The Antiquary, Rob Roy, Ivanhoe* (1820),
Kenilworth (1821), *The Pirate* (1822), *The Fortunes of Nigel* (1822), *Peveril of the Peak*
(1822), *Quentin Durward* (1823), *St Ronan's
Well* (1824), *Redgauntlet* (1824), *Woodstock*
(1826) and *Anne of Geierstein* (1829); the
TALES OF MY LANDLORD employed the fiction
that they were by Jedediah Cleishbotham,
schoolmaster of Gandercleugh, who based
them on manuscripts of stories told by the
landlord of the Wallace Inn and written by his
assistant Peter Pattieson: *The Black Dwarf*
(1816), *Old Mortality, The Heart of Midlothian,
The Bride of Lammermoor, A Legend of Montrose, Count Robert of Paris* (1832) and *Castle
Dangerous* (1832). The remainder appeared
under the titles *Tales from Benedictine Sources*
(*The Monastery* and *The Abbot* (both 1820));
Tales of the Crusaders (*The Betrothed* and *The
Talisman* (both 1825)); and CHRONICLES OF
THE CANONGATE (*The Two Drovers, The Highland Widow* and *The Surgeons Daughter* (published together, 1827) and *The Fair Maid of
Perth* (1828)). There are several reasons for
Scott's desire for anonymity: a love of mystery,
a sensitivity to criticism and a feeling that
novel-writing was not a fitting occupation for a
man in his social position. The 'secret' of his
authorship was revealed at a public dinner held
in the Assembly Rooms, Edinburgh, in February 1827).

The publication of the novels made Scott a
national figure and he enjoyed the friendship
of the leading writers of his day. In 1818 he was
created a baronet and he helped to supervise
the celebrations for George IV's visit to Edinburgh in August 1822. The intricacies of
Scott's business relationship with Ballantyne
and Constable and their English agents, Hurst
Robinson and Company, drew him into their
financial crash of 1826 and in January 1826 he
was declared bankrupt, a fate he had avoided
on a similar occasion in 1813. In the ensuing
settlement Scott agreed to pay off his debt
through his writing, declaring, according to
Lord COCKBURN, 'this right hand shall work it
all off!' The debt was finally repaid shortly
before his death.

Scott's work as an antiquary and editor is
also noteworthy. Early in his career he edited
for Constable *The Works of John Dryden* (1808)
and *The Works of Jonathan Swift* (1814), and
his biography of Napoleon was well received.
He founded the BANNATYNE CLUB in 1823 and

was a frequent contributor to learned journals,
publishing papers on subjects from Scotland's
history. He also wrote, less successfully, for the
theatre, including *Halidon Hill* (1822), *Mac-
duff's Cross* (1823), *The Doom of Devorgoil* and
Auchindrane (1830).

The latter years of Scott's life were plagued
by recurring illnesses and during the winter of
1831 he toured the Mediterranean in a frigate
put at his disposal by the government. With his
health failing, he returned to Scotland in July
1832 and died at Abbotsford that same year on
21 September. His wife had died on 14 May
1826. In 1820 his daughter Sophia had married
JOHN GIBSON LOCKHART, the author of the
seven-volume *Memoirs of the Life of Sir Walter
Scott* (1837–8) which, despite its inaccuracies, is one of the great literary biographies
in English. Scott has been the subject of
numerous biographies and critical works and
his achievement marks him as a man of genius
and a writer of sensitivity, with a unique understanding of Scotland, its history and its people.

During his lifetime Scott was also known as
'the Great Unknown' and 'the Wizard of the
North'.

WORKS: trans., Gottfried Bürger, *The Chase, and
William and Helen, Two Ballads from the German*
(1796); trans., Johann Wolfgang von Goethe, *Goetz
of Berlichingen* (1799); ed., *The Minstrelsy of the
Scottish Border*, 3 vols. (1802–3); *The Lay of the Last
Minstrel* (1805); *Ballads and Lyrical Pieces* (1806);
ed., *Memoirs of Capt. George Carleton* (1808); ed.,
*Memoirs of Robert Carey and Fragmenta Regalia, by Sir
R. Naunton* (1808); ed., *Original Memoirs Written
during the Great Civil War* (1806); *Marmion* (1808);
ed., Joseph Strutt, *Queenhoo Hall, and Ancient Time*
(1808); ed., *The Works of John Dryden, with Notes
and a Life of the Author* (1808); ed., *A Collection of
Scarce and Valuable Tracts*, 3 vols. (1809); ed., *The
Life of Edward, Lord Herbert of Cherbury* (1809); ed.,
English Minstrelsy (1810); *The Lady of the Lake*
(1810); ed., *The Poetical Works of Anna Seward*
(1810); ed., *Memoirs of Count Grammont* (1811);
ed., *Secret History of James the First* (1811); *The
Vision of Don Roderick* (1811); ed., Horace Walpole,
The Castle of Otranto (1811); ed., *A Collection of
Scarce and Valuable Tracts*, 7 vols. (1812); *The Bridal
of Triermain* (1813); *Rokeby* (1813); ed., Sir Philip
Warwick, *Memoirs of the Reign of King Charles I*
(1813); *The Border Antiquities of England and Scotland*
(1814–17); *Waverley* (1814); ed., *The Works of
Jonathan Swift with Notes and a Life of the Author*
(1814); *The Field of Waterloo* (1815); *Guy Mannering*
(1815); *The Lord of the Isles* (1815); ed., *Memoirs of
the Somervilles* (1815); ed., Samuel Rowland, *The
Letting of Humours Blood in the Head Vaine* (1815);
The Antiquary (1816); *Paul's Letters to his Kinsfolk*
(1816); *Tales of my Landlord*, 1st series, *The Black
Dwarf* and *Old Mortality* (1816); *Harold the Dauntless*
(1817); ed., with Robert Jamieson, *Burt's Letters
from Scotland* (1818); *Rob Roy* (1818); *Tales of my*

Landlord, 2nd series, *The Heart of Midlothian* (1818); *Provincial Antiquities of Scotland* (1819–26); *Tales of my Landlord*, 3rd series, *The Bride of Lammermoor* and *A Legend of Montrose* (1819); *Ivanhoe* (1820); *Tales from Benedictine Sources*, consisting of *The Abbot* and *The Monastery* (1820); ed., Richard Franck, *Northern Memoirs* (1821); *Kenilworth* (1821); *Lives of the Novelists* (1821–4); ed., *Chronological Notes of Scottish Affairs from 1688 to 1701* (1822); *The Fortunes of Nigel* (1822); *Halidon Hill* (1822); ed., *Military Memoirs of the Great Civil War* (1822); *Peveril of the Peak* (1822); *The Pirate* (1822); *Quentin Durward* (1823); *Redgauntlet* (1824); *St Ronan's Well* (1824); *Tales of the Crusaders*, consisting of *The Betrothed* and *The Talisman* (1825); *Woodstock* (1826); *Chronicles of the Canongate*, 1st series, *The Highland Widow, The Two Drovers* and *The Surgeon's Daughter* (1827); *The Life of Napoleon Buonaparte* (1827); *Chronicles of the Canongate*, 2nd series, *The Fair Maid of Perth* (1828); *Religious Discourses* (1828); *Tales of a Grandfather*, 1st series (1828); *Anne of Geierstein* (1829); *History of Scotland*, 2 vols. (1829–30); ed., *Memorials of George Bannatyne* (1829); *Tales of a Grandfather*, 2nd series (1829); *The Doom of Devorgoil* (1830); *Essays on Ballad Poetry* (1830); *Tales of a Grandfather*, 3rd series (1830); *Letters on Demonology and Witchcraft* (1831); *Tales of my Landlord*, 4th series, *Count Robert of Paris* and *Castle Dangerous* (1832)

EDITIONS: H. J. C. Grierson, ed., *Letters*, 12 vols. (London, 1932–7); J. G. Tait, ed., *Journal*, 3 vols. (London, 1939–46); W. E. K. Anderson, ed., *The Journal of Sir Walter Scott* (Oxford, 1972); J. C. Corson, ed., *Notes and Index to Sir Herbert Grierson's Edition of The Letters of Sir Walter Scott* (Oxford, 1979); P. H. Scott, ed., *The Letters of Malachi Malagrowther* (Edinburgh, 1981); D. Hewitt, ed., *Scott on Himself* (Edinburgh, 1981)

REFERENCES: J. G. Lockhart, *Memoirs of the Life of Sir Walter Scott Bart.*, 7 vols. (London, 1837–8); J. Buchan, *The Life of Sir Walter Scott* (London, 1932); H. J. C. Grierson, *Sir Walter Scott* (London, 1938); A. J. Cockshut, *The Achievement of Sir Walter Scott* (London, 1965); T. Crawford, *Scott* (Edinburgh, 1965 rev. 2/1982); F. R. Hart, *Scott's Novels: the Plotting of Historical Survival* (Virginia, 1966); A. M. Clark, *Sir Walter Scott: the Formative Years* (Edinburgh and London, 1969); A. N. Jeffares, ed., *Scott's Mind and Art* (Edinburgh, 1969); E. Johnson, *Sir Walter Scott: the Great Unknown*, 2 vols. (London, 1970); D. D. Devlin, *The Author of Waverley* (London, 1971); A. Bell, ed., *Scott Bicentenary Essays* (Edinburgh, 1973); D. Brown, *Sir Walter Scott and the Historical Imagination* (London, 1979); G. Tulloch, *The Language of Sir Walter Scott* (London, 1980); A. N. Wilson, *The Laird of Abbotsford, a View of Sir Walter Scott* (Oxford, 1980); P. H. Scott, *Walter Scott and Scotland* (Edinburgh, 1981)

Scott, William Bell (1811–90). Poet and artist. He was born on 12 September 1811 in Edinburgh and was educated at the HIGH SCHOOL OF EDINBURGH and the Trustees' Academy. In 1840 he moved to London, where he supported himself by painting, and after a brief period teaching in Newcastle he returned to London to involve himself in the government's organization of schools of art. Most of his artistic work was executed for private patrons and he supervised the decoration of several large houses with scenes from literature, including a series of designs from THE KINGIS QUAIR at Penkill Castle in Ayrshire. Scott was a member of the Pre-Raphaelite group and a close friend of Algernon Swinburne (1837–1909) and Dante Gabriel Rossetti (1828–82). During his lifetime Scott published five collections of largely derivative verse and his illustrated editions of the work of Byron, Keats and Shelley were deservedly popular in their day. He died on 22 November 1890 in Ayrshire.

WORKS: *Hades and the Transit of the Mind* (1838); *The Year of the World* (1846); *Memoir of David Scott* (1850); *Poems* (1856); *Albrecht Dürer: his Life and Works* (1869); *Poems* (1875); *Ballads and Studies from Nature Sonnets* (1875); *The Little Masters* (1879); *A Poet's Harvest Home* (1882)

Scottish Arts Council. The government's main agency for supporting the arts in Scotland; it is an independent body and not a branch of the Civil Service. From 1947 until 1967 it was the Scottish Committee of the Arts Council of Great Britain. In 1967 the Scottish Committee became the Scottish Arts Council, with virtual autonomy over the allocation of its block grant-in-aid. It forms part of the Arts Council of Great Britain and shares the aims of its Royal Charter: (1) to develop and improve the knowledge, understanding and practice of the arts; (2) to increase the accessibility of the arts to the public throughout Great Britain; and (3) to advise and co-operate with government departments, local authorities and other bodies on any matters concerned directly or indirectly with these objects. The Scottish Arts Council consists of 22 members appointed by the Arts Council of Great Britain, subject to the approval of the Secretary of State for Scotland.

Scottish Chapbook. A literary magazine published and edited by CHRISTOPHER MURRAY GRIEVE between August 1922 and December 1923. The magazine's rallying call, 'Not Traditions – Precedents!', reflected Grieve's new-found support for the revival of Scots as advocated by the Vernacular Circle of the London Burns Club. Until then he had been of the opinion that the use of English was the only way forward for the Scottish writer, and his change of attitude towards the Club and the language required a change of name; in the first issue he published part of a playscript *Nisbet: an Interlude in Post-War Glasgow*, written under the pseudonym 'Hugh M'Diarmid', and in the third issue he published the lyric 'The Water-gaw' under the same pseudonym, which was later altered to 'Hugh MacDiarmid', the name by which Grieve is best known. Although the magazine had only a short life, it was a vital link in Grieve's concept of a SCOTTISH RENAISSANCE of letters.

Scottish Chaucerians. The name given, frequently and inaccurately, to the 15th- and 16th-century Scottish poets whose work was influenced to some degree by the poetry of Geoffrey Chaucer (c 1340–1400). The poets usually associated with the description are ROBERT HENRYSON, JAMES I, WILLIAM DUNBAR and GAVIN DOUGLAS, but while it is true that they experimented with the courtly, aureate, highly Latinized style of Chaucer, they were not merely imitators of it. All admitted their debt to Chaucer, none more sincerely than Henryson, but the title 'Scottish Chaucerians' suggests a limitation, or a lack of originality in their poetry; the expression 'Scots makars' is now preferred, 'makar', or 'maker', the Scots word for poet, being a truer reflection of their innovatory style.

Scottish Committee of the Arts Council of Great Britain. *See* SCOTTISH ARTS COUNCIL.

Scottish Enlightenment. The period of intellectual growth in Scotland, which is generally considered to have begun in the years following the ACT OF UNION of 1707 and to have reached its conclusion in 1832 with the death of Sir WALTER SCOTT. It coincided with the 18th-century Enlightenment in Europe, the period that saw remarkable innovations in the study of the sciences, medicine and the arts, and the growth of a new understanding among intellectuals of the triumph of reason over tradition and faith. In Scotland the Enlightenment was confined to the major cities, Edinburgh, Glasgow and Aberdeen, and it found its most forceful expression in Edinburgh among the legal, ecclesiastical and literary circles that blossomed during the second half of the 18th century. The Act of Union provided the first impetus. Unlike the removal in 1603 of the court of JAMES VI to London, it did not create a social and intellectual wilderness within the

country. Many leading landed politicians foresook Scotland for London but others stayed on and drifted to Edinburgh to form an élite of 'literati', as they chose to style themselves, who dominated the principal appointments in the law, the Church and the University.

Finance, too, played a part. The construction of Edinburgh's New Town, with its architecture blessed by the smile of Reason, may have echoed the ideals of the age, and created 'THE ATHENS OF NORTH', but it was carried out to satisfy the needs of Edinburgh merchants anxious to emulate London, and more importantly to attract finance and trade to the city. The arrival of that new wealth allowed the University, long in a decayed state, to flourish: it could afford the latest scientific apparatus and new buildings and was therefore able to attract to its staff some of the leading thinkers and teachers of the day. In the arts the educational policy was to encourage the teaching of a wide range of subjects and to underpin that learning with the study of moral philosophy.

Although the study of science, natural history and medicine was encouraged, philosophy reigned supreme and provided the intellectual backbone to the Enlightenment in Scotland. In particular the leading minds studied the science of man, that is the study of man and society and the rules and regulations that bound one to the other. DAVID HUME (ii), the greatest philosopher of the period and a thinker whose ideas transcended the temporal bounds of the Enlightenment, moved from that discussion of the sympathetic mechanisms which govern social obligations to a study of religion and history and the evolution of society from rudeness to refinement. Many of his ideas were developed by ADAM SMITH, whose study THE WEALTH OF NATIONS argued against government intervention in economic affairs and promoted instead the case for improvement through man's inherent desire to better his position. Hume's and Smith's examinations of man's place in society provided the intellectual base for the Enlightenment but neither worked in isolation. ALLAN RAMSAY and HENRY MACKENZIE wrote on the moral requirements of the sentiments in, respectively, THE GENTLE SHEPHERD and THE MAN OF FEELING; the scientist John Gregory attempted to discover the physiological seat of man's sympathetic mechanisms, and HUGH BLAIR preached sermons which sought a way to find man's proper place in a world that was rapidly changing.

The rigour of their intellectual thought, which, to a large extent, was promulgated in debating clubs like the SELECT SOCIETY and the POKER CLUB, was allied to a nostalgic pride in Scotland's past. Histories of Scotland were written by WILLIAM ROBERTSON and WILLIAM TYTLER, antiquarian studies were fostered and, through Allan Ramsay's anthologies THE EVER GREEN and THE TEA-TABLE MISCELLANY, interest in Scots poetry was heightened. But coupled to that sense of nationhood was a feeling of shame in the use of Scots. Many writers of the period, including Hume, went to great lengths to exorcise 'SCOTICISMS' from their work, and elocution classes were established in Edinburgh and Glasgow. The past may have been ideal for the purposes of study, but it was rude and violent; the men of the Scottish Enlightenment looked to the future for order, elegance and British reasonableness. It would be wrong, though, to regard the Enlightenment as a time when things Scottish were subordinated totally to the new philosophy. Both ROBERT FERGUSSON and ROBERT BURNS were products of the Enlightenment, educated men who chose to write in Scots, and their poetry is now considered to have been the high-water mark of the age, remembered while the pallid vapours of the blind poet THOMAS BLACKLOCK are forgotten.

The great law lords, Kames, Monboddo and Hailes, were proud both of their learning and of their use of Scots in court. Kames was an agrarian improver, agriculture being another science that flourished during the 18th century and which added to the sense of change. Other men who should be remembered are the philosopher ADAM FERGUSSON, the architect ROBERT ADAM and the painter Sir HENRY RAEBURN. Like the scientists Joseph Black (1728–99) and James Hutton (1726–97), they worked within a Scottish idiom and yet were aware of the forces of change that gave their work a less provincial appeal.

By the end of the 18th century most of the leading men of the Enlightenment were dead and it was left to Sir WALTER SCOTT to pull together their two contrasting interests by way of the historical novel. His works trace the development of Scotland from the chaos of the 17th century to the more hopeful years of improvement and prosperity. The age of Scott was the last flowering of the Enlightenment

and it also saw the foundation of Edinburgh's two great magazines, representing opposing political interests, the *Edinburgh Review* (*see* EDINBURGH REVIEW (ii))), which supported the Whigs, and BLACKWOOD'S MAGAZINE, which supported the Tories. The confident neo-classical tone of their essays and reviews encouraged a wide readership, inspired by the contributors' use of plain language unadorned by technical or literary jargon. It had been noted by many visitors to Edinburgh that intellectual though its society might be, its conversation was always to the point, one of the intellectual standpoints of the Scottish Enlightenment being that subjects ought to be reduced to first principles. That philosophy informs the early 19th-century Edinburgh journals and is one of the reasons for their success.

The swansong of the Scottish Enlightenment was aided by the Napoleonic wars when Europe was cut off and Edinburgh became a place of learning to be visited; but by 1832, the year of Scott's death, the distinctive period of the Enlightenment in Scotland was at an end. Arguments about the effectiveness of the general education offered by the Scottish universities heralded the Royal Commission of 1825, which argued convincingly against the traditional administration of the four Scottish universities. THOMAS CARLYLE, one of the last great Scottish thinkers, moved to London in 1829, the year in which FRANCIS JEFFREY abandoned the editorship of the *Edinburgh Review*. Literature became more provincial and the school of sentimentality flourished, eventually giving way to the KAILYARD writers of the late 19th century. Industrialization altered the economy and offered new careers to educated men and women, and Scotland became, as a result of the standardization of industrialism, a more integrated part of the United Kingdom. All these related factors contributed to the demise of the long period of the Scottish Enlightenment.

REFERENCES: S. A. Grave, *The Scottish Philosophy of Common Sense* (Oxford, 1960); G. E. Davie, *The Democratic Intellect* (Edinburgh, 1961); A. Chitnis, *The Scottish Enlightenment* (London, 1967); J. Rendall, *The Origins of the Scottish Enlightenment* (London, 1978)

Scottish Gaelic Text Society (SGTS). A publishing society founded in 1937 for the purpose of editing and printing scholarly editions of the texts of the major Gaelic writers.

Scottish National Dictionary (*SND*). A dictionary of the Scottish language from 1700 to the present day, begun in 1929 and completed in 1976. Its editors were William Grant and his successor, David Murison, and its instigator was the lexicographer WILLIAM ALEXANDER CRAIGIE, who in 1919 put forward plans for a series of dictionaries that would cover different periods of English and Scottish history. The *Scottish National Dictionary* was compiled on the historical principles of the *Oxford English Dictionary*, which decree that each word be supported by copious quotations as examples. In its ten volumes it deals with the origins of 50,000 words used in spoken and literary Scots and records their historical development and geographical distribution. Its companion dictionary, the *Dictionary of the Older Scottish Tongue*, covers Older Scots to 1700 and will be completed by the end of the century.

Scottish Renaissance. The term applied to the 20th-century revival of interest in Scottish literature, inspired largely by CHRISTOPHER MURRAY GRIEVE, who wrote under the pen-name 'Hugh MacDiarmid'. It had its origins in a renewal of the use of the vernacular in poetry at the turn of the century and less tangibly in the new desire for nationhood felt by many Scots after World War I. Although the word 'renaissance' was used by newspaper critics such as WILLIAM JEFFREY and WILLIAM POWER to describe the work of poets writing in Scots in the 1920s, it is generally agreed that the term 'Scottish Renaissance' owes its life to Denis Saurat, Professor of English at the University of Bordeaux. In the April 1924 issue of the *Revue anglo-américaine* he referred to the writers currently composing poetry in Scots as 'le groupe de "la Renaissance écossaise"', a phrase that was taken up by Grieve and used increasingly thereafter to describe the writers concerned with the revitalization of Scots and its use as a literary language.

Grieve was the driving force behind the philosophy of the movement. Between 1920 and 1922 he edited three issues of the anthology *Northern Numbers*, 'being representative selections from certain living Scottish poets', in which he introduced work in Scots by writers who were to become associated with the movement: MARION ANGUS, HELEN BURNESS CRUICKSHANK, ALEXANDER GRAY, WILLIAM JEFFREY, WILLIAM SOUTAR and LEWIS SPENCE. At the same time, though, Grieve was an active opponent of the Vernacular Circle of the London Burns Club, which was attempting to revive Scots for literary purposes. '"Braid Scots" is, and will remain, the special preserve of the *tour de force* and the *jeu d'esprit* – a backwater of the true river of Scottish national expression.' (*Dunfermline Press*, 25 November 1922). But in the same year that he made this judgement he revised his opinions in a dramatic way. In the first edition of the SCOTTISH CHAPBOOK he introduced his readers to the work of 'Hugh M'Diarmid' and subsequent issues carried many of his early lyrics including 'The Watergaw' which Grieve explained had been written by his friend M'Diarmid out of an interest in Scots philology. Grieve's promotion of Scots was not the action of a sentimental preservationist; he insisted that 'the Scots Vernacular is a vast store-house of just the very peculiar and subtle effects which modern European literature in general is assiduously seeking' (*Scottish Chapbook*, March 1923, p.210). The rationale that he imposed on the renaissance movement was that the Scottish language could be welded on to the European avant garde to provide Scotland with a new literature, and he continued the debate in a series of invigorating critical articles published in the *Scottish Educational Journal* between 1925 and 1927.

Debates about the use of Scots, about whether or not it was a synthetic language and even about its correct title – 'LALLANS' being preferred – have continued throughout the century to the present day, but there is little doubt that Grieve's example inspired many poets to reconsider their attitudes towards Scots. Many, having spoken Scots in childhood as part of their heritage, were encouraged to develop it as a literary language and a a later group of poets was also inspired by the movement's aims. Amongst them may be mentioned J. K. ANNAND, ROBERT GARIOCH SUTHERLAND, MAURICE LINDSAY, A. D. MACKIE, ALEXANDER SCOTT (ii), TOM SCOTT, and SYDNEY GOODSIR SMITH. By the 1930s the poetic aims of the movement had been embraced by novelists like NEIL M. GUNN and ERIC LINKLATER and the playwright ROBERT MCLELLAN. Also associated with Grieve in his early days were the composer FRANCIS GEORGE SCOTT and his cousin the artist William Johnstone (1897–1981).

During the 1950s and 1960s the Scottish Renaissance movement attracted its share of opponents who believed that the wheel had come full circle and that there was an editorial bias towards writing in Lallans; but despite their protestations it has to be said that Grieve remained true to his ideals. Despite the narrowness of outlook of some of its later proponents, the Scottish Renaissance movement brought about, in the broadest sense, a reappraisal of literature in Scots, a revision of KAILYARD attitudes and a new approach to the country's literary traditions.

REFERENCE: D. Glen, *Hugh MacDiarmid and the Scottish Renaissance* (Edinburgh and London, 1964)

Scottish Studies, School of. An institute within the University of Edinburgh, established in 1951 with the object of integrating all aspects of academic studies related to Scotland. The following main areas of study were identified by the school's founders in a document submitted to the Senatus of the University of Edinburgh on 10 May 1950: (*a*) Archaeology; (*b*) A compilation of information upon which maps of prehistoric and historic Scotland could be based; (*c*) The collection of place-names from both documentary and oral sources, and the organization of a place-name archive; (*d*) The collection of oral traditions of all parts of Scotland and the organization of an equivalent folklore archive for these; (*e*) Study of the structure of the European and other affinities of music in Scotland; (*f*) The integration of intensified field studies in social anthropology with the rest of the work of the School; (*g*) The co-ordination of the study of Scots law in relation to the other studies of the school. One of the chief activities, and the one for which it is best known, has been the study of Scotland's folk culture; research fellows from the School have been responsible for the recording and collection of a wide variety of material from Scotland's oral tradition, Gaelic and Scots, and for the discovery of many notable traditional singers and tradition bearers.

Scottish Text Society (STS). A publishing society founded in 1882 for the purpose of editing and printing authoritative scholarly editions of older Scottish literary texts. The Society's primary concern has been the publication of medieval and Renaissance texts, although it has also published the works of ALLAN RAMSAY and ROBERT FERGUSSON.

Scougal, Francis. Pen-name of FELICIA MARY FRANCES SKENE.

Seasons, The. A poem by JAMES THOMSON (i), published in four books between 1726 and 1730. *Winter*, the first book, was published in 1726 and it was followed in turn by *Summer* (1727), *Spring* (1728) and *Autumn* (1730), the cycle being completed by a 'Hymn to Nature'. The work represents the pinnacle of the Augustan tradition and although its over-elaborate language and facile moralizing make for uneasy reading today, it still remains remarkable for Thomson's observation of nature in all its many moods. In *Winter*, the best of the poems, a telling comparison is made between the warmth of the farmhouse and the bitter cold outside as a shepherd dies in a snowdrift. That, and Thomson's delight in minute description, allows the work to stand comparison with other, earlier poems of natural description in the Scottish tradition, such as THE TESTAMENT OF CREISSEID of ROBERT HENRYSON, with its picture of the fury of winter, the prologues to books XII and XIII to the ENEADOS of GAVIN DOUGLAS, and *Of the Day Estivall* by ALEXANDER HUME, set on a summer's day. But whereas those poets revel in natural description and construct a cheerful intimacy with nature, Thomson's work tends to be more objective and classically restrained. The cyclical pattern of the seasons provides a pattern which enables him to explain the ever-changing nature of life and of the parts played by man and beast and encourages him to try to account for God's ways to man. Scientific change and classical mythology are both part of that pattern and are accurately expressed in the work. Thus Thomson's vision finds its unity in the inevitable and unceasing cycle of the seasons and in a secure belief in God's divine mercy. The work is a celebration of nature and a hymn of praise to the harmony that is found within it. The entire work, written in Miltonic blank verse, was a source of inspiration to several Scottish poets, including ALASDAIR MAC MHAIGSTEIR ALASDAIR and EOGHAN MACLACHLAINN, both of whom also wrote within the strong Gaelic tradition of nature poetry.

REFERENCE: R. Cohen, *The Unfolding of the Seasons* (London, 1970)

Select Society. A debating society formed in Edinburgh on 22 May 1754 at the instigation of the artist Allan Ramsay (1713–84), the eldest son of the poet ALLAN RAMSAY. Its aims were 'the pursuit of philosophical inquiry and the improvement of the members in the art of speaking'. Among its first members were ALEXANDER CARLYLE, DAVID HUME (ii), ADAM SMITH and JAMES BURNETT Lord Monboddo, but its membership grew to include most of the leading *literati* of the Edinburgh of the SCOTTISH ENLIGHTENMENT. The society met every Wednesday in the Advocates' Library, and although debate was its primary business, it also aimed at promoting excellence through the award of prizes for 'the arts, sciences and manufactures'. A later goal was the perfection of its members' elocution, and in 1761 the actor Thomas Sheridan was hired to provide lessons in the proper articulation and pronunciation of 'the English tongue'. The club ceased its activities in 1763.

Selkirk, J. B. Pen-name of JAMES BROWN.

Sempill, Francis (c1616–1682). Poet. He was born at the ancestral home of Beltrees in Renfrewshire, the son of ROBERT SEMPILL (ii). Little is known about his life except that he studied law, probably in Europe. In 1677 he was appointed Sheriff-Depute of Renfrewshire and he died on 12 March 1682. During his lifetime he enjoyed a reputation as a poet and wit, and although few of the pieces ascribed to him by literary historians are certain to have come from his pen, he did write a lively autobiographical poem, *The Banishment of Poverty by James, Duke of Albany*. His name has been linked with the poems 'Blythesome Wedding', and 'Maggie Lauder', which is supposed to have given WILLIAM TENNANT the inspiration for his comic poem ANSTER FAIR.

EDITION: J. Sempill, ed., *The Poems of the Sempills of Beltrees* (Edinburgh, 1849)

Sempill, Sir James (1566–1625). Courtier. He was the son of John Sempill and Mary Livingstone, who were special favourites of MARY, Queen of Scots; he himself was closely associated with the court of JAMES VI, with whom he shared an education under GEORGE BUCHANAN. He assisted James in the preparation of the BASILICON DORON (1599) and he wrote a number of satirical verses against the Catholic Church, notably *The Packman's Pater Noster*, first published in 1669, in which a packman scores several telling points in an argument with a priest. Sempill spent some time in London but he returned to Scotland in 1603 after the Union of the Crowns. His son ROBERT SEMPILL (ii) succeeded to the family estate of Beltrees.

WORKS: *Sacrilege Sacredly Handled* (1619); *Paranesis ad Scotos* (1622); R. Sempill, rev., *A Pick-Tooth for the Pope or the Packman's Pater Noster* (1669)

EDITION: J. Sempill, ed., *The Poems of the Sempills of Beltrees* (Edinburgh, 1849)

Sempill, Robert (i) (c1530–95). Balladwriter. Very little is known about his life and his prolific output of ballads and satires contains nothing of an autobiographical nature. It is certain, however, that he was not a member of the Sempill family of Beltrees. Part of his early life may have been spent in Paris and he was there again in 1572 at the time of the St Bartholomew's Day Massacre, but for most of his life he seems to have lived in Edinburgh, where he associated himself with the reformers' cause, writing broadsides and political satires from the press of ROBERT LEKPREVIK. His dogmatism reflects the temper of the times and his work, which was mainly of a religious propagandizing disposition, betrays crude, hectoring energy, typical of which is his long poem *The Legend of the Lymmaris Lyfe*, a scurrilous attack on Patrick Adamson, Archbishop of St Andrews. His only other work of any consequence is 'The sege of the Castell of Edinburgh', which casts an interesting light on events in Edinburgh during the Reformation. Critical reaction to Sempill's work has often depended on the religious persuasions of the critic, but his work as a writer of ballads is leavened at times by his vigorous, though coarse wit, which is seen to advantage in poems like 'The Flemyng Bark' and 'Crissel Sandilandis'.

EDITIONS: T. G. Stevenson, ed., *The Sempill Ballatis* (Edinburgh, 1872); J. Cranstoun, ed., *Satirical Poems of the Time of the Reformation*, 2 vols., STS (Edinburgh and London, 1889–93)

Sempill, Robert (ii), of Beltrees (c1595–c1665 Poet. He was the son of Sir JAMES SEMPILL, a courtier and the author of the anti-Catholic poem *The Packman's Pater Noster*, which Robert improved upon and arranged for its eventual publication in 1669. He was educated at the University of Glasgow and was involved on the Royalist side during the Civil War, but little is known about his life. His lasting monument is his poem 'The Life and Death of Habbie Simpson, the Piper of Kilbarchan', written in the stanza form later christened 'STANDARD HABBIE' by ALLAN RAMSAY. Sempill invented a six-line stanza that enabled him to mix visual description in the first four lines with a pithy satirical or ridiculing comment in the last two; the form was later used to good effect by Ramsay, ROBERT FERGUSSON and ROBERT BURNS. Although 'Habbie Simpson' is not a great poem, its intrinsic merit lies in the graphic description of country life and Sempill's dry comments on the piper's abilities. To Sempill has also been attributed the sequel to 'Habbie Simpson', 'Sawney Briggs, Nephew to Habbie Simpson and Brother to the Laird of Kilbarchan', though it could equally well have been written by his son FRANCIS SEMPILL. 'Habbie Simpson' and several other poems appeared in the CHOICE COLLECTION OF COMIC AND SERIOUS SCOTS POEMS (1706–11), published by JAMES WATSON.

WORKS: rev., Sir James Sempill, *A Pick-Tooth for the Pope or the Packman's Pater Noster* (1669); *The Life and Death of Habbie Simpson, the Piper of Kilbarchan* (1698)

EDITION: J. Sempill, ed., *The Poems of the Sempills of Beltrees* (Edinburgh, 1849)

Shairp, J(ohn) C(ampbell) (1819–85). Poet and critic. He was born on 30 July 1819 at Houston House, West Lothian, the son of an army officer. He was educated privately and at Edinburgh Academy, and in 1836 he matriculated at the University of Glasgow where he studied classics. In April 1840 Shairp won the Snell Exhibition to Balliol College, Oxford, where he remained until 1845, having won the Newdigate Prize for Poetry in 1842. Between 1846 and 1856 he taught at Rugby School, but he returned to Scotland in 1857 to take up the Chair of Latin at the University of St Andrews, becoming Principal of United College in 1868. As a teacher Shairp was a supporter of the move towards specialization in the Scottish universities. His last public appointment was as Professor of Poetry at Oxford, a post he held until his death on 18 September 1885.

Early in his career Shairp became interested in the Lake poets and their influence can be felt in his one collection of poems, *Kilmahoe and Other Poems* (1864). His critical essays were published in *Studies in Poetry and Philosophy* (1868) and his Oxford poetry lectures in *Aspects of Poetry* (1881). In this day, Principal Shairp, as he liked to be known, was a well-known and attractive literary figure and while at Oxford he was close to Matthew Arnold (1822–88) and Cardinal Newman (1801–90). But many remember him only for his priggish attack on ROBERT BURNS in his study of the poet published in 1879 and for his often anthologized poem 'The Bush Abune Traquair'.

WORKS: *Charles the Twelfth* (1848); *The Wants of the Scottish Universities and Some Remedies* (1856); *Uses of the Study of Latin Literature* (1857); *Kilmahoe and Other Poems* (1864); *John Keble* (1866); *Studies in Poetry and Philosophy* (1868); *Culture and Religion* (1870); ed., *Life and Letters of James David Forbes* (1873); *On Poetic Interpretation of Nature* (1877); *Robert Burns* (1879); *Aspects of Poetry* (1881)

EDITION: J. Veitch, ed., *Sketches in History and Poetry* (Edinburgh, 1887)

REFERENCE: W. A. Knight, *Principal Shairp and his Friends* (London, 1888)

Sharp, William ['Fiona Macleod'] (1855–1905). Poet and novelist. He was born on 12 September 1855 in Paisley, the son of a merchant. He was educated at Glasgow Academy and at the University of Glasgow, but his father's death in 1876 curtailed his education and he was sent to Australia to test his prospects. Between 1877 and 1890 he worked in London, intermittently in a bank but more successfully as a journalist and editor. Much of that period was spent in travel in Europe and North America, and until his death, on 6 December 1905 in Sicily, he led a peripatetic life, often using Argyll in Scotland as a base.

During his period in London Sharp became associated with the Pre-Raphaelites, and his first collection of fairly derivative verse, *The Human Inheritance, The New Hope, Motherhood and Other Poems*, appeared in 1882. His other collections are *Earth's Voices* (1884) and *Romantic Ballads and Poems on Phantasy* (1888). He also edited a number of editions of English poetry in the Canterbury Poets series, and for a time worked as art critic of the GLASGOW HERALD; but this literary hack work interfered with his own writing and he spent the winter of 1890–91 in Rome, where he produced his literary *alter ego*, his feminine Celtic soul, 'Fiona Macleod'. Under her name he wrote a series of visionary novels set in the ancient Celtic world, a collection of poems, songs and fragments, *From the Hills of Dream* (1901), and two verse dramas, *The House of Usna* and *The Immortal Hour* (1905).

Sharp went to a good deal of trouble to

conceal the identity of 'Fiona Macleod' even to the extent of composing a mock biography for *Who's Who*. And she was not just a *nom de plume:* there is evidence in Sharp's autobiographical writings to suggest that he was attempting to resolve his vision of the ancient world from a feminine viewpoint. His interest in Celticism had its origins in his childhood forays into the Highlands; in 1894 he was involved with PATRICK GEDDES in the Celtic movement in Edinburgh and he also enjoyed the friendship and support of William Butler Yeats (1865–1939). In his 'Fiona Macleod' novels Sharp attempted to rewrite Celtic folklore and traditions in popular fiction, but this method led to the creation of an unbelievable never-never-land of faery and fable. Under his own name he wrote three novels, *The Sport of Chance* (1888), *Wives in Exile* (1898) and *Silence Farm* (1899), as well as several collections of short stories. A memoir of his life was published by his wife in 1910.

WORKS: *The Human Inheritance, The New Hope, Motherhood and Other Poems* (1882); *Earth's Voices: Transcripts from Nature; Sopistra and Other Poems* (1884); ed., *The Poetical Works of Sir Walter Scott* (1885); ed., *The Songs and Sonnets of Shakespeare* (1885); ed., *The Sonnets of this Century* (1886); ed., *For Song's Sake and Other Stories* (1887); *Life of Percy Bysshe Shelley* (1887); *Life of Heinrich Heine* (1888); *Romantic Ballads and Poems on Phantasy* (1888); ed., *American Sonnets* (1889); *The Children of Tomorrow* (1889); *Life of Browning* (1890); *Sospiri di Roma* (1891); *A Fellowe and his Wife* (1892); *Flower o' the Vine* (1892); *The Life and Letters of Joseph Severn* (1892); *Pagan Review* (1892); *Vistas* (1894); *The Gipsy Christ and Other Tales* (1895); *Ecce puella and Other Prose Imaginings* (1896); *Fair Women in Painting and Poetry* (1896); ed., *The Poems of Matthew Arnold* (1896); *Wives in Exile: a Comedy in Romance* (1898); *Silence Farm* (1899); ed., *The Poems of Swinburne* (1901); *The Progress of Art in the Nineteenth Century* (1902); ed., *The Poems of Eugene Lee-Hamilton* (1903); *Literary Geography* (1904); as Fiona Macleod: *Pharais, A Romance of the Isles* (1894); *The Laughter of Peterkin* (1895); *The Mountain Lovers* (1895); *The Sin-Eater and Other Tales* (1895); *The Washer of the Ford* (1895); *Green Fire* (1896); *The Dominion of Dreams* (1899); *By Sundown Shores* (1900); *The Divine Adventure* (1900); *Iona* (1900); *From the Hills of Dream, Threnodies, Songs and Later Poems* (1901); *The Winged Destiny: Studies in the Spiritual History of the Gael* (1904); *The House of Usna* (1905); *The Immortal Hour* (1905)

EDITIONS: Mrs William Sharp, ed., *The Works of Fiona Macleod*, 7 vols. (1910–12); Mrs William Sharp, ed., *Selected Writings of William Sharp*, 5 vols. (1912)

REFERENCES: F. Alaya, *William Sharp: 'Fiona Macleod'* (Cambridge, Mass., 1936); S. C. Fiechter, *Von William Sharp zu Fiona Macleod* (Tübingen, 1936)

Sharpe, C(harles) K(irkpatrick) (1781–1851). Antiquary. He was born on 15 May 1781 at Hoddam, Dumfriesshire, and was educated in Edinburgh and at Christ Church, Oxford, where he graduated in 1806. In 1803 he began a lifelong friendship with Sir WALTER SCOTT, contributing two ballads to the third volume of THE MINSTRELSY OF THE SCOTTISH BORDER (1803), and giving advice about the origin of several ballads, especially 'The Twa Corbies'. Sharpe had a reputation for his waspish caricatures and satires, and his letters, which were published in 1888 by Alexander Allardyce, demonstrate his weakness for scandal, though they present a vivid picture of literary society in his lifetime. An indefatigable collector of antiquities and ballads, he edited and illustrated editions for the BANNATYNE CLUB and the ABBOTSFORD CLUB, and he enjoyed the friendship of DAVID LAING and THOMAS THOMSON. The latter part of his life was spent in seclusion in Drummond Place, Edinburgh (where he amused his friends by printing his visiting card 'C ♯'). In his youth Sharpe wrote a number of poor poems and a drama, which remained unpublished.

WORKS: *Metrical Legends and Other Poems* (1807; ed., *Extracts from the Household Book of Lady Marie Stewart* (1815); ed., *A Ballad Book* (1823); ed., *A Paint of the Life of Lady Margaret Cunninghame* (1827); ed., *A Memorial of the Conversion of Jean Livingstone, Lady Waristoun* (1827); *The Wizard Peter* (1834); ed., *Surgundo* (1837); *A Historical Account of the Belief of Witchcraft in Scotland* (1884)

EDITIONS: A. Allardyce, ed., *Letters from and to Charles Kirkpatrick Sharpe*, 2 vols. (Edinburgh, 1888); C. E. S. Chambers, ed., *The Letters of Walter Scott and Charles Kirkpatrick Sharpe to Robert Chambers, 1821–1845* (Edinburgh, 1904)

Shirley. Pen-name of JOHN SKELTON.

Sibbald, Sir Robert (1641–1722). Antiquary and physician. He was born on 15 April 1641 in Edinburgh and was educated at the HIGH SCHOOL OF EDINBURGH and the University. On graduating he studied medicine at Leiden before returning in 1662 to Scotland, where he devoted much of his life to the study of botany. One of the founder-members of the Royal College of Physicians (1681) he was its president in 1685, and he held other important posts, including physician to Charles II, first Professor of Medicine in Edinburgh and Geographer Royal for Scotland. In 1667 he was largely instrumental in the establishment of a botanical garden in Edinburgh. Sibbald's principal publications as an antiquary are concerned with Scotland's geography, history and sociology: he wrote works on Fife and Kinross and on Orkney and Shetland, as well as *Scotia illustrata* (1685), a largely unsuccessful attempt to compile a description of Scotland, the country and its people.

WORKS: *An Account of the Scottish Atlas* (1683); *Nuncius Scoto-Britannus* (1683); *Scotia illustrata* (1685); *Nova phalainologia* (1692); *An Essay Concerning the Thule of the Ancients* (1693); *Auctarium musaei balfouriani* (1697); *Memoria Balfouriana* (1699); *Provision for the Poor in Time of Dearth and Scarcity* (1699); *Commentarius in vitam Georgi Buchanani* (1702); *The Liberty and Independency of the Kingdom of the Church of Scotland* (1702); *In Hippocratis legum* (1706); *Introductio ad historiam rerum a Romanis gestarum* (1706); *History and Description of Stirlingshire Ancient and Modern* (1707); *The History, Ancient and Modern of the Sheriffdoms of Fife and Kinross* (1710); *Miscellanea* (1710); *Tractatus varii ad Scotiae antiquae et modernae* (1710); *Commentarius in Agricolae expeditiones* (1711); *Memoirs of the Royal College of Physicians at Edinburgh, a Fragment* (1837)

Sìleas [Cicely, Giles] **na Ceapaich** [Macdonald, MacDonnell] (c1660–c1729). Poet. She was probably born in Glen Roy, the daughter of Gilleasbuig Mac Mhic Raghnaill, chief of the MacDonalds of Keppoch. She married into the Gordon family and lived most of her life in Banffshire, where her husband Alexander Gordon was a factor to the Duke of Gordon. Very little is known about her life, although from the evidence of her poetry it is clear that her husband (d 1720) predeceased her and that she was dead by 1729. She is buried with her husband at Mortlach, Banffshire. 19th-century commentators tended to criticize her later religious poetry for its Catholic, pro-Rome sentiments, but her hymns have a simplicity of literary style and imagery which effectively express her feelings of piety and reverence for the Church. Her best work is a dignified lament addressed to the widow of the Clan chief of Glen Garry, 'Alasdair á Gleann Garadh'. Like many other Scottish poets of her day she poured scorn on the ACT OF UNION, writing several rousing pro-Jacobite songs such as 'Do dh' arm Rìgh Seumas'. Her poems were translated and edited with a critical introduction by Colm O Baoill in 1972 for the SCOTTISH GAELIC TEXTS SOCIETY.

Sillar, David (1760–1830). A friend of ROBERT BURNS, who wrote to him the 'Epistle to Davie' (*see* EPISTLES OF ROBERT BURNS).

He was the schoolmaster in Tarbolton before the permanent post was given to John Wilson (*see* 'DEATH AND DR HORNBOOK'), and he was also a member of the Tarbolton BACHELORS' CLUB. Sillar's *Poems* were published in 1789 by JOHN WILSON (ii), of Kilmarnock but they enjoyed little success. After Burns's death he was one of the founder-members of the Irvine Burns Club.

Silver Darlings, The. A novel by NEIL M. GUNN, published in 1941; it takes its title from the herring – the 'silver darlings'. Like much of Gunn's previous work, it is firmly rooted in the fishing and crofting communities remembered from his boyhood, and it is concerned with the aftermath of the Highland CLEARANCES, a theme Gunn had already treated in *Butcher's Broom* (1934). Driven from the land by the landlords, the crofting people struggle to earn a living from fishing; their love–hate relationship with the sea, potently stated in the first chapter, becomes the leitmotif for the novel. Catrine loses her husband, Tormad, to the sea and, pregnant, moves north to Dunster where she attracts the attention of Roddie Sinclair, a fishing skipper. The next section deals with the journey from boyhood to manhood of her son Finn, his growing fascination with the sea and his rivalry with Roddie. Finn becomes a fisherman, saves his crew by a daring climb up a stormbound cliff and after several adventures ends up in the Western Isles. There he learns compassion and self-control, and on his return to Dunster he can look forward to a new life. His initiation into manhood, through trials both physical and emotional, is complete.

Although the land- and sea-scapes are vividly described and Gunn was at pains to research the historical background carefully, it is through Gunn's skilful handling of the narrative and through Finn's heroic encounters with a host of trials and tribulations that *The Silver Darlings* takes on the mantle of the epic. The novel has been reprinted several times and was made into a film in 1946.

Simpson, William (1758–1815). A friend of ROBERT BURNS, who wrote to him the 'Epistle to William Simpson of Ochiltree' (*see* EPISTLES OF ROBERT BURNS). He was the schoolmaster in Cumnock, Ayrshire. Burns's verse epistle was written in response to a flattering verse letter from Simpson and it is a good exposition of the poet's craft.

Sinclair, Catherine (1800–64). Novelist. She was born on 17 April 1800 in Edinburgh, the daughter of Sir JOHN SINCLAIR of Ulbster. She was her father's secretary until his death in 1835, when she became an independent author, at first writing children's books, the most popular of which was *Holiday House*. Later she wrote a succession of light romantic novels and her travel books on Shetland, northern Scotland and Wales show a keen eye for scenery and local colour. Renowned as a philanthropist in Edinburgh, Catherine Sinclair supported several local missions and charities to the poor. She died on 6 August 1864.

WORKS: *Modern Accomplishments* (1836); *Modern Society* (1837); *Hilland Valley* (1838); *Holiday House* (1839); *Scotland and the Scotch* (1840); *Shetland and the Shetlanders* (1840); *Modern Flirtations* (1841); *Scotch Courtiers* (1842); *Charlie Seymour* (1844); *Jane Bouverie* (1846); *The Journey of Life* (1847); *The Business of Life* (1848); *Sir Edward Graham* (1849); *Lord and Lady Harcourt* (1850); *The Kaleidoscope of Anecdotes and Aphorisms* (1851); *Beatrice* (1852); *Popish Legends* (1852); *London Homes* (1853); *Memoir of Sir John Sinclair Bart.* (1853); *The Cabman's Holiday* (1855); *Cross Purposes* (1855); *Torchester Abbey* (1857); *Anecdotes of the Caesars* (1858); *Sketches and Stories of Scotland and the Scotch* (1859); *Sketches and Stories of Wales and the Welsh* (1860); *Letters for Children* (1862); *The Bible Picture Letter* (1863); *The Mysterious Marriage* (1875)

Sinclair, Sir John, of Ulbster (1754–1835). Statistician and agrarian reformer. He was born on 10 May 1754 in Thurso, the son of a Caithness landowner. He was educated at the HIGH SCHOOL OF EDINBURGH and the University, and later studied law at Oxford. In 1770 he took over the management of his family estates and began his lifelong interest in agricultural improvement, including the proper rotation of crops and the husbandry of sheep. His *Code of Agriculture* was published in 1817, but his best-known work is in statistics: following the success of his *History of the Public Revenue of the British Empire* (1785), he became responsible for the preparation of the first *Statistical Account of Scotland*, in 29 volumes, which was completed in 1799. Sinclair used a network of ministers throughout Scotland to provide uniform information about their parishes for inclusion in the work. He was created a baronet in 1786 and was twice president of the Board of Agriculture, which he helped to found in 1793. In his later years his secretary was his daughter, the novelist CATHERINE SINCLAIR.

WORKS: *Disputatio juridica* (1775); *Consideration of Militias and Standing Armies* (1782); *Lucubrations during a Short Recess* (1782); *Observations on the Scottish Dialect* (1782); *Thoughts on the Naval Strength of the British Empire* (1782); *Hints Addressed to the Public* (1783); *History of the Public Revenue of the British Empire* (1785); *Specimen of the Statistical Account of Scotland* (1791); ed., *The Statistical Account of Scotland*, 29 vols. (1791–9); *General View of the Agriculture of the Northern Counties and Islands of Scotland* (1795); *Hints on Vegetation* (1796); *Cursory Observations on the Military System of Great Britain* (1799); *Essays on Miscellaneous Subjects* (1802); *Hints Regarding Cattle* (1802); *Observations on the Propriety of Preserving the Dress, the Language, the Poetry, the Music and the Customs of the Ancient Inhabitants of Scotland* (1804); *Code of Health and Longevity* (1807); *A Dissertation on the Authenticity of the Poems of Ossian* (1807); *Materials Collected for Drawing up an Account of the Husbandry of Scotland* (1810); *Observations on the Bullion Committee* (1810); *An Account of James Small* (1811); *An Account of the Improvements Carried out by Sir John Sinclair Bart.* (1812); *An Account of the Systems of Husbandry Adopted in the More Improved Areas of Scotland* (1812); *General Report of Scotland* (1812); *An Account of the Highland Society of London* (1813); *General Report of the Agricultural State of Scotland* (1814); *The Pyramid Statistical Inquiry* (1814); *Hints Regarding the Agricultural State of the Netherlands* (1815); *The Code of Agriculture* (1817); *Collection of Papers on Political Subjects* (1819); *Hints on Circulation* (1822); *Miscellaneous Papers* (1825); *The Late Prosperity and the Present Adversity of the Country Explained* (1826); *Correspondence* (1831); *Thoughts on Parliamentary Reform* (1831)

REFERENCE: R. Mitchison, *Agricultural Sir John* (London, 1962)

Singer, James Hyman ['Burns Singer'] (1928–64). Poet. James Hyman Singer, who wrote under the name 'Burns Singer', was born on 29 August 1928 in New York, the son of Michael Singer a Polish–Jewish immigrant and Bertha Singer who had been born in Greenock. In 1932 his family moved to Glasgow and, apart from a period of wartime evacuation in Aberdeenshire, it remained Singer's home until 1945, when, following a short period at the University of Glasgow, he moved to London. He spent three years in Europe, much of it in Germany, where he met the abstract painter Wols whom Singer named later as an important influence on his work. He returned to Glasgow in 1949 to study zoology and became a marine scientific assistant at the Scottish Home Department's marine laboratory in Aberdeen. In 1955 he left to become a freelance journalist in London, and he married Marie Battle in 1956. In 1960 he moved to Cambridge where he renewed his interest in marine biology; he was appointed to a

Leverhulme Fellowship in Plymouth in June 1964, and he died there on 8 September 1964.

Singer's only collection of poetry published during his lifetime, *Still and All*, appeared in 1957; a *Collected Poems*, edited by W. A. S. Keir was published in 1970. His best poems, such as 'S. O. S. Lifescene', are remarkable for their complex scientific imagery and for their sustained narrative strength. He was a prolific critic and a perceptive admirer of the poetry of Hugh MacDiarmid (CHRISTOPHER MURRAY GRIEVE); he also wrote an important book on fishing, *Living Silver* (1957).

WORKS: *Still and All* (1957); *Living Silver* (1957); ed., with Jerzy Peterkiewicz, *Five Centuries of Polish Poetry* (1960)

EDITIONS: W. A. S. Keir, ed., *Collected Poems of Burns Singer* (London, 1970); A. Cluysnaar, ed., *Selected Poems of Burns Singer* (Manchester, 1977)

Skelton, Sir John ['Shirley'] (1831–97). Man of letters. He was born in Peterhead, Aberdeenshire, where his father was Sheriff-Substitute. He was educated at the University of Edinburgh where he studied law. Although he was admitted a member of the FACULTY OF ADVOCATES, his interests lay in writing and, so as not to jeopardize his professional career, he adopted the pseudonym 'Shirley' (from Charlotte Brontë's novel of the same name). Under that guise he became a regular contributor to BLACKWOOD'S MAGAZINE, with which he maintained a lifelong contact as a contributor of essays and reviews. His essays, which ranged from Scottish historical studies to reminiscences of his friends among the Pre-Raphaelites, were published in *Essays of Shirley* (1882) and *The Table Talk of Shirley* (1895). MARY, Queen of Scots, remained a lifelong interest and he espoused her cause in *The Impeachment of Mary Stuart* (1876), *Maitland of Lethington and the Scotland of Mary Stuart* (1887) and *Mary Stuart* (1893). Among his other publications of note were *The Crookit Meg: a Story of the Year One* (1880), a largely autobiographical study of Peterhead; and a collection of verses, *Songs by a Western Highlander* (1881). Skelton occupied several important positions in the Local Government Board of Scotland and he wrote several professional tracts on the role of local government in preventing poverty in Scotland. He was knighted in the year of his death.

WORKS: *Early English Life in the Drama* (1857); *Thalatta!* (1862); *John Dryden 'in Defence'* (1865); *Spring Songs* (1865); *The Great Lord Bolingbroke* (1868); *The Boarding Out of Pauper Children in Scotland* (1876); *The Impeachment of Mary Stuart* (1876); *Essays on Romance* (1878); *The Crookit Meg: a Story of the year One* (1880); *Songs by a Western Highlander* (1881); *Essays of Shirley* (1882); *Essays on History and Biography* (1883); *Maitland of Lethington and the Scotland of Mary Stuart* (1887); *The Handbook of Public Health* (1890); *The Administration of the Public Health Act* (1891); *Mary Stuart* (1893); *The Table Talk of Shirley* (1895); *Charles I* (1898)

As Shirley: *Nugae criticae* (1862); *A Campaigner at Home* (1865); *Alpine Resting Places* (1883); *An Arcadian Summer* (1889); *Among the Summer Isles* (1891)

Skene, Felicia Mary Frances ['Francis Cougal'] (1821–99). Novelist. She was the daughter of James Skene of Rubislaw (1775–1864), a close friend of Sir WALTER SCOTT and the sister of the historian WILLIAM FORBES SKENE. She was born on 23 May 1821 at Aix-en-Provence and much of her childhood was spent abroad, particularly in Athens, where she lived between 1838 and 1845. For the rest of her life she lived in Oxford and she was an early promoter of penal reform, becoming one of the first prison visitors appointed by the government. Nursing was also an interest and she corresponded with Florence Nightingale (1820–1910) during the Crimean War. Many of her contributions to BLACKWOOD'S MAGAZINE were on those two subjects, but she also wrote about her travel experiences of earlier life in *Wayfaring Sketches* (1847), and her poems, which were collected in *Isles of Greece and Other Poems* (1843), attracted some praise. Among her novels only *Hidden Depths* (1866), with its realistic descriptions of the poor and criminal in Victorian society, has any real merit. She also wrote a number of devotional works, the best-known of which was *The Divine Master* (1852). She died on 6 October 1899 in Oxford.

WORKS: *The Isles of Greece and Other Poems* (1843); *The Lesters* (1847); *Wayfaring Sketches* (1847); *The Inheritance of Evil* (1849); *Use and Abuse* (1849); *The Tutor's Ward* (1851); *The Divine Master* (1852); *The Ministry of Consolation* (1854); *Hidden Depths* (1866); *Penitentiaries and Reformatories* (1866); *A Memoir of Alexander, Bishop of Brechin* (1876); *A Life of Alexander Lycurgus* (1877); *The Shadow of the Holy Week* (1883); *A Strange Inheritance* (1886); *Awakened* (1888); as Francis Scougal, *Scenes from a Silent World* (1889)

REFERENCE: E. C. Rickards, *Felicia Skene of Oxford* (London, 1902)

Skene, William Forbes (1809–92). Historian. He was born on 7 June 1809 at Inverie, Knoydart, the second son of James Skene of Rubislaw (1775–1864) who was a close friend of Sir WALTER SCOTT. He was educated at the HIGH SCHOOL OF EDINBURGH and his parents fostered his childhood interest in Gaelic by allowing him to be tutored privately in a Gaelic-speaking household at Laggan in Inverness-shire. The rest of his education was gained at Frankfurt, where he acquired a thorough knowledge of German, and at the University of St Andrews. After graduating he trained as a lawyer and he practised in Edinburgh until his death on 29 August 1892. Skene's claim to fame as a historian lies in his tireless research into the original documents of Scottish history; his *Celtic Scotland: a History of Ancient Alba*, published in three volumes between 1876 and 1880, threw new light on the period between ST COLUMBA and the reign of MALCOLM III (Malcolm Canmore). He also wrote on Irish links with Scotland, with particular regard to the OSSIAN poems of JAMES MACPHERSON, and he provided textual notes to the BOOK OF THE DEAN OF LISMORE. In 1881 he succeeded JOHN HILL BURTON as Her Majesty's Historiographer for Scotland.

WORKS: *The Highlands of Scotland, their Origin, History and Antiquities* (1837); *The Four Ancient Books of Wales* (1868); *Essay on the Coronation Stone of Scone* (1869); ed., *The Chronicles of the Picts and Scots* (1869); ed., *Johanis de Fordun, Chronica gentis Scotorum*, 2 vols. (1871); *Celtic Scotland: a History of Ancient Alba*, 3 vols. (1876–80); *A Humorous Story for Children* (1883); *A Gospel History for the Young* (1884)

Skinner, John (1721–1807). Songwriter. He was born on 3 October 1721 at Balfour in the parish of Birse, Aberdeenshire. His father was the local schoolmaster and it was from him that Skinner received his early education, before matriculating at Marischal College, Aberdeen, in 1734. Thereafter he followed the profession of schoolmaster in the Aberdeenshire parishes of Kemnay and Monymusk, where he came under the patronage of the laird Sir Archibald Grant. In 1740 he was appointed a family tutor in the Shetlands, by which time he had been received into the Episcopalian Church. His first charge was at Longside, Aberdeenshire, where he remained from 1742 until shortly before his death on 16 June 1807 in Aberdeen. Although he was well loved in the area, his life as a parish priest was not without a period of suffering. After the 1745 Jacobite uprising he

was suspected of Jacobite sympathies and his church was burned to the ground. His resistance to the government's measures to curb Episcopalianism after the Jacobite rebellion led to his imprisonment in Aberdeen in 1753. Skinner's son, John, (1744–1816) followed his father into the Church and eventually became Bishop of Aberdeen.

Among Skinner's many theological publications, his *Ecclesiastical History of Scotland* (1788) is a lucid, well-argued account of the progress of the Episcopalian Church in Scotland from the Reformation to the reign of Charles II. It as a songwriter, though, that Skinner is best remembered, especially for *Tullochgorum*, a spirited song celebrating political and social unity, based on the folk-tune of the same name; Robert Burns considered it to be 'the best Scotch song ever Scotland saw'. His humourously pathetic poem 'The Ewie wi' the Crookit Horn' may have inspired Burns to write his two poems to Mailie, a pet sheep. The two men corresponded in verse after Burns's northern tour of 1787 and Skinner sent several songs for inclusion in THE SCOTS MUSICAL MUSEUM by JAMES JOHNSON.

WORKS: *A Preservative against Presbytery* (1748); *A Dissertation on Jacob's Prophecy* (1757); *Tullochgorum* (1769); *An Ecclesiastical History of Scotland* (1788); *The Contented Old Couple* (1796); *The Ewie wi' the Crookit Horn* (1796); *Lizy Liberty* (1796); *Amusements or Leisure Hours* (1809); *A Garland from the Vernacular* (1921)

EDITION: H. G. Reid, ed., *Songs and Poems of John Skinner* (Peterhead, 1859)

Skirving, Adam (1719–1803). Songwriter. A tenant farmer in East Lothian, he enjoyed a reputation among the farming community as an athlete and wit. His claim to fame rests on his composition of the song *Hey, Johnnie Cope*, which was written after the Jacobite victory at the Battle of Prestonpans in 1745. With its spirited tune and exaltation over the defeat of the government army under Sir John Cope, Skirving's song enjoyed, and has continued to enjoy, a wide popularity. His other song of note is *Tranent Muir*.

Smellie, William (1740–95). Printer and antiquary. He was born in Edinburgh and was educated at the village school of Duddingston and at the HIGH SCHOOL OF EDINBURGH. He was apprenticed to a printer in 1752 but his diligence earned him the permission to attend classes at the University, where he won several prizes for his botanical studies. In 1765 he set up a printing business on his own account and six years later, with Andrew Bell and Colin MacFarquhar, he printed the first edition of the ENCYCLOPAEDIA BRITANNICA for which he wrote most of the articles. Smellie was a founder-member of the Society of Antiquaries in 1780 and he also assisted in the preparation of the first statistical account of Scotland, by Sir JOHN SINCLAIR. During the visit of ROBERT BURNS to Edinburgh in 1786 the two men became close friends; as well as introducing the poet to the delights of the drinking and debating club, the CROCHALLAN FENCIBLES, Smellie printed the Edinburgh edition of Burn's poems for WILLIAM CREECH. Smellie contributed many articles on literary and scientific subjects to the leading journals of his day and his memoirs, Literary and Characteristic Lives (1800), is an agreeably anecdotal record of the Edinburgh of the SCOTTISH ENLIGHTENMENT. He died on 24 June 1795 after a long illness.

WORKS: Thesaurus medicus, 4 vols. (1778–85); An Account of the Institution and Progress of the Antiquaries of Scotland (1782); An Address to the People of Scotland (1784); The Philosophy of Natural History, 2 vols. (1790–99); Literary and Characteristic Lives of J. Gregory M.D., Lord Kames, David Hume and Adam Smith (1800)

Smiles, Samuel (1812–1904). Biographer and social reformer. He was born on 23 December 1812 in Haddington, East Lothian, and was educated there at the burgh school, where one of his closest friends was Jane Welsh (see CARLYLE, JANE WELSH), the future wife of THOMAS CARLYLE. At the age of 14 he was apprenticed to two local doctors and continued his education at the Grammar School until 1829, when he matriculated at the University of Edinburgh. By 1833 Smiles was in Haddington again and he remained there in medical practice until 1838, when he spent the summer gaining a medical degree at the University of Leiden.

In the same year he was appointed editor of the Leeds Times. Smiles had started his literary career by writing on medical matters, but in Leeds he interested himself in the political philosophy of Richard Cobden (1804–65), who believed in free trade allied to gradual social change through education; this interest resulted in the publication of Self-Help (1859), an immensely popular work, which was trans-

lated into seventeen languages. The sequels to it were Character (1871), Thrift (1875), Duty (1880) and Life and Labour (1887); Smiles also write a life of the engineer George Stephenson (1857) and Men of Industry and Invention (1884), among other improving tracts. He was interested in the development of the railways, acting as secretary to several companies in the north of England and later as secretary to the South Eastern Railway Company. His Autobiography was published in 1905, a year after his death on 16 April 1904 in London.

WORKS: Physical Nature and Education of Children (1836); History of Ireland (1843); Life of George Stephenson (1857); Self Help (1859); Lives of the Engineers (1861); Industrial Biography (1863); Boulton and Watt (1866); Huguenots in England and Ireland (1867); Character (1871); A Boy's Voyage Around the World (1871); Thrift (1875); Thos. Edward, Cobbler and Naturalist (1876); Geo. Moore, Merchant and Philanthropist (1878); Robt. Dick, Baker and Geologist (1878); Duty (1880); Naysmith (1883); Men of Industry and Invention (1884); Life and Labour (1887); A Publisher and his Friends (1891); Jasmin: Hairdresser and Poet (1891); Josiah Wedgwood (1894); T. Mackay, ed., Autobiography (1905).

REFERENCE: A. Smiles, Samuel Smiles and his Surroundings (London, 1956)

Smith, Adam (1723–90). Political economist. He was probably born only a few days before his baptism on 5 June 1723 in Kirkcaldy, Fife, and not long after the death of his father who had been Controller of Customs there. His early education was at the burgh school of Kirkcaldy and in 1737 he matriculated at the University of Glasgow, where he showed an early leaning towards mathematics and philosophy, which was then taught by Francis Hutcheson (1694–1746). In 1740 the award of a Snell Exhibition took him to Balliol College, Oxford, but by 1746 he had returned to live in Edinburgh, where he earned a living by giving lectures on such diverse subjects as jurisprudence and philosophy. Through their success and his growing friendship with members of the Edinburgh literati – HUGH BLAIR, ADAM FERGUSON, WILLIAM ROBERTSON were especial friends – he was appointed to the Chair of Logic at Glasgow in 1751. In the following year he became Professor of Moral Philosophy in the same university, a post he held until 1764, when he left Scotland to spend two years in Paris and Geneva as tutor to the 3rd Duke of Buccleuch. On his return in 1766 he lived quietly in Kirkcaldy for ten years, during which period he wrote his influential study, *An Inquiry into the Nature and Causes of the Wealth of Nations* (1776).

In 1778 Smith became a Commissioner of Customs in Edinburgh and lived at Panmure House in the Canongate; he remained a well-known member of the city's intellectual society until his death, on 17 July 1790. After his death his executors, the scientist Joseph Black (1728–99) and the geologist James Hutton (1726–97), issued Smith's remaining unpublished philosophical and scientific fragments in *Essays on Philosophical Subjects* (1795).

Smith's economic theory relied on the simple belief that government should never interfere with free-market practices; his argument was backed up by a comprehensive range of 'curious facts', which helped to increase the political impact made by *The Wealth of Nations*. His theories underpin the doctrine of capitalism and they influenced Victorian attitudes to the free-trade movement; they are also the basis of modern political economy. Smith's other main work, *The Theory of Moral Sentiments* (1759), is the sum of the philosophy he had learned at Glasgow under Hutcheson – namely that happiness is quantitative; it also emphasizes the part played by 'feelings' in determining man's moral behaviour. In the latter respect it offers a view of 'sentiment' similar to that later expressed by HENRY MACKENZIE in his novel THE MAN OF FEELING.

WORKS: *The Theory of Moral Sentiments* (1759); *An Inquiry into the Nature and the Causes of the Wealth of Nations* (1776); D. Stewart, ed., *Essays on Philosophical Subjects* (1795)

EDITIONS: H. W. Schneider, ed., *Adam Smith's Moral and Political Philosophy* (London, 1970); R. H. Campbell and A. S. Skinner, eds., *An Inquiry in the Nature and Causes of the Wealth of Nations* (Oxford, 1976); D. D. Raphael and A. L. Macfie, eds., *The Theory of Moral Sentiments* (Oxford, 1976); R. L. Meek, D. D. Raphael and P. G. Stein, eds., *Lectures on Jurisprudence* (Oxford, 1977); E. C. Mossner and I. S. Ross, eds., *The Correspondence of Adam Smith* (Oxford, 1977); W. P. D. Wightman and J. C. Bryce, eds., *Essays on Philosophical Subjects* (Oxford, 1980)

REFERENCES: T. D. Campbell, *Adam Smith's Science of Morals* (London, 1971); S. Hollander, *The Economics of Adam Smith* (London, 1971); A. S. Skinner and T. Wilson, eds., *Essays on Adam Smith* (Oxford, 1975)

Smith, Alexander (1830–67). Poet and essayist. He was born on 31 December 1830 in

Kilmarnock, Ayrshire, the son of a pattern designer. He followed his father's trade in Glasgow until 1854, when he was appointed Secretary to the University of Glasgow. By then his own reputation as a poet had been tarnished by his allegiance to the 'Spasmodic' poets, who included P. J. Bailey (1816–1902) and Sydney Dobell (1824–74). Their mannered, feverish, heroic poems had been savaged by WILLIAM EDMONSTOUNE AYTOUN in BLACKWOOD'S MAGAZINE. Smith's *City Poems*, published in 1857, show a surer handling of the over-sensuous imagery that intruded on his earlier work, and it contains, in 'Glasgow', his vivid description of the city of his boyhood. Smith's reputation was enhanced by *A Summer in Skye* (1865), one of the most durable Scottish travel books, made memorable by his lovingly described pictures of Glasgow in the early days of heavy industrialization and of the natural beauty of the Isle of Skye. Equally directly, yet imaginatively, expressed are his essays, collected in *Dreamthorp* (1863), which contains a fine evocation of Edinburgh in the depths of winter. *Last Leaves*, a later collection, was published after his death on 5 January 1867. Smith also wrote two minor novels, *Alfred Hagart's Household* and *Miss Dona M'Quarrie*, both of which betray an overdependence on the urgent, voluptuous imagery that characterized so much of his early work.

WORKS: *A Life Drama* (1853); with Sydney Dobell, *Sonnets on the War* (1855); *City Poems* (1857); *Edwin of Deira* (1861); *Dreamthorp* (1863); *A Summer in Skye* (1865); *Alfred Hagart's Household* (1866); *Miss Dona M'Quarrie* (1866); *Last Leaves* (1868)

EDITION: W. Sinclair, ed., *The Poetical Works of Alexander Smith* (London, 1909)

Smith, Iain Crichton (Iain Mac a'Ghobhainn) (*b* 1928). Poet and novelist. He was born on 1 January 1928 on the island of Lewis and was educated there at the Nicolson Institute, Stornoway, and at the University of Aberdeen. He graduated in 1949 but his career was interrupted by a period of National Service in the Army Education Corps between 1950 and 1952. Until 1977, when he became a full-time writer, he was a teacher in schools in Clydebank and Oban. He has won several literary prizes and was made an OBE in 1980.

Smith is bilingual in English and Gaelic; he publishes his Gaelic work under the name 'Iain Mac a'Ghobhainn', and he has made several translations of Gaelic poetry into English, including *Poems to Eimhir* (1971) from *Dain do Eimhir* (1943) by SOMHAIRLE MACGILL-EAIN. This duality in his linguistic background has given rise to several tensions in his writing, especially to a tendency to remake his Gaelic work in English. His first collection of Gaelic short stories and poems, *Burn is Aran* (1960), is now considered a minor masterpiece, *An Dubh is an Gorm* (1963) contains short stories later reworked in English, and his novel *An t-Aonaran* (1976), published in English as *The Hermit*, goes to the heart of a theme that is central to his fiction – the misfit in society. That, and the isolation and pain of exile run through his novels in both languages. *Consider the Lilies* (1968) portrays the tragic nobility of an old woman forced to face up to the events of the CLEARANCES and is written in spare, elegant language, reminiscent of Smith's best poetry. Two of his most notable poems, 'Old Woman' and 'Sunday Morning Walk' explore a sense of exasperation with the past and the helplessness and despair brought about by death and decay. Religion and the lost world of childhood also play a significant part in the subject matter of his poetry. *The Permanent Island* (1975) contains translations of poems taken from *Biobuill is Sanasan Reice* (1965) and *Eadar Fealla-dha is Glaschu* (1974); his poetry in English has been collected in *Selected Poems* (1970, 1982) and *Love Poems and Elegies* (1972).

As with all his writing, Smith's poetry is marked by an exactness of line and rhythm and a sense of harmony, which enable him to pull together contrasting conceits. Smith is intensely aware of the recession in his native Gaelic culture and of the threat to the language's well-being: this is nowhere more coherently expressed than in his 25-part poem *Shall Gaelic Die?*, a translation of *Am Faigh a Ghaidhlig Eas?*; he returned to this theme in 'Deer on the High Hills', a meditation in which the deer becomes a metaphor for the grace that transcends man's mutability.

Deer on the high hills, in your halfway kingdom,
uneasy in this, uneasy in the other,
but all at ease when earth and sky together
are mixed are mixed, become a royalty
none other knows, neither the migrant birds
nor the beasts chained to their instinctive courses.

The sense of speculation and the aetherial luminosity of the half-hidden deer serve only to underline the insecurity of the poet–narrator with his feet of clay rooted in

the world of everyday affairs. This poem is also, in part, a homage to the 18th-century Gaelic poet DONNCHADH BÀN MAC AN T-SAOIR.

Smith has written radio drama and one-act plays in English and Gaelic, and his most recent work includes *My Last Duchess* (1971), *Goodbye Mr Dixon* (1974), *A Field Full of Folk* (1982), and two collections of short stories, *The Hermit* (1977) and *Murdo* (1981).

WORKS: *The Long River* (1955); *Burn is Aran* (1960); *Thistles and Roses* (1961); *Deer on the High Hills* (1962); *An Dubh is an Gorm* (1963); *Biobuill is Sansan Reice* (1965); *The Law and the Grace* (1965); *Modern Gaelic Verse* (1966); *The Golden Lyric: an Essay on the Poetry of Hugh MacDiarmid* (1967); *At Helensburgh* (1968); *Consider the Lilies* (1968); *Ben Dorain by Duncan Ban MacIntyre* (1969); *From Bourgeois Land* (1969); *The Last Summer* (1969); *Iain am Measg Nan Reultan* (1970); *Maighstirean is Ministearan* (1970); *Selected Poems* (1970); *Survival Without Error* (1970); *My Last Duchess* (1971); *Poems to Eimhir translated from Sorley MacLean* (1971); *Love Poems and Elegies* (1972); *An t-Adhar Ameireaganach* (1973); *The Black and the Red* (1970); *Rabhdan is Rudan* (1973); *Eader Fealla-dha is Glaschu* (1974); *Goodbye Mr Dixon* (1974); *Hamlet in Autumn* (1974); *The Notebooks of Robinson Crusoe* (1975); *The Permanent Island* (1975); *An t-Aonaran* (1976); *The Hermit and Other Stories* (1977); *An End to Autumn* (1978); *River, River* (1978); *On the Island* (1979); *Murdo* (1981); *A Field Full of Folk* (1982); *Selected Poems 1955–1982* (1982)

REFERENCES: R. Fulton, *Contemporary Scottish Poetry: Individuals and Contexts* (Loanhead, Midlothian, 1974); E. Morgan, 'The Raging and the Grace', *Essays* (Cheadle Hume, 1974)

Smith, James (1765–c1808). A friend of ROBERT BURNS, who wrote to him the 'Epistle to James Smith' (*see* EPISTLES OF ROBERT BURNS), which deals with Burns's affair with Elizabeth Paton. Burns treated Smith as a confidant, disclosing to him information about his sexual relationships; Smith was the first to be told of Burns's marriage to JEAN ARMOUR. He died shortly after emigrating to Jamaica.

Smith, Sydney Goodsir (1915–75). Poet. He was born on 26 October 1915 in Wellington, New Zealand, and went to live in Edinburgh as a young man when his father was appointed to the Chair of Forensic Medicine at the University in 1927. Educated at the universities of Edinburgh and Oxford, Smith taught English to Polish troops during World War II. By 1940 he was writing verse in Scots; although it was not his native tongue, Smith evolved a poetic language based largely on the cadences of spoken Scots, reinforced with a vocabulary garnered from the Middle Scots makars. However artificial it might appear in theory, Smith's language is always vibrantly alive and rich with the demotic strengths of spoken speech. The themes relate to such central issues as nationalism, love, freedom and disenchantment, and his work is enriched by his ability to contrast mood and emotion. Thus, although in UNDER THE EILDON TREE, a sequence of 24 poems dealing with the world's greatest loves and their relationship to the poet's own loves, elegy is the dominant mood, Smith's natural good-humoured exuberance is never far away as may be seen in the bawdy Elegy XIII. *Under the Eildon Tree*, which was first published in 1948, is generally considered to be Smith's best sustained piece of writing, but his later lyrics, in collections such as *So Late into the Night* (1952) and *Figs and Thistles* (1959), are no less powerful with their emotional intensity and subtle inner rhythms.

Smith was also a poet of Edinburgh, in the tradition of ROBERT FERGUSSON, and his long poem *Kynd Kittock's Land* (1965) is a loving description of his adopted city in all its different moods; like his 18th-century forebear, Smith had little difficulty in observing the contrasting faces of wealth and poverty in Scotland's capital city. As a dramatist he wrote the verse play *The Wallace* (1960) which owes its strength more to the passion of its author's nationalism than to the play's dramatic structure and sophistication. His comic novel *Carotid Cornucopius* was described by CHRISTOPHER MURRAY GRIEVE as 'doing for Edinburgh no less successfully what Joyce did for Dublin', but although in places it is outrageously funny, Smith's word-play is eventually oversubtle and over-ambitious.

Smith's work as an editor includes an edition of Burns's THE MERRY MUSES OF CALEDONIA, with JAMES BARKE, and a collection of essays on the bicentenary of Fergusson's birth. One of his last works was 'The Riggins o Chelsea', a comic poem in three stanzas which summarizes Smith's sense of the ridiculous and displays his endearing ability to employ it at his own expense. Before his death on 15 January 1975 he had come to be regarded as the most important writer in the second generation of the SCOTTISH RENAISSANCE.

WORKS: *Skail Wind* (1941); *The Wanderer and Other Poems* (1943); *The Deevil's Waltz* (1946); *Carotid*

Cornucopius (1947); *Selected Poems* (1947); *Under the Eildon Tree* (1948); *The Aipple and the Hazel* (1951); *A Short Introduction to Scottish Literature* (1951); *Robert Fergusson, 1750–1744: Essays by Various Hands* (1952); *So Late Into the Night* (1952); *Cokkils* (1953); *Omens* (1955); *Orpheus and Eurydice* (1955); *Figs and Thistles* (1959); *Gavin Douglas, a Selection from his Poetry* (1959); ed., with James Barke, *Robert Burns, The Merry Muses of Caledonia* (1959); *The Vision of the Prodigal Son* (1960); *The Wallace* (1960); ed., with Kulgin Duval, *Hugh MacDiarmid: a Festschrift* (1962); *Kynd Kittock's Land* (1965); *A Choice of Burns's Poems and Songs* (1966); *Fifteen Poems and a Play* (1969); *Gowdspink in Reekie* (1974); *Collected Poems* (1975)

REFERENCES: E. Gold, *Sydney Goodsir Smith's 'Under the Eildon Tree'* (Preston, 1975); H. MacDiarmid, *Sydney Goodsir Smith* (Edinburgh, 1963); *For Sydney Goodsir Smith* (Loanhead, Midlothian, 1975)

Smith, Walter Chalmers ['Orwell'; 'Hermann Knott'] (1824–1908). Poet. He was born on 5 December 1824 in Aberdeen and was educated there at the Grammar School and at Marischal College, from which he graduated in 1841. Thereafter he studied for the ministry of the Free Church of Scotland and he was ordained in 1850. His first charge was in London but he returned to Scotland two years later and was, in succession, minister of Orwell, Kinross-shire, the Roxburgh Free Church in Edinburgh, the Free Tron Church in Glasgow and, from 1876, the Free High Church in Edinburgh. Under the pseudonym 'Orwell' he published a collection of nature poems, *The Bishop's Walk* (1861), but for some reason he altered his *nom de plume* in 1872 to Hermann Knott. His later work was published under his own name. Most of his work is little more than light verse and the subject matter is touched by his evangelical leanings, but Smith possessed a sure ear for rhyme and metre and in his conversational poems he proved his knowledge of the cadences of Scotland's regional dialects. After retiring he lived in Dunblane where he died on 20 September 1908.

WORKS: *The Bishop's Walk* (1861); *Olrig Grange* (1872); *Baldred Hall* (1874); *Hilda Amongst the Broken Gods* (1878); *Raban, or Life Splinters* (1880); *North Country Folk* (1883); *Kildrostan* (1884); *Thoughts and Fancies for Sunday Evening* (1887); *A Heretic* (1890); *Poetical Works* (1902); *Sermons* (1909)

Smollett, Tobias (George) (1721–71). Novelist. Tobias George Smollett was born at Dalquharn, a farm in the Vale of Leven in Dunbartonshire, on the Bonhill estates of his grandfather Sir James Smollett. He was educated at Dumbarton Grammar School and the University of Glasgow, which he left with a qualification in medicine in 1739. The following year he moved to London in the hope of finding a producer for his youthful tragedy *The Regicide*. Disappointed in his lack of literary success and running into financial difficulties, Smollett gained a position as a ship's surgeon in the Cartagena expedition against the Spanish in the West Indies. The campaign was a fiasco and when the squadron docked in Jamaica Smollett took his leave of the navy and settled on the island until 1744, when he returned to London. There he made fresh attempts to have his play staged, without success, and he lived in some obscurity having failed, too, to build up a medical practice. During the Jacobite uprising of 1745 Smollett's sentimental patriotism was expressed in his moving poem on the BATTLE OF CULLODEN, 'Tears of Scotland', and at that time he published two controversial satires in the style of Juvenal, *Advice* (1746) and *Reproof* (1747), both of which involved him in disputes with some of the leading literary men of the day. His prickly temperament was to lead to a quarrel with DAVID MALLOCH, his fellow countryman who had also settled in London, and in 1759 he was imprisoned for a libellous attack on Admiral Knowles in the *Critical Review*.

Financial difficulties loomed large in Smollett's life and he was forced into literary hack work and translation. In 1762 he edited *The Briton*, a magazine established to champion the government of Lord Bute against the attacks of John Wilkes (1727–97); among his translations are those of *Gil Blas* (1749) by Alain-René Lessage (1688–1747) and *Don Quixote* (1755) by Miguel de Cervantes (1547–1616), and between 1761 and his death he edited the works of Voltaire. He wrote a history of England (1757–8) and in 1766 he published his caustic description of the terrors and lack of comfort of being abroad, *Travels through France and Italy*, a book which caused his rival Laurence Sterne (1713–68) to dub him 'Smelfungus'. His final work of non-fiction of note was his satire on political life, *The History and Adventures of an Atom* (1769), in which the leading politicians of his day are attacked under the thin disguise of Japanese pseudonyms.

Increasing ill health forced Smollett to spend his last years abroad and he died at Livorno in Italy on 21 October 1771. Smollett

made several visits to Scotland, the most notable being in 1756 during which he met the leading *literati* at Edinburgh and was invited to address Allan Ramsay's SELECT SOCIETY. He visited Glasgow and Loch Lomond on other occasions, the last being in 1766, and in 1750 he received a medical degree from the University of Aberdeen.

Smollett's first novel, *Roderick Random* (1748) was an immediate success and comparisons were made with the work of Henry Fielding (1707–54), whose novel *Joseph Andrews* had been published in 1742. Autobiographical in content, the novel follows the adventures of Roderick Random, a Scot in London, as he meets a succession of figures from the underworld who proceed to help him to lose his fortune. As Roderick's star wanes he is forced to travel abroad and is redeemed by the love of Narcissa and the good sense of his uncle Tom Bowling. *Roderick Random* falls short of being a true picaresque novel, but it is remarkable for Smollett's delineation of life in the navy, drawn from his own experiences, and for his evocative description of life in 18th-century London. *Peregrine Pickle* (1751) covers similar territory in the eponymous hero's adventures during a Grand Tour of Europe. The farcical episodes tend to fade towards the end as financial difficulties plunge Peregrine from one hectic downfall to the next, before he finds true happiness with Emilia. There followed two less successful novels, *Ferdinand, Count Fathom* (1753), and *Sir Launcelot Greaves* (1762), whose hero is similar to Don Quixote.

Smollett's final novel, *Humphry Clinker* (1771), was written out of the tour he had made of Scotland in 1766. This, the best loved of his novels, is written in epistolary form as a party of travellers wanders through the Britain of George III. The group is varied enough to present a multiple viewpoint: Matthew Bramble a warm-hearted Welsh squire, Tabitha his uncharitable sister, Jeremy Melford an Oxford man, his romantically impressionable sister Lydia, Winifred Jenkins a Welsh maid, and the vivid creation of the Scots Lieutenant Obadiah Lismahago. Humphry Clinker plays a subordinate role as Bramble's long-lost illegitimate son. Although the charm of the novel lies in the characters' reactions to the countryside through which they pass and to the people they meet, Smollett was careful to keep social satire at a distance and his writing is suffused with a controlled sentiment and a rare clarity of detail.

Smollett's writing is characterized by his leanings towards comedy and his sense of the absurd, especially in the posturings of his principal characters and the niceties of English social life. Much of his material came from his own life and from his powers of observation, and although he may have lacked the narrative strength of his contemporaries Fielding and Samuel Richardson, his unmannered style contributed greatly to the development of the Augustan novel.

WORKS: *Advice: a Satire* (1746); *Reproof: a Satire* (1747); *The Adventures of Roderick Random* (1748); *The Regicide, or James I of Scotland* (1749); *The Adventures of Peregrine Pickle* (1751); *A Faithful Narrative of the Base and Inhuman Arts that were Lately Practised upon the Brain of Habbakkuk Wilding* (1752); *A Essay upon the External Use of Water* (1752); *The Adventures of Ferdinand, Count Fathom* (1753); *The Reprisal, or the Tars of Old England* (1757); *A Complete History of England from the Descent of Julius Caesar to the Treaty of Aix-la-Chapelle*, 3 vols. (1757–8); *The Adventures of Sir Launcelot Greaves* (1762); *A Continuation of the Complete History* (1766); *Travels through France and Italy* (1766); *The History and Adventures of an Atom* (1769); *The Expedition of Humphry Clinker* (1771); *Ode to Independence* (1773)

REFERENCES: O. Smeaton, *Tobias Smollett* (Edinburgh, 1897); D. Hannay, *Life of Smollett* (London, 1898); L. L. Martz, *The Later Career of Tobias Smollett* (New Haven, Conn., 1942); G. M. Kahrl, *Tobias Smollett, Traveler-Novelist* (Chicago, 1945); L. M. Knapp, *Tobias Smollett, Doctor and Man of Letters* (Princeton, N. J., 1949); M. A. Goldberg, *Smollett and the Scottish School* (Albuquerque, New Mexico, 1959); R. Giddings, *The Tradition of Smollett* (London, 1967); D. Grant, *Tobias Smollett: a Study in Style* (Manchester, 1977); A. Bold, ed., *Tobias Smollett* (London, 1982)

Sorley, C(harles) H(amilton) (1895–1915). Poet. He was born on 19 May 1895 in Aberdeen, the elder of twin boys. His father was William Ritchie Sorley, Professor of Moral Philosophy at the University of Aberdeen, and his mother was the daughter of George Smith, an Edinburgh journalist. In 1900 Sorley's father was appointed Knightbridge Professor of Moral Sciences at the University of Cambridge. Sorley was educated at King's College Choir School and in 1908 he won a scholarship to Marlborough College, where he started writing poetry strongly influenced by the Wiltshire countryside. In December 1913, having won a place at University College, Oxford, he spent seven months in Germany and learned the language while attending a seminar at the University of Jena. At the outbreak of World War I in August 1914 he returned to Britain and was gazetted as a second lieutenant in the Suffolk Regiment.

Sorley had an ambivalent attitude towards the war and towards Germany. Although he was one of the first officers in Kitchener's Army his decision was fired neither by jingoistic patriotism nor by hatred of Germany. In his first war poem, the sonnet 'To Germany', he shows a subtle understanding of the brutalization of war and of a people led blindly by their rulers. War, for him, was a necessary evil. In March 1915 his battalion was moved to France, he was promoted captain and four months later was in action on the Western Front. He was killed by a sniper's bullet at the Battle of Loos in October 1915.

Sorley's collection *Marlborough and Other Poems* was published posthumously in January 1916 and although it contains much of his juvenilia it became an instant success, owing to the inclusion of his war poems. Of these, his sonnets to death, the last, 'When you see Millions of the Mouthless Dead' being written immediately before his own death, and the often anthologized 'All the Hills and Dales Along' are perhaps the best-known. Because he died at such an early age Sorley had no opportunity to develop his powers, yet his war poetry reveals him as a poet of maturity and marked potential. His *Poems and Selected Letters* appeared in 1978, with an introduction by Hilda D. Spear.

EDITIONS: W. R. Sorley, ed., *The Letters of Charles Sorley* (Cambridge, 1919); H. D. Spear, ed., *The Poems and Selected Letters of Charles Hamilton Sorley* (Dundee, 1978)

Soutar, William (1898–1943). Poet. He was born on 28 April 1898 in Perth, the only child of John Soutar, a joiner, and his wife Margaret Gow Smith. He was educated at primary school and between 1912 and 1916 at Perth Academy, where he started writing poetry for the school magazine. In 1916 the Military Service Act came into operation and Soutar joined the Royal Navy, serving in the Atlantic before being demobilized on 1 February 1919. During his war service he first showed the symptoms of the illness that was to be diagnosed later as spondylitis or ossification of the spine. In April 1919 he went up to the University of Edinburgh to study medicine but he transferred in the same year to the Faculty of

Arts to read English literature. He graduated in 1923 and returned to Perth, where his deteriorating physical condition prevented him from working or taking up a profession. By 1929 he had lost the use of his legs and despite intensive medical treatment his condition worsened; on 3 November 1930 he became a permanent, bedridden invalid.

While still at university Soutar published, anonymously, a first collection of verse, *Gleanings by an Undergraduate* (1923). Most of the poems were romantic pastiche and he followed up their publication with a similar collection, *Conflict*, in 1931. By then he had started writing in Scots and he published his first collection of Scots verse, *Seeds in the Wind* for children, in 1933 (revised and enlarged, 1943). The poems for children, or 'bairnrhymes', were influenced by Soutar's knowledge of traditional folk-song and singing games, and the beast fables such as 'The Herryin o Jenny Wren' and 'The Whale' are written in a rigorous ballad form. The language of all the poems in the collection is simple and direct and possesses a colloquial quality lacking in his English verse. Throughout his life he continued to write poetry in Scots for children, claiming in a letter to Hugh MacDiarmid (CHRISTOPHER MURRAY GRIEVE) that 'if the Doric is to come back alive, it will come first on a cock-horse'. *Riddles in Scots* was published in 1937 and his 'whigmaleeries', a collection of 36 sardonically humorous short poems for children, appeared in the posthumous *Collected Poems* (1948).

In 1935 Soutar published *Poems in Scots*, which contains 'Song', a symbolic acceptance of his own fate, and 'Tryst', a subjective expression of unfulfillable sexual longing. He also wrote a series of political and social satires, 'Topical Tropes', which were never published. After his two early collections Soutar brought out six further volumes of poetry in English; the *Collected Poems* (1948), edited and introduced by Hugh MacDiarmid, is incomplete. Although his poetry in English lacks the verbal wit and power of his work in Scots, his nature poems show an intense delight in sensuous beauty and an exact and sympathetic observation of nature. In his later poems he returned to metaphysical speculation, contrasting the idea of universal law with that of man's free will. He also composed a series of 'miniatures' or epigrams and short descriptive poems. In the 'Themes and Variations' collection he remade

into Scots the translated work of a number of European poets.

Soutar enjoyed the friendship of many of his contemporaries, including the artist James Finlayson, who drew for him the unicorn which was to become his symbol, and the poets WILLIAM MONTGOMERIE, HELEN BURNESS CRUICKSHANK and Hugh MacDiarmid. Through his wide circle of friends he maintained an interest in Scottish nationalism and he was a committed pacifist. From 1930, the year in which he became bedridden, he kept a journal and commonplace book, and for the period 5 July 1943 until 14 October, when he knew that he was dying, he kept a private diary, published as *Diaries of a Dying Man*. These diaries provide an intimate insight into Soutar's attitudes, his relationship to his poetry and his political thought. He died on 15 October 1943.

WORKS: *Gleanings by an Undergraduate* (1923); *Conflict* (1931); *Seeds in the Wind* (1933, rev. 2/1943); *The Solitary Way* (1934); *Brief Words* (1935); *Poems in Scots* (1935); *A Handful of Earth* (1936); *Riddles in Scots* (1937); *In the Time of Tyrants* (1939); *But the Earth Abideth* (1943); *The Expectant Silence* (1944)

EDITIONS: H. MacDiarmid, ed., *Collected Poems* (London, 1948); A. Scott, ed., *Diaries of a Dying Man* (Edinburgh and London, 1954); W. R. Aitken, ed., *Poems in Scots and English* (Edinburgh and London, 1961)

REFERENCE: A. Scott, *Still Life: William Soutar 1898–1943* (Edinburgh, 1958)

Spalding, John (*fl* 1650). Historian. He was an ecclesiastical lawyer attached to the church of St Machar in Aberdeen. His *History of the Troubles and Memorable Transactions of Scotland*, an accurate and fair account of the events of Charles I's reign in Scotland, is memorable for Spalding's ability to incorporate original texts and documents into the body of his thesis and is considered to be one of the main source books for the period. It was edited for the BANNATYNE CLUB by WILLIAM FORBES SKENE in 1829 and again in 1850 for the SPALDING CLUB, the publishing society named for the book's author.

EDITION: J. Stuart, ed., *Memorialls of the Trubles in Scotland*, 2 vols., Spalding Club (Aberdeen, 1850)

Spalding Club. A publishing society founded in Aberdeen in 1839 for the purpose of editing and printing works of Scottish historical interest. One of its founders was the historian and record scholar JOSEPH ROBERTSON. It was named after the 17th-century historian JOHN SPALDING. The club went into abeyance in 1871 but was revived in 1886 as the New Spalding Club.

Spark, Muriel Sarah (*b* 1918). Novelist. She was born in Edinburgh and was educated at James Gillespie's School for Girls. During World War II she worked for the Political Intelligence Department of the British Foreign Office. She remained in London after the war to become the General Secretary of the Poetry Society and editor of the *Poetry Review* between 1947 and 1949. Since then she has lived as a full-time writer in Rome and New York. In 1954 she became a Roman Catholic, and her later novels have been associated with the English Catholic tradition in fiction.

Although the majority of Muriel Spark's work is set outside Scotland, in places that seem to be as much of the creation of the mind as of geographical location, she has written of the importance to her artistic growth of her childhood spent in Edinburgh (K. Miller, ed., *Memoirs of a Modern Scotland* (London, 1970)). From that experience came her sixth novel, *The Prime of Miss Jean Brodie* (1961), a penetrating study of the dynamics of Calvinism, set in an Edinburgh girls' school. The central character, Jean Brodie, is a monstrous creation, descendant in name and personality of the 18th-century WILLIAM BRODIE, who led two lives – respectable deacon by day and outlaw by night. A similar dichotomy leads Miss Brodie to espouse an absurd combination of ideals, ranging from an admiration of Mussolini's fascist Italy to progressive education, which she practises on her charges. Unable to act out her own philosophy, she encourages her schoolgirls to be her surrogates. The result is tragedy and the destruction of her ideals by the girl who resembles her most, Sandy Stranger. It is Sandy who sees in Jean Brodie's vision of the *crème de la crème* (her pupils) and the rest (the other girls in the school who do not come under her charge) a parallel to the Calvinist dogma of the elect and the damned. Thus it is Sandy who brings about Jean Brodie's destruction and who, fully alive to the consequences, enters a convent, almost in reparation for her actions. Muriel Spark's vision of Edinburgh is stylishly conceived and the dialogue is handled deftly with a sure ear for the different rhythms of middle-class speech. The novel was made into an equally successful play and film.

Muriel Spark's fascination for the moral ambiguities surrounding good and evil surfaces in other characters, notably Dougal Douglas in *The Ballad of Peckham Rye* (1960), Mrs Pettigrew in *Memento Mori* (1959) and Patrick Seton in *The Bachelors* (1961). Their diablerie suggests a vision of the devil as a terrible human familiar who is nevertheless a figure of fun, a creation also found in the literature of ROBERT BURNS, JAMES HOGG and ROBERT LOUIS STEVENSON. Critics have argued about Muriel Spark's 'Scottishness' as if it were a commodity, but as she has made clear she remains tied to the country of her birth both by her upbringing and its various influences, and also by her sense of exile from them.

WORKS: ed., with Derek Stanford, *Tribute to Wordsworth* (1950); *Child of Light: a Re-Assessment of Mary Shelley* (1951); *The Fanfarlo and Other Poems* (1952); with Derek Stanford, *Emily Bronte: her Life and Work* (1953); *John Masefield* (1953); ed., with Derek Stanford, *My Best Mary: the Letters of Mary Shelley* (1953); ed., *The Brontë Letters* (1954); *The Comforters* (1957); *The Go-Away Bird* (1957); ed., with Derek Stanford, *The Letters of John Henry Newman* (1957); *Robinson* (1958); *The Very Fine Clock* (1958); *Memento Mori* (1959); *The Ballad of Peckham Rye* (1960); *The Bachelors* (1961); *The Prime of Miss Jean Brodie* (1961); *Voices at Play* (1961); *The Girls of Slender Means* (1963); *The Mandelbaum Gate* (1965); *Collected Poems 1* (1967); *Collected Stories 1* (1968); *The Public Image* (1968); *The Driver's Seat* (1970); *Not to Disturb* (1971); *The Hothouse on the East River* (1972); *The Abbess of Crewe* (1974); *The Takeover* (1976); *Territorial Rights* (1979); *Loitering with Intent* (1981)

REFERENCES: D. Stanford, *Muriel Spark* (London, 1963); K. Malkoff, *Muriel Spark* (New York, 1968); P. Kemp, *Muriel Spark* (London, 1974); A. Massie, *Muriel Spark: a New Assessment* (Edinburgh, 1979)

Speculative Society. A debating society founded on 17 November 1764 by six students of the University of Edinburgh for the purpose 'of improvement in Literary Composition and Public Speaking'. The founder members were WILLIAM CREECH, Allan Maconochie, Alexander Belshes of Invermay, John Bruce, John Bonar and John Mackenzie. The society, which is still in existence, has attracted to its membership most of the literary and legal figures connected with Edinburgh including FRANCIS JEFFREY and HENRY THOMAS COCKBURN, Sir WALTER SCOTT, ROBERT LOUIS STEVENSON and Hugh MacDiarmid (CHRISTOPHER MURRAY GRIEVE). In 1769 the Society's Hall was built on a vacant plot within the area of Old College and it has remained an integral part of the buildings of the University. A caricature of a meeting of 'Spec', as it is known by its members, can be found in PETER'S LETTERS TO HIS KINSFOLK by JOHN GIBSON LOCKHART.

REFERENCE: W. Watson, ed., *The History of the Speculative Society, 1764–1904* (Edinburgh, 1905)

Spence, (James) Lewis (Thomas Chalmers) (1874–1955). Poet. He was born on 25 November 1874 at Broughty Ferry near Dundee and was educated at the University of Edinburgh, where he studied dentistry. His studies were interrupted by his impatience to turn to writing and in 1899 he became a sub-editor with THE SCOTSMAN. Between 1906 and 1909 he worked for *The British Weekly*, which, under WILLIAM ROBERTSON NICOLL, had done much to espouse the cause of the KAILYARD school of writing. Spence returned to Edinburgh to take up a freelance career and his interests turned to world mythologies, an area in which he became an acknowledged expert on the folklore and anthropology of Central and South America. Among his numerous books on the subject, *Myths and Legends of Mexico and Peru* (1913), *An Encyclopaedia of Occultism* (1920), *An Introduction to Mythology* (1921) and *The Magic Arts in Celtic Britain* (1945) are the most influential and best-known.

Spence also turned to writing verse in Scots and he was one of the first Scottish poets in the 20th century to experiment with the use of archaic Scots words and phrases in his work. Although his efforts were praised by Hugh MacDiarmid (CHRISTOPHER MURRAY GRIEVE) for their foundations in 'exquisite sensory and intellectual equipment', the early friendship between the two men was destroyed by bitter argument in later life about the part played by Spence in the SCOTTISH RENAISSANCE movement. As were many other writers of that period, Spence was attracted by the politics of nationalism and he was one of the founder-members of the National Party of Scotland in 1928. He was the first member to contest a parliamentary seat and he also wrote many articles and essays on the theme of Scottish independence.

Although Spence recognized the importance of the makars in the revitalization of Scots poetry, most of his own work never rose higher than soft-centred romantic glances at Scotland's past. Most of his earlier poetry, much influenced by *fin-de-siècle* decadence, was written in English; he also wrote several short stories and stage plays. He died on 3 March 1955 in Edinburgh.

WORKS: *Le Roi d'Y* (1900); *The Mythologies of Ancient Mexico and Peru* (1907); *The Civilisation of Ancient Mexico* (1910); *A Dictionary of Mythology* (1910); *A Dictionary of Medieval Romance and Romance Writers* (1913); *Myths and Legends of Mexico and Peru* (1913); *Songs Satanic and Celestial* (1913); *Myths and Legends of the North American Indians* (1914); *The Occult Causes of the Present War* (1914); *Hero Tales and Legends* (1915); *Myths and Legends of Ancient Egypt* (1915); *Myths and Legends of Babylonia and Assyria* (1916); *Legends and Romances of Britanny* (1917); *Mexico of the Mexicans* (1917); *The Story of William Wallace* (1919); *An Encyclopaedia of Occultism* (1920); *Legends and Romances of Spain* (1920); *An Introduction to Mythology* (1921); *The Gods of Mexico* (1923); *The Phoenix and Other Poems* (1923); *The Problem of Atlantis* (1924); *Atlantis in America* (1925); *The History of Atlantis* (1926); *Plumes of Time* (1926); *Weirds and Vanities* (1927); *The Mysteries of Britain* (1928); *The Mysteries of Egypt* (1929); *The Magic and Mysteries of Mexico* (1930); *The Archer in the Arras* (1932); *The Problem of Lemuria* (1932); *Boadicea, Warrior Queen of the Britons* (1937); *Legendary London* (1937); *Cornelius Agrippa* (1939); *Will Europe follow Atlantis?* (1942); *The Occult Sciences in Atlantis* (1943); *The Outlines of Mythology* (1944); *The Magic Arts in Celtic Britain* (1945); *The Religion of Ancient Mexico* (1945); *The Fairy Tradition in Britain* (1948); *The History and Origins of Druidism* (1949); *Let's See Auld Reekie* (1951); *Second Sight* (1951); *Collected Poems* (1953)

Spottiswood, Alicia Ann, Lady Scott (1810–1900). Poet and songwriter. She was born on 24 June 1810 at Westruther, Berwickshire, into an old-established Borders family with Jacobite leanings. In 1836 she married Lord John Scott, the brother of the 5th Duke of Buccleuch and although she chose to be known socially as Lady Scott she is remembered by her maiden name for the composition of Scottish songs such as *Annie Laurie* and *Durrisdeer*. Through her interest in the collection of traditional songs and antiquities she became the friend of C. K. SHARPE, and she enjoyed a reputation as a skilled, if somewhat eclectic, antiquary. In all she wrote 69 original songs and poems, often reworking crude originals. This is the case with *Annie Laurie*, which was written by William Douglas of Fingland in Kirkcudbright to the tune 'Kempie Kaye'; in 1835 Alicia Ann Spottiswood recast the words, added a third verse and reworked the air into a more melodious tune. After her husband's death in 1860 she returned to her family house and took over the running of the estates. She died on 12 March 1900.

Spottiswoode, John (1565–1639). Historian. He came from a distinguished Episcopalian family: his father was a prominent minister and his brother James was Bishop of Clogher in Ireland. Spottiswoode started his career as an assistant to his father in Calder and his growing reputation at court led to his appointment as Archbishop of Glasgow in 1603. In 1615 he became Archbishop of St Andrews. As a Privy Councillor under Charles I and Lord Chancellor under Charles II he was an influential administrator and did much to introduce a moderate form of church government in Scotland. His *History of the Church of Scotland* (1655) covers ground similar to that of DAVID CALDERWOOD; although he lacked Calderwood's accuracy, Spottiswoode had a pleasant prose style and, unusually for his day, avoided extremes of religious partisanship. He died in London in 1639 and was buried in Westminster Abbey.

WORKS: *A True Relation of the Proceedings against John Ogilvie* (1615); *Refutatio libelli de regimine ecclesia scoticanae* (1620); *De pace inter evangelicos procuranda* (1643); *The History of the Church of Scotland* (1655)

EDITION: M. Russell, ed., *History of the Church of Scotland, by the Right Rev. John Spottiswoode*, 3 vols. Spottiswoode Club (Edinburgh, 1851)

Stables,   William   ['Gordon   Stables'] (1840–1910). Writer of boys' adventure fiction. He was born on 21 May 1840 at Aberchirder, Banffshire, and was educated there and at the University of Aberdeen, where he studied medicine. While a student he first indulged his taste for travel by sailing on a whaler to Greenland, and on becoming a doctor he joined the Royal Navy as a ship's surgeon. Ill health forced him to retire in 1871, but he spent a further two years in the Merchant Marine. In 1875 he returned to Britain to live at Twyford in Berkshire, where he took up writing adventure stories for boys under the name of 'Gordon Stables'. During his lifetime he published over 100 adventure books with titles like *Wild Adventures in Wild Places* (1881), *The Hermit Hunter of the Wilds* (1890) and *Kidnapped by Cannibals* (1900), all of which placed great reliance on self-sufficiency and manly courage in the face of impossible odds. In later life he took up caravaning as a hobby and his *Cruise of*

the Land Yacht Wanderer (1886) is a delightful evocation of the joys of the wandering life. He also wrote on natural history and was an early proponent of wild-life protection. He died on 10 May 1910 in Berkshire.

WORKS: *Medical Life in the Navy* (1868), *Cats* (1876); *The Domestic Cat* (1876); *Friends in Fur* (1877); *Jungle Peak and Plain* (1877); *Canine Medicine and Surgery* (1879); *Wild Adventures in Wild Places* (1881); *Our Home in the Silvery West* (1883); *Tea* (1883); *Wild Adventures Round the Pole* (1883); *Aileen Aroon* (1884); *O'er Many Lands on Many Seas* (1884); *Our Friend the Dog* (1884); *Stanley Grahame* (1884); *Turkish and Other Baths* (1884); *Kenneth MacAlpine* (1885); *The Cruise of the Land Yacht Wanderer* (1886); *Rota vitae* (1886); *Born to Wander* (1887); *Harry Milvaine* (1887); *Health upon Wheels* (1887); *From Squire to Squatter* (1888); *In the Daring Days of Old* (1888); *In Touch with Nature* (1888); *Jack Locke* (1888); *Harry Wilde* (1889); *Hints about Home and Farm Favourites* (1889); *By Sea and Land* (1890); *Exiles of Fortune* (1890); *The Hermit Hunter of the Wild* (1890); *The Mystery of the Millionaire's Grave* (1890); *Rocked in the Cradle of the Deep* (1890); *The Cruise of the Crystal Boat* (1891); *The Girl's Own Book of Health and Beauty* (1891); *Leaves from the Log of a Gentleman Gipsy* (1891); *'Twixt School and College* (1891); *Born to Command* (1892); *The Boy's Book of Health and Strength* (1892); *From Greenland's Icy Mountains* (1892); *Our Humble Friends and Fellow Mortals* (1892); *Two Sailor Lads* (1892); *Children of the Mountain* (1893); *The Dog* (1893); *Facing Fearful Odds* (1893); *Hearts of Oak* (1893); *Just like Jack* (1893); *As we Sweep through the Deep* (1894); *A Mother's Book of Health* (1894); *Westward with Columbus* (1894); *The Wife's Guide to Health and Happiness* (1894); *From Ploughshare to Pulpit* (1895); *How Jack Mackenzie Won his Epaulettes* (1895); *On the Rescue* (1895); *Shireen and her Friends* (1895); *To Greenland and the Pole* (1895); *Born to be a Sailor* (1896); *The Cruise of the Rover Caravan* (1896); *For Honour not Honours* (1896); *For Life and Liberty* (1896); *The Rose of Allandale* (1896); *Shoulder to Shoulder* (1896); *Travels by the Fireside* (1896); *Deeds of Daring* (1897); *Dogs' Ailments* (1897); *Every Inch a Sailor* (1897); *A Fight for Freedom* (1897); *For Cross or Crescent* (1897); *In the Land of the Lion and the Ostrich* (1897); *A Life on the Ocean Wave* (1897); *The Pearl Divers* (1897); *Frank Hardinge* (1898); *A Girl from the States* (1898); *The Island of Gold* (1898); *The Naval Cadet* (1898); *Off to the Klondyke* (1898); *'Twixt Day Dawn and Light* (1898); *Annie o' the Banks of Dee* (1899); *Courage True Heart* (1899); *A Pirate's Gold* (1899); *Remember the Maine* (1899); *Alisdair Adair* (1900); *England's Hero Prince* (1900); *Kidnapped by Cannibals* (1900); *Old England on the Sea* (1900); *On War's Red Tide* (1900); *For England's Flag* (1901); *Fresh-Air Treatment* (1901); *In Far Bolivia* (1901); *With Cutlass and Torch* (1901); *The Cruise of the 'Vengeful'* (1902); *In Forest Lands* (1902); *In Quest of the Giant Sloth* (1902); *In Ships of Steel* (1902); *In the Great White Land* (1902); *Rob Roy Macgregor* (1902); *Sable and White* (1902); *Sweeping the Seas* (1902); *Chris Cunningham* (1903); *The Cruise of the 'Arctic Fox'* (1903); *How to be Healthy and Strong* (1903); *An Island Afloat* (1903); *Midship-*

mite Curly (1903); *The Shell Hunters* (1903); *Valour and Victory* (1903); *Young Peggy Macqueen* (1903); *Hearthstone Talks on Health and Home* (1904); *In Regions of Perpetual Snow* (1904); *Practical Kennel Guide* (1904); *Heroes of the Empire* (1905); *The Meteor Flag of England* (1905); *The City at the Pole* (1906); *Leaves from the Log of a Sailor* (1906); *War on the World's Roof* (1906); *Wild Life in Sunny Lands* (1906); *Household Pets* (1907); *The Ivory Hunters* (1907); *A Little Gipsy Lass* (1907); *The Voyage of the 'Blue Vega'* (1907); *First Aid to Dogs* (1908); *From Slum to Quarterdeck* (1908); *The Boy's Book of Battleships* (1909); *From Pole to Pole* (1909); *The Parents' Guide to Children's Ailments* (1909); *The Cruise of the Snowbird* (1910); *On Special Service* (1910); *For Money or Love* (1914); *The Sauciest Boy in the Service* (1914); *Shadowed for Life* (1914); *For England Home and Beauty* (1936)

Standard Habbie. A verse form used by several Scottish poets during the 18th century and especially by ALLAN RAMSAY and ROBERT FERGUSSON. It was called 'Standard Habbie' by Ramsay from its earliest use in the poem 'The Life and Death of Habbie Simpson, the Piper of Kilbarchan' by ROBERT SEMPILL (ii), of Beltrees.

> Kilbarchan now may say alas!
> For she hath lost her game and grace,
> Both Trixie and the Maiden Trace:
> But what remead?
> For no man can supply his place,
> Hab Simpson's dead.

The stanza was easy to write and was particularly suited to satire and social comment. It was used in several versions with particular ease by ROBERT BURNS.

Sterling, John (1806–44). Editor and man of letters. Of Irish descent, he was born on 20 July 1806 at Kames Castle on the Isle of Bute. His childhood was spent in London and Wales and he was educated at the University of Glasgow and at Trinity College Cambridge. He was to have studied for the English Bar but the ill health that was to dog him for the rest of his life prevented him from following a strenuous career. With Frederick Denison Maurice (1805–72), a philosopher friend from Cambridge, he bought the *Athenaeum*, a literary magazine, as editor of which he came into close contact with the leading literary figures of his day. Chief among these was THOMAS CARLYLE, to whom Sterling owes his place in literary history: after Sterling's death on 18 April 1844 Carlyle set about writing his amiable biography, *Life of John Sterling* (1851), which is remarkable for its intimate vision of the sub-

ject's life. Much of Sterling's life was spent abroad in a quest for good health, but between 1834 and 1835 he acted as curate to his Cambridge friend Julius Hare (1795–1855) who was rector of Herstmonceux. Among Sterling's publications are a novel, *Arthur Coningsby* (1833), and several long poems, heavily influenced by the Lake poets, which were mostly published in BLACKWOOD'S MAGAZINE.

WORKS: *Fitzgeorge* (1832); *Arthur Coningsby* (1833); *Poems* (1839); *The Election* (1841); *Stafford* (1843); *Letters to a Friend* (1848)

EDITION: J. C. Hare, ed., *Essays and Tales of John Sterling* (London, 1848)

REFERENCE: T. Carlyle, *Life of John Sterling* (London, 1851)

Stern, Stuart. Pen-name of HUGH C. RAE.

Stevenson, Robert Louis (Lewis Balfour) (1850–94). Novelist and poet. He was born on 13 November 1850 in Edinburgh. His father was Thomas Stevenson who, like his own father Robert Stevenson, was engineer to the Board of Northern Lighthouses; his mother was Margaret Isabella Balfour, the daughter of the minister of Colinton in Edinburgh. During his childhood Stevenson was a constant invalid and his closest companion was his nurse 'Cummy', Alison Cunningham, who gave him a solid religious grounding in the stories of the Old Testament and in the history of the COVENANTERS. These, together with his father's stories, gave full rein to his imagination and in later life his childhood fantasies found expression in *A Child's Garden of Verses* (1885).

At the age of seven Stevenson moved with his parents from their damp house in Inverleith Place to 17 Heriot Row, and between 1861 and 1863 he was educated at Edinburgh Academy, until his ill health forced the family to travel abroad. He spent a short period at an English public school before completing his education privately in Edinburgh; in 1867 he matriculated at the University, where he studied engineering. While a student he began a lifelong friendship with Charles Baxter, and also enjoyed the company of Walter Simpson, the son of the discoverer of chloroform, Sir James Y. Simpson, and Walter Ferrier, the son of Professor JAMES FREDERICK FERRIER.

During his period at Edinburgh Stevenson abandoned his plans to become a lighthouse engineer, preferring instead to study law. He also spent considerable time exploring the city and became a habitué of the brothels and taverns of the Old Town and Leith Walk. He travelled abroad and in 1873 visited Suffolk, where he fell in love with Fanny Sitwell who was later to marry the critic Sidney Colvin (1845–1927). In Edinburgh another close friend was his cousin the artist R. A. M. 'Bob' Stevenson, and their iconoclastic opinions led to a breach with Stevenson's parents. Although there was to be a reconciliation, that quarrel, together with Edinburgh's harsh climate, its moral stiffness and his own need to write, made it increasingly difficult in later life for Stevenson to remain in Scotland.

In 1875 Stevenson became an advocate and met for the first time the critic and editor W. E. Henley (1849–1903), with whom he collaborated in four lack-lustre plays: *Deacon Brodie, or The Double Life* (1880, revised 1888), *Admiral Guinea* (1884), *Beau Austin* (1884) and *Macaire* (1885). He spent a considerable time in France with Bob Stevenson at the artists' colony at Fontainebleau, and it was at Grez that he met Fanny Osbourne, an American woman, married and ten years his senior, whom he was to marry in May 1880 after pursuing her to California. During a period of penury there, he wrote an account of their first days of married life in a mining camp in *The Silverado Squatters* (1883). They returned to live in Edinburgh but Stevenson's ill health again forced them to winter in Europe. Later Stevenson and Fanny settled in Bournemouth, where they remained until 1886 when Thomas Stevenson died in Edinburgh. His father's death marked Stevenson's final break with the city, for he moved to live in America, on Saranac Lake in the Adirondack Mountains.

Stevenson began his literary career by contributing essays and criticism to the *Cornhill Magazine* edited by Leslie Stephen (1832–1904) and to Henley's *London Magazine*. His account of a canoe trip in France and Belgium with Walter Simpson, *An Inland Voyage*, was published in 1878 and his reputation was consolidated in 1879 with two further non-fiction books: *Travels with a Donkey*, Stevenson's vivid description of a journey he made with a donkey, Modestine, through the Cevennes; and *Edinburgh: Picturesque Notes*, in which he recorded his ambivalent views about the city of his birth. His essays, short stories

and pieces of travel and autobiographical writing were collected in *Virginibus puerisque* (1881), *Familiar Studies of Men and Books* (1882), *The New Arabian Nights* (1882), *The Merry Men* (1887), *Memories and Portraits* (1887), *Across the Plains* (1892), *Island Nights Entertainments* (1893) and *In the South Seas* (1890).

Stevenson's first novel, *Treasure Island*, which began life as *The Sea Cook*, was completed in 1881 after a summer holiday spent in Braemar. It was published initially in *Young Folks' Magazine* as a serial, and in book form in 1883. With its plot of pirates and hidden treasure in the South Seas, *Treasure Island* is generally considered to be a children's adventure story, but it has been enjoyed equally by adults, and the characters of the pirates Long John Silver and Billy Bones are memorable creations. It was followed by another adventure serial, *The Black Arrow* (published as a book in 1888), and by a historical novel, *Prince Otto* (1885).

The success of the adventure novels gave rise to one of Stevenson's best-loved works, KIDNAPPED, published in 1886. Set against the background of the aftermath of the 1745 Jacobite rebellion and the events of the Appin murder (*see* JAMES STEWART of the Glens) is the story of David Balfour, a Lowland teacher's son, and his adventures with the romantic Highlander ALAN BRECK STEWART; Stevenson concentrates on the conflicting loyalties and contradictions that bind the two men together. David Balfour also appeared in a sequel, *Catriona* (1893). Shortly before *Kidnapped* was published, Stevenson had written one of his most popular novels of that period, THE STRANGE CASE OF DR JEKYLL AND MR HYDE (1886), which deals with the double life led by a conservative London doctor, Jekyll, and the pure evil of his *alter ego*, the murderer Mr Hyde. At the heart of the story is the conflict in Dr Jekyll's conscience as his professional respectability battles with the illicit pleasures he enjoys as Mr Hyde, after discovering a drug that allows his personality to be split.

Stevenson's interest in history and in the psychology of evil found further expression in THE MASTER OF BALLANTRAE (1888), the story of a lifelong feud between James, the rightful Master of Ballantrae, and his younger brother, Henry, who, believing James dead in the 1745 rebellion, succeeds to his estate and his intended wife Alison. The novel ends in the destruction of the House of Durrisdeer and in the death of both brothers. In *The Master of Ballantrae*, as in many of his short stories, Stevenson offered a fine delineation of Scottish landscape and evocation of Scottish character; these qualities are also evident in what might have been his greatest work, the unfinished, novel WEIR OF HERMISTON, which was published in 1896 after his death. It contains one of the most awesomely drawn figures in Scottish fiction: Lord Hermiston, the Lord Justice Clerk (based on ROBERT MACQUEEN, Lord Braxfield, the 'hanging judge'), who is drawn into conflict with his son Archie. The culmination of the novel was to have been Archie's wrongful arrest for murder and his death sentence at the hands of his father. In the fragment that survived the story unfolds like a ballad and its main strength is Stevenson's rich use of language, especially the dialogue in Scots.

In the summer of 1888 the Stevensons chartered a yacht, the *Casco*, to cruise the southern Pacific in a search for a region and climate that would be congenial to Stevenson's health. After considering Tahiti and Honolulu and finding them unsuitable, they arrived in December 1889 at Upolu, Samoa, the island that was to be his home until his death on 3 December 1894. There he built a house on the estate of VAILIMA and from his experiences he wrote two novels, *The Wrecker* (1892), with his stepson Lloyd Osbourne, and *The Ebb Tide* (1894), and one of his best short stories, *The Beach of Falesa*. He also wrote the historical novel *St Ives* (1897), which was completed by Sir Arthur Quiller-Couch. Stevenson's ability to draw characters and evoke landscape and his mastery of language make his short stories an important part of his literary output; among the finest are those with the theme of diabolic possession – *Thrawn Janet* and *Markheim*.

Stevenson was one of the best-loved writers of his generation and his lifelong battle against ill health and his early death in the South Seas have created a romantic legend around his life and career.

WORKS: *The Pentland Rising* (1866); *An Inland Voyage* (1878); *Edinburgh: Picturesque Notes* (1879); *Travels with a Donkey* (1879); with W. E. Henley, *Deacon Brodie, or The Double Life* (1880); *Not I and Other Poems* (1881); *Virginibus puerisque* (1881); *Familiar Studies of Men and Books* (1882); *Moral Emblems* (1882); *The New Arabian Nights* (1882); *Penny Whistles* (1883); *The Silverado Squatters* (1883); *Treasure Island* (1883); with W. E. Henley,

Admiral Guinea (1884); with W. E. Henley, *Beau Austin* (1884); *A Child's Garden of Verses* (1885); *The Dynamiter* (1885); with W. E. Henley, *Macaire* (1885); *More New Arabian Nights* (1885); *Prince Otto* (1885); *Kidnapped* (1886); *Some College Memories* (1886); *The Strange Case of Dr Jekyll and Mr Hyde* (1886); *Memoir of Fleeming Jenkin* (1887); *Memories and Portraits* (1887); *The Merry Men* (1887); *Ticonderoga* (1887); *Underwoods* (1887); *The Black Arrow* (1888); *The Master of Ballantrae* (1888); *The Misadventures of John Nicholson* (1888); with Lloyd Osbourne, *The Wrong Box* (1889); *Ballads* (1890); *Father Damien* (1890); *In the South Seas* (1890); *Across the Plains* (1892); *The Beach of Falesa* (1892); *A Footnote to History* (1892); with Lloyd Osbourne, *The Wrecker* (1892); *Catriona* (1893); *Island Nights Entertainments* (1893); *The Ebb Tide* (1894); *The Amateur Emigrant* (1895); *Weir of Hermiston* (1896); *St Ives* (1897)

EDITIONS: S. Colvin, ed., *The Works of Robert Louis Stevenson*, 29 vols., Edinburgh Edition (Edinburgh, 1895–8); E. Gosse, ed., *The Works of Robert Louis Stevenson*, 20 vols., Pentland Edition (London, 1906); *The Works of Robert Louis Stevenson*, with an introduction by Andrew Lang, 25 vols., Swanston Edition (London, 1911); *The Works of Robert Louis Stevenson*, 26 vols., Vailima Edition (London, 1922–3); S. Colvin, ed., *The Works and Letters of Robert Louis Stevenson*, 35 vols., Tusitala Edition (London, 1923–4); *The Works and Letters of Robert Louis Stevenson*, 3 vols., Skerryvore Edition (London, 1924–6); J. A. Smith, ed., *Collected Poems of Robert Louis Stevenson* (London, 1950)

REFERENCES: G. Balfour, *The Life of Robert Louis Stevenson* (London, 1901); D. Daiches, *Robert Louis Stevenson* (Glasgow, 1947); J. A. Smith, ed., *Henry James and Robert Louis Stevenson: a Record of Friendship and Criticism* (London, 1948); J. C. Furnas, *Voyage to Windward* (London, 1952); D. Butts, *R. L. Stevenson* (London, 1960); E. M. Eigner, *Robert Louis Stevenson and the Romantic Tradition* (Princeton, 1960); R. Kiely, *Robert Louis Stevenson and the Fiction of Adventure* (Cambridge, Mass., 1964); J. Pope-Hennessy, *Robert Louis Stevenson* (London, 1974); J. Calder, *RLS: a Life Study* (London, 1980)

Stewart. The royal house of Scotland. The first Stewart king of Scotland was Robert II (1316–90), the son of Walter, the sixth High Steward of Scotland and Marjorie the daughter of ROBERT I (Robert the Bruce). Between 1370 and 1603 eight Stewarts (Robert III, JAMES I–VI and MARY) occupied the throne of Scotland; from 1603 to 1714 five occupied the throne of England, and later Great Britain (James I, Charles I and II, James II, and Anne). The male line ended in 1807 with the death of Prince Henry Benedict, the brother of CHARLES EDWARD STUART.

Stewart, Alan Breck (*d* 1789). Jacobite adventurer, the foster-brother of JAMES STEWART of the Glens. He fought in the

Jacobite rebellion of 1745 and with James was wrongly accused of the Appin murder of Colin Campbell of Glenure (1708–52) on 14 May 1752. James was hanged for the murder, but Alan fled into exile and died in France in 1789. Alan Breck Stewart appears with his brother in the novels KIDNAPPED and *Catriona* (1893) by ROBERT LOUIS STEVENSON.

Stewart, David, of Garth (1772–1829). Soldier and historian. He served with the 42nd Highlanders, the Black Watch, in the West Indies campaigns of 1794 and 1795 and later in the Napoleonic campaigns in Spain and Egypt. In June 1814 he retired on half pay and turned his attention to the history of the Scottish regiments and the clan system, research that led to the publication of *Sketches of the Character, Manner and Present State of the Highlanders of Scotland, with Details of the Military Service of the Highland Regiments* (1822). Although it was attacked for the author's Jacobite sympathies, the book was one of the first objective studies, treated in an unromantic way, of the history of the Scottish Highlands. Stewart was a friend of Sir WALTER SCOTT and was associated with him in the preparations for George IV's visit to Edinburgh in 1822. He acquired the family estate of Garth in Perthshire after the death of his older brother in 1823 but resumed his military career in 1825, after being promoted major-general. Appointed Governor-General of St Lucia in 1829, he died there of fever in the same year on 18 December.

Stewart, Dugald (1753–1828). Philosopher. He was born on 22 November 1753 in Edinburgh, the son of the Professor of Mathematics in the University. By the time he was 19, having completed his education at the HIGH SCHOOL OF EDINBURGH and the University, Stewart was assisting his father, becoming a full-time teacher in 1774. In the University he was given the opportunity of displaying the virtuosity and flair for extempore speaking that were to be the hallmarks of his academic career, and he quickly made a name for himself as a brilliant teacher. In 1785 he became Professor of Moral Philosophy, having changed posts with ADAM FERGUSON; he held the chair until his retirement in 1810. Although he was highly regarded as a teacher and included among his pupils JAMES MILL, FRANCIS JEFFREY, HENRY THOMAS COCKBURN and WALTER SCOTT, as well as the politicians Lords Palmerston, Lansdowne and Russell, his philosophical work was shallow and he chose to neglect the work of DAVID HUME (ii), preferring a diluted version of the 'Common-Sense' school of THOMAS REID. However, like ADAM SMITH he taught political economy in his philosophy classes and held advanced liberal views, which earned him local censure during the French Revolution. For his services to the Whig Party he was awarded the sinecure of the specially created post of Gazette Writer to Scotland, and his last years were spent at Kinneil House near Bo'ness where he died on 11 June 1828.

Stewart stands at the watershed of the SCOTTISH ENLIGHTENMENT, between the Golden Age and the age of Sir Walter Scott, and was a leading and influential figure in the Edinburgh of his day. He was a prolific writer and editor, and among his works are biographies of Reid, Adam Smith and WILLIAM ROBERTSON. His most authoritative philosophical works are *Philosophy of the Human Mind*, 3 vols. (1792–1827) and *Outlines of Moral Philosophy* (1793).

EDITION: W. Hamilton, ed., *The Works of Dugald Stewart*, 2 vols. (Edinburgh, 1854–8)

Stewart, James, of the Glens (*d* 1752). The illegitimate son of the Laird of Ardshiel and half-brother of the leader of the Clan Stewart of Appin in the 1745 Jacobite rebellion. He was evicted from his farm at Glenduror by Colin Campbell of Glenure, following the forfeiture of the Stewart and Cameron lands to the Campbells. When Glenure was murdered in 1752 Stewart and his foster-brother ALAN BRECK STEWART were wrongly accused of the crime and James was hanged at Ballachulish on 8 November 1752. The Appin murder case and both James of the Glens and Alan Breck feature in KIDNAPPED and *Catriona* (1893) by ROBERT LOUIS STEVENSON.

Stewart, J(ohn) I(nnes) M(acintosh) ['Michael Innes'] (*b* 1906). Novelist. He was born on 30 September 1906 in Edinburgh and was educated at the Edinburgh Academy and Oriel College, Oxford. His subsequent career as an academic took him to the universities of Leeds and Adelaide and the Queen's University of Belfast before he became a Fellow of Christ Church, Oxford. Under the pseudonym 'Michael Innes' he has written a large number of detective novels whose hero, Inspector Appleby, is an intellectual; most of the plots are held together by essentially cultivated characters set against a stereotyped, middle-class background. He has also written novels about university life and middle-class manners, including the quartet of Oxford novels, *A Staircase in Surrey (The Gaudy, Young Patullo, A Memorial Service and Astrolabe)*. His critical work includes an edition of Florio's translation of Montaigne (1931), *Character and Motive in Shakespeare* (1949) and introductions to the work of several English writers, including Rudyard Kipling, Thomas Hardy and Joseph Conrad.

WORKS: ed., *Montaigne's Essays* (1931); *Character and Motive in Shakespeare* (1949); *Mark Lambert's Last Supper* (1954); *The Guardians* (1955); *James Joyce* (1957); *A Use of Riches* (1957); *The Man who Wrote Detective Stories* (1959); *The Man who Won the Pools* (1961); *Eight Modern Writers* (1963); *The Last Tresilians* (1963); *Thomas Love Peacock* (1963); *An Acre of Grass* (1965); *The Aylwins* (1966); *Rudyard Kipling* (1966); *Vanderlyn's Kingdom* (1967); *Joseph Conrad* (1968); *Cucumber Sandwiches* (1969); *Avery's Mission* (1971); *Shakespeare's Lofty Scene* (1971); *Thomas Hardy* (1971); *A Palace of Art* (1972); *Mungo's Dream* (1973); *The Gaudy* (1974); *Young Patullo* (1975); *A Memorial Service* (1976); *The Madonna and the Astrolabe* (1977); *Full Term* (1978); *Our England is a Garden* (1979); *Andrew and Tobias* (1980); *The Bridge at Arta* (1981);
as Michael Innes: *Death at the President's Lodging* (1937); *Hamlet Revenge!* (1937); *Lament for a Maker* (1938); *Stop Press* (1939); *The Secret Vanguard* (1940); *There Came both Mist and Snow* (1940); *Appleby on Ararat* (1941); *The Daffodil Affair* (1942); *The Weight of the Evidence* (1944); *Appleby's End* (1945); *From London Far* (1946); *What Happened at Hazel Wood* (1946); *A Night of Errors* (1948); *The Journeying Boy* (1949); *The Hawk and the Handsaw* (1950); *Operation Pax* (1951); *A Private View* (1952); *Christmas at Candleshoe* (1953); *Appleby Talking* (1954); *The Man from the Sea* (1955); *Appleby Plays Chicken* (1956); *Appleby Talks Again* (1956); *Old Hall New Hall* (1956); *The Long Farewell* (1958); *Hare Sitting Up* (1959); *The New Sonia Wayward* (1960); *Silence Observed* (1961); *A Connoisseur's Case* (1962); *Money from Holme* (1964); *The Bloody Wood* (1966); *A Change of Heir* (1966); *Appleby at Allington* (1968); *A Family Affair* (1969); *Death at the Chase* (1970); *An Awkward Lie* (1971); *The Open House* (1972); *Appleby's Answer* (1973); *Appleby's Other Story* (1974); *The Mysterious Commission* (1974); *The Appleby File* (1975); *The Gay Phoenix* (1976); *Dead Man's Shoes* (1977); *Honeybath's Harem* (1977); *The Ampersand Papers* (1978); *Going it Alone* (1980); *Lord Mullion's Secret* (1981)

Stewart, John, of Baldynneis (c1539–c1606). Poet. John Stewart, the son of Lord Innermeith and a distant cousin of JAMES VI, was educated at the University of St Andrews.

Thereafter he may have studied in Paris but he first comes to attention when he became involved in a lengthy, and frequently violent, altercation over family property following the death of his father. In April 1580 his brother, who had succeeded to the family title, settled on him the lands of Baldynneis near Dunning in Perthshire. He became a courtier at James's court and was considered one of the most original of the CASTALIAN BAND of poets who surrounded the young king. Following the precepts of James's rules of prosody, contained in the REULIS AND CAUTELIS, he composed a number of wittily alliterative poems and sonnets in the Spenserian form. These were dedicated to James in a collection entitled *Rapsodies of the Author's Youthfull Braine* (1556), in which the king was characterized as 'brycht purpour Pean' (the Apollo figure); the book represents the high point of the formal Castalian tradition. His major work, though, is his translation of Ariosto's *Orlando furioso*, which employs a richly ornate language, used at its best in the scenes of action and natural description. Stewart's adherence to the Master of Gray, a court favourite who fell from grace, led to his own banishment from court and his last days were spent on his Perthshire estates.

EDITION: T. Crockett, ed., *The Poems of John Stewart of Baldynneis*, STS (Edinburgh and London, 1913)

Stewart, John Roy. The English name of IAIN RUADH STIÙBHART.

Stirling, Jessica. Pen-name of HUGH C. RAE and Peggy Coghlan.

Stirling-Maxwell, Sir William (1818–78). Historian. He was born on 8 March 1818 at Kenmure, Stirlingshire, and was tutored privately before entering Trinity College, Cambridge, in 1835. On graduating he visited Spain and thus began a lifetime's interest in, and affection for, the country, its people and its art and literature. Stirling-Maxwell was a pioneering critic of Spanish art, and his *Annals of the Artists of Spain*, published in three volumes in 1848, not only introduced the British public to the art of Spain but also focused attention on the work of Velazquez. In 1849 he inherited the family's estates in Scotland and Jamaica, and from then until his death on 15 January 1878 he lived the life of a country gentleman with political and antiquarian interests: he was Tory MP for Perthshire from

1852 and he built up a substantial library, including many volumes in Gaelic, which he had learned in childhood. In his public career he interested himself in the future of the Scottish universities, being Lord Rector of St Andrews in 1862, Aberdeen in 1870 and Edinburgh in 1872. His antiquarian interests led to his concern for the official collection of historical documents. Although much of his writings on Spain and the Middle East have since been superseded, Stirling-Maxwell is remembered by scholars for his early investigations and for the sense of enthusiasm that pervades all his writing.

WORKS: *Annals of the Artists of Spain*, 3 vols. (1848); *The Cloister Life of the Emperor Charles V* (1852); *Don John of Austria* (1883)

Stiùbhart, Iain Ruadh (John Roy Stewart) (1700–52). Poet. He was born at Knock, Kincardine, into an old landed family whose property had been ceded to the Dukes of Gordon during the 17th century. He served as a lieutenant and quartermaster in the Royal Scots Greys, but resigned from the army when he refused to be transferred to another regiment, the Black Watch. Suspected of being a Jacobite, he was imprisoned in Inverness in 1736, but he escaped to join the French army in Paris. He served on the French side at the Battle of Fontenoy in April 1745 and later that year joined the Jacobite army of Prince CHARLES EDWARD STUART at Blair Atholl in Perthshire. During the ensuing campaign he commanded a regiment, and his courage and military ability made him a favourite with the soldiers and clan chiefs alike. After the BATTLE OF CULLODEN he escaped again to France, where he ended his days in 1752. Iain Ruadh was a poet of some ability and his songs and laments for the Jacobite cause are a good measure of the passions aroused in the Highlands by the 1745 rising. His lament for the dead at Culloden 'O gur mor mo chuis mhulaid' is his best-known work.

EDITION: E. E. Mackechnie, ed., *The Poems of John Roy Stewart* (Glasgow, 1947)

Stone of Destiny [Stone of Scone]. A stone sacred in Scottish history as the ancient coronation stone of the kings of Scotland. It is also known as the Stone of Scone and in Gaelic as *Lia Fail*, and it is supposed to have been brought from Ireland in the tenth century to rest in Scone in Perthshire, the capital of the king-dom of Alba. Tradition claims that it is the stone that Jacob used as a pillow at Bethel and that it later became the pedestal of the Jewish Ark of the Covenant; thereafter it is supposed to have been taken by one of Moses' followers' Gathelus, to Ireland by way of Syria and Egypt. The stone was removed to England by Edward I in 1296 and still rests below the coronation throne in Westminster Abbey, although it was briefly removed in 1950 by a group of Scottish nationalists. The stone is once supposed to have carried the inscription: '*Ni fallat fatum Scoti quocumque locatum invenient lapidem regnasse tenentur ibidem*: If Destiny prove true then Scots are known to have been kings wherever men find this stone.'

Strange Case of Dr Jekyll and Mr Hyde, The. A novel by ROBERT LOUIS STEVENSON, published in 1886. The central character, Dr Henry Jekyll, haunted by his consciousness of a double identity within himself, experiments with a drug that will separate his personality into good and evil. The evil aspect, which is intended to absorb all his wicked instincts, is a hideous physical manifestation whom he calls Mr Edward Hyde. In that guise evil is allowed to rule and Hyde begins to commit a number of crimes, culminating in a murder. Increasingly unable to control his metamorphoses Jekyll finds Hyde becoming the dominant charcter, and to save himself from public exposure is forced to take his own life. Although Stevenson tended to overwrite the Gothic transformation scenes as gentle doctor becomes evil monster, the novel is a chilling examination of man's capacity for evil. The inspiration for the theme of the divided personality is supposed to have come from the story of WILLIAM BRODIE, an 18th-century Edinburgh deacon who was a robber by night and a sober citizen by day.

Stuart, Alice V(andockum) (*b* 1899). Poet. She was born in Rangoon, of Scottish parents, and she was educated at St Hilda's School, Edinburgh. After graduating from Somerville College, Oxford, she taught for several years in England and Scotland before settling in Edinburgh as a tutor to foreign students. She was an early promoter of poetry readings and a founder-member of the Scottish Association for the Speaking of Verse. Two influences find their ways into Alice Stuart's poetry: the atmosphere of the ballads and a Georgian Romanticism, especially in her nature poetry.

Her best work is contained in *The Unquiet Tide* (1971).

WORKS: *The Far Calling* (1944); *The Dark Tavern* (1953); *David Gray: the Poet of 'The Luggie'* (1961); *The Door Between* (1963); *The Unquiet Tide* (1971); ed., with Charles Graves, *Jubilee Anthology of the Scottish Association for the Speaking of Verse* (1974)

Stuart, Charles Edward ['The Young Pretender', 'Bonnie Prince Charlie'] (1720–88). He was born on 31 December 1720 in Rome, the son of Prince James Francis Edward, *de jure* James VIII, and Princess Clementina Sobieski. He had a military education and on 19 August 1745 he landed at Glenfinnan, Argyllshire, to raise a JACOBITE rebellion in his father's name. After a short stay in Edinburgh, he defeated a government army under Sir John Cope at the Battle of Prestonpans on 21 September 1745 and marched into England. His army was drawn mainly from the Highlands, and when the English Jacobites failed to offer support he decided to retreat after reaching Derby. The government army was defeated again at the Battle of Falkirk on 17 January 1746 but the final defeat came at the hands of the Duke of Cumberland when the Jacobite army was routed at the BATTLE OF CULLODEN on 16 April 1746. Charles escaped to France after hiding in the Highlands and Western Isles in the protection of loyal clansmen. He spent the rest of his life in France and Italy; he married Princess Louisa of Stolberg in 1772 but they parted without issue 11 years later. He died on 31 January 1788 in Rome.

Although Charles, or 'Bonnie Prince Charlie', remains a romantic figure in Scottish history, he was an ineffectual military commander, and the failure of the Jacobite rebellion marked the beginning of the subjugation of the Highlands and the destruction of the clan system. Charles Edward Stuart figures in Scott's novels WAVERLEY and *Redgauntlet*.

Stuart, Gilbert (1742–86). Historian. He was born in Edinburgh and educated at the HIGH SCHOOL OF EDINBURGH and the University, where he studied law. Although his father George Stuart, Professor of Humanity and Roman Antiquities in the University, hoped that his son would be called to the Scottish Bar, Gilbert Stuart's inclinations were towards the life of a man of letters. The publication of his successful *Historical Dissertation concerning the English Constitution* (1764) gave him the

confidence to move to London, where he was employed by the publishers of the *Monthly Review*. In 1773 he returned to Edinburgh to edit the short-lived *Edinburgh Magazine and Review*, but he was given to writing scurrilous reviews attacking the *literati* of Edinburgh and by 1782 he was in London again, having been unsuccessful in his attempts to gain a chair at Edinburgh. Believing that WILLIAM ROBERTSON, Principal of the University of Edinburgh, was opposed to his appointment, Stuart pursued him with bitter attacks on his work and character. Another historian, ROBERT HENRY, was similarly persecuted by Stuart on the publication of his *History of England*. Although he was an able scholar and an entertaining and incisive writer on historical and legal subjects Stuart allowed himself to be swayed too frequently, by personal animosity, and his talents were largely wasted in Grub Street attacks on his opponents. He died after a short illness on 13 August 1786 at his father's house in Musselburgh.

WORKS: *Historical Dissertation Concerning the English Constitution* (1764); *View of Society in Europe in the Progress from Rudeness to Refinement* (1778); *Observations concerning the Public Law and the Constitutional History of Scotland* (1779); *History of the Establishment of the Reformation of Religion in Scotland* (1780); *History of Scotland from the Establishment of the Reformation till the Death of Queen Mary* (1781)

Sutherland, Robert Garioch ['Robert Garioch'] (1909–81). Poet. Robert Garioch Sutherland, who wrote under the name 'Robert Garioch', was born on 9 May 1909 in Edinburgh. He was educated at the HIGH SCHOOL OF EDINBURGH and, between 1927 and 1931, at the University. Until his retirement in 1964 he taught in schools in Edinburgh, London and Kent, and between 1971 and 1973 he was Writer in Residence at the University of Edinburgh. He also worked as a 'lexicographer's orraman' for the *Dictionary of the Older Scottish Tongue*. During World War II he served with the Royal Signals in the desert war in North Africa and was a prisoner-of-war in Italy and Germany from 1942 until 1945. His experiences were recounted in *Two Men and a Blanket* (1975), a straightforward, yet ironic, study of the boredom and deprivations many soldiers had to face while in captivity.

Most of Sutherland's poetry is in Scots; he was influenced by the collection *Poems in Two Tongues* (1928) by A. D. MACKIE, and he himself admitted that, like ALLAN RAMSAY, his writing in Scots was a protest against the encroaching anglicization of the Scots tongue. There was, though, a quality to his use of language that sprang directly from his use of a living Scots as a child. Sutherland's first collection, *17 Poems for 6d* (1940), was shared with the Gaelic poet SOMHAIRLE MACGILL-EAIN; it was followed after the war by *Chuckies on a Cairn* (1949). A *Selected Poems* was published in 1966.

The best-known of Sutherland's poems are those dealing with his native city of Edinburgh, and short, pithy pieces like 'Glisk of the Great', 'In Princes Street Gairdens' and 'An Alabaster Box' are exasperated satires on the foibles of the ruling fathers. Sutherland used his comic muse to attack all forms of public hypocrisy and he always took it upon himself to espouse the cause of the underdog. ROBERT FERGUSSON influenced his poetry and his attitudes to Edinburgh, and that debt is acknowledged in 'To Robert Fergusson' and 'At Robert Fergusson's Grave'. There is a more sombre voice in 'Garioch's Repone til George Buchanan' and 'Sisyphus', poems which question the role of the teaching profession. In his later collections, *The Big Music* (1971) and *Doktor Faust in Rose Street* (1973), his philosophical range is extended in the title poems, and in 'The Muir', a long poem on the nature of perception, he speculated on the atomic theory. The *Collected Poems* was published in 1977.

Sutherland also wrote a short play about Edinburgh, *The Masque of Edinburgh* (1954), and was an active translator. He reworked from the Latin *Jepthes* and *Baptistes* by GEORGE BUCHANAN and translated the work of Somhairle MacGill-Eain and Guillaume Apollinaire (1880–1918); but his most intimate translations into Scots are from the poetry of Giuseppe Belli, a Roman poet whom Sutherland felt to have similar aims to his own in dealing with the society of his native city. Sutherland died on 26 April 1981 in Edinburgh.

WORKS: with Somhairle MacGill-Eain, *17 Poems for 6d* (1940); *Chuckies on a Cairn* (1949); *The Masque of Edinburgh* (1954); trans., George Buchanan, *Jepthah and the Baptist* (1959); *Selected Poems* (1966); *The Big Music* (1971); *Doktor Faust in Rose Street* (1973); ed., *Made in Scotland: an Anthology of Poems* (1974); *Two Men and a Blanket* (1975); *Collected Poems* (1977)

Swan, Annie S. (1859–1943). Novelist. She was born near the village of Coldingham, Berwickshire, and was brought up in Edinburgh and at Gorebridge, Midlothian. In 1883 she married James Burnett Smith, a schoolmaster, and they lived near Markinch in Fife until 1885, when Smith entered the University of Edinburgh to study medicine. They lived in London between 1896 and 1908 when they moved to Hertford. During World War I Annie S. Swan worked for the Ministry of Food in Britain and, towards the end of the war, in America; her husband served with the Black Watch. Following her husband's death in death in 1927 she returned to live in Scotland and died there on 17 June 1943.

Annie S. Swan began her writing career as a schoolgirl by winning a Christmas story competition in the *People's Journal*. Although her first novel, *Ups and Downs*, was published in 1878, it was not until 1883 that she made her name with *Aldersyde*, a Border romance in the style of MARGARET OLIPHANT. This was followed by a sequel, *Carlowrie* (1884), and by further novels of middle-class manners, *A Divided House* (1885) and *The Gates of Eden* (1887). Thereafter she concerned herself with the manufacture of light, romantic novels and serials for pulp magazines. She was closely connected with the popular press publishing activities of WILLIAM ROBERTSON NICOLL, and she was the main contributor to his women's magazine *The Woman at Home*. Her autobiography, *My Life*, was published in 1934 and her letters were edited in 1945.

WORKS: *Ups and Downs* (1878); *Bess* (1880); *Grandmother's Child* (1882); *Into the Haven* (1882); *Katie's Christmas Lesson* (1882); *Tom's Memorable Christmas* (1882); *Aldersyde* (1883); *For Lucy's Sake* (1883); *Marion Forsyth* (1883); *Mistaken* (1883); *A Year at Coverley* (1883); *The Better Part* (1884); *Carlowrie* (1884); *Mark Desborough's Vow* (1884); *Adam Hepburn's Vow* (1885); *A Divided House* (1885); *Holidays at Sunnycroft* (1885); *Warren Chase* (1885); *Freedom's Sword* (1886); *Robert Martin's Lesson* (1886); *Thankful Rest* (1886); *Thomas Dryburgh's Dream* (1886); *The Gates of Eden* (1887); *Jack's Year of Trial* (1887); *The Straight Gate* (1887); *Briar and Palm* (1888); *Doris Cheyne* (1888); *Hazell and Sons, Brewers* (1888); *Miss Baxter's Request* (1888); *The Secret Panel* (1888); *St Vida's* (1889); *A Vexed Inheritance* (1890); *Climbing the Hill* (1891); *Maitland of Laurieston* (1891); *Who Shall Serve?* (1891); *A Bachelor in Search of a Wife* (1892); *The Guinea Stamp* (1892); *A Bitter Debt* (1893); *Courtship and Marriage* (1893); *Homespun* (1893); *A Foolish Marriage* (1894); *A Lost Ideal* (1894); *Love gives Itself* (1894); *The Bonnie Jean* (1895); *Elizabeth Glen* (1895); *A Victory Won* (1895); *Kinsfolk* (1896); *Memories of Margaret Grainger* (1896); *A Stormy*

Voyager (1896); The Curse of Cowden (1897); Mrs
Keith Hamilton (1897); The Ne'er do Well (1897);
Wilful Winnie (1897); Not Yet (1898); Wyndham's
Daughter (1898); A Son of Erin (1899); An American
Woman (1900); A Blessing in Disguise (1902); The
False and the True (1902); From a Turret Window
(1902); Good out of Evil (1902); Love Grown Cold
(1902); An Only Son (1902); The Secret of Dunstan
Mere (1902); Stephen Glyn (1902); A Mask of Gold
(1906); Nancy Nicolson (1906); Love unlocks the
Door (1907); Ann Hyde (1908); The Broad Road
(1908); Hester Lane (1908); The Inheritance (1909);
The Magic of Love (1909); The Old Moorings (1909);
Margaret Holroyd (1910); The Mystery of Barry In-
gram (1910); Rhona Keith (1910); What Shall it
Profit? (1910); The Last of their Race (1911); Songs of
Memory and Hope (1911); The Bridge Builders
(1913); The Fairweathers (1913); The Farrants
(1913); Love's Crown (1913); Prairie Fires (1913);
Corroding Gold (1914); A Favourite of Fortune
(1914); The Girl who Helped (1914); Meg Hamilton
(1914); Letters to a War Bride (1915); The Stepmother
(1915); The Homecoming of the Boys (1916); The
Woman's Part (1916); Young Blood (1917); Hands
across the Sea (1919); America at Home (1920); The
Ruling Passion (1920); Woven of the Wind (1920);
Christian's Cross (1921); Love's Miracle (1922);
Shadowed Lives (1923); Macleod's Wife (1924); A
Maid of the Isles (1924); Wrongs Righted (1924);
Across the Path (1925); Grannie's Little Girl (1925);
Closed Doors (1926); Elsie Thorburn (1926); The
Pendulum (1926); Mary Garth (1927); Love the Mas-
ter Key (1928); Twice Tried (1928); The Burden
Bearers (1929); A Wild Harvest (1929); The Forerun-
ners (1930); A House on the Rock (1930); The
Marching Feet (1931); The Luck of the Livingstones
(1932); The Maclure Mystery (1932); The Shore
Beyond (1932); Christians against the World (1933);
The Last of the Laidlaws (1933); The Little Stranger
(1933); Ursula Vivian (1933); A Winsome Witch
(1933); My Life (1934); The Pride of Fiona MacRae
(1934); The Purchase Price (1934); Between the Tides
(1935); The Bondage of Riches (1935); Dorothea Kirk
(1935); A Homing Bird (1935); The Way of Escape
(1935); We Travel Home (1935); The Ayres of Stud-
leigh (1936); The Land I Love (1936); An American
Wife (1937); A Breaker of Hearts (1937); A Daughter
of Destiny (1937); For Love of Billy (1937); Peggy
Fordyce (1937); The Road to Damascus (1937); Seed
Time and Harvest (1937); The Enchanted Door
(1938); The Family Secret (1938); The Greater Freedom (1938); The Head of the House (1938); The
White House of Marisaig (1938); A Witch in Pink
(1938); Double Lives (1939); Fiona MacRae (1939);
Love the Prodigal (1939); These are our Masters
(1939); A Trust Betrayed (1939); The Uninvited
Guest (1939); The Elder Brother (1940); The Outsider
(1940); Proud Patricia (1940); The Secret of Skye
(1940); The Third Generation (1940); The Dark
House (1941); Dreams Come True (1941); The Mischief Makers (1941); Rebel Hearts (1941); The
Younger Brother (1941); The Family Name (1942);
Who are the Heathen? (1942)

Sylvander. The name adopted by AGNES
M'LEHOSE for ROBERT BURNS during their epistolary relationship of 1787 to 1891.

Sym, Robert (1752–1835). Lawyer and man
of letters. He was born on 29 February 1752 in
Glasgow. After an education at the University
of Glasgow, he served his legal apprenticeship
with an uncle before being admitted a WRITER
TO THE SIGNET in 1775. His nephew was JOHN
WILSON (iii) and to that family relationship
Sym owes his place in literary history as the
character 'Timothy Tickler' in the 'NOCTES
AMBROSIANAE' published each month in
BLACKWOOD'S MAGAZINE between 1822 and
1835. A tall, thin man, who delighted in
taking long walks whatever the state of the
weather, Sym was a popular, though slightly
eccentric figure in the Edinburgh of his day.

T

Tait's Edinburgh Magazine. A literary magazine founded in 1832 by the Edinburgh bookseller William Tait (1793–1864) in an attempt to capture some of the market for periodicals that had been created by the *Edinburgh Review* (see EDINBURGH REVIEW (ii)) and BLACKWOOD'S MAGAZINE. Like the former it adopted the Whig interest in politics but it failed to match its rival's supremacy in attracting authors of note, and its declining readership lead to its demise in 1846.

Tales of a Grandfather. A history of Scotland to the Jacobite rebellion of 1745 by Sir WALTER SCOTT, published initially in two series in 1828 and 1829. It was written for his grandson James, son of JOHN GIBSON LOCKHART, and a further series, published in 1830, dealt with the history of France. Of the history's intention Scott confided to his *Journal* on 7 August 1827 his desire 'to find my way between what a child can comprehend and what shall not yet be absolutely uninteresting to the grown reader'.

Tales of my Landlord. The title of four series of novels by Sir WALTER SCOTT, published between 1816 and 1831. The first series contained *The Black Dwarf* and OLD MORTALITY; the second, THE HEART OF MIDLOTHIAN; the third, THE BRIDE OF LAMMERMOOR and A LEGEND OF MONTROSE and the fourth, *Count Robert of Paris* and *Castle Dangerous*. In the prologue to *The Black Dwarf* Scott adopted the conceit, which was continued in the succeeding novels, that the tales had been written down by one Peter Pattieson from stories told to him by the landlord of the Wallace Inn at Gandercleugh, and then reworked and sold to the publisher by the village schoolmaster and parish clerk, Jedediah Cleishbotham.

Tam o' Shanter. A narrative poem by ROBERT BURNS, first published in the *Edinburgh Magazine* of March 1791 and subsequently in the second volume of the *Antiquities of Scotland* by Francis Grose. The poem was written originally to accompany the drawing of ALLOWAY KIRK in Grose's volume and was based on a local folk-tale in which a farmer, Tam o' Shanter, on his way home after carousing in Ayr, encounters a witches' and warlocks' coven with the Devil in Alloway Kirk. When the farmer shouts out in praise of Maggie, a witch with a short smock or 'sark', he is pursued and saved only by his horse crossing running water at the River Doon (for the complete story, see Burns's letter of June 1790 to Grose).

Tam o' Shanter is Burns's only narrative poem and it demonstrates a sure handling of the free-flowing octosyllabic couplets. He kept to the facts of the folk-tale but his deft changes of mood, especially in the contrast between the cosy world of the tavern and the horrors of devilry in Alloway Kirk, give the poem a tone which is at once full of suspense and yet not without comedy. The scene in the kirk, written in a vital, racy language, is one of the poem's highlights, with its description of 'Auld Nick' boasting all the properties attributed to him by country superstition, and the mock-Gothic horror of the witches' dance. The poem reaches a fitting climax in the breathlessly told story of the chase and Tam's escape. The eight lines in the middle of the poem written in a heightened literary English have been a subject of contention between critics but are generally agreed to have been included 'to set the sternness of objective fact against the warm, cosy and self-deluding view of the half-intoxicated Tam' (D. Daiches, *Robert Burns* (London, rev. 2/1966)).

Tannahill, Robert (1774–1810). Poet and songwriter. He was born on 3 June 1774 in Paisley, the son of a silk weaver. Lacking any formal education, he interested himself in the collection of traditional songs. He helped to found a Burns Club in Paisley in 1803, for which he composed a number of songs set to traditional airs. Although his poems were printed in 1807, he failed to find either a patron or a publisher to support him, and in a fit of depression he drowned himself in the Paisley canal on 17 May 1810. As so often happens, his fame spread after his death and he has long been celebrated as Paisley's 'civic bard'. Most of his songs are in the popular sentimental vein of his day; the most enduring is *Jessie, the Flower o' Dunblane*. The standard edition of his works was published in 1876.

WORKS: *The Soldier's Return: a Scottish Interlude in Two Acts* (1807); *Poems and Songs* (1815)

EDITION: D. Semple, ed., *The Poems and Songs and Correspondence of Robert Tannahill, with Life and Notes* (Paisley, 1876)

Tarbat, 1st Viscount. *See* MACKENZIE, GEORGE (i).

Taylor, Launcelot. Pen-name of JOHN ARMSTRONG.

Taylor, Rachel Annand (1876–1960). Poet. Rachel Annand was born in Aberdeen and was educated there at the University. After graduating she married Alexander Cameron Taylor and lived in Dundee and, later, in London, where she died on 15 August 1960. Much of her verse has a Pre-Raphaelite quality; she was also much influenced by Hugh MacDiarmid's insistence on the importance to Scottish literature of WILLIAM DUNBAR, and her study *Dunbar the Poet and his Period* (1931), despite its flaws and her insistence on Dunbar's lack of learning, helped to promote Dunbar's case as a major poet of his period. In 1943 she was awarded the honorary degree of LLD by her *alma mater*.

WORKS: *Poems* (1904); *Rose and Vine* (1908); *The House of Fiammetta* (1909); *Aspects of the Italian Renaissance* (1923); *The End of Fiammetta* (1923); *Leonardo the Florentine* (1927); *Dunbar the Poet and his Period* (1931); *Renaissance France* (1949)

Tea-Table Miscellany, The. An anthology of Scottish songs and ballads made by ALLAN RAMSAY and published in 1724, 1725, 1727, 1732 and 1737. Its full title is *The Tea-Table Miscellany: a Collection of Choice Songs, Scots and English.* Ramsay made his selection from a number of sources, but in so doing he chose to anglicize many of the songs to make them more acceptable to a genteel audience. Nevertheless, he made it plain that the ballads were meant to be sung, and *The Tea-Table* was responsible for an almost patriotic interest in Scotland's ballad traditions. Among the less corrupted texts in the collections are good versions of *Waly Waly, Fair Willy drown'd in Yarrow, Barbara Allan, The Gaberlunzie Man* and *The Bonny Earl of Moray.* Ramsay's work inspired several similar ballad collections during the 18th century but he was also responsible for the habit of publishing songs and ballads without their tunes, though he did give an indication of what tunes might be used. Shortly after the publication of the first two volumes of *The Tea-Table,* William Thomson, without reference to Ramsay, published *Orpheus caledonius,* a set of simple figured bass accompaniments to many of the songs.

Tennant, William (1784–1848). Poet and scholar. He was born on 15 May 1784 in Anstruther, Fife, and was educated at the University of St Andrews between 1799 and 1801. An accident in childhood left Tennant lame and his early years were spent at home, a period he used to further his study of Hebrew, Arabic and Persian. Between 1813 and 1834, when he was appointed Professor of Oriental Languages at St Andrews, he worked as a schoolmaster in various parts of Scotland. Ill health forced him to retire in 1848 and he died that same year on 14 October in Anstruther.

Tennant published his *Synopsis of Chaldaic and Syriac Grammar* in 1840 and it remained a standard textbook for many years. He was a prolific poet but most of his work has been long forgotten: he wrote two historical verse dramas, *Cardinal Beaton* (1823) and *John Baliol* (1825), and a long poem couched in heroic terms, *The Thane of Fife* (1822). His monument is the successful ANSTER FAIR, a long poem about country people celebrating a traditional festival; written in English, with a Scots accent never far away in its comic rhymes, it is also notable for its stanza form, which may have suggested the *ottava rima* used by Lord BYRON in his *Don Juan.* Tennant's other work of note, dedicated to Sir DAVID LYNDSAY, is *Papistry Storm'd,* a spirited description of the destruction of St Andrews Cathedral.

WORKS: *Anster Fair* (1812); *The Dominie's Disaster* (1816); ed., *The Poems of Allan Ramsay* (1819); *The*

Thane of Fife (1822); *Cardinal Beaton* (1823); *John Balliol* (1825); *Papistry Storm'd* (1827); *Critical Remarks on the Psalms of David* (1830); *Synopsis of Chaldaic and Syriac Grammar* (1840)

REFERENCE: M. F. Conolly, *Memoir of the Life and Writings of William Tennant* (London, 1861)

Testament of Creisseid, The. A poem by ROBERT HENRYSON. It tells the story of Creisseid's fate after her desertion by Diomeid, and her subsequent torment and death from leprosy. Although his poem is not strictly a sequel to Chaucer's *Troylus and Cryseyde*, Henryson made generous reference to Chaucer in the prologue and employed a Chaucerian rhymeroyal throughout, albeit overlaid with heavy alliteration and a frequently harsh, consonantal language. Although there is an implicit reliance on Chaucer, *The Testament* is neither imitative nor conventional but an original work of sustained tragedy.

The poem has a variation on the traditional spring opening: instead of 'lustie May' the weather is unseasonably that of late winter, with a cold northern wind, misty clouds and a heavy frost. The 'doolie sessoun' is emphasized too by the poet's hoary old age and his infirmity before the elements, thus establishing a bleak mood for the telling of the tragedy. Having praised Chaucer, Henryson takes 'ane uther quair' to discover Creisseid's fate. Creisseid, deserted by Diomeid, returns to her father, Calchas, and in a mood of desperation reproaches Venus and Cupid for having led her to trust in physical beauty. In a dream sequence the gods appear as planets before Creisseid to offer their judgement on her blasphemy. Saturn, the oldest planet, condemns her to lose her beauty by striking her with leprosy. In this condition Creisseid is passed one day by Troylus and his entourage. Something in her bearing reminds him of the woman he once loved and he throws her his purse. On learning the identity of her benefactor Creisseid returns to him the ruby ring which was his first gift and after her death Troylus raises a marble tomb to her memory. Creisseid's tragedy is that Fortune has cut her off from the pleasures of her former life and although she warns other women against unfaithfulness, a traditional courtly love motif, she realizes that her tragedy initially was brought about by blaspheming the gods. There is little Christian comfort in the poem: Creisseid has paid the price for daring to pit herself against the all-pervasive power of Fortune.

EDITION: D. Fox, ed., *The Testament of Creisseid* (London, 1968)

REFERENCE: J. MacQueen, *Robert Henryson: a Study of the Major Narrative Poems* (Oxford, 1967)

Thirty-nine Steps, The. A novel by JOHN BUCHAN, published serially in BLACKWOOD'S MAGAZINE in 1915 under the pseudonym 'H. de V.'. It was published in book form in October 1915 and it became an immediate success, selling 25,000 copies between its publication and the end of the year. Buchan had written his first thriller (or 'shocker' as he called them), *The Power-House* in 1913 but it was *The Thirty-nine Steps* that established his reputation. The hero, Richard Hannay, is a South African mining engineer on leave in Britain, who is drawn into a series of adventures with the Black Stone Gang. Much of the action takes place in Galloway where the Gang poses a threat to British security until Hannay unravels the secret of the coded message about the 39 steps. Two of Buchan's favourite motifs are present in the novel: that civilization is a thin veneer which can be breached by evil and disorder, and that courage and responsibility are necessary to maintain its highest standards. Richard Hannay, who appears in five other novels, is based on Field Marshal Lord Edmund Ironside whom Buchan had met in South Africa.

Thom, William (1798–1848). Poet. He was born in Justice Port, a slum area of Aberdeen, at the end of 1798. The death of his father forced him to leave school at the age of ten, to work in a cotton-weaving factory in a trade that he followed until 1828 when he married and moved to Dundee. In 1831 his marriage broke up and he formed a relationship with Jean Whitecross, a Kirriemuir woman, who bore him four children before her death in 1840 and shared with him the financial difficulties caused by the recession in the cottonweaving industry during the 1830s. Between 1840 and 1844 Thom lived in Inverurie, Aberdeenshire, with Jean Stephens by whom he had three daughters.

Thom started writing poetry in Aberdeen and several of his poems were published in the *Aberdeen Journal* and the WHISTLE-BINKIE series, but it was during his Inverurie years that he enjoyed his greatest creativity. In January 1841 his popular and subsequently often anthologized poem 'The Blind Boy's Pranks' was published in the *Aberdeen Herald* and this was followed by an equally popular poem 'The Mitherless Bairn'. A collection, *Rhymes and Recollections of a Handloom Weaver*, was published in 1844 and Thom moved to London, where he was lionized in literary and social circles as the 'weaver poet'. Second and third editions of *Rhymes and Recollections* appeared in 1845 and 1847 but Thom dissipated the proceeds from his writing and he died in poverty in Dundee in 1848.

Like many others of his day, Thom lacked any formal education and, despite his comic gifts and firm use of language, he also allowed himself to be swayed by undiscerning critics who preferred his sentimental verse to his grotesque satires, such as 'Chants for Churls' written at the time of THE DISRUPTION in the Church of Scotland in 1843. One of his best poems is 'Whisperings for the Unwashed', a passionate protest against the misery and squalor of factory life. The poems were edited with a biography by William Skinner in 1880.

EDITION: W. Skinner, ed., *Rhymes and Recollections of a Handloom Weaver, with a Biographical Sketch* (Aberdeen, 1880)

REFERENCE: R. Bruce, *William Thom: the Inverurie Poet* (Aberdeen, 1970)

Thomas of Erceldoune [Thomas the Rhymer; Thomas Learmont] (*c*1220–*c*1297). Poet and seer. He lived at Erceldoune (Earlston) in Berwickshire and his name is mentioned in such documents as the cartulary of the Trinity House of Soltra. Among the many predictions attributed to him are the death of Alexander III, the BATTLE OF BANNOCKBURN and the accession of JAMES VI to the throne of Great Britain. They earned for him the nickname of 'True Thomas'. He is the reputed author of a romance of Tristram which Sir WALTER SCOTT held to be genuine and edited from a French source in 1804. The romantic myth of Thomas and his 'ladye gaye', the Queen of Faerie, with whom he spent seven years in elfland, has its origins in the 15th century. *The Romance and Prophecies of Thomas of Erceldoune* was edited in 1875 by JAMES A. H. MURRAY.

Thomson, Derick. The English name of RUARAIDH MACTHÓMAIS.

Thomson, George (1757–1851). Music publisher and song collector. He was born in Limekilns, Fife, and became Chief Clerk to the Board of Trustees for the Encouragement of Art and Manufacture in Scotland, which had been established after the ACT OF UNION to promote Scottish trade. He played in the orchestra at the St Cecilia Concerts in Edinburgh, at which he admired the Italianate interpretations of Scottish songs performed by singers such as Tenducci and Urbani. In 1792 he began work on collecting Scottish songs and contracted the help of ROBERT BURNS, who contributed 25 songs to the first volume of *A Select Collection of Original Scotish Airs* (1793). For his work, which lasted until his death, Burns received little payment and Thomson made significant alterations to the words and tunes of many songs, as well as to their settings, most significantly to the song known as SCOTS WHA HAE. After Burns's death Thomson attempted to conceal his editorial alterations by obliterating much of their correspondence. To the six volumes of the *Select Collection* (1793–1841) Burns contributed 114 songs. Thomson enlisted several leading European composers, including Haydn, Beethoven, Weber and Hummel, to write settings for the songs but the series was not a success. In 1839 Thomson retired from public life and spent some time in London before he died on 18 February 1851 in Leith.

Thomson, James (i) (1700–48). Poet. He was born on 11 September 1700 at Ednam in Roxburghshire, where his father was the parish minister; his childhood was spent in the neighbouring parish of Southdean. He was educated at Jedburgh and at the University of Edinburgh, where he studied divinity. Criticism of his ornate prose style in the composition of sermons drove him from Edinburgh in 1725 and he moved to London to become tutor to the son of the Earl of Haddington. He met Alexander Pope (1688–1744) and JOHN ARBUTHNOTT, and was introduced to DAVID MALLOCH, with whom he was to collaborate in *The Masque of Alfred* (1740) for which he wrote the patriotic song *Rule Britannia*. Thomson wrote several plays for the stage, none of which has stood the test of time, although, in their day, *Sophonisba* (1730) and *Tancred and Sigismunda* (1745) were not without their admirers. Through his literary work Thomson gained the patronage of Lord Chancellor Talbot and accompanied his son on a Continental tour. He later received a pension of £100 a year, together with the sinecure of Surveyor-General to the Leeward Islands. He retired from public life in 1740 and settled in Richmond, Surrey, where he died on 27 August 1748.

Thomson's literary reputation ultimately rests on his long poem THE SEASONS, the first part of which, *Winter*, appeared in 1726; *Summer* appeared in 1727, *Spring* in 1728, and *Autumn* in 1730, the year in which the whole poem was first published. It was revised at various times throughout Thomson's life. With its evocative and elaborate descriptions of scenery, animals, plants and natural phenomena, intermingled with folk-tales and a moral commentary, *The Seasons* challenged the Augustans' artificial view of nature and may be said to qualify Thomson as an early precursor of the Romantic movement. It is marred in several passages by Thomson's intricate and tortured rhythms and by his tendency to indulge in an over-ornate language, the 'fishy race' being preferred to 'fish', for instance. Apologists for Thomson have linked the aureate style to that of the Scottish makars and it is possible to hear in Thomson's onomatopoetic passages echoes from the ENEADOS by GAVIN DOUGLAS. Thomson also wrote a self-centred allegory, couched in Spenserian stanzas, called *The Castle of Indolence* (1748).

EDITION: J. L. Robertson, ed., *The Complete Poetical Works of James Thomson* (London, 1908)

REFERENCES: A. D. McKillop, *The Background of Thomson's Seasons* (London, 1942); D. Grant, *James Thomson: Poet of the Seasons* (London, 1951); R. Cohen, *The Unfolding of 'The Seasons'* (Baltimore, 1969)

Thomson, James (ii) ['B.V.'] (1834–82). Poet. James Thomson, who also wrote under the initials 'B.V.' (Bysshe Vanolis, a pseudonym from the names of Shelley and Novalis) was born on 23 November 1834 at Port Glasgow. His father was a merchant seaman and his mother, who came from Galloway, was a disciple of the Secessionist EDWARD IRVING. In 1842 the family moved to London and following the death there of both his parents, Thomson was brought up in the Royal Caledonian Asylum and educated at the Royal Military Asylum, Chelsea, where he trained to become an army schoolmaster. His first posting was in 1851 to Ballincollig, County Cork, where he fell in love with Matilda Weller, the

daughter of an armourer-sergeant, who in life and death was to exert a powerful emotional influence on Thomson's life. Her death in 1853 temporarily unhinged him and led to bouts of drinking and depression which were to characterize the rest of his career. The remainder of his army service was spent in Plymouth, Aldershot, Dublin and at the Curragh in Ireland, but his increasing alcoholism led to his dismissal from the army in 1862. Thomson then turned to a variety of careers: journalism (1862–4); business (1864–9); secretary to the Champion Gold and Silver Mines Company in Colorado (1872–3); and war correspondent in Spain during the Carlist Wars (1873). The last years of his life were spent in lodging houses and his drinking eventually led to his death from intestinal haemorrhaging on 8 June 1882.

Thomson's chief outlet for his work was the *National Reformer*, published by his friend Charles Bradlaugh (1833–91), the reformer and free thinker, who also gave Thomson employment as a journalist. His other writings appeared in obscure magazines such as *Cope's Tobacco Plants*, and much of his life was spent in a struggle to have his work published. His principal work is *The City of Dreadful Night*, a long poem published in instalments in the *National Reformer* in 1874 and in a collection with other poems in 1880. In this powerful, though pessimistic work the modern city becomes a symbol for man's isolation in a universe in which God does not exist. Despair and horror set the tone for Thomson's portrayal of man beset by nightmare and hallucination, and forced to live in the desolation and pain of life without purpose. The poem is enriched by Thomson's ability to impose a free-flowing rhythm on the verse, and by his use of an unadorned vocabulary. In happier mood he wrote a number of poems illustrating London life and manners, such as 'Sunday up the River' and 'Sunday in Hampstead'.

EDITIONS: A. Ridler, ed., *Poems and Some Letters of James Thomson* (Oxford, 1963); W. D. Schaefer, ed., *The Speedy Extinction of Evil and Misery* (London, 1967)

REFERENCE: B. Dobell, *The Laureate of Pessimism* (London, 1910)

Thomson, Thomas (1768–1852). Historian in the field of record scholarship. He is remembered for his work in arranging and indexing the Scottish national records, which, until his appointment as Deputy Clerk Register in 1806, had suffered from generations of neglect. He also contributed scholarly introductions to editions published by the BANNATYNE CLUB and succeeded Sir WALTER SCOTT as its president in 1832.

Tickler, Timothy. Pen-name of ROBERT SYM.

To a Louse. A poem written by ROBERT BURNS, 'on seeing one on a lady's bonnet at church'. In the opening stanzas, in swift descriptive touches Burns expresses his indignation at seeing the louse on the lady's bonnet; he then develops the theme to contrast the squalor of the louse with the lady's social pretensions. The final stanza contains the frequently quoted lines: 'O wad some Pow'r the giftie gie us,/To see oursels as others see us.'

To a Mouse. A poem written by ROBERT BURNS 'on turning her up in her nest with the plough, November 1785'. In a poem that bridges the gulf between the worlds of man and animal with compassion and understanding, Burns compares the plight of the mouse with his own problems. The seventh stanza contains the frequently quoted line: 'The best laid schemes o' Mice an' Men gang aft a-gley.'

Todd, Ruthven ['R. T. Campbell'] (*b* 1914). Poet. He was born on 14 June 1914 in Edinburgh, the son of American parents. He was educated at Fettes College, Edinburgh, and the Edinburgh School of Art. For two years after graduating he worked as a farm labourer on Mull before returning to Edinburgh to work as a journalist. In 1935 he moved to London and that was to be his home until 1947 when he returned to his parental home in the United States. There he was variously employed as a visiting professor at the University of New York, Buffalo, and as a small-press publisher. Between 1950 and 1956 he ran the Weekend Press which was then one of America's foremost literary presses.

Under the pseudonym of R. T. Campbell, Todd wrote several adventure novels, but he is best known as a poet and for his editing of the works of William Blake (1757–1827). His best work is to be found among his early poetry, especially in those pieces that anticipate World War II. 'It was easier' counterpoints the ease of peace with the harsh reality of war, in which the visionary poet can hear only 'the moan/Of the black planes and see their pendant bombs'. Although Todd left Scotland at the age of

31 and was destined not to return, his concern for things Scottish continues to inform much of his work. In particular he is fascinated by the pull of ancestry: 'Personal History', written for his son, is as much a family chronicle as it is an introduction to an awareness of history's immensity. And like other poets who have exiled themselves from Scotland he shows a keen awareness of the colours of light and shade in the Scottish countryside.

WORKS: *Proems* (1938); *The Laughing Mulatto* (1939); *Over the Mountain* (1939); *Poets of Tomorrow* (1939); *Ten Poems* (1940); *Until Now* (1942); ed., Alexander Gilchrist, *Life of William Blake* (1942); *Poems for a Penny* (1942); *The Acreage of the Heart* (1943); *The Planet on my Hand* (1944); ed., William Blake, *America, a prophecy* (1947); ed., William Blake, *Poems* (1947); ed., Richard and Samuel Redgrave, *A Century of British Painters* (1947); ed., Christopher Smart, *A Song to David* (1947); *In Other Worlds* (1951); *Love Poems for the New Year* (1951); *Indian Spring* (1954); *A Masterpiece of Shells* (1954); *Indian Pipe* (1955); ed., *Selected Poems of William Blake* (1960); *Funeral of a Child* (1962); *Garland for the Winter Solstice* (1962); *The Geography of Faces* (1964); ed., *Blake's Dante Plates* (1968); *The Lost Traveller* (1968); *John Berryman 1914–1972* (1972); *Lament of the Cats of Rapallo* (1973); *McGonagall Remembers Fitzrovia in the 1930s* (1973)
as R. T. Campbell: *Unholy Dying* (1945); *Take thee a Sharp Knife* (1946); *Adventure with a Goat* (1946); *Bodies in a Bookshop* (1946); *Death for Madame* (1946); *The Death Cap* (1946); *Swing Low Sweet Death* (1946); *Loser's Choice* (1953)

Tranter, Nigel (*b* 1909). Novelist and historian. He was born on 23 November 1909 in Glasgow and was educated in Edinburgh at George Heriot's School. After training as an accountant he became a full-time writer in 1936; he is one of Scotland's most prolific writers with over 100 books to his credit. Among his novels those on Scottish historical subjects stand out, their hallmark being Tranter's knowledge of the events and personalities of Scotland's past. He has written fictionally about many notable characters, including ROBERT I (Robert the Bruce) in a trilogy published between 1969 and 1971. The architecture of Scotland has been his main non-fiction interest and is the subject of *The Fortalices and Early Mansions of Southern Scotland* (1935) and the five-volume *The Fortified House in Scotland* (1962–71). Tranter has also taken an interest in public and political affairs and he has been chairman of the Scottish Committee of International PEN and of the National Book League in Scotland.

WORKS: *The Fortalices and Early Mansions of Southern Scotland* (1935); *Trespass* (1937); *Mammon's Daughter* (1939); *Harsh Heritage* (1940); *Eagles Feathers* (1941); *Watershed* (1941); *The Gilded Fleece* (1942); *Delayed Action* (1944); *Tinkers Pride* (1945); *Man's Estate* (1946); *Flight of Dutchmen* (1947); *Island Twilight* (1947); *Colours Flying* (1948); *Root and Branch* (1948); *The Chosen Course* (1949); *Fair Game* (1950); *The Freebooters* (1950); *High Spirits* (1950); *Tidewrack* (1951); *Bridal Path* (1952); *Cheviot Chase* (1952); *Ducks and Drakes* (1953); *The Queen's Grace* (1953); *The Night Riders* (1954); *Rum Week* (1954); *Rio d'Oro* (1955); *There are Worse Jungles* (1955); *The Long Coffin* (1956); *The Enduring Flame* (1957); *Macgregor's Gathering* (1957); *Balefire* (1958); *Spaniard's Isle* (1958); *The Stone* (1958); *Border Riding* (1959); *The Clansman* (1959); *The Man Behind the Curtain* (1959); *The Flockmaster* (1960); *Nestor the Monster* (1960); *Spanish Galleon* (1960); *Birds of a Feather* (1961); *The Deer Poachers* (1961); *Kettle of Fish* (1961); *The Master of Gray* (1961); *Drug on the Market* (1962); *Gold for Prince Charlie* (1962); *Something Very Fishy* (1962); *The Fortified House in Scotland*, 5 vols. (1962–71); *The Courtesan* (1963); *Give a Dog a Bad Name* (1963); *Chain of Destiny* (1964); *The Pegasus Book of Scotland* (1964); *Silver Island* (1964); *Outlaw of the Highlands* (1965); *Past Master* (1965); *Pursuit* (1965); *A Stake in the Kingdom* (1966); *Fire and High Water* (1967); *Lion Let Loose* (1967); *Tinker Tess* (1967); *Land of the Scots* (1968); *The Steps to the Empty Throne* (1969); *The Path of the Hero King* (1970); *The Price of the King's Peace* (1971); *The Queen's Scotland: the Heartland (Clackmannan, Perth and Stirlingshire)* (1971); *Portrait of the Border Country* (1972); *The Queen's Scotland: the Eastern Counties (Aberdeen, Angus and Kincardineshire)* (1972); *The Young Montrose* (1972); *Montrose: the Captain General* (1973); *The Queen's Scotland: the North-East (Banff, Moray, Nairn, East Inverness and Easter Ross)* (1974); *The Wisest Fool* (1974); *The Wallace* (1975); *Lords of Misrule* (1976); *The Captive Crown* (1977); *A Folly of Princes* (1977); *The Queen's Scotland: Argyll and Bute* (1977); *Macbeth the King* (1978); *Margaret the Queen* (1979); *Portrait of the Lothians* (1979); *David the Prince* (1980); *Nigel Tranter's Scotland* (1981); *True Thomas* (1981)

Tremayne, Sydney (*b* 1912). Poet. He was born on 15 March 1912 and was educated at Ayr Academy. Between 1929 and 1974 he worked as a journalist in England before returning to Scotland to live in Wester Ross. In Tremayne's poetry there is a freshness of observation of natural life and a recognition of man's place in the environment. Typical of his work are poems such as 'Outpost in Winter', 'The Hare' and 'Earth Spirit', which recognize the subtle complexity of man's relationship with nature.

WORKS: *For whom there is no Spring* (1946); *Time and the Wind* (1948); *The Hardest Freedom* (1951); *The Rock and the Bird* (1955); *The Swans of Berwick* (1962); *The Turning Sky* (1969); *Selected and New Poems* (1973)

Tretis of the Tua Mariit Wemen and the Wedo, The. A poem by WILLIAM DUNBAR. *The Tretis* opens and closes with a description of the natural beauty and the sights and sounds of a warm summer's night. After midnight on Midsummer's Night the poet is walking alone when he comes across three high-born ladies, who are known to him, sitting in an arbour drinking wine. They are dressed in bright colours and garlanded with beautiful flowers, but as the wine loosens their tongues they start to discuss their love lives. The poet hides to listen to their stories. The first woman prefers freedom to marriage: she is married to a senile old man and only his wealth binds her to him. The second woman is married to a young man who appears to the world to be a virile lover but is in fact impotent. The widow then prays for heavenly inspiration to help her to tell her story and to correct the values of the two wives, but she too is a dissembler, who has disposed of two husbands: one a cough-ridden packman and the second a wealthy, but down-trodden, merchant. Although she abused her last husband by cuckolding him and attacking his own family, his death allows her to maintain public respectability as a widow, while wearing gay cloths under her mourning and attracting numerous lovers in private. As dawn breaks the women leave their arbour and the poet retires to write down their 'pastance most mery'. Dunbar's poem ends with his asking his audience which woman they would take for a wife: 'quhilk wald ye waill to your wife, gif ye suld wed one?'

The Tretis contains many of the conventions of the *Roman de la rose* and its philosophy of courtly love, in which the love affair is usually adulterous. In that tradition the two married women and the widow could take lovers outside their marriages, but Dunbar is unsympathetic and at times satirical in his description of their behaviour. It is that criticism that has led scholars (T. Scott, *Dunbar: a Critical Exposition of the Poems* (Edinburgh, 1966), pp.206–11) to find in *The Tretis* a satirical attack both on women and the institution of medieval marriage. The poem is written in unrhymed alliterative metre and this looser structure is suited to Dunbar's frank telling of a bawdy story.

Tulloch, John (1823–86). Divine. He was born on 1 June 1823 in Perthshire and was educated in St Andrews at Madras College and the University. After a period as a minister in Dundee, he came to prominence in 1853 with an essay on Theism and he became an influential speaker and writer on the 16th-century Reformation in the Scottish Church. He was later principal of St Mary's College, St Andrews, and Professor of Theology. Among his books are *Leaders of the Reformation* (1859), which contains biographical sketches of Calvin, Luther and JOHN KNOX, *English Puritanism and its Leaders* (1861) and *Rational Theology and Christian Philosophy in England in the Seventeenth Century* (1872), a sympathetic treatment of the Cambridge Platonists. Tulloch was an important figure in the Church of Scotland and an upholder of liberal values; he also contributed many articles on literature, history and philosophy to the leading periodicals and newspapers of his day. He died in Torquay on 13 February 1886 and was buried in the grounds of the Cathedral of St Andrews. A biography, *Memoir of the Life of John Tulloch*, by MARGARET OLIPHANT was published in 1888.

WORKS: *Theism* (1855); *The Light of the World* (1857); *Leaders of the Reformation* (1859); *English Puritanism and its Leaders* (1861); *Beginning Life* (1862); *The Christ of the Gospels* (1864); *Rational Theology and Christian Philosophy in England in the Seventeenth Century* (1872); *Religion and Theology* (1875); *The Christian Doctrine of Sin* (1876); *Pascal* (1878); *Luther and other Leaders of the Reformation* (1883); *Modern Theories in Philosophy and Religion* (1884); *Movements of Religious Thought in Britain* (1885); *Theological Controversy, or The Function of Debate in Theology* (1885); *Sundays at Balmoral* (1887)

REFERENCE: M. Oliphant, *Memoir of the Life of John Tulloch* (London, 1888)

Tusitala. The name given to ROBERT LOUIS STEVENSON by the inhabitants of the Polynesian island of Upolu, Samoa, on which he lived between 1889 and his death in 1894. It means 'Teller of Tales': Polynesian literature and history existed only in the oral tradition and the title was given to Stevenson as a mark of respect for his position in the island community.

Twa Dogs, The. A poem by ROBERT BURNS, completed in February 1786 and placed first in the KILMARNOCK EDITION of his works published in the same year. It belongs to the Scottish tradition of beast fables in which animals take on human characteristics in a comic or mock-heroic style. Written in octosyllabic couplets, 'The Twa Dogs' is a con-

versation between Caesar, a gentleman's dog, and Luath, 'a gash an' faithfu' tyke', in which Burns attacks the ignorance of the wealthy and, especially, their ill treatment of the poor. The poem also contains an unsentimentally realized description of the pleasures of the rustic life.

Tweedsmuir of Elsfield, Lord. *See* BUCHAN, JOHN.

Tyrie, James (1543–97). Divine. A native of Perthshire, he was educated at the University of St Andrews and at Louvain, France, where he joined the Society of Jesus in August 1563. Thereafter he entered the Jesuit college at Clermont where he remained for 25 years, eventually becoming its rector. He died on 20 March 1597 in Rome. A man of piety and learning who was well versed in ecclesiastical history, Tyrie is best remembered in Scotland for his disputation with JOHN KNOX over the indivisibility of the Church. His final answer, written in Scots, was published in 1573 as *The Refutation of ane answer made· by Schir Johne Knox to ane latter send be James Tyrie.* There are sympathetic portraits of Tyrie in the lives of Knox and ANDREW MELVILLE written during the 19th century by THOMAS McCRIE.

EDITION: T. G. Law, ed., *Catholic Tractates of the Sixteenth Century*, STS (Edinburgh and London, 1901)

Tytler, Alexander Fraser, Lord Woodhouselee (1747–1813). Historian. He was born on 15 October 1747 in Edinburgh, the son of WILLIAM TYTLER of Woodhouselee. He was educated at the HIGH SCHOOL OF EDINBURGH and spent two years at an academy in London, before matriculating at the University of Edinburgh. He was called to the Scottish Bar on 23 Janurary 1770 and practised as an advocate, being appointed Judge-Advocate in 1790, and to the Court of Session in 1802, taking the title 'Lord Woodhouselee'. As well as practising law Tytler pursued another career: he was appointed Professor of History at the University of Edinburgh in 1780 and was praised by Lord Cockburn for his 'elegant and judicious' lectures. He published several historical texts and a *History of the Royal Society of Edinburgh* (1787). He was a member of the group of contributors to THE MIRROR and THE LOUNGER, and in later life he published several legal texts, edited a collection of the works of

ALLAN RAMSAY and wrote a life of HENRY HOME, Lord Kames. After his death on 5 January 1813 his youngest son, PATRICK FRASER TYTLER, followed in his footsteps as an eminent historian.

WORKS: *Disputatio juridica* (1769); ed., *Piscatory Eclogues of Phineas Fletcher* (1771); *Plan and Outline of a Course of Lectures on Universal History* (1782); *A History of the Royal Society of Edinburgh* (1787); *Essay on the Principle of Translation* (1797); *Essay on Military Law and the Practice of Courts Martial* (1800); ed., *The Poetical Works of Allan Ramsay* (1800); *Remarks on the Genius and Writings of Allan Ramsay* (1800); *Elements of General History Ancient and Modern* (1801); *Memoirs of the Life and Writings of Henry Home of Kames* (1807); *An Historical and Critical Essay on the Life and Character of Petrarch* (1810); *Considerations on the Present Political State of India* (1815); *Travels in France during the Years 1814–1815* (1816).

Tytler, James ['Balloon'] (?1747–1805). Writer and scientist, commonly known as 'Balloon'. He was born in Brechin, the son of a minister. His education as a medical student at the University of Edinburgh was halted by a lack of funds and he became an apothecary in a shop in Leith. Debt forced him to leave Edinburgh but he returned in 1772 to take up residence in the debtors' sanctuary in Holyrood. There he edited a number of unsuccessful newspapers and journals and worked on the second edition of the ENCYCLOPAEDIA BRITANNICA. His interests turned to ballooning in 1784 and in August that year he became the first man in Britain to navigate a Montgolfier hot-air balloon, reaching a height of 350 feet. Among his literary works are several essays on historical matters and a number of songs in the folk tradition. In 1792 he published a journal, *The Historical Register or Edinburgh Monthly Intelligencer* in which he advocated ideas for parliamentary reform which were in advance of their time. Forced to flee the country, he settled in Salem, Massachusetts, where he died in 1805.

Tytler, Patrick Fraser (1791–1849). Historian. He was born on 30 August 1791 in Edinburgh, the son of ALEXANDER FRASER TYTLER, Lord Woodhouselee, and the grandson of WILLIAM TYTLER. He was educated at the HIGH SCHOOL OF EDINBURGH and at the University, where he studied law, being called to the Scottish Bar in July 1813. Having private means he turned to the life of a man of

letters on his father's estate of Woodhouselee, south of Edinburgh. In 1814 he toured Europe with the historian ARCHIBALD ALISON and his first literary efforts were published in BLACKWOOD'S MAGAZINE. With Sir WALTER SCOTT, he helped to establish the BANNATYNE CLUB, for which he edited one book, *The Memoirs of the War in Scotland and Ireland, 1689–1691*, by Major General Hugh MacKay.

It was Scott who suggested that Tytler should write the *History of Scotland* on which his reputation rests. Although it was attacked by several critics for his high Church stance, Tytler's history demonstrates his sound use of state documents and his unmuddled, analytical mind. The history covers the period from the reign of Alexander III to the Union of the Crowns of Scotland and England in 1603. Tytler was a tireless advocate for the proper care of state papers and it was he who persuaded the government to allow the publication of public records. Among his minor works are a study of JAMES CRICHTON of Cluny, 'THE ADMIRABLE CRICHTON', and *Lives of the Scottish Worthies* (1831–3).

For a time Tytler lived in London and towards the end of his life he travelled on the Continent in pursuit of better health. He died on 24 December 1849 at Malvern and is buried in Greyfriars' Churchyard in Edinburgh.

WORKS: *Life of James Crichton of Cluny* (1819); *An Account of the Life and Writings of Sir Thomas Craig of Riccarton* (1823); *Life of John Wicklyff* (1826); *History of Scotland*, 9 vols. (1828–43); *Lives of the Scottish Worthies*, 3 vols. (1831–3); *A Historical View of the Progress of Discovery of the more Northern Coasts of America* (1832); *Life of Sir Walter Raleigh* (1833); *Life of King Henry VIII* (1837); *England under the Reigns of Edward VI and Mary* (1839); *Memorable Wars of Scotland* (1861)

REFERENCES: J. W. Burgeon, *Memoir of Patrick Fraser Tytler* (Edinburgh, 1859); J. Small, *Biographical Sketch of Patrick Fraser Tytler* (Edinburgh, 1864)

Tytler, Sarah. Pen-name of HENRIETTA KEDDIE.

Tytler, William (1711–92). Historian. He was born on 12 October 1711 in Edinburgh and was educated at the HIGH SCHOOL OF EDINBURGH and the University. He became an accomplished lawyer and was made a WRITER TO THE SIGNET in 1744. He acquired the estates of Woodhouselee to the south of Edinburgh, which were later to become the property of his equally eminent descendants, ALEX-

ANDER FRASER TYTLER and PATRICK FRASER TYTLER. Tytler was a member of the SELECT SOCIETY and through his friendships with that group he became a contributor to THE LOUNGER. But the work that excited the most attention was his spirited defence of MARY, Queen of Scots, in *Inquiry, Historical and Critical into the Evidence against Mary Queen of Scots* (1759). It was reprinted several times and, with the later publication of a supplement on Mary's marriage to Bothwell, marked Tytler as one of the earliest apologists for Mary's life and career; the works earned him much sympathy and respect. In 1783 he published *The Poetical*

Remains of James I, King of Scotland, and he was the discoverer of James's long poem THE KING-IS QUAIR in the Bodleian library, Oxford, although this version was transcribed for him by an Oxford student. Tytler died at the age of 81 and his prescription for longevity has often been quoted: 'short but cheerful meals, music, and a good conscience'.

WORKS: *Inquiry, Historical and Critical into the Evidence against Mary Queen of Scots* (1759); *The Poetical Remains of James I, King of Scotland* (1783); *An Account of the Fashionable Amusements and Entertainments of Edinburgh in the Last Century* (1792)

U

Under the Eildon Tree. A poem of 24 related elegies by SYDNEY GOODSIR SMITH, written in 1948 and revised in 1954. The myth of THOMAS OF ERCELDOUNE binds together the poet's obsessive celebratory contrast of his own passions with those of the world's great lovers: Orpheus and Eurydice, Dido and Aeneas, Burns and Highland Mary. For Smith, love is a complex emotion and the elegies range from the exaltation of consummated passion to the degradation of rejection and despair. The poem is enriched by Smith's feeling for rhythmic balance and by his own energetic sense of humour.

Union, Act of. *See* ACT OF UNION.

Uphalieday. Twelfth Night or Epiphany, the last day of the Christmas festivities. It was celebrated at the Scottish court with plays and pageants; ANE PLEASANT SATYRE OF THE THRIE ESTAITIS by Sir DAVID LYNDSAY was first performed in Linlithgow on Uphalieday 1540.

Up-helly-aa [Aphelli]. A festival to mark the end of YULE, held on the last Tuesday of January in Lerwick, Shetland. It has its origins in the burning of tar barrels which were dragged through the streets of Lerwick. In 1882 a committee was formed to regularize the proceedings, and it introduced the burning of the Norse longship that has come to be the central part of the festival. The burning and the parade that accompanies it are followed by a night of dancing and revelry in the halls of the town under the direction of the Guizer Jarl, the central figure in the ceremony.

Urquhart, Fred (*b* 1912). Novelist. He was born on 12 July 1912 in Edinburgh, the son of a chauffeur. His early childhood was spent there and in Perthshire; between 1921 and 1925 he lived in Wigtownshire and was educated at Stranraer High School. When he was 13 he returned to Edinburgh and after leaving school in 1927 he worked as a bookseller in the city until 1935. Most of Urquhart's life has been spent in the book trade in London: he worked as a literary agent, editor and publisher's reader until he retired in 1974, and he has lived in Sussex since 1955.

Urquhart's first novel, *Time will Knit*, was published in 1938 and it is a thinly disguised autobiographical account of his adolescent years in Edinburgh. It was followed by *The Ferret was Abraham's Daughter* (1949), *Jezebel's Dust* (1951) and *Palace of Green Days* (1979). It is as a short-story writer, though, that he found his true *métier*; his work is notable for his accurate delineation of Scots speech and for his unromantic evocation of country life and manners. His stories have been collected in *The Dying Stallion* (1967) and *The Ploughing Match* (1968). Urquhart's work as an editor is no less noteworthy: he has edited three collections of Scottish short stories: *Scottish Short Stories* (1957); *No Scottish Twilight* (1947), with MAURICE LINDSAY; and *Modern Scottish Short Stories* (1978), with Giles Gordon.

WORKS: *Time will Knit* (1938); *I Fell for a Sailor* (1940); *The Clouds are Big with Mercy* (1946); *Selected Stories* (1946); ed., with Maurice Lindsay, *No Scottish Twilight* (1947); *The Last G.I. Bride Wore Tartan* (1948); *The Ferret was Abraham's Daughter* (1949); *The Year of the Short Corn* (1949); *The Last Sister* (1950); *Jezebel's Dust* (1951); *The Laundry Girl and the Pole* (1955); ed., *Scottish Short Stories* (1957); ed., *W.S.C.: a Cartoon Biography of Winston Churchill* (1955); ed., *The Cassell Miscellany* (1958); *The Dying Stallion* (1967); *The Ploughing Match* (1968); ed., with Giles Gordon, *Modern Scottish Short Stories* (1978); *Palace of Green Days* (1979); *A Diver in China Seas* (1980); *Proud Lady in a Cage* (1980); ed., *The Book of Horses* (1981)

Urquhart, Sir **Thomas** (*c*1611–1660). Man of letters and translator. He was probably born in 1611 in Cromarty, the son of a substantial landowner. He was educated at King's College, Aberdeen, and he spent some years in Europe before returning to Scotland in 1636 in the hope of taking over his father's estate. A devout Episcopalian, he took Charles I's side against the COVENANTERS and fought on the Royalist side at the Battle of Turriff in 1639. His support of the king forced him to flee to London and he was knighted for his services to the Crown on 7 April 1641. While in London he pursued again the classical studies he had begun in Europe, and he published a collection of fashionable aphorisms, *Epigrams: Divine and Moral*, in 1641. The following year his father died, leaving the estate in semi-bankruptcy, but Urquhart returned north to take up residence in the tower of Cromarty; there he wrote *Trissotetras* (1645), a study of trigonometry based on the invention by JOHN NAPIER of logarithms. The coronation of Charles II at Scone in 1651 encouraged Urquhart to take up the Royalist cause again, but after the Battle ofnWorcester (3 September 1651) his estates were forefeited and, after a brief imprisonment, he left for Europe, where he died in 1660, supposedly as the result of an uncontrollable outburst of laughter on hearing of the Restoration.

Despite the loss of his possessions, Urquhart was able to salvage his writings, which consisted of three books, bizarrely titled in Greek: *Pantochronochanon* (1652), in which he fancifully traced his ancestry to a prince of the third century BC, Esormon of Achaia, a 16th-generation descendant of Adam; *Ekskubalauron* (1652), or as it is better known, *The Discoverie of a most Exquisite Jewel*, an attack on the Scottish clergy, which contains the famous essay on the need for a universal language; he returned to these themes in *Logopandecteison* (1653). *The ... Jewel* is perhaps best remembered, though, for Urquhart's ribald, mock-heroic account of his lifelong hero, the soldier–scholar JAMES CRICHTON of Cluny ('THE ADMIRABLE CRICHTON').

The verbal wit that Urquhart employed in his essay on Crichton comes to the fore in the work on which his literary reputation rests, the translation into English of the first three books of *Gargantua and Pantagruel* by François Rabelais (c1494–1553), which were published in three volumes (two in 1653 and a third in 1693). Although he did not attempt to follow faithfully the difficult, and at times obscure, French original, Urquhart entered into the spirit of Rabelais with his own bawdy, colloquial and idiomatic language. For many years Urquhart's was the standard translation and it remains still a monumental work, which amply matches the wit and gusto of Rabelais' original. The first two books were published in 1653 and the third in 1693 after Urquhart's death.

WORKS: *Epigrams: Divine and Moral* (1641); *Trissotetras* (1645); *The Discoverie of a most Exquisite Jewel* (1652); *Pantochronochanon* (1652); *Logopandecteison* (1653); ed., *The Works of Rabelais*, 3 vols. (1653, 1693)

EDITIONS: D. Herd, ed., *Tracts of the Learned and Celebrated Antiquarian Sir Thomas Urquhart* (Edinburgh, 1774); G. Maitland, ed., *The Works of Sir Thomas Urquhart*, Maitland Club (Edinburgh, 1834); R. Boston, ed., *The Admirable Urquhart: Selected Writings* (London, 1975)

REFERENCE: F. C. Roe, *Sir Thomas Urquhart and Rabelais* (Oxford, 1957)

V

Vailima. The estate on the island of Upolu, Samoa, where ROBERT LOUIS STEVENSON lived from the early part of 1890 until his death on 3 December 1894. He purchased it soon after his arrival on the island in December 1889 and a house was built, slowly taking shape to become a substantial dwelling by late 1891, with Stevenson as the paterfamilias of a household that included his wife Fanny, her children, his mother and a changing group of itinerant friends and relations. By the end of his life the estate extended to 400 acres and had been cultivated, with moderate success, to grow cocoa, coffee and vanilla. Vailima took its name from a native word meaning 'five streams' although, in reality, there were only four.

Veitch, John (1829–94). Philosopher and poet. He was born on 24 October 1829 at Peebles, the son of a soldier and veteran of the Peninsular War. He was educated locally and at the University of Edinburgh. At the time of THE DISRUPTION he became a member of the Free Church, and his religious leanings took him next to New College, Edinburgh, to study theology. Veitch was never licensed as a preacher, preferring to keep himself by private tutoring before returning to academic life in 1856 as assistant to Sir WILLIAM HAMILTON (iii), the Professor of Logic and Metaphysics at Edinburgh. In 1860 Veitch was appointed to the Chair of Logic at St Andrews, and then at Glasgow, a post he held until his death on 3 September 1894, dividing his time equally between his place of work and his native Peebles. Although Veitch added little to Scottish philosophy he wrote studies of Hamilton and DUGALD STEWART and he was considered to be one of the last apologists for his Edinburgh mentor.

Veitch was an ardent Borderer, steeped in the history and folklore of his native country, and his verse shows a fine feeling for the sights and sounds of the Border hills and valleys he knew so well. His critical study *The Feeling for Nature in Scottish Poetry* (1887) attempts to provide an all-embracing romantic framework for Scottish nature poetry.

WORKS: *Memoir of Dugald Stewart* (1857); *Memoir of Sir William Hamilton* (1869); *Hillside Rhymes* (1872); *The Tweed and Other Poems* (1875); *Hamilton* (1879); *The Feeling for Nature in Scottish Poetry* (1887); *Knowing and Being* (1889); *Merlin and Other Poems* (1889); *Dualism and Monism* (1895); *Border Essays* (1896)

REFERENCE: M. R. L. Bryde, *Memoir of John Veitch* (Edinburgh, 1896)

W

Walker, Patrick (1666–1745). Biographer. He was a native of Lanarkshire who became an ardent supporter of the COVENANTERS at an early stage in his life. In 1684 he was arrested and taken to Edinburgh, where he was sentenced to deportation to North America but he effected an escape to the south-west, where he joined the CAMERONIANS. With the Revolution Settlement of 1689 and the accession to the throne of William and Mary, Walker's extreme views seem to have moderated and he lived out the rest of his days in Edinburgh. There he became a well-known local figure, and he appears in Scott's novel THE HEART OF MIDLOTHIAN as 'a packman at the Bristo Port'.

For one who kept such a personal record of the events of the Covenanting opposition, very little of Walker's character creeps into his writings, and consequently the facts of his life are shadowy and obscure. His first work, a life of the Covenanter Alexander Peden, appeared in 1724 and he went on to write lives of the other leading Covenanters John Semple, John Welwood, Richard Cameron, Donald Cargill and Walter Smith. Although, as an apologist for his subjects, he paints a highly coloured and partisan view of their lives and acts, there is little doubt that Walker was a good witness of the main actions of the Covenanting opposition. His eye for detail and his ability to summon up whole episodes and conversations give his biographies a vigour and raciness unusual for his times.

EDITION: D. H. Fleming, ed., *Six Saints of the Covenant, Lives of Peden, Semple, Welwood, Cameron, Cargill, Smith, by Patrick Walker*, 2 vols. (London, 1901)

Wallace. A poem by BLIND HARRY in 12 books, running to 11,877 lines, which presents in heroic terms the life of the Scottish patriot Sir WILLIAM WALLACE and the story of his struggle against the English. In relating the history of Scotland's resistance to the English in the 13th and 14th centuries *Wallace* has a similarly patriotic purpose to THE BRUCE by JOHN BARBOUR; it was obviously Harry's intention that Wallace should emerge as a patriot –hero in the same mould as ROBERT I (Robert the Bruce). Although Harry altered historical fact to suit his own literary invention, such as the march to St Albans and the battle at Biggar (both book VI), the poem remains the best source of information about Wallace's life. Harry would have had access to the SCOTICHRONICON of WALTER BOWER and the ORYGYNALE CRONYKIL OF SCOTLAND by ANDREW OF WYNTOUN, but he also mentions a fictitious work in Latin by John Blair, Wallace's schoolfriend: 'He was the man that pryncipall wndirtuk/That fyrst compild in dyt the Latyne buk/Off Wallace lyff.' (book V, 539–41)

The opening books introduce Wallace, the second son of Sir Malcolm Wallace of Elderslie, at the age of 18, the traditional age for heroes to begin their adventures. After his murder of two English soldiers Wallace appears as a fighter of heroic proportions and books III – VI are notable for their vivid and accurate scenes of battle. In book VI Wallace is created Guardian of Scotland, and from that point Harry develops his theme of Wallace, the legendary hero, the patriotic martyr, who has been appointed to save his country from the oppression of the English. Even the reverses that Wallace faces in books IX – XII cannot destroy that image. Towards the end Wallace is a more mature figure, and there is a quiet dignity in his lament for his friend Sir John Graham after the Battle of Falkirk (book XI, 559–82). Book XII recounts Wallace's betrayal by Menteith into the hands of Edward I, but Harry glosses over the facts of Wallace's barbarous execution by the English, preferring instead to concentrate on the hero's saintly demeanour: 'and fair was his endyng,/Quhill spech and spreyt at-anys all can fayr/to lestand blys, we trow, for euirmayr.' (Book XIII, 1404–6)

Wallace is a poem of pride in nationhood and the hero is presented in stylized terms that matched the mood of the old landed gentry's opposition to the pro-English politics of JAMES III. It was written in about 1477 with the encouragement of Harry's friends Sir William Wallace of Craigie, Sir James Liddale of Creich and Master John Blair, minister of Maybole in Ayrshire, who may have been included in the poem as the 'author' of the 'Latyne buk'. The poem existed in a single manuscript copy of 1488 by John Ramsay; it was printed by WALTER CHAPMAN and Andrew Myllar in 1509 and a revised edition, *The Actis and Deidis of Schir William Wallace*, was printed by ROBERT LEKPREVIK in 1570. It became one of the most enduringly popular of the early Scottish poems and in 1722 an anglicized version was published by WILLIAM HAMILTON (i) of Gilbertfield. Its publication influenced in later years ROBERT BURNS, JAMES HOGG and William Wordsworth (1770–1850); *see Prelude*, 1, 214–20. It was edited for the SCOTTISH TEXT SOCIETY by Matthew P. McDiarmid as *Hary's Wallace* (1968–9).

Wallace, Sir William (*c* 1270–1305). Scottish patriot. He was the second son of Sir Malcolm Wallace of Elderslie in Renfrewshire. He became involved with Sir Andrew de Moray in the resistance against Edward I of England whose army they defeated at the Battle of Stirling Bridge on 11 September 1297. Wallace's subsequent capture of Berwick and his raids into northern England confirmed his position as a leader and by 1298 he had been knighted and created Guardian of Scotland by John Balliol. His success was short-lived as he lacked the support of the nobility and on 11 July 1298 he was defeated by Edward at the Battle of Falkirk. Following the collapse of the resistance against the English, Wallace was taken to London, tried as a traitor and barbarously executed on 23 August 1305. Wallace succeeded as a military strategist by using guerilla tactics, and his struggle for Scottish freedom from the administration of Edward I made him a national hero. Many of the facts of his life come from WALLACE, a long poem by BLIND HARRY.

Wandering Willie's Tale. The story told by the blind fiddler, William Steenson, in *Redgauntlet* (1824) by Sir WALTER SCOTT, concerning his grandsire's relationship to the house of Redgauntlet. Prevented, by Sir Robert Redgauntlet's death, from obtaining a receipt for his rents, Steenie Steenson is lured by a stranger into a haunted chamber in Redgauntlet Castle. There he meets a ghostly Sir Robert and other spectres and manages to claim his receipt and to preserve the sanctity of his own soul. *Wandering Willie's Tale* is a flawless supernatural short story in its own right, but it is also integrated into the central theme of *Redgauntlet*, the symbolic journey of Darsie Latimer to discover his own destiny and to retrieve his legal rights.

Wardlaw [née Halket], **Elizabeth,** Lady (1677–1727). Poet. She was born in April 1677 in Fife, the daughter of Sir Charles Halket of Pitfarraine. On 13 June 1696 she married Sir Henry Wardlaw of Pitcruivie. Lady Wardlaw is best remembered as the supposed author of the ballad 'Hardyknute', which she claimed to have discovered as a fragment in a vault in Dunfermline. It was published in 1719 as a traditional ballad and in 1724 ALLAN RAMSAY published it in THE EVER GREEN. The authenticity of the ballad was called into question in 1765 when it appeared in *Reliques of Ancient English Poetry* by Bishop Thomas Percy (1729–1811), and the controversy gave rise to false speculation that Lady Wardlaw might also have reworked the ballad 'Sir Patrick Spens'.

Watson, James (*d* 1722). Publisher. He was born in Aberdeen, the son of Charles II's printer in Scotland. On his father's death in 1695 he expanded the family business, which occupied premises opposite St Giles in Edinburgh, and soon established a reputation as an accurate and elegant printer with interests in Scottish literature and contemporary affairs. He published the *Edinburgh Gazette* and was the printer of the *Edinburgh Courant*, but much of his life was spent in defending his printing monopoly against the claims of the widow of Andrew Anderson the former Royal Printer; in 1700 he was imprisoned for printing a pamphlet, *Scotland's Grievance Respecting Darien*, which attacked the English government's attitude to the DARIEN SCHEME.

Watson's art as a printer reached its zenith in the publication of his *History of the Art of*

Printing (1713), but Watson is best remembered for the publication in three parts of the CHOICE COLLECTION OF COMIC AND SERIOUS SCOTS POEMS (1706, 1709, 1711). The anthology included a mixture of traditional songs, the work of the makars and contemporary poetry. Watson's intention was to provide a wide range of material on which a Scottish literary tradition could be based; his motives were both nostalgic and patriotic, in response to his nationalistic feelings about the 1707 ACT OF UNION. The *Choice Collection* remained a standard work and was later emulated by ALLAN RAMSAY in THE TEA-TABLE MISCELLANY, DAVID HERD in ANCIENT AND MODERN SCOTTISH SONGS and Sir WALTER SCOTT in THE MINSTRELSY OF THE SCOTTISH BORDER.

WORKS: ed., *Choice Collection of Comic and Serious Scots Poems both Ancient and Modern*, 3 vols. (1706–11); *Specimens of Types* (1706); *The History of the Art of Printing* (1713); *Rules and Directions to be Observed in Printing Houses* (1721)

REFERENCE: J. S. Gibb, *James Watson: Printer, Notes of his Life and Work, with a Hand-list of Books and Pamphlets Printed by him* (Edinburgh, 1896)

Watson, John ['Ian Maclaren'] (1850–1907). Novelist. He was born on 3 November 1850 in Manningtree, Essex, the son of a Receiver of Taxes. In 1854 the family went to Scotland to live in Perth, where Watson received his early education and a solid grounding in the evangelical beliefs of the tightly knit family circle. Between 1862 and 1872 he was educated at Stirling High School, the University of Edinburgh and at the Free Church of Scotland's New College in Edinburgh. His career as a minister in the Free Church was distinguished: in 1873 he was called to the parish of Logiealmond in Perthshire, and between 1877 and 1880 he was in Glasgow, but most of his life was spent as minister in Sefton Park, Liverpool, where he took a leading part in the establishment of University College, later the University of Liverpool. His public church duties included the Presidency of the National Free Church Council and he played an important role in the foundation of Westminster College, Cambridge; his appointment as Principal was to have been ratified on the day of his death, 6 May 1907; he died while he was on a lecture tour of America.

Watson wrote several contentious religious tracts placing Christ as the centre of theology and preaching: *The Mind of the Master* (1896),

The Life of the Master (1901) and *The Doctrines of Grace* (1900) enjoyed the widest circulation. But he is best known as 'Ian Maclaren', the creator of *Beside the Bonnie Brier Bush* (1894), a collection of sentimental rural sketches, or 'Idylls' as Watson preferred to call them. Immensely popular in their day, the idylls follow the lives and hopes of the people of Drumtochty, an idealized Scottish village that was probably based on Watson's charge at Logiealmond. There is no central narrative thread and the stories unfold in the lengthy conversations of the villagers as they touch on subjects ranging from the trivial to the sanctimonious. Although Watson strove to find a sincere means of expressing a community's attitude to divinity, too many of his sketches border on the ludicrous with their elegiac themes and preoccupation with death: a gifted boy dies 'beside the bonnie brier bush' of the title. Further idylls, equally mawkish and imbued with the spirit of the 'kirkyard', appeared in *The Days of Auld Lang Syne* (1895) and in *Afterwards and Other Stories* (1899). His novel of life in Drumtochty, *Kate Carnegie and those Ministers* (1896) belongs, as do the 'idylls', to the KAILYARD school of rural sentimentality. He also published some sketches of Glasgow life in *St Jude's* (1907).

Watson was a popular and gifted preacher and public speaker, and between 1896 and 1907 he gave three lecture tours of North America, where his books were equally successful. WILLIAM ROBERTSON NICOLL, who first encouraged Watson to write the Drumtochty stories, published a memoir in 1908.

WORKS: *The Order of Service for Young People* (1895); *The Cure of Souls* (1896); *The Mind of the Master* (1896); *The Upper Room* (1896); *Companions of the Sorrowful Way* (1898); *The Potter's Wheel* (1898); *Doctrines of Grace* (1900); *The Life of the Master* (1901); *Homely Virtues* (1903); *The Inspiration of Our Faith* (1905); *The Scot of the Eighteenth Century* (1907); *God's Message to the Human Soul* (1907); as Ian Maclaren: *Beside the Bonnie Brier Bush* (1894); *The Days of Auld Lang Syne* (1895); *A Doctor of the Old School* (1895); *Kate Carnegie and those Ministers* (1896); *Afterwards and Other Stories* (1899); *Rabbi Saunderson* (1899); *Church Folks* (1901); *Young Barbarians* (1901); *His Majesty Baby, and some Common People* (1902); *St Jude's* (1907); *Graham of Claverhouse* (1908)

Watson, Robert (c1730–81). Historian. He was Professor of History at the University of St Andrews and became its Principal in 1777, the year he published the book for which he is best remembered, *The History of Philip II of Spain*. It was translated into several European languages and remained a standard work until it was superseded by William Hickling Prescott's *History of the Reign of Philip II King of Spain* (1855).

WORKS: *History of the Reign of Philip II* (1777); *History of the Reign of Philip III* (1793)

Watson, Roderick (*b* 1943). Poet. Roderick Watson was born on 12 May 1943 in Aberdeen and was educated at the Grammar School and the University before undertaking post-graduate work at Peterhouse, Cambridge, between 1966 and 1969. Since 1971 he has taught at the University of Stirling. He has written on the poetry of Hugh MacDiarmid (CHRISTOPHER MURRAY GRIEVE), the subject of his research, and this has had a profound effect on his own work; the influence may be felt especially in a poem such as 'True History on the Walls', where family history is balanced with a historical perspective.

WORKS: with James Rankin, *28 Poems* (1964); *Poems* (1970); with Valerie Simmons and Paul Mills, *Trio* (1971); ed., with Maurice Lindsay and Alexander Scott, *Scottish Poetry 7–9* (1974–6); *True History on the Walls* (1976); *Hugh MacDiarmid* (1976); with Martin Gray, *The Penguin Book of the Bicycle* (1978)

Watt, William (1793–1859). Poet and songwriter. He was a native of East Kilbride, a village near Glasgow. After a rudimentary education he became a handloom weaver and his life was destined to be a long struggle against illness and poverty. He married in 1832 and reared a large family, and it was to support them that he turned to publishing in broadsides the songs that he had written as a young man. For the most part they are simple, artless compositions, suffused with a homely sentimentality and taking romantic and patriotic themes as their subject. His poems, published in 1835 and 1844, are scarcely better but he will be remembered for his lively delicately rhymed comic song *Kate Dalrymple*. Watt died in poverty on 26 April 1859.

EDITION: *Poems on Sacred and Other Subjects, and Songs Humorous and Sentimental* (Glasgow, 1860)

Waverley. The first of the novels of Sir WALTER SCOTT, published anonymously in 1814, with the subtitle ''Tis Sixty Years Since'. Scott had begun it several years earlier and it was completed during the summer of 1813 while he was in residence at ABBOTSFORD. It at once

displayed the duality of Scott's attitude towards Scotland's history: on the one hand he believed in the solid Hanoverian virtues of the Union, on the other he maintained a romantic attachment to Jacobitism and a nostalgia for the past. Against that background he mingled fictional people with historical events and personalities to build up a comprehensive picture of the past. Edward Waverley, a romantically inclined British army officer, is stationed in Scotland in 1745. While visiting the Baron Bradwardine, a Jacobite sympathizer and a friend of his uncle, Waverley attracts the attention of the baron's daughter Rose. But events take him north to meet two Highland warriors, Donald Bean Lean and Fergus Mac Ivor Vich Ian Vohr; he falls in love with Fergus's sister Flora, and owing to mounting suspicion within his regiment about his political sympathies, Waverley is cashiered and throws in his lot with the Jacobite cause of Prince CHARLES EDWARD STUART. At the Battle of Prestonpans his chivalrous behaviour to the English Colonel Talbot earns Waverley's pardon, and he returns to the Hanoverian fold, renounces the Jacobite cause and having been rejected by Flora marries Rose who has remained constant to him.

As was to prove typical of Scott's fiction, the minor characters are no less interesting, both for their observations on the central action and for the richness of their spoken Scots, than the principals. Among their number in *Waverley*, the following are particularly memorable: Duncan Macwheeble, Bradwardine's factor; the Laird of Balmawhapple who quarrels with Waverley; and David Gellatly, the 'half-crazed simpleton', into whose mouth Scott placed such beautiful lyrics as 'False love and hast thou played me 'thus', based on a traditional song, and 'Young men will love thee more fair and more fast', the words of which hint at Bradwardine's part in beating the Laird of Balmawhapple on Waverley's behalf. *Waverley* is one of Scott's most assured novels with a secure plot structure and a careful linking of fantasy to historical reality. Several of his later novels, until the secret of his authorship was made public in 1827, were inscribed 'by the author of Waverley'. Scott's historical novels as a group came to be known as 'the Waverley novels'.

Wealth of Nations, The. The shorter title to Adam Smith's treatise on political economy, *An Inquiry into the Nature and Causes of the*

Wealth of Nations, which was published in 1776. It was composed in the years following Smith's return from France in 1766 and it was influenced by his meetings in Paris with Jacques Turgot (1721–81), a leading member of the school of Physiocrats, who believed in free-market practices and that the land was the only source of wealth. Smith's work falls into five parts, each of which deals with particular economic issues. Part I discusses the theory of price and postulates wages, rent and profit as being the determination of its value. Part II deals with capital, its accumulation, and its disposal for the greater benefit of society. Part III is a history of economics in western Europe. Part IV is a detailed attack on mercantilism and provides the main thrust of Smith's advocacy of free trade as being the best means of increasing man's wealth. And Part V is a discussion of the optimum extent of the state's involvement in different aspects of public life, such as defence, the law and administration.

So that his economic analysis might not appear too obscure, Smith offered a series of 'curious facts' written in plain language to help his readers to grasp his argument readily. As a result, the book made an immediate impact and may be said to have marked the beginning of modern political economy. Smith's advocacy of free trade, and his views that government should not interfere in the market-place and that prosperity owes its existence to man's dynamic need to better himself underpinned British government thinking throughout the 19th century and became the lode-star of Victorian capitalism. The range of Smith's thinking and his ability to provide an analysis reinforced by hard fact make *The Wealth of Nations* the single most influential work in the early history of British economics. Its impact was felt until the 20th century when the government was forced to intervene in the nation's economy with the very kind of controls and restrictions Smith had condemned.

Wedderburn. Three brothers, James (*d* 1553), John (*d* 1556) and Robert (*d* 1557), who were responsible for the compilation and collection of the sacred and secular songs and ballads in the work commonly known as the GUDE AND GODLIE BALLATIS. They were natives of Dundee where their father was a prosperous merchant, and all studied at St Leonard's College in St Andrews, where they gained their first interest in the aims of the Reformation move-

ment. James spent some time in Dieppe and Rouen, working for his father, and on his return to Dundee he acquired a reputation for his construction of mystery play on the beheading of John the Baptist, and a comedy *Dionysius the Tyrant*, which were performed regularly in the city. The spirited attacks on the Catholic Church which informed both plays and James's increasingly reckless assaults on the clergy and on spiritual corruption within the Church led to his banishment to Rouen where he died in 1553.

John had been a friend of the martyr Patrick Hamilton (1504–28) and was an early recruit to the group of reformers which was centred on St Andrews. Like his older brother he too was forced into exile for his beliefs, and lived for a time with the Protestant community at Wittenberg in Germany before returning to Scotland during the regency of the Earl of Arran.

Robert, the youngest brother, was the most distinguished scholar of the trio and although he became a priest, his growing impatience with the Church and its stubbornness in the face of reform meant that he too was forced to take the path of exile. In all probability he spent much of the rest of his life in the company of his brother John. Recent scholarship has proved that Robert was the author of THE COMPLAYNT OF SCOTLAND, one of the most important early prose works in Scots.

The book for which they are best known, the *Gude and Godlie Ballatis*, was mainly the work of John and Robert, who had access to German vernacular translations of Latin hymns and psalms. The compilation was completed by John but it was not published until 1567 after all three brothers were dead. The inclusion of secular ballads and satirical songs was probably the work of James. According to the historian DAVID CALDERWOOD parts of the book were extant and in general use long before the work was published in its entirety.

EDITION: A. F. Mitchell, ed., *A Compendious Book of Godly and Spiritual Songs*, STS (Edinburgh and London, 1897)

Weekly Magazine, or Edinburgh Amusement, The. A magazine founded and edited by WALTER RUDDIMAN and first published on 7 July 1768. It was the first weekly journal to appear in Scotland and it continued in being until 10 June 1784 with only one break, for a year between 11 July 1782 and 3 July 1783. Each week it provided a news digest, articles on a variety of literary and scientific subjects and poetry, and within a year of its first publication it had become the premier journal in Scotland. In 1777, to avoid payment of the stamp duty enforced on newspapers, the news digest was published separately as *Ruddiman's Weekly Mercury*. By far the most enduring contributor to *The Weekly Magazine* was ROBERT FERGUSSON whose poems were published from February 1771 to December 1773.

Weir of Hermiston. An uncompleted novel by ROBERT LOUIS STEVENSON, on which he was engaged at the time of his death in 1894. The fragment was published in 1896 with an editorial note by Sidney Colvin summarizing the subsequent story as Stevenson had planned it. His notes came from Mrs Strong, Stevenson's step-daughter and amanuensis, and from Sydney Lysaght, with whom Stevenson had discussed the novel. The central character is Adam Weir, Lord Hermiston, the Lord Justice Clerk and a 'hanging judge', whom Stevenson based on the 18th-century judge ROBERT MACQUEEN, Lord Braxfield. Weir's wife, whom he has terrorized throughout their married life, dies young, leaving a delicate son, Archie, to a far from tender upbringing. Archie loathes and fears his father and is repelled by the aggressive manner in which he bullies a prisoner, Duncan Jopp, before sentencing him to death. Archie attacks his father in public and is ordered to remove himself to the family's Border seat of Hermiston. There his companion is Kirstie, the housekeeper, through whom he meets and falls in love with her niece Christina (young Kirstie) Elliot, sister to the 'Black Elliot' brothers, who are heirs to the old Border reivers. Archie is warned off a close involvement with Christina by Kirstie and by a house guest, his friend and fellow advocate Frank Innes. The fragment ends with Archie giving grave offence to Christina by telling her that the relationship must come to an end. From Stevenson's notes it would seem that the plot was to have unfolded through Frank Innes's seduction of Christina, blame falling on Archie who murders Innes in a duel. The process of the law sees Archie arrested, tried and sentenced to death by his own father, only to be saved by the Black Elliots and allowed to emigrate to America with Christina. The strain of the proceedings overwhelms Lord Hermiston who collapses and dies.

Although there are serious flaws in the summary, it is obvious that Stevenson's plot would have led to a final confrontation between Archie and his father and that capital punishment was to have been an issue. Lord Hermiston is a monstrous creation whose mocking relationship with his sensitive son is awesomely portrayed by Stevenson, writing at the height of his powers, especially in the scene of confrontation between father and son after Jopp's execution.

Whistle-binkie. *Whistle-binkie, or The Paper of the Party, being a Collection of Songs for the Social Circle* was a series of collections of sentimental poems and songs published in 1832, 1853, 1878 and 1890 by David Robertson of Glasgow. Most of the work was mawkishly pathetic and resounded with the sentimentality into which Scots vernacular verse had sunk in the mid and late 19th century. Among the contributors were ALEXANDER RODGER, JAMES BALLANTINE and WILLIAM THOM, and the collections enjoyed a wide popularity in Scotland for their simple, easily remembered rhyming poems and songs, the best known of which was the nursery rhyme 'Wee Willie Winkie' by William Miller (1810–72). The *Scottish National Dictionary* takes the derivation of 'whistle-binkie' from Jamieson's *Etymological Dictionary of the Scottish Language*: 'one who attends a penny-wedding but without paying anything, and therefore has no right to take any share of the entertainment; a mere spectator, who is, as it were left to sit on a bench by himself, and who, if he pleases, may whistle for his own amusement'. But it is also suggested by Charles Mackay, a friend of Robertson (*Through the Long Day* (London, 1877)), that the derivation is from Gaelic: *Duine uasal* 'a gentleman' and *beannachaidh* 'a blessing', thus, 'the blessing given to the newly wedded couple by the superior or chief'.

Whyte-Melville, George John (1821–78). Novelist and poet. He was born on 19 January 1821 in Strathkinness, Fife. He was educated at Eton and in 1839 he received a commission in the 93rd Highlanders, transferring later to the Coldstream Guards. During the Crimean War he commanded a regiment of Turkish irregular cavalry and retired with the rank of major. Whyte-Melville devoted most of his life to the pursuits of a country gentleman and the best of his 28 novels deal with his first love, hunting; in all his work there is an emphasis on aristocratic manners and chivalry. *The Queen's Maries* (1862) is a serious attempt to deal, fictionally, with the story of MARY, Queen of Scots, and her ladies-in-waiting (*see* THE QUEEN'S MARIES). After the breakdown of his marriage in 1847 Whyte-Melville lived in Gloucestershire and he was killed in a hunting accident on 5 December 1878.

WORKS: *Tilbury Nogo* (1854); *Kate Coventry* (1856); *The Arab's Ride to Cairo* (1857); *The Interpreter* (1858); *General Bounce* (1860); *Holmby House* (1860); *Good for Nothing* (1861); *Market Harborough* (1861); *The Queen's Maries* (1862); *The Gladiators* (1863); *The Brookes of Bridlemere* (1864); *Cerise* (1866); *The White Rose* (1867); *Bones and I* (1868); *Songs and Verses* (1869); *Contraband* (1871); *Sarchedon* (1871); *Satanella* (1872); *The True Cross* (1873); *Uncle John* (1873); *Katerfelto* (1875); *Sister Louise* (1876); *Rosine* (1877); *Digby Grand* (1878); *Riding Recollections* (1878); *Roy's Wife* (1878); *Black but Comely* (1879)

Wilkie, Sir David (1785–1841). Artist. The son of the minister of Cults, Fife, he was educated locally and at the Trustees' Academy, Edinburgh, between 1799 and 1804. He moved to London in 1805 and although he worked as a portrait painter he began a series of other works – those for which he is best known – the intricately detailed depictions of social life in Scottish country villages such as *The Village Politicians* (1809) and *The Penny Wedding* (1818). In 1807 Wilkie met JOHN GALT, whose writing was much influenced by Wilkie's fine delineation of Scottish character and landscape. One of the most popular painters of his day, Wilkie became the King's Limner in Scotland in 1823 and the King's Painter in Ordinary in England in 1830. He was knighted in 1836. His paintings of Scottish rural life and character and those touching on historical subjects place him in the same rank as Galt and Sir Walter Scott for recording the life of a bygone Scotland.

Wilkie, William (1721–72). Poet, who was nick-named the 'Scottish Homer'. He was born on 5 October 1721 at Dalmeny, the son of a farmer. He was educated at the University of Edinburgh but was forced to leave without taking a degree when his father died. Despite that drawback Wilkie continued his studies alone and was rewarded by being licenced as a preacher in the Church of Scotland on 29 May 1745. His first charge was at Linlithgow, but he was able to secure the patronage of the Earl of

Lauderdale eight years later, and he was given the sole living of the parish of Ratho in Midlothian. There he was able to pursue his various intellectual interests but he grew into something of an eccentric and his abstracted style of preaching commended itself to neither congregation nor patron. In 1759 he moved to the more congenial ambience of the University of St Andrews as Professor of Natural Philosophy and it was in that city that he died on 10 October 1772.

Wilkie owes his sobriquet to his long poem *The Epigoniad*, written in heroic couplets and based on the fourth book of the *Iliad*. It scarcely earns Wilkie the title of Homer, but he was highly esteemed during his lifetime and the nickname stuck more out of respect for his learning than for the qualities of the poem. More successful and enduring are his animal fables of 1768 which include 'The Hare and the Partan', a poem in commendable Scots, much admired by ROBERT FERGUSSON who was Wilkie's student at St Andrews.

WORKS: *The Epigoniad* (1757); *Fables* (1768)

Williams, Gordon ['P. B. Yuill'] (*b* 1934). Novelist. He was born on 20 June 1934 in Paisley, the son of a policeman. He left school when he was 15 and became a reporter with the local newspaper; between 1952 and 1954 he carried out his National Service with the Royal Air Force. On returning to civilian life he became a journalist again and after the success of his early novels he settled in London as a full-time writer. With Terry Venables he writes popular television crime fiction series under the name 'P. B. Yuill'.

Many of Williams's novels are autobiographical, reflecting aspects of his own life and experience. *From Scenes Like These* (1968) is a vividly realized portrayal of a working-class boyhood in the west of Scotland, and *The Upper Pleasure Garden* (1970) accurately summons up the atmosphere of the rootlessness of provincial life. But it would be unfair to Williams to see his work merely as visions of his own experience. In *From Scenes Like These* the hero Duncan Logan is disfigured by the drunkenness and mindless violence that characterizes his boyhood, and realizes ultimately that there can be no escape for him and no outlet for his talents. The analysis of violence in terms of the Scottish urban experience and the novel's study of moral degeneration is typical of the Scottish fiction of the 1960s; but it was the last of Williams's novels set in Scotland.

London became the focus of his attention in *Big Morning Blues* (1974), and his most successful novel to date, *Walk Don't Walk* (1977), records an absurdly picaresque tour round America by a best-selling British novelist. In it, the wry humour that had never been far below the surface in the early novels explodes in a series of ribald episodes and bizarre happenings all related in a fast-moving, hilarious narrative. With his acute sense of observation and depth of characterization, Gordon Williams is rightly considered the most innovatory of the post-war Scottish novelists.

WORKS: *Last Day of Lincoln Charles* (1965); *The Camp* (1966); *The Man Who had Power over Women* (1967); *From Scenes Like These* (1968); *The Siege of Trencher's Farm* (1969); *The Upper Pleasure Garden* (1970); with Terry Venables, *They Used to Play on Grass* (1971); *Big Morning Blues* (1974); *The Duellists* (1977); *The Straw Dogs* (1977); *Walk Don't Walk* (1977)

Wilson, Sir Daniel (1816–92). Historian. He was born on 2 June 1812 in Edinburgh and was educated at the HIGH SCHOOL OF EDINBURGH and the University. After graduating he worked in London but he returned to Edinburgh in 1842. He was appointed Professor of History and English Literature at Toronto University in 1853 and lived in Canada until his death on 6 August 1892. He was knighted for his services to education in 1888 and in Canada he is remembered as a reformer of the country's universities and as an upholder of non-denominational education. Wilson's most lasting work was on the antiquities of his native city: his *Memorials of Edinburgh in Olden Times* (1847) is a meticulously documented history which he illustrated with his own sketches; his other work of importance on that subject is his *Reminiscences of Old Edinburgh* (1878). He also wrote among other critical works a study (1869) of Thomas Chatterton (1752–70) and *The Archaeology and Prehistoric Annals of Scotland* (1851).

WORKS: *Memorials of Edinburgh in Olden Times*, 2 vols. (1847, rev. 2/1891); *Oliver Cromwell and the Protectorate* (1848); *The Archaeology and Prehistoric Annals of Scotland* (1851); *Prehistoric Man* (1862); *Prehistoric Annals of Scotland* (1863); *Chatterton* (1869); *Caliban: the Missing Link* (1873); *The Present State and Future Prospects of the Indians of British North America* (1874); *Spring Wild Flowers* (1875); *Reminiscences of Old Edinburgh* (1878); *William Nelson: a Memoir* (1889); *The Lost Atlantis* (1892)

Wilson, John (i) (1720–89). Poet. He was born on 30 June 1720 at Lesmahagow in Lanarkshire. He showed an early aptitude for learning at the parish school and on the death of his father in 1734 he took up a long and ultimately successful career in teaching in order to maintain his family. However, his interest in poetry, which had flowered at the same time, proved to be a barrier to progress and he was only offered an appointment at Greenock Grammar School on condition that he abandon 'the profane and unprofitable art of poem-making'. His appearance before the school authorities is the subject of an elegant poem in heroic couplets written by Douglas Dunn: 'John Wilson in Greenock 1786' (*St Kilda's Parliament* (1981)). His best-known work and one that belies the strictures of the school's managers is *The Clyde*, a long descriptive poem, in Romantic mood, portraying the River Clyde and its surrounding countryside. He died on 2 June 1789 at Greenock.

WORKS: *Earl Douglas, or Generosity Betrayed* (1764); *The Clyde* (1764)

Wilson, John (ii) (1754–1821). Printer, active in Kilmarnock. He published *Poems, Chiefly in the Scottish Dialect*, by ROBERT BURNS, known also as the KILMARNOCK EDITION. The book sold out within a month but caution led Wilson to abandon plans for a second edition, which was later brought out by the Edinburgh publisher WILLIAM CREECH. Wilson also published the poems of JOHN LAPRAIK and the earliest Ayrshire newspaper, the *Ayrshire Advertiser*.

Wilson, John (iii) ['Christopher North'] (1785–1854). Novelist, poet and editor. He was born on 18 May 1785 in Paisley, Renfrewshire. His father was a wealthy gauze manufacturer and his mother, Margaret Sym, was a descendant of JAMES GRAHAM, Marquis of Montrose. Wilson was privately educated by a Church of Scotland minister in the neighbouring parish of Mearns and, on the death of his father in 1795, at the University of Glasgow. Between 1803 and 1807 he was a Gentleman-Commoner at Magdalen College, Oxford, where he won the Newdigate Prize for Poetry in 1806 and gained a reputation as a prodigious athlete. A well-built, burly man, Wilson retained a lifelong interest in walking tours and athletic pursuits.

On his graduation Wilson moved to his small estate of Elleray in the Lake District, which he had bought with his patrimony; during his time in the country he was a close associate and friend of the Wordsworths and Thomas de Quincey. In 1811 he married Jane Penny, the daughter of a Liverpool merchant, but three years later he lost the greater part of his fortune owing to his uncle's mismanagement of the estate. He was forced to take up residence with his family in Edinburgh where he was admitted to the FACULTY OF ADVOCATES.

Wilson started writing poetry during his period at Elleray; his work was palely derivative of the Lake school and in 1812 he published his first collection, *Isle of Palms and Other Poems*. Although the volume attracted some attention when it was published, the title poem, which tells the story of a young couple shipwrecked in a pastoral, pre-Satanic Eden, is overlong and cloyed with vapid sentimentality. This was followed in the same year by *The Magic Mirror*, which was addressed to Sir Walter Scott, and in 1816 Wilson published a third long poem, *The City of the Plague*.

Despite their weaknesses, the two 1812 publications gained for Wilson a reputation in Edinburgh's literary society; his acquaintance with WILLIAM BLACKWOOD led to his becoming an intimate of Blackwood's saloon at 17 Princes Street, where he met, among others, JOHN GIBSON LOCKHART, who was also studying law. In October 1817 he joined with Lockhart and JAMES HOGG in editing the first issue of BLACKWOOD'S MAGAZINE, which contained the notorious 'CHALDEE MANUSCRIPT' and critical attacks on Leigh Hunt. Although Wilson was forced to flee temporarily to Elleray in the ensuing uproar he continued to be a contributing editor to *Blackwood's*; he wrote several notable series, such as the 'NOCTES AMBROSIANAE', between 1822 and 1835, in which he took the persona of 'Christopher North', and 'Lights and Shadows of Scottish Life' (collected 1822), stories of country life which are precursors of the KAILYARD school of rural sentimentality. He published two novels, *The Trials of Margaret Lyndsay* (1823) and *The Foresters* (1825); both are celebrations of the intelligently pious peasantry and its progress from squalor and tribulation to an innocent, earthly paradise.

Wilson's influence on *Blackwood's Magazine* was considerable and he used his editorial powers to promote high Tory politics and an idyllic, parochial simplicity in literature. His feelings towards his friends and fellow contributors were ambiguous, especially towards James Hogg whom he would praise in one issue and then lampoon in the next.

In 1820 Wilson was appointed to the Chair of Moral Philosophy at the University of Edinburgh, in succession to Dr THOMAS BROWN; his election being due to the pro-Tory Town Council who made all professional appointments. Lacking any formal qualifications, Wilson relied on notes supplied by his friend from Glasgow days, Alexander Blair, who was Professor of Rhetoric and Belles Lettres at University College, London, between 1831 and 1834, and on the strength of his own eloquent rhetoric. He held the post until 1851, when ill health forced him to retire, and he died on 3 April 1854. His eldest daughter, Margaret Ann, married the nephew of SUSAN EDMONSTOUNE FERRIER, JAMES FREDERICK FERRIER, who edited his father-in-law's works; his youngest daughter, Jane Emily, married WILLIAM EDMONSTOUNE AYTOUN, Professor of Rhetoric and Belles Lettres in the University of Edinburgh.

WORKS: *A Recommendation of the Study of the Remains of Ancient Grecian and Roman Architecture Sculpture and Painting* (1807); *Lines Sacred to the Memory of the Rev. James Grahame* (1811); *The Isle of Palms and Other Poems* (1812); *The Magic Mirror* (1812); *The City of the Plague* (1816); *Lights and Shadows of Scottish Life* (1822); *The Trials of Margaret Lyndsay* (1823); *The Foresters* (1825); *Poems* (1825); with John Gibson Lockhart, *Janus, or the Edinburgh Literary Almanack* (1826); *Blind Allan* (1840); *The Land of Burns* (1840); *The Recreations of Christopher North* (1842); *The Noctes Ambrosianae*, 4 vols. (1843); *Scotland Illustrated* (1845); *Specimens of the British Critics by Christopher North* (1846); *Essays Critical and Imaginative*, 4 vols. (1866)

EDITION: J. F. Ferrier, ed., *The Works of Professor Wilson*, 12 vols. (Edinburgh, 1855–8)

REFERENCES: M. Gordon, *A Memoir of Christopher North*, 2 vols. (Edinburgh, 1862); E. Swann, *Christopher North* (Edinburgh and London, 1934)

Wingate, David (1828–92). Poet. He was the son of a Hamilton coalminer and followed his father into the pits at an early age in childhood. By attending evening classes he rose in life to become a colliery manager and was able to retire early to devote himself to writing. His poems and songs enjoyed a huge following in his day; with their homespun sentiments, religious motifs and artless rhymes they have long since been forgotten. Many of them were published in BLACKWOOD'S MAGAZINE, to which Wingate was a regular contributor.

WORKS: *Poems and Songs* (1862); *Annie Weir* (1866); *Lily Neil* (1879); *Poems and Songs* (1883); *Selected Poems* (1890)

Winzet, Ninian (c1518–1592). Religious propagandist. He was a Renfrew man who was probably educated at the University of Glasgow. He was ordained in 1540 and later became a master in the Grammar School of Linlithgow. A resolute opponent of the Reformation, Winzet was one of the few articulate Catholic pamphleteers, and when his *Certane Tractatis for Reformation of Doctryne and Maneris in Scotland* appeared in 1562 he was forced to leave Scotland and settle in Antwerp. From there he continued to attack JOHN KNOX in a good-humoured satirical strain, and he is noteworthy as being one of the few participants in the debate who wrote in Scots. In 1565 he was at the University of Paris and, after being offered sanctuary in a number of French monasteries, he was made Abbot of Ratisbon. He died on 21 September 1592.

WORKS: *Certane Tractatis for Reformatioun of Doctryne and Maneris in Scotland* (1562); *The Last Blast of the Trompet of Godis Worde aganis the usurpit Auctoritie of Iohne Knox* (1562); *The Buke of the Four Scoir thre Questions* (1563); *Ane Brief Gathering of the Halie Signs* (1565); *Flagellum sectariorum* (1582)

EDITION: J. K. Hewison, ed., *Certain Tractates by Ninian Winzet*, 2 vols., STS (Edinburgh and London, 1888–90)

REFERENCE: J. H. Burns, *Ninian Winzet* (Edinburgh, 1959)

Wizard of the North, the. One of the names by which Sir WALTER SCOTT was known during his lifetime. In the 'CHALDEE MANUSCRIPT', which was published in the October 1817 edition of BLACKWOOD'S MAGAZINE, he appears as 'the great magician which hath his dwelling in the old fastness, hard by the River Jordan, which is by the Border'.

Wodrow, Robert (1679–1734). Historian. He was librarian to the University of Glasgow, and from 1703, after his ordination, he was minister of Eastwood near Glasgow. He is best known as an early historian and chronicler of the COVENANTERS and their opposition in the reigns of Charles II and James II. Much of his work was done in the FACULTY OF ADVOCATES library in Edinburgh. His two-volume *History of the Sufferings of the Church of Scotland from the Restoration to the Revolution* (1721–2) earned the respect of later historians for its basis in the principal archives of the period.

EDITIONS: W. J. Duncan, ed., *Collections upon the Lives of the Reformers and Most Eminent Ministers of the Church of Scotland*, 2 vols., Maitland Club (Edinburgh, 1834–5); *Analecta, or Materials for a History of Remarkable Providences mostly Related to Scotch Ministers and Christians*, 4 vols., Maitland Club (Edinburgh, 1842–3); T, McCrie, ed., *Correspondence of Robert Wodrow*, 3 vols. (Edinburgh, 1842–3)

Wodrow Society. A publishing society founded in Edinburgh in 1841 'for the publication of the works of the fathers and early writers of the Reformed Church of Scotland'. It was named after ROBERT WODROW, the historian who did so much to collate the papers relating to the period of the Covenanting opposition during the 17th century. Amongst the Society's principal publications are editions of David Calderwood's *The History of the Church of Scotland* (1842–9) and David Laing's edition of John Knox's *History of the Reformation . . . within . . . Scotland* (1848). The society ceased to publish in 1851.

Woodhouselee, Lord. *See* TYTLER, ALEXANDER FRASER.

Wright, Tom (b1923). Dramatist. He was born on 8 March 1923 in Glasgow. He left school at the age of 14 and worked as a messenger boy and later a glass embosser. During World War II he served with the army in Europe and the Far East; he then returned to glass embossing in Glasgow and in 1964 he became a mature student at the University of Strathclyde. Later he became the University's first Fellow in Creative Writing.

Wright's early career as a dramatist was restricted by the lack of directors in Scotland willing to present work by Scottish writers, and his first play, *The Mask*, was not produced until 1960. The production of *There was a Man* at the Traverse Theatre in Edinburgh was a breakthrough for him proving that there was a market for the one-man play, in this case a sidelong glimpse at the life and work of the poet ROBERT BURNS. Although the theatre may not always have provided Wright with a platform, television did. He has been one of the principal contributors to the drama output of Scottish Television and BBC Scotland, for which he adapted the uncompleted novel WEIR OF HERMISTON by ROBERT LOUIS STEVENSON; his adaptation was later published as a novel. Other adaptations include ROB ROY by Sir WALTER SCOTT and *Doom Castle* by NEIL MUNRO; and in 1973 his vision of ANE PLEASANT SATYRE OF the THRIE ESTAITIS by Sir DAVID LYNDSAY was produced at the Edinburgh International Festival. In all his dramatic works, whether for the stage or for television, Tom Wright has proved himself a master of Scots dialogue, with an ability to maintain historical tensions through the interrelation of his characters, all of whom exist as flesh-and-blood figures and not as cardboard cutouts.

Writer to the Signet. A Scottish solicitor who is a member of one of the ancient legal bodies in Scotland, the Society of Writers to Her Majesty's Signet. The royal signet, or seal, was assigned to the COURT OF SESSION and the solicitors who practised there were thus incorporated. The other legal societies for Scottish solicitors are the Society of Solicitors in the Supreme Court, the Royal Faculty of Procurators in Glasgow and the Society of Advocates in Aberdeen. The Signet Library near the law courts in Edinburgh, founded in 1722, is one of Scotland's leading libraries.

Wyntoun, Andrew of. *See* ANDREW OF WYNTOUN.

Y

Young, Andrew (1885–1971). Poet. He was born on 29 April 1885 in Elgin and was educated at the HIGH SCHOOL OF EDINBURGH and the University. His formal education was completed as a theological student at New College, Edinburgh, and he was ordained a minister of the United Free Church of Scotland in 1912, his first charge being in the village of Temple, Midlothian. During World War I he was attached to the YMCA in France and in 1918 he left Scotland to become minister of the English Presbyterian Church at Hove in Sussex. In 1936 there began his conversion to the Church of England and after a period as a curate in Plaistow, Sussex, he became Vicar of Stoneygate in the same county from 1941 until his retirement in 1959. His last years were spent in Yapton near Arundel, where he died in 1971.

Young's very earliest short volumes of verse, *Songs of Night* (1910), *Boaz and Ruth* (1920) and *Thirty-One Poems* (1922), reveal him as a poet whose vision embraces not only an accurate description of nature and natural objects, but also of the part they play in the Christian scheme of life, death and regeneration. Inherent in all his works is an almost mystical belief in the sanctity of nature and all its creatures. The publication of *Winter Harvest* in 1933 and of his first *Collected Poems* in 1936 confirmed his reputation as a poet in the tradition of Thomas Traherne (1637–74) and Henry Vaughan (1622–95), able to delineate the English countryside economically and accurately and to interpret its wonders in terms of a resolute Christian faith. Young's main statement of his religious beliefs is contained in his verse play *Nicodemus* (1937) and in his long poem *Out of the World and Back* (1958), which traces the journey of the soul from the dark night of despair to the ecstasy of a reunion with God: 'New eyes would see/The invisible world'.

A botanist of some note, Young published four prose books on the botany, history and folklore of the British Isles, including *The Poet and the Landscape* (1962), a series of portraits of British pastoral poets as seen in their rural settings. In 1952 he was awarded the Queen's Medal for poetry.

WORKS: *Songs of Night* (1910); *Boaz and Ruth* (1920); *The Death of Eli* (1921); *Thirty-One Poems* (1922); *The Adversary* (1923); *The Bird-Cage* (1926); *The Cuckoo-Clock* (1929); *The New Shepherd* (1931); *Winter Harvest* (1933); *The White Blackbird* (1935); *Collected Poems* (1936); *Nicodemus* (1937); *Speak to the Earth* (1939); *A Prospect of Flowers* (1945); *The Green Man* (1947); *A Retrospect of Flowers* (1950); *Collected Poems* (1950); *Into Hades* (1952); *A Prospect of Britain* (1956); *Out of the World and Back* (1958); *Quiet as Moss* (1959); *Collected Poems* (1960); *The Poet and the Landscape* (1962)

REFERENCES: L. Clark and R. G. Thomas, *Andrew Young and R. S. Thomas* (London, 1964)

Young, Douglas (1913–73). Poet and dramatist. He was born on 5 June 1913 at Tayport, Fife, and his early childhood was spent in India. He was educated at Merchiston Castle School, Edinburgh, the University of St Andrews, where he read classics, and (1934–8) New College, Oxford. After his graduation he became a lecturer in Greek at the University of Aberdeen, where he remained until 1941. He joined the Scottish National Party, and because he refused to be conscripted during World War II, was imprisoned in Edinburgh. Between 1947 and 1968 he taught at University College, Dundee, and at the University of St Andrews, before being appointed Professor of Classics at McMaster University in Canada. He became Professor of Greek at the University of North Carolina at Chapel Hill in 1970, only three years before his death, on 23 October 1973.

Young published three collections of poetry: *Auntran Blads: an Outwale o Verses* (1943), *A Braird o Thristles* (1947) and *Selected Poems* (1950). Most of his work was written in Scots and there is a classical control in his best lyrics, 'For a Wife in Jizzen' and 'Requiem'. He also translated into Scots a selection of work by the Gaelic poets SOMHAIRLE MACGILL-EAIN and GEORGE CAMPBELL HAY. In 1966 his translation of Aristophanes' *The Birds* into Scots (*The Burdies: a Comedy in Scots Verse by Aristophanes and Douglas Young*) was produced at the Edinburgh International Festival; he also wrote *The Puddocks: a Verse Play in Scots frae the auld Greek o Aristophanes* (1957). As an editor he produced the *Saltire Modern Poets Series* with MAURICE LINDSAY and *Scottish Verse, 1851–1951* (1952). His Greek textual work is noteworthy and he contributed to the translations of Aeschylus and Theognis.

WORKS: *Auntran Blads: an Outwale o Verses* (1943); *A Braird o Thristles* (1947); *Plastic Scots and the Scottish Literary Tradition* (1947); ed., with Maurice Lindsay, *Saltire Modern Poets Series* (1947); ed., *Selected Poems* (1950); *Scottish Verse, 1851–1951* (1952); *The Burdies: a Comedy in Scots Verse by Aristophanes and Douglas Young*, (1975); *The Puddocks: a Verse Play in Scots frae the auld Greek o Aristophanes* (1957); *Theognis. Ps.-Pythagorus. Chares. Anonymi Aulodia. Fragmentum teliambicum. Post E. Diehl.* (1961); *Edinburgh in the Age of Sir Walter Scott* (1965); *Scots Burds and English Reviewers* (1966); *Edinburgh in the Age of Reason* (1967); *Venus with a Vengeance: the Hippolytus of Euripides in English Verse* (1968); *St Andrews: Town and Gown,* *Royal and Ancient* (1969); *Scotland,* (1971); *Aeschylus: the Orestia Translated into English Verse from a Scientifically Conservative Greek Text* (1974)

REFERENCE: C. Young and D. Murison, eds., *A Clear Voice: Douglas Young, Poet and Polymath* (Loanhead, Midlothian, n.d.)

Young Pretender, the. *See* STUART, CHARLES EDWARD.

Yuill, P. B. Pen-name of GORDON WILLIAMS.

Yule (from Old Norse *jól*). A festival celebrating the Winter Solstice, which later became the Christian festival of Christmas. Traditionally Yule began on Christmas eve and ended on UPHALIEDAY or Twelfth Night; the holiday period was known as the DAFT DAYS, and is celebrated in a poem of the same name by ROBERT FERGUSSON. During the 16th century in Edinburgh the festivities were presided over by an Abbot of Narent or Misrule and there is a vivid picture of the grotesque revels in *The Abbot* by Sir WALTER SCOTT. It was also a period of guizing when THE GOLOSHAN, a traditional Christmas mumming play, was performed. The celebration of Christmas was long frowned upon by the post-Reformation Church.

Z

Zeluco. A novel by JOHN MOORE published in 1786 with the sub-title, 'Various views of Human Nature, Taken from Life and Manners, Foreign and Domestic'. It tells the story of the crimes committed by Zeluco, a vicious Sicilian nobleman whose life is corrupted by lust, cruelty and revenge. His childhood is marked by several cruel acts; as he grows into manhood his wickedness culminates in the enforced marriage, by treachery, of a beautiful and virtuous girl who is finally driven into madness. Zeluco is then himself killed in circumstances that mirror the uneven tenor of his own life. Although the sadistic and scandalous scenes link the novel to Gothic tales of horror, *Zeluco* is saved from the excesses of that genre by Moore's psychological insights into the central character's monstrous behaviour. The novel is notable, too, for Moore's vivid descriptions of the Mediterranean, which he gained from his own travels, and also for his polished and caustic literary style. The minor characters are not without interest, especially the servants, Targe and Buchanan, two Scots who squabble remorselessly and intolerantly over the character of MARY, Queen of Scots. Moore's social criticism led him to include a detailed attack on the horrors of Negro slavery, and a hostile satire on the Roman Catholic church.

Zion's Flowers. A collection of stories from the Old Testament rendered into verse by the poet ZACHARY BOYD, first published in 1644. *Zion's Flowers, or Christian Poems for Spiritual Edification* begins with 'The Fall of Adam' and ends with 'The History of John Baptist'; also included are two original pieces of verse, 'The Popish Powder Plot' and 'The World's Vanities'. Although Boyd's work was a creditable attempt to make the scriptures more widely available to the public, it was marred by his frequently ridiculous style of versification, of which the following is a typical example:

> There was a man called Job,
> Dwelt in the land of Uz;
> He had the gift of the gob;
> The same case happen us!